Mastering

Microsoft FrontPage 2002
Premium Edition

Mastering™
Microsoft® FrontPage® 2002
Premium Edition

Peter Weverka

and

Molly E. Holzschlag

SYBEX®

San Francisco • Paris • Düsseldorf • Soest • London

Associate Publisher: Cheryl Applewood

Acquisitions and Developmental Editor: Kathy Yankton

Editor: Suzanne Goraj

Production Editor: Elizabeth Campbell

Technical Editor: Susan Glinert Stevens

Book Designer: Maureen Forys

Graphic Illustrator: Tony Jonick

Electronic Publishing Specialist: Kris Warrenburg, Cyan Design

Proofreaders: Nanette Duffy, Laurie O'Connell, Nancy Riddiough, Suzanne Stein

Indexer: Jack Lewis

CD Coordinator: Christine Harris

CD Technician: Kevin Ly

Cover Designer: Design Site

Cover Illustrator/Photographer: Jack D. Myers

Library of Congress Card Number: 2001094266

ISBN: 0-7821-4003-3

Software License Agreement

Terms and Conditions

The media and/or any online materials accompanying this book that are available now or in the future contain programs and/or text files (the "Software") to be used in connection with the book. SYBEX hereby grants to you a license to use the Software, subject to the terms that follow. Your purchase, acceptance, or use of the Software will constitute your acceptance of such terms.

The Software compilation is the property of SYBEX unless otherwise indicated and is protected by copyright to SYBEX or other copyright owner(s) as indicated in the media files (the "Owner(s)"). You are hereby granted a single-user license to use the Software for your personal, noncommercial use only. You may not reproduce, sell, distribute, publish, circulate, or commercially exploit the Software, or any portion thereof, without the written consent of SYBEX and the specific copyright owner(s) of any component software included on this media.

In the event that the Software or components include specific license requirements or end-user agreements, statements of condition, disclaimers, limitations or warranties ("End-User License"), those End-User Licenses supersede the terms and conditions herein as to that particular Software component. Your purchase, acceptance, or use of the Software will constitute your acceptance of such End-User Licenses.

By purchase, use or acceptance of the Software you further agree to comply with all export laws and regulations of the United States as such laws and regulations may exist from time to time.

Reusable Code in This Book

The authors created reusable code in this publication expressly for reuse for readers. Sybex grants readers permission to reuse for any purpose the code found in this publication or its accompanying CD-ROM so long as the authors are attributed in any application containing the reusable code, and the code itself is never sold or commercially exploited as a stand-alone product.

Software Support

Components of the supplemental Software and any offers associated with them may be supported by the specific Owner(s) of that material but they are not supported by SYBEX. Information regarding any available support may be obtained from the Owner(s) using the information provided in the appropriate read.me files or listed elsewhere on the media.

Should the manufacturer(s) or other Owner(s) cease to offer support or decline to honor any offer, SYBEX bears no responsibility. This notice concerning support for the Software is provided for your information only. SYBEX is not the agent or principal of the Owner(s), and SYBEX is in no way responsible for providing any support for the Software, nor is it liable or responsible for any support provided, or not provided, by the Owner(s).

Warranty

SYBEX warrants the enclosed media to be free of physical defects for a period of ninety (90) days after purchase. The Software is not available from SYBEX in any other form or media than that enclosed herein or posted to www.sybex.com. If you discover a defect in the media during this warranty period, you may obtain a replacement of identical format at no charge by sending the defective media, postage prepaid, with proof of purchase to:

SYBEX Inc.
Customer Service Department
1151 Marina Village Parkway
Alameda, CA 94501
(510) 523-8233
Fax: (510) 523-2373
e-mail: info@sybex.com
WEB: HTTP://WWW.SYBEX.COM

After the 90-day period, you can obtain replacement media of identical format by sending us the defective disk, proof of purchase, and a check or money order for $10, payable to SYBEX.

Disclaimer

SYBEX makes no warranty or representation, either expressed or implied, with respect to the Software or its contents, quality, performance, merchantability, or fitness for a particular purpose. In no event will SYBEX, its distributors, or dealers be liable to you or any other party for direct, indirect, special, incidental, consequential, or other damages arising out of the use of or inability to use the Software or its contents even if advised of the possibility of such damage. In the event that the Software includes an online update feature, SYBEX further disclaims any obligation to provide this feature for any specific duration other than the initial posting.

The exclusion of implied warranties is not permitted by some states. Therefore, the above exclusion may not apply to you. This warranty provides you with specific legal rights; there may be other rights that you may have that vary from state to state. The pricing of the book with the Software by SYBEX reflects the allocation of risk and limitations on liability contained in this agreement of Terms and Conditions.

Shareware Distribution

This Software may contain various programs that are distributed as shareware. Copyright laws apply to both shareware and ordinary commercial software, and the copyright Owner(s) retains all rights. If you try a shareware program and continue using it, you are expected to register it. Individual programs differ on details of trial periods, registration, and payment. Please observe the requirements stated in appropriate files.

Copy Protection

The Software in whole or in part may or may not be copy-protected or encrypted. However, in all cases, reselling or redistributing these files without authorization is expressly forbidden except as specifically provided for by the Owner(s) therein.

For Professor John Frink

—Peter Weverka

Acknowledgments

A big book on a short schedule is never a solitary venture. Our thanks go to the many people involved in making this one a reality.

We would especially like to thank Kathy Yankton for giving us the opportunity to write this book and for skillfully steering it along. Thanks as well go to Cheryl Applewood for getting us started on the book, Elizabeth Campbell for speeding it through production, and Teresa Trego for standing in for Elizabeth now and then. We owe a big debt of gratitude to copy editor Suzanne Goraj for doing such a good job with the manuscript and Susan Glinert Stevens for going over our words for technical accuracy. Thanks as well go to Indexer Jack Lewis for his work.

Thanks go to Kris Warrenburg for her skillful layout, and also to the proofreaders: Nanette Duffy, Laurie O'Connell, Nancy Riddiough, and Suzanne Stein

We would be remiss if we didn't thank all the different authors, past and present, who helped write this book, so thank you Daniel Tauber, Brenda Kienan, Bill Rodgers, and Charles Hornberger.

Contents at a Glance

Contents

Introduction

FrontPage 2002 is no mere HTML editor. It offers an interface that gives both the novice and the professional a powerful tool for creating Web sites. Whether your goal is easy creation of single Web pages or the planning, building, and maintenance of a big site that will be tended by a whole team of Webmasters, FrontPage 2002 can meet your needs, and *Mastering Microsoft FrontPage 2002 Premium Edition* is your indispensable guide to maximizing FrontPage 2002's potential.

Is This Book for You?

This book is an excellent choice for novices and intermediate readers alike. Written in plain English and filled with practical examples and step-by-step exercises, *Mastering Microsoft FrontPage 2002 Premium Edition* will take you where you want to go with Web site development—and quickly! It will get you started using all of the features of FrontPage 2002 in no time. You'll rapidly be able to create dazzling effects just using FrontPage's basic tools, its themes (prepackaged looks), and a selection of its components, which can add functions to your site with no programming whatsoever.

If you already have the basics under your belt, you'll find that this book will help you produce and maintain a powerful Web site presence in no time flat, with insider tips that might otherwise take you forever to stumble onto. *Mastering Microsoft FrontPage 2002 Premium Edition* offers strategic advice on designing a successful site, making the most of typography, assigning and managing site creation and maintenance tasks, and even promoting your site and measuring its success.

This book includes a variety of advanced chapters that will help bring you to the domain of the professional developer. With advanced graphics techniques, you'll learn how to create graphics the way the best designers in the business do. Back-end and project management information will give you a solid conceptual foundation for what, beyond software, is necessary for creating Web sites. Finally, we walk you step by step through the production of Web sites so you can see how FrontPage 2002 really works.

Throughout this book, you'll find pointers to handpicked Web sites of all kinds that we know will provide you with additional information on every topic in this book. We'll tell you where to find Web-friendly color palettes, images, animations, sound files, and ActiveX controls you can use, as well as more tips on publishing a terrific Web site and announcing it to the world.

How This Book Is Organized

This book is organized into six parts containing 33 chapters. Part I, *Building Basic FrontPage Web Sites*, sets the stage for future work by introducing sound Web design principles and then leading you through the FrontPage interface. It teaches you how to create basic pages with FrontPage, introduces you to working with text and type, and gears you up to manage tasks and then publish a site right to the Web.

Part II, *Creating Sophisticated Designs*, introduces how to incorporate design elements and media such as graphics, animation, image maps, sound, video, and music into your site. It covers using FrontPage's Cascading Style Sheets features to apply a consistent look to your site, and discusses how to implement effective forms and use frames well. You'll be introduced to special effects, and address perhaps the most important design concern of all: Browsers are not equal! Chapter 16 shows you how to take into consideration the ins and outs of designing for multiple browsers using FrontPage 2002.

Part III, *Advanced Web Graphic Design*, homes in on various aspects of graphic production for the Web. You'll get situated with an understanding of important design concepts, move on to a wealth of information about today's hottest design software that will complement the work you do in FrontPage, and finish up with production techniques that will get and keep you organized and your sites moving along admirably.

Part IV, *Taking Your Web Site to the Top*, shows you how to integrate Microsoft Office into your site, and how to take advantage of FrontPage's handy components—which let you incorporate effects that typically require programming know-how, even if you have no programming experience at all. Then you'll learn how FrontPage manages important programming elements such as JavaScript, Dynamic HTML (DHTML), and databases. The section finishes up with a tutorial on how to maintain and promote your site for the long term.

Part V, *Back-End Applications and Professional Management*, helps you put on the Web developer cap. In this section of the book, you'll learn about server extensions, SharePoint Team Services, and back-end technologies such as CGI and Perl, take an in-depth look at Active Server Pages and databases, and read about another software application that's akin to FrontPage: Microsoft's Visual InterDev.

Part VI, *Step-By-Step FrontPage Sites*, wraps up the book by putting the rubber to the road. This section's four chapters walk you through the actual creation of four types of sites, a personal Web page, a small business site, a community site, and a large-scale site. Each of these chapters has plenty of professional tips and provides visual references throughout the process.

You'll also find five appendices at the back of the book. Appendix A steps you through customizing FrontPage, Appendix B guides you in choosing and installing the correct server software so your installation of FrontPage will go smoothly, Appendix C demystifies installing and troubleshooting TCP/IP, Appendix D explains the Microsoft Clip Organizer, and Appendix E offers a comprehensive HTML reference.

A Complete, Updated HTML Reference

At www.htmlreference.com, you'll find a complete, easy-to-use online reference to HTML 4 including the Netscape and Internet Explorer extensions and style sheet attributes.

What's New in FrontPage 2002

FrontPage 2002 has improved on its predecessor, FrontPage 2000, in many important ways. Moreover, you can do the following in FrontPage 2002:

- Create shapes, AutoShapes, and lines for your Web pages with the Drawing tools on the Drawing toolbar.

- Include a search engine, weather forecasts, news headlines, and other amenities on a Web page with the new Web Components.

- Use SharePoint technology to create a Web site on which colleagues can have discussions, work as a team on different files, and conduct surveys.

- Switch from Web page to Web page by clicking page tabs.

- Quickly format a table with the AutoFormat command.

- Do tasks in the task pane, a panel that appears on the side of the screen when you give certain commands.

- Cut, copy, and paste from many different sources with the Office Clipboard.

- Create link bars so that visitors to your Web site can go from place to place easily.

- Create inline frames—frames that appear in the middle of a page, not on the top, bottom, or sides.

- Generate usage-analysis reports that show who visits your Web site, what kind of browsers they use, and more.

- Quickly format text you pasted from different sources.

- Publish only a handful of Web pages to your ISP instead of the entire Web site.

- Work on your Web site and publish it to the Internet at the same time.

- Make a document library available to others over the Web (with SharePoint technology).

- Display the contents of a database on a Web page.

- Use Microsoft Photo Editor to touch up JPEG and GIF graphics.

All of these features make FrontPage 2002 an impressive Web site management package. With FrontPage, you can move seamlessly from building an effective site to maintaining the site, and because of the FrontPage interface, you can work without having to overcome a steep learning curve. Whether your site is large or small, and whether you are an HTML novice or an old pro, you'll find out why FrontPage is just the application you need to manage your site.

Conventions Used in This Book

Mastering Microsoft FrontPage 2002 Premium Edition uses various conventions to help you find the information you need quickly and effortlessly. Tips and Warnings, shown here, are placed strategically throughout the book to help you zero in on important information in a snap.

Here you'll find insider tips and shortcuts—quick information meant to help you use FrontPage more adeptly.

Here you'll find cautionary information describing trouble spots you may encounter when using the software.

A simple kind of shorthand used in this book helps to save space so that more crucial matters can be discussed. For example, directions to "pull down the File menu and choose Save" appear as "select File ➜ Save."

Long but important or interesting digressions are set aside as bordered text, called *sidebars*.

These Are Called Sidebars

In boxed text like this, you'll find background information and side issues—anything that merits attention or adds to your knowledge base, but can be skipped in a real pinch.

Special *Mastering What's Online* sidebars tell you exactly where on the World Wide Web you can find out more about the topic at hand or where to find the home page being described. The URL for the home page of interest at the moment appears in a special font: `www.tauberkienan.com`.

What's on the CD?

The accompanying CD features a 30-day trial version of FrontPage 2002, so you can try out the techniques you've learned!

Let's Get Started!

Enough about what's in the book—we're sure you want to get going! It's just a turn of the page and you'll be off to a great start learning how to create Web sites with Front-Page 2002.

 Visit the Microsoft FrontPage Web site, `www.microsoft.com/frontpage/`.

Part I
Building Basic FrontPage Web Sites

In This Part

Introduction to
Web Design

FRONTPAGE

Chapter 1

We know you're itching to get busy using FrontPage 2002, but before you do, take the time to plan your site, develop its *look and feel* (its visual presence), and get a sense of what successful sites look like. Yes, laying the groundwork for a Web site requires time, but take it from us: The time you spend now to plan ahead will save many hours or even days in the long run.

This chapter explains how to go about planning a Web site. It explores a number of Web site dos and don'ts to help you build a site that looks great and works well, too. This chapter points the way to Web sites that demonstrate a high regard for design. It introduces some ways that FrontPage and the tools that come with it can help you along. After you read this chapter, you'll be ready to create your own successful Web site. Topics include:

- Why learn about Web design?

- Planning your Web site

- Web site dos and don'ts

- Exploring successful page designs

Planning Your Web Site

The importance of planning a Web site cannot be stressed enough. Many people don't realize how important planning ahead really is. Planning a Web site is akin to drawing plans for a new house. If you jump in and begin building, you inevitably will have to do tasks all over again, or you may lack the right tools and materials. Even the most careful planners have to change course or modify their plans. Proper planning, however, reduces and in some cases removes the frustrations that occur when you undertake a big project such as building a Web site.

Here are the basic steps in planning a Web site:

1. Set goals and get organized.

2. Define your target audience.

3. Create a folder structure (also known as *site mapping*).

4. Create a *storyboard* (sketch) of the Web pages you intend to create.

5. Design and refine the look and feel of the site.

If all this sounds complicated, don't worry! The next handful of pages explains each step in detail. You will master the concepts and get tips on how to make the planning process a success.

Step 1: Set Goals and Get Organized

To start designing your Web page, you must first think through what your site's goals and mission are. To inform? Promote? Educate? Research and report? Maybe you are in this for entertainment purposes. Make sure that your goals are clear to you, and if yours is a company site, make sure that the goals you establish for your site are in line with the company's values and mission. Most companies—indeed, many departments within bigger companies—have a mission statement from which they work. You can check your goals against those mission statements and even write one for the site.

What's Your Mission?

To write a mission statement for your site, consider these questions:

- What product or service do you or your company offer, either generally or through the site?

- What three to five goals do you (or your company) plan to achieve? (Will the site inform, entertain, sell, promote, distribute, or research and report? Most sites are geared toward accomplishing a combination of these goals.) Think for the short- *and* long-term here. Your needs today might be different from your long-term plans.

- What few words or simple phrases can describe your image or the image you want your site to project?

- What audience or user base should the site reach?

- How will the site itself help to reach the target audience or achieve the overall goals you have established?

- What sorts of content or technologies are available for use in the site? Be sure to take into account your budget and the appropriateness of material as it pertains to your audience and goals.

- How will you and/or your company achieve success for your Web site?

Go ahead and pull these thoughts together into a cohesive written statement that describes your site's mission. Keep it short—one paragraph or a few brief sentences are fine. If one part of the statement seems to conflict with another, go back and prioritize. Always keep in mind aims that will serve your overall goals.

As you go on to actually plan your site, check and double-check to make sure that your tactics suit your strategy and that your content and design fulfill the mission you've set out, whatever it may be. As you plan and execute your site, remembering your goals is a vital part of getting and remaining organized.

Organize Your Assets!

Now, organize your assets. Pull together existing documents and images that you want to work with. If yours is a personal site, gather the artwork and stuff you've written. If you intend to build a company site, assemble logos, company information, and product descriptions. You may need to create new content and write new material. If so, jot down a few ideas for now and do the writing later. You're just in the planning stage.

Think about the message you want to convey to fulfill your mission and which types of images or text are appropriate. If your site's goal suggests fun and lightheartedness, then chatty, informal language and whimsical graphics fit the bill. On the other hand, formal, concise language and smooth, elegant graphics are more appropriate for a corporate site.

Do the Shuffle

After your mission and strategy are clearly laid out and your materials are in hand, shuffle those materials around a bit. Put like things together into groups and eliminate instances of repetition. Try taping pages to a big whiteboard and shuffling the pages until you see some kind of organization take shape. Put the whole business into a giant chart. Very likely, a site plan will begin to emerge, but don't get too attached to any aspect of the plan just yet. Instead, ponder the plan and fiddle with it. You may need to create new material to go with the material you already have. You can never do too much organizing and planning, and the bigger your site will be, the more planning you need to do. In the next step, you can start to nail things down more formally.

Mastering What's Online

Many people mistakenly believe that everything on the Web is "in the public domain." It isn't. Make sure you have the legal right to use materials you find on the Web (or anywhere else) and plan to include in your Web site. Some copyright and legal resources include:

- The Internet Legal Resource Guide at www.ilrg.com

- The Copyright Web Site at www.benedict.com

- The Nolo Press Self-Help Law Center at www.nolo.com

- United States Copyright Office at www.loc.gov/copyright/

Step 2: Define Your Target Audience

Dozens, if not hundreds or thousands, of people will visit your Web site every day. A Web site should clearly convey what its message is—promoting wonder widgets, publishing the results of research, showing off a resume, or describing the marvels of the local soda pop machine.

But how do Web sites—or any media, for that matter—convey a message? The first step is understanding who will receive the message. Without understanding who your audience is, you'll miss the mark. You need to consider viewers' backgrounds, experiences, interests, and tastes. You need to ask why they will visit your Web site. And you would do well to know your audience's age, its geographical location, and what it expects of a Web experience.

People who build a Web site to make a personal statement or express their creative side sometimes think they can bypass Step 2 and design their Web sites to suit their own tastes and preferences, not an audience's. But if you neglect the audience, you put a cap on the number of people who will frequent your site. No one will know what your site is really for. To reach far and wide for an audience, carefully consider all the planning steps discussed in this chapter.

How do you gather information about an audience? Well, if you're working in a professional environment, someone has very likely collected information about the people who use your company's products and services. Find out if any demographic studies have been done, and, if any have been done, use the information to put together a portrait of your client base. If no information is available or you are not working in a professional environment, use the following "Demographic Survey" as your guide.

Demographic Survey

Describe your current and intended future audience in detail. Be sure to include information about:

- Age
- Gender
- Financial status
- Educational background
- Geographical location
- Marital status

What else do you know about your audience? Does it consist of friends and relatives? Business buddies or clients? What are its major interests and concerns? Jot down a few notes about who you want your site to reach and who you want it to reach down the road.

Thinking through Step 2 is important. If you miss your target audience, you miss an opportunity to provide individuals with an experience they might really want or need.

Consider this: Gadgets that make a Web site fun to an audience that wants to be entertained only serve to annoy and distract serious researchers and technical professionals who want information. Similarly, graphics and multimedia can be exciting on a Web site that is hosted on a corporate intranet, where employees can access the site by way of a speedy *local area network (LAN)*—but in a professional setting like that, are snappy graphics and active media really necessary? Many would find them distracting.

The key to successfully communicating with an audience is to identify the audience and then determine how to serve that audience. You can tailor almost every aspect of a Web site to the target audience—from the way you organize information to the kinds of fonts and images you use.

Mastering What's Online

As you define your target audience, you can learn a lot about demographics and how to get demographic information by visiting these sites:

- Census Information—If you live outside the United States, you can search for census information using your favorite search engine; census information for the U.S. can be found at www.census.gov.

- CIA World Factbook—The Central Intelligence Agency, wouldn't you know it, offers many country profiles and all kinds of interesting tidbits: http://www.odci.gov/cia/publications/factbook.

- The Internet Advertising Resource Guide—This guide will help you understand more about the importance of planning and knowing your audience: www.admedia.org.

- Info Please—Starting here, you can find almanacs for the United States and various other countries: www.infoplease.com.

- KnowX—This public records search can help you find all kinds of interesting information for free or at a very low cost: www.knowx.com.

Later in this chapter, you'll see how Web sites use design and navigational elements to accomplish their purposes. Meanwhile, make your own tour of Web sites and decide for yourself what works and what doesn't. As you do so, imagine the design decisions that other Web site creators made when they were putting together their Web sites.

If your audience wants the newest gizmo, go ahead and design for the latest and greatest, but if your audience includes people in underdeveloped countries who have slow Internet connections and older browsers, be sure to take that into consideration. The point is to consider your audience's browser capabilities and design your Web site accordingly. See Chapter 16 for more details.

Step 3: Create a Folder Structure

The next step is to arrange your content into a filing system of sorts. If your site is to include a small amount of HTML code and few image files, you can store all the files in a single folder. Complex sites require you to manage files more carefully. You may need to organize your files into folders and subfolders to make identifying files and maintaining your Web site easier.

Setting up a folder structure for files, sometimes called *site mapping*, is a piece of cake—provided you do it in advance. Developing a logical folder structure is an essential part of planning a Web site. Typically, a Web page consists of more than one file, and you must specify the correct path to each file you reference in a Web page. On a Web page that includes a graphic, for example, you must specify the folder where the graphic is stored. Hyperlinks connect the Web pages in a Web site. By carefully placing Web pages in the right folders, you can be sure that the hyperlinks that connect pages to one another always reach their targets. If, halfway through the job of creating a Web site, you create new folders, move files, or change filenames, you end up with hyperlinks that don't work and empty boxes on Web pages where graphics are supposed to be. Consider this illustration, which you have no doubt seen before in your adventures on the Internet. This Web site developer moved a graphic to different folder, so X's and empty boxes appear where graphics are supposed to be.

You can use the information you gleaned from "Step 1: Set Goals and Get Organized" in this step. Organize your folders and subfolders into a top-down structure in much the same way that you organize the folders and subfolders on your hard disk.

To help map your folder structure, first draw a box (you can use a pen and paper, or work in the imaging software of your choice) to represent your home page. Below that, draw a horizontal line and sketch boxes under it to represent the subfolders where groups of material will be kept. You can place smaller groups within subfolders at a deeper level.

As you do all of this, consider again which pages can be linked, and don't place copies of the same page in two different subfolders. Note, too, that every page and file that will make up your site must go in one folder or another; keep fooling with your folder structure until you can make that happen neatly. Choose short and descriptive names for folders and subfolders. For example, instead of "Joblistings," go with "Jobs."

If yours is a large site, create separate folders for elements other than the primary HTML files. In a site with many graphics, developers often create a subfolder for all the images in the site. You can also create subfolders for specific kinds of content.

Step 4: Create a Storyboard

Now create a storyboard, or sketch, of your home page and each page it will link to. Include in your storyboard all of the elements you're considering (text, images, buttons, hyperlinks). And don't be afraid to make adjustments. By the way, you needn't be an artist to create a storyboard. The goal is to organize your Web site, not design it. If your original concept doesn't flow nicely, scrap it and start again. Better to find out now that you need to start all over than to find out when you're halfway through the design stage.

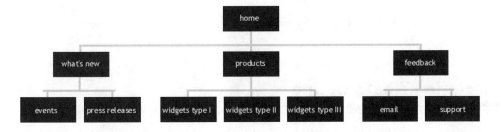

After you come up with a general site plan and folder structure, you may notice that your content falls into certain types. If so, it might be possible to take advantage of Web page templates and spare yourself the trouble of designing the site page by time-consuming page. FrontPage, for example, offers templates for presenting graphics. To create a Web page from a template, see Chapter 2 and Chapter 3.

Remember that the *Web* in World Wide Web is there for a reason—because hyperlinks connect Web sites into a vast web, or network of interconnected sites. Hardly anyone reads an entire Web site in the same way, for example, that they read a novel. Web surfers typically jump to an item that interests them and then move on just as quickly to something else. Surfers may enter your Web site at any point by way of a link from another site.

Visitors must be able to move around a Web site quickly and easily so they can find what they seek with a minimum of fuss and bother. If your Web site is difficult to navigate, visitors will quit in frustration and probably not bother coming back. Provide people with aids to navigation—a navigation bar, for example, with simple text links or buttons. Provide one-click access to key sections of your Web site from the home page or from other key pages. Make sure that the navigational elements are easy to find and use.

The difference between an exciting Web site and a dull one has less to do with the complexity or technical sophistication of the Web site than the quality of the site's content *and* its presentation. Design each page so that it stands alone and yet is part of the Web site as a whole. Consider what *palette*, or combination of colors, you want to use, which fonts will work best, and where to place items such as:

- Navigational elements—for example, a navigation bar with buttons, or text links to other pages

- Identifying banners, logos, and so on

- Illustrations and other types of artwork

- Text of all types

- A notice of ownership or copyright that you want to include

Mastering What's Online

A great way to get a grip on Web designs that work is to look at Web designs that *don't* work:

- Cruise through Web Pages That Suck at `www.webpagesthatsuck.com`.

- To see some surprising examples of bad style, check out the Bad Style Page at `www.disi.unige.it/ftp/person/CosciaE/pub/Bad_Style_Page.html`.

- Look (for as long as you're able) at Clay Shirky's Worst Page on the World Wide Web at `www.panix.com/~clays/biff`.

- For more finger-pointing fun, check out Yecch!!!, a Web site that presents parodies of Web sites, at `www.yeeeoww.com/yecch/yecchhome.html`.

Step 5: Develop a Look and Feel

The next step is to work on the look and feel of your Web site. Among Web page designers, the term *look and feel* refers to the overall visual representation of a Web site, the combination of color, graphics, fonts, and text that convey the site's meaning.

You've already done your planning and created a storyboard, so you know what the basic elements of your site are. Now your task is to work those elements into a sophisticated—and integrated—visual design.

FrontPage 2002 can help you do this because it provides a range of outstanding site templates (see Chapter 3). Figure 1.1 shows some of the FrontPage 2002 templates. In order to maintain flexibility and control over your site, being able to visualize the end product from the very beginning is important.

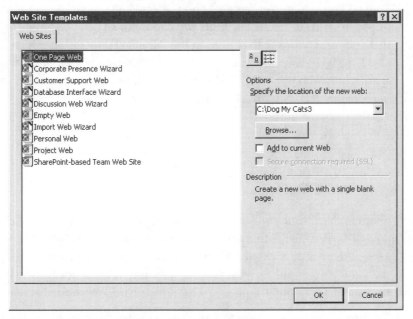

Figure 1.1 *FrontPage 2002 offers a large variety of site templates.*

A few paragraphs in a computer book can't replace years of experience in Web page design, but you can take several important steps to ensure that a consistent look and feel evolves on your Web site. Here is a list of elements to take into consideration as you develop the look and feel of your Web site:

Space and balance   This is the amount of space the elements on your page occupy as well as the amount of empty, or "white," space that appears around elements. Visitors to a Web page like to see plenty of empty space along with other elements. A healthy balance between elements and empty space makes a page easy to read, keeps the page from being cluttered, and makes for a relaxed presentation.

Color   We'll look at color throughout this book—particularly when we study text, fonts, and tables. To start with, however, consider what colors mean and which colors will work best on your Web site. If you are building a personal home page and you happen to be a splashy, bright person, then splashy, bright colors are what you need. But if your Web site tackles a serious topic, muted colors are in order.

Fonts   Fonts, like color, say a lot about the personality of a Web site and the impact it wants to make. The fonts you choose must be appropriate to the message that you want your site to convey. In the following illustration, which font is suitable for a Web page announcing a party, a funeral, or a sale? Fonts should be used sparingly. A Web page with 20 different fonts looks unprofessional and is confusing. Chapter 6 takes a close look at how to handle fonts.

April 16, 2001
April 16, 2001
April 16, 2001

Shapes   Next time you surf the Web, notice the number of rectangles. Look at advertising banners—they are always rectangular! So are most page headers, buttons, and other page elements. Rectangles are okay, but because they are so common and you very likely want your site to stand out, consider other shapes for your site as well. Ovals and triangles, for example, give a Web site a distinctive look.

Texture   Think about how texture can set the tone for your Web site and how to work texture into your site, if you feel that texture can be useful. Unusual textures call attention to themselves, however, and they can make a site harder to view and read. Be sure to select a subtle texture that doesn't obscure or muddle the text.

Special effects   Is your site going to benefit from special effects, such as animations or mouseovers (also known as rollovers)? If you think so, start thinking about special effects now, and use a light hand! Overblown special effects are rampant on the Web. Don't overrun a perfectly good site with a horde of bouncing, jumping, and blinking elements. Chapter 15 looks at special effects in detail.

Consistency   Think about how your site will look from page to page. Using a single color scheme throughout a Web site is a good way to achieve consistency. Another way is to place the same navigation aids on all the pages.

Variation   Should every page be the same color? Not necessarily. Depending on your site map, you can make subtle changes at different levels and still maintain consistency. Later in this chapter, when we pay a visit to the Web site of San Francisco's Exploratorium, you will see how to balance variation and consistency.

Developing a look and feel is a major part of Web design. Many people who build Web pages are not designers, so they aren't aware of the kinds of concerns that are outlined in the previous section of this book. Study these issues well and you'll gain insight into how to create Web pages that are visually interesting.

Web Designer's Toolbox

Use these URLs and books to gain a better understanding of how to design Web sites:

- Builder.com. CNET's Developer site has vast resources and snappy articles to help you gain a better understanding of design as well as Web technology: `www.builder.com`.

- Netscape's DevEdge. Learn how to design Web sites from this site sponsored by Netscape, maker of the popular Netscape Navigator Web browser: `developer.netscape.com`.

- Webreview.com. A great site for those who have a real hunger for all that's new in the Web design and development world, the site offers articles, departments, community, and live events: `www.webreview.com`.

- The Web Design Community. Specializing in helping the novice get acquainted with the world of Web Design, this Microsoft Network community also offers articles, chats, events, and newsgroups for intermediate and advanced Web designers, too: `communities.msn.com/webdesign`.

- The Web Design Group. Create sites accessible to *all* browsers with the help of their tools, articles, links, and discussion: `htmlhelp.inet.tele.dk`.

- The Web Developer's Virtual Library. This site is a constantly growing resource on every aspect of Web development and design: `www.wdvl.com`.

- One book you'll want on your shelves is *Web Pages That Suck* (Sybex, 1998). This is a full-color, humorous look at learning good design by checking out designs that, well, suck! Written by Vince Flanders and Michael Willis.

Web Site Dos and Don'ts

While you design your Web site, remember that you have about two seconds to grab readers' attention. Two seconds! That's the conventional wisdom in advertising and publishing circles, anyway. You can't go wrong if you follow these basic tips for designing an eye-catching page with links that work:

- Make the title short, catchy, descriptive, and accurate. And then be sure to fulfill its promise. If you call your page "Thousands of Yummy Recipes," it had better be that.

- Provide clues at the top of the page about what the page contains; don't expect visitors to scroll down the page to find out.

- Break up your page into more than one page if your page is longer than three "screenfuls."

- Balance white space, large and small images, different shapes, and blocks of text to give your page interest and variety. A sense of balance is key; don't let your page design get lopsided.

- Don't overload a Web page with extraneous doodads.

- Use text and link colors that complement rather than clash with the background.

- Be sure that anything that looks like a button behaves like one.

- Don't create two links with the same name that go to two different places, or two links with different names that go to the same place. Always offer a way back from one link to the originating page if the link is within your Web site.

- Make your links descriptive; avoid the generic. "Click Here!" isn't all that intriguing.

- Use well-compressed images.

- Use thumbnails as links to larger images.

- Remember that the people who access Web pages use different browsers with different capabilities.

- Keep filenames short and make them consistent with one another.

- Tell people the size of downloadable files to help them decide whether to download them.

- Get permission to use text and images that were created by someone else.
- Create a link to the e-mail address of the Webmaster.

Exploring Successful Page Designs

The best way to get ideas and to create a winning Web page is to study examples. In that spirit, these pages take a look at a few especially well-designed Web pages and point out what makes them so terrific. Most of these pages make use of basic HTML to achieve stunning results. To show you what you might one day aspire to, you'll also review a few pages with more complex and challenging effects—such as tables, frames, and forms (covered in Part II of this book).

If you want to see exactly what a Web designer did to create a Web page, launch your Web browser, view the page of interest, and select the option for viewing HTML code from the browser's menu bar. In Navigator, select View ➜ Source. The HTML code of the page you're looking at will appear in a separate window.

Mastering What's Online

A great way to study Web page design is to look at a Web site made by a successful Web designer. You may find it useful to check out Organic at www.organic.com, Razorfish at www.razorfish.com, Brainbug at www.brainbug.com, and Design inSites at designinsites.com. Be sure to check out the pages of their clients as well, as clients often get more attention from designers than the designers' own home pages get.

Simple, Friendly, and Clear

Using simple HTML and colorful graphics scanned from original watercolor paintings, The Tea Shop (Figure 1.2) is a very friendly site with clear intent, well-organized content, and an appealing look and feel that supports the message of the site. Visitors are made to relax and imagine that they're in an exotic tea shop breathing in the lovely scents of different teas and herbs.

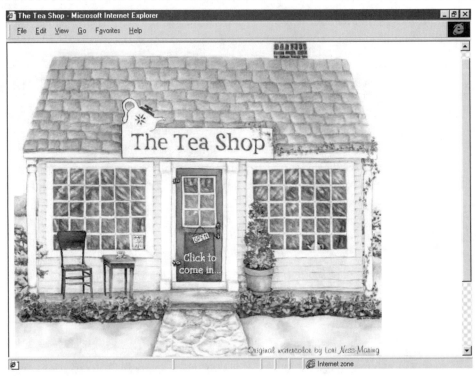

Figure 1.2 *Relax and enjoy a cuppa in the warm and friendly atmosphere of The Tea Shop.*

Visitors can learn about teas from around the world, including Ceylon, Japan, China, and India. Want to buy some tea? You can order right online. The Tea Shop also offers a selection of books, gifts, and accessories related to teas. And, if you want to get in touch, you can send tEa-mail!

The Tea Shop is a fine example of a from-the-heart design that emphasizes warmth and ease rather than focusing on the slick and complex.

Mastering What's Online

Take a break at The Tea Shop: www.theteashop.com.

Terrifically Clickable

In keeping with its reputation as a stunning and visionary museum, San Francisco's Exploratorium offers an excellent Web site filled with online exhibits that are beautiful to see and fun to navigate (see Figure 1.3). The Web site uses color bars to make for a clean, comfortable design. A background GIF is used to create the color bars—this popular technique (explained in Chapter 9) can be highly effective in adding color and intrigue to a page.

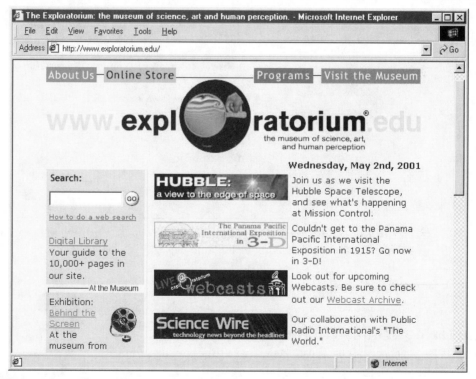

Figure 1.3 *The Exploratorium's home page*

The page shown in Figure 1.4 is from another page on the Exploratorium Web site. Comparing this figure to Figure 1.3, you can see that the Web site is consistent from page to page and the site maintains a consistent look and feel. Notice that the buttons have plenty of eye appeal and you can tell at a glance where clicking them will take you.

Figure 1.4 *This page at The Exploratorium's Web site is consistent in layout with the parent site, but it has its own unique flair and feel.*

Mastering What's Online
Venture to the Exploratorium's home page at www.exploratorium.edu.

A Selective Color Palette

Donna Kossy's Kook's Museum is a beautifully designed Web site (Figure 1.5). In keeping with the carnival-like atmosphere of the site, Donna uses bright colors and quirky graphics. No matter where you go in the site, you know you're lost in the Kook's

Museum, because all the Web pages have a consistent look and feel. This Web site is an excellent example of how a selective color palette sets the right tone for a Web site.

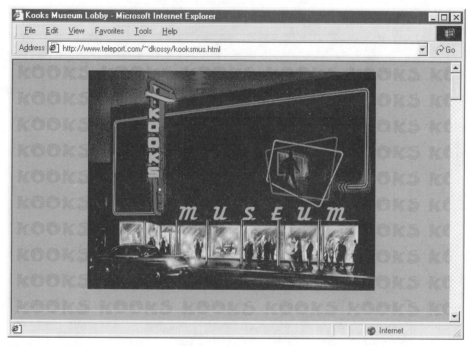

Figure 1.5 *The Kook's Museum is a fine example of the use of attractive colors on a Web site.*

Mastering What's Online
To visit the Kook's Museum, aim your Web browser at: www.teleport.com/~dkossy/newsoluprob.html.

Clean Columns

Addicted 2: Stuff (Figure 1.6) is a stylish and funny home page. The creators did not build the site for money, but it looks as good as or better than many big-budget commercial sites. The page is made up primarily of text. The columns are achieved through the use of tables, but you wouldn't necessarily know that because table borders have been turned off, a technique you'll be using a lot when you create Web pages. (Chapter 11 explains how to use tables to lay out a Web page.) Using tables for layouts is one of the best ways to create a cross-platform, cross-browser Web page that is stable and attractive.

Figure 1.6 *Borderless tables are a very convenient way to lay out a Web page.*

Fully Functional Frames

GroundZero, a Web design firm in New York City, uses *frames* quite wonderfully in its Web site (Figure 1.7). Frames are an HTML feature with which you can divide a browser window into smaller windows or frames.

When frames were introduced, everybody jumped on the frames bandwagon and crowded their Web pages with too many frames. Now that the novelty has worn off, however, frames are being used as navigational aids—and used well in most cases. Frames are used well on the GroundZero site both as a navigation aid and to show visitors the GroundZero portfolio. (Chapter 12 explains frames.)

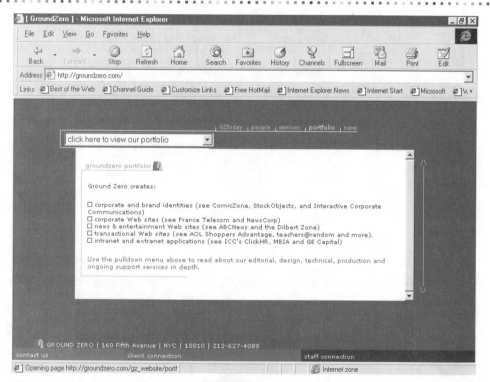

Figure 1.7 *Frames can be very useful as navigation links.*

An Effective Button-Style Navigation Bar

A *button bar* may well be the best way to give visitors to a Web site the means of going from page to page. The navigation bar shown in Figure 1.8 is from the IRS's daily newsletter, a surprisingly non-stodgy piece of publishing from everybody's favorite government agency.

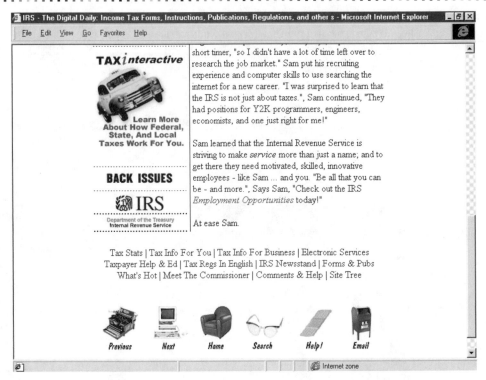

Figure 1.8 *The button bar at the bottom of the IRS's page is clearly clickable.*

You can use FrontPage's Navigation view to generate navigation bars automatically. See Chapter 15 for more information.

The sites you've just seen should inspire you when you design a Web site of your own. Web design isn't an easy task, contrary to some people's opinions. It challenges your technological know-how as well as your sense of aesthetics. We like to think of Web site design as an opportunity for personal growth! One of the greatest things about FrontPage 2002 is that it will make the growth process easier on you. FrontPage 2002 offers a variety of ways to be creative on your own, and, barring that, the program provides a toolkit for people who are not creatively inclined.

Visiting Web sites regularly is important. Your ideas about what makes a good and bad design will become more refined and you'll gain a clearer idea of what you want *your* site to be like!

Mastering What's Online

David Siegel is a master Web designer whose site is jam-packed with tips, information, examples, and links to other sites that you may find helpful in your Web-designing adventures. His home page, `www.dsiegel.com`, is itself an example of good design.

Up Next

Now that you have a sense of basic design and planning concepts, no doubt you're anxious to begin working with FrontPage itself. In Chapter 2, you'll do exactly that.

Get ready to explore FrontPage's interface and actually step through some procedures that will help you familiarize yourself with the way the software works.

Exploring
FrontPage 2002

FRONTPAGE

Chapter 2

This chapter introduces you to the workings of FrontPage—it gets straight to the business of creating Web sites. You discover how FrontPage can help you build Web sites and how to create a Web site on your own or with a template. You also explore the different views—the ways to do and examine your work. This chapter explains how to create Web pages, open a Web site you want to work on, delete a Web site, and quit FrontPage. Topics include:

- Understanding the big picture

- Starting FrontPage

- Creating a new Web site

- Getting familiar with the different views

- Adding new pages to a Web site

- Opening a Web site

- Deleting a Web site

- Exiting FrontPage

Web Pages, Web Sites, and HTML

The Web sometimes seems like a vast and confusing place, and publishing a Web site can seem like a daunting task. It helps to realize that the Web isn't really a "place" at all, but rather files stored on computers called *Web servers*, all of which are hooked together with phone lines and other types of network connections. When you surf the Web using a *Web browser* such as Netscape Navigator or Microsoft Internet Explorer, you merely access files stored on the Web servers.

The files themselves are called *Web pages*. The text, pictures, and other elements that you see on your computer screen as you explore the Web are stored on Web pages. A *Web site* is simply a collection of Web pages that are linked together and offer information about the same topic. The first step in creating a Web site is to create the Web pages. (Well, the first step is really to plan your Web site—ponder its look and feel and consider what you want it to communicate. Chapter 1 describes all of that.)

Underneath the text-and-picture pages you see on your computer screen when you surf the Internet is the skeletal system of every Web page: the *Hypertext Markup Language*, or *HTML*. HTML is computer code that consists of *tags*. The tags define how Web pages look. Web browsers interpret the tags so that you can see text, pictures, and what-all on a Web page. For example, one HTML tag (<B>) creates bold text; another HTML tag (<IMG>) inserts an image onto a page. When you view a Web page using a Web browser, the browser translates the HTML tags into attractive, clearly laid-out pages. Figure 2.1 shows the HTML tags that produce the Web page shown in Figure 2.2.

Next time you are surfing the Web, take a peek at the HTML tags that produce the Web page you are looking at. To see the tags, choose View ➜ Source in your browser.

HTML tags can be kind of scary. Not so long ago, Web page creation was reserved for individuals with a technical background who understood HTML tags. For that reason, many people shied away from learning HTML and relied on professionals to build Web pages. Fortunately, you no longer need to learn HTML in detail to create Web pages, because FrontPage can help you build a Web site even if you know nothing about HTML and don't care to learn it.

A working knowledge of HTML can be a great asset, especially when you are troubleshooting a Web page and you have to "get under the hood" and correct problems. At its most basic, HTML is not difficult to understand, but becoming fluent in HTML takes time. Appendix E of this book describes HTML tags.

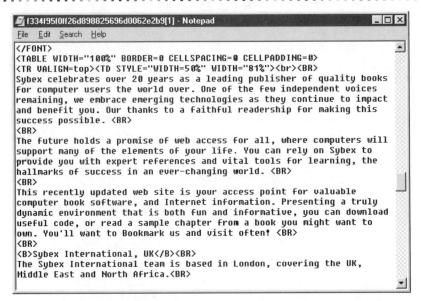

Figure 2.1 *Behind every Web page is the skeletal system of the Web: HTML.*

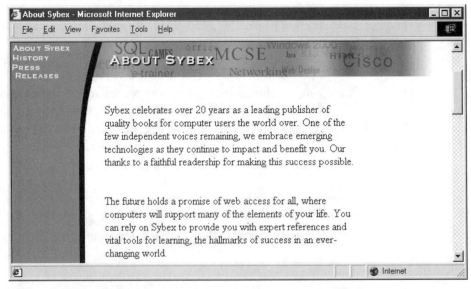

Figure 2.2 *The Web browser translates HTML tags into text and images.*

You can create a great Web site right now without learning a single HTML tag. You've got everything you need already—good concepts regarding design and an excellent tool to work with. You're ready to go to work! Soon, you'll have a complete Web site to call your very own.

Mastering What's Online

For a good HTML authoring reference, see www.htmlhelp.com.

What Is FrontPage?

So, there's the Web, which is full of Web sites, which are made up of Web pages, which are created using HTML. Where does FrontPage fit in? FrontPage is a *Web authoring* or *Web publishing* program. Web publishing programs put the power of Web site creation in everyone's hands—including those who don't want to or don't have the time to learn HTML.

In FrontPage, you create Web pages in much the same way as you create documents in a word processing program. The following illustration, for example, shows how similar FrontPage and Word really are. By using the FrontPage menus and toolbar buttons, you enter and format text, pictures, and other page elements in much the same way as you enter and format these items in Word.

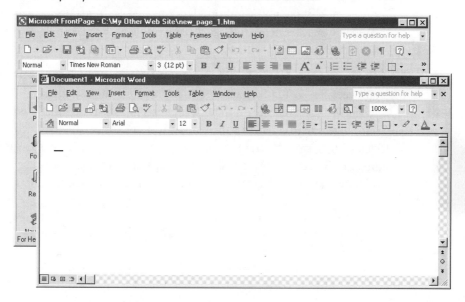

FrontPage generates the HTML tags in the background. You need never concern yourself with them. However, if you want to go into the HTML view and make changes, you can do that as well.

FrontPage Builds Web Sites Big and Small

You can use FrontPage to build many different kinds of Web sites:

A Personal Web Site   A popular type of public Internet site, the personal Web site is all about *you*. It can describe your interests, your friends, and your family, or offer hyperlinks to your favorite Web sites. Many Web-development professionals got their start by creating a personal Web site. The personal Web site is a chance to be creative. Being a user-friendly program, FrontPage is a good choice for this small but exciting type of Web site.

A Small Business Site   If you have a home-based or small business and your advertising budget is small, a Web site is a great way to spread the news about your product. FrontPage can help you create a Web site for a small business. By making use of the FrontPage templates, you can set up a professional storefront without having to spend months learning techniques and technologies.

A Corporate Web Site   Large companies want their Web sites to provide product information, customer support, consumer-relations information, and even online shopping. FrontPage is useful in a corporate setting because its powerful tracking features make it possible for more than one person to make changes and updates to Web site pages. And FrontPage is compatible with and can be integrated with many other software products.

A Corporate Intranet   A corporate *intranet* is an internal company network that employees can surf in the same way that they surf the Internet. A Web site on an intranet is like a Web site on the Internet except for the fact that it is available only to employees who can access the company network. Because an intranet is protected from curious Web surfers, internal company information such as sales figures, human resources communications, and department resources can be transmitted company-wide. FrontPage has tools for creating customized intranets.

FrontPage Is a Collaborative Software Program

You can use FrontPage in collaboration with these Microsoft applications:

Microsoft Office XP   FrontPage 2002 shares menus and toolbars with Office XP. Files that were created in Word, Excel, and PowerPoint can be made into Web pages. What's more, users of Office products can export their work from other Office programs to a FrontPage Web site.

Visual InterDev   Visual InterDev is a high-powered management and programming tool for database applications. High-end developers use Visual InterDev to manage sites. Chapter 29 explains how Visual InterDev and FrontPage can work together.

Microsoft Internet Explorer   Use the Internet Explorer Web browser to surf the Web and to preview your site before it goes live (you'll see how to preview Web pages in Chapter 3).

Mastering What's Online

You can find detailed information and news about the products discussed previously at the following Web sites:

- Microsoft Office: www.microsoft.com/office
- Visual InterDev: msdn.microsoft.com/vinterdev
- PhotoDraw: www.microsoft.com/office/photodraw
- Microsoft Internet Explorer: www.microsoft.com/ie

FrontPage Web-Building Basics

The best way to learn a new skill is to just do it! Because you already have a fair idea of how the Web works and you understand what a powerful tool FrontPage is, you are ready to jump in feet-first.

On the following pages, you will start FrontPage and create a new Web site. Along the way, you'll become familiar with the FrontPage interface and learn how to add new pages to a Web site.

If you haven't yet installed FrontPage on your computer, turn to the installation instructions in Appendix A.

Starting FrontPage

Starting FrontPage requires the same steps as starting most other Windows programs. To start FrontPage in one easy step, from the Windows Start menu select Programs ➜ Microsoft FrontPage. FrontPage starts (see Figure 2.3).

Figure 2.3 *FrontPage, ready to go*

Like most computer programs, FrontPage includes a main menu and toolbars for completing tasks. Where it differs, however, is the *Views bar* along the left side of the window. As "FrontPage Views" explains later in this chapter, you can click an icon in the Views bar to embark on tasks or discover something new about your Web site.

How to Get Help within FrontPage

For quick FrontPage assistance, turn to the FrontPage Help system. The Help system identifies unfamiliar menu items and toolbar buttons, and provides general overviews and step-by-step instructions for FrontPage operations. To access FrontPage Help, select Help ➜ Microsoft FrontPage Help. To get context-sensitive help, click the Help button available in many FrontPage dialog boxes, or press Shift+F11 and then click the item of interest.

Creating a Web Site with Templates

If you're not sure how to begin building a Web site or you need a complete Web site fast, FrontPage gives you plenty of help in the form of templates. A *template* is a ready-made Web site where all that is required of you is entering text where the placeholder text is and, if you wish, inserting new graphics where the placeholder graphics are now. The idea is for you to customize the ready-made pages with your own text and designs.

Sometimes creating a Web site from a template falls into the "more trouble than it's worth" department. Yes, the template takes care of much of the formatting. And the pages in the Web site are linked together very nicely. The problems start when you make the Web site your own. After you enter your own text and the graphics, the Web pages often need tweaking. You have to reformat pages and move text around. You end up having to do the same tasks that you would do if you created the Web site without a template.

FrontPage provides templates for many different purposes—a Customer Support Web site, a Personal Web site, and a Project Web site. There's also the One Page Web site for creating a Web site that comprises a single page and an Empty Web site for creating the structure of a Web site but nothing more.

You can create your own templates by either modifying an existing template or creating one from scratch. See Chapter 3.

As Chapter 1 explained, you can do yourself a favor by creating a new folder for each new Web site you create. Doing so makes organizing the different files in the Web site easier. After you create a new folder, follow these steps to create a Web site from a template:

1. Choose File ➜ New ➜ Page Or Web. As shown in Figure 2.4, the New Page Or Web task pane appears on the right side of the screen.

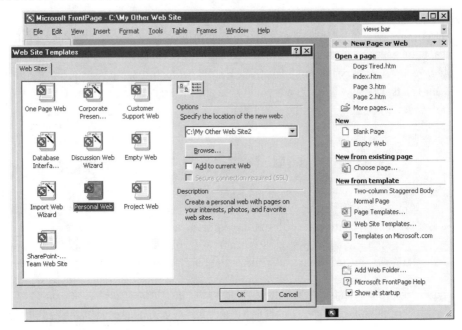

Figure 2.4 *Creating a Web site from a template*

2. Look under New From Template in the task pane, and click the Web Site Templates hyperlink. As shown in Figure 2.4, the Web Site Templates dialog box appears. It lists templates that are available to you. You also see one or two wizards, but we'll get to those in a bit. For the sake of an example, Personal Web is a good choice. Using that template, you can create a Web site to describe your personal interests.

3. Click to highlight the Personal Web icon.

4. On the right side of the dialog box, enter the folder where you want to store your new Web site. To do so, type the path to the folder (or click the Browse button, locate, and select the folder) in the New Web Location dialog box, and click the Open button. If you intend to store your Web site on a company intranet, get the URL for the network administrator and enter it in the text box.

5. Click OK. FrontPage does a bit of thinking, and in a moment or two your new Web site is ready.

When you create a new Web site, FrontPage generates a local URL for it (URL stands for Uniform Resource Locator, another name for a Web site address). The URL points to an address on your computer. The address is a stand-in for the Internet address to which you will eventually upload your Web site.

The name of the folder where you stored your Web site appears in the FrontPage title bar. But where are the Web pages? Follow these steps to view the home page of the Web site you just created:

1. Click the Folders button in the Views tab. As shown in Figure 2.5, you see the name of the folder where you stored your Web site in the Folder List. Notice that FrontPage created a handful of subfolders to store the many files that make up your Web site.

2. Double-click the file named `index.htm`. The home page of your new Web site loads into the main window.

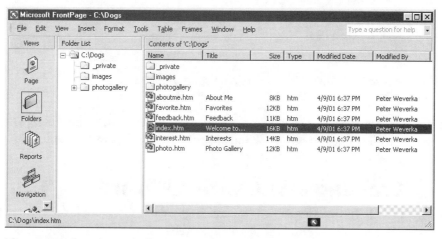

Figure 2.5 *Opening a Web site in Folders view*

Later in this chapter, "FrontPage Views" introduces you to the different ways of viewing Web sites. Each view is meant to help you with a different aspect of Web site creation, management, and maintenance. For now, just look at the Views bar in the FrontPage window to see the different views you can use—Page, Folders, Reports, Navigation, Hyperlinks, and Tasks. For example, select Folders to see the folders in your Web site (see Figure 2.6).

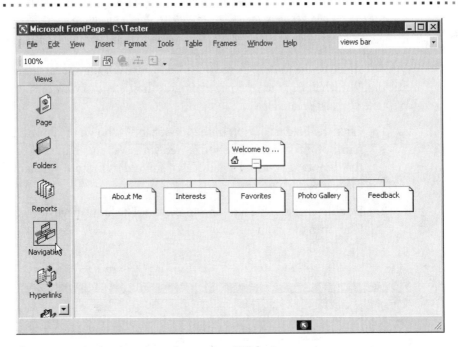

Figure 2.6 *Navigation view of a personal Web site*

You'll be doing a whole lot more with this down the road, but let's move on to learning other ways to view and create Web sites in FrontPage 2002.

Creating a Site with a Wizard

FrontPage provides wizards for creating its two most complex templates, the Corporate Presence Web site and the Discussion Web site. A *wizard* is a series of dialog boxes that ask you questions about something you want to create—in this case, a Web site. After you tell the wizard what you want, the wizard generates the Web site.

FrontPage offers these wizards:

- The Corporate Presence Web Wizard builds an entire corporate site by asking you what kind of information you want to present on the site.

- The Discussion Web Wizard creates a FrontPage *discussion group,* a Web site that hosts a public forum where visitors can post articles and respond to articles that others have posted.

- The Import Web Wizard is for gathering files and documents for a Web site.

- The Database Interface Wizard is for creating a Web site that enables visitors to query, sort, and add records to a database table.

Follow these steps to create a Web site with a wizard:

1. Choose File ➜ New ➜ Page Or Web. The New Page Or Web task pane opens.

2. Under New From Template, click the Web Site Templates hyperlink. The Web Site Templates dialog box appears (refer to Figure 2.4).

3. Choose the Corporate Presence Web Wizard and click OK. The first Wizard dialog box appears.

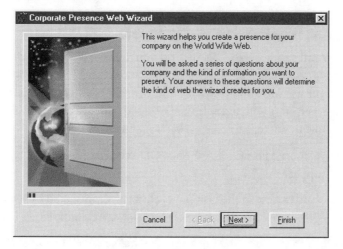

4. Read the introduction and click the Next button to advance to the next panel, where you can specify which pages you'd like to have included in your Web site. Customize these by removing or adding a check next to the page description. When you're ready, click Next.

5. You'll now be asked for a descriptive title for your Web site. Make it a sensible title—something that relates to the subject you're working on.

6. In each subsequent panel, read and follow the wizard's directions. To proceed to the next panel, click Next. To go back to a previous panel, click Back.

7. When you reach the final panel, the Next button appears grayed out. To finish creating the Web site, click the Finish button. The wizard uses the information you provided to generate the Web site.

When the Web site is complete, you can open and view it in Page view by clicking Folders in the Views bar and then clicking the index.htm file (refer to Figure 2.5). Now you can open the pages and start customizing.

Web sites created using FrontPage templates and wizards contain all sorts of unique FrontPage features. A few of these features—for example, keyword site searches and discussion groups—work only if the site is published on a Web server.

Creating an Empty Web Site

If you're not sure where to begin, or if you'd like to see examples of how typical Web sites are structured, FrontPage templates and wizards are the way to go. But if you know your way around FrontPage and you want to start from scratch, more power to you. You can start with a single blank Web site and take it from there.

Follow these steps to create a Web site from scratch:

1. Choose File ➜ New ➜ Page Or Web. The New Page Or Web task pane appears.

2. Under New in the task pane, click the Empty Web hyperlink. You see the Web Site Templates dialog box. The Empty Web template is highlighted.

3. In the Specify The Location Of The New Web text box, either type the path to the folder where you want to store your new Web site or click the Browse button and select the folder in the New Web Location dialog box.

4. Click OK.

The next step is to start adding the Web pages. See "Adding Pages to a Web Site" later in this chapter.

Importing an Existing Web Site into FrontPage

Suppose you created a Web site with another software program and now you want to do your Web work in FrontPage. It can be done. You can import the Web site into

FrontPage and thereby transform the site into a FrontPage Web site. To do the trick, you use the Import Web Wizard, which can import any Web site file that is stored on your computer, on a network that your computer is connected to, or on the World Wide Web itself.

When you import a Web site into FrontPage, the Web site is unchanged. Really, you copy the Web site into a new folder and place it under the auspices of FrontPage when you import a Web site.

Take note of where the Web site is located and follow these steps to import it:

1. Chose File ➜ Import. The Import dialog box appears.

2. Click the From Web button. You see the Import Web Wizard dialog box (see Figure 2.7). It asks where you want to import the Web pages from.

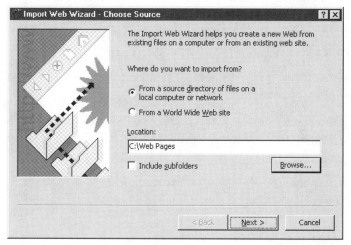

Figure 2.7 *Here you specify the location from which a Web site will be imported.*

3. Specify the location of the Web site you want to import. If the site is currently stored in a folder on your computer or local network, click the From A Source Directory Of Files On A Local Computer Or Network button. In the Location text box, type the path to that folder, or click the Browse button to select a folder from a list of folders on your computer and local network. To import files stored in the site's subfolders, click the Include Subfolders check box.

If the site is available on the World Wide Web, click the button labeled From A World Wide Web Site, and in the Location text box, type the site's URL.

4. Click Next. Which dialog box appears next depends on the location of the Web site files. If the site is stored on your computer or network, the Import Web Wizard – Edit File List dialog box appears. If the site is stored on the Web, the Import Web Wizard – Choose Download Amount dialog box appears.

5. In the Import Web Wizard – Edit File List dialog box, the Files list box lists all the Web site files contained in the location you specified. To exclude one or more files, press the Ctrl key while clicking the names of the file(s), and then click the Exclude button. To start over with a complete file list, click the Refresh button.

   or

   In the Import Web Wizard – Choose Download Amount dialog box, specify the download options you want the wizard to use. The dialog box enables you to control the number of levels (the successive depth of subfolders) to import and the total file size of the imported files. You can also choose to import only the site's Web pages and its image files.

6. In either dialog box, click Next. The Import Web Wizard – Finish dialog box appears.

7. Click the Finish button. The Import Web Wizard imports the files you selected into your Web site (this may take a moment, especially if you're importing a big Web site).

You can now use FrontPage to update and maintain your Web site. When you're ready to start working on your Web site, turn to Chapter 3.

Keep It Contained

For the Import Web Wizard to properly import a Web site, the site's files must be contained within a single main folder (it's okay if the main folder contains subfolders). If the site's pages are not contained in one folder, you need to import the pages by using the Import Web Wizard, and then import the rest of the pages individually (you'll see how in the section called "Importing Web Pages for Your Web Site" later in this chapter). Because the imported site's file system will no longer fit the site's original structure, importing a site in this manner risks creating *broken hyperlinks*. (*Hyperlinks* are bits of highlighted text or images in a Web page. You click these to jump to different locations.) You'll learn how hyperlinks work in Chapter 4, and how to detect and fix broken hyperlinks in Chapter 24.

FrontPage Views

Like other programs, FrontPage has a main menu and toolbars along the top of the screen for giving commands. And, also like most programs, you will find a status bar along the bottom of the screen that provides helpful information. Where FrontPage differs from other programs, however, is the Views bar. Use it to change views of the Web site you are working on. To change views, click an icon in the Views bar.

Each view presents a different type of information about the Web site you are working on and enables you to work with the site in a different way. This section looks at each view in detail.

You can also change views by choosing an option on the View menu.

Page View

Think of *Page view* as the "editor" view. In Page view, you see one page—the one you're working on (see Figure 2.8). You can make changes or adjustments to the items on a page in Page view.

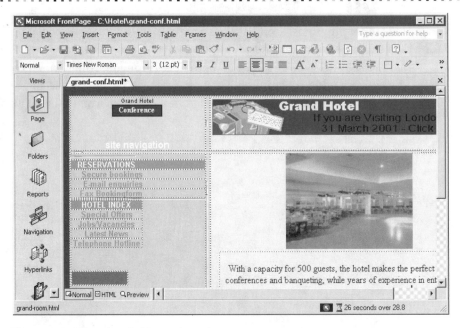

Figure 2.8 *Page view in Normal mode*

One of the most powerful aspects of Page view is that you can click a tab—Normal, HTML, or Preview—along the bottom of the screen to switch *modes*. Page view offers these modes:

Normal This is the standard mode, the one in which you enter text and graphics. The view shows roughly what the page will look like in a Web browser. Dotted lines show where page elements begin and end.

HTML In this mode, you can actually get to the heart of the matter: the HTML code. You can make changes directly to the code or see how the code has been altered by changes made in the visual editor. (See Figure 2.9.)

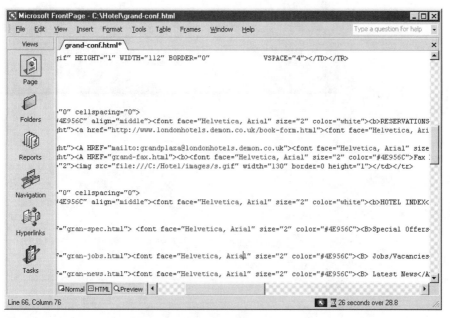

Figure 2.9 *FrontPage's Page view in HTML mode*

Preview   Preview mode is where you see what your page will look like after it is published on the Internet. Here, you see the final results of the page, with no code or editing marks. (See Figure 2.10.)

Page view is especially helpful because you can not only make visual alterations but can also work behind the scenes with the HTML code. And when you're done, you can check out the way the page will look in Preview mode. Page view is also where you'll spend most of your FrontPage time. Get well acquainted with this view.

Yet another way to see what your Web page will look like in a browser is to open it in a browser window. FrontPage offers a command for doing just that, the File ➜ Preview In Browser Command. Choose that command and your default browser will open and you'll see the Web page there.

Figure 2.10 *FrontPage's Page view in Preview mode*

Folders View

In *Folders view* (shown in Figure 2.11), the screen is split in two panes. The Folder List pane shows a hierarchical list of folders inside the Web site you are working on. The Contents pane shows a detailed list of pages and files in the folder that you selected in the Folder List pane.

The Folder List side of the window works much like Windows Explorer. Click the plus sign (+) next to a folder to see its subfolders. To collapse a folder and make its subfolders disappear, click a minus sign (−). Use Folders view to manage and rename files, create new folders, and move Web pages to different subfolders (you'll see how shortly).

When you change the name or location of a file, FrontPage automatically updates all hyperlinks to the file. Therefore, you don't have to worry about links becoming inoperative when you move files.

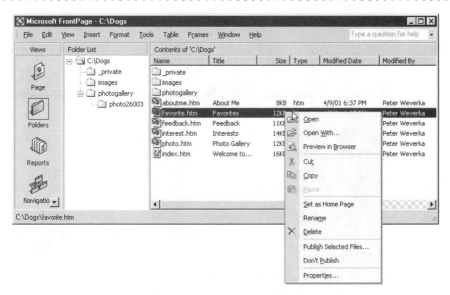

Figure 2.11 *Folders view is for managing the files in a Web site.*

Each FrontPage Web site is equipped with two standard folders: the _private folder and the images folder. The _private folder (note the underscore character before the word "private") is a good place to store pages you don't want other people to see—for example, in-progress work—because visitors to your Web site can't see or access it. And you can use the _private folder to shield Web pages from the FrontPage text-indexing component, the component by which visitors can search your Web site. (FrontPage components are prepackaged interactive elements you can add to your site without having to do any programming. Find out more about them in Chapter 15.)

Another way to keep a file in your Web site from actually being published on the Internet is to right-click it in Folders view and choose Don't Publish on the shortcut menu.

The images folder is the best place to store Web graphics. Keeping Web pages and graphic files in separate locations makes managing the elements of a Web site a little easier. Web graphics are a topic of Chapter 9.

Here is a rundown of the file management tasks you can do in Folders view:

Opening a file   Double-click the filename. The file opens in Page view.

Seeing the contents of a folder   Double-click the folder's name. Its contents appear—where else?—in the Contents pane of the window.

Renaming a file   In the Contents pane, right-click the file and select Rename on the shortcut menu. Then type a new name where the old name was and press Enter.

Creating a new folder   In the FrontPage menu, choose File ➜ New ➜ Folder. A new folder appears in both panes. Type a new folder name in the space provided and press Enter. You now have a new folder, ready to use.

Moving a page into a folder   Click and drag the page to the target folder (in either pane). The page moves to its new location. You can also right-click a page, choose Cut on the shortcut menu, right-click a folder, and choose Paste.

Sorting the file list in the Contents pane   Click one of the header labels at the top of the pane. For example, to sort the list alphabetically by name, click the Name label.

Deleting a file   Click the filename and press the Delete key. The Confirm Delete dialog box appears. Click Yes and your file is history.

View a file's properties   Right-click the filename and choose Properties from the shortcut menu. The Properties dialog box appears. From there, you can change the title of a Web page (on the General tab), enter a comment (on the Summary tab), and assign categories (on the Workgroup tab). Categories make finding a file easier. Comments can be read in Folders view.

Reports View

Switch to *Reports view* when you want to get statistics or learn more about your Web site. When you first switch to Reports view, you land on the Site Summary screen (see

Figure 2.12), a screen that presents hyperlinks that you can click to generate reports. Do one of the following to generate a report:

- Click a hyperlink on the Site Summary screen.

- Choose View ➔ Reports, select a submenu name, and choose a report on the submenu that appears.

- Click the Reports button, choose an option from the drop-down menu, and choose a report name from the submenu (refer to Figure 2.12).

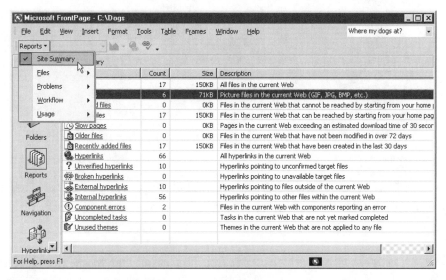

Figure 2.12 *Switch to Reports view to learn more about your Web site.*

The Description column on the Site Summary screen tells you what each report does. To return to the Site Summary screen, click the Reports button and choose Site Summary on the drop-down menu.

Navigation View

In *Navigation view* (Figure 2.13), you can see at a glance how visitors will find their way around your Web site. What's more, by building a *navigational structure* in Navigation view, you also create *navigation bars,* the rows of text hyperlinks or buttons that visitors click to move from Web page to Web page. Chapter 15 explains how to build a navigational structure and use navigation bars.

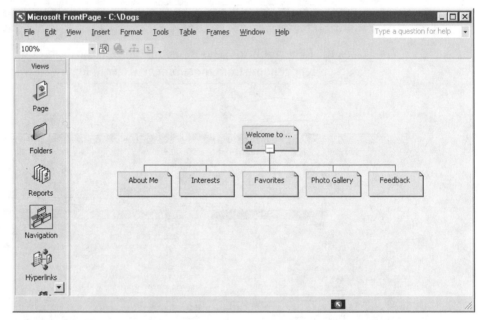

Figure 2.13 *Navigation view shows the structure of your Web site.*

If you're ever asked to create a site map for a client, you can use Navigation view to generate the map. Simply import the site into FrontPage using the Import Web Wizard and switch to Navigation view. You can print a site map when in Navigation view. To do so, choose File ➜ *Print.*

Hyperlinks View

In *Hyperlinks view* (shown in Figure 2.14), you can see which pages in your Web site a certain page is linked to. Being able to see hyperlinks is very convenient when you want to examine hyperlinks to see how the pages in your Web site are linked together.

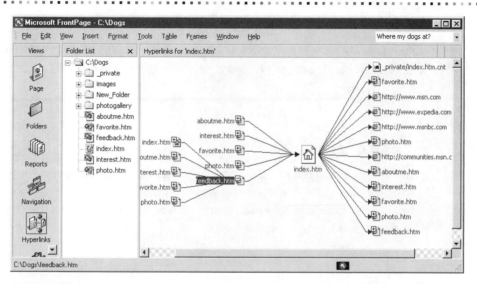

Figure 2.14 *In Hyperlinks view, you can see very clearly how pages are linked.*

To choose which Web page to examine in Hyperlinks view, start by choosing View ➜ Folder List to display the Folder List pane (see Figure 2.14). From there, select the Web page whose hyperlinks you want to examine.

A fast way to open the Folder List pane is to click the Toggle Pane button on the Standard toolbar. If the Navigation pane, not the Folder List pane, appears, open the drop-down menu on the Toggle Pane button and choose Folder List.

The left side of the window shows links to the page; the right side shows links from the page to other pages in your Web site. Pages with hyperlinks show a plus sign (+). By clicking the plus sign, you can branch out and examine more links.

Right-click the screen in Hyperlinks view and choose options from the shortcut menu to examine links in different ways:

See page titles instead of filenames Choose Show Page Titles on the shortcut menu. Sometimes identifying pages by title is easier than identifying them by filename.

See links to graphics as well as other pages Choose Hyperlinks To Pictures on the shortcut menu.

Examine hyperlinks with the same target page   Choose Repeated Hyperlinks to find out when hyperlinks go to the same Web site.

If you came to Hyperlinks view to look for broken hyperlinks, you came to the wrong place. Switch to Reports view and choose View ➔ Reports ➔ Problems ➔ Broken Hyperlinks to generate a Broken Hyperlinks report.

Tasks View

In *Tasks view*, you can maintain a to-do list of items that need doing for your Web site to be complete. Tasks view is especially useful when more than one person is working on a Web site, because the entire team can maintain the list. Chapter 7 describes Tasks view and how to enter tasks on the list.

Tasks						
Status	Task	Assigned To	Prio...	Associated ...	Modified Date	Description
● Not Started	Hurry Up	Peter Wev...	High		4/10/01 8:49:3...	The Cats page has to be done by Th...
● Completed	Investigate th...	Roger Ra...	Low		4/10/01 8:51:0...	Case links need investigating

Adding Pages to a Web Site

After you create a FrontPage Web site (especially if it is only one page long), the next step is to start adding more Web pages. To create a new page, you can rely on a template or simply attach a blank page to your Web site. For that matter, you can import a Web page from another Web site. Keep reading.

Creating a Blank Web Page

Create a new blank page when you want to start from scratch and do all the layout work yourself. Follow these steps to attach a blank Web page to your template:

1. Switch to Folders view. To do so, click the Folders button in the Views pane.

2. Click the New Page button or press Ctrl+N. A placeholder filename is high-lighted on the Contents tab in Folders view. The filename is "new_page_1,"

unless you are starting from a blank Web site. In that case, the placeholder file is called "index."

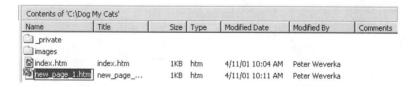

3. Type a filename for your new page. The filename should be short, descriptive, easy to remember, and have the `.htm` or `.html` extension.

4. Press Enter.

After you finish creating a new Web page, be sure to select it, choose File ➜ *Properties, and enter a title for the page on the General tab of the Properties dialog box. When you view a Web page in a browser, the page's title appears on the title bar at the top of the screen. Unless you enter a title, people who visit the Web page you created will see its filename, not a title, in the title bar of their browser windows.*

Creating a Web Page from a Template

By creating a Web page from a template, you save yourself from doing some of the layout work. You get a Web page that was laid out and developed by a professional. All you have to do is enter your own text and graphics where the placeholder text and graphics are on the page.

Follow these steps to create a new Web page from a template:

1. Choose File ➜ New ➜ Page Or Web. The New Page Or Web task pane opens.

2. Under New From Template, click the Page Templates hyperlink. The Page Templates dialog box appears (see Figure 2.15).

3. Select a page. The Preview box shows roughly what each page looks like.

4. Click OK.

Pages created with a template come with placeholder text and, in some cases, sample graphics to help you get an idea what a completed page is supposed to look like. Replace the generic text with your own words of wisdom and make the other layout changes as you see fit.

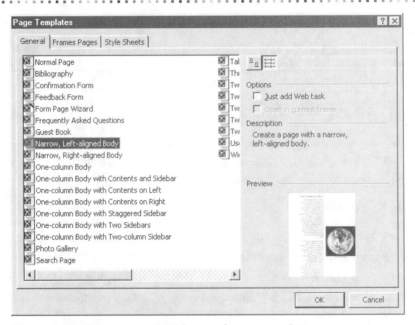

Figure 2.15 *Creating a new Web page from a template*

The dotted gridlines that surround the text in most templates are the boundaries of *invisible tables* (tables without any border specifications). Invisible tables form the framework in which the table is laid out. Chapter 11 explains how to work with tables.

Importing Web Pages for Your Web Site

Import a Web page if you've already created (or have access to) a finished Web page and you want to attach it to the Web site you are working on. For that matter, you can import more than one page at a time or import an entire folder. Pages you import can be stored on your computer, a local network, or the World Wide Web.

You can actually import any type of file from a Web site into your FrontPage Web site—not just HTML files, but also graphics files, sound files, text files, and so on. Earlier in this chapter, "Importing an Existing Web Site into FrontPage" explained how to import a Web site you created with another software program.

Follow these steps to import a Web page into your Web site:

1. Choose File ➜ Import. You see the Import dialog box.

2. To import a file or files that are stored on your computer or local network, click the Add File button. The Add File To Import List dialog box appears.

    or

    To import an entire folder that's stored on your computer or local network, click the Add Folder button. The File Open dialog box appears.

    or

    To import a file or folder that is currently located on the World Wide Web, click the From Web button. The Import Web Wizard – Choose Source dialog box appears. (For help with using the Import Web Wizard, refer to "Importing an Existing Web Site into FrontPage" earlier in this chapter.)

3. If you are importing files, select the files you want to import in the Add File To Import List dialog box and click the Open button. Back in the Import dialog box, the files you selected appear in the Import list.

    or

    If you are importing a folder, select the folder you want to import and click the Open button. Back in the Import dialog box, files in the folder you selected appear in the File list.

In the File list, the local URL of each file you want to import appears in the URL column. To change where FrontPage stores a file, select the file and click the Modify button. In the Edit URL dialog box, enter a new location for the file. For example, if you are importing an image named `face.gif` *and you want the image to be stored in the images folder, type* **`images/face.gif`** *in the text box. Click OK to close the dialog box. The new URL appears in the Import list.*

4. In the Import dialog box, click OK. FrontPage imports the file(s) you chose. When the import process is finished, the dialog box closes.

· · · · · · · · · · · · · · · · · ! ·

Fixing Imported Files

It goes without saying that importing a Web page into the Web site you are working on saves work. But, sad to say, not all Web pages land flawlessly in FrontPage after you import them. FrontPage is very picky about HTML. For your Web page to work properly, certain HTML tags have to be present. If you import a Web page, switch to Page view, and discover that the page isn't displaying properly (if you see a blank page, for example, when you know there is supposed to be information on it), investigate the page's HTML source code. To do so, click the HTML tab at the bottom of the Page view window and do the following:

- Verify that the first and last tags of the file are, respectively, <HTML> and </HTML>.
- Verify that the <TITLE> tag is between the <HEAD> and </HEAD> tags.
- Verify that the body of the page is between the <BODY> and </BODY> tags.

If you notice that one of these tags is missing or out of place, go ahead and make corrections. Then switch back to the Page view and see if that fixes the problem. Chapter 4 describes how to read a page whose HTML codes are showing.

Opening a FrontPage Web Site You Created

When you start FrontPage, the program opens the Web site that was open when you last closed the program. Follow these steps, if need be, to open a Web site you created:

1. From the FrontPage menu bar, select File → Open Web. The Open Web dialog box appears. Folders where Web sites are kept are marked with a circle.

2. Locate and select the folder where you keep the Web site you want to open.

3. Click the Open button.

The fastest way to open a Web site is to choose File ➜ *Recent Webs, and then, on the submenu, select a Web site. The submenu lists the last four Web sites you worked on. You will find the same list of Web sites at the top of the New Page Or Web task pane.*

Deleting a Web Site

Suppose you need to delete a Web site. It can be done, but before you do it, remember that a Web site can't be recovered after you delete it. You can't visit the Recycle Bin and resuscitate it, for example. If the Web site you want to delete is worth anything whatsoever, make a backup copy before you delete it.

Follow these steps to delete a Web site you created in FrontPage:

1. Open the condemned Web site and switch to Folders view.

2. Find the topmost folder, right-click it, and choose Delete on the shortcut menu. You see the Confirm Delete dialog box.

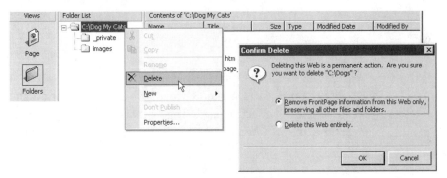

3. Choose an option button and click OK:

Remove FrontPage Information From This Web Only   Deletes the Web site, but preserves the files. In other words, the Web site as an entity is gone, but the graphics and Web pages with which it was made remain on your computer.

Delete This Web Entirely   Removes all files in the Web site from your hard disk.

After you delete a Web site, it is gone for good. FrontPage does not include an Undelete or Undo command in case you change your mind. If you nix a Web site by mistake, you'll just have to start over.

Quitting FrontPage

More than one Web site can be open at the same time. When more than one is open, each has a button on the Taskbar. Click a Taskbar button to switch from one Web site to another. To close a Web site, either click its Close button (the X in the upper-right corner of the FrontPage window) or choose File ➜ Close Web.

Follow these steps to close FrontPage and call it a day:

1. Choose File ➜ Exit or press Alt+F4.

2. If you didn't save your work before giving the Exit command, a dialog box asks whether to save it. Click Yes or No.

As mentioned earlier, the last Web site you worked on appears onscreen when you start FrontPage, but if you prefer not to see the last one you worked on, choose Tools ➜ Options, select the General tab in the Options dialog box, and uncheck the Open Last Web Automatically When FrontPage Starts check box.

Up Next

With all this interface exploration done and understood, you're ready to move on and actually edit pages. In Chapter 3, you discover how to work with Page view in order to create simple but effective pages. Page view is where you'll spend most of your FrontPage time, at least when it comes to adding and modifying page elements.

Working in Page View

FRONTPAGE

Chapter 3

hapter 2 took you on a tour of the FrontPage interface and showed you how to create a Web site. You looked briefly at Page view. In this chapter, you look more deeply into Page view, the central command post for almost all FrontPage 2002 tasks. Think of Page view as a program within a program. In Page view, you concentrate on the different pages that make up the site. Page view is where you enter and format text, create hyperlinks, insert pictures, and work with all the other elements that go into a Web page.

The majority of your FrontPage time is spent in Page view. Sometimes, however, you need to open a Web page that's *not* part of a Web site you are currently working on. That's okay, too. FrontPage can accommodate a number of scenarios, as you'll soon see. Topics include:

- Getting familiar with Page view

- Getting started

- Opening a Web page

- Setting page properties

- Using the text-editing tools

- Saving your work

- Printing a Web page

Opening the Web Page You Want to Work On

After FrontPage is up and running, the next step is to open the Web page you want to work on. FrontPage offers a number of different ways to open a Web page. With each of these techniques, the Web page opens in Page view (see Figure 3.1):

- Click Folders, Navigation, or Hyperlinks in the Views bar to switch to Folders, Navigation, or Hyperlinks view. Then double-click the icon for the page you want to open.

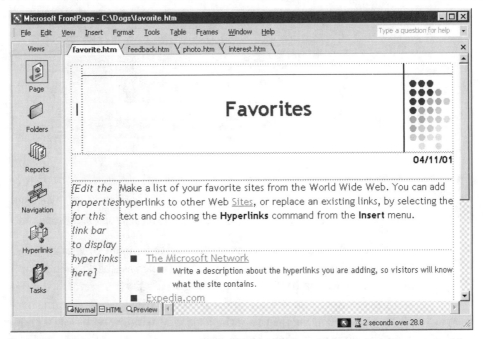

Figure 3.1 *Use Page view to edit and format Web pages. This example was created from the Personal Web template.*

- Choose File → Recent Files and select a Web page on the submenu. The last eight files you worked with appear on the submenu.

- Choose File ➜ Open (or Ctrl+O). Then, in the Open File dialog box, locate the Web page that you want to open and either double-click it or select it and then click the Open button. Go this route if you want to open a Web page that is on a network.

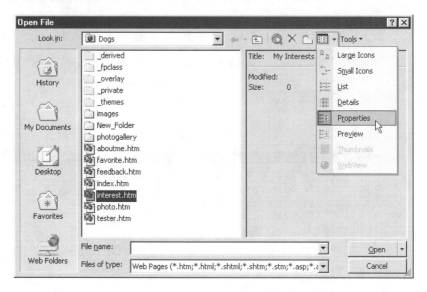

 Sometimes identifying a Web page by its name is difficult in the Open File dialog box, but you can find out a page's title in the dialog box. To do so, open the drop-down menu on the View button and choose Properties. The title of the page you selected appears on the right side of the dialog box.

If the Web page you open was created with a template or wizard, it will include place-holder text, and possibly a few design elements such as a background graphic, a page banner, and a navigation bar. If you're building a Web site from scratch, the page is empty.

You can open and work on more than one Web page at the same time. FrontPage places a new tab along the top of the Page view window each time you open a new page. To switch from page to page, either click a tab or open the Window menu and choose a different page.

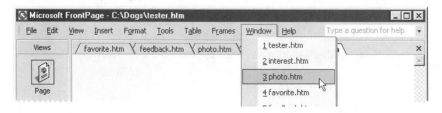

Converting Other Documents into Web Pages

FrontPage can open files in several different formats, and, in so doing, convert copies of those files into Web pages. Being able to convert files this way makes transforming files you've already created much, much easier.

FrontPage can convert the following document formats into Web pages:

- Microsoft Word documents
- Microsoft Works documents
- WordPerfect documents
- Microsoft Excel and Lotus 1-2-3 spreadsheets
- Rich Text Format (.rtf) files
- Text (ASCII) files

Chapter 20 explains how to integrate Office files into a Web site.

Introducing the Web Page Toolbars

Take a look at the FrontPage screen. You are likely to recognize a few buttons and tools, especially if you're a user of a Microsoft Office program. In Page view, FrontPage works very much like Microsoft Word, as far as entering and formatting text goes.

To hide or display a toolbar, do either of the following:

- Choose View ➜ Toolbars and then select the name of the toolbar you want to hide or display on the submenu.

- Right-click any toolbar (or the menu bar) and choose the name of the toolbar you want to hide or display.

Here's a quick rundown of the toolbars that matter when you are in Page view and you are entering text or formatting a Web page:

Standard toolbar   This toolbar offers buttons for standard tasks, including creating, opening, saving, and printing pages, in addition to tasks specific to Web publishing, such as creating hyperlinks and inserting images.

Formatting toolbar   This toolbar offers buttons and drop-down lists for common text-formatting tasks. Chapter 4 explains many of the buttons on this toolbar.

DHTML Effects toolbar   This toolbar allows you to add special effects such as *mouseovers* to your page. Chapter 15 explains special effects.

Pictures toolbar   This toolbar helps you control how images appear in your Web pages. It also enables you to transform images into image maps (images that contain several clickable hotspots). Chapter 9 explains graphics.

Tables toolbar   The buttons on this toolbar help you create and lay out tables. On Web pages, tables serve double duty. Besides being a means of presenting data, they are useful for laying out Web pages. Chapter 11 describes tables.

Understanding Properties

Each Web page you create or open contains general settings that govern how the page works and, in some cases, how it looks. FrontPage refers to these settings as *properties*. Properties are controlled by way of the Page Properties dialog box (see Figure 3.2).

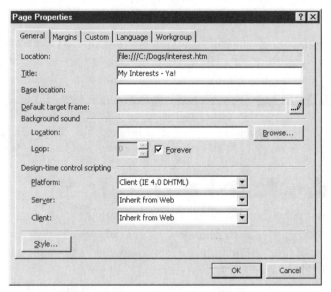

Figure 3.2 *The Page Properties dialog box lets you control general page settings.*

To access the Properties dialog box, choose File ➜ Properties or right-click an empty part of a Web page and choose Page Properties on the shortcut menu. The Page Properties dialog box includes four tabs, each of which controls a different set of properties. Most of the properties are addressed in upcoming chapters, but here is a brief overview of the tabs:

The General tab   Provides general information about the page, including the page's URL and title, which you can change by entering a new title in the Title text box. You can also set the page's default target frame, the one that is assigned to the page by default, or specify a background sound (adding background sound is covered in Chapter 10). Other features include setting scripting controls.

The Margins tab   Offers options for changing the margins of the Web page.

The Custom tab   Controls the META tags in the page, the tags that describe the Web page. Often META tags include keywords to help search engines index the page and Web surfers find it. For more information about META tags, turn to Chapter 24.

The Language tab   Determines which character will appear when the page is viewed in a Web browser. Selecting character sets for languages is covered in Chapter 24.

The Workgroup tab   Helps you set up the Web page as part of a workgroup. You can name the workgroup yourself or select from a list of pre-specified groups. Each group can be assigned to an individual by name, who is responsible for the group. What's more, you can set the status of each page. In this case, "status" refers to the development stage of a page. For example, if the page is fully coded, the next step in the creation process might be to have it copyedited. You can set this as the status.

Using the Text-Editing Tools

Graphics, multimedia, and interactive effects tend to grab the spotlight, but text is what keeps the Web moving forward. In Page view, FrontPage is essentially a text editor. Page view offers all sorts of tools for manipulating text and making it do precisely what you want it to do.

Like its Microsoft Office teammates, FrontPage has powerful text-editing features. You can cut and paste, drag and drop text, find and replace, spell-check a Web site, and even call upon a thesaurus to help in your writing. The following pages examine the text-editing tools.

Moving and Copying Text

Because so much of Web publishing involves plain old writing and document design, you'll surely want to move and copy text here and there as you build Web pages. Front-Page takes advantage of two Windows operations that you probably already know and love: *copying or cutting and pasting* and *dragging and dropping*.

When you copy or cut and paste, you place the text you copied or cut on the *Clipboard*. Use the Clipboard method of cutting or copying text when you want to copy or move text long distances or to different Web pages. The Clipboard can hold as many as 24 items—items you cut or copied from FrontPage or another Office program.

Follow these steps to move or copy text with the Clipboard:

1. Select the text you want to move or copy. To do so, click and drag over it with the mouse.

2. Move or copy the text to the Clipboard:

   Moving   Choose Edit ➔ Cut, press Ctrl+X, click the Cut button on the Standard toolbar, or right-click the text and Cut on the shortcut menu. The text is removed from the Web page.

Copying Choose Edit ➜ Copy, press Ctrl+C, click the Copy button, or right-click and choose Copy.

3. Click where you want to move or copy the text.

4. Paste the text from the Clipboard:

Paste text you just cut or copied Choose Edit ➜ Paste, press Ctrl+V, click the Paste button on the Standard toolbar, or right-click and choose Paste.

Paste text you cut or copied earlier Display the Clipboard task pane (see Figure 3.3). To do so, choose Edit ➜ Office Clipboard or press Ctrl+C twice. Then locate the text or other item you want to move or copy and click it in the Clipboard task pane.

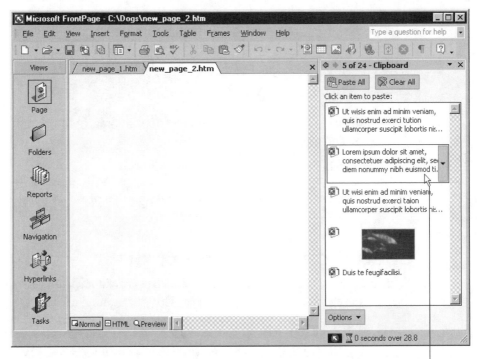

Click an item in the Clipboard task pane to paste it.

Figure 3.3 *Pasting an item from the Clipboard on a Web page*

After you copy or move text, you see the Paste Options button. This button and its drop-down menu are designed to help you format text that you moved or copied. Text keeps its formatting when it is cut or copied, but you can click the Paste Options button and choose an option on the drop-down menu to format the text a different way:

Keep Source Formatting   The text retains its formatting (what normally occurs if you don't choose an option from the drop-down menu).

Keep Text Only   The text is stripped of its formatting. It adopts the formatting of surrounding text.

The other way to move or copy text is to drag and drop it by following these steps:

1. In Page view, highlight the text to be copied or moved.

2. Copy or move the text:

    Move it   Drag the text to a new location. To drag, hold down the mouse button and drag the mouse across the screen.

    Copy it   Hold down the Ctrl key as you drag.

 You can cut, copy, and paste (or drag and drop) any Web page element, including images and tables.

Checking for Spelling Errors

To ensure that your site looks professional, always check for spelling errors. The spell-checker is so easy to use, you have no excuse for not running it.

 In Page view, the spell-checker examines a single page—the one that appears onscreen. If you want to spell-check your entire Web site, switch to any view besides Page view and choose Tools → Spelling (or press F7). Then, in the Spelling dialog box, select the Entire Web option button and click Start.

Follow these steps to check for spelling errors:

1. Choose Tools ➔ Spelling, or press F7. You'll see the Spelling dialog box. The first instance of a misspelled word or a word that is not in the spelling dictionary appears in the Not In Dictionary text box (see Figure 3.4).

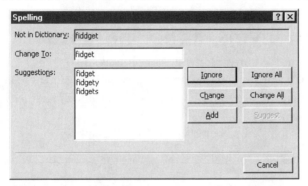

Figure 3.4 *The Spelling dialog box tells you what's wrong and how to fix it.*

2. FrontPage suggests a correct spelling in the Change To text box and lists other close approximations in the Suggestions list box. To accept the spelling suggestion, click the Change button. To change all instances of the misspelled word at once, click the Change All button.

    or

    To ignore the supposedly misspelled word and move along, click the Ignore button. To ignore all instances of the same word, click the Ignore All button.

    or

    To add the word to the dictionary so FrontPage won't hassle you about it in the future, click the Add button.

3. After you click one of the buttons, the next misspelled or unrecognized word appears in the Not In Dictionary text box. Repeat step 2 until the spell check is complete.

4. Click OK to close the dialog box.

Running the smell-checker is no substitute for carefully proofreading your Web pages. The spell-checker doesn't really catch misspellings—it catches words that are not in its dictionary. If you write, "Nero diddled while Rome burned," the spell-checker will not catch the error, because, although Nero fiddled, diddled is also a legitimate word in the spell-checker's dictionary. The moral: Don't expect the spell-checker to catch all your smelling errors.

Finding Synonyms in the Thesaurus

Use the thesaurus to find synonyms for words or phrases and thereby improve your writing. A *synonym* is a word whose meaning is the same as or similar to another word. Use the thesaurus when you need a fresh word but can't think of another way to express a thought or concept.

Follow these steps to fish for a better word in the thesaurus:

1. Click inside the word or highlight the phrase for which you need a synonym.

2. Choose Tools ➜ Thesaurus (or press Shift+F7). The Thesaurus dialog box appears with the word or phrase you selected in the Looked Up text box. Different meanings for the word or phrase appear in the Meanings list box. FrontPage suggests the closest synonym and lists alternatives in the accompanying list box.

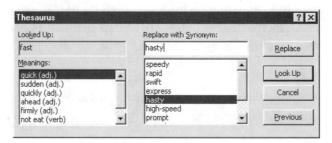

3. If the meaning you want is not already selected in the Meanings list box, click a different word. You get a new set of synonyms in the list box to the right.

4. If the synonym you want to use doesn't appear in the Replace With Synonym text box, click the synonym you want in the accompanying list box, and then click the Replace button. The Thesaurus dialog box closes, and the highlighted word or phrase in your page is replaced with the synonym you chose.

Finding Text

When you build your Web site, you occasionally lose track of a word or phrase and have to find it. For that matter, you sometimes have to find and replace a word or phrase. Maybe you spelled a company's name incorrectly or misspelled the name of a city. The Find command makes finding text easy, and if you decide to replace what you have found, you can do that as well.

If you happen to know which Web page the missing text is on, open the Web page and switch to Page view. To search a select few Web pages, switch to Folders view and select the Web pages you want to search. Follow these steps to find a missing text or phrase:

1. Starting in any view, choose Edit ➜ Find (or press Ctrl+F). The Find And Replace dialog box appears (see Figure 3.5).

2. In the Find What text box, type the character, word, or phrase you want to find. If you searched for a phrase since you last opened FrontPage and you want to search for it again, open the Find What drop-down menu and select the word or phrase.

3. Select a Find Where option. Choose All Pages to search all the pages in your Web site; Selected Pages to search pages you selected in Folders view; or Current Page if you are in Page view and you want to search the page that is onscreen.

4. Choose among these options to help narrow your search:

    Match Case   Searches for words with upper- and lowercase letters that match exactly the words you entered in the Find What text box.

    Find Whole Words Only   Normally, a search for "rip" finds that word as well as "ripple" and "trip," for example. Select this option and you only get "rip."

    Find In HTML   Select this option to search for HTML codes.

5. Click the Find Next button (if you're searching a single page) or the Find In Web button (if you're searching more than one page or the entire Web site).

Double-click to go to the page.

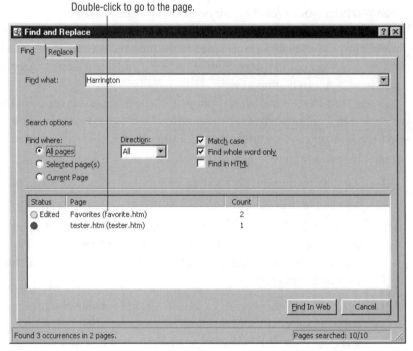

Figure 3.5 *Searching an entire Web site for a word, phrase, or HTML code*

If you're searching a page, the cursor jumps to and highlights the first instance of the thing you are looking for. You can click the Find Next button to continue your search.

If you're searching a handful of pages or all the pages in your Web site, the names of pages where the thing you are searching for can be found appears in a list at the bottom of the dialog box. Double-click a page to open it to the word or phrase you are looking for.

Suppose you want to replace the text you have found? Keep reading.

Replacing Text

Replacing text works like finding text, the only difference being that FrontPage can replace the text with a word or phrase of your choice. Follow these steps to find and replace text:

1. Choose Edit ➜ Replace (or press Ctrl+H). The Replace tab of the Find And Replace dialog box appears.

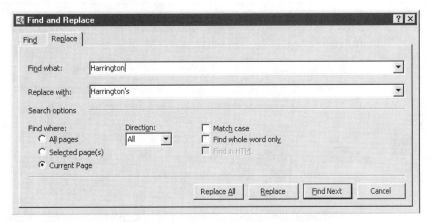

2. Enter and find the word or phrase that you want to replace (the previous section in this chapter explains how).

3. In the Replace With text box, enter the text you want to replace the found text.

4. Click the Find Next button (if you're searching a single page) or the Find In Web button (if you're searching more than one page).

5. To replace the text, click the Replace button. Voilà! The highlighted text is instantly replaced with the text you specified.

To replace all instances of the text in one step, click the Replace All button. If you make a mistake, you can undo the replace by selecting Edit ➜ Undo or using the key combination Ctrl+Z to undo all instances of the changed items.

Saving Your Web Pages

Saving your work is, of course, the most important part of any computer project. After all, you want to preserve your creative efforts, right? Save your work often and you'll be glad you did, if and when your computer goes down with a "slipped disk."

Each Web page is a file unto itself and must be saved from time to time. When you click the Save button, you save the Web page you are working on, not all the Web pages that are open. How you save a Web page depends on how the page was originally created or opened. Here are instructions for saving Web pages:

Saving a Web page for the first time   Click the Save button. The Save As dialog box appears. If necessary, go to and select the folder where you want to save your Web page. Then enter a name in the File Name text box and click the Save button.

 When you save a Web page for the first time, be sure to click the Change Title button and enter a title for your Web page in the Set Page Title dialog box. The title you enter will appear in the title bar of visitors' browser windows when they open the Web page.

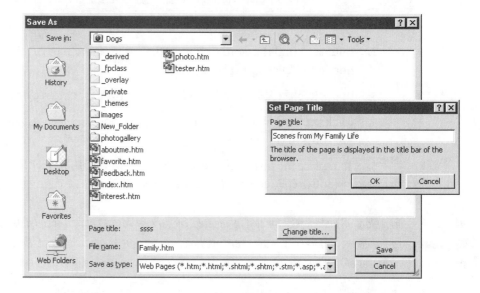

Saving a Web page in the Web site you are working on   Click the Save button (or press Ctrl+S). That's all there is to it.

Saving a Web page to a different Web site   Choose File ➜ Save As. In the Save As dialog box, go to the Web site where you want to save the file, select a folder, and click the Save button.

Saving a Page that Includes Embedded Files

When you insert a graphic or multimedia file into a Web page and then save the page, you see the Save Embedded Files dialog box. You see the dialog box because FrontPage wants to know where to save the file. When you are done negotiating the Save Embedded Files dialog box, a reference to the graphic or multimedia file is placed in your Web page so that the file's contents can be displayed on the Web page in Web browsers.

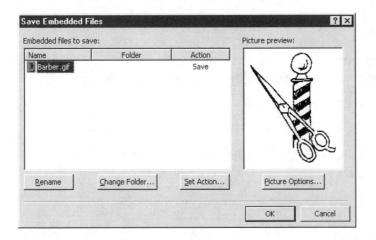

The Embedded Files To Save area of the dialog box lists each embedded file in the Web page you are saving. The Folder column lists the location where each file will be saved (the same location as the Web page you are saving unless you choose a different folder), and the Action column lists the action about to be taken on each file. (If the Folder column is blank, the file is saved in the topmost folder of your Web site.)

You can do a few things using this dialog box:

- To rename a file, select it and click the Rename button. The filename is highlighted. Type a new filename and press Enter.

- To save the file in a folder apart from the topmost folder in the Web site, click the Change Folder button, choose a new folder in the Change Folder dialog box, and click OK.

- To control how the file is saved, click the Set Action button. The Set Action dialog box appears. In this dialog box, you can save the file (the default setting); not save the file, but maintain the reference in the Web page; or, if you're saving an edited version of the embedded file, overwrite the current version of the file. Choose an option by clicking the appropriate option button and then click OK. (These options will make more sense when you learn how to use graphic and multimedia files, as discussed in Chapter 9 and Chapter 10.)

Saving a Web Page as a Template

As you know if you ever created a Web page from a template, a template is a pre-designed page that you can use as the starting point for creating Web pages. Suppose you take the trouble to design a Web page you particularly like. Maybe the page has a company logo that you would like to have appear on other Web pages. To make your design available when you create Web pages in the future, you can save your Web page as a template.

Templates you create yourself appear in the Page Templates dialog box, the dialog box that you see when you create a Web page from a template. You can choose your own template as well as one of the templates that FrontPage provides.

Follow these steps to save a Web page you designed as a template:

1. Open the Web page.

2. Choose File ➜ Save As. The Save As dialog box appears.

3. Open the Save As Type drop-down menu and select FrontPage Template (*.tem).

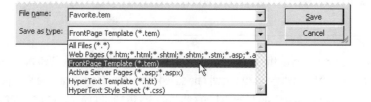

4. Click the Save button. You see the Save As Template dialog box.

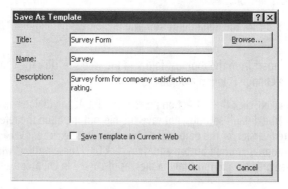

5. In the Title text box, type a descriptive name for the template. The name you type will appear in the Templates dialog box, so enter a descriptive name.

6. In the Name text box, enter a short, one-word name (the filename is constructed out of the word you choose).

7. In the Description text box, briefly describe the template's layout or function. This will remind you and other Web team members how to use the template.

8. Click OK.

If the page contains images, the Save Embedded Files dialog box appears. Read the sidebar "Saving a Page that Includes Embedded Files" for information on how to use the options in this dialog box. Or, if the page does not contain images, FrontPage simply saves the page as a template.

9. Change the template as necessary, and then click the Save button on the toolbar to save the changes. Or, from the menu bar, select File ➜ Close to close the newly saved template.

The next time you create a new page based on a template, the name of your custom template will be listed in the Page Templates dialog box.

FrontPage templates you create yourself are kept in the `C:\Windows\Application Data\Microsoft\FrontPage\Pages` *folder. If you need to delete your template, go there and delete it.*

Previewing a Page

In Page view, the page you are currently working on looks much as it will look when a visitor to your Web site sees it in his or her Web browser. But to see exactly what a Web page will look like after you publish it on the Web, you must *preview* your page.

You can preview your page by using the Preview tab or by launching it in a browser. Better read on.

Viewing a Page with the Preview Tab

As long as Microsoft Internet Explorer (version 3 or later) is installed on your computer, a Preview tab appears in the lower-left corner of the screen when you are in Page view. Click this tab and you can see how the page you are staring at will look when it is viewed with Internet Explorer. The Preview tab is very handy for quick back-and-forth previewing.

Viewing a Page with a Web Browser

The Preview tab is nice enough, but suppose you want to see what a Web page will look like in a full-fledged Web browser or a Web browser other than Internet Explorer. In that case, preview your Web page in a Web browser. We recommend using this method because you can check out the page in Netscape Navigator, Internet Explorer, and other browsers as well. (See Chapter 16 for details about browser-specific features and considering which to include or not include.)

Follow these steps to preview a Web page in a Web browser:

1. Choose File ➜ Preview In Browser. The Preview In Browser dialog box appears, as shown in Figure 3.6. The Browser area of the dialog box lists the different browsers installed on your computer.

Figure 3.6 *Choose a browser to preview your Web page.*

2. In the Browser list box, select the name of the browser you want to use.

3. In the Window Size area, click the button next to the screen resolution that you want the browser window size to approximate.

We recommend first previewing Web pages using the lowest possible resolution (640 × 480) to see how your page will look to Web surfers who use small or low-resolution monitors. Then you can check the page at other resolutions.

4. To have the Editor save page changes each time you preview the page, select the Automatically Save Page check box.

5. Click the Preview button. A Web browser opens and displays the Web page.

If you want to make changes to the pages you're previewing, return to FrontPage. Make your changes in Page view, save the page, and go to the Web browser again. To see the updated page in the browser, you have to reload it by clicking the Reload button (in Netscape Navigator) or the Refresh button (in Internet Explorer). You can keep switching back and forth between the browser and FrontPage in this way as you fine-tune your Web page.

To quickly preview a Web page with the settings you chose last time around in the Preview In Browser dialog box (refer to Figure 3.6), click the Preview In Browser button on the Standard toolbar or press Ctrl+Shift+B.

Downloading Netscape Navigator and Internet Explorer

Netscape Navigator and Internet Explorer are by far the most popular Web browsers. If you want to be a serious or even a semi-serious Web site developer, you need both browsers. You need to see what your Web pages look like in both places. As of this writing, 60 percent of Web surfers use Internet Explorer, 35 percent use Netscape Navigator, and the other 5 percent use other browsers.

Fortunately, you can download Netscape Navigator and Internet Explorer for free over the Internet. To download the programs, go to these Web sites:

- Netscape Navigator: home.netscape.com/download

- Internet Explorer: www.microsoft.com/windows/ie

Printing Your Web Pages

If you need paper copies of Web pages to distribute at a meeting or fax to a colleague, you can make quick printouts using FrontPage. By default, FrontPage prints pages with the title at the top and page numbers at the bottom of the page. Each page prints with half-inch margins. To change the header, footer, or margins, choose File ➜ Page Setup. In the Page Setup dialog box, enter new header, footer, or margin values and then click

OK. Keep in mind, however, that margin changes you make in the Page Setup dialog box affect page margins in browser windows as well.

To see how a Web page will look before you commit it to paper, choose File ➜ *Print Preview.*

Open the page that you want to print in Page view and follow these steps to print Web pages:

1. Choose File ➜ Print, or press Ctrl+P. The Print dialog box appears.

2. If the name of the printer you want to use is not already visible in the Name list box, select it.

FrontPage uses the printer's default settings to print the page. If you want to change the page's orientation (vertical or horizontal), specify a different paper size or source, or change the graphic resolution, click the Properties button. In the Properties dialog box, change the necessary settings, and then click OK to return to the Print dialog box.

3. If you want to specify a print range (number of pages to print) in the Print Range area, click the Pages option button, and in the accompanying text boxes, type the range. For example, if the current page fits on five pieces of paper, but you want to print only the first two pages, enter **1** in the From text box and **2** in the To text box.

4. In the Number Of Copies text box, type the number of copies you want to print.

5. Click OK.

Up Next

At this point, you should be familiar with some basic Web design principles and the FrontPage 2002 interface. Now that you're comfortable using Page view, it's time to start actually creating Web pages! Chapter 4 teaches you how to do just this.

Creating Basic Pages

FRONTPAGE

Chapter 4

Ready to have some fun? We hope so, because in this chapter, you see how easy it is to enter text and place images on a Web page, as well as do the formatting and "jazzing up" work. This chapter shows how to enter a title and choose colors and themes for Web pages. Starting here, you leave Web page design theory behind and discover how to build the pages for your Web site. You learn how to decorate a Web page with graphics and ruled lines, as well as choose a background color or theme for your pages. Finally, this chapter explains how to insert a hyperlink into a Web page. Topics include:

- Placing text on Web pages

- Entering paragraphs and line breaks

- Working with images

- Drawing ruled lines

- Putting a background on a page

- Choosing and applying a theme

- Inserting hyperlinks in Web pages

FrontPage offers toolbar and menu commands for most of the formatting tasks you will tackle in this chapter, but we also present a handful of fancy HTML tricks that involve inserting pieces of code, called tags, into Web pages. You can apply the HTML tricks you learn in this chapter to nearly anything you want to do with your Web pages.

Titling a Web Page

In Web page parlance, the *title* of a page has nothing to do with what appears at the top of the page itself. No, the title is what appears *in the title bar* of the browser window, as shown in the following illustration. This title also appears on the Forward and Back drop-down menus (in Internet Explorer) and the Go drop-down menu (in Netscape Navigator)—the menus that Web surfers make use of when they want to jump to Web pages they visited before. Most search engines index pages by giving weight to the title of a Web page, so choosing a good title for pages is important if you want your pages to be found in Web searches.

Giving a Web page a clear, descriptive title is very smart. Many search engines give special credence to words in the title, so the accuracy of a title helps users to find your Web pages. The title also appears in the search engine's hit list (the index of search results a user gets), and even in bookmark lists. See the discussion of META tags in Chapter 24 for tips on coaxing search engines into recognizing your site and titling the page effectively.

Giving your page a title is easiest to do when you save it. The first time you save a Web page, the Save As dialog box appears (see Figure 4.1), and you are prompted to give your Web page a name as well as a title. Click the Change Title button and enter a title in the Set Page Title dialog box.

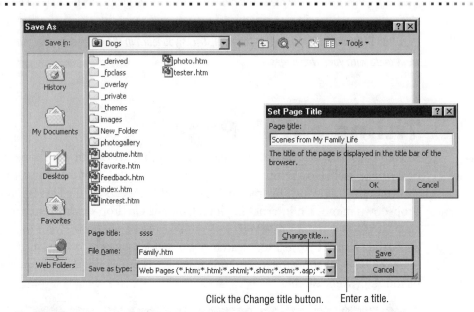

Click the Change title button.   Enter a title.

Figure 4.1 *You can give a Web page a title when you save it for the first time.*

No matter what title a Web page has, you can change it by following these steps:

1. Open the Page Properties dialog box (see Figure 4.2). To open it in Page view, choose File ➔ Properties. In the Folders or Navigation view, select the page and choose File ➔ Properties. If you start in Folders or Navigation view, you get a simplified version of the Page Properties dialog box (see Figure 4.2). No matter—you can title a Web page starting either place.

2. On the General tab, enter a title in the Title text box.

3. Click OK.

Your page now has a distinguishable title.

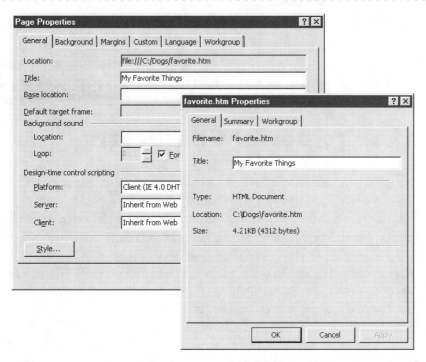

Figure 4.2 *Which Page Properties dialog box you see depends on whether you are in Page view (left) or Folders or Navigation view (right).*

Entering Text on a Web Page

To enter text in a Web page, open the Web page and begin typing in Page view. Entering text on a Web page is very much like entering text in a word-processed document. You can also copy or cut text from a text file, a Microsoft Word file, an e-mail message, or another Web page, and then paste it into the page you're working on (Chapter 3 explains how to move and copy text).

Of course, entering text is one thing, and arranging it on the page is another. Besides typing it straight in, consider these strategies for entering text on a Web page:

Entering text in text boxes   A text box is like a mini-page inside another page. After you enter text in a box, you can drag the text box wherever you want on the page and in so doing position the text where you want it to be.

Using tables to lay out text   Chapter 11 explains how you can make text land on Web pages where you want it to land by entering the text in tables.

Using styles to make pages consistent with one another   By assigning styles to text, you can make sure, from Web page to Web page, that headings and paragraph text look the same and are laid out the same way. Chapter 5 discusses styles.

Using Special Characters

A few symbols, known as *special characters*, are commonly used in day-to-day editing. The registered symbol (®), for example, denotes a type of trademark; the copyright symbol (©) denotes ownership. Letters such as *è* and *ñ* are required if you decide to sprinkle a foreign-language word or two in the text. These symbols and letters don't appear on the keyboard. To enter them, word processors provide a special menu or dialog box.

Unfortunately, you can't simply enter a special character or unusual letter in Front-Page because the character or letter doesn't translate into HTML. Therefore, it doesn't show up on Web pages. Fortunately, HTML provides special codes called *escape characters* for generating special characters and letters that are not found on the keyboard. These aren't tags, precisely, but bits of code that tell a Web browser what to display.

FrontPage makes entering special characters and oddball characters fairly easy by way of the Insert ➜ Symbol menu command. Follow these steps to enter a special character:

1.   In Page view, click where you want the character to go.

2.   Choose Insert ➜ Symbol. The Symbol dialog box appears.

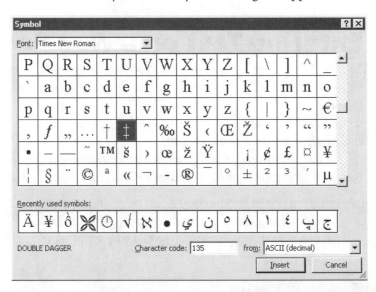

3. Locate the symbol you want to insert, click it, and then click the Insert button. The symbol appears in your document.

4. Click Close to close the dialog box and return to the Page view window when you're done.

Making Paragraphs Work

Words turn into sentences and sentences have a habit of turning into paragraphs. When you reach the end of one line, text *wraps,* or moves down to, the next line. Press Enter to create a new paragraph.

In HTML, the language of the Web, paragraph breaks don't mean quite the same thing that they do on the printed page. Short of entering a few blank spaces, for example, indenting the first line of a paragraph is impossible. On most Web pages, white space marks the end of one paragraph and the beginning of the next. Fastidious designers sometimes create the illusion of indents and other conventions of the printed page. The next few pages explain how fastidious designers do it.

By the way, a *paragraph* in FrontPage is simply all the text that comes before a paragraph break. A heading is a paragraph. So is a single line of text. Why do you need to know this? Because when you give a paragraph-formatting command, your command applies to all the text in the paragraph.

Paragraphs wrap from one line to the next, but where one line ends and the next begins usually has to do with browser settings and screen settings. Unless you press the Enter key or use another technique for breaking lines, lines break according to viewers' screen resolution and browser settings. Keep that in mind as you enter paragraphs on your Web pages.

Inserting a Paragraph Break

In Page view, inserting a paragraph break is as simple as pressing the Enter key. Front-Page inserts a paragraph break, which is then marked in HTML by the <P> tag. If you click the HTML tab in Page view and examine the source code of your Web page, you will see a <P> at the end of each paragraph where you pressed the Enter key. The <P> tag inserts a blank line and enters a line of blank space between one page element and the next.

Breaking a Line

Line breaks, represented as <BR> in HTML, can be used to format text when you want to end one line and continue it on the following line, without inserting a blank line between the items you're delineating. For example, suppose you are formatting the text of a poem, a recipe, a masthead, or table of contents and you want a break but not a chasm of white space to appear between lines. Figure 4.3 shows a poem in Preview mode formatted with paragraph breaks, and the same poem below it, formatted with line breaks.

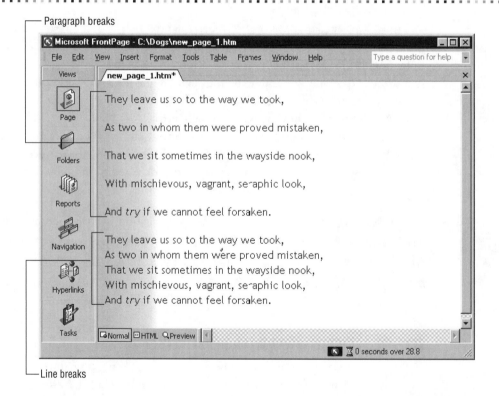

Figure 4.3 *Paragraph breaks insert a line of white space between units of text, but line breaks simply break lines.*

To insert a line break, follow these steps:

1. In Page view, click where you want the line break to appear.

2. Choose Insert ➜ Break. The Break dialog box appears.

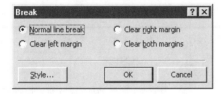

3. Select the Normal Line Break option button.

4. Click OK.

You can insert a line break quickly by holding down the Shift key and pressing Enter.

As a glance at the Break dialog box shows, you can break a line in several different ways. Figure 4.4, for example, shows an image with a caption. The first example is a normal line break, the second clears the left margin, the third clears the right margin, and the last example clears both margins. To format line breaks around images, choose Insert ➜ Break and select one of these options in the Break dialog box:

Select This…	To Do This…
Normal Line Break	Insert a regular line break between the image and the text.
Clear Left Margin	Move the next line of text down until it clears the left margin of the image.
Clear Right Margin	Move the next line of text down until it clears the right margin of the image.
Clear Both Margins	Move the next line of text down until it clears both margins of the image.

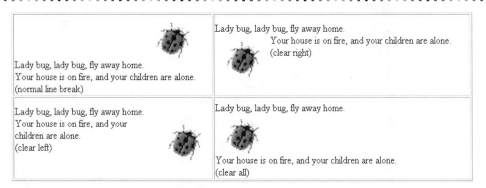

Figure 4.4 *FrontPage offers more than one way to break a line.*

Aligning Paragraphs

Figure 4.5 demonstrates the different ways that you can align text. Starting in Page view, follow these steps to tell FrontPage how you want to align the text:

1. To align a single paragraph, click the paragraph. To align multiple consecutive paragraphs, highlight all or part of the paragraphs to be aligned.

2. Click an Alignment button on the Standard toolbar or choose Format ➜ Paragraph and, in the Paragraph dialog box, select an option on the Alignment drop-down list.

Most, but not all, browsers can display justified text. A browser that can't display justified text left-aligns the text instead.

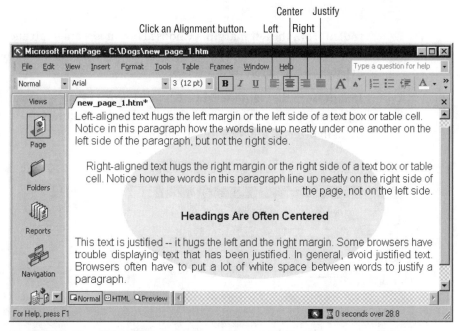

Center   Justify

Click an Alignment button.   Left |Right|

Figure 4.5 *The different ways to align text on a Web page*

Indenting Paragraphs

Yes, it is possible to indent a paragraph from the left margin or right margin of a Web page. Remember: A paragraph in FrontPage means any amount of text—a word, a heading, a Faulkneresque five-hundred-word strung-together sentence. To indent a paragraph or paragraphs, follow these steps:

1. Click the paragraph if you want to indent it; to indent more than one paragraph, select all or part of each one.

2. Do one of the following:

   Indent from the left margin by clicking the Increase Indent button   You will find this button on the Formatting toolbar. Click it (or press Ctrl+M) and the paragraph(s) indent by 50 pixels from the left margin. You can click the button as many times as necessary to increase the amount of the indentation.

To "unindent" a paragraph, click the Decrease Indent button (or press Ctrl+Shift+M).

Indent from the left margin   Choose Format ➜ Paragraph and, in the Indentation area of the Paragraph dialog box (see Figure 4.6), enter a measurement in pixels in the Before Text text box.

Indent from the right margin   Choose Format ➜ Paragraph and, in the Indentation area of the Paragraph dialog box (see Figure 4.6), enter a measurement in pixels in the After Text text box.

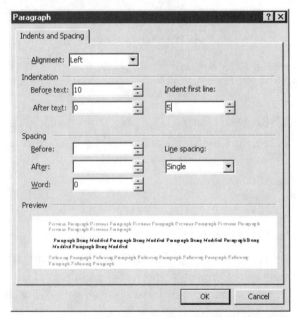

Figure 4.6 *The Paragraph dialog box presents one way to handle paragraph indentations.*

Centered paragraphs can't be indented. If you want a paragraph to be off-center, change its alignment to either left- or right-aligned (see the previous section, "Aligning Paragraphs") and then indent it.

The Paragraph dialog box (refer to Figure 4.6) calls for you to enter measurements in pixels. A *pixel* (the term stands for "picture element") is a tiny dot that, together with thousands of other tiny dots, makes up the images you see on the computer screen. Most people's computer screens are either 640 × 480 or 800 × 600 pixels. If you indent by 50 pixels on a 640 × 480 screen, you indent by about one-twelfth the width of the screen; indent by 50 pixels on a 800 × 600 screen and you indent by about one-sixteenth the width of the screen.

Style sheets afford you much more control over the alignment and indentation of paragraphs. See Chapter 13 for more information about using style sheets.

Entering Nonbreaking Spaces

Plain spaces that you enter by pressing the spacebar are considered extraneous by most Web browsers. If you put in a bunch of blank spaces one after another to try to format text, only one blank space will show up. Therefore, if you are serious about entering blank space, enter a *nonbreaking space*. FrontPage enters the HTML code   in your document, and that code tells the browser to indeed display blank spaces onscreen.

Like word processors, Web browsers wrap text from one line to the next at spaces. They do not, however, wrap text at nonbreaking spaces; that's why they're called nonbreaking.

Suppose you work for ABC Computers and the company prefers that lines never break between "ABC" and "Computers." Type "ABC Computers" on a Web page and the words may fall on one line, but if you enter a nonbreaking space between the words, "ABC Computers" will always appear on the same line. Similarly, phone numbers look bad if they are broken across two lines, but you can prevent that from happening with a nonbreaking space.

To insert a nonbreaking space, start in Page view and follow these steps:

1. Click to place the insertion point at the spot in the text where you want the nonbreaking space to be.

2. Click the HTML tab to see the HTML code in the Web page.

3. Type the following: ** **

Making Multiple Paragraph Breaks

Although you can stack line breaks (<br>), you can't stack paragraphs (<P>). Place several <P> tags in a row, and most Web browsers will ignore everything after the first single <P> tag. If you need to enter a lot of blank space on a Web page, use one of these methods:

- Combine one <P> tag and several <br> tags:

    <P>

- Stack as many <br> tags as you want:

- Press Enter several times in a row in Page view to produce code that looks like this:

    <P> </P>

    <P> </P>

    <P> </P>

    <P> </P>

- This code tells the Web browser to leave several lines of white space, by creating a paragraph whose only character is a nonbreaking space.

This last method is particular only to WYSIWYG editors like FrontPage.

Understanding the HTML behind Your Web Page

So you have a Web site and at least one Web page. You're ready to begin placing images on Web pages, and eventually you'll be manipulating those images. But before we show you how to do those things, we feel you need to be able to view and understand the *way* your text and images are put on the page.

Besides showing you what your pages will look like, Page view allows you to work directly with the underlying HTML code—the code that tells the browser where to put text, images, and other media. Besides viewing pages, as we describe in Chapter 3, you can also peek under the virtual hood and enter HTML code yourself. What's more, you can enter HTML code that is not directly supported by FrontPage, check your work, and even make changes to a page's code.

To view the HTML code and perhaps edit it, switch to Page view and then click the HTML tab. The HTML source code for the document appears (see Figure 4.7). Now you can make changes by typing new or modified HTML directly into the page. You can also delete extraneous or unwanted HTML by highlighting the unwanted code and pressing the Delete key.

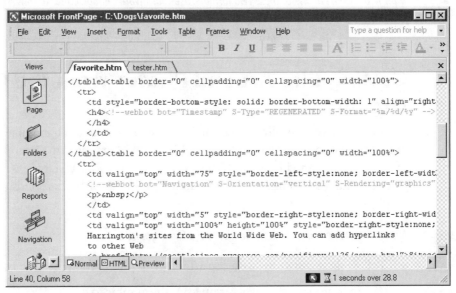

Figure 4.7 *Looking under the hood at the HTML code*

Be careful: It is very easy to turn your functioning Web page into a nonfunctioning page by deleting necessary code. This can result from something as simple as removing just one tag that you don't realize is required by FrontPage. This is why it's good to get some background in HTML. If you're interested in doing more "hands on" work, check out Mastering HTML 4 *(2nd ed.) from Sybex (1999).*

When you are done and want to switch back to Normal view, simply click the Normal tab at the bottom of the Page view window. The contents of the window change to reflect the HTML editing you did.

Working with Graphics

The Web consists of much more than just text. Today's Web site is designed to have a handful of graphics. To make Web pages more compelling, you can include a clip art image from the Microsoft Clip Organizer, a graphic stored on your computer, or a graphic from the Internet. Better keep reading.

Graphics must be in the GIF or JPEG format to be viewed using most Web browsers. If the images you want to use aren't in one of these two formats, use your favorite image editor to convert them to GIF or JPEG files.

Getting Clip Art and Photos from the Clip Organizer

Not everyone is artistically inclined and can create or scan and manipulate images to put on their Web pages. For that reason, Microsoft offers the Clip Organizer, a library of digital clip art and photographs that you can use on your Web pages. The Clip Organizer contains clip art images, photographs, buttons, lines, backgrounds, and animated graphics.

Appendix D explains how to manage files in the Clip Organizer.

Follow these steps to place a clip art image or photograph on a Web page:

1. In Page view, click where you want the graphic to go.

2. Choose Insert ➔ Picture ➔ Clip Art or click the Insert Clip Art button on the Drawing toolbar. The Insert Clip Art task pane appears (see Figure 4.8).

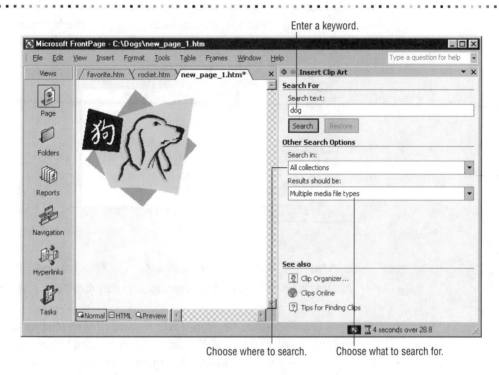

Figure 4.8 *Inserting a clip art image or photograph on a Web page*

3. In the Search Text box, enter a keyword that describes the kind of graphic you want.

4. Open the Search In drop-down list and check or uncheck boxes to tell Front-Page where to search for graphics.

My Collections Graphics you have placed in the Favorites folder and any other folder you created (Appendix D explains what the Favorites folder is and how to create your own folders).

Office Collections Folders with graphics you installed when you installed FrontPage.

Web Collections   Folders on the Design Gallery Live Web site, a Web site that Microsoft maintains. You must be connected to the Internet to search Web collections.

To search a folder and all its subfolders, double-click the folder's check box. You can tell when all the subfolders will be searched because three overlapping boxes appear where normally you see one check box.

5. Open the Results Should Be drop-down list and choose what kind of graphic (or multimedia file) you want. By clicking the plus sign (+) next to Clip Art, Photographs, Movies, or Sound, you can be more selective and choose what kind of file you want. Here, GIF and JPEG graphics are being sought.

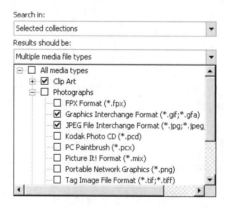

6. Click the Search button.

7. Scroll to and click an image to insert it in the Web page.

If the graphic you need doesn't show up in the Insert Clip Art task pane, click the Modify button and start all over.

If you really like a piece of clip art and anticipate using it again, open its drop-down menu in the Insert Clip Art task pane and choose Copy To Collection on the drop-down menu. Then, in the Copy To Collection dialog box, select the Favorites folder or another folder of your choice and click OK. Appendix D explains the different folders in the Clip Organizer.

After a graphic has landed on the page, you can drag it to a new location. To delete an image if you decide that you don't want it, click to select it and then press the Delete key.

If you can't drag an image and it stubbornly stays in the same place, display the Pictures toolbar and click the Position Absolutely button.

Putting Your Own Clip Art and Photographs on a Web Page

Chances are, you keep more than a few clip art images and photographs on your computer or on the network that your computer is connected to (if your computer is connected to a network). Remembering that GIF and JPEG graphics are the best choice for a Web page because all browsers can display them easily, follow these steps to place an image of your own on a Web page:

1. In Page view, click where you want the graphic to go.

2. Choose Insert → Picture → From File. The Picture dialog box appears.

In the Picture dialog box, open the drop-down menu on the Views button and choose Preview. That way, the dialog box shows you what the images look like.

3.   Select the graphic you want to place on your Web page.

4.   Click the Insert button.

Your image is there, displayed in the Page view window. You can drag it to a new location if you so desire. And if the image refuses to be dragged elsewhere, display the Pictures toolbar and click the Position Absolutely button.

Grabbing images from other people's Web pages is easy enough, but the legal ramifications of doing so aren't so simple. If the images are clearly marked as being public domain, and you are very confident that this is true, feel free to use them as you like. Otherwise, the author of the image holds copyright on it—and there are no exceptions to this rule of intellectual property. If you can't live without an image, send its owner an e-mail message and ask permission to use it.

Borrowing Graphics You Find on the Internet

You can copy a graphic you discover on the Internet to your computer and use it on your own Web pages—provided, of course, that the graphic is not copyrighted and does not belong to someone else. Follow these instructions to borrow a graphic you discover in the course of your adventures as a Web surfer:

- In Internet Explorer: To copy a graphic in Internet Explorer, right-click it and choose Save Picture As. You see the Save Picture dialog box. Find and select the folder where you want to save the graphic (and give it a new name, if you so desire). Then click the Save button.

- In Netscape Navigator: To copy a graphic in Netscape Navigator, right-click it and choose Save Image As. You see the Save File dialog box. Find and select the folder where you want to store the graphic file, and click the Save button.

The next section in this chapter explains how to copy a graphic to the images folder in your Web site. From there, you can make it a part of your Web site very easily.

Importing Many Graphics for Use in Your Web Site

Importing a graphic means to move it to a Web site folder so you can use it later on. Not that you will use the graphic necessarily, but you will have easy access to it if you do decide to put it on a Web page.

Follow these steps to import a graphic or graphics so you can use them later on:

1. In the Views bar, click the Folders icon to switch to Folders view. Now you can see the folders and files in your Web site.

When you create a Web site, FrontPage gives you a folder called "images." Storing graphics there is a good idea. That way, you know where the graphics you want to use are located. You can, however, import graphics into any folder by selecting the folder in step 2.

2. In the Folder List, click the images folder to display its contents. The files in the images folder appear on the Contents side of the window.

3. Choose File → Import. The Import dialog box appears.

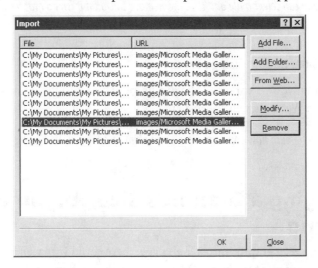

4. To add a single file to the images folder, click the Add File button. The Add File To Import List dialog box appears. Use it just like any other Open dialog box to locate and select the graphic you want to import. When you're done, click Open to return to the Import dialog box, where you see the name of the file you just selected.

or

To copy the entire contents of a folder to the images folder, click the Add Folder button. The File Open dialog box appears. Locate the folder on your hard drive or local network and select its icon. When you're done, click Open to return to the Import dialog box, where you'll see the names of all the files in the folder you just selected.

or

To add files from a Web site, click the From Web button. The Import Web Wizard appears. Simply follow the wizard through the necessary steps to import the file(s) you want right off the Web.

5. Repeat step 4 as often as you like until you've selected all the images you need.

The Import dialog box is for importing all kinds of documents, not just graphics. When you import the contents of a folder, for example, you get all its files, whether or not they are graphic files. In the Import dialog box, you can select a file and click the Remove button if it isn't a graphic file and you don't care to import it.

6. In the Import dialog box, click OK.

Now that you've imported all your graphic files into the images folder, putting the graphics on Web pages will be a snap.

See Chapter 9 to learn how you can create original images for your Web page.

Changing a Graphic's Size, Alignment, and Spacing

After you insert a graphic into a Web page, there could very well be something about the graphic you want to change. Maybe you'd like to change its size or realign it. Maybe you would like to place a border around it. Chapter 9 explains how to use FrontPage tools to alter images.

To tinker with a graphic's properties, click to select the graphic and then open the Picture Properties dialog box (see Figure 4.9). FrontPage offers no fewer than four different ways to open the Picture Properties dialog box:

- Choose Format ➜ Properties.
- Double-click the graphic.
- Right-click and choose Picture Properties.
- Press Alt+Enter.

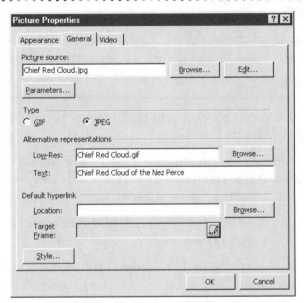

Figure 4.9 *Go to the Picture Properties dialog box to tinker with a graphic's properties.*

The General tab of the Picture Properties dialog box offers commands for:

Type Change the graphic type from GIF to JPEG or vice versa.

Low-Res Some people configure their browsers to show low-resolution, black-and-white graphics in place of normal ones. To satisfy these users, click the Browse button under Type and choose a low-resolution or black-and-white graphic in the Select Alternate Picture dialog box.

Text In the Text box, enter a description of the graphic. Someone who visits your Web page and moves the mouse over the graphic will see the text you enter.

It's very important to include alternate text for any image that will be visibly displayed. The reason for this is that many people accessing the Web cannot see or choose not to see images. Individuals in remote areas are often at the mercy of restricted bandwidth or older computer systems, necessitating text-only browsing, or browsing without images. Still others prefer fast access to information, so they will browse with the auto image-loading feature in their browser turned off.

Default Hyperlink   These options (Location and Target Frame) have to do with frames, the subject of Chapter 12.

Style button   Modify any sheet information included with the text by clicking the Style button. A new dialog box pops up, and you can make changes to the styles there (see Chapter 13 for more information on style sheets).

Click the Appearance tab of the Picture Properties dialog box to tell FrontPage where you want the graphic to be on the page. Here are your options:

Wrapping Style   Choose the None, Left, or Right option to tell FrontPage what to do when text runs up against the graphic. Text can run around its left or right side. The None option leaves white space on either side of the graphic.

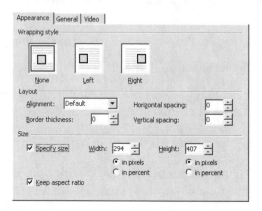

Layout Alignment   Choose alignment for the graphic. You can align the image according to the browser's default behavior (most browsers use Baseline as the default), in which case choose the Default setting. To choose another alignment, however, open the Alignment drop-down list and choose an option. Table 4.1 explains what the options are.

Table 4.1 Layout Alignment Options in the Picture Properties Dialog Box

OPTION	WHAT IT DOES
Left	Places the graphic on the left side of the browser window, with text or other elements wrapped around the right side of the graphic.
Right	Places the graphic on the right side of the browser window, with text or other elements wrapped around the left side of the graphic.
Top	Aligns the top of the graphic with the top of the tallest element on the same line.
Texttop	Aligns the top of the graphic with the top of the tallest character on the same line.
Middle	Aligns the middle of the graphic with the middle of the surrounding text.
Absmiddle	Aligns the middle of the graphic with the middle of the largest item on the current line (stands for "absolute middle").
Baseline	Aligns the bottom of the graphic with the imaginary line on which the surrounding text rests. Use this option to place a small image on a line of text.
Bottom	Aligns the bottom of the graphic with the bottom of the surrounding text (this is another name for baseline).
Absbottom	Aligns the bottom of the graphic with the bottom of the current line of text (stands for "absolute bottom").
Center	Center the graphic horizontally in the browser window.

Horizontal and Vertical Spacing   You specify that the browser leave a margin of white space around your graphic by entering a number (in pixels) in the Horizontal and Vertical text boxes (10 is a good start; you can experiment from there).

Border Thickness   You can have a solid border appear around an image. If you'd like your image to include a border, type a number (in pixels) in the Border Thickness text box. Entering 0 (or leaving the text box empty) prevents the border from appearing at all. Borders around images can make a page look tight and cluttered, so leaving this setting empty or specifying 0 is the recommended way to go.

If you're concerned about the visual appearance of your pages (as well you should be!), be sure to place white space around your graphics. This is especially true when the surrounding text wraps around a graphic. If the text is too close to the graphic, the page will appear cramped and be difficult to read.

Size   Specifying the size of an image allows the browser to load the page more efficiently, because it can draw a placeholder while it is fetching the image itself. FrontPage automatically sets the image size when you first insert it, but if you want to resize the image, you can do so.

Changing the size of a graphic in the Picture Properties dialog box is unwise. If you want to make a graphic larger or smaller, change the physical size of the image in an image editor before you place it on a Web page. You can do this in almost any image editor. One of the rare exceptions to this good rule of thumb is when using single pixel GIFs to fix table widths or create visual rules. See Chapter 9 for more information.

Using Ruled Lines

Horizontal rules are pretty much what they sound like: horizontal lines that separate one part of a Web page from another. You can insert ruled lines beneath document heads, between parts of a memo or article, or anywhere else you please. There are basically two kinds of ruled lines: horizontal rules created through the <HR> tag in HTML, and graphics that look like lines (and act to divide space) but don't share their HTML properties. Many of the decorative ruled lines that you have seen on the Web are probably graphics. Figure 4.10 shows several different ruled lines; the two at the bottom are graphic images.

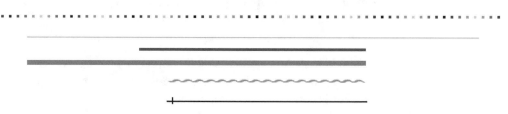

Figure 4.10 *The two objects at the bottom of this picture are actually images, while the other three are ruled lines.*

Standard HTML-based horizontal rules include a line of white space before and after the line itself, and their properties include height, width, and the option of 3-D shading. When you insert a horizontal rule, you get an engraved line that's centered on the page and occupies 100 percent of the width of the window. You can then change the look and properties of this line; additional lines you create after adjusting the properties of that line will continue to look like it until you reset their properties.

Drawing a ruled line in Page view is quite easy. In the following pages, you find out how to draw a line, adjust the properties of a line and in so doing alter its appearance, and use a graphic image as a ruled line.

Inserting a Ruled Line

Follow these steps to drop a ruled line onto a Web page:

1. In Page view, click where you want the ruled line to appear.

2. Choose Insert ➜ Horizontal Line. A horizontal line appears across the page.

That's easy enough, isn't it?

Too Many Lines Spoil the Web Page

You might be tempted to put fancy, flashy, engraved, colorful, beveled dividing lines all over your Web pages. Don't do it!

Dropping ruled lines onto a page is easy, but many a Web site developer forgets the purpose of ruled lines: helping people read and comprehend the message of the Web site. Instead of using ruled lines, try a few other tricks. Generally, white space works as well as a ruled line when it comes to dividing one part of a Web page from another. When working with blocks of text, you might also try using different alignments (left, right, and center) in combination. Consider using different text colors to make one paragraph stand out. Or indent text and tables to help distinguish different parts of a page.

Chapter 1 offers advice for designing Web pages. Ruled lines are fine, but use them sparingly.

Changing the Look of a Ruled Line

In our opinion, the plain, engraved, ruled line you get by default breaks up a page too dramatically. To soften the line, change its thickness, give it a different color, or change its properties. Follow these steps to do so:

1. Either double-click the line or right-click it and choose Horizontal Line Properties. You see the Horizontal Line Properties dialog box.

If you selected a theme for your Web site, you can't change the look of a ruled line. Sorry. The line is part of the theme and can't be changed.

2. Enter new measurements in the Width and Height text boxes to change the length and height of the line. Make these choices as well:

   • To enter a measurement relative to the window, click the In Percent option button.

   • To enter a measurement in pixels, click the In Pixels option button.

3. By default, ruled lines appear in the center of the page, but you can make them run to the left or right margin by selecting the Left or Right option button under Alignment.

4. If you want the line to stand out more, choose a new color from the Color drop-down menu.

5. If you'd like to remove the beveling (the 3-D shading) from your line, place a check mark in the Solid Line (No Shading) check box.

6. For advanced users who are using style sheets (see Chapter 13), you can modify the rule with style information. Click the Style button to open the Modify Style dialog box. Use this box to change the rule.

7. Click OK.

About Pixels and Percentages

When you're choosing the size for a Web page element, you're often given two choices for the unit of measure: *percentage* or *pixels*. Percentage means that the measurement is drawn to occupy a certain portion of the available screen size—usually the screen's width.

Pixels are actually (and generally) a unit of projected light. There's no precise size for pixels; a pixel is just a dot of light on a screen. Televisions and computer screens both use pixels as their basic unit of measure, although the pixels on a TV screen are generally much bigger than those on computer screens. The higher the resolution of the medium, the smaller the pixels are.

When you're using pixels as your unit of measure, you should realize two things: One pixel is pretty small, but it's not invisible; and pixels are different sizes when viewed on screens of different sizes or resolutions. The lowest resolution screens these days are 640 pixels by 480 pixels (640 × 480). In recent years, screens with a resolution of 800 × 600 and even 1024×768 pixels have become more common. Some high-end computers come with screens of much higher resolution; they'll have lots more pixels.

In designing Web pages, you ought to consider the size of screen you'll generally design for (this goes back to what sorts of machines you expect your audience to have). You'll also want to consider this in choosing a pixel size for elements that appear on your pages.

Using a Graphic as a Ruled Line

As you know, when you create Web pages you are actually creating HTML codes; you just don't see it that way while you're doing the deed. Instead of typing in the code—the HTML instructions for how a page should look—you create the text, images, and other objects, making them look as you want them to appear to users. All the while, little HTML elves work behind the scenes to write the code that allows those instructions to be carried out by the user's browser software. A simple ruled line is just that—simple. It does not show up as a string of teddy bears holding hands, a multi-colored zigzag line, or anything very fancy at all. You might wonder how to create such nifty effects. The answer is simple: These are not really ruled lines, but graphics masquerading as ruled lines.

Using graphics for ruled lines involves different HTML. Horizontal rules in HTML are represented by the <HR> tag, which can include other attributes (such as height and color—we described creating and modifying a ruled line like this in the previous sections.)

You can insert an image that *acts* and *looks* like a ruled line quite easily. In fact, the Clip Organizer comes with an assortment of images intended for this purpose. It's best to start with an image that's pretty long and narrow, but even that's not a prerequisite. You can use an image of your own or a line from the Clip Organizer.

Getting a Ruled Line from the Clip Organizer

Follow these steps to get a ruled line from the Clip Organizer:

1. In Page view, click where you want the line to appear.

2. Choose Insert ➔ Picture ➔ Clip Art, or click the Insert Clip Art button on the Drawing toolbar. The Insert Clip Art task pane appears. To search for ruled lines, leave the Search Text box blank and look in categories instead.

3. Open the Search In drop-down menu, and, by choosing categories, tell Front-Page that you want to look for ruled lines. Web Collections offers ruled lines in these categories: Dividers & Decorations and Web Dividers.

Earlier in this chapter, "Getting Clip Art and Photos from the Clip Organizer" explained in detail how to search in the Insert Clip Art task pane. Appendix D explains the Clip Organizer.

4. Open the Results Should Be drop-down menu and select Clip Art in the All Media Types folder.

5. Click the Search button. Ruled lines and other decorations appear in the task pane (see Figure 4.11).

6. Click a ruled line to enter it on the Web page.

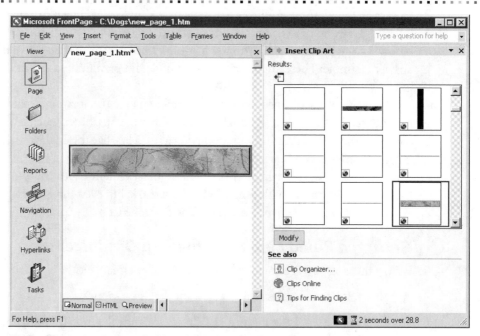

Figure 4.11 *Getting a ruled line from the Clip Organizer*

Using a Ruled Line of Your Own

You can create your own images to use as graphical lines. For that matter, you can find them in clip art collections on the Web. Either way, you can insert a ruled line you've stored on your computer into a Web page by following these steps:

1. In Page view, choose Insert ➜ Picture ➜ From File or click the Insert Picture From File button on the Drawing toolbar. The Picture dialog box appears.

2. Locate and select the ruled line graphic. Be sure to open the drop-down menu on the Views button and choose Preview to get a good look at the lines.

3. Click the Insert button.

Earlier in this chapter, "Importing Many Graphics for Use in Your Web Site" explained how to keep graphics on hand in the images folder so you can find them easily when you need them for a Web site. Try putting a few ruled lines in the images folder and using them as you need them. You'll save time that way.

Making Changes to a Ruled Line

The easiest way to make changes to a ruled line is to select it and drag a selection handle. Selection handles are the black squares that appear on graphics and lines. Drag a top or bottom handle to change a line's height; drag a side handle to change its length.

Beyond that, you can open the Picture Properties dialog box to change the size of a ruled line. Select the line and do any of the following to open the Picture Properties dialog box:

- Choose Format ➜ Properties.
- Double-click the graphic.
- Right-click and choose Picture Properties.
- Press Alt+Enter.

On the Appearance tab, enter Width and Height settings to change the size of the ruled line. For example, if you'd like your graphical line to take up 90 percent of the width of the window, click the In Percent option button (under Width), and then type 90 in the Width text box. If you'd like the line to be a certain number of pixels wide, click the In Pixels option button, and then type a number in the Width text box. You can adjust the height of your image in the same way.

If your image looks a little funny or is not what you had in mind, keep playing with it by repeating the steps above until you get it right.

To quickly change the alignment of a ruled line, select it and click one of these alignment buttons on the Formatting toolbar: Align Left or Align Right.

Creating Backgrounds for Web Pages

The background of a Web page really sets the tone. A subdued background, a flashy background, a bright background—and let's not forgot no background at all—tell you a lot about a Web site or a Web page. Read on to find out how to choose background color for a Web page, use a graphic in the background, and decorate a page or Web site with a *theme,* a ready-made design from Microsoft.

Choosing a Background Color

Being able to choose a single background color for a Web page is great—but it's also a potential design pitfall. Take care when designing pages that you choose simple, harmonious color schemes. Not many people, for example, bother to read a Web page with orange text superimposed over a bright-green golf course.

If you chose a theme for your Web site, you can't change the background color.

Follow these steps to choose a background color for a Web page:

1.   In Page view, choose Format ➜ Background or right-click and choose Page Properties. You see the Background tab of the Page Properties dialog box (see Figure 4.12).

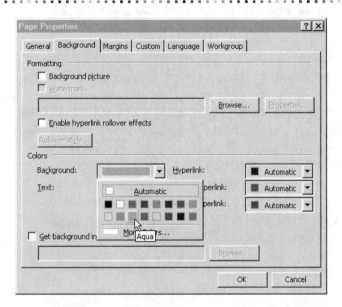

Figure 4.12 *Use the Background tab of the Properties dialog box to change the color of your pages.*

2. Open the Colors/Background drop-down menu and choose a color. To choose a color apart from the default colors, select More Colors at the bottom of the drop-down menu. The More Colors dialog box appears. Choose a color there and click OK.

Choosing a color from outside the default range can be problematic for older browsers. The default color palette in FrontPage is made up of a series of colors referred to as "browser-safe" or "Web-safe" colors. These colors are well suited to different browsers, computer platforms, and hardware types. It's always best to stick with a browser-safe color selection.

3. Click OK to apply the background color you just chose.

Choosing a Background Graphic for Web Pages

Choosing a background graphic is quite similar to specifying a background color. The graphic you choose should be subtle and serve the purpose its name suggests—a background for the text on the page. Web browsers that can display background images *tile* the graphic. As shown in Figure 4.13, the graphic is repeated over and over until it fills the browser window completely (no matter what size the user's browser window is). If you've ever changed your Windows Desktop wallpaper, you're probably familiar with the concept of tiled images.

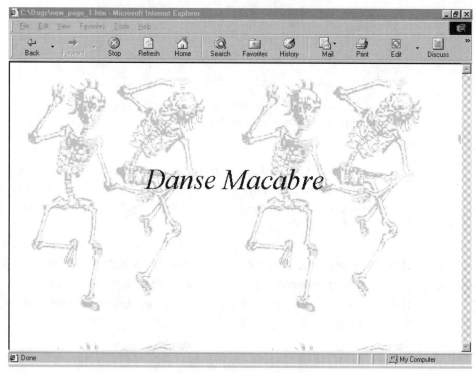

Figure 4.13 *Example of a tiled background graphic*

Follow these steps to choose a background graphic for a Web page:

1. In Page view, choose Format ➜ Background or right-click and choose Page Properties. The Background tab of the Page Properties dialog box appears (refer to Figure 4.12).

2. Click to enter a check mark in the Background Picture check box.

3. In the Background Image text box, type the full path name of the location for the background image you want to use, or click the Browse button and select the graphic you want to see in the Select Background Picture dialog box.

4. If you're using a large image for your background (an image that takes up a screenful or so of page real estate), consider placing a check mark in the Watermark check box to make the graphic stationary. Watermarks don't scroll along with any text or other page elements in the latest browsers; instead, they remain anchored on the page while everything else scrolls by.

5. Click OK.

Double-check the graphic to make sure it is a suitable background for the page. To do so, save your Web page and click the Preview tab in Page view. While you're at it, choose File ➜ Preview In Browser to see what the page looks like in a genuine Web browser.

Choosing a Theme for Web Pages and Web Sites

A *theme* is a collection of page design elements that have a given look and feel. You can save yourself a lot of design time by choosing a theme for a Web page or for your entire Web site. The professional artists at Microsoft created the themes that come with Front-Page. When you choose a theme, you get a professional-looking Web page or Web site.

Themed pages have a banner image and a navigation bar at the top. Each has an attractive background. To get you started, themes include labels so you know what you are dealing with. Your job is to replace the labels with genuine text.

You can choose from among the many themes and base the design of your site on whichever seems appropriate. The only disadvantage to themes is that they are not original designs. If you're going for practical, that's fine, but if you want your Web site to stand out, you need to use or refine your design skills, or get a professional to help with the look and feel of your site.

You don't *have* to use themes. You can change horses in the middle of the theme, or you can start with a theme or two or more and then do away with themes on your pages altogether. Furthermore, you can select a theme for an entire Web site or a single page.

Follow these steps to apply a theme to a single Web page or an entire Web site:

1. If your goal is to apply a theme to a single page, open that page (if you want to apply a theme to the whole site, go straight to step 2).

2. In Page view, choose Format ➜ Theme. The Themes dialog appears (see Figure 4.14).

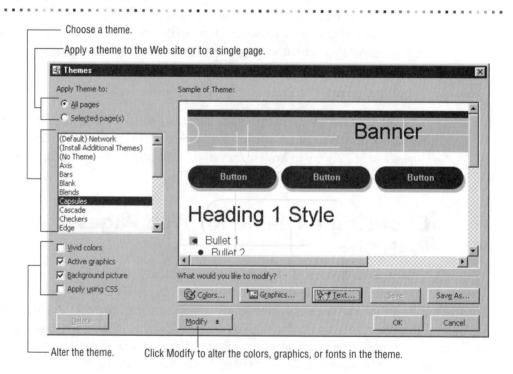

Choose a theme.

Apply a theme to the Web site or to a single page.

Alter the theme.

Click Modify to alter the colors, graphics, or fonts in the theme.

Figure 4.14 *The Themes dialog box allows you to select and modify themes.*

3. Under Apply Theme To, choose the All Pages option button to apply the theme throughout your Web site; choose Selected Page(s) to apply a theme to a single page.

4. Browse the list of themes that appears along the left side of the dialog box and select one you like. A preview of that theme appears in the window's right side so you can see what you're in for.

5. Make sure the All Pages button is checked.

 You can modify the look of any given theme to include a background color instead of a background image, to include colors that are more vivid or less vivid, or to use animated ("active") buttons and images. To adjust these properties, select (or deselect) the check boxes marked Vivid Colors, Active Graphics, or Background Pictures. Advanced users interested in adding style sheet information to control the appearance of the page can check the Apply Theme Using CSS check box, too.

6. Click OK when you are ready to apply a theme to the entire Web site.

If you regret applying a theme, follow the same procedure for applying the theme, but in step 4, instead of choosing a theme, select No Theme.

If you'd like to remove the banners and buttons and such that are on your page and start with more or less a clean slate, just select the bits you want to remove with your mouse and then press the Delete key.

Creating Your Own Theme

To create your own theme, open the Themes dialog box (see Figure 4.14) and select the theme that most resembles one you want to create. Then click the Modify button. Five new buttons appear in the Themes dialog box—Colors, Graphics, Text, Save, and Save As.

Click the Colors, Graphics, or Text button and a Modify Theme dialog box appears. In the Modify Theme dialog box, you can choose a new color for part of a theme, new graphics, and new fonts. When you are done choosing colors, graphics, and fonts, click the Save As button and enter a name for your new theme in the Save Theme dialog box. Next time you choose a theme for a Web site or Web page, you can choose your new theme in the Theme list.

Including Hyperlinks on Web Pages

Hyperlinks, or just plain *links*, probably constitute the biggest difference between the Web and other media. You can't click on a map on TV, an author's name in a magazine, or a song title in a book and expect to go anyplace.

As you're undoubtedly aware if you've been on the Web for even 15 minutes, a link can point to any address on the Internet. Click a link and you go to another Web page, another place on the same Web page, or another Web site altogether. Sometimes you click a link to download a file, hear a sound, or play a video. Click certain links and your e-mail software opens so you can send an e-mail message.

The following pages explain how to create hyperlinks to these places:

- A different page in your Web site (that is, to the top of the page)

- A specific location on a different page on your Web site (the middle of the page, for example)

- A different place on the same Web page (somewhere further down the page)

- Another Web page on the Internet

- A *mail-to hyperlink* (a hyperlink that opens the clicker's default e-mail program so he or she can send you an e-mail message)

First, however, a few basic instructions for creating hyperlinks.

Creating a Hyperlink: The Basics

No matter what kind of hyperlink you want to create, follow these basic steps:

1. In Page view, select the item that will serve to launch the hyperlink. You can select a word, a phrase, or a graphic.

2. Choose Insert ➔ Hyperlink, click the Hyperlink button on the Standard toolbar, or press Ctrl+K. The Insert Hyperlink dialog box appears (see Figure 4.15).

3. Click the ScreenTip button and enter a phrase or a short sentence in the Set Hyperlink ScreenTip dialog box that describes the who, the what, or the where of your hyperlink. When a visitor moves the pointer over your completed hyperlink, he or she will see the text you enter and decide whether to click the link.

where you will find a list of my favorite things.

Click this link to learn about my favorite things.

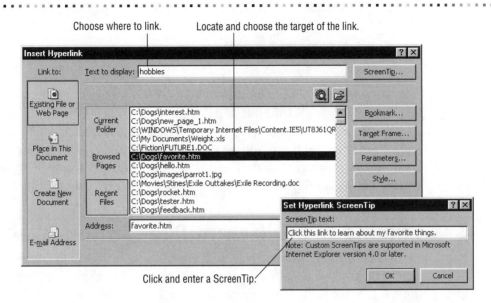

Figure 4.15 *Creating a hyperlink*

4. Under Link To, choose what kind of hyperlink you want to create:

Different page in your Web site   Click the Existing File or Web Page icon under Link To, and then locate the Web page you want to link to. See "Linking to a Different Page in Your Web Site" later in this chapter for details.

Different place on the same Web page   Click the Bookmark button. In the Select Place In Document dialog box, select a bookmark. See "Linking to a Different Place on the Same Web Page" later in this chapter for details.

Specific location on a different page on your site   Locate the Web page you want to link to, and then click the Bookmark button. In the Select Place In Document dialog box, select a bookmark. See "Linking to a Specific Place on a Different Web Page" later in this chapter for details.

Another Web page on the Internet   Enter the address of the Web page in the Address Text box. See "Linking to a Web Page on the Internet" later in this chapter for details.

> **Mail-to link**   Under Link To, click the E-Mail Address icon. Fill in the Edit Hyperlink dialog box and click OK. See "Creating Links to E-Mail Addresses" later in this chapter for details.

5. Click OK.

After you create a hyperlink, be sure to test it. To do so, click the Preview tab in Page view, and then click the link. If it doesn't work or if it goes to the wrong location, click the Normal tab in Page view, then right-click the link and choose Hyperlink Properties on the shortcut menu. You see the Edit Hyperlink dialog box, where you can alter the link (it works exactly like the Insert Hyperlink dialog box shown in Figure 4.15). To remove a link, click the Remove Link button in the Edit Hyperlink dialog box.

Linking to a Different Page in Your Web Site

Read "Creating a Hyperlink: The Basics," the previous section in this chapter, to get a general idea of how to create a hyperlink. In the Edit Hyperlink dialog box (refer to Figure 4.15), do the following to create a link to a different page in your Web site:

- Click the Existing File or Web Page icon under Link To.

- Click the Current Folder button, locate the Web page you want to link to, and select it. As long as the Current Folder button is selected, the Insert Hyperlink dialog box works like an Open dialog box. You can click the Up One Folder button, open the Look In drop-down menu, or click the Browse For File button to navigate on your hard drive and locate the Web page.

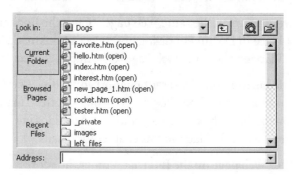

If you opened the Web page recently, try clicking the Recent Files button to see a list of files and select the Web page there.

Creating a Bookmark so You Can Link to a Specific Place

Suppose you want to create a hyperlink, not to the top of a Web page, but to a place in the middle of a Web page. To link to a specific location, either on the page where the hyperlink is located or on a different page on your Web site, you have to mark the target of the hyperlink with a bookmark. Later, when you create the link, FrontPage gives you the opportunity to choose a bookmark to link to. Someone who clicks the link will go, not to the top of the page, but to the bookmark you created in the middle of the page.

Follow these steps to create a bookmark that can be used to create a hyperlink:

1. Open the Web page where you want to place a bookmark and click on the location where you want others to go when they click the hyperlink. In other words, click the spot that others will see when they activate a hyperlink.

2. Choose Insert ➜ Bookmark or press Ctrl+G. The Bookmark dialog box appears.

3. Enter a name for your bookmark in the Bookmark Name text box and click OK.

A small flag appears next to the text you selected in step 1, indicating that this text has been bookmarked.

To delete a bookmark, select Insert ➜ *Bookmark. In the Bookmark dialog box, select the bookmark you want to delete and click the Clear button. Click the Go To button to go to a bookmark in your Web page.*

Linking to a Different Place on the Same Web Page

To link to a different place on the same Web page, read "Creating a Hyperlink: The Basics," earlier in this chapter, to get a general idea of how to create a hyperlink. If necessary, read "Creating a Bookmark so You Can Link to a Specific Place" as well. It explains bookmarks and how to mark the target of a hyperlink with a bookmark.

Knowing that the place to which you want to link has been bookmarked, select the hyperlink text or graphic, click the Bookmark button, or choose Insert ➜ Hyperlink, and, in the Insert Hyperlink dialog box (refer to Figure 4.15), click the Place In This Document icon under Link To. You see a list of the bookmarks on the Web page. Select the bookmark that marks the target of your hyperlink and click OK.

Linking to a Specific Place on a Different Web Page

Before you can link to a place on the middle or bottom of a different page in your Web site, you must mark the place with a bookmark. (See "Creating a Bookmark so You Can Link to a Specific Place" earlier in this chapter. Read as well "Creating a Hyperlink: The Basics," earlier in this chapter, if you need instructions about hyperlinks and how to open the Insert Hyperlink dialog box.)

In the Insert Hyperlink dialog box (refer to Figure 4.15), do the following to create a hyperlink to a specific place on a different Web page:

1. Click the Existing File or Web Page icon under Link To.

2. Click the Current Folder button. Using the tools in the dialog box, locate the Web page with the bookmark you want to link to.

3. Click the Bookmark button. The Select Place In Document dialog box opens. It lists the names of bookmarks in the Web page you selected.

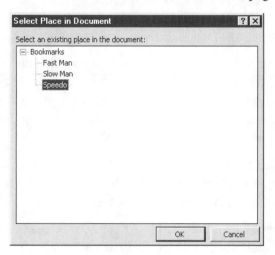

4. Select a bookmark and click OK.

Linking to a Web Page on the Internet

To link to a Web page on the Internet, read "Creating a Hyperlink: The Basics," earlier in this chapter, to get a general idea of how to create a hyperlink. Then, in the Insert Hyperlink dialog box, enter the URL of the page with which you want to link in the Address text box. FrontPage offers these shortcuts for entering the URL:

- Click the Browse The Web button to open your Web browser, and then go to the Web page you want to link to. When you return to the Insert Hyperlink dialog box, the address of the Web page appears in the Address box. The Browse The Web button is the small button with a picture of a globe on it.

- Choose a URL from the Address drop-down menu.

- Click the Browsed Pages button to see a list of pages you visited in the last 90 days, and select the page if you can remember it.

Relative vs. Absolute Hyperlink Addresses

Not that you have to be too concerned about it, because FrontPage handles hyperlinks in the background, but there are only two kinds of hyperlink addresses: *relative* and *absolute*.

Relative addresses contain only a filename, its extension, and possibly its location within the file directory. The URL of a relative address points to a file that resides on the same Web server as your Web site. For example, when you're linking from one page to another within the same folder on your Web site, you can simply point to its file-name: `figs.html`. If you're in your main folder and you want to link to a graphic in the images folder, you can point to that with a relative address, too. It would look like this: `images/figs.gif`.

Using relative addresses is a good practice when you're linking items on the same Web site, because relative addresses make it much easier for you to maintain a Web site. If you've used relative addresses, you can move files from one folder on a Web server to another without having to make major changes to your HTML.

On the other hand, if you were to spell out the entire URL, such as `http://www.mysite.com/figs.html`, you'd be using an absolute address instead. Absolute addresses start with `http://`, `ftp://`, or another *protocol* type. (A protocol is an agreed-upon way of doing things. HTTP is the name of the protocol for Web pages, for example.) The protocol is then followed by the rest of a full URL. The term *absolute* indicates that not only the name of the doc-ument on a server is given, but the full, exact, honest-to-john location of the entire server itself is also spelled out.

Generally, links that point to *local* resources—items on the same server—use relative links, while links that point out into cyberspace use absolute links.

Creating Links to E-Mail Addresses

After Web addresses, the most common type of address you'll want to provide a link to is your e-mail address. When someone clicks the link, his or her default e-mail software opens. Your e-mail address is entered automatically in an e-mail message, as is a subject for the message.

Follow these steps to create a link to an e-mail address:

1. In Page view, type something to indicate that the link will lead to you—your name, the words **Webmaster, mail me, feedback**, or whatever you like. Type it wherever you want it to appear on the page, and then highlight it.

2. Choose Insert ➔ Hyperlink, press Ctrl+K, or click the Insert Hyperlink but-ton. The Insert Hyperlink dialog box appears.

3. Under Link To, click the E-Mail Address icon. As shown in Figure 4.16, the Insert Hyperlink dialog box offers new options for creating a mail-to link.

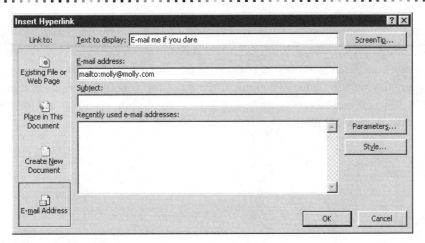

Figure 4.16 *Creating a mail-to hyperlink*

4. In the text box E-Mail Address, type your full e-mail address, which should look like this: **user@site.com**. FrontPage places the words *mailto:* before the address.

5. In the Subject text box, enter a subject for the message.

You don't have to enter a subject, but by doing so, you spare others the trouble of entering it. What's more, when others send you e-mail messages, you will recognize the subject and know what the messages are about.

6. Click OK.

Now, when your page is loaded onto the Web and someone clicks the link to your e-mail address, they'll be able to send you a message and tell you how cool you are.

Up Next

If you're a bit tired at this point, take heart. You've learned a *lot* in this chapter—how to work with text, images, and links, and how to use the specialty FrontPage feature, themes.

The next chapter, "All About Text," will take you from the basics learned here to more sophisticated techniques you can use to lay out text. This is an important part of design. After all, your text is critical—it's a primary aspect of the message you're sending to your site visitors. Proper formatting of text will help you refine your pages, adding impact as well as maximizing the visitor's ability (and desire) to read your carefully prepared content.

All about Text

FRONTPAGE

Chapter 5

Sure, you can type text onto a Web page, but you want your pages to look fancier than word-processed documents. Many people actually hire professional editors to ensure that their written work is presented well. While you don't have to go to that trouble to make your pages worth reading, you can use the tools FrontPage gives you to spruce up your text.

In this chapter, we'll learn how to use text styles and paragraph styles, how to use headers effectively to label a Web page, and how to create lists to organize your ideas. While we discuss how to manipulate each text attribute individually, remember that a well-designed page integrates these elements into a unified design. Topics include:

- The importance of text

- Working around browsers

- Using text styles and paragraph styles

- Composing lists: bulleted, numbered, and definition

- Making headlines

Communicating with Text

Even a site that consists mostly of images includes textual elements, and the construction of these is as important as any image. For instance, the Museum of Modern Art's Web site offers exhibits filled with images, but text is there as well to make for a powerful design (see Figure 5.1).

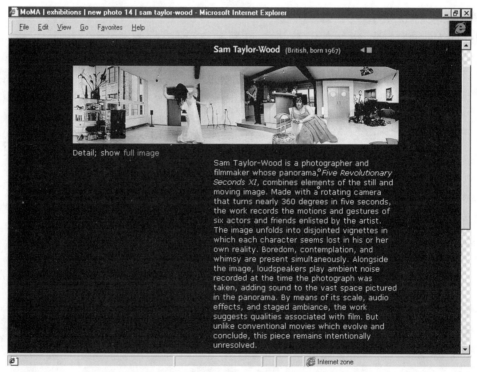

Figure 5.1 *Even if images are your site's focus, you still need to work well with text.*

Chapter 6 and Chapter 13 cover the design-oriented aspects of text. This chapter, however, teaches the basic attributes of text on Web pages.

Chapter 6 and Chapter 13 cover text in more detail. This chapter, however, teaches the basic attributes of text on Web pages.

While your project may not be as ambitious (or as image-driven) as an overview of art history, you should hold your work to high standards. After all, you're going to be putting it on the Web, where countless millions of people have access to it.

Mastering What's Online

Visit the Museum of Modern Art (MOMA), New York, at www.moma.org/.

Making a page look terrific is all well and good, but it's not going to get you anywhere if that page isn't *readable*. All too often, people forget that they're supposed to be presenting *content*—that's the point of having a Web page in the first place. Put too much gigantic, blinking, scrolling, orange text on top of a neon purple background, and most Web surfers will simply flee in horror. They'll miss your message—and what, then, was the point of all your hard work?

In general, the same rules that apply to writing apply to text on the Web. There are some special issues, though, and you'll want to keep them in mind. These tips, while not steadfast rules, are a good set of guidelines to work from:

- Readability is key.

- On Web pages, reserve underlining for links. Italics is the proper format for book titles, and works well for emphasis in general.

- Limit your use of italic type; in particular, ask yourself if entire paragraphs really need to appear in italics. It can be difficult to read, particularly on a computer screen.

- When you're emphasizing a word, choose either bold or italic type. Using too many different styles at once makes text look ***weird***.

- Reserve large, bold type for headlines, which should properly stand out from the rest of the page.

Now let's find out how to put text to work.

Five Steps to Better Content

Here's a checklist of questions and concepts to help you make your text terrific:

Audience   Do you know your audience? Have you defined them well enough so you can write to them and make the content not only understandable but also appropriate? For example, if you're writing for children, your words are going to be decidedly different than they would be if you're writing for adults. A Web page written for sports enthusiasts is remarkably different from one written for classical music lovers. Get to know your audience, and they'll stick around your Web page longer and get to know you!

Intent   What is the *intent* of your message? In other words, do you want to sell, to entertain, or to inform? The intent of a message significantly influences the manner in which you prepare your content.

Clarity   Once you do have an idea of who you're writing for (audience) and what you're writing about (intent), it's important that your content is clear. Are there words you don't need, or areas where you need to be more descriptive? Your Web site visitors will need to know your intent on each page within your site. Are you using words that make this clear?

Voice   Voice is an important part of writing that has to do with the tone and general feel of the words. Consider the way you speak to others. When you speak to authority figures, you have one means of talking. When you speak with children, you use a different voice. The same thing is true of written text; the voice you use should be appropriate to the people reading your text. Proper voice is impossible to achieve without knowing your audience. Once you do, write to them using a method that captures the message you want to express. Are you being casual, using lots of jargon? Or do you need to be more formal, as in a corporate setting?

Web Style   Writing for the Web is a precise art. It's important to understand that people don't hang around terribly long on a Web site unless the content is interesting enough for them to do so. Using short, concise sentences while maintaining an appropriate voice is part of writing for the Web with style. Think in "capsules," or short bursts of text. This makes a page interesting and easy to read.

Understanding the Purpose of Text

It's been said that "content is king." Just what is *content*, though? Is it images and media? Written copy? Content is whatever will serve your audience best. Content is what will bring people to your Web site and keep them coming. If your text information is weak in both written and visual form, it will dramatically reduce your Web site's efficacy.

We'd like to make one thing clear in this chapter: It's not simply the way your text looks that's important to a good Web page; what it does while it's looking good is just as critical. Contrary to what some Webmasters seem to believe, text is not just that stuff that fills in the space between flashing animated GIFs and blinking Java applets. As discussed in Chapter 1, it doesn't matter what kind of gadgets you have, or how flashy your design is, if your site doesn't have good content.

Just as you pay less attention to speakers who mumble or ramble on and on, people pay less attention to text that isn't letter-perfect. Remember that people are actually going to read the words you put on your pages, and that a lot of people really *do* care about things such as spelling, punctuation, and grammar. Not paying attention to these important concerns will cause your site to look amateurish and unprofessional.

Want to check your spelling? In Page view, choose Tools ➜ *Spelling (or press F7). The FrontPage spell-checker will start, and it'll check all the words on your page while skipping the links and other HTML.*

Just as you check your pages to make sure there are no broken links or missing images, you should check your text to make sure that it's grammatically correct and free from typos and spelling errors. Enlist a friend to help you; we certainly know what it's like to work on a page for so long that the words all look the same.

Don't forget to check your page titles, headings, and captions for spelling errors and incorrect capitalization.

Mastering What's Online

To learn more about English usage, enlist the help of a good copyeditor—or learn how to become one—at The Slot (www.theslot.com). Or you could try the classic editor's guidebook, Strunk and White's *The Elements of Style*, at www.bartleby.com/141. The editors of *Wired* magazine have published a very useful guide, *Wired Style: Principles of English Usage in the Digital Age*, edited by Constance Hale (Hardwired, 1997). Of course, you could always go buy the book, so to speak, and get yourself a copy of *The Chicago Manual of Style* or *The AP Style Handbook*. The Indispensable Writing Resource (www.quintcareers.com/writing) lists dozens of other books and Web sites that you might find helpful.

Working with Browser Defaults

When you're getting ready to work with text in your page design, you should be aware of how your efforts are going to show up on the other end: the Web browsers your readers are surfing with. While there are as many different kinds of browsers as there are kinds of cheese, a few basic rules apply when you are dealing with browsers.

Your basic Web surfer is probably using some version of either Netscape Navigator or Microsoft Internet Explorer; only about 5 percent of the Web population use any other browser. Both of these browsers, as well as many of the others, use two kinds of fonts to present text: proportional and fixed-width.

Each character in any font consists of a letter, number, or symbol together with a certain amount of surrounding white space. Proportional and fixed-width fonts differ in the amount of space taken up by each character. The *proportional* font is called that because, like the text on this page, each character is a different width and therefore takes up an amount of space proportional to its size. The amount of space a word occupies on a line depends on *which* letters it contains, not on *how many* letters it contains. Here, ten letter *w*'s and ten letter *i*'s are shown in Times Roman, a proportional font. Notice how the *w*'s take up far more space than the *i*'s.

wwwwwwwwww

iiiiiiiiii

The factory default for most browsers' proportional font is Times New Roman, 10- or 12-point. Proportional fonts are generally used for most body text and headlines, because they are usually much easier to read.

 Point size *is a measurement of how big the letters in a word appear on the page. In old-fashioned, hand-set type, one point is equal to 1/72 of an inch (meaning that 72-point type is one inch high). In digital type, point size is more relative. Some fonts (such as Courier or Bookman Old Style) appear bigger than other fonts (like Times or Garamond), even when they're set to the same point size. This is generally due to how wide the characters are or how the type is spaced.*

Fixed-width fonts, on the other hand, employ letters that all occupy an equal amount of space. Imagine that each character occupies a little square of space. In a fixed-width font, that square is the same size for all characters, yet there is usually more white space in the square for the *l* than there is for the *m*. When we look at ten *i*'s and *w*'s in a fixed-width font, Courier New, they take up the same amount of space:

wwwwwwwwww

iiiiiiiiii

Courier or Courier New, which looks suspiciously like old typewriter or telegram text, is the default font for most people's fixed-width fonts.

Fixed-width fonts are used to emulate computer code, quoted e-mail messages, mathematical and scientific equations, and so on. Because it is a fixed-width font, Courier New is also a popular choice for e-mail and Telnet programs.

Now, having said all this, there's still the chance that the folks at home have completely reconfigured their default font faces and sizes. Most Web browser software programs, in particular Netscape Navigator and Microsoft Internet Explorer, afford the user a lot of opportunity to customize the way their interface to the Web looks and acts. Users can, for instance, customize the default font faces and sizes used to display text on the Web. Nearsighted people can set their default text size to 14- or 16-point for easier reading; others may choose to use a smaller font size to fit more text per square inch on the screen. And anyone at all can decide to up and change their default font faces, which can give a totally different look to pages that maximize the distinction between proportional and fixed-width fonts.

Some browsers even allow users the option of using Times New Roman, a decidedly proportional font, for their fixed-width font, simply because they like the way it looks. One of the things we'll explore in this chapter is how to maximize your control over which font faces and sizes your users see, so that your pages will appear the same on every screen—or as close as you can get. This is why you should learn as much as you can about typography: to ensure that your audience sees the page *you* designed.

Using Text and Paragraph Styles

In computing parlance, *text style* is a generic term for specially formatted text. Bold is one example of a text style; underlined is another. Manipulating the weight of text, as in bold type, and the orientation, as in italic type, serves to emphasize words. Watch out for overemphasis, however, as described in the sidebar "Blinking Red Eyes."

Text style is a standard term used by most word-processing and page layout software to mean the way formatting (bold, italic, etc.) is applied to text; in FrontPage, text styles are also referred to as font styles. Paragraph style describes how HTML formatting affects the way a paragraph is treated by a Web browser—note the Paragraph Style drop-down menu on the Formatting toolbar, the leftmost menu. Style sheets, described in Chapter 13, are a relatively recent invention and should not be confused with text or paragraph styles.

Blinking Red Eyes

Did you ever wonder why it is that newspaper headlines are so easy to read? Well, they're bigger than the stories they describe, and they're bold.

Unfortunately, some folks with Web pages have taken this little fact of life to mean that all the text on their pages should be pretty big, and bold—and italic, and red, and flashing (courtesy of the <BLINK> tag).

Have you ever gotten an e-mail message written ALMOST ENTIRELY IN CAPITAL LETTERS? Did you actually read the whole thing? Didn't it feel like someone was shouting at you?

The thing about emphasis is that, in order for it to do its job—that is, make part of the text stand out from the whole—it needs to *stand out* from the whole. If all the text on a page is bold, italic, and large, then you'd need to make your point in really tiny letters in order for it to garner notice.

Your eye has to do some work in order to read at all. A nice serif font in 12-point type is not only perfectly readable, but very easy on the eye (see in Chapter 6). However, the more doodads you add to that type, the more difficult it is to read.

In other words, if all the text on your page is bold, then nothing stands out; the non-bold text on such a page almost recedes away from the eye, which has to work much harder to read a page composed entirely of bold and italic letters.

When you're designing a page, make sure that the text stands out from the background, rather than clashing with it; make sure the words that need to be *emphasized* have a chance at **standing out** from the rest of the text; and make sure that people can tell the headlines from the text.

Formatting Text for Emphasis

If you want to add emphasis to your pages with bold, italic, or underlined text styles, FrontPage will be happy to oblige you. Just follow these steps:

1. In Page view, highlight the text you want to format for emphasis.

2. Click the appropriate button on the Formatting toolbar: **B** for bold, *I* for italic, or <u>U</u> for underlined. Your text is emphatically changed.

To remove this formatting, just repeat the steps above, and the text style reverts to normal. Remember to use caution when choosing to underline text. As we mentioned, it confuses people to see underlined words that are not links on a Web page.

Using Other Physical Text Styles

There are other text styles that you can use to modify your type. Physical text styles descibed in Table 5.1, allow you to manipulate text in a very precise way in order to draw attention to that type for the following purposes.

Table 5.1 Physical Text Styles

Physical Text Style	What It Does	How to Achieve It
Strikethrough	~~Draws a horizontal line through~~ selected words. May be useful if you want to show corrections.	Choose Format ➜ Font; in the Font dialog box's Effects area, click Strikethrough.
Overline	Draws a line across the top of text.	Choose Format ➜ Font; in the Font dialog box's Effects area, click the Overline check box.
Blink	Makes words flash on and off on the screen, which can be very annoying. Luckily, we can't reproduce this effect in print.	Choose Format ➜ Font; in the Font dialog box's Effects area, click the Blink check box.
Superscript	Shrinks selected letters or words and raises them slightly above the line that surrounding text sits on. Used for text such as footnotes and equations, as in $E=MC^2$.	Choose Format ➜ Font; in the Font dialog box's Effects area, click Superscript.
Subscript	Shrinks selected letters or words and lowers them slightly below the line that surrounding text sits on. Used most often in chemistry and mathematics, as in H_2O.	Choose Format ➜ Font; in the Font dialog box's Effects area, click the Subscript check box.
Keyboard	Makes text appear in a font that `looks like typewriter text`. Although this is technically a physical style, the way it will appear on screen depends on the fonts that users have installed and specified as defaults.	Choose Format ➜ Font; in the Font dialog box, click the Keyboard check box.

Use these styles with caution. A lot of strikethrough text, for example, might seem clever at the time you're using it, ~~but have you ever tried to actually read several lines of text that were struck through~~? This warning goes double for blink. It's true that flashing text is a uniquely digital phenomenon, but once you've seen the word NEW!!! blinking on and off a hundred times, you've seen it a million times.

Using Logical Text Styles

Logical text styles, in the wild, wild Web of yesteryear, told a browser that a piece of text was somehow *different* from regular old text, but the interpretation of this difference was left up to the browser software. Now Internet Explorer and Netscape Navigator are good at interpreting text styles.

In addition to the browsers we've mentioned, there are other types of browsers such as Braille browsers, text-to-speech browsers, and telephone-based browsers—all of which use the <EM> and <STRONG> tags to emphasize passages with volume, stridency, pauses, and the like. The visual design focus that many Web designers lean toward often doesn't consider browsers that work for the disabled.

When decisions were being made about basic HTML code, there were a lot of people at bat for all kinds of logical text styles, from `<strong>` to `<person>` (which, believe it or not, was supposed to indicate a proper name).

There actually was a logic in developing HTML tags this way—the idea of logical styles had to do with the underlying cross-platform nature of the Web; it was thought that allowing the browser software to have some say in how to interpret a tag helped to make the original Web cross-platform. Also, the Web was not originally intended as a true publishing medium, but as a means for scientists and researchers—who did not care about fancy layout—to share information about research, academics, and hobbies. Cool fonts, fancy layout options, and the like were considered frivolous and irrelevant— and to some old-school types, they still are.

Little did the code standard-makers realize how infrequently their painstaking inventions would be used. Let's take a quick look at these logical styles—while you may never find a use for them, someone may ask you to, or you may find yourself updating an old relic of a page that does use them.

You can apply any of these text styles by following these steps:

1. In Page view, select the text you want to change.

2.   Choose Format ➔ Font. The Font dialog box appears (see Figure 5.2).

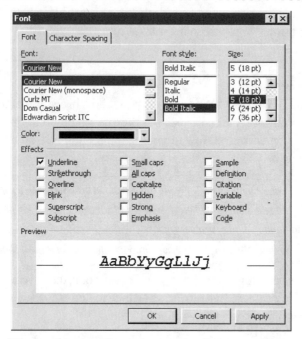

Figure 5.2 *The Effects check boxes in the Font dialog box let you choose from a number of logical text styles.*

3.   Click any of the Effects check boxes in the Font dialog box, and the Preview text at the bottom of the dialog box changes to reflect your choices.

4.   Click OK.

Table 5.2 explains what these styles actually do. Because these are logical styles, different browsers interpret these tags in different ways. In the following table, the "What It Looks Like" column indicates how the listed styles are interpreted by popular browsers such as Microsoft Internet Explorer and Netscape Navigator.

Table 5.2 Logical Text Styles

LOGICAL TEXT STYLE	WHAT IT'S USUALLY USED FOR	WHAT IT LOOKS LIKE
Citation `<cite>`	Quotations in papers and essays	*Italic text*
Sample `<samp>`	Samples of scripts, output from programs, and the like.	`Fixed-width font, slightly smaller than regular text`
Definition `<dfn>`	Definitions of words in online glossaries	*Italicized text* in Explorer; normal text in Navigator
Code `<code>`	Examples of computer code	`Fixed-width font`
Variable `<var>`	A variable or program argument	*Italicized text*
Keyboard `<kbd>`	Emulating keyboard or typewriter text; a fixed-width or monospace font	`Fixed-width font, slightly smaller than regular text`

Although many of these tags look similar, you may find them useful for their original purpose, in particular if you're working with example code on your Web pages. Generally speaking, however, you won't be using logical text styles too often.

Using Paragraph Styles

What's the difference between *text* style and *paragraph* style? Simply put, text style can be applied to a few words, a single word, or even a single letter anywhere on a page, while paragraph style affects an entire paragraph. As you'll recall from Chapter 4, a paragraph in HTML is a unit of text followed by a line break or a paragraph break; it is not the unit of composition that you learned about in school. HTML paragraphs can be single lines of text or even single words. (But don't tell that to an English teacher!)

Technically, headings, lists, block quotes, and other formatting styles are paragraph styles, but for our purposes there are three kinds of paragraph styles: Normal, Formatted, and Address. (We'll cover headings and lists in upcoming sections.)

Normal style is what it sounds like: regular words on a page. You can apply any kind of text style—such as bold, code, or subscript—to normal text. Any time you want to remove text styles and make text normal, just do this:

1. In Page view, select the text you want to change back to normal.

2. On the Formatting toolbar, open the Style menu and choose Normal (it's the default, so it may already be selected).

Ta-da! Your text is normal—at least style-wise. Normal is the default paragraph style FrontPage uses for text as you type. You don't actually have to change most text into Normal style, unless you want to change it *back* to Normal from some other paragraph style.

Normal style, as a paragraph style, can contain any number of text styles, such as bold, italic, typewriter, and the like. If you want to remove text formatting from your paragraphs, select the text you'd like to make plain and choose Format ➜ *Remove Formatting (or press Ctrl+Shift+Z). All text styles are removed from your selection.*

Formatted style paragraphs look like typewriter text, but the HTML code behind them is not the same as the logical styles we discussed earlier in this chapter. In normal HTML, formatting done with multiple spaces or multiple line breaks is pretty much ignored. In preformatted paragraphs, the formatting of the text is preserved.

To choose the Formatted paragraph style, just follow these steps:

1. In Page view, highlight the paragraphs you want to change.

2. Open the Style drop-down menu on the Formatting toolbar and choose Formatted.

Your text appears like typewriter text, with all the spacing preserved. This is especially nice for things like ASCII art, text-based tables, poems, and other blocks of text designed in a text editor with spaces used for formatting.

You may want to specify that text is formatted before you paste in a big chunk of formatted text from an e-mail message or text editor window. Just select the Formatted style before you paste in the text to guarantee that your plain-text formatting will be preserved.

Address style was initially intended to indicate the name and contact e-mail address of the Webmaster or administrator of the page. In most Web browsers, address-style text is displayed in italic font. Once upon a time, the Address style may have been considered valuable because of the possibility of standardization of Web pages. If all pages on the Web used the <ADDRESS> tag to indicate the page's owner, it would have been trivial to employ search engines to locate and file away that information. These days, the Address style is rarely used for its intended purpose, although with the increasing popularity of style sheets, some of the old logical styles may see a resurgence in popularity. To format a paragraph as Address style, just follow these steps:

1. In Page view, highlight the paragraph(s) you want to change to Address style.

2. Open the Style drop-down menu on the Formatting toolbar and choose Address.

Your text is italicized; it is also recognized as Address-style text by any Web browsers or indexing programs that care to note it.

Margin of Defeat

You can arrange elements and white space on a page in many ways; just keep in mind that white space *is* one of the elements on your page. The more things you cram together, the less likely someone is to stop and read the pages.

When you're laying out type in FrontPage, wouldn't it be convenient if you could somehow change the margins? There are several ways to get your content to spread out into the gutter of the page:

- Use paragraph indents and vary the alignment of chunks of text to create a look that's different from the regular old block of text on a page (see Chapter 4).

- Use tables without borders to divide up the space on the page—try using empty table cells to create extra room to maneuver in (see Chapter 11).

- Use the HTML tag <blockquote> around the text that requires margins. Or set the margin information in the <body> tag, using margin attributes. To learn how to do this manually, visit www.microsoft.com/ workshop/author/dhtml/reference/objects/BODY.htm.

- Delve into the world of Cascading Style Sheets (see Chapter 13).

Using Lists

You're undoubtedly familiar with the use of lists to display related tidbits of information. You can use three different kinds of lists on Web pages: bulleted lists, numbered lists, and definition lists. You can use any kind of list on your page, in combination with practically every kind of paragraph formatting other than headings.

Lists are particularly good for Web pages because they break up space, which makes reading easier, and they highlight specific points of interest with short, simple language—the best kind for the Web.

Using Bulleted Lists

Bulleted lists are good for lists in which each item should stand out, but the order the items are listed in does not matter. Bulleted lists look like this:

- Tom
- Dick
- Harry

Creating a Bulleted List

To create a bulleted list, follow these steps:

1. In Page view, type (or paste) your plain-text list on the page. Enter each entry in the list on its own line.

2. Highlight the items in the list.

3. Click the Bullets button.

Your list is now riddled with bullets.

Changing the Style of Bullets

Not all browsers are up to this challenge, but many can display different kinds of bullets, such as solid circles, open circles, or solid squares. Follow these steps to change the way the bullets in a list look:

1. Create a bulleted list (as described in the preceding section) or display a page containing a bulleted list.

2. Highlight the list items whose bullets you want to change.

3. Right-click the highlighted list and choose List Properties. The List Properties dialog box appears (see Figure 5.3). The Plain Bullets tab is selected.

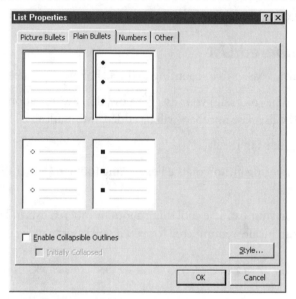

Figure 5.3 *Choosing a new kind of bullet*

4. Click the kind of bullet you want to use for the selected list item(s), and then click OK.

If you chose a theme for your Web page or Web site (see Chapter 4), which bullets appear is governed by the theme you chose. You can't change bullets if you're operating under a theme.

Using Numbered Lists

Numbered lists are good to use when the order of the items in the list is important. Step-by-step procedures in this book, for example, might not be as easy to follow if the steps weren't numbered in lists.

Numbered lists look like this:

1. Lather

2. Rinse

3. Repeat

Read on to count your blessings.

Creating a Numbered List

Making a numbered list is easier than counting to three. Follow these steps:

1. In Page view, type (or paste) your list. For now, don't worry about numbering the items in the list. The numbers will be added automatically.

2. Highlight the items in the list.

3. Click the Numbering button on the Formatting toolbar. (Faster than counting on your fingers!)

Numbers appear on your list. The cool thing about numbered lists in FrontPage is that the items are automatically renumbered for you if you insert a new entry in the list.

Renumbering Lists

FrontPage automatically renumbers your lists for you, even if you don't want it to. Suppose that within a numbered list of directions, you want to insert a small map. If you press Enter within the list, you'll insert a paragraph break, and with it, extra numbered lines. Trying to get your list items to maintain their proper numbers around elements inserted in the middle of the list can be an incredible pain. You can end up with a list that has every item numbered 1, because FrontPage assumes that it's supposed to start a new list after every inserted image.

The solution? Insert *line breaks*, rather than paragraph breaks, before and after images if you want to put them in the middle of your list.

If you do need to renumber a list, though, just delete any extraneous lines, select the entire list, open the Style drop-down menu on the Formatting toolbar, and choose Numbered List. Your list is renumbered.

Changing the Style of Numbering

You may want to get fancy and use letters (A, B, C, or a, b, c) or Roman numerals (I, II, III or i, ii, iii) to number a list instead of standard Arabic numerals. Follow these steps to change numbering styles in a list:

1. Create a numbered list (as described in the preceding section) or display a page containing a numbered list.

2. Right-click the list and choose List Properties on the shortcut menu. The List Properties dialog box appears (see Figure 5.4). The Numbers tab is selected.

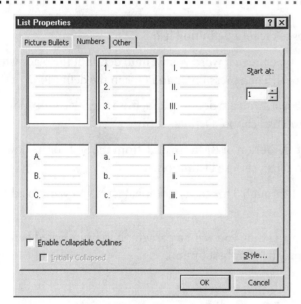

Figure 5.4 *The Numbers tab of the List Properties dialog box lets you play the numbers.*

3. Click the kind of number you want to use.

4. Click OK.

Your choice of number style now appears in your numbered list.

Using Definition Lists

Definition lists offer you the option to show each list item with associated text indented on the line beneath it. The most common use of a definition list is to show terms with their definitions—hence the name definition list. Here is an example of a definition list.

```
Apple
      A red round fruit that keeps doctors away.
Carrot
      An orange fruit to dangle in front of others as an enticement.
Potato
      A tuber that French friars are fond of.
```

Follow these steps to create a definition list:

1. In Page view, type the first word you want to define at the place where you want it to appear. Then press Enter and type in the definition.

2. Highlight the word you are defining and, from the Style drop-down list on the Formatting toolbar, choose Defined Term.

3. Highlight the definition of the term and, from the Style drop-down list on the Formatting toolbar, choose Definition.

4. Repeat steps 1 through 3 for each additional term you want to add to the definition list.

Keep in mind that any time you want a paragraph to be indented beneath other text, a definition list may be your best option.

Including Headings

Just like headlines in newspapers and magazines, *headings* (also called headers, headlines, or heads) on Web pages often denote a title for a page or story. They also break text into smaller, more readable sections, allowing people to find what they seek more easily (just as we've done in this book).

The principle for using headings on Web pages is exactly the same as in traditional print: Headings are larger than regular text, they often appear in bold type, and they're usually offset from the preceding and following text by a blank line of space.

Often, in print, the amount of blank space that follows a heading is less than that above it; this helps the reader's eye create more of a connection between the heading and the text it is introducing. HTML and FrontPage both place the same amount of blank space before and after a heading. However, you can change this by using a method such as style sheets, which are covered in Chapter 13.

You can use a heading to announce the title of your page, or you can use headings of different sizes for different levels of emphasis. For example, again in this book, the headings for chapter titles are in the largest type size, while each section of the chapter gets a smaller head, and the headings for subsections get increasingly smaller as the subsections become sub-subsections.

In HTML, there are six sizes of headings. Not all of these would make really effective headlines; the sixth, or smallest, heading size is tiny and is smaller than the body text. Headings 1 through 6 are shown in Figure 5.5.

To create a heading using FrontPage, just follow these steps:

1. In Page view, click anywhere in the heading.

2. Open the Style drop-down menu on the Formatting toolbar and choose a headings style (Heading 1 to Heading 6).

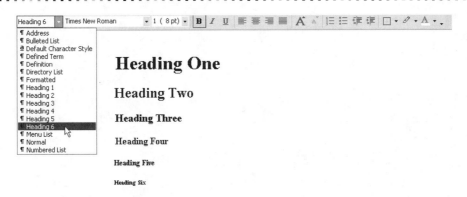

Figure 5.5 *Changing styles for a heading*

Because headings are considered to be a type of paragraph style in HTML, applying the heading formatting to even a single word selected from the middle of a paragraph turns the entire paragraph into a heading. If you want a word in the middle of a paragraph to be big and bold, you need to apply that formatting as a separate text style, rather than trying to make a heading appear in the middle of your text.

Up Next

Now that you know how to work with basic text, it's time to add power and impact to that text. This is done through the use of *typography*. As you'll see in Chapter 6, by using proper type, or *font* styles, your pages can begin to approach a sophisticated, professional level of design.

Fantastic Fonts

FRONTPAGE

Chapter 6

In this chapter, you get a short course in basic typography for the Web. We'll demonstrate different kinds of type and explain when to use each kind. Then we'll look at how to use FrontPage and HTML tricks to present different kinds of type. We'll also look at how to add color to text and links. A list of typographic dos and don'ts is included. Topics include:

- Kinds of type
- Selecting a font face
- Changing font sizes
- Using color with text and links

Typography and the Web

Early in HTML's life, there really wasn't much you could do with it to *design* your Web pages. Instead, you had to work within the constraints of the language. HTML, after all, was never intended to be a page design or layout language.

However, the demands of designers and audiences, as well as the competitive nature of browser developers, have changed all that. HTML has changed from a simple document-formatting language to a skeletal system for Web page design and layout. Now HTML offers more flexibility and options to the Web page designer.

One area in which the changes in HTML have influenced design is *typography,* also known as *fonts.* Handling type is still filled with challenges, but Web designers have more typographic options based in HTML than ever before. This chapter focuses on type that you can create with HTML, or "HTML-based" type. (Chapter 13 covers the use of the font tag and Cascading Style Sheets, another aspect of typography on the Web.)

You can always opt to replace type with a graphic—and this is often a good choice for headers or logos. However, the more type options you include in the HTML, the faster your pages will appear in viewers' Web browsers. This is one of the reasons the growth of type technology in HTML is so important. What's more, type can be indexed by search engines, but type that you enter as part of a graphic cannot be indexed.

Entire volumes—including many good ones—have been written about the power of typography and the manipulation of text on the page. The use of typefaces on the Web might be a relatively new concern, but it's an extremely important one. Besides serving as decorative elements, typefaces help send a powerful message about who you are and what you do.

Looking at Types of Type

There are so many different kinds of type that they've been grouped into categories to help designers keep track of them. The Web isn't as sophisticated as the printed page, at least as far as typefaces are concerned. On the Web, there are hard and fast rules about which kinds of type can be used, and why you'd want to use one kind over another.

There are five categories of type that are important to the Web:

Serif This is a standard, familiar group of fonts that are identified by *serifs,* which are tiny horizontal strokes, or "feet," on the individual letters (*serif* in Latin means "stroke"). Serif fonts are said to be the easiest to read, but this may not be true for the screen. While the jury is still out, it can confidently be said that serif fonts are often the default fonts used in software programs. In general, serif fonts are excellent for body text, the explanatory text that appears below headings.

> Times New Roman is a classic example of a serif font.

Sans serif   A very common group to Web design is the *sans serif* category. These font families have no tiny horizontal strokes (feet). Fonts in this category are considered easy to read. Sans serif fonts are very popular for body text on the Web.

> Arial is the preeminent sans serif font.

Monospaced   In this font group, each character and the white space around it takes up the same amount of horizontal space, similar to the fixed-width text described in Chapter 5. Like fixed-width text, monospaced fonts are often referred to as *typewriter* fonts, because they resemble the monospaced type produced by that venerable old machine, the typewriter. In Web design, monospaced type is used mostly as a decorative element.

```
Courier New is a monospaced font.
```

Script   This category includes fonts designed to look like handwriting. Script fonts are very difficult to read in large doses. Therefore, they should not be used for body text. Script can be used most effectively for short headers or decorative elements.

> *Brush Script MT is an example of a script font.*

Decorative   This group is identified as having special decorative features such as dots, scrolls, and other designs. As the name indicates, you should use decorative type only for headers or decoration.

> Chiller is an example of a decorative font.

Many designers spend their entire lives learning how to design with and create type. This is a good indication of how powerful a design element it is! Choose the right typeface and your work will have the impact you're after. Choose a clashing or inappropriate typeface, and your work will be unattractive—or worse, boring!

Adding Fonts to a Page

When you don't specify a font face, most Web browsers use Times, a serif font, for "normal" text, and Courier, a monospaced font, for preformatted and other code-like text. In FrontPage, you can use any font that is installed on your machine on your Web page, but be forewarned: If a person looking at your site doesn't have the font you used on his or her machine, the text will appears in whatever the viewer has chosen as a default font face.

Despite the warning, don't shy away from using different fonts. Fonts are a big part of Web page design, and anyone who chooses to override the designer's font choices will likely miss out on a terrific design! As a Web designer, you can control a viewer's experiences through the magic of typography—and that means specifying fonts.

Follow these steps to choose a font for text:

1. In Page view, select the text whose font you want to change.

2. Open the Font drop-down menu on the Formatting toolbar and select a font (see Figure 6.1). Notice how each font name shows what the font looks like.

When you select a font, FrontPage inserts the HTML code `<FONT FACE="fontname">`. This code tells the browser that loads the page to check and see whether the font is on the user's computer; if it isn't, the browser uses the default font instead of the one you chose.

Another way to choose a font is to select the text and choose Format ➜ Font. In the Font dialog box (see Figure 6.2), choose a font and click OK.

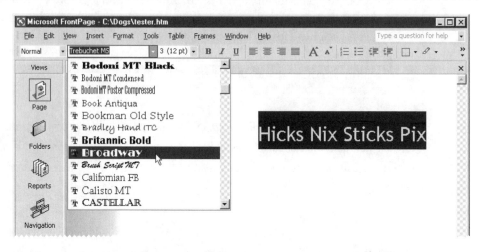

Figure 6.1 *The drop-down Font menu*

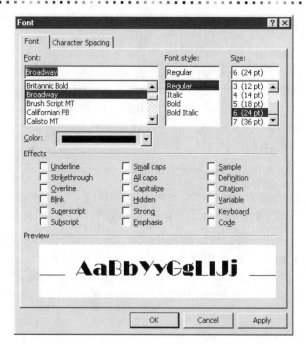

Figure 6.2 *Choosing a font in the Font dialog box*

Managing Web Fonts

At this point, you might be thinking to yourself, "Cool! Lots of categories, lots of fonts to choose from, and it's real easy to do!" Unfortunately, there's more to it than that.

As we warned earlier, the problem is that in order for an HTML-based font to be seen, a font you choose for text *must reside on the visitor's computer*. In other words, if a font you want for your Web page isn't installed on Jane Doe's computer, she will see the default font instead of your font. If you use a fancy, decorative font such as Whimsy on your pages, chances are very few people will see it because very few computers have the Whimsy font. Where you want visitors to see Whimsy, they will see their default fonts. Whoosh! Your nice design is gone.

The following pages describe a couple of workarounds for this problem. One technique is to use fonts that are installed on almost everyone's machine. Unfortunately, that means using only two fonts: Times and Courier. You can use a technique called *stacking* fonts (something that FrontPage doesn't do automatically, but you can do yourself), or a new technology known as *font embedding*. Or you can request that your visitors download a specialty set of fonts from Microsoft known as *core* fonts. Keep reading.

Stacking Fonts for Cross-Platform Typography

Arial is a font native to Windows machines. Rarely, however, is it found on a Macintosh. And unless Arial is resident on a Mac, the Mac's browser will simply display the default font, which is normally Times Roman. Imagine how quickly the Times Roman for Arial substitution can disrupt a design!

Fortunately, HTML allows you to *stack* font faces. Stacking means to provide a list of acceptable fonts to use as substitutes. You can use any font you want as a substitute, but you need to keep in mind that a different set of fonts is found on Macintosh and PC computers. In order to stack fonts effectively, you really need to understand the categories of type and know which popular fonts fit into each category. The browser looks for the first font you name in the stack, and if it doesn't find it, it moves on to the next named font, and so forth. To stack fonts, you have to get into the HTML itself, because FrontPage cannot stack fonts for you.

Despite the fact that you have to do a little hand-coding work here, there's a big advantage to stacking fonts. You gain more control than you have when the browser does the thinking for you. You can put as many font names as are appropriate and reasonable into a stack. This way, the browser looks for your preferred font first, and if it doesn't find it, then it looks for a similar font that you have specified. Helvetica, for example, is a sans serif font that is commonly found on Macs and is very similar to Arial, so you can include Helvetica in your font stack for people who view your Web page on a Macintosh.

First, let's look at font stacking in HTML. Later, you'll see how to stack fonts using FrontPage.

How Font Stacking Works in HTML

Here's how you make a bit of text appear in the Arial font using FrontPage's HTML:

```
<FONT face="arial">
Through the eyes of a child<br>
love paints a rainbow<br>
With each passing day<br>
the colors unfold<br>
A story of enchantment<br>
that touches my heart.<br>
</FONT>
```

This poem appears in Arial—provided that Arial is installed on the computer of the person looking at the HTML code through his or her browser.

Because Macs don't usually have the font, you can go ahead and stack a sans serif font that is common on Macs, such as Helvetica, like so: `<FONT face="Arial, Helvetica">`.

While there is conceivably no limit to the way you stack fonts, there are two simple and stable options for body text. If you want a serif font, you can set the font stack to include the serif of your choice, such as Garamond, followed by Times (which is available on Mac and PC). The opening tag and attributes will look like this: `<FONT face="Garamond, Times">`.

For a sans serif body, choose the sans serif font of your choice, such as Verdana. Follow it up with Arial, which is available to people whose computers run Windows, and then with Helvetica, which is available to Mac users: `<FONT face="verdana, arial, helvetica">`.

In order to accommodate both machines, you can create HTML code that looks like this:

```
<FONT face="verdana, arial, helvetica">
Through the eyes of a child<br>
love paints a rainbow<br>
```

```
With each passing day<br>
the colors unfold<br>
A story of enchantment<br>
that touches my heart.<br>
</FONT>
```

With this coding, the browser looks for Helvetica if it cannot find Verdana or Arial.

Older browsers do not read font names in stacks. However, you can add another option to the stack to accommodate them:

```
<FONT face="arial, helvetica, sans serif">
Through the eyes of a child<br>
love paints a rainbow<br>
With each passing day<br>
the colors unfold<br>
A story of enchantment<br>
that touches my heart.<br>
</FONT>
```

If the older browser cannot find Arial or Helvetica, it seeks out the first sans serif font it can find on the resident machine and uses that.

Table 6.1 shows the fonts that are always native to Windows and Macintosh computers. By "native" we mean that these fonts are shipped with the Windows operating system or the Macintosh OS. Anyone can load any font onto his or her machine, but you can be absolutely sure that the fonts listed in this table are available.

Table 6.1 Native Windows and Macintosh Fonts

WINDOWS	WINDOWS (CONT'D)	MACINTOSH
Arial	Courier	Chicago
Arial Black	Courier New	Courier
Arial Narrow	Garamond	Helvetica
Arial Rounded MT Bold	MS Serif	Monaco
Book Antiqua	MS Sans Serif	New York
Bookman Old Style	Times New Roman	Palatino
Century Gothic	Verdana	Times
Century Schoolbook		

You can see from this table that *only two fonts,* Times and Courier, are native to Windows and Macintosh! This is unnerving, to say the least. However, if you understand cross-platform font limitations and know the difference between serif and san serif fonts, you can gain some control over standard HTML documents.

Even if you want to use a fancy decorative font that isn't available on most machines, you can stack alternatives and be sure that everyone sees a stylish typeface. Consider this example:

```
<FONT face="whimsy ICG, garamond, times, serif">
Through the eyes of a child<br>
love paints a rainbow<br>
With each passing day<br>
the colors unfold<br>
A story of enchantment<br>
that touches my heart.<br>
</FONT>
```

This way, if the person doesn't have Whimsy, the next best font, Garamond, is used, and if Garamond isn't available, the browser will look for Times, which the site visitor is very likely to have.

Stacking Fonts in FrontPage

Now that you know how the stacking technique works, follow these steps to do it in FrontPage:

1. In Page view, select the text you want to modify.

2. Open the Font drop-down menu on the Formatting toolbar and select your first choice in fonts. Behind the scenes, FrontPage enters the necessary HTML for controlling fonts.

3. Click the HTML tab to switch to see the HTML code. Your next step is to enter your second-choice font, the one that will be displayed on the screens of visitors who don't have your first-choice font.

4. Click between the name of your first-choice font and the closing quotation mark ("), enter a comma (,), enter a blank space, and type the name of your second-choice font. Now the HTML code should look something like this:

```
<font face="Gill Sans MT, Arial">
```

5. Repeat step 4 to enter a third-choice and even a fourth-choice font.

6. For extra safety, you can add the sans serif value to accommodate older browsers. If you do so, your HTML code will look something like this:

```
<font face="Gill Sans MT, Arial, Helvetica, sans serif">
```

Be sure to save your file to record the font stack you entered. You now have a cross-platform means of displaying fonts. Your visitors may not see your first choice, but they'll at least see a font style that you've created for your site.

Embedding Fonts

Another way to get around the problem of displaying fonts correctly is to embed fonts in a Web page. Embedding a font means to make it a part of your Web page so that visitors to the page download the font file at the same time as they download the page. With the font file on their computers, visitors to your Web page have the information they need to display the page as you meant it to be displayed.

Both Internet Explorer and Netscape Navigator have methods by which to offer embedded fonts. In Internet Explorer, font embedding is delivered using a font format known as OpenType. In Netscape, font embedding is dealt with using a technology developed by Bitstream known as TrueDoc.

While there is a lot of general interest in the idea of font embedding, it's currently being used only in test cases or experimental design sites. Embedding itself is not a new concept, however. You can already embed TrueType fonts within documents that have embraced the TrueType standard, notably Microsoft Office applications and many programs for the Macintosh.

In those cases, you simply use the font you want, give the document to someone via e-mail or disk, and they can see the font—and print it. It seems like a logical step to extend the TrueType specification to the Web, but this is not yet a standard.

Embedded Fonts

For Bitstream's TrueDoc, check out www.bitstream.com/.

Microsoft covers the OpenType format at www.microsoft.com/truetype/.

Microsoft Core Fonts

Microsoft is more than willing to give away fonts so that Windows and Mac users can have the same fonts on their computers. You can add these core fonts to your own collection, and if you're a font-maniac showing off a home page, you can ask your visitors to download the Microsoft Core fonts.

On a commercial site, it's never wise to tell visitors what they need to properly view the site. You should design commercial Web sites that will receive a lot of visitors by using the cross-browser design techniques found in Chapter 16. You can include some recommendations on a Help page, but don't rely on this for your commercial visitors.

Mastering What's Online

The Microsoft Core Fonts collection includes serif, sans serif, monotype, and decorative fonts. To download these fonts, visit www.microsoft.com/typography/fontpack/.

Using Font Tips and Tricks

If you want more fonts, there are plenty on the Web that you can download and install for free—but the more fonts you have, the more choices you have! Not to mention the fact that installing too many fonts means taking longer to choose a font on drop-down menus and dialog boxes. Remembering what each font looks like can be difficult.

One thing you might do to make font choices less confusing is create a font reference in your favorite word processing program. To do so, write a sentence or two, copy it numerous times, and then apply the different fonts on your computer to each sentence. You can group the fonts alphabetically or by category, with all of the script fonts in one section, the handwriting fonts in another, and the heavy, decorative fonts in still another.

Windows offers a means of examining the different fonts on your computer. Click the Start button, choose Settings ➜ Control Panel, and, in the Control Panel, double-click the Fonts icon. You see a list of the fonts on your computer. Double-click a font name to examine it up close in the window that appears.

Just because you have a font doesn't mean you should use it—and just because you have 57 fonts doesn't mean you should use all of those, either! Using a light hand with fonts is *always* the best trick of all.

Here are some other helpful guidelines:

- Using more than two or three fonts on a page makes it look cluttered and confusing. Figure 6.3 shows an example of mixed fonts that works, and Figure 6.4 shows one that doesn't. Note that both examples use not only more than one font face, they also mix alignments, sizes, colors, and styles (bold and italic).

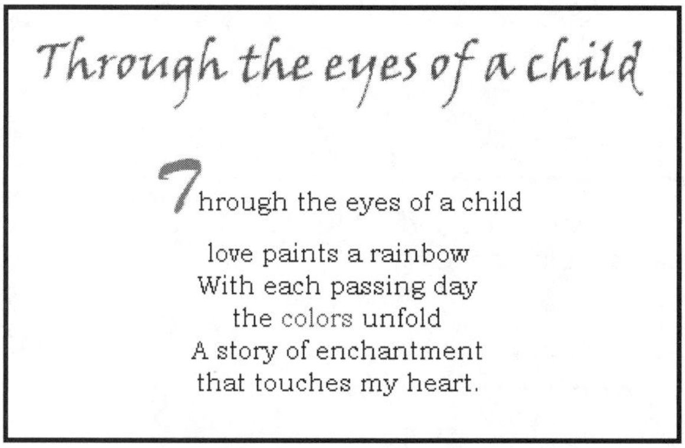

Through the eyes of a child

*T*hrough the eyes of a child

love paints a rainbow
With each passing day
the colors unfold
A story of enchantment
that touches my heart.

Figure 6.3 *Mixing fonts well means using a light hand.*

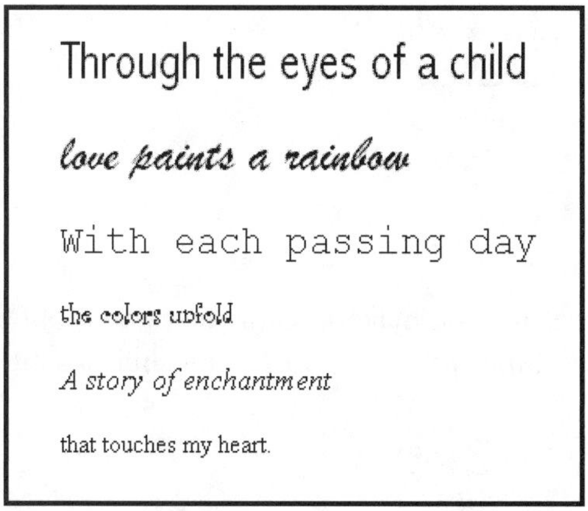

Through the eyes of a child

love paints a rainbow

With each passing day

the colors unfold

A story of enchantment

that touches my heart.

Figure 6.4 *Too many fonts can spoil the soup.*

- When choosing a font, contrast can make a page look very professional. To create contrast, choose a font for headers that is different from the font you use in the body text. For example, you can choose a sans serif font for your headers, and a serif font for your body text (see Figure 6.5), or vice versa (see Figure 6.6). Either way can work well, but be consistent!

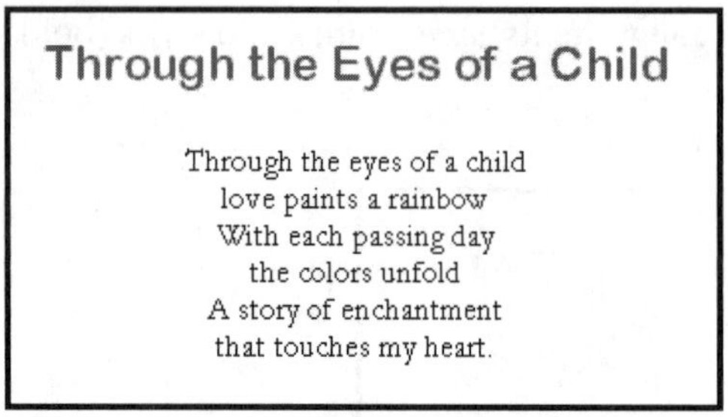

Through the Eyes of a Child

Through the eyes of a child
love paints a rainbow
With each passing day
the colors unfold
A story of enchantment
that touches my heart.

Figure 6.5 *A sans serif font for headers and a serif font for body text is a professional mix.*

Through the Eyes of a Child

Through the eyes of a child
love paints a rainbow
With each passing day
the colors unfold
A story of enchantment
that touches my heart.

Figure 6.6 *A serif font for headers and a sans serif font for body text looks good too, but be consistent!*

- Limit your font color palette, and make sure that text stands out from the background without clashing with it. More on colors in just a bit.

A Font Resource

You can get a lot of information about fonts, and download specialty fonts as well, by visiting Web Wonk at www.dsiegel.com/tips/.

Changing Font Size

Just as different fonts can add variety and interest to a page, so can different font sizes. You've already learned that headings come in different sizes. As you will recall, headings come in sizes from 1 to 6, where size 1 is very large and size 6 is very small.

Similarly, text sizes in HTML range from size 1 to size 7, although the scale goes the other way: size 1 text is rather small, while size 7 is large. "Regular size" type, or the default setting, is size 3, which generally corresponds to 12-point type. Size 4 is generally 14 points, and so it goes on up to size 7, which translates to 36 points. At the other end of the scale, tiny size 1 type is generally displayed at 8 points—small print indeed. This numeric method is referred to as *absolute*. However, because different browsers interpret information in their own unique ways, and because there are many variables—such as customizing default fonts or changing the resolution on one's monitor—font sizing in HTML is not very specific or accurate.

You can see the different font sizes in Figure 6.7, where the base font is size 3.

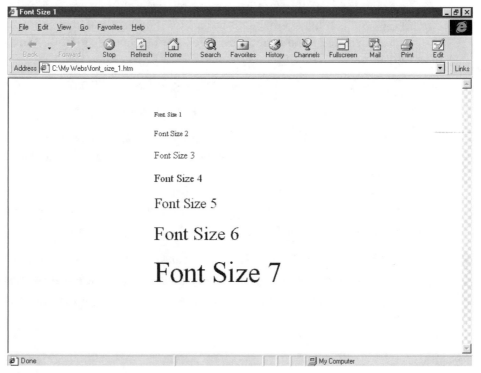

Figure 6.7 *HTML uses seven different font sizes.*

Font sizes are also *relative* to the default font size settings in the visitor's browser software. Nearsighted folks, or people with Really Big Monitors, may have set their default font size to 14 or larger; keen-eyed people may set their default font size to 10, to fit more text on the screen. What this means is that the font size you set will not be based on 12 points, but on the user's own private standard.

Because users can change their browser's font size settings, all HTML font sizes are really relative, but some are more relative than others. FrontPage uses two different scales to handle font size:

- The absolute type scale specifies font sizes as ranging from 1 to 7. When you choose an option from the Font Size drop-down menu on the Formatting toolbar, you choose an absolute font size.

- The relative scale uses a numeric scale based on plus and minus values. This method tells the browser to knock the point size up or down a notch from the base font size (3 on the absolute scale).

In the absolute scale of 1 to 7, size 3 is the default font size; it's also known as the *base font* size. The other font sizes on the relative scale then use 3 as the "zero" setting. These seven settings act the same as the 1 to 7 point scale used by FrontPage. The +1 size, for instance, is the same as font size 4 (3+1). The code for these fonts looks rather similar:

Relative type scale   `<FONT SIZE=+1>14 point</FONT>`

Absolute type scale   `<FONT SIZE=4>14 point</FONT>`

Each of these pieces of code produces text the same size; to use relative sizes instead of absolute sizes, you'd simply open the HTML view in Page view and make the changes there.

The relative size that is the most important is the base font size. If you set the base font size (usually equivalent to size 3) to size 5, for instance, all the + and – settings would be based on size 5 rather than size 3.

Absolute or relative: Which is better? This depends upon your preference—and your audience. In most cases, stick to the absolute method. However, if you know that your audience tends to modify their browser defaults (such as an audience with known vision difficulties), you may opt for the relative method.

To set an absolute font size:

1. In Page view, select the text whose size needs changing.

2. Do one of the following:

   - From the drop-down sizing menu on the formatting toolbar, select the numeric size you want (see Figure 6.8).

   - Click the Increase Font Size or Decrease Font Size button (or press Ctrl+> or Ctrl+<) as many times as necessary to get the size you want.

   - Choose Format Font to open the Font dialog box and select a font size there.

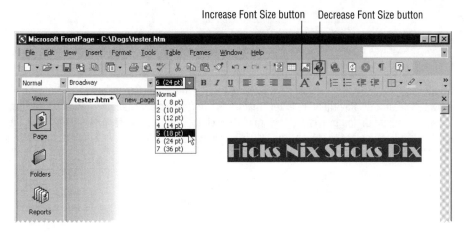

Figure 6.8 *Changing the size of text*

To choose a relative font size for text, you can go right into the HTML and add your changes by following these steps:

1. In Page view, select the text whose size needs changing.

2. Open the Font Size drop-down menu on the Formatting toolbar and select a size. Behind the scenes, FrontPage enters the necessary HTML codes.

3. Click the HTML tab to see the codes.

4. Place your cursor in front of the numeric value that describes the font size, enter a plus (+) or minus sign (–), and then enter the relative numeric value that you want the font size to be.

5. Save your file.

Nifty Font Size Effects

So you can make some pieces of text bigger than others—what's the big deal? You can achieve a polished look by mixing the font sizes on a page, or you can make your page look weird and haphazard (we don't recommend the latter). Here are some ways you can use different font sizes to great effect:

- **Initial caps**   Increasing the font size of the first letter in a paragraph makes for an eye-catching effect.

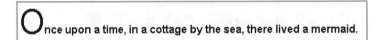

- **Small caps**   Small capital letters can also add a touch of elegance to a Web page. Note, however, that older browsers cannot display them. To enter small capital letters, select the letters and choose Format ➜ Font. Then, in the Font dialog box, check the Small Caps check box. In news reports, small capital letters are often used in the dateline at the start of the article, as shown in this illustration. Small capital letters do not appear in font sizes above 12 points.

> KEY WEST, FLA. APR 22 (UPI) - A storm of unparalleled intensity slammed into the coast of Florida yesterday afternoon.

- **Varied font size**   To make letters of varying size, change the size of each letter in a word. If you're careful, varying font sizes makes for a nice graphic effect. They call attention to words or sentences—but don't use them too many times, because they can be a distraction.

- **Address information smaller than other text**   The address information on a Web page, which is usually found at the bottom of the page, is often a bit smaller than body text. You can also make captions and sidebars a smaller font size.

Choosing Colors for Text

Text in different colors makes for a nice visual contrast. It makes pages more interesting. Besides choosing colors for text, you can choose colors for hyperlinks, both the color of links themselves and the color of links that a visitor has clicked.

Be sure to use a text color that contrasts sharply with the background; black text on a white page and white text on a black page are two obvious examples. In either case, choosing a color for hyperlinks that contrasts with the background, contrasts with other text on the page, and stands out is essential.

What's more, sometimes highlighting portions of a page by using an additional font color that is different from the color assigned to text and links is necessary. Some pages look elegant with headings set in their own color, for example. But you want to be sure not to confuse your visitors with too many colors. As with typefaces and font sizes, a light hand is always the most effective.

When choosing a color scheme, remember your audience. If you're creating a lively page about gardening, you might opt for pale yellow text on a dark green background, with light green or gold hyperlink colors for the entire site. On the other hand, if your site is a post-industrial wasteland of punk bands, skateboards, and splatterpunk fiction, you might go for a more grisly look with a black background, silver text, and blood-red links.

No matter the color palette you choose, colors should be consistent throughout a site. For example, you should use the same text and link colors on the main page as you do on any of the internal pages.

You can control the hyperlink color and default text color of a Web page as long as you haven't applied a theme to the page. If your page uses a theme, you'll have to turn it off before you can make changes to the background properties. See Chapter 4 for more about themes.

Mastering What's Online

These two sites present good examples of designs whose color schemes suit their audience: HotWired and Salon. HotWired, at www.hotwired.lycos.com/, uses a neon array of bright, mind-bending colors to challenge the paradigms of the technocracy (and the patience of the people who actually try to read the stuff).

Salon, an online features magazine for highbrows, uses a traditional print color scheme of black body text on white pages. Not only do links appear in color, so do headlines, initial caps, and introductions, usually by using dark red, blue, brown, or some other stately color to attract attention to part of a page. Salon's Web pages are worth looking at—and reading—at www.salon.com/.

Choosing the Default Text Color for a Web Page

The default text color is the one that is assigned to all text on the page, except for any text that has been assigned a different color by way of the Font Color button or the Font dialog box. For the default text color, choose the color you want for the majority of the text.

Follow these steps to choose the default text color for a Web page:

1. In Page view, choose Format → Background. The Background tab of the Page Properties dialog box appears (see Figure 6.9).

Choose hyperlink colors.

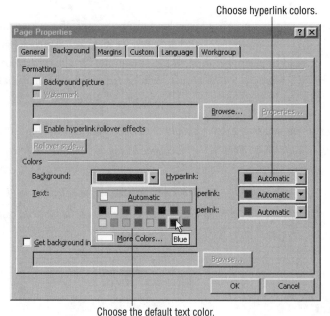

Choose the default text color.

Figure 6.9 *In the Page Properties dialog box, you can change the default text color and hyperlink colors, among other things.*

2. Open the Text drop-down menu and choose a color for text.

Notice the More Colors option at the bottom of the drop-down menu. Click that option and you see the More Colors dialog box, where you can select among numerous colors. Many are tempted to open this dialog box and choose an offbeat color, but remember: The basic color choices offered to you as menu options may not be very exciting, but they do offer a distinct advantage over colors you create yourself—they're standard. No matter which platform or what kind of awful, low-resolution color monitor a visitor to your site uses to surf the Web, visitors see pretty much the color you choose, if you stick to basic colors.

Other Typographical Issues

Entire books have been written on typography. Indeed, entire courses of study are devoted to learning how to present text on a page. We've looked at what you can do with type on the Web using FrontPage 2002, but let's touch on some other typographical issues you may hear mentioned in your travels with type:

Anti-aliasing   This feature, found in graphics programs, makes images and text blend smoothly into the background. As you know, what you see on a computer screen is made of thousands upon thousands of pixels. Because pixels are square, the edges of images and text can look jagged when they land on a background. Anti-aliasing smoothes the edges of images and text so they are not jagged. The feature does this by creating a transition zone between the foreground and background image or text and blending the colors in the transition zone.

Kerning and Tracking   Most computer fonts employ *proportional spacing*; that is, the space between each letter in a word is adjusted depending on the size and shape of each unique letterform. Typographers often adjust the way lines of type are spaced. *Kerning* refers to adjusting the space between pairs of letters, while *tracking* refers to adjusting the spacing of an overall line. Page design and imaging programs such as Adobe Photoshop, Adobe Illustrator, Adobe PageMaker, and Quark XPress include tools for kerning and tracking. If you design a block of text using one of these programs, you could create an image based on this picture-perfect type.

Margins   Part of what makes a page look either lovely or cluttered is the space between text or images and the edge of the page, or the space between columns (which you can create through the use of tables, as discussed in Chapter 11).

Vertical Spacing   Balancing the white space between paragraphs, between images and their captions, and between headlines and stories can help unify the overall look of a page. Chapter 9 describes how to adjust the space between text and images, and Chapter 4 discusses the use of horizontal rules to divide space. However, be aware that simple white space is rarely overused.

Changing Font Colors

While the main body of your text will generally be all one color, you may want to change the colors of headings, captions, addresses, particular words, or whatever else you feel like sprucing up.

Another effective way to use color on your pages is to assign an entire paragraph a slightly different color from the rest of the text to make the reader's eye jump to it. In Salon Magazine, the online magazine we referred to earlier, black text is used on most pages, but occasionally the editors splash dark red on a paragraph to make it stand out.

Manipulating text colors on your pages can create lovely effects, especially in combination with tables, background colors, and a mix of paragraph alignments or indents. Beware of overuse, however. Too many colors of text on a page can make it look busy—and worse, make it difficult to read.

Follow these steps to change the color of a piece of text:

1. In Page view, highlight the text whose color you want to change.

2. On the Formatting toolbar, open the drop-down menu on the Font Color button and choose a color (see Figure 6.10). To use the default color, choose the Automatic option on the drop-down menu.

Figure 6.10 *Choosing a font color for text*

Another way to assign a color to text is to select it, choose Format ➜ Font to open the Font dialog box, and select a color there from the Color drop-down menu.

Choosing a Color for Hyperlinks

You probably know that links are traditionally a brighter color than the rest of the page, but you may not be aware that hyperlinks actually have *three* color attributes:

Hyperlink color   The color of a new link—one that a visitor to a Web site has never before clicked.

Visited hyperlink color   The color of a link the visitor has clicked. The visited hyperlink color is meant to inspire déjà vu. The visitor knows that he or she has visited the link before, and the link's color assures the visitor that that is the case.

Active hyperlink color   The color of a link the visitor is in the act of clicking. The link changes color while the visitor is clicking it and holding the mouse button down.

Follow these steps to choose a color for hyperlinks, visited hyperlinks, and active hyperlinks:

1. In Page view choose Format ➜ Background. The Background tab of the Page Properties dialog box appears (refer to Figure 6.9).

2. Open the Hyperlink, Visited Hyperlink, and Active Hyperlink drop-down menus and choose a color that appeals to you. If you select Default, no color is chosen, and the colors that appear on the user's screen when he or she views your page will be determined by the default browser settings that the individual user has set.

You won't see visited and active link colors in action until you've loaded your page into a Web browser and tested your links.

Up Next

Believe it or not, you now have enough skills to create a fine-looking page! In order to help bring you to the next level, we're going to focus first on how to manage your things-to-do list, helping you organize the various pieces of the basic Web sites you can now create.

Chapter 7 will not only help get your work organized, but also get you in position to move toward publishing your pages.

Managing Tasks

FRONTPAGE

Chapter 7

Creating a great Web site is a lot of work, even with FrontPage's wizards and shortcuts giving you a hand. In a Web site that consists of many pages, keeping track of everything you must do is challenging. To help you manage and maintain your Web site, FrontPage offers *Tasks view*.

A *task* is an item associated with a particular Web site that represents an action that needs doing. Think of the Tasks view as a planning organizer that happens to be a part of your Web site. FrontPage wizards create some tasks for you automatically. The Corporate Presence Wizard, for example, creates tasks that remind you which pages to customize. You can also add your own tasks to the Tasks view whenever you want. To see a lists of tasks, all you have to do is click the Tasks icon, the last icon on the Views bar. This chapter explains how to manage and work with tasks that you create, team members create, or FrontPage itself creates. Topics include:

- Understanding Tasks view

- Creating a new task

- Modifying and deleting tasks

- Using the Tasks view in a Web team or workgroup setting

Creating a New Task

Before you create a new task, you need to know that FrontPage distinguishes between two types of tasks:

Linked task   A task that is associated with a particular page or file. By creating a linked task, you can click a task name in Links view and go straight to the Web page. Writing a paragraph of text for a specific Web page is an example of a linked task.

Unlinked task   A task associated with a Web site, not a particular part of it. An unlinked task is associated with a Web site in general, not with a particular Web page or file. Entering a copyright notice or a text-link navigation bar on every page in a Web site is an example of an unlinked task. Unlinked tasks are also known as *general tasks*.

The following pages explain how to create linked and unlinked tasks.

As "When FrontPage Wizards Create Tasks" explains later in this chapter, FrontPage creates tasks for you automatically when you create a Web site from a template. Don't be surprised, therefore, if you discover a full Tasks list after you create a Web site from a template.

FrontPage gives you an opportunity to create tasks automatically as part of creating other things. For example, you can create a link to a new page without actually creating the page; instead, you create a task that reminds you to create the page later. You can also create tasks in the course of doing routine chores. When you verify hyperlinks, for example, you can create a task that reminds you to fix broken hyperlinks.

Creating a Linked Task

Follow these steps to create a task that is linked to a particular Web page on your Web site:

1.   Choose or open the Web page with which the task is to be linked. To do so in Page view, open the Web page; in Folders view, Navigation view, or Hyperlinks view, select the Web page. (Chapter 2 explains views).

2. Choose File ➜ New ➜ Task, choose Edit ➜ Tasks ➜ Add Task, or open the drop-down menu on the New Page button and choose Task.

The New Task dialog box appears (see Figure 7.1). The figure shows the dialog box after it has been filled in. Notice that the dialog box lists the Web page with which the task is associated.

Figure 7.1 *Creating a new task*

3. In the Task Name text box, enter a brief phrase to identify or describe the task. You can include spaces, but try to keep the task name to three words or fewer to accommodate space limitations in the Tasks list. You can enter a long description later, as step 6 demonstrates.

4. In the Priority area, click an option button—High, Medium, or Low—to describe how important the task is.

5. To assign the task to someone else, enter his or her name in the Assign To text box or choose it from the drop-down menu.

6. If you'd like to describe the task in more detail, enter a few words in the Description text box. The words you enter will appear in the Description column of the Tasks list.

7. Click OK.

Click the Tasks icon in the Views bar or choose View ➜ Tasks to see the task you entered on the Tasks list.

Creating an Unlinked Task

An unlinked (or general) task is one associated with the Web site, not a particular Web page. Follow these steps to add an unlinked task to the Tasks list:

1. Switch to Tasks view. To do so, either click the Tasks icon on the Views bar or choose View ➜ Tasks.

2. Open the New Task dialog box (refer to Figure 7.1). FrontPage offers three ways to open this dialog box in Tasks view:

   - Choose File ➜ New ➜ Task.

   - Open the drop-down menu on the New Page button and choose Task.

   - Right-click a blank area and choose Add Task on the shortcut menu.

3. In the Task Name text box, briefly describe the task. Make sure your description is short enough to fit on the Tasks list.

4. In the Priority area, click the High, Medium, or Low option button to describe how important the task is.

5. To assign the task to someone else, type that person's name in the Assign To text box or choose a name from the Assigned To drop-down menu.

6. Optionally, enter a description in the Description text box to explain what the task is. Doing so can be helpful, for example, if you are assigning the task to another team member.

7. Click OK. The task you created appears at the bottom of the Tasks list.

If you need to change a task you created, double-click its name in the Tasks list. You'll see the Task Details dialog box appear, where you can change whatever you please.

Because an unlinked task isn't associated with a Web page, your headway on an unlinked task can't be monitored automatically. You must manually mark the task complete when the time comes. To do so, right-click the task in the Tasks list and choose Mark Complete on the shortcut menu.

Spell-Check and Page-Creation Tasks

Suppose you're spell-checking your Web site, you decide to spell-check all the pages, and the Spelling dialog box produces a bunch of errors (see Figure 7.2). If you aren't ready to deal with this tedium right now and you want to put off today's task until tomorrow, you can check the Add A Task For Each Page With Misspellings check box and click the Start button. This way, instead of running a spell check, the Spelling dialog box enters spell-check tasks on the Tasks list. You get one task for each page in which a misspelled word is found.

Status	Task	Assigned To	Prio...	Associated ...	Modified Date	Description
● Not Started	Fix misspelled ...	Peter Wev...	Med...	My Interests...	4/23/01 5:37:3...	Misspelled words: yes CarPoint.com a...
● Not Started	Fix misspelled ...	Peter Wev...	Med...	Hello	4/23/01 5:37:3...	Misspelled words: hello spaelling erorr
● Not Started	Fix misspelled ...	Peter Wev...	Med...	My Favorite ...	4/23/01 5:37:3...	Misspelled words: thisö spalling errur E...
● Not Started	Fix misspelled ...	Peter Wev...	Med...	Feedback	4/23/01 5:37:3...	Misspelled words: ss
● Not Started	Fix misspelled ...	Peter Wev...	Med...	new_page_...	4/23/01 5:37:3...	Misspelled words: Danse

Click to make spell-checking pages a to-do task.

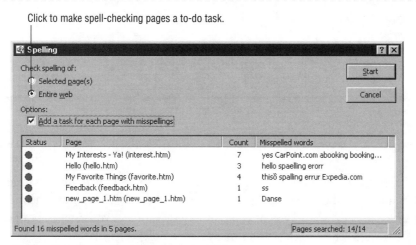

Figure 7.2 *Spell-checking an entire Web site*

Similarly, suppose you need to create a Web page from a template but you don't have the time at present to do all the donkeywork. Instead of creating the page, you can create a task to remind yourself that a Web page needs creating. FrontPage offers a special command for doing just that. In the Page Templates dialog box, create the page as you normally would, but click the Just Add Web Task check box as well. After you click OK in the dialog box, the page is created, and a task to remind you to start work on the page is added to the Tasks list.

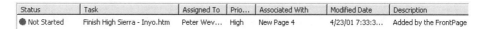

In Chapter 2, "Creating a Web Page from a Template" explains how to create a Web page in the Page Templates dialog box.

When FrontPage Wizards Create Tasks

When you create a Web site with a wizard, you will usually find a Tasks list full of tasks. FrontPage creates them automatically to help you get a grip on all the tasks you must do to make your Web page complete. This illustration shows the list of tasks you get when you create a Web site with the Corporate Presence Wizard.

Tasks						
Status	Task	Assigned To	Prio...	Associated ...	Modified Date	Description
● Not Started	Customize Home Page	Peter Wev...	High	Home	4/23/01 7:58:3...	replace generic text with something m
● Not Started	Customize News Page	Peter Wev...	High	ACME News ...	4/23/01 7:58:3...	add your own public relations text
● Not Started	Customize Products...	Peter Wev...	High	ACME Produ...	4/23/01 7:58:3...	create data sheets for your own prod
● Not Started	Customize Services ...	Peter Wev...	High	ACME Servic...	4/23/01 7:58:3...	describe your service offerings
● Not Started	Customize Feedbac...	Peter Wev...	Med...	ACME Feedb...	4/23/01 7:58:3...	adjust input areas in the form
● Not Started	Customize TOC Page	Peter Wev...	Med...	ACME Table ...	4/23/01 7:58:4...	describe sections in more detail
● Not Started	Customize Search P...	Peter Wev...	Med...	ACME Searc...	4/23/01 7:58:4...	explain how to search for common top

Each task points out something that needs to be done to finish a page in the newly created Web site. You don't have to complete the tasks right away. The purpose of the Tasks list is to remind you of what needs to be done so you can go about doing other things and return to the tasks when you're ready.

In Chapter 2, "Creating a Site with a Wizard" explains how to, well... do just that.

Reading the Tasks List

When you click the Tasks icon on the Views bar or choose View ➔ Tasks to switch to Tasks view, a Tasks list appears. For example, Figure 7.3 shows a typical Tasks list. In general, tasks are displayed in rows, with information about the tasks shown in columns:

- The *Status* of the task designates the task as Not Started, In Progress, or Completed. Initially, all tasks are assigned a status of Not Started.

- The *Task* column lists the name of each task. (Every task has to have a name.)

- The *Assigned To* column lists the name of the person assigned to complete the task. (By default, the user who created the task is responsible, but you can assign the task to someone else if you want.)

- The *Priority* column indicates whether the task is given High, Medium, or Low priority.

- The *Associated With* column shows which Web page is associated with the task, if the task is associated with a page.

- The *Modified Date* column indicates when the task was last addressed (until you go to work on a task, this will be the date that the task was created).

- The *Description* column shows detailed information about each task (whether that information was entered by a wizard or by an individual).

Click a column heading to sort, or rearrange, the list entries.

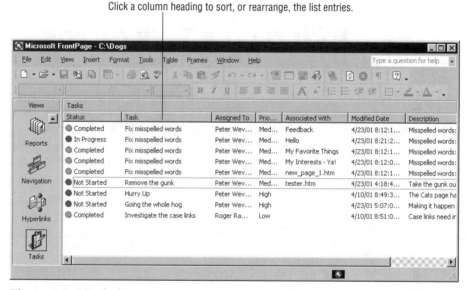

Figure 7.3 *A Tasks list*

To hide or display completed tasks on the list, right-click a blank area on the Tasks list and choose Show History on the shortcut menu. When the Show History command is selected, Completed as well as Not Started and In Progress tasks appear; when the command is not selected, only Not Started and In Progress tasks show up on the list.

Depending on the screen resolution of your monitor, you might not be able to see all of the columns in the Tasks list at once. If this is so, you can scroll horizontally to see additional columns. What's more, you can sort columns to arrange the tasks on the list in different ways.

By default, tasks are listed in the order they were created. But by clicking the column heading you want to use as sort criteria, you can arrange the list in Status, Task

Assigned To, Priority, or Associated With order. To sort tasks by priority, for example, click the Priority heading. The Tasks list rearranges itself and sorts all the tasks in the list (in ascending order) as you specified. Click a second time to reverse the order to descending. To restore the default order, click once on the Modified Date column heading, and the Tasks list displays the tasks in the order in which they were entered on the list or last addressed.

Embarking on a Task on the Tasks List

The beauty of the Tasks list is that it always spells out precisely what tasks need doing to complete your Web site. After you click the Tasks icon on the Views bar or choose View ➔ Tasks to switch to Tasks view, you'll see the tasks in all their splendor.

FrontPage makes it very easy to start work on a linked task that is associated with a Web page (earlier in this chapter, "Creating a New Task" explained the difference between linked and unlinked tasks). Tasks that are associated with Web pages show a Web page name in the Associated With column of the Tasks list, as shown in this illustration.

Status	Task	Assigned To	Prio...	Associated With	Modified Date	Description
● Not Started	Fix misspelled words	Peter Wev...	Med...	Feedback	4/23/01 8:12:1...	Misspelled words:
● Not Started	Fix misspelled words	Peter Wev...	Med...	My Favorite Things	4/23/01 8:12:1...	Misspelled words:
● Not Started	Fix misspelled words	Peter Wev...	Med...	My Interests - Ya!	4/23/01 8:12:0...	Misspelled words:

Select a task that is associated with a Web page and follow any of these instructions to start work on it:

- Double-click the name of the task to open the Task Details dialog box. From there, click the Start Task button.

- Right-click and choose Start Task on the shortcut menu.

- Choose Edit ➔ Tasks ➔ Start Task.

And if the task isn't associated with a particular Web page? Then go to it without choosing the Start Task command!

If you have indeed completed the task at hand, you can mark it as complete (see "Marking a Task as Complete" to learn how to do this).

To find out more about a task, double-click it. The Task Details dialog box appears. It lists all the information you entered when you created the task.

Managing Tasks on the Tasks List

The Tasks list is an excellent way to see whether tasks are complete, what needs completing, who has been assigned to different tasks, and what the tasks are. Following are instructions for managing the Tasks list. Read on to find out how to change a task description, mark a task as complete, and delete a task from the Tasks list.

Modifying a Task Description

Sometimes you want to modify some details about a task. Perhaps you need to change its priority rating, assign it to someone else, or update its description. Follow these steps to modify a task description:

1. Choose View ➔ Tasks or click the Tasks icon on the Views bar to see the Tasks list.

2. Double-click the task you want to modify. The Task Details dialog box appears (see Figure 7.4). Does this dialog box look familiar? It's the spitting image of the New Task dialog box (refer to Figure 7.1).

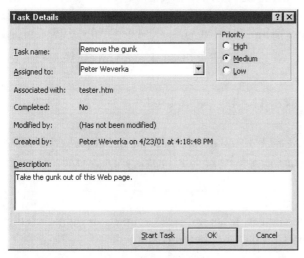

Figure 7.4 *Change your description of a task in the Task Details dialog box.*

With most tasks, there are four fields that you can change: the Task Name text box, the Assigned To text box (which displays the name of the person to whom the task is assigned), the Priority area, and the Description text box. (Any tasks that were added by a wizard have a fixed task name that you can't change. And with completed tasks, you can change only the description.) The other fields can't be changed directly, but to get around this you can always just create a new task.

3. Change any of the fields by typing in the appropriate text boxes.

4. Click OK.

Marking a Task as Complete

You can mark tasks as completed whenever you want, but there's no going back. After a task is marked as completed, you can't change its status. Therefore, you should mark a task as completed only when *everything* needed to finish it has been done. For example, if several team members are responsible for completing a given task, the task should not be marked as completed until all team members have finished their contributions. Similarly, if a team has finished working on a Web page but the page needs to be reviewed and approved, do not mark the task as complete until the page has been reviewed, any last-minute corrections have been made, and the page is approved for posting.

Follow these steps to indicate that a task has been really, truly completed:

1. Choose View ➜ Tasks or click the Tasks icon on the Views bar to go to the Tasks list.

2. Select the task that has been completed.

Remember: After you have marked a task complete, it's done. Be sure you've finished a task before marking it as complete. If you prematurely mark a task complete, you have to delete it and create a new task from scratch to replace it.

3. Either choose Edit ➜ Tasks ➜ Mark Complete or right-click the task and choose Mark Complete on the shortcut menu.

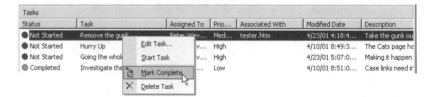

By the way, if you undertake some kinds of tasks—editing a Web page, for example—and choose the Save command, FrontPage asks whether the task is complete and should be removed from the Tasks list. Click Yes or No in the dialog box that appears and be on your merry way.

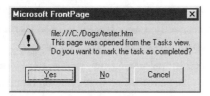

Deleting a Task from the Tasks List

By right-clicking a blank spot on the Tasks list and deselecting the Show History command on the shortcut menu, you can remove Completed tasks from the Tasks list. Removing Completed tasks is fine and dandy, but even with the Completed tasks removed, a list can still be crowded with tasks. To keep the Tasks list from getting too long, you might want to delete tasks that you have no intention of completing as well as Completed tasks.

There's no way to undelete a task. Even the Undo command won't work. Be very sure that you really want to delete the task, because there are no second chances.

To delete a task, follow these steps:

1. Choose View ➜ Tasks or click the Tasks icon on the Views bar to switch to Tasks view.

2. Select a task and do one of the following to delete it:

   • Press the Delete key.

   • Right-click the task and choose Delete Task on the shortcut menu.

   • Choose Edit ➜ Delete.

3. In the Confirm Delete dialog box, click Yes.

That's it! The task is gone, never to return. You can now switch to another view in FrontPage or continue to work on other tasks.

Using the Tasks View in a Team Setting

As you've seen throughout this chapter, FrontPage keeps track of who created each task and who is assigned to each task. You can also see who last modified a page linked to a task (and the time of the modification as well). These tracking features make using FrontPage 2002 in a workgroup or Web-team setting a project manager's dream.

To work properly as a team, you need to make sure that each person logs into the network correctly (under his or her own username) and that your Web site is set up correctly, with the proper permissions in place for each member of the team. In organizing a team or workgroup to work on a Web site, the most fundamental consideration is whether to assign team members to areas of the site (a decentralized approach) or assign tasks to team members (a centralized approach).

There are pros and cons either way:

- In a decentralized approach, individuals (or smaller teams) "own" one area. The decentralized approach provides for an increased sense of pride, responsibility, and accountability.

- In a centralized approach, one key player has greater control over the big picture and team members carry out various functions in a more assembly-line-like manner. The centralized approach can be very efficient.

As team leader or manager, you need to decide which approach to take, make assignments, and set permissions accordingly. You may want to assign and set permissions for a whole area of the site or a specific area to a given person, or you may want to assign and set permissions on a task-by-task basis. Again, Chapter 24 covers setting permissions; you must set appropriate permissions before you can assign tasks to individuals.

Remember to set permissions for team members who are to check other people's work. For example, if you have a review team or quality assurance person who has to check the work of others, permissions must be granted accordingly.

Assigning a Task to a User

By default, FrontPage assigns a task to the person who created it. You may want to assign tasks differently, however. You can assign any user to a task. Follow these steps:

1. Choose View ➜ Tasks or click the Tasks icon on the Views bar to see the Tasks list.

2. Double-click the name of the task that needs reassigning. The Task Details dialog box appears.

3. In the Assigned To text box, either type the name of the person who will do the task or choose a name from the drop-down menu. (See the sidebar "On User-names and FrontPage" for tips and cautions.) You can use a group name here.

4. Click OK.

Whenever you create a new task (regardless of how you go about creating it), you can quickly assign it to a user other than yourself by entering that person's name in the New Task dialog box's Assigned To text box.

Anyone who has the correct permissions can complete a task, whether or not it was originally assigned to that person.

On Usernames and FrontPage

When you first switch on a computer that is connected to a network, Windows displays a login dialog box, with text boxes for your username and password. It's best and simplest all the way around if you use that same username here. Usernames are usually only one word long.

Note that you will not be forced to use a username from the list of users and groups assigned to the Web site as a whole. This means that you have to make certain the correct username is listed for each task. It's helpful to make a list of usernames for your team members and distribute it to ensure that everyone is using this list consistently.

Tracking Modifications

Knowing who completes or modifies a task is of great concern to you, the team leader. FrontPage keeps track of the last person who worked on a task along with the last time he or she saved the file. This information is recorded in the Tasks list's Modified By field, in FrontPage's Tasks view.

If you want to know who last worked on a task and when, follow these steps:

1. Chose View ➜ Tasks or click the Tasks icon in the Views bar to switch to Tasks view.

Make sure that everyone working on a task has used the correct username and has logged in properly.

2. Double-click the desired task. The Task Details dialog box appears. Note especially the information listed in the Created By and Modified By fields. (If the task is already completed, the Modified By field will have been replaced with a Completed By field. If the task is an unlinked task, the Modified By field will always say "Has not been modified.")

3. Click OK.

Mastering What's Online

In some ways, FrontPage's Tasks view acts like scaled-down project management software.

Microsoft Project is a full-featured project manager program you can use in addition to FrontPage; read more about this popular application at the Microsoft Project home page (www.microsoft.com/project).

Up Next

Now that you've learned not only how to create and modify pages in FrontPage, but also basic Web site management skills, it's time to try out the next logical step: making your site live on the Internet!

Don't worry if you feel as though your site isn't ready for prime time. We're going to work on advanced design concepts in upcoming sections of the book. However, it is time to get your feet wet with the aspects of FrontPage that you'll need to use when you do feel confident about your site. So, let's move on to Chapter 8.

Publishing Your Pages

FRONTPAGE

Chapter 8

Web pages don't amount to a lot until they are published on the World Wide Web. Without being published, they sit on your computer, unread and unloved. So far, this book has been concerned with using FrontPage and designing Web pages, but this chapter shows you how to publish your labor of love on the Web so that Web surfers the world over can admire it. We'll also make sure you are familiar with making changes so that you can regularly update your Web pages with ease. Topics include:

- The stages of Web publishing

- Choosing an Internet service provider or Internet presence provider

- Publishing to the World Wide Web

- Publishing to a local intranet

- Making changes to your Web site

- Deleting published Web sites

What Is "Publishing"?

To be a part of the World Wide Web, your FrontPage Web site must be *published* (or uploaded) to a Web server. And to publish a Web site, you need an account with an *Internet service provider* (*ISP*) or have access to a company Web server. (Later in this chapter, "Choosing an Internet Service Provider" offers advice for choosing an ISP.)

Publishing, in Web terminology, means to copy all the files that make up a Web page or a Web site to the proper computer. Without FrontPage, publishing a Web is a complex task that requires a thorough knowledge of *FTP* (*File Transfer Protocol*), file permissions, and other technology skills.

After you've specified the name of the Web server to which you will publish your Web site, provided FrontPage with a URL (Uniform Resource Locator, the address assigned to you by your ISP), and provided other basic information, publishing a Web site is easy. In other words, publishing is easy after you do it the first time. You can forever after publish changes and new pages with the click of a button.

What's more, if you have access to a company intranet, you can create a Web site and set it up in such a way that everyone whose computer is connected to the company's in-house network can browse your Web site. Or you can restrict access to the Web site so that only people who have permission to visit it can visit it.

Types of Web Sites

As far as the Web publishing process is concerned, three important types of Web sites are worth knowing about:

Internet   An Internet site is a typical public site that all people with Internet access can visit.

Intranet   An intranet site is part of a network. Only people working in-house at a company can access it. Company networks employ the same technologies as the Internet, but intranet material is private and accessible only to those with access privileges.

Extranet   An extranet is used when a company wants to exchange internal, intranet-based information with subcontractors, vendors, and other outsiders without allowing access to all internal data. Extranets are proprietary and private Web sites that allow access to specific external entities.

The Stages of Publishing

When software manufacturers create a product, they go through two stages: alpha testing and beta testing. *Alpha testing* refers to the tests that the manufacturers run themselves while the software is being developed. *Beta testing* is broader-based testing by a larger group of interested parties, sometimes including outsiders. When beta testing is finished, the product is ready to be shipped to the manufacturer or otherwise presented for public consumption.

Your Web site will go through both of these stages before it is launched. When you create Web pages and your Web site, think of yourself (and the site) as being in the alpha stage. Instead of publishing your site on a Web server, you are simply publishing it to your own computer. The only person who visits your site is you (and the team, if others are helping you build the site). As you work on your Web site, you should constantly test it on different Web browsers and refine your design and content as necessary. (Chapter 16 explores Web browsers, which browsers are in use, and how you can design your pages to accommodate different browsers' capabilities.)

Use the techniques we showed you in Chapter 1 for creating a storyboard and structure, working out navigational elements, and building a prototype. Show your work to a small group of colleagues if you like—it doesn't hurt to get feedback along the way.

When your site is more or less together, prepare to enter *beta* testing. Round up some good people who can test your Web site and give you detailed feedback. It's a good idea to set up or borrow space on a temporary Web server called a *staging server*. (You can simply use a secret directory on your normal Web server if you like.)

Distribute this temporary URL only to beta testers and ask them to let you know what they think. Keep your Web site on the staging server during the testing and refining stage. Very likely, your Web site will go through several revisions, and you will publish different versions as you gather more feedback (and recruit more beta testers, if necessary). When you've resolved the beta testers' issues to your satisfaction, beta testing is finished—and you're ready to publish your Web site to its final location.

You can assign beta testing to a select group of coworkers if yours is a company site, or you can hire freelance editors and reviewers to look at it. Whether you have a company site or personal site, you may be able to get volunteers by posting a request to a Usenet newsgroup such as comp.infosystems .www.authoring.html *or a newsgroup devoted to the same subject that your Web site is devoted to. Be sure to keep your postings short, relevant, and specific. Don't post to more than two or three newsgroups; be familiar with the newsgroup and what is normally posted there; read the newsgroup diligently after you post to follow up any questions or comments; and don't post your announcement more than once. Any other approach is a violation of Usenet etiquette, will earn you a bad reputation, and will discourage beta testers.*

Weighing Your Web Publishing Options

Now that you know the publishing process, let's look at how to get your Web site onto a remote Web server. As we mentioned earlier, you need an Internet connection to publish on the Web. You also need access to a Web server, either a company Web server (if the company with which you are associated has its own servers) or the Web server at your ISP. These pages look at how to choose an ISP and how to register a domain name.

Mastering What's Online

Within limits, you can publish on the Web for free. Geocities (`www.geocities.com/`) offers free Web home pages and e-mail on the Web. Many other free Web services are available; to find a long list, go to Yahoo! (`www.yahoo.com/`) and search for *Free Web Pages*. Note, however, that some free Web page services focus less on customer service or will offer you only a tiny amount of space. Others operate on a shoestring. Almost all place advertisements somewhere on your Web pages. For a truly professional site, you're going to have to purchase service.

Choosing an Internet Service Provider

Assuming you have an e-mail account for sending and receiving e-mail, you might first investigate whether the company that you use to exchange e-mail also provides Web site hosting services. If yours is a small Web site, sticking with the company that provides e-mail services may be the best way to go. If yours is a larger site, you probably require more server space and perhaps more attention from the people who run the ISP that hosts your site, and the cost of hosting your site will go up accordingly. Shop around. Your best bet is to ask around, to look in print publications including the local phone book, and to search the Web for local and national providers.

Mastering What's Online

The World Wide Web is a good place to start looking for ISPs. Try starting with Budgetweb (`www.budgetweb.com/`), The Blade (`www.theblade.org/`), and a big, famous list at The List (`www.thelist.com/`). Another way to find ISPs online is to start at Yahoo! (at `www.yahoo.com`)—enter **ISPs** in the Search box, and drill down to investigate the different ISPs. Yahoo! lists them by region, by U.S. states, and by country.

After you make a list of likely candidates, go to their home pages and investigate further. For example, DNAI (`www.dnai.com`) is a good local ISP in the San Francisco Bay Area. Many ISPs even let you sign up online.

What to look for? Well, local ISPs typically offer more personal service and lower overall fees than national ISPs. National ISPs, on the other hand, can sometimes provide more consistent service than local ISPs because they have the resources to stay up during temporary emergencies caused by power outages and equipment failures.

Phone ISPs and ask questions. What's most important to you, of course, depends on the purpose, content, and audience of your site. Here are some things to focus on:

Reliability   Does the ISP have on-site technicians? Are they there around the clock? How often are backups performed? How will the technicians handle power outages, earthquakes, bad weather conditions, and other potential disruptions to service?

Disk space   How much disk space is allocated for Web sites? Usually 5 to 20MB will be included in the basic monthly fee; find out what the ISP charges for more if you need it. Remember that sites get bigger as they grow older and include more content. Remember, too, that one AVI file can take as much disk space as 1,000 HTML files, so how much disk space you need depends on what sort of content you'll publish.

The FrontPage Server Extensions   Are they installed? If not, will the ISP install them? (Some of the advanced features of FrontPage just won't work without them, as we explain later in this chapter.)

Scripting   Can they handle any scripts your site might use?

Live content   Are they set up to handle any sort of live content you plan?

Traffic levels   What if your site goes through the roof? How much traffic can the ISP manage successfully? Also, will it charge extra for heavy traffic should you be lucky enough to experience it?

Databases   Does the ISP support databases? If so, can technicians help you get your database into the format that the ISP supports? And can the ISP deal with Active Server Pages (ASPs)?

Transactions   Does the ISP offer a secure server for online transactions? Does it charge extra for using it? What sort of technical and customer service support is provided for online transactions, if any?

Domain name   Does the ISP allow you to have your own domain name? (Most do, but you should check, just in case.)

Consulting vs. hosting   How much consulting or general assistance does the ISP provide? Is it actually an *Internet presence provider (IPP)*? Are there stepped-up package deals—for example, design plus hosting at one price, design plus hosting plus concept development at another?

Besides Internet service providers, you can also obtain hosting services from an Internet presence provider. IPPs offer a range of services, including developing concepts, design, implementation, and hosting. They can also help with site promotion and managing online transaction systems. Obviously, you pay more for the services of an IPP, but paying a professional is sometimes worthwhile, especially if yours is a commercial Web site.

Customer service   What is the ISP's reputation for customer service? Ask about this and pay attention to your own experiences with the ISP. Are its representatives helpful and polite? Do they answer questions quickly and accurately? Do they answer the phone and respond to messages in a timely way? Actions speak louder than words. How does the treatment you receive compare to what the ISP says its customer service policy is?

Cost   What's all this going to set you back? Be sure to ask about any extra expenses hidden in the potential use of databases, extra disk space, high traffic, and so on.

Any additional offerings   What sets this service apart? Ask the ISP this question outright and then make your assessment by comparing Company A's answers to Company B's answers and by comparing what each company says to what you actually experience in the course of your investigations. Does the ISP fulfill the stated or implied promises of its marketing hype? Does it seem, after all your questioning, to be a good, reliable company? What makes it stand out in a way that's useful to you?

Registering a Domain Name

A business Web site, to look professional, must have its own domain name. Using a virtual domain name, one that is actually the domain name of the ISP with a little identifier tacked on, such as `www.ispco.com/~joe`, is like having a P.O. box as the company address—it just points out that you are small-time stuff. A custom domain name is easier to type and remember. Rupert's URL for a site hosted at Best would be `www.best.com/~rupert/`, for example, but if Rupert gets a custom domain name, his URL becomes `www.rupert.com`. With the `www.rupert.com` address, Rupert's customers won't know whether Rupert has his own Web server or an ISP. What they will know is that Rupert's business is professional and credible. And they'll also remember his address better. Perhaps most beneficial of all, domain names can be transferred from one ISP or IPP to another, so if Rupert decides to switch to a different ISP, he can take www.rupert.com along with him.

Getting a domain name is inexpensive and relatively easy. The hard part is finding out whether the domain name you want is already taken. All domain names that end in .com or .org must be registered through InterNIC (www.internic.net/). Geographical domains such as .uk, .jp, and .us are handled by individual country registries. Your domain name for a U.S. business should end in .com; but if you're nonprofit, your domain name should end in .org. To register a domain name, InterNIC requires the name of a contact person, a telephone number, and an address.

To see if the domain name you want is available, visit InterNIC's "whois" service at www.internic.net (see Figure 8.1). By following the instructions on the page, you can check for a domain name's availability. Another quick trick is to use your browser to try to access a site with the domain name you want. Just type the name as though you were entering a real URL and see if you turn up anything.

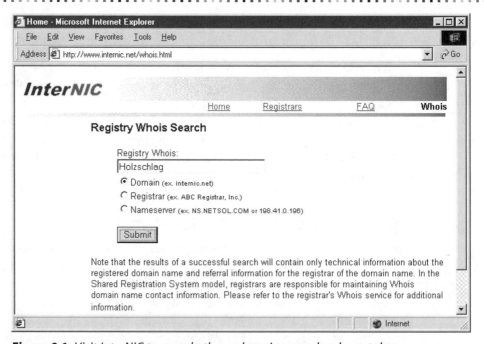

Figure 8.1 *Visit InterNIC to see whether a domain name has been taken.*

In researching potential domain names via InterNIC, don't type in a URL or machine name—just type the domain name (for example, `rupert.com`). Don't be surprised if your first choice is already taken. There are only so many words in the language. Remember, domains can contain only letters, numbers, and a hyphen; other punctuation (including spaces) is not allowed. In addition, domain names can be only 26 letters—and after the period and three letters for `.com` or `.org`, that leaves you only 22 letters. You'll have to be creative. For example, if your site promotes fresh produce, you are quite likely to find that `freshproduce.com` and `vegetables.com` are taken; but `rutabagas.com` or `vegco.com` *might* not be.

After you find an available domain name you like, you'll have several forms to fill out. Rather than do this yourself, the easiest way to register a domain name with Inter-NIC is through your ISP or IPP. The typical setup fee can range from $20 to $200. In addition, InterNIC charges $70 for the first two years, and then $35 per year after that; these fees are not negotiable. Your ISP or IPP may charge a monthly fee or yearly fee on top of the setup fee and in addition to the InterNIC charges. As usual, our advice is to shop around; many ISPs and IPPs will register a domain name for a small setup fee when you sign up, as an incentive, and won't charge any fees after that.

A convenient place to investigate domain names is Register.com (at `www.register.com`*). Enter a name you want and click the Check It button. At Register.com, you can find out who owns names and whether all the suffixes—.org, .net, .tv, .cc, .ws—are taken.*

Publishing Your Web Site for the First Time

Now let's look at how to actually publish your FrontPage Web site to a Web server for the first time. In this discussion, there are two types of Web servers: those with the FrontPage Server Extensions, and those without. The procedures for publishing to each vary a bit. It will help somewhat if you know in advance whether the machine to which you'll be publishing has the FrontPage Server Extensions. But if you don't know, you'll be notified along the way and adjustments will be made automatically, so you can in fact start out assuming that the FrontPage Server Extensions are there.

If you're still in the alpha or beta stages of designing your Web site, you can use these publishing techniques to put your Web site on a staging server. Then finish your site and be sure that testing is complete. Be sure that every link works (see Chapter 24). Be sure as well that you've tested your site by using as many browsers as possible (see Chapter 16). Are all of your tasks completed (see Chapter 7)? Are your pages spell-checked (see Chapter 3)? After you've actually published your Web site, you can begin maintaining and promoting the site (see Chapter 24).

Table 8.1 lists which features depend on the FrontPage 2002 Server Extensions. If the Server Extensions are not available on the Web server to which you publish your Web site, the features shown in the table will not work. What does that mean in real terms? It means that a visitor to your Web site will not be able to use the feature; instead, he or she will see an HTTP 404 error in the Web browser window. Chapter 25 explains the FrontPage Server Extensions in detail.

Table 8.1 Features That Require FrontPage Server Extensions

MINIMUM REQUIREMENT	FEATURE
FrontPage 2002 Server Extensions	Custom Link Bars
	File Uploading
	Shared Border Background Properties
	Top 10 List Component
	Usage Analysis Reports

Table 8.1 continued Features That Require FrontPage Server Extensions

FRONTPAGE 2000 SERVER EXTENSIONS	Categories Component
	Database Interface Wizard
	Database Results Wizard
	Nested Subwebs
	Send to Database Form Handler
	StyleSheet Links to Multiple Files or Asp Files
PRE–FRONTPAGE 2000 SERVER EXTENSIONS	Confirmation Field
	Discussion Form Handler
	Field Set
	Hit Counter
	Registration Form Handler
	Save Results Form Handler
	Search Form
	Server-Side Image Maps Created with FrontPage
Microsoft SharePoint Services	Discussion Board
	Document Library
	Lists
	List and Document Library Views
	List Forms
	SharePoint Team Web Site Wizard
	Survey

Because in an intranet setting you usually have physical access to the computers involved (as well as the appropriate permissions), you can install the FrontPage Server Extensions to the server manually if they're not available. But if your ISP's remote Web server doesn't have the Extensions, you'll have to contact your ISP and persuade them to install those Server Extensions designed for their operating system and Web server.

Publishing to a Server with FrontPage Server Extensions

Because FrontPage 2002 can automatically detect whether the FrontPage Server Extensions are installed (and compensate if they're not), it's quite safe to assume that they are and proceed as if they are. The following pages explain how to publish to your ISP's Web server on the Internet and how to publish on a company intranet for the first time.

After you publish your Web site for the first time, doing it the second and subsequent times is considerably easier. The first time, you have to declare the address where the Web site is published and do one or two other things. Later in this chapter, "Publishing a Web Site the Next Time Around" explains how to publish after you have done it initially.

Before you get too revved up, make sure your computer is connected to the Internet and that you know the full URL for the machine to which you'll be publishing your Web site—the target server. You can get this information from your ISP. After you have it, you can publish your Web site to the Internet for the first time:

1. With the Web site you want to publish open in FrontPage, choose File ➜ Publish Web. The Publish Destination dialog box appears (Figure 8.2).

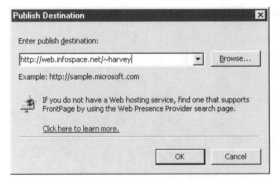

Figure 8.2 *The Publish Destination dialog box*

If you have already published this Web site to a Web server, the Publish Destination dialog box does not appear; you see the Publish Web dialog box instead. However, if you want to publish the Web site to a different Web server, click the Change button in the Publish Web dialog box to display the Publish Destination dialog box (refer to Figure 8.2)

2. In the Enter Publish Destination text box, enter the URL of the target Web server and click OK. If yours is a custom domain name, you may have to use your ISP's machine name instead of your custom domain name while publishing your Web site. The technical support people at your ISP can help you determine the proper name to use. You see the Publish Web dialog box.

If the FrontPage Server Extensions are not installed on the Web server to which you want publish your Web site, you can't go past Step 2. A dialog box tells you as much. Click OK in the dialog box and start all over by publishing your Web site to an FTP site. See "Publishing to an FTP Server" later in this chapter.

3. Click the Publish button. The dialog box closes and the publishing process begins in FrontPage. If the Server Extensions are installed, the installation process proceeds and uploading starts. A dialog box shows the progress of the upload.

   A large Web site can take five minutes or more to publish. Go get coffee or something, because even after the progress counter in the status bar reaches 100 percent, you have to wait while FrontPage updates the target Web server at the remote location. When your upload is finished, a dialog box tells you that your new Web site has been successfully published.

4. Click the first hyperlink in the dialog box, Click Here To View Your Published Web Site, to view the Web site in a browser window.

   The Web pages that make up that Web site should appear; be sure to test all of their features.

Publishing to an FTP Server

If FrontPage Server Extensions are not installed on the Web server to which you want to publish your Web site, you can still publish your Web site via FTP. FTP (File Transfer Protocol) is the protocol for copying files to and from remote computers over the Internet or a network. Follow these steps to publish your Web site using FTP:

1. Open the Web site you want to publish and choose File ➜ Publish Web. You see the Publish Destination dialog box (refer to Figure 8.2).

If you have already published this Web site to a Web server, you see the Publish Web dialog box instead of the Publish Destination dialog box. Click the Change button if your goal is to publish your Web site to a different Web server. You see the Publish Destination dialog box (refer to Figure 8.2).

2. In the Enter Publish Destination text box, type the address of the folder into which the files should be uploaded and click. Your ISP can provide the address of the folder. Do not enter the letters *ftp* in the address name. FrontPage will enter them for you later on.

3. In the Name and Password Required dialog box, enter your username and password and click OK. Again, your ISP can provide this information if you have forgotten it.

4. In the Publish Web dialog box, click the Publish button. The upload begins. If any of the pages you are publishing require the FrontPage Server Extensions, the Publishing FrontPage Components dialog box appears and lists which components require the extensions. You can click Cancel and change the problematic page so that it does not require the Server Extensions (see Table 8.1), or you can click Continue to continue publishing the Web site (including the page that does not function correctly). The Transferring Files dialog box appears.

When the upload is complete, a dialog box tells you as much.

5. Click the first hyperlink in the dialog box, Click Here To View Your Published Web Site, to view the Web site in a browser window.

Publishing is a success! You'll want to test your Web site in several browsers (see Chapter 16) and make sure that you remember to fix pages that aren't working (see Chapter 24).

Other Ways to Upload a Web Site via FTP

FrontPage isn't the only program with which you can upload a Web site to an FTP site. The Windows operating system comes with a program called the Web Publishing Wizard for uploading Web sites. And you can acquire FTP programs from the Internet as well.

Web Publishing Wizard is part of the Windows operating system (although it is not installed as part of a standard installation on some editions of Windows). To see if Web Publishing Wizard is installed on your computer, click the Start button and choose Programs ➜ Accessories ➜ Internet Tools ➜ Web Publishing Wizard. The program is fairly easy to use, but it doesn't offer all the options that FrontPage does. It's all or nothing with Web Publishing Wizard. Either upload all the Web pages in a Web site or none of them.

A shareware program, CuteFTP, and a freeware program, WS_FTP, are probably the most popular programs for uploading Web sites. Go to Download.com (www.download.com), a Web site that offers computer programs, and download them to your computer if you want to give them a try.

Publishing Your Web Site on an Intranet

To publish a Web site on an intranet, start by finding out the name of the machine you want to publish the Web site on. The name of the Web server you select will be the designated computer's name on your intranet. You probably have to ask the network administrator for the name of the machine and perhaps for permission to publish the Web site there.

Then you can follow the same procedure outlined in the section before this one ("Publishing to a Server with FrontPage Server Extensions"). When you come to the Publish Destination dialog box, enter the path to the Web server in the Enter Publish Destination text box.

Publishing a Web Site the Next Time Around

After you have published a Web site the first time, publishing it the second and subsequent times is considerably easier. You don't have to provide the address information. All you have to do is select a destination. And you can pick and choose which pages to upload, which saves you from having to wait while all the pages are uploaded.

Suppose you want to upload a page or two to the Web server. You can do that in Folders view without having to fool with the Publish Web command. In Folders view, right-click the name of the file you want to upload and choose Publish Selected Files on the shortcut menu.

Connect to the Internet and follow these steps to publish a Web site you have published before:

1. With the Web site you want to publish open in FrontPage, choose File ➔ Publish Web. The Publish Web dialog box appears (see Figure 8.3).

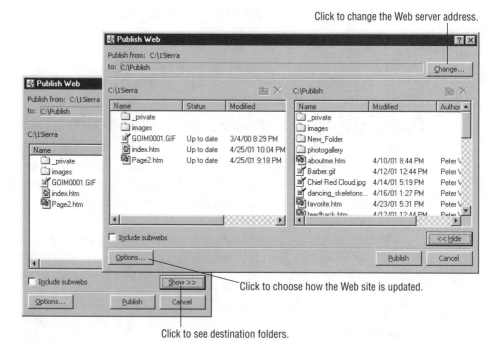

Figure 8.3 *Publishing a Web site you have published before*

The URL of the Web server you want to send the files to should appear in the To box of the Publish Web dialog box. If it doesn't appear, click the Change button to open the Publish Destination dialog box. There, either choose the URL from the Enter Publish Destination drop-down menu or enter a new URL. The section "Publishing to a Server with FrontPage Server Extensions" earlier in this chapter explained how to enter new URL Web server addresses.

2. Click the Show button, if necessary, to expand the dialog box and see the destination folders on the Web server as well as the Web site folders on your computer (refer to Figure 8.3).

3. Choose which pages to upload. By default, all new pages in the Web site are uploaded to the Web server, as are all pages that have changed since the last time you uploaded the Web site. You can do the following to decide for yourself which pages are uploaded:

Prevent a page from being published   Right-click the page in the Publish Web dialog box and choose Don't Publish on the shortcut menu. Pages that are not published show a red *X* by their names. Be sure to right-click the page's name and deselect the Don't Publish command when you want to publish the page again. You can do that in the Publish Web dialog box or in Folders view.

Upload all the pages Click the Options button in the Publish Web dialog box. On the Publish tab of the Options dialog box, check the All Pages, Overwriting Pages Already On Destination option button.

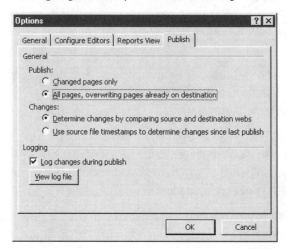

Tell FrontPage how to determine which pages to upload As we mentioned, all new pages are uploaded to the Web server by default, but you can decide how to determine which pages are new by clicking the Options button and opening the Options dialog box. Under Changes, the Determine Changes By Comparing Source And Destination Webs option tells FrontPage to give precedence to the source file every time. By choosing the other option, Use Source File Timestamps To Determine Changes Since Last Publish, you can keep the file that has been edited most recently on the Web site.

You can also publish pages by dragging and dropping them from the left, or source, side of the Publish Web dialog box to the right, or destination, side.

4. Click the Publish button to upload your Web site to the Web server. A dialog box tells you how the upload is progressing, and another invites you to click to view your Web site on the Internet.

5. Click the Click Here To View Your Published Web Site hyperlink to view your Web site in a browser window.

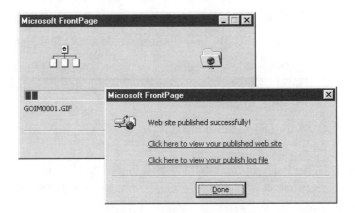

When you publish to a location you've published to before, the old files are erased from that server and replaced with the new files. Before you do this, make certain that this is your intention. The last thing you want to do is accidentally erase your important documents.

Deleting Remote Web Pages That You've Published

Okay, the day might come when you need to delete a Web page or Web site. Perhaps it was just a test Web site. Perhaps the company has folded. Perhaps it's a remote copy that's outdated and you're about to replace it. Bottom line: you need to kill the pages. How? Simply delete the Web site on the remote Web server.

A deleted Web site cannot be resurrected. The Undo command won't work, and there's no Recycle Bin or Trashcan from which to recover the files. Make sure you mean it when you kill a Web site—deleted Web sites are really, truly, absolutely gone. By keeping a copy of the site locally, however, you can republish it in place of the Web site you've deleted.

Follow these steps to delete a Web on a remote server:

1. With the Web site you want to delete open, choose File ➜ Publish Web. The Publish Web dialog box appears (refer to Figure 8.3).

2. If necessary, click the Show button to see the folders on the Web server.

3. On the right side of the dialog box, locate and select the file(s) and folder(s) you want to delete. To delete the entire Web site, click the first item and Shift-click the last to select all item.

4. Click the Delete button or right-click and choose Delete on the shortcut menu.

To delete a Web site this way, the server that holds the site must have the FrontPage Server Extensions installed. If it doesn't, you'll have to delete the files manually on the remote Web server—a procedure that varies depending on the computer's operating system.

Up Next

Now that you know how to publish your FrontPage Web sites to an intranet and onto the Web, you've learned all of the basics and finished Part I! Give yourself a pat on the back. But don't relax for too long: Your competitors are jazzing up their sites with advanced features like multimedia, tables, and frames. To find out about these features, Part II will tell you everything you need to know—starting with a lot of information about graphics, animation, and image maps.

Part II
Creating Sophisticated Designs

In This Part

Designing Graphics
for the Web

FRONTPAGE

Chapter 9

Once upon a few short years ago, a Web site was mainly very plain text on a very dull gray background, with few images in sight. Well, the times they sure have a-changed, and these days Web sites are rich, lively, highly visual presentations. From drawings to photographs, artistic treatments of text, and even animations, the Web is alive with color, texture, and motion.

In this chapter, you'll learn to create and modify visual elements for your Web page. You'll find out how to take your site from the simple and basic to the lively and colorful ranks of the sophisticated. Topics include:

- Understanding imaging programs and file formats
- Working with Microsoft Photo Editor
- Creating images with the FrontPage Drawing tools
- Creating image maps

A Look at Imaging Programs

To create images, you need an imaging program. As a certified user of FrontPage, you can take advantage of two means of creating or embellishing images: the Drawing tools and Microsoft Photo Editor, both of which are explained in this chapter. Photo Editor comes with Office XP. The Drawing tools can be found on the Drawing toolbar (click the Drawing button or choose View ➜ Toolbars ➜ Drawing to see it).

However, many imaging programs, also referred to simply as *graphics software*, demand attention. Different graphics software packages work for different folks. Which one works for you depends on your work habits and what sorts of imaging tasks you do.

If you are or aspire to be a graphic designer, you should know about Adobe Photoshop and Adobe Illustrator, which are considered industry standards. A less costly alternative from the Adobe family is Adobe ImageReady. Fans of Macromedia products also enjoy Macromedia Fireworks, a graphics software package built just for the Web. Corel-DRAW! is a popular product, and even more popular among personal Web page enthusiasts is Jasc's PaintShop Pro, a low-cost shareware program that packs a powerful punch and offers many of the same features as the more expensive alternatives. Another suite of popular Web graphics tools is available from Ulead. Be sure to visit the sidebar in this section for a list of Web sites where you can download demos of these programs.

Choose the package you find most suitable for your budget and needs, and you'll be well equipped to create your own images especially for the Web. And, once you have the program in hand, the real work begins!

Mastering What's Online

To take a look at Adobe's offerings, visit www.adobe.com. Macromedia's Fireworks can be found at www.macromedia.com. CorelDRAW! and related software is a short jump away, at www.corel.com, as is Jasc's PaintShop Pro, at www.jasc.com. Finally, visit www.ulead.com for a look at these lower-cost but punch-packing packages.

GIFs and JPEGs

It's important to know that almost all graphics on the Web exist in one of two file formats: *GIF* or *JPEG*. These two file types are supported by most browsers, which accounts for their popularity. While many other graphics formats exist, support for GIF and JPEG is the most comprehensive.

On the Web, small files are good files, and the GIF and JPEG formats make small files, but they do it in different ways. Obviously, you want the graphic files from which your Web pages are made to be small in size so that pages load faster. And you want the graphic files to be small without sacrificing clarity. To make an informed decision about what kind of graphic file format to use, you need a little background in the GIF and JPEG formats.

GIF (Graphics Interchange Format) was originally designed to display graphics on CompuServe, the online service. An 8-bit file format, it can contain a maximum of 256 unique colors within an image. When an image is saved as a GIF file, any color that is not one of the select 256 is converted into one of the select 256. Sticking to 256 colors keeps the file sizes down but it can also cause a loss of image quality. Therefore, GIF is not a great option for storing photographic images, in which subtle gradations usually require more than 256 colors. Still the GIF format is terrific for simple images without many subtleties—images with big blocks of solid color, geometric shapes, or text that is being handled as an image (see Figure 9.1). In fact, you can reduce GIFs below the maximum 256 colors, so if you have very few colors, your graphic files are greatly reduced in terms of their file size.

Figure 9.1 *Use the GIF format for simple shapes of solid colors.*

The JPEG file format was named after the people who invented it, the *Joint Photographic Experts Group*. JPEG files start by allowing an image to include over 16 million colors, which is actually more than the human eye can see. JPEG does not reduce file size by reducing color range, as GIF does. Instead, the JPEG format uses a built-in file reduction technique called *lossy compression*.

When you save a file in JPEG format, you can actually control how much the file is compressed—which is important in Web work because, as you know, small files are good files. However, the more a file is compressed, the worse its quality gets. Figure 9.2 shows a JPEG photograph saved at a "minimum" compression. At this most bloated of compression ratios, the file is 17 kilobytes in size. Figure 9.3 shows the same photograph, saved as a JPEG with a high compression—it's only 9 kilobytes in size and, for use on the Web, is of nearly identical quality. Unlike GIF files, JPEGs are well suited for storing photographic images or other art in which subtle gradations of color is found.

Figure 9.2 *The original JPEG file (compare this to Figure 9.3)*

Figure 9.3 *This file was saved at high compression, and then magnified to demonstrate the degradation in the image's integrity (compare this to Figure 9.2).*

Using Microsoft Photo Editor

Microsoft Photo Editor is a means of touching up photos and graphics. The program comes with Office XP. You can't capture images with Photo Editor, but it is a great way to crop, tweak, and otherwise manipulate bitmap graphics. A bitmap graphic is one that is composed of pixels. Photo Editor works with the following bitmap graphic formats:

- GIF (Graphics Interchange Format)
- JPG, JPEG (Joint Photographic Experts Group)
- BMP (Microsoft Windows Bitmap)
- PNG (Portable Network Graphics)
- PCD (Kodak Photo CD)
- PCX (PC Paintbrush)
- TIF, TIFF (Tagged Image File Format)

These pages explain the basics of Photo Editor as well as the rudiments of editing graphics: how to change their size and shape, choose corners for them, change their appearance, and change their texture.

Getting Up and Running with Photo Editor

To start Photo Editor, click the Start button and choose Programs ➜ Microsoft Office Tools ➜ Microsoft Photo Editor. You see the Photo Editor screen shown in Figure 9.4. When it comes to the basics, Photo Editor works much like other programs. Choose menu commands or click buttons on the toolbar to get things done. Here are the basics of handling files:

Opening a File   Click the Open button on the toolbar or choose File ➜ Open. Then, in the Open dialog box, find the graphics file you want to work with and click the Open button. The Open dialog box offers handy buttons for learning about a graphic before you go to work on it. Click the Properties button to open the Properties dialog box and find out a graphic's resolution and size. Click the Preview button to open the Preview dialog box and get a better look at a graphic.

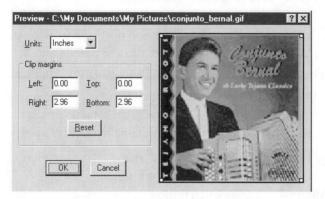

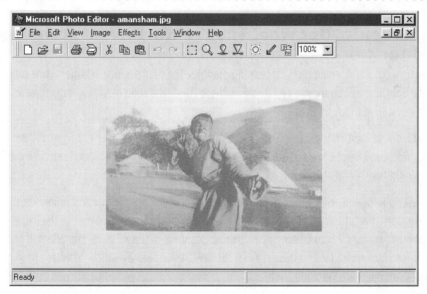

Figure 9.4 *Welcome to the Microsoft Photo Editor*

To quickly open a file you have been working on recently, open the File menu and choose its name at the bottom of the menu. The bottom of the menu lists the last four files you worked on.

Working on More than One File   You can open and work on more than one file at a time. To switch from file to file after you've opened more than one, click the Window menu item and choose the name of the file you want to go to.

Saving a File   Click the Save button or choose File ➜ Save to save a file you have been working on. To save it under a new name (and retain the original), choose File ➜ Save As and save it under a new name in the Save As dialog box.

Closing a File   Either choose File ➜ Close or click the Close button (the X) in the window. Be careful not to click the Close button in the upper-right corner of the Photo Editor window. Click that button and you close Photo Editor, not the graphic you have been working on. To close a graphic, click the second Close button, the one directly below the button that closes Photo Editor.

Creating Graphics (for What They're Worth) and Scanning with Photo Editor

Photo Editor offers a couple of feeble tools for creating graphics. The program doesn't offer a text tool or drawing tools. In fact, the only kind of graphic you can create in Photo Editor is a solid block. You can, however, scan graphics into Photo Editor and then touch them up.

To create a solid block of color, choose File ➜ New or click the New button. You see the Blank Picture dialog box. In the Resolution, Width, and Height text boxes, choose a resolution and size for the block. Then click the Color button and choose a color in the Color dialog box.

To scan a picture or photograph, click the Scan button or choose File ➜ Scan Image and follow the on-screen directions. If you have more than one scanner, choose File ➜ Select Scanner Source and choose the name of the scanner in the dialog box that appears. Photo Editor only recognizes scanners that are TWAIN-compliant. If your scanner isn't listed, either you need to reinstall it or it doesn't meet the TWAIN standard by which software programs and image-capturing devices communicate with one another.

Changing the Size of, Rotating, and Cropping Graphics

The most basic way to change the look of a graphic is to change its size, rotate it, or crop it. *Crop* means to cut away parts of a graphic. Nine times out of ten, the photographs you see in newspapers and magazines were cropped either to make them fit on the page better or to make them look better.

Following are instructions for resizing, rotating, and cropping.

Resizing a Graphic

Choose Image ➜ Resize. You see the Resize dialog box. Enter new measurements for the graphic in the Width and Height text boxes. If you want to make the graphic wider or higher, check the Allow Distortion check box before you enter width and height measurements. We recommend checking the Smooth check box. By doing so, you permit Photo Editor to add a pixel here or there to make the graphic look better.

Rotating a Graphic

Photo Editor offers two ways to turn a graphic on its head:

- Click the Rotate 90 button as many times as necessary to rotate the graphic into the right position. Each time you click the button, the graphic rotates by 90 degrees.

- Choose Image ➜ Rotate. You see the Rotate dialog box. Choose an option to rotate the graphic (and watch the Image box to see what your choice will do). By entering a number in the By Degree text box, you can rotate the graphic by a degree other than 45, 90, or 180.

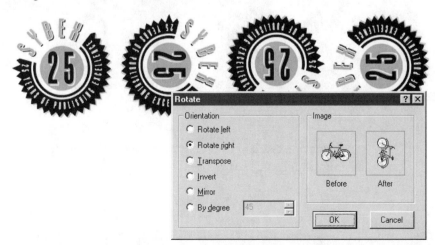

Cropping a Graphic

To crop a graphic, select the part of the graphic you need and then give the Crop command. Follow these steps to crop a graphic:

1. Select a part of the graphic by using one of these techniques:

   • Click the Crop button and drag your mouse crosswise over the part of the graphic you want.

   • Choose Edit ➜ Select All (or press Ctrl+A) to select the entire graphic, and then drag a selection handle on a corner or side of the graphic to change the part of the graphic that is selected.

 Press the Escape key if you select part of a graphic and want to start all over.

As shown in Figure 9.5, dotted lines show you what part of the graphic has been selected.

2. Right-click and choose Crop on the shortcut menu.

Select the part of the graphic you want.   Give the Crop command.

Figure 9.5 *Crop a graphic to select only the parts that you need.*

If you don't care for the way you cropped the graphic, choose Edit ➜ Undo Crop or press Ctrl+Z and start all over.

On the subject of cropping, Photo Editor offers a neat technique for cropping in an oval shape instead of a rectangular one. To crop in an oval shape, select the part of the graphic you want to crop. Then choose Image ➜ Crop, and, in the Crop dialog box, select the Oval option button (you'll find it in the Crop Margins area) and click OK.

Choosing Corners and Mat Styles for Graphics

One way to spruce up a graphic and give it a little character is to change its corners. Instead of conventional square corners, you can opt for round or cut corners. Similarly, you can make a graphic stand out by giving it a mat background. Matting in Photo Editor is like the matting behind a framed picture—it provides a little empty space to set the picture off.

To change the corners or matting of a graphic, choose Image ➜ Crop to open the Crop dialog box. Then choose options in the dialog box:

Mat Margins   In the Left, Right, Top, and Bottom text boxes, enter measurements to tell Photo Editor how much matting to place around the graphic.

Corners   For each corner—Top-Left, Top-Right, Bottom-Left, and Bottom-Right—choose the Square, Round, Cut, Fillet, or Ear option from the drop-down menu. In the Size text box, enter a measurement to determine how large to make the corners. Figure 9.6 demonstrates different corner styles.

Figure 9.6 *Different corner styles, from left to right: round, cut, fillet, and ear*

Photo Editor's Two Indispensable Tools

Before you learn anything more about Photo Editor, make the acquaintance of two indispensable tools—the Zoom command and the ruler.

Use the Zoom command to make graphics larger or smaller on-screen. To zoom in or out, either choose an option on the Zoom drop-down menu or click the Zoom button and then click on your graphic at the point where you want to enlarge it. Each time you click, you enlarge the graphic by twice the size it was previously. At the bottom of the Zoom drop-down menu is a command called Fit To Window. Click it and the graphic grows as large as the window permits it to grow.

To display or hide the ruler, choose View ➜ Ruler. A ruler appears on the top and left side of the graphic to show precisely how large the graphic is. Which unit of measurement do you prefer: centimeters, inches, or pixels? Choose View ➜ Measurement Units ➜ and Cm, Inches, or Pixels on the submenu to change the unit of measurement shown on the ruler.

Adjusting a Graphic's Overall Appearance

To change the overall look of a graphic, experiment with its brightness, contrast, and gamma settings. These settings determine how light or dark an image looks. *Gamma* refers to the contrast between the different dark areas of a graphic. The higher the brightness setting, the brighter the graphic looks. The higher the contrast setting, the more colors stand out. You can have a lot of fun with these settings, especially when you are dealing with black-and-white graphics.

To change a graphic's brightness, contrast, and gamma settings, click the Image Balance button or choose Image ➜ Balance. You see the Balance dialog box. Drag the sliders to change settings. To change settings for a particular color channel, choose Red, Green, or Blue from the drop-down menu.

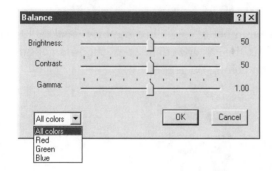

To radically change the look of a graphic, try turning it into a black-and-white or monochrome graphic. You can do that by choosing File ➜ Properties and, in the Properties dialog box, choosing Gray Scale (8 bit) or Monochrome (1 Bit) from the Type drop-down menu.

Touching Up a Graphic

The first six commands on the Effects menu give you ample opportunities for tweaking a graphic. These commands do any number of things to graphics, and when you use them in combination, you can create interesting effects or otherwise amuse yourself on a rainy day. Following is a rundown of the first six commands on the Effects menu.

Some of the commands on the Effects menu only work on JPEG graphics.

Sharpen and Soften   Respectively, these commands make an image look more severe or fuzzier. Use these commands to give a graphic more or less luster.

Negative   Renders a negative image. In other words, all colors are assigned their opposite.

Despeckle   Idealizes an image by removing so-called specks, or stray dots of color. After you choose Effects ➜ Despeckle, choose the Small, Medium, or Large option button in the Despeckle dialog box to tell Photo Editor what constitutes a speck. On the Sensitivity slider, choose how much color change is necessary in an area for it to be considered a speck.

Posterize   Reduces the number of colors in a graphic to make it look more like a poster. Under Resample in the Posterize dialog box, choose an option. The fewer bits you choose, the fewer colors you get.

Edge   Renders the image in outline form. In the Edge dialog box, choose to outline all edges with a thin or thick line, or outline horizontal or vertical edges.

Changing the Texture of a Graphic

The last eight commands on the Effects menu change the texture of an image. Here, for example, is the Chalk and Charcoal command at work. It gives you a charcoal-and-chalk rendition of your graphic.

No matter which of the eight commands you choose, you see a dialog box similar to the one in Figure 9.7. The dialog box offers sliders for altering the graphic. After you have fiddled with the sliders, click the Preview button. The After box shows what effects your choices have. You can drag the box in the Preview screen to examine different parts of your graphic. Click the Apply button when you are satisfied with the appearance of your choices.

Drag to examine a part of your graphic.

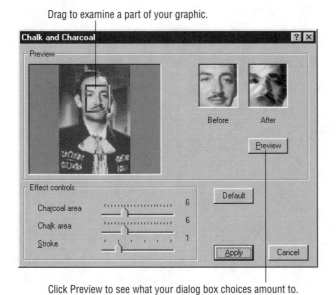

Click Preview to see what your dialog box choices amount to.

Figure 9.7 *Photo Editor offers dialog boxes like this one for changing the texture of graphics.*

Using the FrontPage Drawing Tools

Click the Drawing button on the Standard toolbar or choose Views → Toolbars → Drawing and you see the Drawing toolbar. It offers many commands for decorating Web pages with shapes and lines. What's more, you can fill the shapes with color and even make shapes cast a shadow or appear in three dimensions. These pages explain the Drawing toolbar and how you can use it to make your Web pages a little fancier.

Drawing a Line or Shape

To draw a line or shape, click a button on the Drawing toolbar and start dragging your mouse across the Web page. From left to right on the Drawing toolbar, FrontPage offers the opportunities to create these items:

AutoShapes Open the AutoShapes pop-up menu and you see a bunch of submenus. Choose a submenu and you find different AutoShapes. This illustration shows all the different AutoShapes you can create. Some of these polygons make very nice Web page buttons and navigational tools.

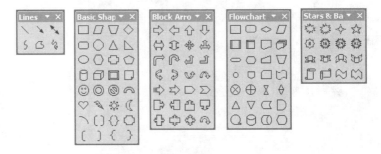

Lines Click the Line button and start dragging to draw a line.

To change the thickness of a line or the lines on a polygon, click to select the line or polygon, if necessary, and then click the Line Style button on the Drawing toolbar and choose an option on the pop-up menu.

Arrows Click the Arrow button and start dragging to draw an arrow. You can change the arrowhead or choose where to place the arrowhead by clicking the Arrow Style button on the Drawing toolbar and making a choice from the pop-up menu.

Rectangles Click the Rectangle button and drag crosswise on-screen to draw a rectangle.

Ovals Click the Oval button and drag on-screen to draw an oval. To draw a circle, hold down the Shift key as you drag.

After you draw a shape or line, it becomes what FrontPage calls an *object*. The techniques for manipulating objects are the same whether you are dealing with a rectangle, oval, or arrow. To use objects successfully on a Web Page, you have to know how to position them on the page, change their size and shape, put borders around them, and overlap them. You also need to know how to select an object. Better read on.

Selecting Lines, Shapes, AutoShapes, and Other Objects

Before you can do anything to an object—change its size or shape, move it, or change its border—you have to select it. To select an object, simply move the pointer over it, wait until you see the four-headed arrow, and click. Shift-click to select several objects at once. You can tell when an object has been selected because small circles called *selection handles* appear. As this illustration shows, most objects have eight selection handles each; a line, however, has only two.

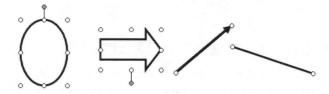

Besides Shift-clicking, you can select more than one object at a time by clicking the Select Objects button and using the pointer to draw a rectangle around the objects you want to select.

Changing the Shape, Size, or Location of an Object

Select an object and follow these instructions to move it, change its size, or change its shape:

Moving an object   Drag the object to a new location. A dashed outline appears where the object will move when you release the mouse button.

Changing an object's size   Gently move the mouse pointer over a corner selection handle. When you see the two-headed arrow, click and drag. Dragging a corner selection handle changes the object's size but maintains its proportions.

Changing an object's shape   Gently move the mouse pointer over a selection handle on the side, top, or bottom. When you see the two-headed arrow, click and start dragging. The object is stretched or crumpled, depending on which direction you drag the handle.

Adding a Background Color or Border to an Object

Select an object, display the Drawing toolbar, and follow these instructions to give your object a background color or a border:

Background color Click the Down arrow next to the Fill Color button and select a color on the Fill Color menu. Choose No Fill to remove the background color.

Color for the border Click the Down arrow beside the Line Color button and choose a color from the drop-down menu.

Creating Shadow and 3-D Effects

To add a little pizzazz to an object such as a polygon or rectangle, you can use tools on the Drawing toolbar to give the object a shadow or another dimension. Check out the shadows on these AutoShapes.

To create a shadow or 3-D effect for an object, select the object in question and then click the Shadow Style or 3-D Style button on the Drawing toolbar and make a selection from the pop-up menu.

Making Objects Overlap

When objects collide, as they do in the following illustration, one inevitably overlaps the other. And when you throw text into the mix, sometimes objects overlap text and sometimes they don't. How can you control whether objects obscure text and which object appears in front of the other?

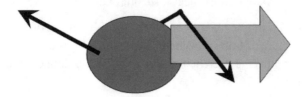

The Order commands can be confusing. The easiest way to handle them is to display the Order toolbar and start clicking buttons. To display the toolbar, drag the line at the top of the Order submenu to make the menu "float."

To handle this problem, select the object, right-click, and choose Order from the submenu (or else click the Draw button on the Drawing toolbar and choose Order). Then choose one of the following commands on the submenu:

- Bring to Front: Places the object atop all other objects.
- Send to Back: Moves the object behind all other objects.
- Bring Forward: In a stack of objects, moves the object higher in the stack.
- Send Backward: In a stack of objects, moves the object further down the stack.

Making Better Image Maps

Just what is an *image map*, anyway? Put very simply, an image map is an image that contains hyperlinks. How is that different from an image that *is* a hyperlink? Generally, an image map contains at least two hyperlinked *hotspots* within its borders. A hotspot is a distinct area of the image that is defined as a hyperlink. For example, a national retail shop may want to provide its Web site users with information about where its stores are located. To do so, the site's designers create a map of the United States with icons that identify each national location of the store (see Figure 9.8). Each of these icons is then defined as a hotspot and is hyperlinked to information about that store.

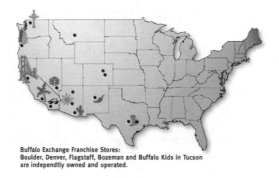

Figure 9.8 *An image map with hotspots*

More than any other graphic you may use on your site, an image map that aids navigation has to be viewable by all. You really must consider color depth and file size carefully. Your map may be the most beautiful image on your site, making use of tens of thousands of colors, but will that work? If those colors don't view well on a 256-color system, or if they blend together when viewed in gray scale, your visitors may lose the visual clues you've so carefully provided them to aid in navigation on your site. If they can't navigate easily, they won't stay long. Read the early sections of this chapter for more information about what to consider when creating images for the Web.

To accommodate users with text-based browsers, or older browsers that may not support image maps, provide a text alternative for navigation. This is usually accomplished with a row of small text-only links at the bottom of a page that are linked to the same areas as your image map.

Creating an Image Map

Unlike many other image-editing programs, FrontPage includes all the tools you need to create image maps. To create an image map, you essentially create the image, then place it on a Web page, and then place the hotspots—the links—in it.

Follow these steps to create and place an image map on your Web page:

1. Either create or obtain the GIF or JPEG graphic that you want to use for the image map.

2. In Page view, click where you want to place the image map.

3. Choose Insert ➜ Picture ➜ From File. You see the Picture dialog box appear.

You can also insert an image in a Web page by dragging it from the images folder.

4. Locate the graphic you want, select it, and click the Insert button. The graphic lands on your Web page.

5. If necessary, display the Pictures toolbar by right-clicking a toolbar and choosing Pictures.

6. Click the Hotspots button—Rectangular Hotspot, Circular Hotspot, or Polygonal Hotspot—for the type of hotspot you want to create (see Figure 9.9).

To create a polygon-shaped hotspot, click the Polygonal Hotspot button and draw the hotspot instead of dragging to create it. When you are finished drawing one line, release the mouse button, and then click and draw the next line. To enclose the polygon, return to the point where you started drawing and double-click.

7. Drag over the part of your graphic where you want to place the hotspot. When you are finished dragging, the Insert Hyperlink dialog box appears.

8. Create the hyperlink (see Chapter 4 if you need help with the Insert Hyperlink dialog box).

When most novices design image maps, they define small hotspot areas. However, most users don't search diligently for those itty-bitty hotspots. It's a far better strategy to create large, easy-to-find hotspots in your image map.

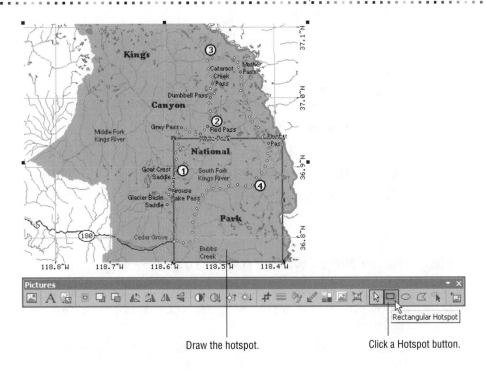

Draw the hotspot.

Click a Hotspot button.

Figure 9.9 *Drawing a hotspot on an image map*

9. Repeat steps 6 through 8 for each additional hotspot you want to add.

Adjusting Hotspots

One problem with image maps is that when links change on the site, or indeed when whole sections of the site go defunct or launch anew, you have to go into the image map and fix up the links. But this becomes a far easier task with a FrontPage-created image map. To add a new hotspot, simply open the image map in Page view and follow the steps outlined in "Creating an Image Map."

Follow these steps to move, resize, or delete a hotspot:

1. Select the image by clicking it. Boxes appear on the image to show you where the hotspots are.

2. Click in the hotspot you want to change. Selection handles appear on the hotspot.

3. Adjust the hotspot:

    • Moving a hotspot: Click anywhere within the box (except on a handle) and drag the hotspot to a new location.

    • Resizing a hotspot: Click and drag one of the handles on the border of the box until the hotspot is the size you prefer.

    • Deleting a hotspot: Press the Delete key.

    • Changing the link: Double-click the hotspot and make changes in the Edit Hyperlink dialog box.

4. Press the Esc key.

Creating Image Maps with Professional Savvy

When producing image maps, keep in mind the following tips for best results:

• Because image maps tend to be larger than other graphics, be sure to keep the file size as small as possible without losing quality.

• Put some space between hotspots. At the same time, make hotspots large enough to accommodate a click in the general area rather than requiring users to hunt them down carefully.

- If you use bullets or other small accent graphics near each item in the image map, be sure those visual accents are located within the hotspot—they provide a target for clicking.

- As a courteous, helpful nod toward those with minimal screen capabilities or those browsing the Web with images turned off, always offer a text alternative to the image map. This can be a small navigation bar of text links placed immediately below your image map, or one placed neatly at the bottom of the page.

Up Next

In this chapter, you learned how to use two popular programs to make and tweak graphics for your Web site. Now you're ready to learn about another aspect of sophisticated design: adding multimedia.

Multimedia—especially audio and video—is becoming quite popular on the Web. Chapter 10 introduces you to audio and video on the Web and teaches you how to add such media to your own pages.

Adding Multimedia

FRONTPAGE

Chapter 10

strike up the band and listen here: You don't have to stick to text and images on your Web site. To lend your site a bit of pizzazz, you can offer video, sound, and music! In days gone by, video and audio on the Web was a limited affair—users had to actually download the files and use special viewers and players to see and hear the stuff. But nowadays a variety of options are available. Tried-and-true downloadable files are still a great way to go because people with advanced browsers can play them automatically without relying on special viewers and players, while people with older browsers can do the download two-step. Meanwhile, newer "streaming" options allow video and sound to appear and play seamlessly with no apparent wait for downloading.

This chapter looks at the various formats and technologies for delivering digitized video and sound over the Web. It also explains how to incorporate video and sound in a Web page. Topics include:

- Looking at common video formats

- Embedding video in a Web page

- Considering common sound formats

- Embedding sound in a Web page

- Playing music in the background

- Using streaming video and sound

Presenting Video on a Web Site

In many ways, video is just another file format. Like other file formats, you can store it on a Web server and serve it to a Web browser—nothing special about that. But depending on the format under which the video file is stored and the software with which the user views it, the user may not be able to see a video clip you so carefully prepared and offered up. Your challenge is to choose the video format best suited to your audience and your presentation needs.

In some cases, video is not the way to go. By means of animated GIFs, you can put moving pictures on a Web page without resorting to the large files that video requires. Basically, an animated GIF is like those paper "flip books" that so amuse kids and adults. Chapter 4 explains how to get animated GIFs from the Clip Organizer. Chapter 21 describes how to animate an image with Dynamic HTML.

Adding video and sound to your site can jazz things up quite a bit. But keep in mind that video for video's sake is no better than gratuitous blinking text. As always, keep in mind your audience's real needs, what equipment your audience has, and how to most effectively get your message across.

You can download a video file from a Web site to your computer by right-clicking it and choosing Save Target As on the shortcut menu. You see the File Download dialog box momentarily, and then the Save As dialog box appears. Choose a folder for the video file and click the Save button.

By the way, rule number one in delivering video and sound via the Web: You must tell visitors the size of the file. Video and sound files can be very BIG, and large files can overload a user's system and bring it crashing down. Not only is crashing someone's computer unfair, it kills all interest in your site in a single, frustrating instant. Do yourself and visitors to your site a favor by letting them know just what they're getting into when they play the video or sound files you offer.

Mastering What's Online

Thousands of sound and video files are available for you to peruse (and sometimes use) at many Web sites. One good site with a large collection of great files is at www.yahoo.com/Computers_and_Internet/Multimedia/Video/Collections/. Apple maintains collections of QuickTime videos at www.apple.com/quicktime.

About Video Formats

If a picture is worth a thousand words, video can be (and often is) worth a thousand or more pictures. A quick video clip can often grab attention and relay your message instantly. Tune into CNN Interactive, for example, and you'll see that video clips complement many stories, from celebrity deaths to the latest doings of a robot orbiting Mars. Keep in mind, though, that a video file can grow to gargantuan proportions; you must take care to keep the file size down and let folks know how big it is before they start to download or play the thing.

Mastering What's Online

News sites are known to incorporate lots of video into their pages. For example, take a look at MSNBC (www.msnbc.com) and CNN Interactive (www.cnn.com). Many movie studios, such as Fox (www.fox.com) and Paramount (www.paramount.com), also offer video previews of new movies.

Plenty of video formats are floating around. A lot of them are perfectly viable, but the problem with presenting a video on a Web site is that not every user can play every file format. For that compelling reason, the best idea by far is to stick to the more popular, commonly used file formats. There are two:

Microsoft Video for Windows files   This file type, which has the extension .avi and is commonly called AVI, can be played on all Windows computers (and that's a heck of a lot of computers). Mac users can also download and use freely available software to play these files, so no one is left out.

QuickTime files   This file type is Apple's video software, but QuickTime players are common on Windows machines, too. The files have the extension .mov or .qt.

Which format to choose is mostly a matter of which format was used to create a file you plan to offer. If your company has a bunch of files of one type or the other in stock, then that format is the one to use. If you are jobbing out the creation of the files to a service, the service probably has systems for creating one type of file or the other, so that will determine your choice. Try to stick to one file type for your entire Web site, if you can. Requiring users to have two players, one for AVI and one for QuickTime files, is a bit inconsiderate.

Mastering What's Online

You can find out all about QuickTime at Apple's QuickTime site at `www.apple.com/quicktime`.

Placing Video on a Page

When it comes to incorporating video into a Web page, you have two basic choices:

Embed the video   An embedded video appears on a page in much the same way as an image does. How the user experiences the video depends on what sort of browser is used.

Create a link to a video   With this technique, the user downloads the file and then a program on the user's computer plays it.

Let's see how these tasks are accomplished.

Embedding Video for Internet Explorer and Netscape Navigator

By embedding video directly into a Web page, you allow visitors to click the image that represents the video and play the video quite seamlessly. No need to download the video file and no need to use any external player software. Most Web site developers want as many users as possible to view their content. In that spirit, we suggest embedding a video in such a way that visitors with both Internet Explorer and Netscape Navigator can view the videos you present. (There is another, simpler method, which we'll get to in the next section, but only users of Internet Explorer are able to play the files created using that method.)

While most users have either Internet Explorer or Netscape Navigator, not all do. Some very old and out-dated browsers simply won't recognize plug-ins or video files, and that's that.

With this method of embedding a video, you actually set things up so that the user's browser employs a plug-in to play the file. A *plug-in* is a helper program that enables a browser to play files it would not otherwise recognize. Both Internet Explorer and Netscape Navigator come with the necessary plug-in for this to work with AVI files. Many users have the plug-in for QuickTime files; those who don't can get it easily. A video file embedded using this technique appears on the Web page as an image;

when the user plays the video file, it simply *plays*—the use of the plug-in is essentially invisible to the user.

Follow these steps to embed a video in such a way that users with Internet Explorer and Netscape Navigator can play it:

1. In Page view, place the cursor where you want the video image to appear.

2. Choose Insert ➜ Web Component. The Insert Web Component dialog box appears (see Figure 10.1).

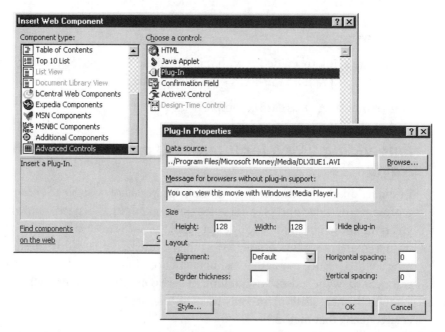

Figure 10.1 *The Plug-In Properties dialog box lets you embed either Windows Media Player or QuickTime videos into a Web page.*

3. Under Component Type, scroll to the bottom of the list and choose Advanced Controls.

4. Under Choose A Control, double-click Plug-In. The Plug-In Properties dialog box appears (refer to Figure 10.1).

5. In the Data Source text box, type the URL for the video you want to include. You can also click the Browse button and, in the Select Plug-In Data Source dialog box, locate and select the video file you want to embed. Be sure to include the proper file extension (`.avi` for a Video for Windows video or `.qt` or `.mov` for a QuickTime video).

6. In the Message For Browsers Without Plug-In Support text box, type the message you want to appear when users of browsers that don't support plug-ins visit the page. (A good choice might be: "Sorry, but your browser does not seem to support either video or the use of plug-ins needed to play this video.")

7. Tell FrontPage about the size and layout of the video image that appears on the page representing the video:

   Size   Specify the height and width of the image, and therefore, the size of the video screen.

The default size, 128 × 128, works just fine for most videos, but as always, you ought to test your page by viewing it with a number of browsers and adjust the size as needed so it looks as good as it can in as many browsers as possible. (See Chapter 16 for more on designing for multiple browsers.)

   Alignment   On the drop-down menu, choose how you want the video to be aligned on the page. (Your choices are the same as they are for images; see Chapter 4 for details.)

   Border Thickness   Specify the width of a border in pixels if you want a border to appear around the video image on the page; leave the text box blank if you don't care for borders.

   Horizontal Spacing and Vertical Spacing   Specify in pixels the amount of white space that you want to appear between the video and any surrounding elements on the page.

8. Click OK. FrontPage makes a copy of the video file and places it in the same folder as the Web page.

Meanwhile, an icon appears on-screen to indicate where you just embedded the video.

To change any of the particulars of the video, double-click its icon (or right-click it and choose Plug-In Properties on the shortcut menu). The Plug-In Properties dialog box appears so you can change settings.

The video you just placed on your Web page is not visible in Page view, but if you view the page in either Internet Explorer or Netscape Navigator, you can see the video image. When a user clicks the image representing the video (assuming the user has a browser that recognizes video and can use plug-ins, which means most users of Internet Explorer or Netscape Navigator), the browser seamlessly and invisibly launches the necessary plug-in and the video plays.

To remove the video, start in Page view, click to select the video image, and then press the Delete key.

Embedding Video for Internet Explorer Only

One method for embedding video into a Web page via FrontPage has a pretty severe handicap: Only visitors with Internet Explorer can view the files. The Internet Explorer–only method may be of interest to people developing an intranet for use within a company that relies exclusively on Internet Explorer as the Web browser of choice. On the whole, however, it's no easier than the previously described method and carries the handicap of limiting your audience to people with the Internet Explorer browser.

As is true of other embedding methods, this one will plop the video right onto your Web page. When a user loads the page, the first frame on the video appears on screen looking much as any other image does. When the user plays the video, it plays right on the Web page. Nice. Too bad this method works only with Internet Explorer.

Follow these steps to embed a video into a Web page so that people with the Internet Explorer Web browser can play it:

1. In Page view, place the cursor where you want the video to appear.

2. Choose Insert → Picture → Video. The Video dialog box appears.

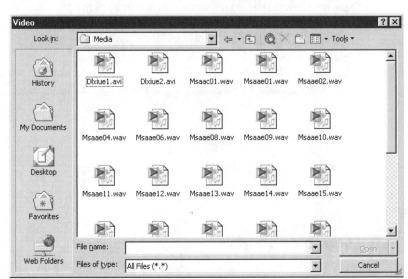

3. Find and select the name of the video file.

4. Click the Open button.

Back on the Web page, you see, masquerading as a simple image, the first frame of the video you just inserted.

When you insert a video using this method, FrontPage uses the same tag that's used to insert actual images. You can format the image (setting such nifty options as its alignment) using the same basic techniques you learned in Chapter 9. You can also control the position of a video on a page by using tables, as Chapter 11 explains.

The only way you can tell that the image on-screen is actually a video is to right-click it and, from the drop-down menu, choose Picture Properties. The Picture Properties dialog box appears. If the item you right-clicked is a video (as opposed to an image), the Video tab is selected. From a user's perspective, when the page is viewed in Internet Explorer, clicking the image causes the video to play.

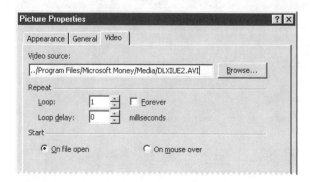

Linking to a Video

An old, tried-and-true, easy-as-pie method for including a video on your site is to place a hyperlink on the Web page that leads to a video file. (This is the way it was done before plug-ins and streaming video.) When a user clicks the link, the linked file is downloaded to the user's computer. Then the user can play the video using the appropriate application. If the file is an `.avi` file, it can be played using Windows; if it is an `.mov` or `.qt` file, the user needs the QuickTime player.

To link a file, see Chapter 4. And remember: Because video files can be very large, it is customary and common courtesy to indicate the size of the file right there next to the link.

Playing Sound and Music on a Web Site

In the right place at the right moment, sound and music can make all the difference. For sites like IUMA.com and CDNOW, which present or sell music over the Web, sound clips are downright necessary—they "show" users the company wares. In addition, sound can give people something to remember your company or product by. Think of all those commercial jingles you end up humming all day! Sound files can also set the stage with mood and tempo for additional multimedia elements.

And, to nab the attention of users in a heartbeat, an appropriate sound file that arrives and plays with the site's splash screen can be a real kick. A sound file like this should be quick, and relevant to the site. A clever example might be a doorbell when you get to the entrance of an online shop. Sound is a relatively low-bandwidth method of adding multimedia features to a Web site.

However, embedding big, downloadable sound files into a Web page without warning visitors first can alienate visitors. You might consider using a *streaming protocol* to deliver sound. For more on that option, see "Streaming Video and Sound" later in this chapter.

About Sound Formats

Computers have been capable of producing and playing sound for far longer than video. Starting way back when, everyone making computer systems developed a file type for sounds and many of them are still around. Not to worry—even if a sound format was originally developed for use on a system unlike your own, software has almost certainly been created to allow all computers to play that file type.

In general, which format your sound files are already in determines which file type you use on your Web site or which platform you will use to develop sound files. Here is a list of the most common sound file formats:

Microsoft WAV files This widely used standard format was developed (big surprise!) by Microsoft, so all Windows computers can play WAV files. WAV files have the .wav extension.

Macintosh Sound files All Macs, as well as most other types of computers, can play sounds stored in the Macintosh Sound format. Macintosh Sound files have the .snd or .mac file extension.

Sun Audio files Almost all Unix-based computers, as well as most other computers, can play sounds stored in the Sun Audio format. These files have the .au extension.

MIDI files These files were originally developed to pass digital information between musical instruments. Later they were used as well to store musical notes in computer files. MIDI files require much less disk space than the other formats discussed here. Because MIDI files actually are not digitized sound, they are not suitable for use in storing nonmusical sounds, such as conversations. MIDI files can be used universally on all computer platforms. They have the .mid or .midi extension.

The most recent versions of both Internet Explorer and Netscape Navigator are quite capable of playing all the formats listed here without the user having to install special software.

In choosing which format to use, convenience is generally the deciding factor. If you have scads of WAV files, make that your standard format. However, if you want to present music on a Web page and the quality of that music is an issue, MIDI is the best choice by far. Using MIDI for music produces much smaller files than any other format discussed here. The drawback to using MIDI, however, is that it doesn't store digitized sound, but rather the sequence of notes used to create the music. That's why it is only useful for music—conversation and other sounds don't occur in "notes" and can't be stored in MIDI files. In fact, MIDI files are usually created by someone sitting at a keyboard playing the music to be stored in the file.

MIDI's unique method of storing music makes it impossible to convert files in other formats to MIDI. Either a file is in MIDI format or it isn't. If you can't use MIDI as the file format because the material is not music (it's spoken voice, for example) or you already have it in another format, we recommend using either WAV or SND.

Playing Sound on a Web Page

The three basic methods for including sound in a Web page are

- Embedding VCR-type controls that allow the user to play the sound at will

- Making a background sound play automatically when the page is loaded

- Creating a link to a sound file so that the user downloads the file and then a program on the user's computer plays it

Read on to learn about the three techniques.

Embedding Sound for Internet Explorer and Netscape Navigator

In the case of an embedded sound or music file, visitors to the Web page can click VCR-type controls and in so doing start the sound, stop it, or change its volume. Visitors do not need to download the sound file or use external player software to hear the sound or music.

Most Web surfers have Internet Explorer or Netscape Navigator, but a handful do not. Some browsers, such as Lynx, simply won't recognize plug-ins or sound files.

Follow these steps to embed a sound file in a Web page:

1. In Page view, place the cursor where you want the VCR-type sound controls to appear.

2. Choose Insert ➜ Web Component. The Insert Web Component dialog box appears (see Figure 10.2)

· ·

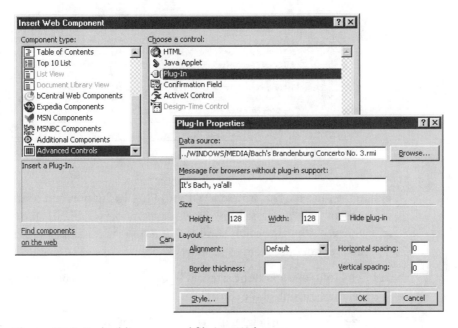

Figure 10.2 *Embedding a sound file in a Web page*

3. Under Component Type, scroll to the bottom of the list and click Advanced Controls.

4. Under Choose a Control, double-click Plug-In. The Plug-In Properties dialog box appears (refer to Figure 10.2).

5. Click the Browse button, and, in the Select Plug-In Data Source dialog box, find and select a sound file and click the Open button. To find out which kinds of files you are dealing with, open the Views drop-down menu, choose Details, and look in the Type column.

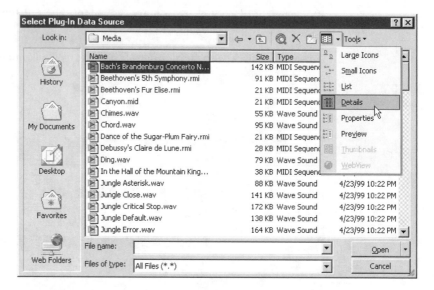

6. In the Message For Browsers Without Plug-In Support text box, type a message for visitors whose browsers do not support plug-ins. (One option is: "Sorry, but our site offers sounds that require the use of a plug-in that your browser does not seem to support.")

7. Tell FrontPage about the size and layout of the VCR-type controls by which visitors can control the sound:

    Size   Specify the height and width of the controls.

    Alignment   On the drop-down menu, choose how you want the controls to be aligned on the page.

    Border Thickness   Specify the width of a border in pixels if you want a border to appear around the controls; leave the text box blank if you don't care for borders.

Horizontal Spacing and Vertical Spacing   Specify in pixels the amount of white space that you want to appear between the controls and any surrounding elements on the page.

8. Click OK. You see the media icon on screen to indicate where you've embedded the sound.

 To alter sound-file settings, double-click the media icon (or right-click it and choose Plug-In Properties). You see the Plug-In Properties dialog box, where you can change the settings.

Preview your Web page in Internet Explorer or Netscape Navigator and you will see the VCR-type controls. More importantly, when a user clicks the Play button on the controls, the sound will play—if the user has a browser that recognizes sound and can use plug-ins.

 For some reason, pages that rely on the use of plug-ins do not always preview correctly when you select File ➜ Preview In Browser from the menu bar. If this happens, simply use a Web browser to view the stuff and everything will be fine.

Setting a Background Sound for Internet Explorer and Netscape Navigator

Background sound can set a tone for a site or help visitors identify a product quickly (as is the case with familiar jingles). If you want visitors to hear music or sound when they come to your Web site, you very likely want *all* visitors to hear it, in which case you need to dig into the HTML code and do a little fiddling. As the next section in this chapter explains, creating a background sound for people who use Internet Explorer is easy, but if you want people who use Netscape Navigator to hear background sounds as well, you need to do a little extra work.

Follow these steps to set a background sound to play automatically when a user loads your page in Internet Explorer *or* Netscape Navigator:

1. Add the sound file to the page in the standard way, as described earlier in this chapter in "Embedding Sound for Internet Explorer and Netscape Navigator."

2. In Page view, double-click the media icon that represents the sound, or right-click it and choose Plug-In Properties. The Plug-In Properties dialog box appears (refer to Figure 10.2).

3. Under Size, enter 2 in the Height text box and 2 in the Width text box. By doing so, you effectively shrink the media icon so that it occupies little space on-screen.

4. Erase anything that appears in the Message For Browsers Without Plug-In Support text box.

5. Click the Hide Plug-In check box (you'll find it to the right of the Width text box). By clicking this check box, you tell FrontPage not to display the Quick-Time or Media Player controls on your Web page. The sound just plays. Visitors to your site don't have the option of clicking a Play button to hear the sound.

6. Click OK. The dialog box closes. The big funky icon is now a small one.

7. Click the HTML tab to view the HTML source code on the page. Now you're going to edit the HTML directly. Doing so is necessary because the FrontPage Plug-In Properties dialog box doesn't directly support all of the features we are using for this procedure.

8. Locate the EMBED tag (that's the HTML tag that was inserted when you added the plug-in). It looks something like this:

   ```
   <embed width="1" height="1" src="welcome.wav" hidden>
   ```

9. Type **autostart="true"** just before the word "hidden." Include the quotation marks as shown, and make sure you have one blank space before `autostart` and after `"true"`.

10. Click the Normal tab.

That's it—you're all set. Now, regardless of whether a user has Internet Explorer or Netscape Navigator, when he or she loads your page, the background sound plays. (You can test this yourself by opening the page with one of those browsers.) If someone loads the page using a browser that does not support plug-ins, the background sound will not play, but the page will function fine silently, and they will never be the wiser.

Setting a Background Sound for Internet Explorer Only

The only reasons to specify a background sound to play automatically when a page loads in Internet Explorer but not Netscape Navigator are

- You are working in an intranet setting in which all users are known to use Internet Explorer.

- You are creating a sound whose intention is to alert Internet Explorer users to something in particular that you don't want users of other browsers to hear— say, the Microsoft jingle, or an exhortation to switch to Netscape Navigator or something. (Just joshing about that last one.)

This method of providing background sound is a bit easier than the one we described in the preceding section, but it leaves out Netscape Navigator users, so think twice about using this method if you want all of your users to hear the fruits of your labor.

Follow these steps to get the job done:

1. In Page view, choose File ➜ Properties. The Page Properties dialog box appears (see Figure 10.3).

2. Under Background Sound, click the Browse button and, in the Background Sound dialog box, find and select a sound file. Then click the Open button. The name of the file appears in the Location text box.

3. Tell FrontPage whether to play the sound a certain number of times or continuously:

   - Continuously: Click the Forever check box.

   - A certain number of times: Deselect the Forever check box and, in the Loop text box, enter the number of times you want the sound to play before stopping.

4. Click OK.

Please don't play background sounds continuously. Doing so is considered very rude.

Enter a background sound.

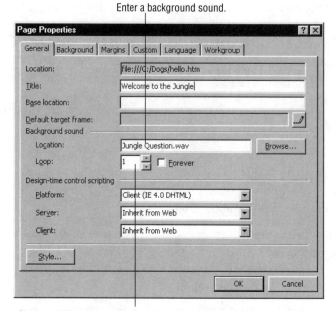

Choose whether the sound plays a certain number of times or continuously.

Figure 10.3 *Designating a background sound for people with the Internet Explorer browser*

Preview the page in Internet Explorer; you should hear the sound play as the page loads.

Linking to a Sound

That old familiar technique, placing a hyperlink on a Web page that goes to a sound file, is a perfectly good (if primitive) method of playing sounds. When a user clicks such a link, the linked file is downloaded to the user's computer, at which time the user can play the sound with an appropriate application—if the file is a WAV file, for example, it can be played using the Windows Media Player. The hyperlink method of playing sound is especially good if the sound file involved is very large, because you don't force a visitor to accept a file that might overwhelm his or her system. Such is the case if your audience includes people who use old browsers or text-only browsers.

To link a file, see Chapter 4. As always, because sound files can be quite large, it is usual, customary, and courteous to indicate the size of the file next to its link.

Streaming Video and Sound

The traditional way to incorporate video or sound in a Web page is to treat video and sound much like a graphic, as described earlier in this chapter. In that case, the stuff is embedded in the page and generally appears as an image (a video still) or a set of sound controls representing the video or sound. (An exception is in the use of background sound, in which case there is no visual representation of the sound on the page.)

When you do incorporate video or sound into a Web page using these methods, the entire video or sound file must be downloaded to the visitor's computer before he or she can see or hear it. This process doesn't always require the user to do something, but it does take a bit of time. Having to wait for a file to download can be a problem if the file is a large one, because the file can then take many minutes to download. Most visitors simply haven't that much patience. They will go on to something else. How to solve this problem? The answer lies in *streaming video and audio*. With this method, the audio or video files "stream" to a visitor's computer in small, bite-size chunks, and the visitor can see or hear the file as it arrives.

Think of it like this: When you turn on your television and tune it to MTV (which is somewhat like tuning into a Web site), you don't have to wait until the entire episode of "Real World" has been sent to your TV before you can watch it. MTV is constantly broadcasting the *data stream* that makes up the television program. Your television tuner grabs the data stream frame by frame and displays it on-screen.

Streaming technology for the Web works on a similar principle. After a user starts to view a video or listen to a sound that is being delivered using a streaming protocol, the server starts sending a data stream—the digitized video or audio—to the player, which then grabs the data stream and plays each frame (or some quantum of audio) as it arrives. If the available bandwidth between your computer and the server becomes too low to support this real-time playing, either frames are dropped out along the way or the video or audio pauses until the data stream catches up. Because streaming video and audio don't require the user to wait for an entire video or sound file to download before he or she can experience it, the user is far more likely to play the video or sound just to find out what it is.

Performing all this magic requires your Web server to have special software. Also, the user's browser needs the help of a special plug-in designed to work with the particular streaming protocol you're offering. For those reasons, including some types of streaming audio and video is more complicated than just embedding a WAV or AVI file in a Web page.

At the very least, you need to check with your server administrator to make sure streaming audio or video support is available. At most, you have to buy and install a special server and authoring tools to create or convert files to the proper format for streaming. Software is available for the streaming of video only, audio only, or for a fully combined multimedia experience.

Programs such as Progressive Network's RealPlayer and VDOnet Corporation's VDOLive Player are popular options; Microsoft's Netshow uses *unicast* technology to send an individual stream that includes VCR-like controls for start, stop, rewind, and fast forward. Users can play the segment at will, just as they can a videotape or cassette. Typically, the streaming video or audio software a user needs in order to experience the stuff is free, and can be easily downloaded, but you have to purchase the authoring software and the server software.

To use streaming video and/or audio with FrontPage, you must first make sure your ISP or in-house Web server can handle the technology. Ask the ISP tech folks or your network administrator. Having done that, your next step is to set up the streaming media software on your server. How to do that varies widely depending on which software you use, so find out what you need to do from the company that provides the software. This process is not terribly simple, but it's necessary and the streaming server software company should provide plenty of support.

You'll have to use the authoring software provided by the streaming software company you're working with to get your content into the correct streaming file format. This stuff does not convert from format to format.

Then, to make streaming stuff available to your users via FrontPage, you can simply follow the steps provided in this chapter for embedding video.

Up Next

Now that you are familiar with how to add text and images as well as video and sound to your pages, it's time to take a look at better methods of controlling the way all of these elements are laid out.

One of the most powerful ways to manage layouts used on the Web today is with HTML tables. Chapter 11 will get you started thinking about and using tables as a way to make your page design more sophisticated.

Using Tables for
Advanced Layout

FRONTPAGE

Chapter 11

On the printed page, tables are used to present data in easy-to-read columns and rows. In the early days of the Web, they were used for the very same purpose. It turns out, however, that tables are one of the most flexible ways to lay out professional-looking pages. Chances are that most of the really beautiful pages you've seen on the Web were laid out using tables. With tables, you can combine text, images, and white space in ways you can't accomplish otherwise.

This chapter looks at how to set up a basic table, and then it delves into some serious table work as you learn how to control the margins, handle spacing, manage colors, and do everything else that's needed to make a refined table. Topics include:

- Creating tables from FrontPage templates

- Placing tables on a page

- Using the Tables toolbar

- Editing table properties

- Adding and removing cells, columns, and rows

- Working with table borders

- Making more room in cells for text

- Coloring tables and creating table backgrounds

What Are Tables?

Tide tables, temperature indices, train arrival and departure schedules, and *Billboard*'s Top 100 music charts are examples of tables. Tables in HTML are just like the tables in books, spreadsheets, and other documents. A table is a way of organizing and presenting information by placing it into rows and columns.

However, the people who design Web pages soon discovered another use for tables—tables can be a convenient way to lay out a Web page. In fact, tables are now the cornerstone of Web page layout. Most layouts, including CNET's (shown in Figure 11.1), wouldn't be possible without tables.

Mastering What's Online

CNET has used table-based layouts for longer than most sites. Visit CNET's site at `www.cnet.com` to see how tables can be used to lay out Web pages. When you're done, drop by `www.builder.com/` for advice about working with all aspects of Web design.

Figure 11.1 *CNET uses tables to create its advanced layout.*

To work well with tables, you'll benefit from knowing a little table terminology. The intersection of each column and row in a table is called a *cell*. Figure 11.2 shows a traditional data table with two columns and nine rows. The top row of the table, called the *table header*, explains the purpose of the table. As you can see, tables present information in such a way that you can easily look up the data you need.

A few cool HTML reference tools...	
Tools	
Netscape Color Reference	An interactive Color Chart for Netscape
HTML Forms Tutor	How to write Forms for Web Pages
Table Tutor	How to make HTML tables.
Frame Tutor	Constructing Framed Sets of Web Pages
GIF Wizard from Raspberry Hill Publishing Inc.	A .gif file size optimizing service. Bandwidth Karma builder

Figure 11.2 *This table demonstrates HTML reference tools.*

Web page designers use tables to present information visually in ways that simple heading-paragraph-break layouts can't. For example, you can use tables to lay out text in columns, integrate text and images, and create wide margins or sidebars. You can use tables to create all kinds of sophisticated page layouts. Figure 11.3 shows another example of how a table can be used to lay out a page. A close look at this page reveals that it is laid out in a three-column table. You can, of course, use tables for their intended purpose to present information, but the focus of this chapter is on how to use tables to lay out Web pages.

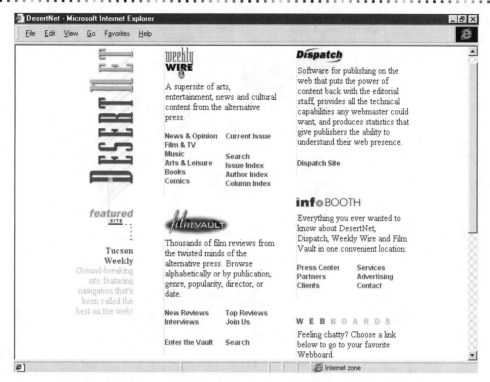

Figure 11.3 *On this Web page, tables are used to create a sophisticated design.*

Creating a Table from a Template

One of the best ways to explore the page design options in FrontPage is to start from a template in which a table is used to create columns and sidebars. Rummage through the templates and you will find about a dozen that take advantage of tables to make sophisticated layouts. Some of the templates are as elegant as the ones you see in newspapers and magazines. These designs wouldn't be possible on the Web without tables.

In Figure 11.4, you can see one of the templates for creating pages that use tables. Figure 11.5 shows the same page with the table borders turned on, so you can see how the page was set up. Many of the templates for creating new pages take advantage of the table motif.

Figure 11.4 *In this template, called "Two-Column Body with Contents on Left," a table is used for layout purposes.*

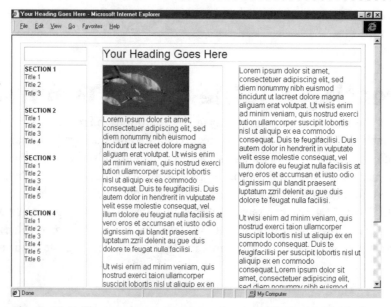

Figure 11.5 *The same template page shown in Figure 11.4 with the borders turned on so you can see where the table cells are.*

Follow these steps to create a Web page from a template in which a table is used for layout purposes:

1. Choose File ➜ New ➜ Page Or Web. The New Page Or Web task pane opens.

2. Click the Page Templates hyperlink. You see the General tab of the Page Templates dialog box, as shown in Figure 11.6.

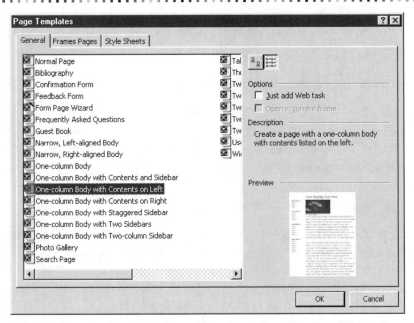

Figure 11.6 *The Page Templates dialog box offers 14 different "table layout" templates.*

3. Select one of the templates that use tables:

   - Narrow, Left-Aligned Body

   - Narrow, Right-Aligned Body

   - One-Column Body

   - One-Column Body With Contents And Sidebar

   - One-Column Body With Contents On Left

- One-Column Body With Contents On Right
- One-Column Body With Staggered Sidebar
- One-Column Body With Two Sidebars
- One-Column Body With Two-Column Sidebar
- Three-Column Body
- Two-Column Body
- Two-Column Body With Contents And Sidebar
- Two-Column Body With Contents On Left
- Two-Column Staggered Body
- Two-Column Staggered Body With Contents And Sidebar

Click one of the templates and you see a preview of the template in the Preview area of the Page Templates dialog box. The preview gives a good idea of how the page looks after it is laid out.

4. Click OK.

After you create a page from the template you selected, the next step is to replace the text, headings, and images with your own material. Feel free to use what you've learned in this book to change fonts and font sizes, the alignment of text, the size of images, and all else that needs changing to make the page truly your own. Throughout this chapter, you learn how to make changes to tables.

You might notice that the text on these template pages is a little funny. "Lorem ipsum dolor sit" isn't written in any specific language; it's the standard dummy text (called greeking) used by page designers when mocking up magazine layouts, advertising text, and the like.

Creating a Table on Your Own

Placing a table on a Web page is as easy as setting the dinner table—just make sure you know how many people you're expecting. You can create a table that takes up the entire page or part of it. And you can change the table later if you change your mind about how big it should be.

Creating a Table with the Insert Table Button

The simplest way to create a table is to follow these steps and use the Insert Table button on the Standard toolbar:

1. In Page view, click where you want the table to be.

2. Click the Insert Table button. A small table menu appears.

3. Click one of the cells to indicate the size of the table you want. If you want a table that is larger than 4 × 5 cells, drag out the menu until it lists the number of cells you want. In this illustration, a table 6 rows × 10 columns is being created.

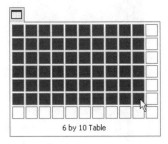

6 by 10 Table

All the default settings for tables are in effect when you create a table with the Insert Table button. Your table probably occupies 100 percent of the screen width and has a 1-pixel border. We say "probably" because, if you created a table since the last time you started FrontPage, the options you chose for that table are in effect. Through this chapter, you find out how to change settings to make tables look the way you want them to look.

Tables are easy to resize, if you just want to adjust them a little. To do so, move your mouse over the right or bottom edge of the table. When the cursor turns into a double-headed arrow, click and drag the wall of the table to resize it, and release the mouse button when the table is the size you want it to be. You can resize individual table cells in the same way.

Creating a Table in the Insert Table Dialog Box

Another way to create a table is to start with the Insert Table dialog box. Go this route and you get to format the table a few different ways. Follow these steps to create a table in the Insert Table dialog box:

1. In Page view, click where you want the table to go.

2. Choose Table ➔ Insert ➔ Table. The Insert Table dialog box appears, as shown in Figure 11.7.

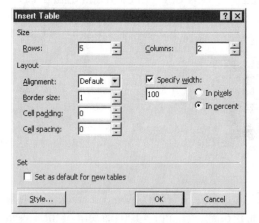

Figure 11.7 *The Insert Table dialog box allows you to choose initial settings for a new table.*

3. Under Size, enter the number of rows and columns you want in the Rows and Columns text boxes.

4. Under Layout, choose options to describe what you want the table to look like:

   Alignment   Open the drop-down menu and choose an option to align your table with the left side, center, or right side of the Web page.

Specify Width   Check this box and enter a measurement for the width of the table (in pixels or by percentage of the Web page) if you want to determine the size of the table on your own. If you uncheck this check box, FrontPage will make the table wide enough to accommodate the content you enter in the cells. To make your table occupy a certain percentage of the window, click the In Percent option button to make it active. To specify the number of pixels your table should occupy, click the In Pixels option button.

Border Size   Enter how many pixels wide you want the outside borders of the table to be. If you want the borders not to show, enter 0 in this text box.

Cell Padding   Enter a measurement in pixels to determine how much space appears between cells. See "Cell Padding, Cell Spacing, and Border Width" later in this chapter for details.

Cell Spacing   Enter a measurement in pixels to determine how close the content can come to the inside border of the cells. See "Cell Padding, Cell Spacing, and Border Width" later in this chapter.

If you want all new tables you create to come up looking like the table you just finished creating in the Insert Table dialog box, check the Set As Default For New Tables check box. Choosing this option is a great way to make sure that pages are laid out the same way or tables all look the same across your Web site.

5. Click OK. Your table appears.

Suppose you made an error when you created your table. To fix it, either right-click the table and choose Table Properties on the shortcut menu or click in the table and choose Table ➡ Table Properties ➡ Table. The Table Properties dialog box appears. It offers many of the same options found in the Insert Table dialog box. Make your changes and click OK.

Drawing a Table and Using the Tables Toolbar

You also have the option of *drawing* a table right onto your Web page by following these steps:

1. Right-click a toolbar and choose Tables or choose View ➜ Toolbars ➜ Tables to display the Tables toolbar.

2. Click the Draw Table button. The pointer turns into a pencil.

3. Drag the pointer to draw the outside boundaries of the table. As you draw, dotted lines show where table lines will appear after you stop dragging.

4. Draw the interior lines of the table.

5. Click the Draw Table button when you are finished drawing the table.

To erase a line you drew with the Draw Table button, click the Eraser button on the Tables toolbar (you'll find it next to the Draw Table button) and drag over the line.

Introducing the Tables Toolbar

You can save yourself a lot of time by learning how to use the buttons on the Tables toolbar. Especially when you are creating a data table, these buttons can be very helpful. Table 11.1 explains what the buttons on the Tables toolbar do. Before you can use any of the options described in the previous section, you need to display the Tables toolbar. To do so, choose View ➜ Toolbars ➜ Tables or right-click a toolbar and choose Tables.

You can click in any blank space on any toolbar and then drag it into the window to make it "float."

Table 11.1 The Tables Toolbar

BUTTON	WHAT IT'S CALLED	WHAT YOU CAN DO WITH IT
	Draw Table	Draw a table or a cell wall.
	Eraser	Erase the borders between cells.
	Insert Rows	Add a row or rows above the selected row or rows.
	Insert Columns	Add a column or columns to the left of the selected column or columns.
	Delete Cells	Delete the selected cells.
	Merge Cells	Combine the selected cells into a single cell.
	Split Cells	Split one cell into many cells.
	Align Top	Align text with the top of the selected cell.
	Center Vertically	Center text vertically in the selected cell.
	Align Bottom	Align text with the bottom of the selected cell.
	Distribute Rows Evenly	Even out the available space between rows.
	Distribute Columns Evenly	Even out the available space between columns.
	Auto Fit to Contents	Make cells large enough to accommodate their content.
	Fill Color	Create a color background for cells.

Table 11.1 continued The Tables Toolbar

None ▼	Table AutoFormat Combo	Choose a new AutoFormat for the table.
	Table AutoFormat	Open the Table AutoFormat dialog box to choose an AutoFormat for the table.
	Fill Down	Enter the data in the first cell you selected into all the other cells you selected in a column.
	Fill Right	Enter the data in the first cell you selected into all the other cells you selected in a row.

Placing Text and Images in a Table

After you create a table, you need to put things in it. You can type or paste text in a table just like you do in any other part of a Web page. Click where you want to enter text and start typing. Text in a table can be manipulated just like any text on a Web page. You can change text styles, fonts, colors, and headings, for example. Manipulating text and images in a table isn't much different from doing it elsewhere on a Web page, but these pages explain a few manipulation tricks that are worth knowing.

You can use the Tab key to move from cell to cell in a table. Press Shift+Tab to move the insertion point back one cell.

Placing images in a table is also no different from placing them on a Web page. Be advised, however, that a table cell expands when you insert an image inside it. The fact that cells expand to accommodate images works for and against you. It works for you because you don't have to bother creating a cell that is the exact size of the image. On the other hand, if you're wedded to a certain height and width for cells in a table, you may have to rethink your plans in order to work with the images you have.

Letting FrontPage Fill in the Text for You

Sometimes when you enter text in a table, you need to enter the same item over and over and over again. For those occasions, FrontPage offers the Fill Down and Fill Right buttons on the Tables toolbar. To take advantage of these commands, all you have to do is enter the first instance of the text you want to enter. Then you click a button and FrontPage does the rest.

For example, suppose you want to enter the word "Yes" into five cells in a row or column. To do so, enter **Yes** in the first cell of the row or column, select the other cells in the row or column, and then click the Fill Right or Fill Down button on the Tables toolbar.

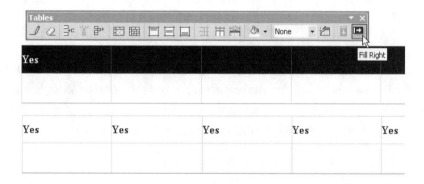

Aligning Text and Images in a Table Cell

Just as you can change the alignment of text on a page, you can change the alignment of text (and images) in a table. As Chapter 4 explains, you can align text and paragraphs with respect to the left margin, the right margin, or the middle of the page. In the context of a table cell, you also have these options, as well as the option of aligning text with respect to the top, bottom, baseline, or middle of a cell. Figure 11.8 shows a table that demonstrates the various text-alignment options.

This text is aligned with the left and top of the cell	
	This text is aligned with the right and bottom of the cell
This text is aligned with the center and the bottom of the cell.	This text is aligned with the left and middle of the cell
This text is larger . . .	And this text shares its baseline

Figure 11.8 *Vertical and horizontal alignments can be combined in many different ways.*

The fastest way to align cells is to select them and click the Align Top, Center Vertically, or Align Bottom button on the Tables toolbar. You don't get as many alignment options on the Tables toolbar, however, as you do in the Table Properties dialog box. Remember that you can use the alignment buttons on the Formatting toolbar to align the text with the left, center, or right side of the cell.

Follow these steps to change the alignment of text in a cell:

1. In Page view, select the cell or cells whose alignment needs adjusting.

2. Either right-click and choose Cell Properties or choose Table ➜ Table Properties ➜ Cell. The Cell Properties dialog box appears.

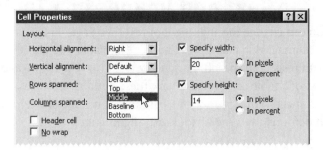

3. Under Layout, open the Horizontal Alignment drop-down list and choose an option: Default, Left, Right, Center, or Justify. If you choose the Default option,

the browser determines how to align the text and applies its default setting for alignments. Usually, the default is left-aligned.

4.   Open the Vertical Alignment drop-down list and choose a vertical alignment: Default, Top, Middle, Baseline, or Bottom. Choose the Default setting and visitors' browsers get to decide how to align the text. On most browsers, the Default settings is Middle.

5.   Click OK.

Text and images in the cell or cells you selected are realigned according to your specifications.

The baseline of text is the imaginary line that the letters rest on. A descender is a part of a letter that falls below the baseline. For example, the stem on a p or q is a descender. (Their counterparts, which reach upward, are called ascenders. The stem on a d or h is an ascender.) If you adjust the vertical alignment of the cells in a row so that the text in each cell is aligned with the baseline, the text will sit on the same imaginary line, regardless of whether the font sizes are the same. You can see this effect illustrated in Figure 11.8.

· ·

The No Wrap Option

Tables on a Web page behave differently than tables on the printed page. On a printed page, the text in a cell always stays in the same place. In a Web browser, however, text is more flexible. The text in a table cell may wrap at any point to the next line, depending on the size of the browser window.

However, you can keep this from happening with the No Wrap option in the Cell Properties dialog box. Text in cells where the No Wrap option is in effect stays put. Lines are not broken to accommodate changes in the size of the table.

Follow these steps to turn on the No Wrap option:

1.   In Page view, select the cell or cells whose text you do not want to wrap from line to line.

2.   Either right-click and choose Cell Properties on the shortcut menu or choose Table ➜ Table Properties ➜ Cell. The Cell Properties dialog box appears.

3.   Under Layout, click the No Wrap check box.

4.   Click OK.

Choosing the No Wrap option doesn't have any immediate visible result. If you want to see it in action, try turning it off and on and previewing the results in a browser window. In the browser, resize the window several times and watch what happens to the text in the table cells.

Creating Table Headers

You can designate one cell, a row, or a column as the *table header*, if you'd like. Table headers, most often found at the tops or on the sides of tables, usually announce the title of a table or explain what is in the rows and columns. Text typed into table headers is bold-faced, but isn't much different otherwise. Different browsers give slightly different treatment to table headers, but the idea is generally the same.

Sometimes the table header is a single cell at the top of the table that straddles several columns. See "Merging Cells" later in this chapter to learn how to merge several cells into a single cell.

Follow these steps to create a table header:

1. In Page view, click in the table cell, select the row, or select the column that you'd like to make into a table header.

2. Either right-click and choose Cell Properties on the shortcut menu or choose Table ➜ Table Properties ➜ Cell. The Cell Properties dialog box appears.

3. Under Layout, click the Header Cell check box to make that option active.

4. Click OK.

Table header text is centered and bold. Any text you type in that cell later will also be centered and bold.

Creating Table Captions

A *table caption* is a special, borderless cell that extends the entire width of the table. It can be used for a table header or as a note at the bottom of a table that defines or explains the table's contents. Although a table caption does not have borders, even if your table does, it shares any background color you apply to your table. Figure 11.9 shows a table with a caption on top.

Mixing Colors

red	yellow	blue
+ yellow	+ blue	+ red
= orange	= green	= purple

Figure 11.9 *This table's caption tells what the table is all about. Notice how the caption doesn't have any borders.*

Follow these steps to place a table caption above or below a table:

1. Click anywhere in the table.

2. Choose Table ➜ Insert ➜ Caption. The table caption cell appears. By default, the caption cell appears at the top of the table.

3. Enter the text of the caption.

If you'd like to change the location of the caption, click in the caption and either right-click and choose Caption Properties or choose Table ➜ Table Properties ➜ Caption. Then, in the Caption Properties dialog box, click the Top Of Table or Bottom Of Table option button.

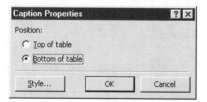

Editing an Existing Table

So you put a table on your page and all of a sudden you realize that you need four columns, not three, and the table needs to be a few rows longer. Perhaps you want the table to occupy more (or less) space on-screen. Or you want to remove the border that you initially put in. Or you want to change the thickness of an existing border. Read on to learn how to change a table you've already created.

Changing the Size of a Table

Cells expand as you enter text or images inside them. Unless you decide otherwise, a table on a Web page is a dynamic thing—it changes size as you enter more content. Nevertheless, you may prefer a table that doesn't change size but maintains a constant size, especially if you want it to occupy a particular percentage of the screen. Fortunately, changing the size of a table you've already created is quite simple.

Follow these steps to change the size of a table:

1. In Page view, either right-click the table and choose Table Properties on the shortcut menu or click the table and choose Table ➜ Table Properties ➜ Table. The Table Properties dialog box appears (see Figure 11.10).

Figure 11.10 *The Table Properties dialog box allows you to edit many table settings.*

2. In the Layout area of the dialog box, check the Specify Width check box, if that's what you want to do. Those options become active (not grayed out).

   or

   If you'd rather have the table resize itself automatically to accommodate new content, uncheck the Specify Width check box.

 You can change the width of a single column by dragging its borderline with the mouse. Move the pointer over the border of a column. When you see the double-headed arrow, click and start dragging.

3. Click the In Pixels or In Percent option button to specify a width by percentage of the browser window or in pixels.

4. Type a number (either a percentage or a number of pixels) in the Specify Width text box.

5. Click the Specify Height check box if you want to establish a set-in-stone height for the table.

6. Click the In Pixels or In Percent option button to specify a height by percentage of the browser window or in pixels. Then type a number (either a percentage or a number of pixels) in the Specify Height text box.

7. If you need to change page alignment of the table, select an option from the Alignment drop-down menu.

8. Click OK.

Your table is resized based on the width and/or height you specified. You can repeat this process until you are satisfied with the table's looks.

Changing the Alignment of a Table

If your table is anything other than 100-percent wide, you can align it on the page with respect to the left margin, the right margin, or the middle of the page. Follow these steps to change the alignment of a table on a Web page:

1. In Page view, either right-click the table and choose Table Properties on the shortcut menu or click the table and choose Table ➜ Table Properties ➜ Table. The Table Properties dialog box appears.

2. Under Layout, open the Alignment drop-down menu and choose Left, Center, or Right.

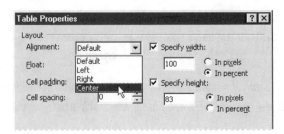

3. Click OK.

Most of the time, tables work best when they are left-aligned on the page, but it's always good to know that you have options.

Remember that `<table align="right">` *does not cause the elements within the table to align right. Instead, it tells the whole table to align to the right, much like* `<img align="right">` *does. In fact, image alignment is quite similar to table alignment.*

Inserting Rows and Columns

From time to time, you have to insert new columns and rows in a table. Not many people are savvy enough to choose the right number of columns or rows when they create a table.

The fastest way to insert a new row or column is to do so using the Tables toolbar. To enter a new row, click the row that you want the new row to go above and then click the Insert Rows button (or right-click and choose Insert Rows). To insert a new column, click in the column that will appear to the right of the new column and then click the Insert Columns button (or right-click and choose Insert Columns).

Follow these steps to insert a new row or column in a table:

1. In Page view, click in the table where you want to insert new rows or columns.

2. Choose Table ➜ Insert ➜ Rows Or Columns. The Insert Rows Or Columns dialog box appears.

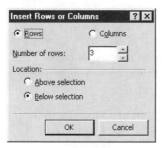

3. Click the Rows option button or the Columns option button. The options in the dialog box change depending on which button you select.

4. In the Number Of Rows (or Columns) text box, enter the number of rows or columns you want to insert.

5. If you're inserting rows, click the Above Selection option button to place the rows above where you clicked in step 1, or click the Below Selection option button to place the rows below that spot.

    or

    If you're inserting columns, click the Left Of Selection option button to insert the rows to the left of where you clicked in step 1, or click the Right Of Selection option button to add the columns to the right of the insertion point.

6. Click OK.

You can repeat these steps as often as needed to keep enlarging your table as you see fit.

Adding a Single Cell

Sometimes, for visual effect, a single cell needs to be added to a table. Figure 11.11 shows a table to which a single cell has been added. Notice, above the extra cell, the funny-looking blank space that's neither a cell nor available space. This sort of placeholder space shows up because tables are only really comfortable when they're rectangular. When there's an awkward number of cells, the rest of the space is filled in with border stuff.

Figure 11.11 *Adding a single cell instead of a row or column lets you make funny-shaped (and funny-looking) tables.*

By default, cells are added to the right of a table (or to the left, if the table is right-aligned). Follow these steps to add a single cell to a table:

1. In Page view, click anywhere in the table.

2. Choose Table ➜ Insert ➜ Cell. Voilà! You have yourself a new cell.

Of course, you can add a bunch of new cells this way, one at a time, but if you want to add whole new rows or columns, you're better off following the instructions in the previous section of this chapter.

Splitting Cells

You can create some interesting effects by splitting cells. Splitting cells means to make two or more cells where they used to be one cell. As shown in Figure 11.12, splitting effectively cuts a cell into pieces so that it forms its own set of mini-columns or mini-rows. In Figure 11.12, the upper-left cell in the table has been split into two rows, while the lower-right cell is split into two columns.

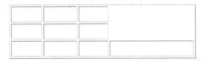

Figure 11.12 *Examples of cell splitting*

Follow these steps to split a cell:

1. In Page view, click in the cell you want to split.

2. Choose Table ➜ Split Cells, right-click and choose Split Cells on the shortcut menu, or click the Split Cells button on the Tables toolbar. The Split Cells dialog box appears.

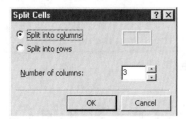

3. In the dialog box, click the Split Into Columns or Split Into Rows option button.

4. By default, a cell divides in two when you split it, but if you'd like to choose another number, type it in the Number Of Columns (or Rows) text box.

5. Click OK. The page reappears, and you'll see that your cell has gone through mitosis in the blink of an eye.

Tables within Tables (within Tables...)

You can place nearly any HTML element within a table, and that includes other tables. Placing one table inside another is called *nesting*. Just click in a cell and insert a table there, and you get a table within a table. The effect is similar to splitting cells, except when you nest one table inside another, you have more freedom to change the background, the borders, the width—just about anything. You could theoretically keep nesting tables until your page became a hall of mirrors.

In general, if you can't achieve what you need by nesting two to three levels deep, you are probably not evaluating your needs accurately. You should be able to achieve virtually anything within three levels of tables. Avoid unnecessary code and overly complex tables, because they take longer for browsers to render and inspire many visitors to click away to a Web site that loads faster.

Generally, nesting tables is useful when *all* the content on your page takes place within the framework of a table and you need to use other tables to place content effectively on a Web page. Nesting is a good example of a task that FrontPage makes easy. Coding tables in HTML by hand isn't fun by any standard, and trying to code a table inside another table by hand can cause migraine headaches.

Splitting a Table in Two

Suppose you need to split a table in two, perhaps to enter a heading or a sentence or three between tables. It can be done. In fact, it can be done very easily by following these steps:

1. Click in the row that is to be the first in the new table.

2. Choose Table ➜ Split Table.

Merging Cells to Form a Single Cell

Merge cells when you want to turn several different cells into a single cell. Typically, merging cells is necessary when you want to fit a large graphic into a table. Or when you want to make room for a long heading that straddles several columns. This illustration shows a table in which the first four cells in the left column have been merged.

Follow these steps to merge two or more table cells and thereby form a single cell:

1. In Page view, select the cells that you want to merge. Here are techniques for selecting cells:

Selecting several cells   Drag over them with the mouse, or click in the first cells you want to select and then Shift-click in the last cell.

Selecting an entire row   Click in the row and choose Table ➜ Select ➜ Row.

Selecting an entire column   Click in the column and choose Table ➜ Select ➜ Column.

You can also select a column or row by moving the pointer directly above the column at the top of the table or to the right side of the row. When you see a fat black arrow, click. Click and drag to select several columns or rows at once.

2. Merge the cells by doing one of the following:

- Choose Table ➜ Merge Cells.

- Right-click and choose Merge Cells on the shortcut menu.

- Click the Merge Cells button on the Tables toolbar.

That's all there is to it.

Removing Rows and Columns

It so happens that sometimes you have more rows or columns than you have data. And when that happens, you need to remove rows or columns. Fortunately, doing so is quite easy. Remember, however, that content in rows and columns you delete is also deleted.

Follow these steps to remove rows or columns:

1. In Page view, select what you want to remove:

   Rows   Either drag the pointer across the rows or choose Table ➡ Select ➡ Row.

   Columns   Click in the column and choose Table ➡ Select ➡ Column.

2. Choose Table ➡ Delete Cells, right-click and choose Delete Cells on the shortcut menu, or click the Delete Cells button on the Tables toolbar.

You can't delete columns or rows by pressing the Delete key. Pressing that key deletes the data in the columns or rows, but not the columns or rows themselves. You can, however, delete columns or rows by selecting them and pressing Shift-Delete.

To delete an entire table, click in the table and choose Table ➡ Select ➡ Table. Then right-click and choose Delete Cells or click the Delete Cells button the Tables toolbar.

Evening Up Your Table

After you've created a table and entered the data, you might decide to make the rows a uniform height and the columns a uniform width. FrontPage offers two commands for doing just that. Follow these steps:

1. In Page view, select the rows or columns you want to make the same size.

2. Choose Table ➡ Distribute Columns Evenly or Table ➡ Distribute Rows Evenly. You can also right-click and choose a Distribute command or click the Distribute Columns Evenly or Distribute Rows Evenly button on the Tables toolbar.

Your table is resized so that the dimensions of the cells in the columns or rows you selected are the same size as the largest cell in that column or row. You can even select an entire table and then follow these steps, if you'd like.

Some Fancy Table Options

Now that you know how to put a table on your page, change its width, alignment, and borders, and add and remove cells, rows, and columns, you're ready to turn the table into something fancy. These pages explain how to space the items in a table with cell padding and cell spacing, splash color on a table, and even add background images to a table and its cells.

Letting the AutoFormat Command Do the Work

Before you learn all the different ways to format a table, consider letting the AutoFormat command do the work. This all-purpose command gives a preformatted table in which the borders, background colors, and fonts have already been applied for you. You don't have to do the layout work yourself.

Follow these steps to format a table with the AutoFormat command:

1. Click in the table that needs formatting.

2. Choose Table ➔ Table AutoFormat or click the Table AutoFormat button on the Tables toolbar. You see the Table AutoFormat dialog box shown in Figure 11.13.

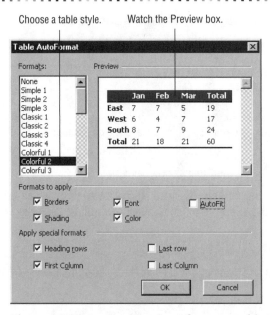

Figure 11.13 *Letting FrontPage format a table in the Table AutoFormat dialog box*

3. Choose a format in the Formats list. The Preview box shows exactly what your choice is.

4. Under Formats To Apply, check and uncheck options to alter the table design and choose different borders, shading, fonts, and colors. If you check the Auto-Fit check box, FrontPage will make each column wide enough to accommodate its largest entry.

5. Under Apply Special Formats, check and uncheck options and watch what happens in the Preview box. Experiment until the table meets your needs.

6. Click OK.

Editing One Cell at a Time

You can make changes that affect only certain cells in your table, although some of the options available for doing this kind of editing are slightly misleading. For instance, using the Cell Properties dialog box, you can specify a pixel or percentage width for a cell. Tables are rectangular, however, so if you make one cell wider, the entire column it's in also increases in width.

Following is a quick rundown of the options in the Cell Properties dialog box (right-click a cell and choose Cell Properties to open it):

- Text alignment options (in the Layout area of the dialog box) allow you to place text at the left side, center, or right side of a cell, on both the horizontal and vertical axes.

- Width options allow you to change the width of a cell, although these specifications affect the entire column in which the cell is found.

- Spanned options let you define how tall or wide a single cell should be. For example, you can set the number of rows spanned to 2 and the number of columns spanned to 3, and the cell would effectively occupy six cells' worth of space.

- Border options, described in the section "Adding Color to Tables," allow you to specify colors for the border of a particular cell.

- Background options, described in the section "Using Table Background Images," allow you to choose a background color or image for a single table cell.

You can experiment with these options to exert even more control over the look and dimensions of your tables.

Cell Padding, Cell Spacing, and Border Width

Cell spacing and cell padding both involve adjusting the amount of white space in a table. *Cell spacing* is the amount of space between a cell's walls and its content; *cell padding* is the amount of space between cells. While different-sized border widths also affect the amount of space between cells, cell padding allows you to fine-tune the layout of the table even when the width of the border is zero.

To give you an idea how cell padding works, here is a table with the default cell padding of 0 and the same table with a cell padding of 10. The table, we think, is easier to read with extra cell padding.

North	East	West	South
14	41	43	30
39	43	83	32
41	98	51	73

North	East	West	South
14	41	43	30
39	43	83	32
41	98	51	73

This illustration shows the same table with cell spacing at 10 pixels, while the cell padding is back to 0 pixels:

North	East	West	South
14	41	43	30
39	43	83	32
41	98	51	73

Here, the table's cell padding and spacing are back to default levels, and the table's border is 10 pixels:

North	East	West	South
14	41	43	30
39	43	83	32
41	98	51	73

Finally, here's the same table with the borders turned off (border size is set to 0):

North	East	West	South
14	41	43	30
39	43	83	32
41	98	51	73

As you can see, the options are almost limitless. You can experiment with different settings for all three options until you find a look that's right for the information you want to present. A lot of cell padding, particularly with borders turned off, is often a good way to present images and text together. Figure 11.14 shows just such a table.

· ·

 a mighty lion

another
mighty lion

Figure 11.14 *In this table, cell padding and spacing provide an ample cushion around text and images.*

Follow these steps to adjust the amount of cell padding, the amount of cell spacing, and the border width of a table:

1. In Page view, either right-click the table and choose Table Properties on the shortcut menu, or click the table and choose Table ➔ Table Properties ➔ Table. The Table Properties dialog box appears (refer to Figure 11.10).

2. To adjust the border size, look under Borders and enter a number (in pixels) in the Size text box (or click the arrows to increase or decrease the number). If you want the border you chose to appear in the gridlines of the table as well as the outside lines, check the Show Both Cells and Table Borders check box.

3. To adjust the cell spacing, go to the Layout area of the dialog box and type a number (in pixels) in the Cell Spacing text box.

4. To adjust the cell padding, go the Layout area of the dialog box and type a number (in pixels) in the Cell Padding text box.

5. Click OK.

You may have to adjust these properties several times before the table looks just so. You can wield great control over your page layout with a little bit of experimentation.

If you're using tables to fit a page to the exact dimensions of a graphic or a specific screen resolution, cell padding and cell spacing can cause trouble by adding space that you do not need. In this case, make sure your cell padding and spacing values are set to 0.

Adding Color to Tables

You learned to add background color to your pages in Chapter 4, and you can do the same thing for tables. Not only can you specify a different background color in your table than the color you used for the main body of the page, you can use a different background color for every single cell, if you like—although that would probably look a mite silly.

Follow these steps to change the background color of a table:

1. In Page view, either right-click the table whose background color you want to change and choose Table Properties on the shortcut menu, or click in the table and choose Table ➔ Table Properties ➔ Table. The Table Properties dialog box appears (refer to Figure 11.10).

To quickly change a table's background color, select all the cells, open the drop-down menu on the Fill Color button on the Tables toolbar, and choose a color from the drop-down menu.

2. In the Background area of the dialog box, open the Color drop-down menu and choose a color for the background of the table.

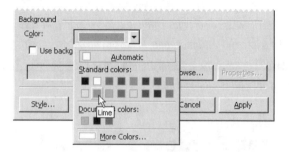

To choose a custom color not shown in the dialog box, click More Colors at the bottom of the dialog box. You see the More Colors dialog box (see Figure 11.15). Click a color there and then click OK. (Be sure to read Chapter 17, which explains how to use color on a Web page and which colors can be viewed by which browsers.)

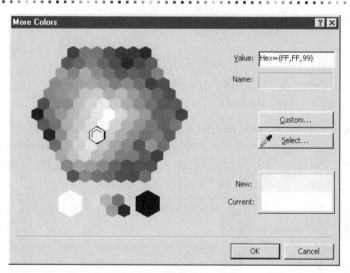

Figure 11.15 *You can choose among many colors in the More Colors dialog box.*

3. Click OK to close the Table Properties dialog box.
Now your table is bright and colorful.

Remember that not all browsers display background colors—and that goes double for table backgrounds, which are a relatively new innovation. Make sure to choose a text color that goes well with the background of the Web page you are working on. You can use the <FONT COLOR=n> tag to specify a different text color in your table than you do on the rest of the Web page.

Coloring the Borders and Gridlines

Besides choosing a color for the background of a table, you can choose one for its borders and gridlines. The gridlines are the interior lines, the ones that demarcate the columns and rows. What's more, you can create a three-dimensional effect for the table by choosing a dark border and light border.

Follow these steps to assign a color to the borders and gridlines of a table:

1. In Page view, either right-click the table whose border color you want to change and choose Table Properties on the shortcut menu, or click in the table and choose Table ➜ Table Properties ➜ Table. The Table Properties dialog box appears (refer to Figure 11.10).

2. Choose options in the Borders area of the dialog box:

Choose a single color for the borders (and the gridlines)   Open the Color drop-down menu and select a color.

Choose colors for a three-dimensional effect   Choose a color from the Light Border drop-down menu and the Dark Border drop-down menu. The light border color appears on the top and left side of the table; the bottom border color appears on the bottom and right side of the table.

Apply the color(s) you choose to the gridlines   Check the Show Both Cells And Table Borders check box.

3. Click OK.

Using Table Background Images

Besides entering a background color for a table, you can enter a background image like the one shown in Figure 11.16. For that matter, you can place a background image in a single table cell. The techniques for entering a background image in a table or a cell are nearly the same.

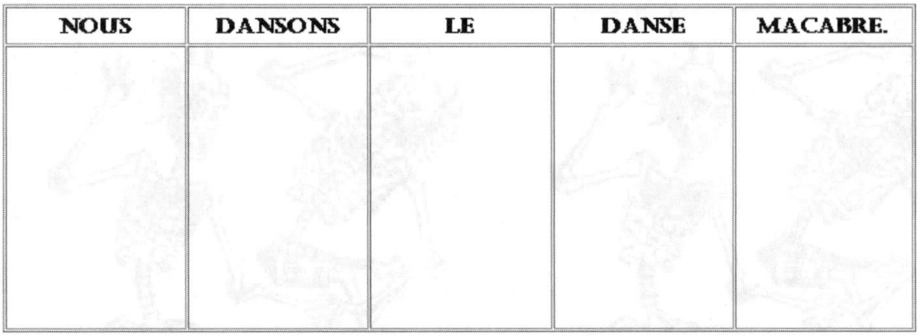

NOUS	DANSONS	LE	DANSE	MACABRE.

Figure 11.16 *A background image in a table*

Follow these steps to insert a background image in a table or in a single cell in a table:

1. Open the Table Properties or Cell Properties dialog box:

   Inserting a background image in a table   In Page view, right-click the table cell where you want to put the image and choose Cell Properties, or else click in the table and choose Table ➜ Table Properties ➜ Table.

   Inserting a background image in a table cell   In Page view, right-click the cell and choose Cell Properties or click in the cell and choose Table ➜ Table Properties ➜ Cell.

2. Check the Use Background Picture check box.

3. Click the Browse button. The Select Background Picture dialog box appears.

4. Find and select the image that you want to use as a background, and click the Open button. Back in the Table Properties or Cell Properties dialog box, the name of the file you chose appears in the Use Background Picture text box.

5. Click OK.

Up Next

One of the best advantages of knowing how to lay out pages using tables is that you can really stretch your creativity. No longer are you limited to standard HTML layouts, which, while effective, tend to restrict the many variations that tables afford.

With a knowledge of table structure, including cells and rows, as well as the tools available within FrontPage to modify that structure, you're going to be able to set a table everyone will be impressed with. Now it's time to move on to another method of layout control: frames.

Fantastic Frames

FRONTPAGE

Chapter 12

Frames make an entire Web site accessible from a single screen. They divide the browser window into individual windows, each of which holds a different page. A page that appears inside a frame can include any element that can be included in a standard Web page. Frames help visitors go easily from page to page in a Web site. And FrontPage is just about the easiest way in the world to get a frames-based page up and running.

This chapter starts by explaining the frames template. It describes how to modify the layout, content, and navigational scheme of a frame. You'll also discover how frames and hyperlinks can work together to make for a dynamic site. Topics include:

- What frames are

- The difference between tables and frames

- Making a navigational frame

- Creating frames with FrontPage templates

- Modifying a framed document

- Targeting links and setting target defaults

- Making frames and forms work together

How Frames Work

When designed properly, frames look great. And they act even better than they look—unlike, say, most children. Children are a pretty good metaphor for frames-based pages because there is a parent page, called a *frames page* in FrontPage parlance, that sets the guidelines for how its children, called *content pages*, act. The whole batch of pages—the frames page and its content pages—is called a *frameset*.

Each frame in a frameset is a separate HTML file. You can create any number of documents to go within a frames-based site. The good news is that assigning pages to frames is easy. All you have to do is click a button and tell FrontPage which page to place inside a frame. The bad news is that FrontPage doesn't create the pages for you. You still have to create the page that goes inside the frame—and you have to be careful about how large you make the page, because it has to fit inside the frame.

The best way to create a frames-based page is to create some of the content pages before you start the frames page, or parent page. Once you place the default pages in the frames page, you can tweak them right there to make sure they look okay after they've been framed.

You get to decide how many frames appear in the window, how big frames are, and how frames act. Figure 12.1 shows an example of a frames-based page divided into three columns. Notice the scroll bars on some of the frames. You can decide whether scroll bars appear on frames. When you click a hyperlink in a frame, the new Web page can appear in the frame itself, in a new window, in a different frame, or in the window where the frames pages is. The determination of which link goes to which frame is called *targeting*. You will learn about targeting later in this chapter.

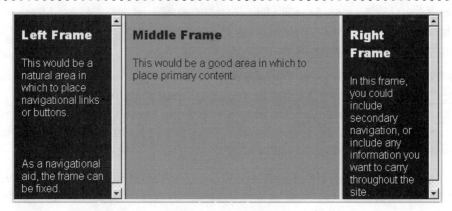

Figure 12.1 *A three-column frames-based page*

Using FrontPage, it's easy to create pages like the one in Figure 12.1. Because each frame presents a different page, each page can have its own background color, text color, and link colors. In the frameset shown in Figure 12.1, all the pages have the same font. The colors were chosen to complement one another rather than clash. Remember as you work with frames that the goal is to present a unified site. As such, frames pages should not clash or conflict with each other.

 Don't use frames pages on your Web site if your Web pages include shared borders or link bars. Shared borders and link bars are, like frames, navigational tools. If you use them along with frames, visitors will have trouble navigating your Web site.

Why Some Folks Hate Frames (and How You Can Ease Their Pain)

Some people just can't stand frames, no matter how well the frames page is designed or how ingeniously it functions. One reason that some people don't care for frames is that they gobble up system resources. Downloading a page with four frames (and the images found therein) takes more time than downloading one page and clicking links to view different pages.

Some folks think frames are just plain ugly. Visually speaking, frames can make the small space on a Web page seem even smaller. One trick to avoiding this is to use borderless frames and keep the number of frames you use to no more than *three*.

Navigational issues are another reason why many dislike frames. When frames were introduced, the Back button on browsers didn't act as users expected it to. Instead of taking them back to the previous frame, the entire frameset was treated as one page, and clicking the Back button sent users back to where they came from—to the Web page they were viewing before they came to the frameset page. A pop-up menu command called Back In Frame allowed you to go back through the history list one frame at a time, but many people never discovered its existence. The Back button problem has been fixed in modern browsers, but the people who dislike frames were permanently traumatized by the disorientation that navigating through frames caused them.

Another reason to hate frames is the reason so many people love them: targeting. Thanks to targeting, clicking a link in a frames site can do three different things: Make a new page appear in any frame in the frames page, make a new page appear in the same window in which the link is found, and open a new window altogether. Some people are put off by the uncertainty of that. What's more, on a poorly designed Web page, clicking a link in a frames page can display a new Web page that doesn't fit well inside a frame.

Others have never gotten the hang of printing or bookmarking a single frame. Still more don't have, or don't plan to use, a browser that supports frames—many browsers for the visually impaired, for instance, aren't frames-compatible.

In other words, it couldn't hurt to offer a non-frames alternative to your site. (The non-frames version obviously should include the same content as the frames version.) Another solution is to offer a Help page that includes instructions for working with frames.

Frames are not the evil, difficult beasts many people think they are. They can, in fact, be extraordinarily useful as a navigation device, and with a bit of nudging, users can benefit greatly from frames.

Uses for Frames

Are frames good for anything? Yes, yes, indeed yes! If visitors to a page on your Web site would benefit from seeing several pages in the same window, frames are an option for you. Here are creative uses for frames:

Tables of contents   These often appear as a long, thin frame on the left side of the window. When you click a link in the table of contents, its target page appears in a larger frame in the same window.

Search engines   The query form appears in one frame, and the results in another, so that the two appear side by side. In this case, you target the links of the query results to appear in a new window.

Button bars   Similar to a table of contents, a button bar or navigation tool set is visible during the whole visit in a frame at the top, bottom, or side of the central navigation area.

Footnotes   Scholarly research papers don't take advantage of the framed footnotes idea nearly often enough. Users click the noted word in the main body of the window and the footnote appears simultaneously in a smaller frame at the bottom of the window.

Guestbooks   Visitors type comments in a form in one frame and, when they click Send, their comments appear in another frame.

Art catalogs   An image is placed in one frame and the text that corresponds to it in another, complete with scroll bars. Frames work beautifully in any instance in which an image is visible on-screen while its related text is being read.

Banner ads   On many sites, banner ads are presented in a separate frame, usually near the top of the page. For some, this solves the problem of how to integrate ads into the design of an overall page.

Multimedia   Use one frame as the container for a sound file, a Shockwave movie, a Java applet, or an inline video clip.

Make a Navigational Frame

One clever use for frames is to create a navigational frame that stays in the same position no matter where a visitor goes on a Web site. The visitor clicks links or buttons in the navigational frame to visit a different part of the site or return to a part he or she has visited before. Links in the navigational frame, of course, are targeted to open up in a different frame, usually the largest frame.

Navigational frames can take many different forms. A full or abridged table of contents can appear in a column-frame along the left side of the window. A button bar can appear in a frame at the top or bottom of the window. The main thing is for the navigational frame to include links—in the form of words, buttons, or icons—that visitors can click in order to move through the site.

Planning a Frames Page

Because there are so many variables, planning a site that includes frames before you start creating the frames is quite important. Planning a frames page goes something like this:

1. Make a rough sketch on paper that shows what the frames page will look like. Include the number of frames you want, how much screen space each frame will occupy, whether frames will have borders and scroll bars.

2. Plan a background, text, and link color scheme for each frame. As you plan, keep in mind what the site as a whole looks like. For example, are you going to use a black background and yellow text in every frame, or just in one part?

3. Create the pages that will fill in the blanks. Ideally, you should at least have a basic page for each frame in your frameset, although creating the content pages before you start the project isn't essential. You can use pages you created months ago as sample pages or create blank pages that you will replace later.

4. Open up FrontPage and get to work putting the thing together!

5. Target your links: Define what will happen when you click each and every link on your page. (You can set defaults for each frame, in which case you need to specify targets only for single links that depart from your default settings.)

After you've planned your frames site, it's time to get to work making it.

Creating Frames Pages from a Template

FrontPage offers many templates for creating framesets. And when you have created a frameset, editing it is fairly easy. You can change the number of frames in the set, alter the arrangement of frames, and do a host of other things to make the frames look just right. To begin with, however, you choose one of the frames templates shown in Table 12.1. Choose the layout that is most similar to the one you sketched when you were planning your Web site. Remember: Frames can be added to and deleted from any template.

Table 12.1 Frame Page Layouts Offered by FrontPage Templates

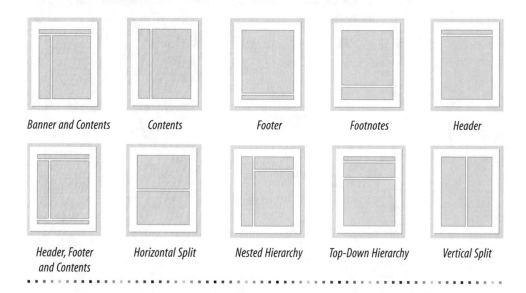

| Banner and Contents | Contents | Footer | Footnotes | Header |

| Header, Footer and Contents | Horizontal Split | Nested Hierarchy | Top-Down Hierarchy | Vertical Split |

There is no easier way to create a frames page than by starting with a template. In the case of forms and tables, starting with a template isn't necessarily the best way to go, but templates are the way to go when it comes to frames. As you get the knack of creating frames pages, you can save your creations under different names and thereby work with templates of your own design. Starting from scratch may seem like a noble goal for the purist, but in the case of templates it ain't worth it.

Follow these steps to create a frames page:

1. Choose File ➜ New ➜ Page or Web. The New Page or Web task plane appears.

2. Under New From Template, click the Page Templates hyperlink. You see the Page Templates dialog box.

3. Click the Frames Pages tab (see Figure 12.2).

4. Select a template. Be sure to read the description on the right side of the dialog box to see precisely what the template is. And glance at the preview image as well so you know what you are getting into.

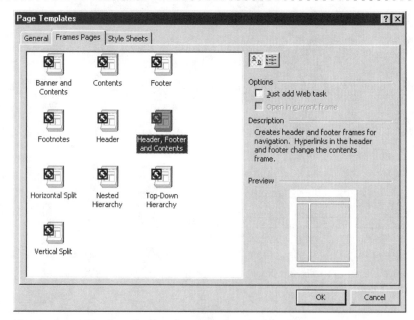

Figure 12.2 *Choose a layout from the Frames Pages tab of the Page Templates dialog box.*

Remember that you can still add or remove frames after you choose a layout—you're going for a general similarity to your ideas here, rather than an exact match.

5. When you find a layout you like, select it and click OK. The layout of your frames page is displayed.

The gray fields that appear are mockups of frames pages. You'll use them to assign individual HTML pages to each frame. Each pane in the frameset is represented by a blank, gray frame with a set of buttons, as shown in Figure 12.3.

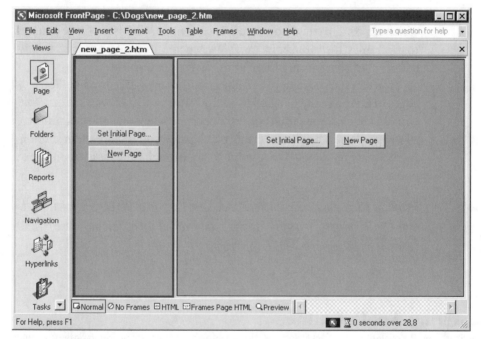

Figure 12.3 *The Contents template. Notice that each frame has two buttons.*

When you work with a frames page, additional tabs appear at the bottom of the window. The No Frames tab shows you what people whose browsers can't handle frames will see when they visit your site. The Frames Page HTML tab shows the HTML for the page that is selected.

To edit a particular frame, click to select it. Click the different frames in your new template and notice how the selected frame is highlighted. Now that you have a frames template to work with, you can get to work. Better read on.

Editing Frames and Frames Pages

FrontPage's design for the frames editing tools is nothing short of brilliant. It's completely obvious when you use this tool that each frame contains a separate document—which is a concept that's tough to grasp for most Web users. Once you attach documents to the frames, they appear in Page view, where you can edit them. The few other frames editors in existence simply aren't this classy or easy to use.

You can start editing your frames page in any order you like. You can attach initial pages that are already finished to all the frames and just tweak them a bit to finish. Or you can attach some initial pages that are partially done one at a time, completing them as you go along. Or you can create blank pages and replace them later on. Your working methods are up to you. We're going to go through each task you might consider doing, one at a time.

FrontPage offers another kind of frame that doesn't appear in the Page Templates dialog box—an inline frame. An inline frame is a sort of scrolling text box that can appear anywhere on a Web page. See "Creating an Inline Frame" later in this chapter.

Mastering What's Online

A classic in frames development is Cocktail, the HotWired site about the history and variations of the mixed drink. Point your browser to www.hotwired.com/cocktail/, and click around a bit. Note in particular the way in which hyperlinks on this site are targeted to appear in different frames depending on the context.

Altering the Frames Page Layout

If the frames page template you chose is just right, you're in luck. You don't have to worry about redesigning the frames page layout. But if you need to add frames to the layout, delete a frame, or adjust the size of a frame, you've come to the right place.

Starting in Page view with the Normal tab selected, follow these instructions to alter the frames page layout:

Changing the size of a frame   Move the pointer over the border between two frames. When you see the two-headed arrow, click and start dragging. You can also right-click the frame you want to resize and choose Frame Properties on the shortcut menu. You see the Frame Properties dialog box. Under Frame Size, enter a Width and Row Height measurement.

Creating a new frame   Click in the frame where the new frame is to appear and choose Frames ➜ Split Frame. The Split Frame dialog box appears. To divide the frame lengthwise, click the Split Into Rows option button. To split the frame vertically, click the Split Into Columns option button.

After you split a frame, you can drag the border between the two halves to resize it, if you don't want the frames to be symmetrical.

Deleting a frame   Click to select the frame you want to delete and choose Frames ➜ Delete Frame. The frame you selected disappears—or rather, because it was part of a larger page, its borders disappear and it is absorbed by an adjoining frame.

You can repeat any or all of these steps to add, resize, and remove frames until the page looks like you want it to. Starting with one of the FrontPage templates, you can achieve any layout you want by splitting, deleting, and resizing frames. Figures 12.4 through 12.7 demonstrate how, starting from a template, you can redesign a frames page.

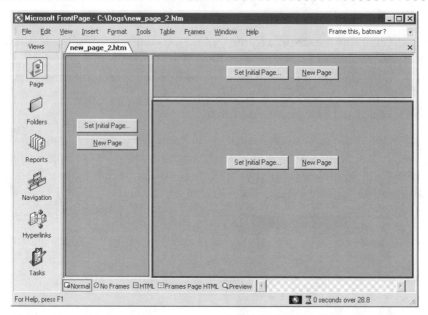

Figure 12.4 *This frames page was created with the Nested Hierarchy template.*

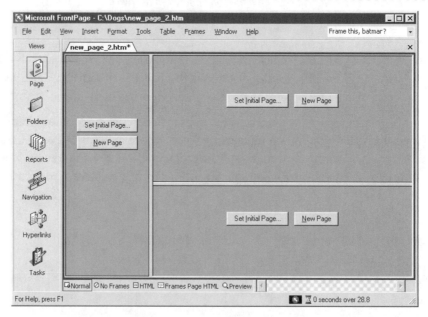

Figure 12.5 *The two frames on the right have been resized by dragging the border between them.*

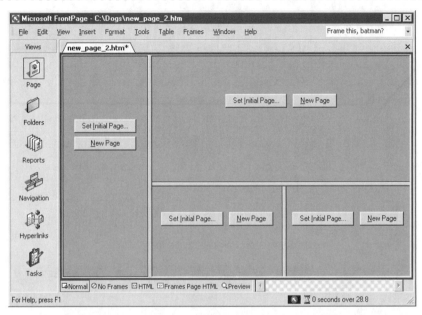

Figure 12.6 *The bottom-right frame in Figure 12.5 was split into the two frames you see here.*

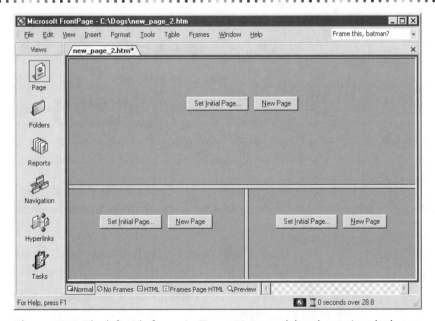

Figure 12.7 *The left-side frame in Figure 12.6 was deleted, creating the layout you now see.*

Attaching an Initial Page to a Frame

The *initial page*, also known as a *default page*, is the page that "belongs" to a frame. When the entire frames page is loaded into a browser window, each frame needs to be filled with something at the outset, and this something is the initial page. No matter what frames get filled as visitors click and backtrack and click again, the initial page will always be the starting point for a frames-based site.

Follow these steps to attach an initial or default page to a frame:

1. With the frames page visible in Page view, click the frame you want to work with.

2. Click the frame's Set Initial Page button. The Insert Hyperlink dialog box appears, as shown in Figure 12.8.

Find and select a Web page for the frame.

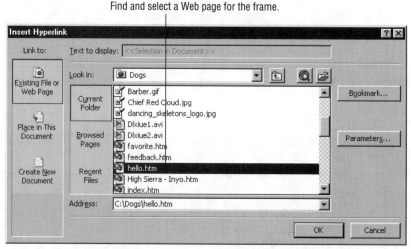

Figure 12.8 *Use the Insert Hyperlink dialog box to attach an initial page to a frame.*

3. Tell FrontPage which page to put in the frame. To **attach a page that you already created**, locate and select the page in the Insert Hyperlink dialog box. FrontPage offers several ways to do this.

   - Click the Current Folder button if the page is stored along with other pages in your Web site.

   - Take advantage of the Look In drop-down menu and Up One Folder button to locate the Web page.

- Click the Browse For File button (the small button near the Bookmark button) to open the Link To File dialog box, where you can find and select a Web page that is stored anywhere on your hard drive.

- Click the Recent Files button and select the Web page in the list of 500 or so files you opened recently.

To **attach a Web page from the Internet**, click the Browse The Web button (the small button near the Bookmark button). Your Browser opens. Go to the Web page you want to link to. Its URL will appear in the Address text box of the Insert Hyperlink dialog box.

Chapter 4 explains the Insert Hyperlink dialog box in detail.

4. Glance at the Address textbox to make sure the right filename or URL appears there, and then click OK to close the Insert Hyperlink dialog box. The Web page that you selected in step 3 is displayed in the frame.

Insert a Web page in each and every frame in your frames page. You can also create a new page right in the frames page, as the next section of this chapter so aptly demonstrates.

Suppose you select an initial page for a frame and change your mind. All is not lost. Follow these steps to choose a different Web page for a frame:

1. Either click the frame and choose Frames ➜ Frame Properties or right-click the frame and choose Frame Properties. You see the Frame Properties dialog box.

2. Click the Browse button. The Edit Hyperlink dialog box appears.

3. Choose a new Web page for the frame. To do so, use the same techniques you used in the first place to choose a Web page in the Insert Hyperlink dialog box (refer to Figure 12.8).

Dropping a Frames Page into a Frame

For a really interesting visual effect, try embedding a frames page in another frames page. In other words, try choosing a frames page as one of the initial pages in a frameset. The frames page will appear as the content of one of the frames.

This technique should be used sparingly, or it can cause clutter and make too many demands on system resources. It can be a nice approach for an initial splash screen page, however. You can set a frames page as an initial frame (see "Attaching an Initial Page to a Frame") and then set that frame's target as parent (see "Creating Target Settings"). Then, when someone clicks a link in that area of your site, the new destination page replaces the frames page as the content of your frame. Try it! You'll like it.

Attaching a New Page to a Frame

If you like, you can create a new page in a frame. In other words, you can start from scratch with a blank slate and fill it with text, graphics, a logo, or other objects. There's no need to create the page ahead of time. You can add a new page to your frameset and stick the page right in the frames template.

Follow these steps to add a new page to a frameset:

1. In Page view, click the frame you want to add a page to.

2. Click the New Page button. A blank page appears in the frame.

That's all there is to that. Now you can start working with the page as you would any other. Later in this chapter, "Editing Pages in the Frames Page" offers tips for working with pages in a frameset.

Saving a Frameset

A frameset is made up of several pages: the frames page, which is the behind-the-scenes page that instructs the frameset how to look and act, and the initial pages, one for every frame in the frameset. When you save a frameset, you save the frameset itself and all its initial pages. If the initial pages haven't been saved yet or saved recently, FrontPage will ask you to save them as well as the frameset when you give the command to save the frameset.

When you save a frameset for the first time, you are asked to enter a filename and title for the frames page. You are asked to do the same for each initial page in the frameset, if you haven't saved it yet. The filename of each initial frame is stored as a URL in the frames page to let it know which initial pages to load.

As you know, a title appears in the Web browser's title bar when someone views a Web page. It isn't absolutely necessary for each initial page to have a title, but having a page title can be helpful when editing a frameset. When you click in a frame, the title bar displays both the title of the entire frameset and the title of the individual frame, so giving your frames a distinct name—even if it's something like *left* or *blue*—can help you distinguish what you're editing.

No matter what state of completion your frameset is in, follow these steps to save a frameset for the first time:

1. In Page view, choose File ➜ Save or click the Save button. The Save As dialog box appears, as shown in Figure 12.9. Pay special attention to the preview area on the right side of the dialog box. It tells you which frame you're saving, or, if all frames are highlighted, that you are saving the frameset.

    First you are asked to save initial pages, if you haven't saved them already. When you've saved them all, you are asked to save the frameset.

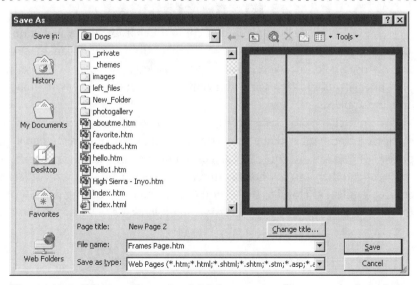

Figure 12.9 *When you're saving initial pages or a frameset, the Save As dialog box appears.*

2. In the File Name text box, enter the filename of the page or frameset that you want to save.

3. If you want to change the title of a page, click the Change Title button, and, in the Set Page Title dialog box, enter a name and click OK.

4. Verify where you're saving the file. If necessary, select a new folder and make sure its name appears in the Save In text box.

5. Click OK. Instead of closing, a new frame or the frameset is highlighted in the Save As dialog box so you can save the next frame or the frameset (if you haven't save it yet).

6. Follow steps 2 through 5 for every frame in your frameset and, finally, for the frameset itself.

7. When you've finished saving the frameset, click OK. At last, the Save As dialog boxes closes.

You can save changes to a page in a frame at any time by clicking in it and then choosing File ➜ Save, pressing Ctrl+S, or clicking the Save button. To save all the Web pages in a frameset, choose File ➜ Save All.

Editing Pages in the Frames Page

As we've said, you can put any kind of content in a frame that you can put in a stand-alone Web page. Editing these pages is just like editing a new, blank page. You can enter text, choose a color for hyperlinks, choose a background color or image, and select a page title. Forms and tables are both right at home in a frame, as are images, plug-ins, and Java applets.

You're welcome to create a complete page and *then* attach it to a frameset. If you do so, however, remember that a frame occupies less space on-screen than a normal Web page does. You can also attach a partially completed or completely blank page to a frameset and then edit it. The only difference is what you see on the screen while you're editing. While it's helpful to see several pages all at once, editing pages within the frameset in FrontPage can be memory-intensive.

To find out more about editing pages, refer to Chapter 4. The principles are all the same, except that, with a frameset, you can work with several pages within the same window. Click in whichever frame you want to work with. All the menu commands and toolbar buttons are available to you.

To view page properties for a frames page, click the frame and choose File ➜ Properties. The Page Properties dialog box appears. Use it to change the page's title, its background, and the color of text and hyperlinks, among other things. Refer to Chapter 4 for details.

Choosing How Each Frame Looks and Acts

By visiting the Frames Properties dialog box, you can tell FrontPage how to make a frame look and act. The Frames Properties dialog box stores information about the layout and functions of individual frames. For example, you can decide whether people who visit your site can resize a frame in their browser windows, whether the frame has scroll bars, what dimensions the frame is, and what portion of the window it occupies. You can also establish margins for a frame to control the distance between the objects in the frame and its borders.

Later in this chapter, "Choosing What All Frame Borders Look Like" explains how to get a uniform look for all the frames in a frameset.

To choose how a frame looks and acts, click in the frame and do either of the following to open the Frame Properties dialog box (see Figure 12.10):

- Choose Frames ➜ Frame Properties.
- Right-click and choose Frame Properties.

Read on to tell FrontPage how to make a frame look and act in the Frame Properties dialog box.

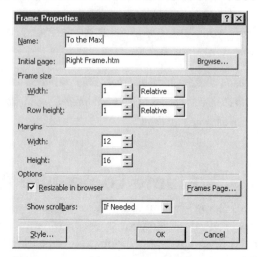

Figure 12.10 *The Frame Properties dialog box lets you adjust the size and margins of a frame.*

Choosing a Frame Size

Frame size is perhaps the most important aspect of a frame. As "Altering the Frames Page Layout" explained earlier in this chapter, you can change the size of frames by dragging their borders with the mouse. Why change the size of frames in the Frame Properties dialog box? Perhaps you want two frames to be the same size or be similar in proportion. Or one frame, for example, may need to be twice as big as another.

Because all the frames in a page are interdependent, you should set one frame's size first, and then base the other frames' sizes on that one.

When you change the size of a frame, adjacent frames change size as well to accommodate the frame whose size you changed. FrontPage offers three ways to decide the size of a frame:

- Relative to the other frames in the same column or row: Go this route when you want one frame to be half or a third as big, for example, as another frame. If you are resizing a frame that happens to be in the same column or row as other frames, you can choose a size relative to the other columns or rows. To do so, choose Relative from the Width drop-down menu and enter a number to indicate how large or small to make the column or row with respect to the other columns or rows. For example, in a two-column frame, entering 2 in the Width text box in one frame and 1 in the Width text box for the other frame ensures that one column is twice as wide as the other.

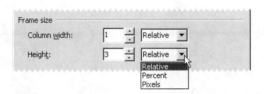

You can actually mix relative sizes with absolute sizes. The frames with relative sizes will divide whatever is left of the window after the frames with absolute sizes are accounted for.

- By percentage of the window: Go this route when you want to distribute frames of various sizes across the window. Open the drop-down menu, choose Percentage, and enter a percentage figure in the text box. If two frames are stacked in a frameset, for example, entering 75 in the Height text box makes one frame occupy three-fourths of the vertical space in the frameset.

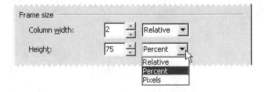

- By pixels: Go this route when you know the exact size in pixels that you want the frame to be. Choose Pixels from the drop-down menu and enter a measurement in pixels in the text box.

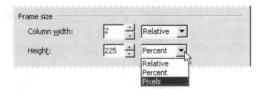

The frameset shown in Figure 12.11 has two columns and two rows (the rows are confined to the right half of the screen and fall one below the other). We decided to

make the leftmost frame 144 pixels wide to accommodate an image of that size. Therefore, we made the column width setting for the remaining two frames Relative, so that
they occupy the remaining screen width, regardless of the size of the browser window.

Figure 12.11 *This frameset has two columns and two rows. The frame on the left spans
144 pixels, and the two right-side frames each occupy 50 percent of the window height.*

We also decided that the two frames on the right of Figure 12.11 should be the
same height. The Height setting for both of these frames is 50 percent. The Height setting for the frame on the left, which occupies 100 percent of the available height, is
automatically set to Relative.

Frame Margins

Frame margins determine the distance between the content and the side of the frame.
The Width margin setting determines the amount of space between the left side of the
frame and the content; the Height margin setting determines the amount of space
between the top border of the frame and the content. Frame margins are measured in
pixels.

Frame margins are particularly helpful for ensuring that content doesn't get lost in
a window or frame when it is resized.

Under Margins in the Frame Properties dialog box (refer to Figure 12.10), enter margin settings in the Width and Height text boxes.

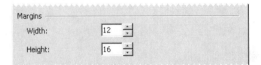

If the page that is housed in the frame already has its own margin settings, those settings are added to the settings that are entered in the Frame Properties dialog box. A page with its own Width margin setting of 3 pixels, if it is augmented by a 3-pixel setting in the Frame Properties dialog box, has a Width margin of 6 pixels.

Letting (or Not Letting) Visitors Resize Frames

In "Altering the Frames Page Layout," earlier in this chapter, you learned how to change the size of frames by dragging their borders. If you click the Resizable In Browser check box in the Frame Properties dialog box (refer to Figure 12.10), visitors to your page can do the same thing. They can move their pointers over the border between two frames and click and drag to change the frame's size. Uncheck the Resizable In Browser check box if you don't want visitors tinkering with a frame.

Don't assume that your page will be viewed by someone with the same screen size, screen resolution, or font sizes that you have. What takes up a single line when you preview it may take up several lines on someone else's screen. Always design with a 640 × 480 screen resolution in mind. In general, you should always let Web surfers change the size of frames. That way, crucial parts of your pages don't get axed on some people's machines.

Choosing Whether Frames Have Scroll Bars

Each frame is perfectly capable of having its own scroll bars, either horizontal, vertical, or both. You can choose from three scroll bar settings: If Needed, Always, and Never. In general, If Needed, the default setting, is the best choice for most pages. The scroll bars show up if they're needed, and they stay out of the way if they aren't.

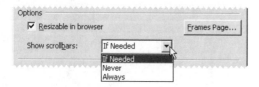

You can choose Never if you're dead certain that no visitor to your Web site will have to scroll to see content in the frame. However, it's dreadfully annoying to see only half a word or two-thirds of a picture on a 15-inch monitor because some clever Web-master with a 17-inch monitor turned off scroll bars in his or her frames.

We can't think of a compelling reason to choose Always. You could select this setting if you believe that the frame you are working on will soon be filled with scroll-happy content. And drawing the scroll bars in before they're needed might save a couple of seconds, since the browser doesn't have to draw them as they are needed.

Choosing What All Frame Borders Look Like

Besides choosing how each frame in a frameset looks and acts (the subject of the last handful of pages), you can do one or two things to tell FrontPage what all the frames should look like. To be specific, you can decide these matters when it comes to all the frames in the frameset:

Frame spacing The amount of gray padding between the frames. The default setting is 2 pixels, but you can make the frames wider than that. The wider you make them, the thicker the gray borders between frames are.

Be advised that frame spacing greater than 5 pixels can play weird tricks on most browsers.

Turning off the borders Frame borders, when turned off, can disguise the fact that a Web site is constructed from frames. Figure 12.12 shows the same frames page you saw in Figure 12.11, but with the borders turned off.

Figure 12.12 *Turning off the borders on a frames page makes the page look entirely different.*

Follow these steps to adjust frame spacing or frame borders:

1. In Page view, click a frame and then choose Frames ➜ Frame Properties. The Frame Properties dialog box appears (refer to Figure 12.10).

2. Click the Frames Page button. The Page Properties dialog box appears.

3. If necessary, select the Frames tab.

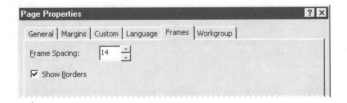

4. In the Frame Spacing text box, type a measurement in pixels for the width and height of the padding between frames.

5. If you'd like to turn off frame borders, uncheck the Show Borders check box; the frame spacing option automatically reverts to 0.

6. Click OK to close the Page Properties dialog box.

7. Click OK in the Frame Properties dialog box.

Your changes may not be evident, or accurately displayed, in the FrontPage window. We suggest previewing your pages in both Internet Explorer and Navigator to make sure the changes display properly.

Creating an Inline Frame

Another type of frame you can include in Web pages is the *inline frame*. An inline frame is a rectangular region, sort of like an image, but instead of holding a picture, it holds another Web page (see Figure 12.13). The advantage of using inline frames is that you can show a file in a specific area of a Web page. Inline frames are great for presenting forms. What's more, you can place an inline frame without having to create a frames page.

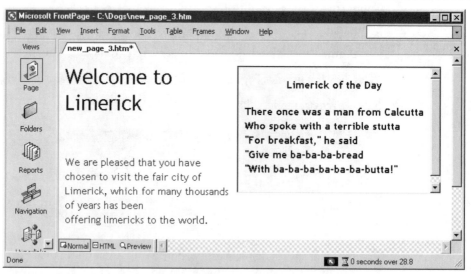

Figure 12.13 *An example of an inline frame*

Follow these steps to create an inline frame:

1. Click roughly where you want the inline frame to go (you'll get the chance later to tinker with the position of the frame).

2. Choose Insert ➜ Inline Frame.

3. Choose a Web page or create a new Web page to put in the inline frame (see "Attaching an Initial Page to a Frame" earlier in this chapter).

After the inline frame lands on the Web page, you very likely have to tinker with it. Here are instructions for doing just that:

Selecting an inline frame   You have to select an inline frame before you can do anything whatsoever with it. To select it, carefully move the cursor to the top of the frame and click when it changes into a pointer. You can tell when an inline frame has been selected because black selection handles appear on its sides and corners.

Changing the size of an inline frame   After the frame has been selected, move the pointer over a black selection handle. When you see the two-headed arrow, click and start dragging. You can also choose Format ➜ Properties (or press Alt+Enter) to open the Inline Frame Properties dialog box (see Figure 12.14). There, under Frame Size, enter measurements in the Width and Height text boxes.

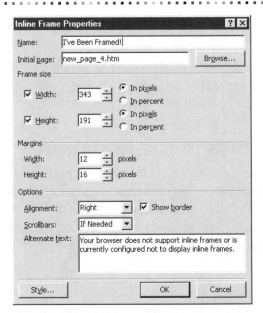

Figure 12.14 *Adjusting the size and position of an inline frame*

Moving an inline frame   After the frame has been selected, try dragging it to a new location. We have discovered, however, that this technique is rather clumsy. Instead, choose Format ➜ Properties (or press Alt+Enter) to open the Inline Frame Properties dialog box (refer to Figure 12.14). Then, under Options, open the Alignment drop-down menu and choose an option that describes where you want the frame to be on your Web page.

Handling the scroll bars   After the frame has been selected, choose Format ➜ Properties (or press Alt+Enter), and, in the Inline Frame Properties dialog box (refer to Figure 12.14), choose an option from the Scrollbars menu to tell Front-Page when to display the scroll bars to Web surfers.

Deleting an inline frame   Select the frame and click the Delete key.

If you chose the wrong page for your inline frame, select it and choose Format ➜ Properties. Then, in the Inline Frame Properties dialog box, enter a new filename in the Initial Page text box.

Setting Targets

What happens when you click a hyperlink in a frames-based page depends on the target of the link. The new page could appear in the same page where the link is located, in a new window on-screen, or in a different frame in the frameset. *Targets* tell the link what to do. And your job is to tell FrontPage what the target is.

Establishing the targets is easier to do after all of the pages in the frameset are in place and you're reasonably sure that you won't have to replace initial pages.

Naming the Frames in the Frameset

Frame names are different from page titles and filenames. They are stored in the frames page along with all the other information about the frameset. Frame names tell the frames page *where* to load each frame, both initially and when a link is targeted there. For instance, in Figure 12.15, the page in the frame on the left has the filename `left.html`, its page title is Left Frame, and the frame itself is named Left. When a link is targeted to load into the frame named Left, the frames page, which works as mission control, loads it into the left-side frame.

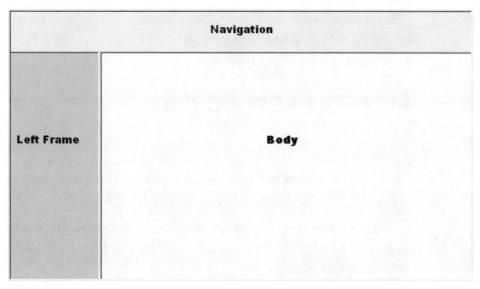

Figure 12.15 *This page has frames named Left Frame, Navigation, and Body.*

FrontPage designates names for each frame when you create a frames page from a template; it also suggests names for each frame you add on your own. You can use the frame names that FrontPage gives you or create names of your own to make the names easier to remember.

Follow these steps to review frame names in the frameset and perhaps change a name or two to make targeting easier:

1. With the frameset visible in Page view, click the frame whose name you want to review or change.

2. Choose Frames ➜ Frame Properties. The Frame Properties dialog box appears (refer to Figure 12.10). The frame name appears in the Name text box.

3. If you so desire, enter a new name.

4. Click OK.

5. Follow steps 1 through 4 for each frame on the frames page.

If you drew a design sketch of your frameset, it might be helpful to write the name of each frame on the sketch so that you can refer to it when you're setting targets.

Avoid these words when naming frames: top, self, parent, and blank. FrontPage uses those words in its default naming scheme for frames. By avoiding those words, you can tell which frame names you invented and which you inherited from FrontPage.

Creating Target Settings

Unless you specify otherwise, clicking a hyperlink in a frame opens the Web page that is the target of the link in the same frame where the link is located. In other words, you click the link and a new Web page appears in the same frame where the link is. You can, however, make the new Web page open in a different frame in the frameset. What's more, FrontPage offers other options for opening a Web page that is the target of a link.

If you already created the hyperlink and you want to change its target page in the frameset, right-click the link and choose Hyperlink Properties. You see the Edit Hyperlink dialog box. Click the Target Frame button and take it from there.

Follow these steps to determine where a Web page is opened after a visitor to your site clicks a hyperlink:

1. With the frameset open in Page view, click the frame you want to insert a hyperlink into.

2. Select the text or image that you want to make into a hyperlink.

3. Choose Insert ➜ Hyperlink or click the Insert Hyperlink button on the Standard toolbar (or press Ctrl+K). The Insert Hyperlink dialog box appears.

4. Create or edit the hyperlink.

Chapter 4 explains in detail how to create hyperlinks and handle the Insert Hyperlink dialog box.

5. Click the Target Frame button. The Target Frame dialog box appears (see Figure 12.16).

Either click a frame...

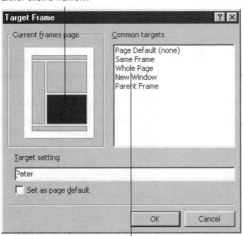

...or choose an option to tell FrontPage how to open the linked Web page.

Figure 12.16 *Choosing in which frame to open a Web page that is the target of a hyperlink.*

6. Choose a target to determine where the Web page appears after its link is clicked:

Appears in a particular frame in the frameset Click a frame in the Current Frames Page box on the left side of the dialog box.

Appears in the default page for the frameset Under Common Targets, choose the Page Default (None) option.

You can choose a default target page for hyperlinks in a frameset. To do so, choose File ➜ Properties and, in the Page Properties dialog box, click the Change Target Frame button (you'll find it to the right of the Default Target Frame text box). In the Target Frame dialog box, select a frame under Current Frames Page.

Appears in the same frame as the link Under Common Targets, choose the Same Frame option.

Appears where the frameset used to be   Choose the Whole Page option. With this option, the Web page replaces the frameset on-screen. People who want to return to the frames page must click the Back button in their browsers.

Appears in a new, second window   Choose the New Window option. With this option, another Web page is opened on-screen and surfers can see the linked page there.

Appears in the parent frame of a nested frameset   Choose Parent frame. With this option, the Web page replaces the parent frame in a nested frameset on the Web page.

To make the target setting you chose in Step 6 the default for all the links in the frame you are dealing with, click the Set As Page Default check box. This way, you set the target for all hyperlinks in the frame—the ones you've already created and the ones you will create. The Set As Page Default option is a timesaving technique. It saves you from having to visit the Target Frame dialog box if all the links in a frame go to the same Web page.

7. Click OK to return to the Insert (or Edit) Hyperlink dialog box.

8. Click OK again.

To make sure that the targets for your links work properly, you must save the Web page, preview your page in a Web browser, and click the link you want to verify. Testing all the links in a frames page to be sure that their target pages open correctly is important. Otherwise, you could end up with frames piling up inside one another. If you link to a frames page, which in turn links to another frames page, and none of these pages have their links targeted outside the window, things can get browser-crashingly cluttered.

Displaying Forms Results in a Frame

One great use for frames is to have a form in one frame, and have the form results displayed in another frame. This enhances the display of search engines and guest books, or any other forms in which users are interested in seeing the results of their input. (To get a head start on using forms, refer to Chapter 14.)

Getting form results to display in a particular frame is no more complex than setting a target for those results. (If you're unsure about the targeting process, refer to the section titled "Creating Target Settings.") Just follow these steps to set a target frame for your form results:

1. With your form page open in Page view (either in the frameset or on its own), right-click inside the form and, from the pop-up menu that appears, choose Form Properties. The Form Properties dialog box appears.

2. In the Form Properties dialog box, click the Target Frame button. The Target Frame dialog box appears.

3. Type the name of your target frame in the Target Settings text box. If you're working with this page while the rest of the frameset is in view, you can click the frame you want in the preview area of the dialog box to choose it.

4. Click OK to close the Target Frame dialog box and return to the Form Properties dialog box, where you'll see the name of your target frame displayed in the Target Frame text box (see "Creating Target Settings," earlier in this chapter, for more details).

5. Click OK to close the Form Properties dialog box.

As always, test, test, test those forms and targets.

Up Next

Now that you're done with this chapter, you can see that working with frames is a bit more complex than some of the other tasks you've undertaken. But frames aren't that difficult! Furthermore, they offer a wide range of options for your site, including navigational and layout structure that would be impossible to achieve in any other way.

It's time to begin to add some style to our virtual soup. Up next is Chapter 13, where you learn how FrontPage manages a special form of HTML to cleverly enhance the layout and design of your pages.

Getting in Style with Cascading Style Sheets

FRONTPAGE

Chapter 13

Cascading Style Sheets can help you control the way that Web pages appear in visitors' browsers. What's more, you can use them as design tools. And, for the sake of consistency, you can use the same Cascading Style Sheet over and over again and in so doing give the Web pages you create a familiar look and feel. This chapter starts by introducing Cascading Style Sheets and style-sheet terminology. Then it looks into when to use Cascading Style Sheets and how to create them in FrontPage. Topics include:

- Understanding style sheets and Cascading Style Sheets

- Using inline style declarations

- Using embedded style sheets

- Linking pages on your site to an external style sheet

What Are Cascading Style Sheets?

To gain more control over the way a document is designed, developers came up with *Cascading Style Sheets* (CSS). This book explains how to add color to a Web page, choose a font, and lay out pages using standard HTML elements, but HTML was not originally intended to do all that. It wasn't meant to be a design tool. No, HTML was meant to format the heading, plain text, and hyperlinks on Web pages.

Because the Web has become an extremely visual environment since its inception, HTML has had to accommodate the need on the part of audiences and developers for bigger, brighter, and faster technologies. Clever developers used HTML to try to meet their needs for more interesting visual design. A perfect example of HTML accommodating sophisticated design is tables, which originally were meant to present technical information. Tables have become the chief means of laying out Web pages.

But the design elements found in HTML are imperfect. So, in order to meet the limitations imposed by HTML, CSS was proposed and eventually adopted as a part of the HTML standard. However, there's a lot of instability on the Web. While CSS is a terrific concept, browser support is a concern. CSS is not backward-compatible. In other words, older browsers don't recognize it. Furthermore, browsers that do support CSS do so inconsistently, and that creates even more challenges for developers.

Netscape 6 and Internet Explorer 5 support CSS—and they do it very well.

Why use CSS? Well, CSS is truly elegant and extremely efficient when it comes to managing the design of a Web page. CSS separates the *content* of a page (stored in an HTML document) from its *presentation* (stored in a style sheet), and this has many advantages. You can change a page's appearance without changing its substance. Furthermore, by using what is known as a *linked* style sheet, you can modify a single style sheet file and in so doing change the appearance of an entire Web site.

FrontPage 2002 lets you apply style sheet rules to individual elements on a page with terrific ease. Themes and other design-oriented features allow you to include style information. A number of templates allow you to set up a page based on style sheet concepts.

Introducing Style Sheets

As you are already aware, FrontPage writes the necessary HTML for you in the background when you create Web pages. When you format a page, FrontPage inserts the HTML to execute your design. HTML, however, is not really a layout language, page-description language, or formatting language. HTML is a markup language that classifies the different parts of a document according to functional roles. HTML tags, for example, mark the title, headings, paragraphs, images, and the author's address in a Web page. But HTML does not and cannot dictate how different elements appear on a given computer screen. Using HTML, you indicate the role each part of a Web page will play. The Web browser on the user's end actually takes care of the visual formatting. The Web is cross-platform and there are many different browsers (as well as many different versions of the same browser). For that reason, you can't guarantee that a WYSIWYG (What-You-See-Is-What-You-Get) editor like FrontPage will produce the same results in every browser window.

HTML does include a few elements and attributes that Web site designers can use to make a document look attractive, including the font element and the various attributes of the horizontal rule element. However, these presentational features are not always recommended because they can cause problems in some browsers, including text-only browsers, text-to-speech browsers, and browsers used by the visually impaired. Instead, style sheets offer a chance for much better (and more complete) control over a document's appearance, in a way that doesn't interfere with the content of a document.

In theory, you can use any style sheet technology with HTML; in practice, the only style sheet technology that is well supported is CSS. This style sheet system was developed by the World Wide Web Consortium (W3C). The W3C is the organization now responsible for developing official standards for HTML and other Web technologies.

Mastering What's Online

To find out more about the World Wide Web Consortium, visit its home page at www.w3.org/. To learn more about the W3C's work on style sheets in general, visit the style sheets page at www.w3.org/Style/. Find a list of CSS specifications, references, tools, tutorials, and recent work at www.w3.org/Style/CSS/. And for an especially well done CSS tutorial (from the Web Design Group), stop by www.htmlhelp.com/reference/css/.

Style Sheet Terms and Concepts

The most important thing to understand about style sheets is the difference between style rules, style sheets, and styles:

- A *style rule* changes the appearance of HTML elements on your page in some way. For example, you can place a border around all level-one headings or make every bold item also be hot pink. To create a style rule, you must first create a style sheet.

- A *style sheet* is a list of style rules. A style sheet can be embedded into a page (known as an *embedded style sheet*) or be stored in a separate file (known as an *external* or *linked style sheet*). A style sheet can be linked to one or more pages on your site.

- A *style,* also known as an *inline style,* is a specific format that you apply to part of a Web page. For example, a particular paragraph can be assigned a border or wider margins by choosing an option on the Style menu. The Style menu is located on the Formatting toolbar. What's more, many FrontPage dialog boxes include a Style button. By clicking that button, you can open the Modify Style dialog box and alter a style to your liking.

FrontPage makes it easy to work with styles through the Style dialog box, and that's a fine way for FrontPage users to go. But if and when you want to employ the full power of style sheets, you'll have to learn how to create a style sheet of your own.

Currently, the most common type of style sheet technology is Cascading Style Sheets. The first official specification of CSS is called level one; we'll use the term CSS1 in our discussion to mean "Cascading Style Sheets, level one." CSS2 is the current style specification under scrutiny by the World Wide Web Consortium.

Mastering What's Online

To read about the latest work being done on style sheets by the World Wide Web Consortium, visit `www.w3c.org/style/`.

What Is a Style Sheet?

A *style sheet* is a collection of rules that affect the appearance of a document. Here's an example of a CSS1 style sheet with one rule.

```
H1 { text-align: center }
```

This rule centers every level-one heading element in an HTML document by default. Later in this chapter, "Embedding a Style Sheet in a Page" and "Structuring an External Style Sheet" explain how to create a style sheet like this one.

A CSS style sheet consists of properties, values, declarations, selectors, and rules:

Property   A browser behavior that can be affected by CSS. For example, font-family, background, border, and text-align are all examples of properties. The properties that can be changed are listed in the CSS specification; there are about 50 of them.

Value   Whatever choice you can set for a property. For example, the font-family property's values can be specific font names such as Arial, Times, and Courier, or a generic name such as serif or sans serif.

Declaration   A property and its value (for example, color: blue is a declaration). FrontPage usually creates declarations for you, but if you become an advanced style sheet user, you might try creating your declarations from scratch. To create a declaration, you start with a property name (be sure to specify it exactly, including any hyphens), followed by a colon, followed by the value for the property. For example, here are a couple of declarations:

```
text-indent: 5%
border: medium double
```

The first adds a 5-percent margin to the first line of a paragraph; the second adds a double border of medium thickness.

Selector   The name of the HTML element to which you want to apply a declaration. For example, if you want to change the behavior of every block quote element, you would use BLOCKQUOTE as your selector. You can use simple selectors (the name of a single HTML element), or more complex contextual selectors (several HTML elements). To use selectors properly, you have to know HTML tags pretty well (see Appendix E for help). Selectors can also contain special attributes known as classes, which are discussed in greater detail in the upcoming section "All about Class."

Rule   A selector plus a declaration. For example, P { margin-left: 20% } is a rule. The selector in this rule is the paragraph element (indicated by P), and the declaration is margin-left: 20%. The property being changed in this declaration is the margin-left property, which normally has a value of 0. In this rule, the left margin for every paragraph is being changed so that it takes up 20 percent of the window's default width.

Note the punctuation in rules. In a rule, the selector is followed by the opening curly brace ({), then the declaration, and then a closing curly brace (}). (Curly braces are sometimes called curly brackets or French braces.) If you create an external style sheet, you need to know this punctuation. If you create an embedded style sheet, FrontPage usually handles the punctuation for you.

You can group declarations and selectors together when creating rules. For example, the code H1, H2 { font-weight: normal } groups two different selectors together to create two rules. Similarly, H1 {background: black; color: white} groups two different declarations together to create two rules. Grouped rules are called *rulesets*.

When you make a ruleset—for example, when you create an external style sheet—be absolutely sure to use semicolons (;) to separate selectors with commas and multiple declarations. A single mistake such as leaving out a comma may cause the ruleset to have a completely different meaning or to just plain not work. FrontPage knows how to group declarations with semicolons, but it doesn't automatically group selectors properly.

By tradition, selectors are in uppercase and declarations are in lowercase. But this is only a tradition; CSS rules are not case-sensitive. When you create a style sheet, you have to type the selectors yourself. FrontPage lets you put selectors in uppercase or lowercase, but (as you'll see later) it uses lowercase for declarations created when you use the Style button.

Using CSS Units

CSS uses several different units of measurement. These units come in two categories: *absolute* units and *relative* units.

The common absolute units are:

- Inches, specified by "in" (for example, 0.5in means half an inch)
- Points, specified by "pt" (for example, 13pt means 13 points)

You can also use centimeters (cm), millimeters (mm), and picas (pc). Some of these are typographical terms: A pica is equal to 12 points, and 72 points is equal to an inch.

In electronic publishing, however, relative units are preferred because they scale better from one medium to another (and you don't have to make assumptions about a viewer's screen size or paper size). Here are the relative units:

- Pixels, specified by "px" (for example, 12px means 12 pixels)

- Ems, specified by "em" (where one em is equal to the width of the letter m in the font you are using)

- Ex-heights, specified by "ex" (where one ex is equal to the height of the lowercase letter x in the current font, so 2ex is twice the height of the letter x)

- Percentages, which are usually relative to the font size (so 200% usually means twice the current font size of the element)

Pixels might not seem to be a relative unit at first glance. But in actuality, pixels can vary tremendously. Take printers: A screen is often 72 pixels per inch, but a printer is typically 300, 600, or 1200 dots per inch. So browsers can scale pixel units appropriately when you print out a document, making pixel a relative term. More importantly, the pixel size measurements for fonts are slightly different on Macintosh platforms than they are on Windows platforms. Still, pixels are the most commonly used method of measuring type on the Web, and are the FrontPage default unit of measurement for style-based type. If you want to be as safe as possible, try to use percentages and ems.

When specifying colors, FrontPage uses the RGB (red, green, blue) color value system. For more details about color units and to see your options, check the CSS1 specification (`www.w3.org/pub/WWW/TR/REC-CSS1#color-units`).

All about Class

Sometimes you want style sheet rules to apply only to certain elements. To fill this need, you can use *class selectors*. A *class* is a name that you assign to one or more elements; you can create style sheet rules that apply only to members of that class.

To create a style sheet rule that selects by class, you simply use a selector name that's a little different. To create a class selector, just use the name you want for the class followed by a period.

You can create classes that apply only to particular HTML elements by combining the element's name with a class selector, or you can create generic classes that can apply to every HTML element. For example, this style sheet creates three classes (the example classes are named *warning*, *note*, and *big*, but you can use any descriptive word you want):

```
<style>
<!--
P { font-family: Verdana, sans-serif }
```

```
P.warning { border: thick double rgb(0,0,0) }
P.note { background-image: url('clouds.gif') }
.big { font-size: 150% }
-->
</style>
```

This style sheet has four rules:

- The first rule applies to every paragraph element (it changes the font face to Verdana or a generic sans-serif typeface if Verdana isn't available).

- The second rule applies only to those paragraph elements in the warning class and gives them a thick black border made of two lines.

- The third rule applies only to those paragraph elements in the note class and adds an image background (assuming the image `clouds.gif` has already been added to the Web page).

- The fourth rule makes the paragraph 50 percent larger than normal, and applies to any HTML element (paragraph, blockquote, table data cell, and so on), but only if that element is in the "big" class.

You apply Class quite often with FrontPage, as you'll see in upcoming examples.

All about Inheritance

Inheritance is a concept that describes how style sheet information is processed. A CSS rule applies a declaration to a particular HTML element. That declaration also applies to any elements nested inside that element. For example, suppose you made paragraphs green by inserting the following rule into a style sheet attached to your page:

```
P { color: green }
```

Consider an element nested inside another element, such as: <P>I am a <I>barrista</I></P>. The word *barrista* will appear both in italics and in green. This is an example of inheritance. The italics element here is said to "inherit" the green property from its *parent* element (in this case, the paragraph element).

Other style properties will also be inherited, such as the font and font size. Some style properties are not inherited from the parent element by the child element. (Check with the CSS specification or a quick reference to see if a property inherits; FrontPage does not always show inheritance properly on screen.)

The best example of inheritance is applying declarations to the body element. For example, the following style sheet sets the text color to white and the background to an image named `marble.gif` or black if the image isn't available:

```
BODY { color: white; background: url(marble.gif) black; }
```

With this style sheet, every element in a document, including every heading and paragraph, inherits the default text color.

Sometimes the value of a property is a percentage that refers to another property, as in this example:

```
P { font-size: 10pt; line-height: 150% }
```

In this example, the line height will work out to 15 points, because it is one-and-a-half times the paragraph's font size of 10 points. Elements nested inside a paragraph element will inherit the 15-point line height.

When more than one rule applies to the same element, it doesn't matter where that rule comes from. Here's how it works: The more direct and specific the source of the rule, the more weight it carries. If the rule comes from a style you chose from the Style menu on the Formatting toolbar, that's very direct. If the rule comes from an embedded or linked style sheet, that's direct (but not as direct as a style you choose from the Style menu). If the rule is applied only through inheritance, then it's indirect and other rules will outweigh it.

When to Use Style Sheets

Are style sheets really worth all of the potential problems and the hassle of learning and applying all that terminology? Well, there are three main advantages to using style sheets:

- You can create effects such as three-dimensional borders and paragraph indents that aren't possible with HTML tags. For example, Figure 13.1 shows a paragraph with a border style applied to it.

- Style sheets can actually speed up the development and downloading time of a Web site because they can be reused and applied to every page on the site. You can define a style once, and apply it all over the place.

- Style sheets are extremely unobtrusive. Browsers that don't support style sheets simply ignore their presence.

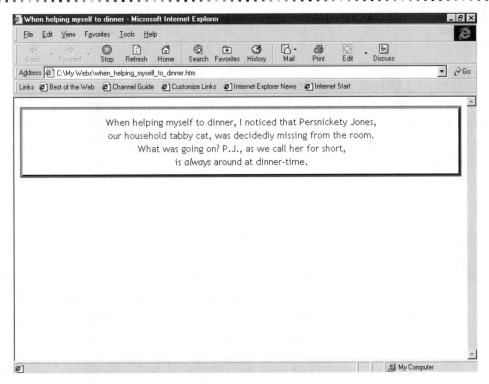

Figure 13.1 *This paragraph was formatted with a border style.*

And now for the disadvantages of using style sheets:

- Style sheets are a somewhat complicated technology to learn, and using them is by no means a requirement of good site design. If you're pressed for time and don't want to learn something new right now, put style sheets on the back burner.

- Older browsers sometimes can't handle style sheets. If a big part of your audience is using older browsers, they won't see your style sheet design at all. Instead, they'll see default fonts and alignment settings. It's not worth the effort to put a lot of time into something that most of your audience won't be aware of.

To learn about browser differences and how to create a page that works with all browsers, see Chapter 16.

Mastering What's Online

For an absolutely essential list of which style sheet properties are safe with which browsers (as well as which properties are dangerous), check out the WebReview Style Sheet Reference Guide, edited by Eric Meyer (www.style .webreview.com/style/). There are also some helpful articles and tutorials here. For some demonstrations of the problems that you may encounter with styles, hop over to Style Sheet Implementation Bugs (www.emf.net/ ~estephen/htmlner/stylebugs.html).

Style sheets promise important advantages to Web authors, particularly those working in corporate intranet environments, where control of software is predetermined. Another strength is that style sheets integrate with other technologies to create special effects. In fact, you may have heard of a grouping of such technologies referred to as Dynamic HTML, or DHTML. Style sheets play a large role in this group of applications, but the same limitations experienced with browsers interpreting current CSS code extend to DHTML, too. So for very broad distribution, style sheets are still a questionable choice.

Some browsers' implementations of style sheets are imperfect and the differences between browsers pose problems, but the management, control, design, special effects, and future importance all make style sheets well worth learning. With a good knowledge of style sheets, there really is an infinite number of effects you can add to a page without using a single graphic image.

Working with Style Sheets in FrontPage

Three types of style sheets are available for use in FrontPage Web pages. To manage styles using FrontPage, you can use a preexisting template, or add style by hand. Either way, the style is controlled based on these three essential style foundations:

- Controlling individual page elements: To control the appearance of an individual page element, you can use *inline styles*. As explained earlier, inline styles are CSS declarations that are attached to a part of a page, such as a heading or a paragraph or the body of the page. While FrontPage is more interested in allowing you to use embedded and linked styles, you can modify styles using the inline method by following some simple directions, as you'll soon see.

- Controlling every element on a page: To control the appearance of every element on a particular page, you can use *embedded style sheets*, which are stored in a special HTML tag at the beginning of a page, as "Embedding a Style Sheet in a Page" explains shortly. This is a terrific way of managing the styles on a single page, and FrontPage enthusiastically supports using styles in this fashion.

- Controlling elements throughout your Web site: To use a single file to control the appearance of your site, you use *external* (also known as *linked*) style sheets, which are style sheets stored in separate files. An external style sheet must be linked to some or all of the pages on your Web site, so that its effects are applied to the selected pages. External style sheets offer you the most bang for your buck in adding stylish effects to a Web site. An external style sheet lets you update your Web site by changing just one file. If you've ever gone through the time-consuming process of editing hundreds of pages to change their appearance, you'll appreciate being able to redesign an entire Web site by changing a single file. FrontPage offers a template to help set up linked style sheets. You can also always write them yourself, and add an appropriate link to all the pages you want to influence with a particular style sheet.

The following pages explain each of these methods.

Applying an Inline Style to a Single Page Element

You can apply an inline style to the following page elements:

- Bulleted lists
- Form fields
- Horizontal rules
- Images
- Java applets
- Numbered lists

- Tables
- Web pages

Follow these steps to apply an inline style to one element on a Web page:

1. In Page view, select the element you want to apply a style to.

2. Right-click the element and choose the relevant Properties option from the drop-down menu. Which Properties options you see depends on which element you are dealing with. For example, if you want to modify the style of a bulleted list, choose List Properties.

3. In the dialog box that appears, click the Style button. As shown in Figure 13.1, the Modify Style dialog box appears.

4. Click the Format button and, from the pop-up menu, choose an option to define the style. Choose the Font option, for example, and the Font dialog box appears so you can choose a font and font size for characters. Choose the Paragraph option and the Paragraph dialog box opens so you can choose from Alignment options or indent the page element in a different way.

5. Click OK to close the Properties dialog box.

If you want to see the way the inline HTML code looks, simply click the HTML Tab from the editing window.

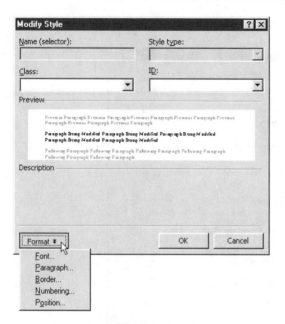

Figure 13.2 *Applying an inline style*

Embedding a Style Sheet in a Page

The styles in an embedded style sheet can be applied to many different elements on a Web page. The first step in creating an embedded style is to create the style itself or modify an existing style. With that done, you can apply the style very easily by choosing it from the Style drop-down menu.

To begin creating a style sheet rule, decide what HTML element you want to change. For example, you can change the behavior of paragraphs (P), level one headings (H1), indented quotes (BLOCKQUOTE), anchors (A), table cells (TD), the entire body of your page (BODY), or any other HTML element. For the purposes of embedded styles, the HTML element you are altering or creating is called the selector (earlier in this chapter, "What Is a Style Sheet?" described selectors.

Follow these steps to create or modify a style and make it a part of the embedded style sheet:

1. In Page view, display the page whose styles need modifying.

2. Choose Format ➜ Style. The Style dialog box appears (see Figure 13.3).

Figure 13.3 *Start in the Style dialog box to create or modify a style*

3. In the Styles list, choose the style, or selector, that you want to modify. If you want to modify a style you created earlier, open the List drop-down menu and choose User-Defined Styles.

4. Click the New button to create a new style, or the Modify button to modify a style that already exists. As shown in Figure 13.4, you see the New Style or Modify Style dialog box. These dialog boxes offers the same options—well, nearly the same options.

If you are creating a new style, open the Style type drop-down menu in the New Style dialog box and choose Paragraph or Character. Paragraph styles apply to all the text in a paragraph. Create Character styles to make it easier to apply complex character formats.

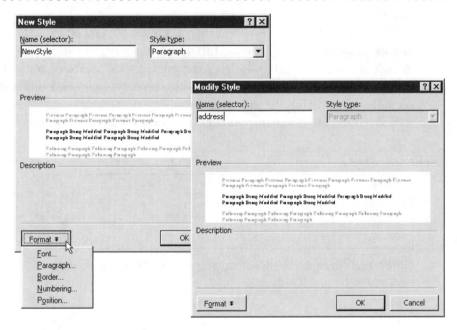

Figure 13.4 *Creating, or modifying, a style*

5. If you are creating a new style, enter a name for the style in the Name (Selector) text box.

6. Click the Format button and, from the pop-up menu, choose an option to define or modify the style. Choose the Border option, for example, to define a border or modify a border style in the Borders and Shading dialog box. If you want all H1 tags to show up in dark blue Arial text, choose Font and then choose options in the Font dialog box. The appropriate dialog box appears.

7. Make your modifications and click OK to return to the New Style or Modify Style dialog box (refer to Figure 13.4).

8. Click OK to return to the Style dialog box (refer to Figure 13.3).

9. Click OK.

Embedded style sheets always start with the <STYLE> start tag and finish with a </STYLE> end tag. FrontPage automatically places these two tags for you, and puts them properly into your document when you're finished with the Style or Modify Style dialog box.

Be aware that older browsers might get confused by embedded style sheets and display the rules on screen. To prevent this from happening, FrontPage properly "comments out" the style sheet by using a comment tag. CSS1-enabled browsers will still obey the style sheet, but other browsers will safely ignore the content they don't understand. To comment out the style sheet, FrontPage puts the `<!--` characters before the style sheet, and the `-->` characters after the style sheet, as you can see in Figure 13.5.

```
<style>
<!--
h1          { font-family: Trebuchet MS; font-size: 18 pt; color: #800000 }
p           { text-align: Left; text-indent: 10; margin: 15 }
-->
</style>
```

Figure 13.5 *To embed a style sheet, you must place your style sheet rules within comment tags.*

Applying Styles throughout a Web Site

In the previous section, you learned how to create an embedded style sheet. This style sheet is attached to a particular page, and its style rules affect every element on that page. But suppose you have a very large Web site and you want to control it with style sheets. You can avoid embedding style information into every single page in the site by simply creating one style sheet and linking to it to the site. To connect a style sheet to your FrontPage Web site, link to an external style sheet using a special `<LINK>` tag.

You can create a style sheet on your own, or you can use a FrontPage 2002 template. There are several templates to choose from, and you can modify any of them, too!

Structuring an External Style Sheet

An external style sheet is simply a text file with your rules and rulesets and no HTML elements at all. Aside from style sheet rules, the only other element that can go in an external style sheet file is comments.

In particular, don't include <HTML> and <HEAD> tags, or any other HTML tags like <STYLE>. In the early days of CSS, some unclear examples of external style sheets encouraged this practice, but style sheets have become much more sophisticated since that time.

Follow these steps to create your own style sheet by hand:

1. Choose File ➜ New ➜ Page or Web. The New Page or Web task pane opens.

2. Under New, click the Blank Page link.

3. You can use a normal page to create your style sheet by typing in your rules or rulesets, one on each line. Alternately, you can paste in a style sheet if you have one somewhere.

Instead of typing your style sheet from scratch, you can create an embedded style sheet using the technique described previously in "Embedding a Style Sheet." Then view the HTML tab, select and cut (Ctrl+X) the style sheet, and paste (Ctrl+V) it into a new page. Don't forget to delete the <STYLE> and </STYLE> tags along with the <!-- and --> comment characters.

4. Save the file with a .css extension. From the menu bar, select File ➜ Save As. Give the style sheet a name such as my_style.css.

If you wish, you can include comments in your style sheet. Comments are simply reminders or notes to yourself or your team members that don't affect the style sheet. CSS has a format for comments that's different from HTML. CSS comments begin with <!-- and end with -->/. For example:

```
<!-- This is a CSS1 comment -->
```

It's a good idea to begin your style sheet with a comment that explains its purpose. Also, any rules that might be complex should be explained with a comment. Here's an example of an external style sheet that uses comments:

```
<!-- CSS1 Style Sheet */
<!-- The ourdefaultfonts.css style sheet contains font settings -->
BODY { background: black; color: white; margin-left: 10%;
       margin-left: 10% }
H1 { text-align: center }
TD { color: white; background: black }
<!-- Because Navigator 4 doesn't inherit properties to tables, you
     must separately define the body rule for a table cell -->
.warning { font-size: larger; font-weight: bolder; text-align:
```

```
     center; color: red; background : yellow; border: thick groove
     gray; }
HR { text-align: center; margin-left: 25%; width: 50%;
     margin-right: 25%; }
```

Most of these rules should be fairly self-explanatory if you love HTML or computer languages. If these rules don't make any sense to you, you probably shouldn't be creating style sheets from scratch on your own. Instead, use one of the templates (described in the following section) or visit one of the recommended Web sites in this chapter that provide style sheet information and resources.

You have a fair amount of flexibility in how you arrange your style sheet rules; the order doesn't really matter much, and you can include extra spaces or returns if you like (whatever makes it easier for you to understand).

Using a Style Template

FrontPage 2002 offers several style sheet templates. Follow these steps to use one of them as an external style sheet:

1. Choose File ➔ New ➔ Page or Web. The New Page or Web task pane appears.

2. Under New from Template, click the Page Templates link. You see the Page Templates dialog box.

3. Select the Style Sheets tab. You see a number of style sheet templates.

4. Choose the template you want and click OK.

After FrontPage opens the style sheet, you see rules and/or rulesets on the page. Make any modifications to the style sheet that you want. Save the page with a name appropriate to your site. Be sure to save it within your Web site or an appropriate folder, along with the pages for your site.

Now that you have an external style sheet, the next step is to link to the sheet from your pages. Better read on.

Adding the External Style Sheet to Your FrontPage Web Site

Now that your CSS file is part of your FrontPage Web site, you can link it into each file quickly and easily by following these steps:

1. Open the page or Web site that you want to apply the style sheet to.

2. Choose Format ➜ Style Sheet Links. The Link Style Sheet dialog box opens (see Figure 13.6).

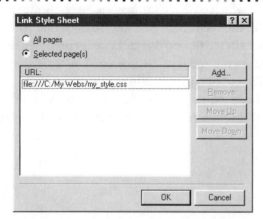

Figure 13.6 *The Link Style Sheet dialog box allows you to link all, a handful, or only one of your pages to a single style sheet.*

3. Select the All Pages or Selected Page(s) option button:

   All Pages Choose this option to apply the style sheet to all the pages in your Web site.

   Selected Page(s) Choose this option if you want only certain pages to be affected by the style sheet. After you choose Selected Page(s), click the Add button. You see the Select Style Sheet dialog box. Each page you select in the dialog box will appear in the Link Style Sheet dialog box.

4. Click OK. FrontPage automatically links the style sheet to the pages you chose.

At this point, you'll want to review your Web site or Web page in a variety of browsers. Because style sheets are still quite bug-ridden, this review will help you to determine how different browsers are managing the style.

Up Next

If style sheets seem confusing and unstable, that's because they are! Why it's taking so long for browsers to fully embrace them is a mystery. Style sheets are a truly elegant and necessary part of Web design—which is one of the reasons we encourage you to learn them, even if you choose to not use them. However, we also hope that you won't get frustrated by the inconsistencies in the technology and give up on style sheets altogether! They are powerful and useful, and if you're interested in professional design for Internet or intranet sites, you'll find opportunities to use them.

In the next chapter, you'll take a turn away from the appearance of a document and concentrate on how you can make your pages more interactive by adding forms and form controls.

Making Interactive Pages with Forms

FRONTPAGE

Chapter 14

Forms present one of the best ways to interact with visitors to your Web site. If you've ever used a search engine, filled out an online survey, ordered products over the Internet, registered to be a member of a site, or entered an online contest, you have filled out an online form.

Forms are designed to collect information and let users interact with a Web site. More important, perhaps, they let you find out who the people who visit your Web site are. Forms are the conduits for online catalogs, search pages, and anything else that requires someone's input. In this chapter, you'll discover how to construct an online form. This chapter explains each element of a form and demonstrates how to collect data from forms. Topics include:

- What forms do and how to create them with the Form Page Wizard

- Editing forms

- Creating text boxes for input

- Adding check boxes, option buttons, and drop-down menus

- Using hidden fields

- Working with Submit and Reset buttons

- Setting up a forms handler

- Creating a confirmation page

What Is a Form?

In the three-dimensional world, a form is a piece of paper with blank lines on which people enter information. The blank lines are labeled in such a way that everyone enters information in the same manner. Forms standardize and simplify the collection of essential data.

Similar to paper forms, forms on the Web standardize and simplify the way in which information is gathered. What's more, an online form can be a simple and fun way to make a Web site interactive. A form can make a visit to a Web site more interesting or helpful.

Suppose, for example, a Webmaster wants to know the favorite color of the people who visit her Web site. She could post a note that reads, "Hey, if you have a favorite color, drop me an e-mail at the address below." She might get a few responses. Probably the responders would pontificate, for example, about the advantages of blue over orange. The Webmaster could also create a survey form in which users click an option button to identify their favorite color, after which the answer is sent to the Webmaster, where a program counts the responses and auto-magically sorts the answers into percentages (6 percent burnt sienna, 40 percent cerulean, and 54 percent puce). Which method of gathering data is more scientific? Which is less trouble? The answer both times is the online form.

Figure 14.1 shows an interactive online form. The form includes every single kind of box and button there is. Most forms are simpler than this one, but no matter—this is meant to show all the different fields you can place on a form: text boxes, check boxes, option buttons, and drop-down lists. Form elements that require input are called *fields*.

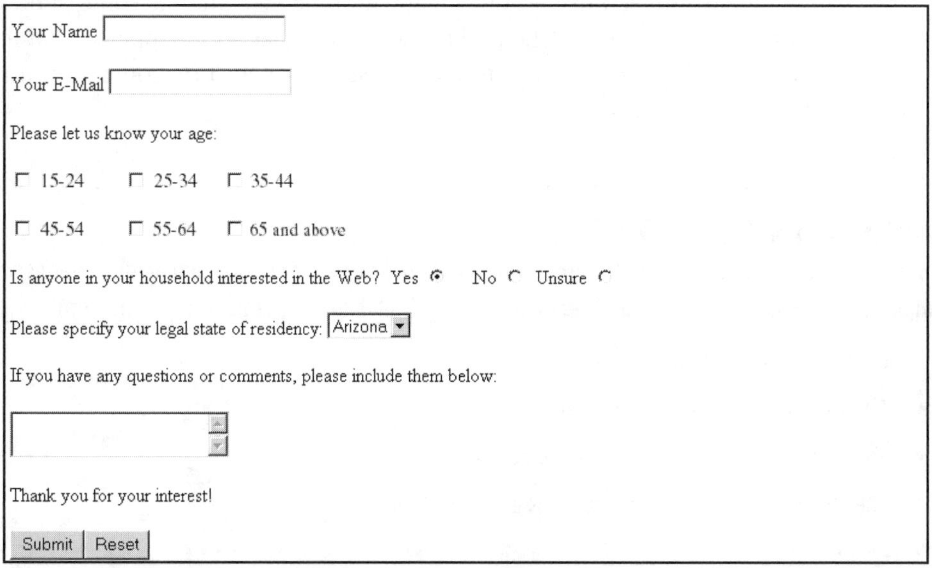

Figure 14.1 *This form has all the fields covered.*

What You Can Do with Forms

Forms can be more than just text boxes and buttons because, except for another form, you can place any Web page element you like inside a form. For example, you can put labels on the form fields and turn the labels into hyperlinks. This way, visitors can click the links to go elsewhere and learn about the choices on the form. Or you can use images or ruled lines in a form to make it user-friendly.

Use forms to gather just about any kind of input you want. For example, you can

- Find out who the visitors to your Web site are

- Ask visitors to fill out a long survey and gather even more information about them

- Supply a feedback form or guestbook to glean visitors' opinions

- Design a Web form as an interface to your company database

- Implement a search tool for searching your site (remember: You can't use a search engine without a box to type search terms into)

- Offer online registration for an event, conference, or contest

- Let the user choose variables (such as color or font) to personalize the site's look

- Create a username and password system to restrict access to your site

You're limited only by your imagination here—although some of these tricks involve scripts that work behind the scenes to make stuff happen. In some cases, programming is required to create a form. (See Chapter 21 for some scripting options that FrontPage supports.)

Mastering What's Online

Many Web sites offer forms to help you retrieve information. Search engines and online dictionaries are classic examples of sites where forms appear. Check out these Web sites to see examples of online forms:

- BigBook (www.bigbook.com)

- Amazon.com (www.amazon.com)

- The United States Post Office (www.usps.gov)

- The MegaConverter (www.megaConverter.com)

What Forms Do

Forms gather *input* from others—input being whatever others type or select in the form itself. Think of a Web form as a dialog box in a software program. When you open a dialog box, you make choices. You click buttons, check check boxes, type text in text boxes, and select options from drop-down lists. All your clicking and typing sends information to the software that enables it to obey your commands. The program either acts on your selections immediately or stores the input for use later on.

The same basic things happen when someone fills out an online form. Consider what happens when someone orders something online or registers as a "member" of a site. After the visitor clicks the Send or Submit button (which is tantamount to clicking OK in a dialog box), the information is whisked away. You see a change in the page you're viewing or the information is sent to a Web server to be used later.

When input is sent off, it is translated into *name-value pairs*. Don't worry—it's not a difficult concept. Suppose, for example, that the *name* of the field is Phone_Number and the *value* that the user enters in the field is 301-555-6789. Thus, the name-value pair is:

```
Phone_Number:301-555-6789
```

After users fill out a form, they usually click a button that sends the input to a *form validator*. This validator (a script, not a person) skims the information to make sure it fits the format specified for the fields on the form. If something isn't quite right, the validator tells the user to adjust his or her input. The user, for example, may have to fill out a text box that was left blank or include an area code in a phone number. When everything's hunky-dory, the data gets relayed to a *form handler*, a little script that can do one of several things with the data:

- Store the input in a text file for later retrieval

- E-mail the input to the Webmaster

- Add the information from the forms to a database

- Post the data directly to a Web page on the site

While the data is being tucked safely away or sent on, most good little form handlers also post a *confirmation page* that tells the user that the input was received and appreciated. The confirmation page also gives the user a link to follow—back to the home page, to the page that led to the survey, or to some other destination. If the form input was posted to another page, the confirmation page generally provides a link to that location.

You've no doubt seen plenty of forms that don't include confirmation pages. You click the Submit button and all is quiet—too quiet. Did anything happen? Did my data go through? Should I send it again? Most Webmasters with sites like these find themselves with a hefty stack of duplicate responses from people who clicked the button again and again and did not receive their confirmation. Later in this chapter, "Offering Confirmation" explains how to set up a confirmation page.

This chapter describes how to create different types of forms, add different kinds of fields to forms, and choose an event handler to process forms. If you're using a Web server with FrontPage Server Extensions (see Appendix B), you can use the built-in handler that comes with FrontPage. If not, contact your Internet service provider to find out how to use existing form scripts or install scripts for handling forms.

Using the Form Page Wizard to Construct a Form

The easy way to get started with forms is to use the Form Page Wizard. Using the wizard, you can create a new Web page and tell FrontPage to put as many fields as you need in it. After you create the page, you can edit it and enter content. You can, for example, cut and paste the form from the wizard page to an existing Web page, redesign the form altogether, or publish it.

Instead of starting with the Form Page Wizard, you can get a head start on a form page by using a FrontPage template. The Feedback Form and Guest Book templates are both accessible from the Page Templates dialog box. Choose File ➔ New ➔ Page Or Web, click the Page Templates hyperlink in the New Page Or Web task pane, and the Page Template dialog box appears. Select either Feedback Form or Guest Book and click OK.

Starting the wizard is quite easy. Of course, you may find yourself scratching your head trying to figure out what some of the options mean, but don't worry—we'll dutifully explain them all as we go along. Follow these steps to use the Form Page Wizard to create a new page with different forms for gathering data:

1. Choose File ➔ New ➔ Page Or Web. The New Page Or Web task pane appears.

2. Click the Page Templates hyperlink. You see the Page Templates dialog box.

3. On the General tab, select the Form Page Wizard, then click OK. The Form Page Wizard appears.

4. Read the first panel (it describes forms) and click the Next button to proceed to the next panel.

5. To start adding forms to the Web page, click the Add button. The Form Page Wizard displays a list of options for form input (see Figure 14.2).

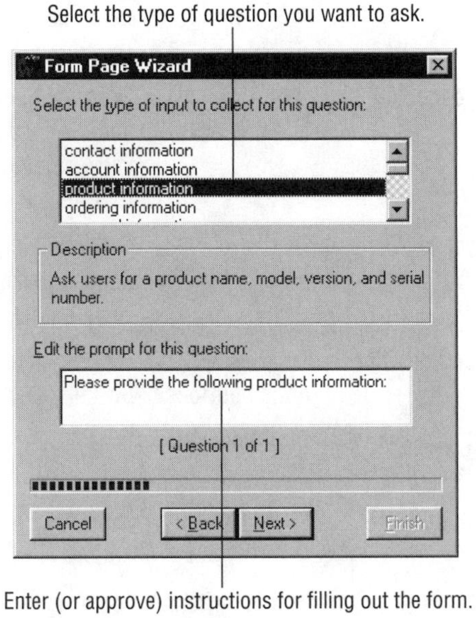

Select the type of question you want to ask.

Enter (or approve) instructions for filling out the form.

Figure 14.2 *You can choose from any number of form field options.*

6. Choose an input type in the Select The Type Of Input To Collect For This Question box. Table 14.1 describes the different input types. Your choice determines what type of input form you get.

Table 14.1 Input Field Types in the Form Page Wizard

INPUT TYPE	DEFAULT PROMPT	INPUT METHOD	DESCRIPTION/PURPOSE
Contact Information	Please provide the following contact information	Text boxes	For soliciting someone's name, job title, telephone number, fax number, and e-mail address.
Account Information	Please provide your account information	Text boxes	For confirming someone's identity. The field asks for a name, password, and password confirmation.
Product Information	Please provide your account information	Drop-down list and text boxes	For gathering information about a product—the name, version number, operating system, and serial number.
Ordering Information	Please provide your account information	Text boxes	For describing a purchased item as well as an address for shipping.
Personal Information	Please identify and describe yourself	Text boxes, option buttons	For obtaining a visitor's name, birthday, and sex.
One of several options	Choose one of the following options	Drop-down list	For selecting a single option.
Any of several options	Select any of the following options that apply	Check boxes	For choosing more than one option.
Boolean	Would you like?	Option buttons	For answering a Yes/No question.
Date	Enter the date of	Text boxes	For entering a date in a standard date format so it can be processed.
Time	Enter the time of	Text boxes	For entering a time in a standard time format so it can be processed.
Range	How would you rate your opinion of?	Option buttons	For rating something with a number.
Number	How much or many?	Text box	For entering a number.

Table 14.1 continued Input Field Types in the Form Page Wizard

INPUT TYPE	DEFAULT PROMPT	INPUT METHOD	DESCRIPTION/PURPOSE
String	Enter your…in the space provided below.	Text box	For soliciting someone's name, job title, telephone number, fax number, and e-mail address. For entering a text string so that it can be processed.
Paragraph	What do you think of?	Scroll box	For entering a long answer to a survey question.

You can read the descriptions in the Form Page Wizard dialog box to get a better idea of the different input types.

7. Modify the Edit The Prompt For This Question text if you think it needs editing. You can enter your own question or edit the text that is already there.

8. Click the Next button to go to the next panel. Figure 14.3 shows the panel for the Contact Information input type.

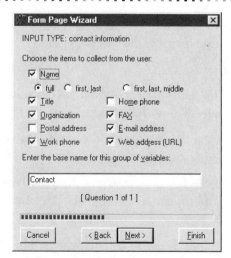

Figure 14.3 Describe the form in this dialog box.

9. Choose options and fill in the text boxes. Which options you see depends on which input type you choose.

Don't concern yourself with making all the right choices in the Form Page Wizard dialog box. As "Editing a Form" explains later in this chapter, you can always go back and change a form.

10. In the Enter The Base Name For This Group Of Variables text box, enter a name for the name-value pair (earlier in this chapter, "What Forms Do" explains name-value pairs). This information is used to transfer the online form data by e-mail or to a database.

11. Click the Next button to return to the dialog box for choosing more forms (refer to Figure 14.2).

12. Repeat steps 5 through 11 to add other forms to your page, if you like.

13. Finalize the forms you will enter on the Web page:

    Delete a form Click the form and then click the Remove button.

    Edit a form Click the form and then click the Modify button. A Form Page Wizard dialog box gives you the opportunity to edit the form.

    Change the order in which the forms appear Click a form and then click the Move Up or Move Down button to change its position on the page.

    Remove all forms Click the Clear List button.

14. Click the Next button when you've finished adding questions and fields to your form. The Presentation Options panel of the wizard appears (see Figure 14.4).

15. Choose Presentation options:

    Presenting the list Click the appropriate button to lay out your table in normal paragraphs, as a numbered list, as a bulleted list, or as a definition list.

    Table of contents If you want the wizard to add a clickable table of contents to the top of your form page, click the Yes option button.

    Aligning form fields in tables If you want to give the wizard the option of using tables to align your form content, click the check box labeled Use Tables To Align Form Fields.

16. Click Next to move to the Output Options panel of the wizard (see Figure 14.5). These options determine how to process the data collected by the form.

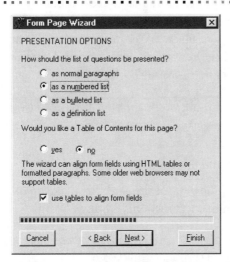

Figure 14.4 *Use these presentation options to format the questions on your form.*

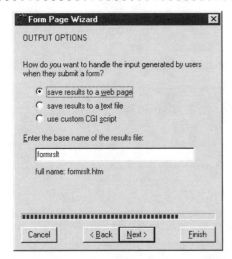

Figure 14.5 *Use this dialog box to declare how you want to process form data.*

17. Choose options for processing the data that the form collects. We discuss these options later in this chapter in "Setting Up a Form Handler." For now, if you know you'll save the survey results as a Web page or a text file, or send results to a custom CGI script, click the appropriate button and type a name for your file in the text box labeled Enter A Name For Your File.

If you choose a custom CGI script to handle your form, the text box is grayed out. Refer to "Setting Up a Form Handler," later in this chapter, for more information.

18. Click the Finish button—and not a moment too soon.

Notice the dashed line around the parts of the page that make up the form itself. You'll learn all about those lines in the next section, "Editing Forms."

Many of the forms generated by the Form Page Wizard include tables for formatting purposes. You can learn more about editing tables in Chapter 11.

This illustration shows a page created with the Form Page Wizard, before it's been edited. You can edit the text of a form field or the questions that introduce forms at any time. Edit the text as you would any other text. Chapter 4 offers instructions for basic text editing and Chapter 6 explains how to change fonts.

Please provide the following contact information:

Name	
Title	
Organization	
Work Phone	
FAX	
E-mail	
URL	

Submit and Reset buttons are added to form pages automatically. Refer to "Adding Submit and Reset Buttons," later in this chapter, to find out how to make these buttons work.

You can see what your form will look like in the Web environment by previewing it in your browser (click the Preview button on the Standard toolbar or choose File ➜ Preview In Browser). Your form won't do anything yet, because you haven't attached it to a form handler, but we'll get to that in the section called "Setting Up a Form Handler," later in this chapter.

Editing a Form

FrontPage makes it easy to edit and create forms on Web pages without resorting to the Form Page Wizard. And after you have created forms, you can modify them or introduce new fields. FrontPage makes it simple to use all types of input fields on Web pages. You use the Forms toolbar or Insert ➜ Form command to create the boxes and buttons. Each form element offers its own Properties dialog box so you can tinker with forms to your heart's content.

The text on your page, whether in or outside a form, can be edited and formatted just like any other text.

Displaying the Form Toolbar

In the following pages, we explain how to use the Form toolbar to create and edit forms. But, you may well ask, where is the Form toolbar? You can't display it in the conventional ways by right-clicking a toolbar and choosing Form or choosing View ➜ Toolbars ➜ Form.

To display the Form toolbar, choose Insert ➜ Form. Then, with the Form submenu on display, gently move the mouse pointer over the top of the menu. When you see the four-headed arrow and the words "Drag to make this menu float," do just that. Click and drag the Form submenu onto the screen. By magic, it turns into a toolbar.

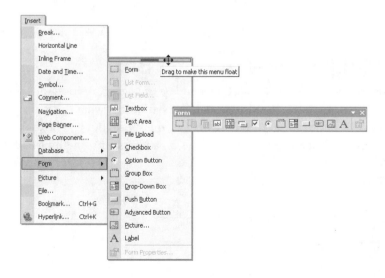

Copying, Cutting, and Pasting Forms and Form Fields

In Page view, you can cut (or copy) and paste just about any HTML element from page to page—and that includes forms. Forms are marked in Page view by dotted lines, as shown in Figure 14.6. Select all or part of a form the same way that you select text—by clicking and dragging. When the part of the form you want to copy is highlighted, press Ctrl+C to copy (or Ctrl+X to cut) the form, code and all, to the Clipboard. Then click where you want that stuff to go, whether it's in the same document or another document, and press Ctrl+V to paste the form components. It's that easy!

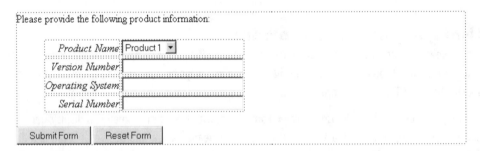

Figure 14.6 *Here you can see the form—it's the part inside the dotted lines.*

Creating a One-Line Text Box

If forms are like high school tests, then *one-line text boxes* are good for short-answer questions (for example: "H_2O is the chemical symbol for what substance?"). Other text boxes work better for multiple choice or essay questions, but text boxes like the following are perfect when all you want is a name, an address, or something else that requires just a few words.

Making a Text Box

Creating and editing a one-line text box is a two-part process. The procedure for creating and editing all fields is similar: First you use the Forms submenu or Forms toolbar to place the element on the page, and then you right-click the element to pop up the dialog box for editing it.

Follow these steps to create a text box in a form:

1. In Page view, click where you want the text box to appear.

2. Choose Insert ➜ Form ➜ Textbox or click the Textbox button on the Form toolbar. A text box appears to the left of the insertion point (the Submit and Reset buttons appear, too). Notice that the area surrounding the text box is enclosed by a dotted line. The line tells you that a form is in the making.

3. Type some text near your box (on either side, or above it, or below it) to indicate its purpose—whether it's for a name, an e-mail address, or what have you.

The text box behaves just like any other element on the page. Click the insertion point before it and start typing, and the text box moves to the right to make way for the text. If you want people to use a particular format for the info in the text box, you can give them an example with your text. Instead of just typing **Name**, you could type **Name (e.g., Franklin D. Roosevelt)** or **Name (e.g., Roosevelt, Franklin)**.

Click your new text box, and little black squares called handles *appear on the edges. You can click and drag a handle to change the width and height of the text box.*

Editing a Text Box

Follow these steps to edit a text box and make it just so:

1. Right-click the text box and choose Form Field Properties (because the text box is, after all, a form field) on the shortcut menu or select the text box and choose Format ➜ Properties (or press Alt+Enter). The Text Box Properties dialog box appears (see Figure 14.7).

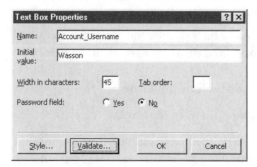

Figure 14.7 *The Text Box Properties dialog box is for editing text boxes.*

2. In the Name text box, enter a name for the text box. Field names can contain only letters and numbers; although you can use underscores, you cannot use spaces. Choosing a name for your form fields is generally helpful when you're sorting the data later on.

3. Enter a default value or name in the Initial Value text box if you want something to appear in the text box when it's loaded onto the page. By entering the most likely value for someone to enter, you spare visitors from having to enter a value. Just make sure that visitors know to enter a value in the text box. Some might see the default text and assume they don't have to enter anything.

4. In the Width In Characters text box, enter the maximum number of characters that people who fill out the text box will be able to enter. The default is 20 characters, which isn't very long.

5. Enter a number in the Tab Order text box in the unlikely event that you want to change the order in which visitors can press the Tab key and move from field to field in the form. Normally, pressing Tab takes you from the first field through to the last in a form, but if you want to establish a different order, enter a number in the Tab Order text box.

For what it's worth, you can enter −1 in the Tab Order to prevent anyone from reaching a text box by pressing the Tab key.

6. Click the Yes option button if you intend to use the field to collect password data. If you click Yes, characters typed in the text box will appear as asterisks.

7. Click OK to close the Text Box Properties dialog box.

Or, if you want to set limits to what your users can type in the text box, hold tight and move on to the next section.

Making Rules for Text Box Validation

Now that you have a text box that does what you want it to, you can make it practically autonomous and freethinking. Okay, maybe not quite—but you make it weed out a lot of blank or improperly filled-in fields by setting validation parameters. If people type unacceptable data into your text box and submit it, a validation script will glance at the data and tell users that something's wrong with what they typed.

Follow these steps to create a validation rule for a text box on a form:

1. If necessary, open the Text Properties dialog box (refer to Figure 14.7) by right-clicking the text box and choosing Form Field Properties on the shortcut menu.

2. Click Validate button to open the Text Box Validation dialog box (see Figure 14.8).

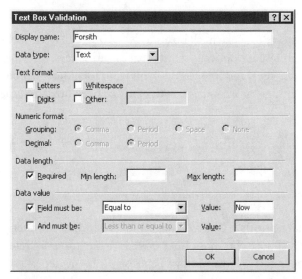

Figure 14.8 *You can limit acceptable input to either numbers or letters by using the Text Box Validation dialog box.*

3. Choose an option from the Data Type drop-down menu:

No Constraints The text box accepts any kind of characters (this is the default option).

Text The text box accepts certain kinds of characters.

Integer The text box only accepts whole numbers.

Number The text box only accepts whole numbers and decimals.

4. If you chose Text, Integer, or Number, type a display name in the Display Name text box. The name you enter will appear in a warning message if someone fills out the form incorrectly. For example, if you want to require an e-mail address, type **E-mail address** in the Display Name text box. The following message will then appear in the warning message: "Please enter a value of the 'E-mail address' field."

5. Choose more options in the Text Validation dialog box (the options are described shortly).

6. Click OK.

Which options are available in the Text Box Validation dialog box depends on which option you choose in the Data Type drop-down menu. Here is a rundown of the different options in the dialog box:

Text Format options Click check boxes to tell FrontPage what sort of characters to accept. The Whitespace option permits spaces, tab spaces, carriage returns (pressing the Enter key), and line feeds. If you want to allow other characters, such as the @ sign, commas, or periods, click the Other check box and type the characters in the box.

Numeric Format options Choose options for separating numbers typed in the text box. You can choose commas or periods for delineating discrete numbers and for separating decimals—the option you choose probably depends on what the data will be used for. For example, if the data will be entered in a database, you might choose the Comma option to create comma-delimited lists.

Required field   If the person filling out the form is required to fill out a field for the form data to be accepted, click the Required check box. (If you're going to require that a field be filled in order to accept a form, make that fact explicit on the page.)

Data Length options   By filling in the Min Length and Max Length text boxes, you can require people to enter a certain number of characters in the text box. Suppose, for example, you're creating a hangman game and the correct answer is 6 characters long. You can make both the minimum and maximum number of characters 6. You might want to set minimums for things such as names (who has a name one character long?) or maximums for questions regarding zip codes.

Data Value options   If you want to set parameters for the data that can or cannot be entered in a field, you can use the Data Value area of the dialog box. Check the Field Must Be check box, choose an option from the drop-down menu, and enter a value in the Value box to describe the parameter. If the value is to fall between two extremes, check the And Must Be check box, choose another option from the drop-down menu, and enter the value of the other extreme.

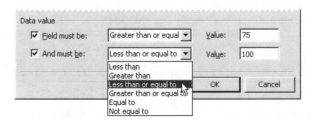

You can use text box validation to run contests and games, to weed out practical jokers, and to make sure that people don't forget to type in their e-mail addresses, among other things.

Preventing Form Failures

You already know that to see how your pages will look on the Internet—with or without forms—you need to preview them in a Web browser. But form pages need to be tested, tested again, and then tested again to make sure they work. Before you launch your Web site, make sure you install the pages on your Web site. Checking to make sure they look right is important, but checking to make sure that they *act* the way they're supposed to is imperative, particularly if you included validation settings or if the form is supposed to do something snazzy. If the form is supposed to store the data sent to it, make sure it does that. If the form is supposed to display a validation screen or send the user somewhere specific, make sure it does that, too. Test the forms yourself, have co-workers test them, and then test them again.

Creating a Scrolling Text Box

One-line text boxes are for short answers to questions, but *scrolling text boxes* are for essay questions. If the purpose of your form is to solicit e-mail messages, gather comments, or encourage people to post to a guestbook, a scrolling text box is what you need. It does what it says—it holds enough text to need its own scroll bars:

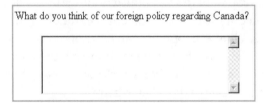

Follow these steps to create a scrolling text box:

1. Click where you want your scrolling text box to go.

2. Choose Insert ➔ Form ➔ Text Area or click the Text Area button on the Form toolbar. A scrolling text box appears on your page.

3. Either right-click the scrolling text box and choose Form Field Properties on the shortcut menu or click the scrolling text box and choose Format Properties

(or press Alt+Enter). The TextArea Box Properties dialog box appears (see Figure 14.9).

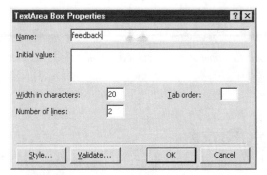

Figure 14.9 *The TextArea Box Properties dialog box lets you adjust the size of scrolling text boxes.*

4. In the Name text box, enter a name for the scrolling text box. Field names can contain only letters and numbers; although you can use underscores, you cannot use spaces. Choosing a name for form fields is generally helpful when you're sorting the data later on.

5. If you want your scrolling text box to appear on your Web page with some text already in it, type this text in the Initial Value text box. For example, you might want to have your text box start out, "I think your page is great because…" if you're asking for feedback.

6. To adjust the size of the scrolling text box, enter a measurement in the Width In Characters and Number Of Lines text boxes.

You can also adjust the size of a scrolling text box by selecting it and dragging one of the black selection handles that appear.

7. Enter a number in the Tab Order text box in the unlikely event that you want to change the order in which visitors can press the Tab key and move from field to field in the form. Normally, pressing Tab takes you from the first field through to the last in a form, but if you want to establish a different order, enter a number in the Tab Order text box.

8. Click OK to close the TextArea Box Properties dialog box. You'll see your new scrolling, scrolling, rocking and rolling text box.

Be sure to type some introductory text for your scrolling text box, such as "Please type your comments here."

If you want to set validation restrictions for your text box, you can click the Validate button in the TextArea Box Properties dialog box. That opens the Text Box Validation dialog box (refer to Figure 14.7) See "Making Rules for Text Box Validation" earlier in this chapter to find out how the dialog box works.

Creating Check Boxes

Check boxes are for questions in which more than one answer can be checked off. By contrast, only one in a set of option buttons (also known as radio buttons) can be selected. Use check boxes on a form when you want to give the responder the opportunity to check off more than one answer.

Dropping check boxes on your page is easier than dropping a stack of plates. Follow these steps to create a check box:

1. In Page view, click where you want the check box to appear.

2. Choose Insert ➜ Form ➜ Checkbox, or click the Checkbox button on the Form toolbar. A check box appears.

3. Either right-click the check box and choose Form Field Properties or click it and choose Properties (or press Alt+Enter). The Check Box Properties dialog box appears (see Figure 14.10).

4. In this dialog box's Name field, type a name for your check box. Choosing a memorable name for your check box is especially important if you're going to have a bunch of them.

5. In the Value text box, enter a value to describe what Checked and Not Checked means. For example, if you want a check mark in the box to indicate "True," type **True**. If you want a checked box to mean, "Yes, please send my name to other companies," type something like **Sell**.

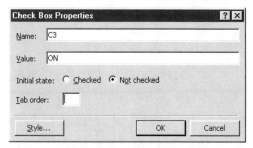

Figure 14.10 *Use the Check Box Properties dialog box to keep track of your check boxes.*

When you use a form with check boxes to store data in a text file, only data from the check box that is checked is recorded, and that poses a problem when it comes time to read the data. Make sure, therefore, that the names and values you choose are meaningful. A line that says Stamp Collecting=Hobby *would be much more decipherable than one that said* SC=ON.

6. Choose an Initial State option to tell FrontPage whether to check the box by default. If you want it to be checked automatically ("Yes, your page is a work of genius, please tell me more"), click the Checked option button. If you want the check box to be blank initially ("Please check this box if you've declared bankruptcy in the last 10 years"), click the Not Checked option button.

7. Enter a number in the Tab Order text box in the unlikely event that you want to change the order in which visitors can press the Tab key and move from field to field in the form. Normally, pressing Tab takes you from the first field through to the last in a form, but if you want to establish a different order, enter a number in the Tab Order text box.

8. Click OK.

You can add check boxes to your heart's content by following these steps. Make sure you label each check box with meaningful text.

Turning On Option Buttons

Option buttons (also known as radio buttons) are like the buttons on a car radio—when you push one of them to select it, it pops in and the others are deselected. Option buttons are good for true-false or multiple choice questions in which only one answer can be made.

Follow these steps to create an option button:

1. In Page view, click where you want the button to go.

2. Choose Insert ➜ Form ➜ Option Button or click the Option Button button on the Form toolbar. An option button appears.

3. Repeat the process to create as many option buttons as you need.

4. Double-click the first option button to display the Option Button Properties dialog box (see Figure 14.11).

Figure 14.11 *The Option Button Properties dialog box lets you name your buttons.*

5. In the Group Name text box, type a name for the entire group of option buttons.

Here's a suggestion for naming a group of option buttons: Use a keyword from the question to which the option buttons belong. That way, when you examine the results of your survey, you will have a better idea of what part of the form the results report on.

6. In the Value field, type a name for this button. If it's a "Yes" button, type **Yes**. If it's a Choice 1 of 5 button—the first of five buttons, each of which presents a different choice—you might type a word from that choice, such as **chocolate**.

7. Click the Selected option button if you want this button to be selected when the page opens (only one option button can be selected in a group of named option buttons). Otherwise, click the Not Selected option button.

8. Enter a number in the Tab Order text box in the unlikely event that you want to change the order in which visitors can press the Tab key and move from field to field in the form. Normally, pressing Tab takes you from the first field through to the last in a form, but if you want to establish a different order, enter a number in the Tab Order text box.

9. Click OK.

10. Follow steps 4 through 9 for the second button. Use the same Group Name and a different Value name. Again, note that only one option button can be selected initially.

You can follow step 1 to create as many option buttons as you like, and then follow steps 4 through 9 for each of them. As long as you use the same Group Name for your buttons, they'll function as a set, but if you change the Group Name, you have a whole new set of buttons on your hands. (Don't forget to write a label for each button.)

You can validate your option buttons and in so doing encourage people to choose wisely among them. Right-click any of the buttons and choose Form Field Properties on the shortcut menu. Then, in the Option Button Properties dialog box (refer to Figure 14.11), click the Validate button. You see the Option Button Validation dialog box. Check the Data Required check box, and, in the Display Name field, type a word for the error message. For example, if you type **City**, *the message will read: "Please select one of the 'City' options."*

Ordering from Drop-Down Menus

For multiple-choice questions that have several possible responses, multiple check boxes work well, especially if you want to let your users choose several (or all) of the possible selections. Another way to go is the drop-down menu. To let your users choose from dozens of options, all of which are indexed in one neat little box, drop-down menus are the way to go:

You can set up drop-down menus so that users can select more than one option at a time, too. Better read on.

Making a Drop-Down Menu

Follow these steps to create a drop-down menu:

1. In Page view, click where you want the drop-down menu to go.

2. Choose Insert ➜ Form ➜ Drop-Down Box or click the Drop-Down Box button on the Form toolbar. A small drop-down menu appears on the page.

3. Double-click the drop-down menu, right-click it and choose Form Field Properties, or click it and choose Format ➜ Properties (or press Alt+Enter). The Drop-Down Menu Properties dialog box appears (see Figure 14.12).

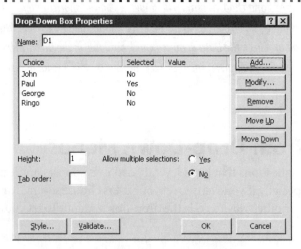

Figure 14.12 *Creating a drop-down menu*

4. In Name field, type a name for the drop-down menu.

5. Click the Add button to enter an option for the menu. The Add Choice dialog box appears.

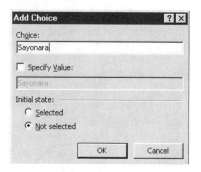

6. In the Choice text box, enter the menu item exactly the way you want it to appear in the drop-down menu. If you would like the value of the item to be different from what appears in the menu, click the Specify Value check box and type the value in its text box. Do this, for example, to make it easier for data-entry people to make choices on the drop-down menu. Rather than choose an item number such as 15115, which is meaningless to most data-entry people, you can enter a descriptive word.

7. In the Initial State area, click the Selected option button if you want this menu item to be pre-selected when your Web page loads; otherwise, leave the default at Not Selected.

8. Click OK to close the Add Choice dialog box. In the Drop-Down Menu Properties dialog box, the choice you added appears.

9. Repeat steps 5 through 8 for as many items as you need to add to your drop-down menu.

10. After you have entered the menu items to your drop-down list, you can do the following:

   • Remove an item: Click the item in the list and then click the Remove button.

   • Change the order of items in the menu: Select a menu item and click the Move Up or Move Down button as many times as necessary. The order changes in the list as you click the buttons.

- Modify an item: Click the item and then click the Modify button. The Modify Choice dialog box appears. Use it as you did the Add Choice dialog box to make the item appear correctly on the menu.

11. In the Height text box, enter the number of items that you want to appear in the menu when the Web page loads. If you want the menu box to display several choices at a time, enter a number greater than 1.

12. Click the No option button in the Allow Multiple Selections area if you don't want users to be able to choose more than one item from the drop-down menu.

13. Enter a number in the Tab Order text box in the unlikely event that you want to change the order in which visitors can press the Tab key and move from field to field in the form. Normally, pressing Tab takes you from the first field through to the last in a form, but if you want to establish a different order, enter a number in the Tab Order text box.

14. Click OK.

If you have a drop-down menu that you need to use several times, you're in luck. You can simply create the menu on one page and then copy and paste it to other pages. You may even be able to borrow such a list from another page that already has one. Just open up the other page, then copy the list, paste it into your own document, and modify it for your use.

Using Validation with Drop-Down Menus

If you want to make sure your users choose *something* (not something in particular, just *something*) from your carefully constructed drop-down menu, enter validation parameters by following these steps:

1. Right-click the drop-down menu you just created and, from the pop-up menu that appears, choose Form Field Validation Properties. The Drop-Down Menu Properties dialog box appears.

2. Click the Validate button. You see the Drop-Down Box Validation dialog box.

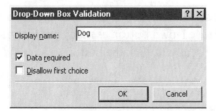

3. Click the Data Required check box if you want to require that users make a choice on the drop-down menu. If you choose to require data, enter a display name for your drop-down menu (such as **Favorite Dog Breed**) in the Display Name text box.

4. If you want to disallow the first (that is, the pre-selected) choice, click the Disallow First Choice check box. Doing so is especially worthwhile if the first item on the menu is "Please select one."

5. Click OK.

Adding Hidden Fields

Hidden fields are data fields that don't show up on Web pages but get sent along with the rest of the data nonetheless. When a user submits the form, the hidden field is sent to you along with the user-entered data. Because the fields are hidden, users can't enter data in them. Their job is to serve as a tagline or reminder to you, the Webmaster.

Hidden fields are particularly useful when you have to process data submitted from several different sources or pages. You can use hidden fields to identify the name of the form, the page that a form came from, or an instruction for a custom CGI script.

Although hidden fields are invisible to the casual user, anyone who views the HTML source for a form page can see them, so don't put confidential information in a hidden field.

Follow these steps to enter a hidden field on a Web page:

1. In Page view, click where you want the hidden field to go.

2. Right-click and choose Form Properties on the shortcut menu, choose Insert ➜ Form ➜ Form Properties, or click the Form Properties button on the Form toolbar. The Form Properties dialog box appears.

3. Click the Advanced button. The Advanced Form Properties dialog box appears (see Figure 14.13).

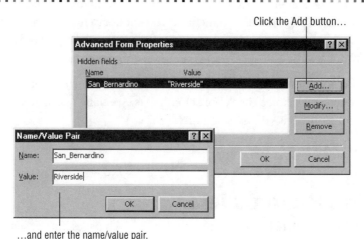

Figure 14.13 *This is where you create those hidden fields.*

4. Click Add to open the Name/Value Pair dialog box (see Figure 14.13).

5. In the Name text box, type a name for the hidden field, and in the Value text box, type a value. Then click OK to close the Name/Value Pair dialog box and return to the Advanced Form Properties dialog box. The name and value you just typed appear in the Hidden Fields list box. You can now add, remove, or modify fields by selecting the appropriate buttons.

6. Click OK to close the Advanced Form Properties dialog box.

7. Click OK again to close the Form Properties dialog box.

You won't see the hidden fields because…they're hidden. Rest assured, however, that they will be sent along with the rest of the input when people submit forms. If you want to see them, click the HTML tab in Page view.

Adding Submit and Reset Buttons

A form isn't complete until you add a Submit button and a Reset button. Users click the Submit button to send the data they entered in the form to your home base. Without a Submit button, a form is nothing more than one of those Dapper Dan dolls that offer a lot of buttons to play with but don't actually do anything. When a user clicks a

Submit button, the data is validated and then whisked away to the form handler (form handlers are explained shortly in "Setting Up a Form Handler"). Many forms also offer a Reset (or Clear) button. Clicking it restores the form to its default settings so that users can begin filling out the form from scratch.

FrontPage 2002 automatically adds a Submit and Reset button to the page when you create a form. Why, then, do you need to know how to create these buttons? Perhaps you're working on a page started in another program, you accidentally deleted the Submit and Reset buttons, or you are creating a form from scratch.

Usually, the Submit and Reset buttons are at the bottom of a form, which may or may not also be the bottom of the Web page as well:

In most forms, the Submit button appears on the left and the Reset/Clear button on the right, but a few forms do it the other way. We remember these forms distinctly because we had to fill them out four or five times in a row—we kept pushing the left button instinctually. The Reset button isn't required. To delete it, just select it and wield your Delete key.

Making a Submit Button

Submit buttons—you can call them Send or whatever you like—are the buttons that get clicked when the user sends the data to the form handler. FrontPage adds these buttons automatically if you use the Insert Form command or create a form with a template, but if you need to add or replace one, follow these steps:

1. Click in the form where you want the button to appear.

2. Choose Insert ➜ Form ➜ Push Button or click the Push Button button on the Form toolbar. A button labeled Button appears on the page.

   Button

3. Open the Push Button Properties dialog box shown in Figure 14.14. To open it, do one of the following:

   - Double-click the button.

- Right-click the button and choose Form Field Properties on the shortcut menu.

- Click the button and choose Format ➜ Properties.

- Press Alt+Enter.

Enter a label for the button.

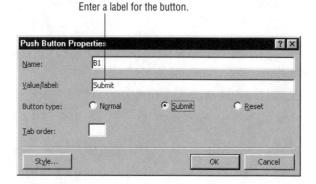

Figure 14.14 You can define buttons as Submit or Reset here.

4. Given that this is a Submit button we're making, either click the Submit option button or type **Submit** in the Value/Label text box. You can, however, type any button name you choose in the Value/Label text box. For example, you can type something more specific, such as **Enter Me in the Contest** or **Bring Home the Bacon**.

5. In the Name field, type a name for your button (such as Submit).

6. Click OK.

Now when your boss says that someone's pushing your buttons, you can assume he means the ones on the company home page!

Making a Reset Button

When a user clicks the Reset button, his or her input is erased and the form's default settings are restored. Follow these steps to create a Reset button:

1. Follow steps 1 through 3 in the previous section, "Making a Submit Button," to create a button and open the Push Button Properties dialog box. (The button is called "Button" when you create it initially.)

2. In the Name field, type a name for the Reset button. For example, you could type **Let Me Start Over**.

3. In the Button Type area, click the Reset option button, and the word Button in the Value/Label field changes to Reset.

4. Click OK.

Using Pictures as Buttons

Those standard gray boxy buttons that you see everywhere are so…standard. Instead of dull gray buttons, you can use pictures for buttons (unfortunately, you can't use pictures for Reset buttons). Creating pictures that are obviously meant as buttons is definitely worthwhile. Having text outside the picture that says, "Click the carrier pigeon to send in your results" helps, but pictures should be concise just the same.

Follow these steps to make a button picture:

1. In Page view, click in your form where you want the image to land.

2. Insert the picture.

Chapter 4 explains how to obtain images from the Microsoft Clip Organizer or import an image from your computer or the Internet.

3. Double-click the picture or right-click it and choose Picture Properties to open the Picture Properties dialog box.

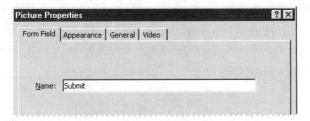

4. On the Form Field tab, enter a name for the picture in the Name text box. If the image is going to act as a Submit button, for example, you might want to name it **Submit**.

5. Click OK to close the Picture Form Field Properties dialog box.

When a user clicks the image, its coordinates are sent to the form handler, which understands it as a Submit button.

Now that you have everything in place, you can turn to the next section, which explains how to set up a form handler to tackle all the behind-the-scenes work.

Chapter 9 explains how to create attractive, graphical buttons that you can use on forms.

Setting Up a Form Handler

When a user clicks the Submit button on a Web page, his or her input is sent to the form handler, and the form handler then processes the results. You can choose from an array of FrontPage-based form handlers, or you can set up the form handler to work with custom scripts installed on your Web site. Here are your choices for form handlers:

- Save results to a file on the server.

- E-mail results to the Webmaster or another person.

- Save results using a custom ISAPI, NSAPI, CGI, or ASP script.

- Use the results to register the user for a restricted Web site (for setting up user-name and password validation, see Chapter 15).

Discussion and registration Web sites are covered in Chapter 15. To work with a custom ISAPI, NSAPI, CGI, or ASP script, contact your system administrator or your ISP's Webmaster or administrator.

All the form handlers described in this section must be used with a server running the FrontPage Server Extensions, with the exception of custom scripts. ISAPI, NSAPI, CGI, and ASP scripts often run on servers other than FrontPage. The first three types run on various flavors of servers, while ASP scripts are most often associated with Microsoft servers.

Working with Custom Scripts

You can set up an ISAPI, NSAPI, or CGI script to do just about anything under the sun. If your Web server doesn't support FrontPage Server Extensions, or if you want more flexibility than FrontPage's scripting extensions can offer, a custom script may be the answer to your prayers.

CGI stands for Common Gateway Interface. ISAPI means Internet Server Application Programming Interface, and NSAPI stands for Netscape Server Application Programming Interface. All three of these types of scripts are used to extend the functionality of Web servers. (Chapter 26 explores CGI scripts in detail.)

However, custom scripts aren't a simple matter of clicking buttons and filling out dialog boxes. If you're not a programmer, you may need one—and a good script from a good programmer (for a good site) can be pricey. If you're dealing with an ISP (as opposed to working with your own or your company's Web server), you may be limited to scripts that your ISP approves and installs for you.

Don't panic, however, because most ISPs offer a set of standard form-processing scripts, and they can tell you how to set up forms so that they access these preexisting scripts—a process that generally involves viewing the HTML and adding a few phrases here and there to the form code.

Check with your system administrator or ISP to find out what your scripting options are before you get your sights set on a complicated form.

Follow these steps to set up a form to work with one of these scripts:

1. In Page view, right-click the form and choose Form Properties from the shortcut menu. The Form Properties dialog box appears (see Figure 14.15).

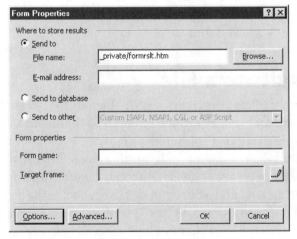

Figure 14.15 *Choose your form handler.*

2. In the Where To Store Results area, click the Send To Other option button.

3. Open the Send To Other drop-down menu and choose Custom ISAPI, NSAPI, CGI, or ASP Script.

4. Click the Options button. The Options For Custom Form Handler dialog box appears.

5. To fill out this dialog box, check with your system administrator (or, if you are the system administrator, fill it out). In the Method drop-down menu, select a method (POST or GET). The URL of your script goes in the Action text box, and the encoding method (if any) goes in the Encoding Type text box.

6. Click OK to close the Options For Custom Form Handler dialog box.

7. Click OK in the Form Properties dialog box.

Because these are instructions for the form's data rather than adjustments to the form itself, you won't *see* any visible result. Be sure to test the heck out of your form to make sure it really does work with your script.

Saving Results to a File

The default setting for handling forms is to save them to a file. You can send results to a text file or an HTML file for later viewing. You can open up the text file and view results whenever you like. Results do look a little funny—raw data files often do. But if you gave memorable names and values to all your fields, you'll be able to make sense of the results. You can crunch these numbers just as you do any others—although automating this process often involves the kind of custom script we talked about in the previous section. If you have a little bit of database or spreadsheet know-how, you can process these results in a database or spreadsheet program, but that topic is beyond the scope of this book.

Follow these steps to set up your form to save input results to an HTML file or text file:

1. In Page view, right-click the form and choose Form Properties on the shortcut menu. The Form Properties dialog box appears (refer to Figure 14.15).

2. In the Where To Store Results area, click the Send To option button, if it's not already selected.

3. Click the Options button to open the Saving Results dialog box (see Figure 14.16).

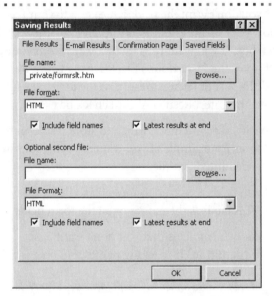

Figure 14.16 *Choosing what type of file to store results in*

4. In the File Format area, open the drop-down menu and choose a file type. Several choices for both HTML and text files are available (the last handful of options on the menu are convenient if the file is going from FrontPage to a script, database, or spreadsheet).

5. Enter a name for the results file in the File Name text box. Make sure the file ends in `.htm` or `.html` for HTML files, or `.txt` for text files.

You can include a directory in the name of the results file, if you want the file to be stored in a particular part of your Web site. If you're using a FrontPage server, you can make the filename something like `private/formresults.txt` *to store the file in the private directory of your FrontPage Web site. To store the file in a particular directory of your FrontPage Web site, click the Browse button. When the Current Web dialog box appears, find and select a folder in which to store the results. The _private folder is a good place for storing form results because others can't view them there.*

6. If for some reason you don't want the field names sent to your file—for example, you're going to post your form results as-is to the Web—deselect the Include Field Names check box. If you want the newest results from your form to appear at the bottom of the form results file, leave the Latest Results At End check box selected. To post the newest results at the top of the file instead of the bottom, deselect the Latest Results At End check box.

7. If you so desire, specify a second file in which to store results in the Optional Second File area. Do so, for example, if you want to save results in both an HTML and comma-delimited text file.

8. To specify which form fields are saved to these files, click the Saved Fields tab (see Figure 14.17). This tab lists the names of all the form fields in the form.

9. Delete the names of any form fields that you don't want to save (for example, the name of the Submit button) by clicking names and pressing the Delete key.

If you delete form field names and realize you'd rather have kept them, don't worry. To restore all the form fields in your form, click Save All, and the deleted names will reappear.

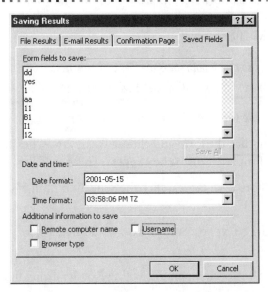

Figure 14.17 *Decide what parts of your form you want to save here.*

10. In the Additional Information To Save area, select any of the check boxes for the data you want added to the form results. FrontPage can add lines for the date and time the form was filled out, the name of the remote machine (alphanumeric or IP address), the username (if you're using FrontPage user registration for users to log into your Web page), and the browser type.

11. Click OK to close the Saving Results dialog box.

12. Click OK to close the Form Properties dialog box.

Don't forget the name of the file you entered in the File Name text box in the Form Properties dialog box (refer to Figure 14.16) because that's where you'll go to fetch the form results. When you're testing your form, be certain to examine this file to make sure the results are satisfactory before you announce your form to the world.

E-mailing Form Results

Another way to examine form results is to have them e-mailed to you. That way, you don't need to remember to check up on your forms, because the results will arrive in your mailbox on a regular basis. Form results are sent as the body of an e-mail message, not as an attachment. You can then save the contents of e-mail messages as text files (and, by extension, as HTML files).

You can set up your form handler so that it both saves the files and e-mails them to you. Just follow the steps detailed in both this section and the preceding one, "Saving Results to a File."

Follow these steps to have form results sent to you by e-mail:

1. In Page view, right-click the form and choose Form Properties on the shortcut menu. The Form Properties dialog box appears (refer to Figure 14.15).

2. In the Where To Store Results area, click the Send To button, if it's not already selected.

3. In the E-mail Address text box, enter the e-mail address where you want the results sent.

4. Click the Options button to open the Saving Results dialog box (refer to Figure 14.16).

5. Click the E-mail Results tab (see Figure 14.18).

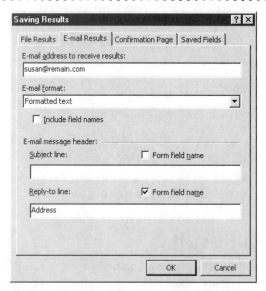

Figure 14.18 *On this tab, arrange to have form results sent to you by e-mail.*

6. Open the E-mail Format drop-down menu and choose a format. Several choices for both HTML and text files are available (the last handful of options on the menu are convenient if the file is going from FrontPage to a script, database, or spreadsheet).

7. To include field names in your e-mail message, make sure the Include Field Names check box is selected.

8. In the Subject Line text box, enter a subject for the e-mail messages you will be sent. If, for example, you want the subject line to announce that the message bears results from an online form, type something like **Results of Customer Survey** in the Subject Line text box.

   or

   If you want the subject line of the message to tell you something about how the form was filled out, you can make the subject line contain results from a form field. Suppose that one of the form fields is a drop-down menu that offers three choices: Compliments, Complaints, and Corrections. You could use one of those words in the subject line. In the E-mail Message Header area, check the Form Field Name check box, and in the Subject Line text box, enter the name of the form field whose results you want to display.

9. If one of the fields in the form asks for the e-mail address of the respondent, the form handler can fill out each e-mail message's reply-to field with the respondent's e-mail address. To make this option active, click the Form Field Name check box in the E-mail Message Header area. Then, in the Reply-To Line text box, type the exact name of the form field that asks for the e-mail address.

In case you weren't aware of it already, e-mail messages include both a From field and a Reply-To field. The From field prints the exact e-mail address of the person who sent the message, while the Reply-To field prints the address that will show up in the To field when you click the Reply button. These can be two different addresses.

10. Click OK to close the Saving Results dialog box.

11. Click OK to close the Form Properties dialog box.

Test this thing a few times to be sure that the e-mail messages sent by the form handler actually make it to the proper e-mail address.

FrontPage 2002 doesn't come "out of the box" ready to support e-mailing form results. To make that option work, the Web server that hosts your Web site must be configured to send mail. If the server is with you, you'll do that; if your site is hosted on your ISP's server, your ISP must make the appropriate settings.

Offering Confirmation

When users click the Submit button, they want to be reassured that *something* happened with all those boxes they filled out. In other words, they want confirmation. Thanking users for their time and giving them a link to click so they can see the data they entered on a new Web page isn't a bad idea. Beyond that, what your confirmation page does is up to you.

You can also include confirmation fields on your Web page to verify the information the user sent. Confirmation fields are great for things such as conference registrations and password requests because users can save or print the results on the confirmation page.

Making a confirmation page is a two-step process. First you make the confirmation page itself (it can include confirmation fields), and then you set up the form page to request that the confirmation page be loaded when a user submits the form. Better read on.

Confirmation fields are only available to Web sites through the use of FrontPage Server Extensions (see Chapter 25 and Appendix A).

Setting Up a Confirmation Page

FrontPage offers two ways to set up a confirmation page:

- With a template: Create a page from a template and choose the Confirmation Form page (go to the Page Templates dialog box to find it). You get a new page with items in brackets. The items in brackets are confirmation fields. Change each confirmation field name so it matches a field name on your form, and then double-click each item in brackets to open and fill in the Confirmation Field Properties dialog box (we explain this dialog box shortly).

- Adding confirmation fields to a page you create: Create a new page and click the page where you want a confirmation field to appear. Then choose Insert ➔ Web

Component. You see the Insert Web Component dialog box. In the Component Type list, scroll to the bottom and select Advanced Controls. In the Choose A Control list, double-click Confirmation Field. You see the Confirmation Field Properties dialog box.

The Confirmation Field Properties dialog box is where you type the name of the field you want to confirm. For example, if a field on your form is called Address and you want the user to see his or her e-mail address on the confirmation page, enter the name of the address field in the dialog box. The name must be exactly the same (including case sensitivity) as it appears in the code for the form.

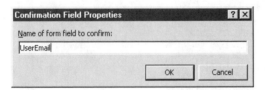

 You can check the name of the form field by viewing your form page in Page view and double-clicking the form field to display the Form Field Properties dialog box.

Making Your Form Call Up the Confirmation Page

Your final task is to set up your original form to call up the confirmation page when a user clicks the Submit button. If you do this correctly, the confirmation page will appear and the user will see the information that he or she entered.

Follow these steps to make your form call up the confirmation page:

1. In Page view, right-click the form and choose Form Properties. The Form Properties dialog box appears (refer to Figure 14.15).

2. Click the Options button. The Saving Results dialog box appears (refer to Figure 14.16).

3. Click the Confirmation Page tab to bring it forward. The dialog box changes to reflect your choice (see Figure 14.19).

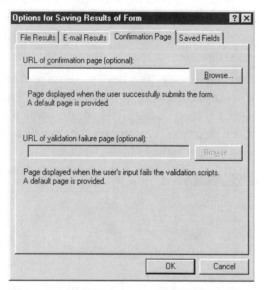

Figure 14.19 *Set up your confirmation page options here.*

4. In the first text box, enter the target URL of the confirmation page (see the previous section, "Setting Up a Confirmation Page," for instructions on making a confirmation page). If your FrontPage Web site is open, you can click Browse to select the file from the available files.

You can specify a validation failure page in the same way that you set up a confirmation page by filling in the bottom half of the Confirmation Page tab (refer to Figure 14.19). This option is available to you only if you've used validation with one of your form fields. Otherwise, it is grayed out.

5. Click OK to close the Saving Results dialog box.

6. Click OK to close the Form Properties dialog box.

Now your users will see your confirmation page when they click the form's Submit button (or the Show Me The Light button, or whatever you called it).

Up Next

If you've been feeling that the tasks in this book are getting more difficult, you're not alone! Working with forms—particularly setting them up to work on a server—can be frustrating for even an experienced Webmaster.

For readers who come to FrontPage 2002 with little page-making experience, there is no doubt that the kind of work we're doing now is significantly more complex than the exercises earlier in the book. The good news is that you've learned how to do a lot of highly technical work without spending years learning how to operate Web servers or learning a language—FrontPage is doing most of the programming work for you.

This pep talk doesn't mean the experience of using FrontPage is going to get any less intricate, though! In Chapter 15, you'll learn how to add some pretty fun Web effects to your pages. While the technology in this book will continue to be sophisticated, you should be feeling confident that, with FrontPage, you can easily accomplish advanced techniques.

Special Effects

FRONTPAGE

Chapter 15

Until recently, you needed a comprehensive knowledge of Web programming to take advantage of the strongest and most flexible features of Web site design. Special programming skills were required to make images display on a page at different times, include a hit counter on a Web page, or create a discussion group. These effects required Web technologies far beyond HTML.

But most people are not programmers, nor do they have the time or desire to become programmers! Still, wouldn't it be nice to implement these special, site-enhancing features without spending money on hiring programmers, or devoting time to learning new technologies?

This chapter explains how to include sophisticated Web-page features on a Web site without resorting to sophisticated technologies. It explains the Web components, special items you can include on Web sites without much trouble. Also in this chapter are various FrontPage and HTML techniques that you can use to spice up Web pages very nicely. Topics include:

- Working with components

- Adding hit counters, hover buttons, and other clever effects

- Including and scheduling pages and images

- Staying organized with search pages, tables of contents, and link bars

- Keeping track with comments

- Registering users and letting them talk to each other

- Creating shared borders for a unified look

Using the Web Components

Web components are prepackaged, preprogrammed elements that you can place on Web sites. Examples of Web components include hit counters, the meters on Web pages that list how many visitors have come to the page, tables of contents, top 10 lists, and Search text boxes. You can insert these handy items into Web pages without having to program at all. What used to take two or three days of programming to create can be accomplished in a matter of minutes. The Web components that come with FrontPage are actually implemented using a number of technologies, including server-side scripts, Java, and JavaScript (see Chapters 21 and 22 for more details). But you don't have to know about Java or JavaScript because FrontPage does the work for you in the background.

Figure 15.1 shows the Insert Web Component dialog box, the starting point for placing a Web component on a Web page. To open this dialog box, choose Insert ➜ Web Component or click the Web Component button on the Standard toolbar.

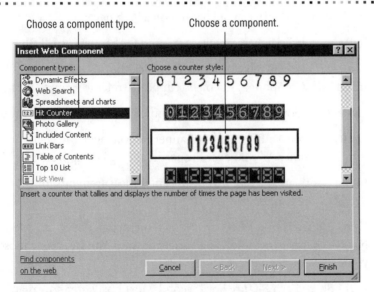

Figure 15.1 *The Insert Web Component dialog box is the starting point for inserting a Web component.*

Be sure to drop by Chapter 21 and Chapter 22 for a look at specific methods of programming effects within Web pages.

Placing an Ad Banner on a Web Page

You've no doubt seen ad banners on Web pages. They usually appear at the top of Web pages and advertise something or other. An ad banner consists of two images that appear one after the other over and over and over again. In effect, an ad banner is a little animated sequence. FrontPage offers a special Web component for placing ad banners on Web pages.

To insert an ad banner, you need GIF or JPEG images. I suggest placing them in the images folder on your Web site so you know where they are before you create the ad banner. Make sure the images are the same size or nearly the same size. What's more, take note of how wide and tall the images are, because you will enter their dimensions when you place the ad banner on your Web page.

Follow these steps to place an ad banner on a Web page:

1. In Page view, click where you want to insert the banner (usually the top of a page).

2. Choose Insert ➔ Web Component or click the Web Component button. The Insert Web Component dialog box appears (refer to Figure 15.1).

3. Under Component Type, select Dynamic Effects if it isn't already selected.

4. Under Choose An Effect, select Banner Ad Manager and click the Finish button. The Banner Ad Manager Properties dialog box appears (see Figure 15.2).

5. In the Width and Height text boxes, enter measurements for the width and the height of the banner.

6. Open the Transition Effect drop-down menu and choose an effect. You can have the banner transition in a variety of ways. You can also choose None if you do not want an effect.

7. In the Show Each Picture For (Seconds) text box, enter how many seconds you want each picture to appear in the ad banner before it yields to the next picture.

8. Click the Add button to tell FrontPage which images to place in the ad banner. In the Add Picture For Banner Ad dialog box, select an image and click the Open button. Repeat this step for each image that will appear in the ad banner. You can include more than two.

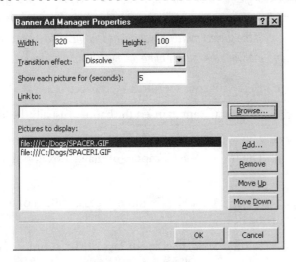

Figure 15.2 *Creating a Banner Ad*

Keeping the total number of images in an ad banner to three is considered the way to go. Beyond three images, you create a mini-movie, not a banner.

9. To change the order in which images appear, select an image in the Pictures To Display box and click the Move Up or Move Down button.

10. If you want the ad banner to also function as a hyperlink, enter a URL in the Link To text box (or click the Browse button and enter the URL by way of the Select Banner Ad Hyperlink dialog box). As a hyperlink, users can click the ad banner and open another Web page.

11. Click OK.

You now have a rotating banner with special effects. Congratulations!

Adding a Hit Counter

Many a Webmaster likes to track the number of visitors to his or her Web site and broadcast this information for all to see. FrontPage makes this a breeze with the Hit Counter Web component. It counts every visit to a Web page and then proudly posts the tally. Several stylish display options are available.

A hit counter may seem like a cool gizmo, but in many circles it is considered the sign of a rank beginner. Take a look at any professional-looking site, and you'll see a complete lack of hit counters. Therefore, it's wise to use this component only if the subject matter of your page lends itself to a hit counter, or if you're creating a personal home page and want the counter more than you want a professional, clean look.

Follow these steps to insert a hit counter into a Web page:

1. In Page view, click where you want to insert the banner (usually the top of a page).

2. Choose Insert ➜ Web Component or click the Web Component button on the Standard toolbar. The Insert Web Component dialog box appears (refer to Figure 15.1).

3. Under Component Type, select Hit Counter. An assortment of hit counters appears in the dialog box.

4. Under Choose A Counter Style, select your favorite hit counter and click the Finish button. The Hit Counter Properties dialog box appears (see Figure 15.3).

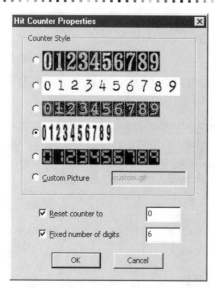

Figure 15.3 *Setting up a hit counter*

5. Select the option button beside the hit counter style that appeals to you most.

6. If you want to start counting from a number other than 0 (cheater!), enter the number in the Reset Counter To text box.

7. By default, hit counters display 5 digits, but you can lower or raise the amount of digits shown by entering a number other than 5 in the Fixed Number Of Digits text box.

 Consider lowering the number of digits in the hit counter to get better control of the layout of the page. Lots of digits can cause the tallied number of visitors to wrap to the next line or even push text and images onto another line. At five digits, you can track up to 99,999 visits to the page. Because only five digits are displayed by default, and these are always the right-most five digits, visitor number 100,000 would actually see 00000. You can always come back to the Hit Counter Properties dialog box and change the number of fixed digits. To reopen the dialog box, double-click the hit counter on your Web page.

8. Click OK. The text *[hit counter]* is inserted in your page to mark the spot where the hit counter is.

To change the look of the hit counter or change the number of digits it displays, double-click *[hit counter]* on your Web page. You see the Hit Properties dialog box (refer to Figure 15.3), where you can make adjustments.

Creating Hover Buttons

Sometimes you visit a Web page and, as you move the mouse pointer over an image, the image changes. It glows or changes color, for example. An image that changes appearance this way is called a *hover button*. With FrontPage's Hover Button Web component, you can add this oh-so-nifty effect (also called a *mouseover*) to your own Web pages.

Follow these steps to create a hover button:

1. In Page view, click where you want the hover button to appear.

2. Choose Insert ➜ Web Component or click the Web Component button. The Insert Web Component dialog box appears (refer to Figure 15.1).

3. Under Component Type, select Dynamic Effects if it isn't already selected.

4. Under Choose An Effect, select Hover Button and click the Finish button. The Hover Button Properties dialog box appears (see Figure 15.4).

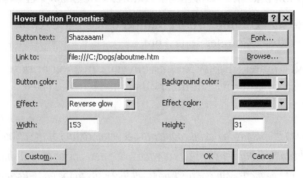

Figure 15.4 *Create special effects for buttons using the Hover Button Properties dialog box.*

5. In the Button Text text box, type the text you want to appear on the face of the button. Change the font, if you like, by clicking the Font button and choosing a different font or font color in the Font dialog box.

6. In the Link To text box, type the URL of the page you want to load when a visitor clicks the button. You can also click the Browse button to open the Select Hover Button Hyperlink dialog box and locate the Web page or file you want to link to.

7. Choose a color for the button:

   Button Color   Open the drop-down menu and choose a color.

   Background Color   Choose a color from this drop-down menu only if you select an image for the button, not a color (from the Button Color drop-down menu). The background color appears behind the image.

To choose a background image for the button, click the Custom button at the bottom of the Hover Button Properties dialog box. Then, in the Custom dialog box, click the Browse button beside the Button text box and locate the image you want in the Select Picture dialog box. If you want an image to appear as well when a visitor hovers over the button, click the Browse button beside the On Hover text box as well and select a second image.

8. Choose what happens when a visitor moves the mouse over the button:

Effect   Open the Effect drop-down menu and choose an effect. (Yes, the effects are hard to figure out, but after you have chosen and tested one effect, you can return to the Hover Button Properties dialog box and choose a different effect. To do so, simply double-click the button in Page view.)

Effect Color   Open the Effect Color drop-down menu and choose the color that you want to appear when a visitor moves his or her pointer over the button. How the color appears depends on which effect you choose.

9. Enter measurements in the Width and Height text boxes to tell FrontPage how big or small to make the button.

The easiest way to change the size of a button is to select it and drag a selection handle, one of the squares that appears in the corners and on the sides of the button.

10. Click OK.

The button you just inserted will be visible; however, the special effects you chose are not visible (not even after you select the Preview tab). You have to preview the page in a Web browser that supports Java to see the full effects of the hover button.

· ·

Sound Effects for Hover Buttons

Sounds as well as sights can call attention to hover buttons. If you so desire, you can play a sound for a visitors who place their mouse pointers over a hover button. And when visitors click the button they can hear a sound as well.

To attach a sound to a hover button, start from the Hover Button Properties dialog box (refer to Figure 15.4). To open this dialog box if it isn't already open, double-click your hover button or right-click it and choose Hover Button Properties on the shortcut menu.

In the Hover Button Properties dialog box, click the Custom button. You see the Custom dialog box. Under Play Sound, enter a sound file name in the On Click text box to play a sound when visitors click the button, and enter a sound file name in the On Hover text box to play a sound when visitors move their mouse pointers over the button. To enter a sound file, click the Browse button and choose a sound file in the Select Sound or Select Hover Sound dialog box.

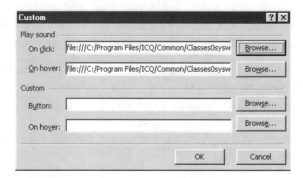

Adding a Marquee

A *marquee* is a line or two of text that scrolls horizontally across the screen. Use marquees to call visitors' attention to something important.

Follow these steps to place a scrolling marquee on a Web page:

1. In Page view, click where you want the marquee to appear.

2. Choose Insert ➔ Web Component or click the Web Component button. The Insert Web Component dialog box appears (refer to Figure 15.1).

3. Under Component Type, select Dynamic Effects if it isn't already selected.

4. Under Choose An Effect, select Marquee and click the Finish button. The Marquee Properties dialog box appears (see Figure 15.5).

5. In the Text text box, type the text for the marquee.

6. Choose how you want the marquee to appear:

   Direction   Choose to scroll the text beginning on the left or right by clicking an option button.

   Speed   Specify the delay (in seconds) before the marquee starts scrolling and how fast in pixels per second to scroll the marquee.

   Behavior   Select Scroll to make the marquee scroll like a stock ticker, Slide to make it scroll into place and rest there, or Alternate to make it scroll and then slide.

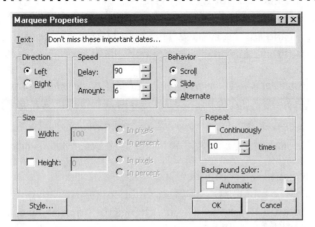

Figure 15.5 *The Marquee Properties dialog box*

7. In the Width and Height text boxes, enter measurements for the marquee if you dare. We suggest sticking with the default measurements.

8. Click the Continuously check box to make the marquee scroll eternally, or click in the Times text box and enter the number of times you want the marquee to scroll before stopping.

9. Select a background color for the marquee scroll box from the Background Color drop-down menu.

You're set to scroll! Click the Preview tab to see the scrolling marquee in action. If you don't like what you see, click the Normal tab, double-click the marquee, and change things around in the Marquee Properties dialog box (refer to Figure 15.5).

The Marquee, like many FrontPage components, is not a standard HTML tag. Therefore, the browser support for it is typically limited to Internet Explorer. See Chapter 16 for more details.

Including a Page within a Page

The Include Page Web component takes the content of one Web page and displays it inside another Web page. That doesn't seem very exciting, but including one page in another can save quite a bit of time. Many Webmasters, for example, like to put standard navigational controls on all the pages in their Web sites. The controls might be buttons, icons, or hyperlinks. Needless to say, typing the text, inserting the images, and creating the links on every page is time-consuming. Worse, if you decide to change anything, you have to load and edit every page. The Include Page Web component means having to enter the stuff that goes on every page only once.

The Include Page Web component is very similar to the Shared Borders component (covered later in this chapter in "Shared Borders for Creating Effects across Multiple Pages" later in this chapter). Use the component when you want to place different content on each of a bunch of individual pages; use Shared Borders when you want to place a piece of content on the edge or edges of many pages.

With the Include Page Web component, you create a navigational bar on one page and then simply insert the Include Page Web component on every page that needs a navigation bar. Changes are also a breeze—just change the original page, indicate that you've updated it, and all of the other pages are updated automatically.

The Include Page Web component is also useful for any part of a Web page that is frequently changed—headlines in a newsletter, entrees on a cafeteria menu, weekly activity schedules, and so on. Put these ever-changing items on a separate, relatively plain page, and then include that page in a more elaborately designed Web page. By doing so, you have only to change the plain page to make changes on several pages. You don't risk marring a perfectly good page by making inadvertent changes.

You can also include other pages in a table cell that appears anywhere on a page. To do so, place a table on the page (see Chapter 11) and use the Include Page Web component to place your included page inside a table cell.

Follow these steps to use the Include Page Web component:

1.   Open the Web page that you will put the "included" page in.

2.   Click where you want the inserted page to go.

3.   Choose Insert ➜ Web Component or click the Web Component button on the Standard toolbar. The Insert Web Component dialog box appears (refer to Figure 15.1).

4.   Under Component Type, select Included Content.

5. Under Choose A Type Of Content, select Page and click the Finish button. The Include Page Properties dialog box appears.

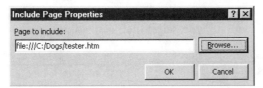

6. Click the Browse button and, in the Current Web dialog box, locate and select the "to be included" page.

7. Click OK.

The Page view window reappears, with the contents of the inserted page now displayed within the current page.

Including Pages or Pictures Based on a Schedule

Like the Include Page Web component (the subject of the previous section in this chapter), the Page Based On Schedule Web component allows you to include one page inside another—except this time the page appears according to a schedule. Similarly, FrontPage offers another component for placing a picture on a Web page according to schedule.

Suppose you want to replace a general navigation bar with a special-event navigation bar during a month in which your Web site promotes a product. Suppose you want a different greeting to appear on your home page at different times of the day. Suppose you want a picture of yourself to appear on your birthday. These tasks are easily done with the Page Based On Schedule Web component or the Picture Based On Schedule Web component.

Follow these steps to include one page in another during a certain time period or a picture on a page during a certain time period:

1. Open the Web page that you will put the included page or picture in.

2. Click where you want the inserted page or picture to go.

3. Choose Insert ➜ Web Component or click the Web Component button on the Standard toolbar. The Insert Web Component dialog box appears (refer to Figure 15.1).

4. Under Component Type, select Included Content.

5. Under Choose A Type Of Content, select Page Based On Schedule or Picture Based On Schedule and click the Finish button. The Scheduled Include Page Properties dialog box or Scheduled Picture Properties appears (see Figure 15.6). These dialog boxes work the same way.

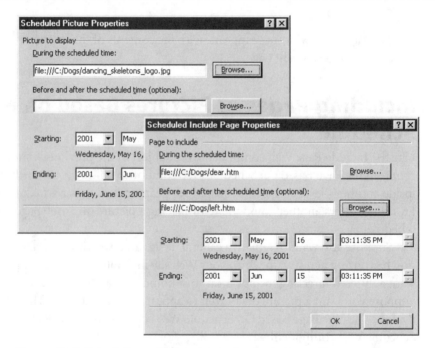

Figure 15.6 *Scheduling a Web page or picture to appear on a page at a certain time*

6. Under Page To Include During The Scheduled Time, enter the filename of a Web page or picture. In other words, enter the name of the Web page or picture that you want to appear during the time period. You can do that by clicking the Browse button and selecting the page or picture in the dialog box that appears.

7. Optionally, enter a Web page file name or picture file name in the Before And After The Scheduled Time text box. The page or picture you enter here will appear in place of the scheduled page or picture before and after the scheduled time period.

8. In the Starting area, enter the starting time for displaying the Web page or picture.

9. In the Ending area, enter the ending time.

10. Click OK.

If the current date falls within the schedule, you see your page or picture on the Web page.

Use the same procedure for any page you want included for a finite period of time. Good candidates for this are announcements that carry a date—such as the date of a meeting, a game, a contest, or promotion.

Including Specified Information throughout the Site

Earlier in this chapter, you discovered how, with the Include Page Web component, you can place the same text and images on several different Web pages and only have to maintain the text and images on one page. Being able to operate from one location like this is a whopping time-saver. It makes maintaining a Web site much, much easier.

Sometimes, though, a word or phrase, not an entire page or image, needs to appear several times in different places. A name, a copyright notice, or piece of "boilerplate" text sometimes has to appear on different pages. To make updating these kinds of words and phrases easier, FrontPage offers the Substitution Web component. With this component, you tell FrontPage which what need substituting, and then you substitute at will.

The words and phrases that may require substituting are called *keywords.* The words and phrases substitute for the keywords are called *values.* By listing keywords and values, you can make sure that your Web site is always up to date. To see how it works, suppose you have a company Web site and the bottom of every page includes a copyright notice. At the start of each year, you have to go from page to page to update the notice—that is, you have to do that unless you take advantage of the Substitution Web component. To save yourself lots of redundant typing time, you make *Copyright YYYY* a keyword and give it the value *Copyright 2001*. Every new year, you enter a new value for the *Copyright YYYY* keyword—*Copyright 2001*, *Copyright 2002*, and so on.

Then, whenever you need to update the copyright notice on all your Web pages, FrontPage does it for you.

FrontPage comes with four defined keywords, but you can define as many as you want. The provided ones are

- *Author*, which is replaced automatically with the name of the author who created the page

- *Modified By*, which is replaced by the name of the author who most recently modified the page

- *Description*, which is replaced by a description of the current page (by default, the title of the page is used as the description)

- *Page URL*, which is replaced by the page's location in the current FrontPage Web site

Remember: The keyword represents changeable text, and the value represents what you want the text to be at the present time. Follow these steps to enter keywords and their values:

1. Choose Tools ➜ Web Settings. The Web Settings dialog box appears.

2. Click the Parameters tab (see Figure 15.7).

Figure 15.7 *Here you can specify keywords and values.*

3. Click the Add button. The Add Name And Value dialog box appears.

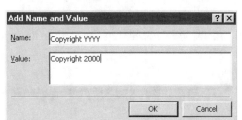

4. In the Name text box, enter a keyword, and in the Value text box, enter its value; then click OK to return to the Web Settings dialog box. The keyword and value you just added are listed.

5. Repeat steps 3 and 4 to enter other keywords and values.

6. Click OK to close the Web Settings dialog box.

As you enter text on Web pages, insert keywords when you come to a place where you want to enter text that will need updating in the future. Follow these steps to enter a keyword:

1. Click where you want to insert a keyword (and hence, its associated value).

2. Choose Insert ➜ Web Component or click the Web Component button on the Standard toolbar. The Insert Web Component dialog box appears (refer to Figure 15.1).

3. Under Component Type, select Included Content.

4. Under Choose A Type Of Content, select Substitution and click the Finish button. The Substitution Properties dialog box appears.

5. Open the Substitute With drop-down menu and choose a keyword.

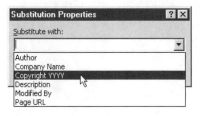 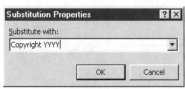

6. Click OK.

When you've changed the value of a keyword (following the steps earlier in this section), open the page in Page view to see that the change has occurred on the page.

Adding a Search Form to a Web Page

You can grant users quick access to whatever they seek on your Web site by offering them a search form. The user has only to type a word or phrase into a text box and press the Search button, and—Poof!—up comes a list of items in your Web site that address that topic.

As with most FrontPage components, you are required to publish your page on a Web server with Front-Page extensions in order for the component to function properly.

Follow these steps to place a search form in your Web site:

1. Click where you want the search form to appear.

2. Choose Insert ➜ Web Component or click the Web Component button on the Standard toolbar. The Insert Web Component dialog box appears (refer to Figure 15.1).

3. Under Component Type, select Web Search.

4. Under Choose A Type Of Search, select Current Web and click the Finish button. The Search Form Properties dialog box appears (see Figure 15.8).

5. Select the Search Form Properties Tab if it's not already selected.

6. If you want, change the defaults for the various labels and buttons by typing in different names in the text boxes. To change the label on the Search For text box, for example, enter Find or Look For in the Label For Input text box.

Figure 15.8 The Search Form Properties dialog box

7. Click the Search Results tab.

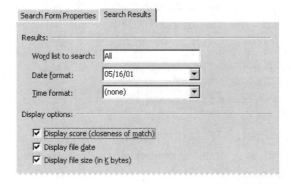

8. If you want, change the defaults and choose a new way to display search results.

9. Click OK.

The dialog box disappears and you see the search form. To preview the form, click the Preview tab. To change the form, double-click it when the Normal tab is selected in

Page view. Doing so opens the Search Form Properties dialog box (refer to Figure 15.8), where you can make your changes.

FrontPage also offers a template for creating a search form. To test-drive it, open the Page Templates dialog box and choose Search Page.

Building a Table of Contents

To help users locate what's on your site in a snap, offer them a table of contents. A table of contents works much like the table of contents in a book. The Table of Contents component creates a list of Web pages that are linked from the Web site's home page.

Follow these steps to create a table of contents:

1. Create an empty page for the table of contents.

2. Choose Insert → Web Component or click the Web Component button on the Standard toolbar. The Insert Web Component dialog box appears (refer to Figure 15.1).

3. Under Component Type, select Table Of Contents.

4. Under Choose A Table of Contents, select For This Web Site and click the Finish button. The Table Of Contents Properties dialog appears (see Figure 15.9).

5. In the Page URL For Starting Point Of Table text box, enter the name of the start page for your table of contents (most likely **index.htm**, the home page of your Web site).

6. Select a font size from the Heading Font Size drop-down menu.

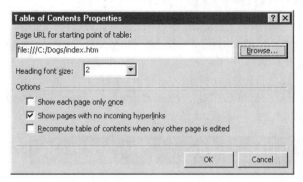

Figure 15.9 *The Table Of Contents Properties dialog box*

7. Under Options, choose which pages to list in the table of contents:

   Show Each Page Only Once   Lists each page on the Web site only once in the table of contents, regardless of how many times it is connected to other pages by a hyperlink.

   Show Pages With No Incoming Hyperlinks   List pages that are not connected to the table of contents page by hyperlinks.

   Recompute Table Of Contents When Any Other Page Is Edited   Tells Front-Page to regenerate the table of contents whenever you edit a Web page. You can always regenerate a table of contents without choosing this option by saving the table of contents Web page.

8. Click OK.

You can also create a table of contents page with a template. In the Page Templates dialog box, go to the General tab and select Table Of Contents.

Site Management Effects

This section looks at effects that can help you manage a Web site—and visitors to the site—more effectively. These effects include time-stamping Web pages, adding comments in your HTML code, and registering site visitors. As you'll soon see, these effects are very helpful in managing a Web site and making it a better place to visit.

Adding Dynamic Date and Time

To lend a Web page a sense of currency or urgency, you might try stamping it with the current time and/or date. Many sites include date-stamps to let visitors know when they were last updated. News sites sometimes include time-stamps to suggest to visitors that the news they present is up to the minute. In the past, date- and time-stamping required knowing sophisticated HTML code and fancy programming techniques, but FrontPage lets you date- and time-stamp Web pages very easily.

This page last updated on 05/16/01 at 07:34 PM Pacific Daylight Time.

Follow these steps to date- and time-stamp a Web page:

1. Click where you want the date- or time-stamp to appear.

2. Choose Insert ➜ Date And Time. The Date And Time Properties dialog box appears (see Figure 15.10).

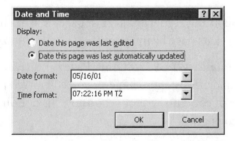

Figure 15.10 *Stamping the date and time when a Web site was last updated*

3. Choose a Date option button:

   Date This Page Was Last Edited   Stamps the page when you or someone else saves it.

   Date This Page Was Last Automatically Updated   Stamps the page when you or someone else saves it, or when a page that is included in this page is saved.

4. In the Date Format drop-down menu, choose a format for the date-stamp.

5. In the Time Format drop-down menu, choose a format for the time-stamp.

To keep a date-stamp or time-stamp from appearing, choose (None) on the Date Format or Time Format drop-down menu.

6. Click OK.

The date- and time-stamp—formatted the way you specified in steps 4 and 5 above—appears on-screen.

Including Comments

So you make your fine, upstanding Web page, and weeks, months, or even years later, you or another team member goes back to it for some reason. Does that person know why you did what you did? Do *you* remember? A good, standard programming practice can and should be applied to the creation of Web pages, and that is to insert comments. *Comments* are lines that aren't executed in the code as part of a program. Comments explain what a particular section of the code or a program is meant to do.

You can put anything you want into a comment because it doesn't appear when a user views the page with a browser. However, anyone who views the source of the Web page (the code) will see the comments you have entered. Watch what you say!

Follow these steps to insert a comment into a Web page:

1. In Page view, click where you want to insert a comment.

2. Choose Insert → Comment. The Comment dialog box appears.

3. Enter your comment.

4. Click OK.

The comment is placed on the page in a different color from the surrounding text (the default color for comments is light gray). When you preview the page in the Preview tab or view it in a Web browser, the comment does not appear. Comments can be seen only when you are editing a page or viewing the source code in a Web browser.

To edit a comment, double-click it to open the Comment dialog box.

Registering Users

Suppose you might want to know who's who in a Discussion Web page (covered later in this chapter) or get a sense of who is visiting a particular part of your Web site. Using the User Registration Web component, you can track who has accessed different parts of your site. How is it done? You require visitors to fill out a form about themselves before they are allowed access to your Web site.

Follow these steps to add a registration form to an existing Web site:

1. With the index, or home, Web page open (the registration form for the Web site is stored on the index Web page), select File ➜ New ➜ Page Or Web. The New Page Or Web task pane appears.

2. Click the Page Templates hyperlink. You see the Page Template dialog box.

3. On the General tab, select User Registration and click OK. A new registration page appears on-screen (see Figure 15.11).

4. Locate the form area of the registration page (it starts with the label Form Submission), right-click it, and choose Form Properties on the shortcut menu. The Form Properties dialog box appears.

5. Click the Options button. The Options For Registration Form Handler dialog box appears.

6. In the Web Name text box, type the name of the Web page you want users to have to register to use.

7. In the URL Of Registration Failure Page (Optional) text box, you can type the filename of a page to display when access to a Web page is denied (this usually happens when someone types the wrong password). Entering a page in this text box is optional.

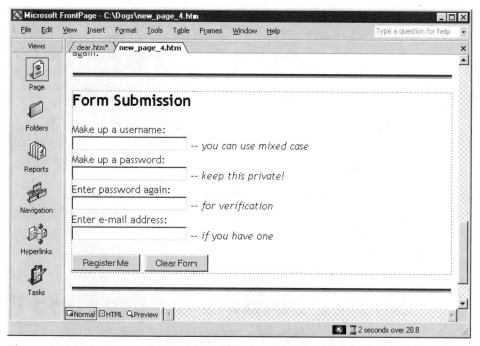

Figure 15.11 *As you customize this registration form,* don't *change any of these text boxes or buttons.*

 Do not change the default entries in the rest of the dialog boxes. They are filled out correctly for the form created by the User Registration template. You need to modify them only if you want to use your own form—with different field names—to register users. That's a big job, and we suggest skipping it unless you're an advanced administrator.

8. Click OK to return to the Form Properties dialog box.

9. Click OK.

10. Choose Edit ➜ Replace. The Replace dialog box appears.

11. In the Find What text box, type [**Other Web**]. This is placeholder text that will appear on the registration page in those locations where the name of the Web page you are requiring users to register for will eventually go.

12. In the Replace With text box, type the name of the Web page requiring registration.

13. Click the Replace All button. The name you provided will replace all the occurrences of [Other Web]. After the replacement is done, a confirmation dialog box appears.

14. Click OK in that dialog box. The Replace dialog box reappears.

15. Click Cancel in the Replace dialog box. The dialog box closes and you are returned to the Page view window, with the user registration page in view.

16. Finally, save the registration Web page.

Before you take this thing live, remember that you need to go around the site and change any links that used to go to the now-protected area so that users must come here first and register. You can use a site-wide search-and-replace to do this; see Chapter 24 for details.

Shared Borders for Creating Effects across Multiple Pages

By means of *shared borders*, you can create effects that appear on many different Web pages. Shared borders allow you to add any graphic or HTML element on the top, bottom, and/or side of a page, making it, in effect, a border. For example, you can create a link bar (as described in an upcoming section) and then make it appear at the top or along the side of every page in a Web site. You can enable shared borders for an entire Web site, so that the same border appears on every page, or you can make the shared border appear only on specific pages.

Here are the two basic steps for creating a shared border:

1. Specify where the shared borders are located. This is, in actuality, what you are doing when you use the shared borders technique—you are positioning a region in which something will appear.

2. Place in the shared border whatever you actually want to appear there—a graphic, piece of HTML code, text, or what have you.

Enabling and Disabling Shared Borders

Follow these steps to enable or disable shared borders:

1. In Page view, choose Format ➜ Shared Borders. The Shared Borders dialog box appears (see Figure 15.12).

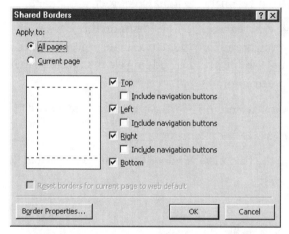

Figure 15.12 *You can place shared borders along the top, bottom, left, or right side of Web pages.*

2. Under Apply To, choose the All Pages option button to place borders on all the pages in your Web site; choose the Current Page option button to place the borders on the page that you were viewing when you chose the Format ➜ Shared Borders command.

3. Click the Top, Left, Right, and/or Bottom check box to place borders where you want them to be on your Web pages. Notice what happens on the preview page as you select check boxes—dotted lines show roughly where the shared borders will go.

4. Click OK.

Exactly what the page looks like depends on what shared borders you enabled, but in general you see the shared borders there with generic comments in them (earlier in this chapter, "Including Comments" explained comments).

Adding Elements to a Shared Border

After you enable shared borders, the next step is to enter the content. You can place text, graphics, or some other HTML element in a shared border. Whatever you place in a shared border will then appear on every page that's been enabled—single pages or all the pages in the Web site. A shared border is a handy place to put a page banner or copyright notice.

Follow these steps to add elements to a shared border:

1. Starting in Page view, either place the cursor on the page where you want to add elements if you are adding them to a single page, or place the cursor on any page in your Web site if you are adding elements into shared borders that all the pages have in common.

2. Place whatever image, text, or HTML you want in the border.

3. Choose File ➜ Save to save your work.

When you return to the Page view window, the stuff you placed in the shared border is quite evident.

Adding a Link Bar

Link bars (sometimes known as *navigation bars*) are a typical element in most Web sites. A link bar usually consists of a set of buttons or text links that appear along the top or side of every page in the site. They provide users with a way to get around. A good, easy-to-use link bar is essential in any Web site. Creating one can be a complex matter that involves site architects, designers, and so on, but with FrontPage, creating a link is a simple matter indeed.

By placing the link bar within a shared border, you can quickly add a link bar to your entire site without having to open and edit every single page. The previous section in this chapter describes shared borders.

Follow these steps to add a link bar to a Web page:

1. With the page of interest open in Page view, click where you want to insert the link bar (if you want to place it within a shared border, click there).

2. Choose Insert ➜ Navigation. The Insert Web Component dialog box appears.

3. Under Choose A Bar Type, select the kind of link bar you want and click the Next button:

   Bar With Custom Links   The hyperlinks on the link bar go to pages inside and outside the Web site. Each hyperlink is a button.

   Bar With Back And Next Buttons   Hyperlinks lead to pages on the Web site; a Back button and a Next button appear on the link bar.

   Bar Based On Navigation Structure   The link bar mirrors the navigational structure of your Web site.

4. Choose a bar style and click the Next button. Be sure to scroll through the lengthy list to find a style that pleases you.

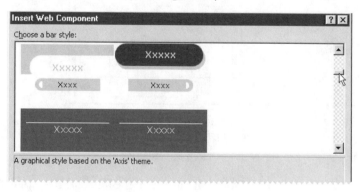

5. Choose an orientation for the link bar and click the Finish button. You see the General tab of the Link Bar Properties dialog box and the Create New Link Bar dialog box (see Figure 15.13).

If you are creating a link bar based on the navigation structure of your Web site, you go straight to the Link Bar Properties dialog box. There, choose a Level option to tell FrontPage which buttons to put on the link bar. The preview graphic in the dialog box shows what your choices mean in real terms.

6. Enter a name for the link bar in the Create New Link bar dialog box and click OK.

7. Click the Add Link button, and, in the Add To Link Bar dialog box, select a Web page that you want a button on the link bar to go to.

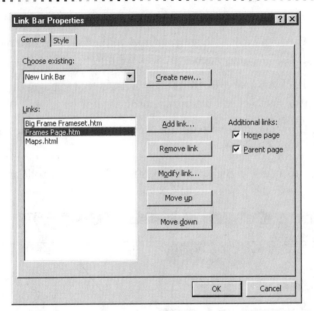

Figure 15.13 *The Link Bar Properties dialog box is your gateway to controlling which links appear on the link bar.*

8. Repeat step 7 for each button on the link bar. You can include two pages in addition to those you select yourself: the Home Page and the Parent Page. Select either or both by clicking their check boxes.

9. After you have entered all the buttons, select links and click the Move Up or Move Down button to establish the order of the buttons on the link bar.

10. Click OK.

To see the link bar, you have to preview the page in a Web browser. Choose File ➜ Preview In Browser.

To edit or alter a link bar after you create it, double-click the link bar. The Link Bar Properties dialog box appears (refer to Figure 15.13). You can click the Style tab to change the appearance of buttons on the link bar. On the General tab, add or remove buttons, or change the order of the buttons.

Extra Web Component Goodies

The Insert Web Component dialog box (refer to Figure 15.1) offers a few extra goodies that are worth knowing about. Choose Insert ➜ Web Component or click the Web Component button on the Standard toolbar to open the Insert Web Component dialog box. Then scroll to the bottom of the Component Type list. As long as your ISP has installed the Microsoft FrontPage Server Extensions, you can take advantage of the Expedia Components, MSN Components, and MSNBC Components.

Select one of the component types and double-click a component on the right side of the dialog box to enter it on a Web page. Following is a rundown of the components you can insert:

Link To A Map   A link that opens a map to a specific location. The map is generated at Expedia.com. When a visitor clicks the link, he or she goes to Expedia.

Static Map   A map of a real location. The map appears on the Web page.

Search The Web With MSN   A text box for searching the Internet by way of the MSN search engine.

Stock Quote   A box for looking up stock quotes.

Various Stuff From MSNBC   Headlines and weather forecasts from MSNBC.

Up Next

At this point, you should feel quite empowered by the various applications FrontPage has allowed you to add to your Web site. Ad banners, hit counters, and user registrations are all examples of advanced technologies that, without FrontPage and its extensions, would be expensive and complicated to set up and manage.

Before we leave our discussion of sophisticated techniques and move on to scripting technologies such as DHTML and JavaScript, we have to study one very important factor in Web design. Designing across the variety of browsers is a challenge that all designers wish there was an easy answer to. It's a complex issue, and one that demands exploration so that you can make informed choices as to what kinds of technologies will be most appropriate for your audience. In Chapter 16, you'll take a close look at browser issues.

Cross-Browser Design

FRONTPAGE

Chapter 16

This chapter covers what different browsers do, what the differences between browsers are, and how to decide who to design for. Some browsers support proprietary features that other browsers don't support—we'll tell you about them. We'll tell you what to do if you want to design for the lowest common denominator. We'll take a look at designing for text-only browsers. And we'll delve into one of the hidden drawbacks of FrontPage: the Internet Explorer–only tags that FrontPage doesn't warn you about. Topics include:

- Designing two versions of a Web site

- Browser-supported features

- Features to avoid

- How to test your site in different browsers

Who's Surfing the Web?

The average visitor who comes to your Web site is probably surfing the Web using a PC with a 28.8 or 36.6 modem. Your average visitor is a middle-class man who can afford a decent computer, probably a Pentium, although possibly not the fastest one on the market. The screen resolution of his computer is most likely set to 640 × 480 or 800 × 600 (whichever resolution was set at the factory), with 24-bit color. He's probably using a version of Internet Explorer, although it might not be the latest version. The hip sister of this fellow is just as likely to drop by. Her computer is a Pentium with Windows 98, 1024 × 768 screen resolution, and millions of colors. And she is using a super-fast DSL connection.

There's a 50-50 chance that the next visitor to your site will be like one of these individuals, but the makeup of the rest of your audience probably falls between the two extremes. Your next visitor could be a teenager surfing on her older brother's abandoned black-and-white Mac Plus, with a 9600 baud modem, using the Lynx Web browser. The visitor after that could be an Internet security expert chugging coffee while she visits your site from a decked-out SGI workstation, using dual T3 lines to download your site lightning fast, and using a browser that just became available for download this morning. And the next visitor could be an 80-year-old physicist and great-grandfather whose browser reads the text on your site aloud while he waters his plants.

After you've designed your pages and put them online, it would be a shame if a large sector of the Internet population isn't able to see them. You already know that your audience is one of the most important considerations to keep in mind during the design process. And your audience comprises not just people, but people with a variety of computing platforms and browser software. These differences in hardware and software affect—in large and small ways—what people see when they visit your Web site. This chapter looks at the ways to make your Web pages accessible to the greatest number of people.

 At the time of this writing, Microsoft is still working on Internet Explorer 6. By the time you read this book, it should be available. Be sure to check up on Internet Explorer 6 to find out which features it does and doesn't support.

What to Design For?

When you're deciding how to plan your Web site, you should be aware of what the browser market looks like, so that you'll know what features to include and exclude. The design decisions you make will probably be based, for the most part, on what kind of audience you're trying to attract and how niche-y that audience is. If you're trying to attract cutting-edge technocrats who decide what's hot and what's not, accommodating people who surf the Web with outmoded software probably doesn't matter to you. On the other hand, if you're designing a site for an audience of die-hard Macintosh users (teachers and graphic designers, for instance), your site needs to look good on Macintosh browsers.

Under certain circumstances you can be sure about the makeup of your audience. If you're designing for your company's intranet, for example, you know which software the staff uses to access the intranet. For that matter, you may have some say in which browser the company chooses. If you're designing channel content, you're probably aiming for the Internet Explorer 5.5 audience or the Netscape NetCaster audience, and you don't need to worry about backward compatibility because people with older software don't look at channels anyway.

Other than the few instances in which you design for a limited or narrowly targeted audience, a wide range of people will visit your site, each with a slightly different combination of software and hardware. It's unlikely that every person who visits your Web pages will use the same platform, monitor resolution, color depth, browser version, and browser settings.

Who uses what kind of software is not simply a matter of being computer-savvy; it's a question of socioeconomics. Many, many people access the Web using public computer labs in schools, universities, and libraries. Many others live in remote areas where costs of computer technology advances are prohibitive. Some machines are outdated and don't have enough RAM and disk space to accommodate new software toys that come down the pike.

Figure 16.1, Figure 16.2, and Figure 16.3 demonstrate how the same Web page can look different when viewed through different Web browsers. Notice in particular how tables and fonts are displayed in Figures 16.1 and 16.2 compared to Figure 16.3. Figure 16.3 shows the unfortunate results of viewing a Web page in a text-only browser. All three figures were shot on a PC with a screen resolution of 800 × 600.

- Figure 16.1 shows the page in Netscape Navigator.

- Figure 16.2 shows the same page in Internet Explorer.

- Figure 16.3 is the attempted view according to Lynx.

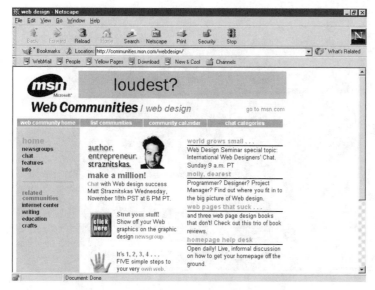

Figure 16.1 *The page as seen in Netscape Navigator*

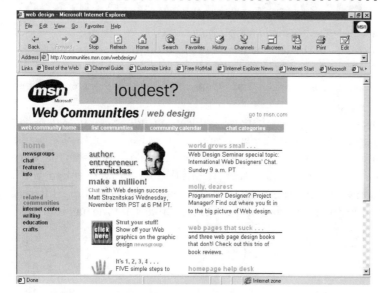

Figure 16.2 *The page as seen in Internet Explorer*

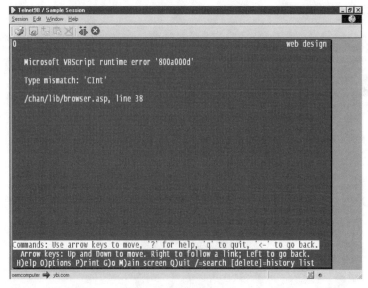

Figure 16.3 *The page is inaccessible in Lynx.*

Who Has What? (And What to Do about It)

But what kind of software *do* people have?

According to BrowserWatch, an organization that tracks browser software usage and popularity, about 68 percent of Web surfers use Internet Explorer, 18 percent use Netscape Navigator, 4 percent use Opera, and the other 9 percent is distributed among other browsers.

However, at last count there were at least *60 different versions of Navigator alone* floating around the Web, as well as 36 versions of Internet Explorer, and 50-odd other browsers besides. If you count international (foreign-language) versions of Netscape Navigator, and the beta versions that haven't yet expired, you approach 200 versions of Navigator alone. All of those versions of all of those different browsers have slightly different views of the Web, and that's not the half of it.

Mastering What's Online

BrowserWatch collects data only from people who visit BrowserWatch's home page, so it's not a scientific survey by any means, although it is a popular benchmark. You can visit this site at `browserwatch.internet.com/`. To view browser statistics at BrowserWatch, go to this address: `browserwatch.internet.com/stats.html`.

You can find many more browser surveys on the Internet. To find them, start at the Yahoo! index of browsers at `www.yahoo.com/Computers_ and_Internet/Software/Internet/World_Wide_Web/ Browsers/Browser_Usage_ Statistics/`.

Five elements come into play when determining what a Web page looks like on a computer screen. Take into account these elements as you design your Web pages:

Resolution   Some computers are 640×480, most are 800×600, others are 1024×768, and still others are 1280×1024. What's more, some Unix workstations are capable of much higher resolutions. Handheld computers, laptops, and very old computers use lower resolutions.

Color depth   Some computers and most printers are black and white, most Windows computers use 256 colors, and newer computers use 16-bit (thousands of colors), or 24-bit (millions of colors).

Platform   Macintosh browsers do look slightly different from their Windows counterparts; graphics are much brighter and tend to dither better, but the font sizes are much smaller.

Browser types   Each browser has its own ideas about what the Web should look like. There are many other browsers (aside from Navigator and Internet Explorer), including Opera, udiWWW, Arena, Amaya, GNUscape, AOL's browser, Lynx, and Mosaic, to name a few. Also, there are text-to-speech browsers, Braille readers, telephone-based browsers (they exist!), and people using Lynx across a Telnet connection.

Individual preferences   All browsers are customizable. People can change the font and font size of text (and sometimes even headings), change the background color of Web pages, decide whether to display images, and impose their preferences in other ways.

With all these different browsers, software platforms, and other variables, what (and who) do you design for? You have these basic options:

- Create a lowest-common-denominator Web site that everyone can view without any trouble.

- Create a site that's compatible with most versions of Navigator and Internet Explorer, and let the rest eat cake.

- Create a site that uses the newest, fanciest features you can come up with, and ignore the majority of Web visitors.

- Use JavaScript to "sniff" out which browser is visiting your site, and deliver any one of numerous styles for each type of browser.

- Allow text to be resized for visitors who are nearsighted.

Oh, there's another option, a nice middle-of-the-road option that offers greater flexibility and makes sure that all the people who visit your Web site get what they want: Create a design to your tastes and make an accessible main page where people can choose to download a text version of the site. This is kind of a "high potency" and "lite-site" option.

Throughout this chapter, you'll see which features are available to which browsers, so that once you decide whom to target, you'll know what you can (and can't) include in your Web designs.

Creating Multiple Versions of Web Pages

To accommodate more Web surfers, creating two versions of your Web pages, one for advanced browsers such as Internet Explorer and Netscape Navigator and one for the rest, is a good idea. The lowest-common-denominator pages would not include ActiveX, style sheets, plug-ins, Java, JavaScript, DHTML, or any new tags and features; the high-tech pages could include just about anything you care to put on them.

If you decide to produce two versions, consider implementing a custom script that detects which browser a visitor has and sends the browser a page it can read. Many sites employ browser-detection scripts that determine whether to send heavy-duty, high-tech versions of Web sites. The script runs ahead and finds out what version of which browser (called *client software*) is requesting the page. Then it sends the appropriate version of the page.

How these scripts are written and handled depends on the server software you're running and what you want to do with your site. Some of these scripts can be implemented with JavaScript, some with CGI scripts. Of course, these scripts aren't foolproof. Some browsers send no information about themselves. Some even misidentify themselves!

Mastering What's Online

If you're looking for scripts, Matt's Script Archive is a good place to start. His scripts are popular and work well. Matt's script collection includes a browser-detection script and links to similar scripts. Point your browser toward `www.worldwidemart.com/scripts/`.

Browser Wars: Who Does What

By now, we hope you've downloaded the *other* browser—if your favorite is Netscape Navigator, get a copy of Internet Explorer, and vice versa. By studying your pages in each browser, you can align tables better, make sure images look just right, and handle text size. On the other hand, if yours is a low-end site (or an alternate, low-end version of your site), you need to know exactly what you can and can't have on your pages.

When you're making a site (or a version of it) that can be used by as many people as possible, knowing exactly what the older (and still popular) browsers are capable of helps a lot. Table 6.1 shows the FrontPage features that different versions of Netscape Navigator and Internet Explorer support.

Table 16.1 FrontPage Features Supported by Netscape Navigator and Internet Explorer

	NN1.1	NN2	NN3	NN4+	NN6*	IE1	IE2	IE3	IE4	IE5+
Absolute Positioning				✓	✓				✓	✓
ActiveX Controls					✓			✓	✓	✓
Animated GIFs		✓	✓	✓	✓			✓	✓	✓
Background Colors	✓	✓	✓	✓	✓	✓	✓	✓	✓	✓
Background Images	✓	✓	✓	✓	✓	✓	✓	✓	✓	✓
Banner Ad Manager		✓	✓	✓	✓			✓	✓	✓

Table 16.1 continued FrontPage Features Supported by Netscape Navigator and Internet Explorer

	NN1.1	NN2	NN3	NN4+	NN6*	IE1	IE2	IE3	IE4	IE5+
Browser Plug-Ins		✓	✓	✓	✓			✓	✓	✓
Channels									✓	✓
Comments	✓	✓	✓	✓	✓	✓	✓	✓	✓	✓
Custom Font Colors		✓	✓	✓	✓	✓	✓	✓	✓	✓
Custom Font Sizes	✓	✓	✓	✓	✓	✓	✓	✓	✓	✓
Custom Font Faces		✓	✓	✓	✓	✓	✓	✓	✓	✓
Forms	✓	✓	✓	✓	✓	✓	✓	✓	✓	✓
Frames		✓	✓	✓	✓			✓	✓	✓
Hover Buttons		✓	✓	✓	✓			✓	✓	✓
Inline Audio/Video			✓	✓	✓			✓	✓	✓
Java		✓	✓	✓	✓			✓	✓	✓
JavaScript		✓	✓	✓	✓			✓	✓	✓
Marquee							✓	✓	✓	✓
Page Transitions									✓	✓
Style Sheets				✓	✓			✓	✓	✓
Tables	✓	✓	✓	✓	✓		✓	✓	✓	✓

There is no Netscape Navigator 5.

Downloading Different Browsers

Netscape and Microsoft charge nothing for downloading their browsers. You can get the software over the Internet for free. Likewise, you can download the Opera and Lynx browsers for free. To download the programs, go to these Web sites:

- **Netscape Navigator** home.netscape.com/download
- **Internet Explorer** www.microsoft.com/windows/ie
- **Opera** www.opera.com/download
- **Lynx** www.falconlynx.com/html/download.htm

Netscape Navigator Features

As Table 16.1 shows, each edition of Navigator greatly expanded the browser's capabilities. The second edition's improvements included frames, Java, JavaScript, animated GIFs, and the introduction of browser plug-ins. Netscape Navigator is still the only major commercial Web browser to include inline support for VRML, and version 6 supports such design innovations as style sheets and layers.

Designing pages that work for the latest version of Netscape Navigator (or Internet Explorer) means that you'll reach a cutting-edge audience, but a lot of educational and public markets still use earlier versions of Netscape Navigator, which doesn't support frames or most high-end gizmos.

Many of Netscape's innovations, such as those in its mail and news programs, don't affect the way your pages will look. Others, such as security features, may affect the way your pages act, and security is one reason why many merchant sites advocate using Netscape secure servers and Netscape browsers. Internet Explorer has caught up with Navigator's security features, so non-beta versions of either browser are generally safe for Internet commerce and other secure transactions.

Microsoft Internet Explorer Features

Microsoft Internet Explorer seemed to be just another Navigator until version 3, which introduced such special effects as ActiveX, designing with font faces and style sheets, and the use of inline frames (also called *floating* frames or *borderless* frames). Microsoft put in more of a browser presence than anyone expected, because free copies of Internet Explorer version 1 shipped with most versions of Windows 95; later versions of the software have shipped with Windows 95 and 98, the Office suite of software, and various other Microsoft CDs.

An alliance between Microsoft and Apple, which included the bundling of Microsoft Internet Explorer with new Apple System Software, and the widely ballyhooed appearance of Internet Explorer as an integral part of Windows 98, have people even more convinced that the software giant is taking control of the browser market. In fact, by a 2 to 1 ratio, more people use Internet Explorer than Netscape Navigator.

Users with old software who hit Microsoft's (fully customizable) Microsoft Network home page after a new version of Internet Explorer is released are instructed to download the new software. The upgrade message is much stronger from Microsoft than it is from Netscape, although both companies' home pages are good examples of designing for both new and old software.

After version 3, Microsoft earned new respect from people who thought that the mammoth company had started too late to be competitive in the browser market. Some of this respect was also tied to the close compatibility of Internet Explorer with FrontPage.

Navigator vs. Internet Explorer: What to Do?

In the past two years, Internet Explorer surpassed Netscape Navigator as the most popular browser, and now the Explorer users outnumber Navigator users by 2 to 1 or higher in some surveys. Overall, both browsers' capabilities are pretty similar these days, except when it comes to tables. The browsers display tables a little bit differently, so a well-designed page can look pretty ugly in the "other" browser, if you're not careful.

When you're designing a site that's "optimized" for one browser or the other, rest assured that most folks are not going to shut down their browser and launch a different browser just to view your site. They're going to mumble to themselves that it probably looks just as dumb in the other browser, look at the content you're offering to decide whether to continue, and keep surfing as usual.

Be sure to check your design in both Navigator *and* Internet Explorer before you launch it. Generally, a little fine-tuning of margins, table settings, and colors renders the display differences negligible, at which point you're free to advocate whatever browser you choose.

Generally, you would do well to give up the idea of total control that some of the more vocal big-deal Web designers endorse. Your pages are going to look different in different environments; you just need to aim to make them look as decent as possible.

If you'd like more details about differences between Macintosh and Windows platforms, and Navigator and Internet Explorer browsers, see David Siegel's page about Browser Offsets at www.dsiegel.com/tips/wonk14/.

Just as Netscape pioneered such things as tables, frames, and plug-ins without so much as a by-your-leave from the standards committees, Microsoft is just as guilty as Netscape for introducing extensions ("IEisms"?), though with greater negative effect. Netscape's introduction of the BLINK tag was merely annoying, and if you couldn't see the blinking words, you weren't missing anything. On the other hand, Internet Explorer 2 introduced several extensions that were incompatible with other browsers, and that the World Wide Web Consortium had no intention of adopting. Of these, <MARQUEE>, <BGSOUND>, and page margins are the most notorious. (Other introductions by Microsoft, like the OBJECT element for embedding different types of information, and the IFRAME element for inline frames, work fine in newer non-Microsoft browsers and are totally supported by the W3C.)

Other Browsers (Including Lynx)

Dozens of other Web browsers are on the market. One relatively popular browser is Cyberdog, which works with the Macintosh. AmigaVoyager, for the Amiga platform, still has a steadfast following, and a handful of others, including Ibrowse, IBM Web-Explorer, and Opera, still haven't fallen off the map.

Most important of all, however, is the fact that Lynx, a text-only browser that is available for nearly every platform under the sun, is still more popular than one might think. People with very low modem speeds (less than 14.4Kbps) can happily wander the Web using Lynx, as can people in countries scattered around the world whose bandwidth scares them away from the graphical Web. Many public terminals in libraries and cyber cafés support Lynx. Lynx is one of the best choices for anyone with a VGA or other black-and-white monitor. Newer versions of Lynx do support both tables and frames (although not everyone has the very latest version of Lynx installed, either).

What People Might Miss

So, people have different machines and different software, and somewhere in Minnesota is a cranky old man surfing the Web at 2400bps with a Web browser built out of twigs, kite string, and gum wrappers. But what does it mean, exactly, when people can't "see" your pages? Do their Web browsers send back a message that says, "That's too high-tech for me?" Not exactly. Do their computers freeze up and die? Yes, sometimes—particularly if your pages are infested with Java and other high-tech gizmos.

Mostly, though, your pages just look different from what you intended. What's so bad about that? Well, suppose your entire site is designed with tables, and Bob in Boise doesn't have a browser that supports tables. He'll see the data scattered all over his page. Or suppose your entire site depends on the background image (please consider adding more content than that to your pages). Some browsers don't load images at all, much less background images, and many people with slow connections have turned off auto-image loading. You need to decide how to present your content in the best-looking way possible to the majority of your target audience.

Tables, Frames, and Style Sheets

Tables have improved flexibility in page design more than any other HTML extension. While some browsers still have problems displaying them properly, you can generally assume that your visitors have access to tables.

So many designers construct poorly executed frames-based pages that a lot of Web surfers hate frames passionately—not to mention the many people who don't have a newer version of Navigator or Internet Explorer handy. Some folks find frames just plain confusing. People who don't know their way around frames sometimes have problems linking to or bookmarking parts of a frameset.

If you're going to make a frames-based site, it's almost always a good idea to make a nonframes version available as well. If a user tries to visit your frames-only site with an older browser or text-only browser, a message will appear saying something like, "This page uses frames, but your browser doesn't support them."

You can easily create a nonframes page that includes links to all the files in the frameset. People can visit and read the nonframes page the old-fashioned way.

Also, if you're going to use style sheets—which boost your speed in designing an entire good-looking site—you need to grab some old browsers to view your site, to ensure that it won't look anemic in the many browsers that don't support them.

Active Content

Users without newer browsers can't view active content such as Java, JavaScript, ActiveX, DHTML, plug-ins, inline multimedia, and the like. So many plug-ins and helper apps have flooded the market, the initial fervor in which many people loaded their browsers with every plug-in around has significantly cooled. Many people maintain their versions of Shockwave, RealAudio, and QuickTime, but few people bother to download every new media item that comes down the pike.

As with frames, it's a good idea to make versions of your site available that don't necessarily depend on Java, JavaScript, or multimedia to get the job done.

FrontPage's Internet Explorer–Only Features

While FrontPage makes it easy to add almost any available feature to your Web pages, it doesn't point out which of these features work only with Microsoft's own browser, Internet Explorer.

Keep in mind that FrontPage features are not necessarily Internet Explorer–only features. Some FrontPage elements work only with servers on which the FrontPage Server Extensions have been installed, but they work nonetheless with most any browser. These features include many of the FrontPage components, including scheduled images and page inclusions, form handling and script confirmation fields, and hit counters. (FrontPage components are covered in Chapter 15; forms are covered in Chapter 14.)

These features, as well as themes, run properly only on FrontPage servers, but they work fine with most browsers.

See Table 8.1 in Chapter 8 for a list of features that require the FrontPage Server Extensions.

Other features that only FrontPage can supply, however, can be viewed properly only with Microsoft Internet Explorer. These currently include all ActiveX/Active Platform components and most of the DHTML effects. While Netscape Navigator can handle some ActiveX (if users install a plug-in) and manage its own brand of DHTML, earlier versions of Netscape Navigator (and Internet Explorer) can't play or view ActiveX controls or IE-style DHTML at all.

JavaScript and VBScript create other interesting browser-specific problems. JavaScript was developed by Netscape; VBScript by Microsoft. Either browser can theoretically handle either language, but code that was written and tested only on one browser often performs erratically when used by the other. In other words, if you create a page that uses JavaScript and test it only with Internet Explorer, Navigator users may find their browser crashing or their machine's performance slowed down by nonstandard or buggy code that worked fine in your version of Internet Explorer. (The reverse is also true.)

It's important to keep in mind that JavaScript doesn't work at all for browsers other than Navigator and Internet Explorer, or older versions of those browsers (Navigator 2 and Internet Explorer 3 are the oldest versions that support it). Also, JavaScript has better backward support in Navigator versions. IE's support for JavaScript didn't fully mature until version 4.

Java, too, only works with newer browsers (Navigator version 2 or later; and Internet Explorer version 3 or later). The FrontPage hover buttons require that a Java applet be inserted on the page. You may not be able to check and see if it works at all until you load your site onto the Web, but if you use hover buttons, you should check its performance (and download time) in both Internet Explorer and Navigator. (That goes for any Java applet, of course.)

In general, Web developers are getting away from using Java on their pages. Java applets typically take time to download, and there are more elegant, cross-browser methods of delivering animations and other effects such as with JavaScript and DHTML.

Problems with the Marquee Tag

In online forums about FrontPage, the most common "problem" people ask about is why their MARQUEE tags don't work with Netscape Navigator. The answer to this is not a problem with Navigator, but with the MARQUEE tag itself. Microsoft introduced the MARQUEE tag as an answer to the scrolling text found in the status bar in early Netscape JavaScript and to the marquee boxes created with simple Java applets.

In Internet Explorer, the marquee text scrolls across the screen. In other browsers, it just sits there—no harm done really, but not very exciting. The detriment of the MARQUEE tag not scrolling isn't much greater than the BLINK tag not blinking, but it still frustrates people who go to the trouble to put it on the page.

Using the MARQUEE tag isn't fatal, but for many folks it isn't very thrilling either, and it isn't standard. A lot of people get very frustrated because their special effects don't work, which proves that taking the time to find out what browsers can do before you get set on special effects that don't work is worthwhile.

Testing, Testing, One, Two, Three

As we've said throughout this book, testing your pages before, during, and after putting them up on the Web (or on your corporate intranet) is imperative. Aside from making sure that your links work, your images are in place, and your pages do what you think they're going to do, you need to test your pages in different environments to make sure that they perform consistently.

Previewing in Different Browsers

When you press the Preview In Browser button on the Standard toolbar (or press Ctrl+Shift+B) for the first time, the *default browser* launches. The default browser is the one that you first installed on your computer or you selected as the default.

FrontPage allows you to preview your site in Internet Explorer, Netscape Navigator, or any other browser that is installed on your system. At the very least, use both Internet Explorer and Navigator to preview each page. Previewing with Lynx isn't a bad idea, either.

The Preview In Browser Dialog Box

If you generally use the Preview button on the Standard toolbar to load your pages into the browser window, you may not be aware of all the available options. The Preview button launches your default Web browser. However, if you use a browser apart from the default to preview pages, the page you want to see will load in that browser next time you click the Preview button.

Follow these steps to preview a Web page in more than one browser:

1. Choose File ➜ Preview In Browser. The Preview In Browser dialog box appears (see Figure 16.4).

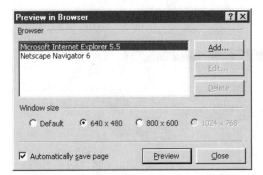

Figure 16.4 *Use the Preview In Browser dialog box to look at your pages in several different Web clients.*

2. Choose a browser from the Browser list.

3. Click the Preview button.

Get in the habit of previewing Web pages in at least Netscape Navigator and Internet Explorer on a regular basis.

You can set the window size of the browser window before you hit the Preview button. In the Window Size area of the Preview In Browser dialog box, click one of the buttons labeled 640 × 480, 800 × 600, or 1024 × 728 to emulate the window size for those screen resolutions. Selecting Default will leave your browser window size the way your browser remembers it from the past.

Getting Other Browsers into FrontPage

The easiest way to help FrontPage detect the browsers on your system is to install them *before* you install FrontPage. Now, you're probably reading this *after* you've installed

FrontPage, so you'll be relieved to hear that you can also add browsers to FrontPage's preview list after installation.

After you've installed an additional browser on your system, follow these steps to get FrontPage to recognize it as a preview option:

1. Open FrontPage, if it's not open already.

2. From the menu bar, select File ➜ Preview In Browser. The Preview In Browser dialog box appears.

3. Click the Add button. The Preview In Browser dialog box appears:

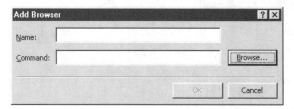

4. Click the Browse button. The Add Browser dialog box appears.

5. Locate and select the executable (`.exe`) file of the Web browser and click the Open button. Back in the Add Browser dialog box, you see the path name of the browser you chose in the Command text box.

6. Type the name of the browser (e.g., Lynx, Mosaic) in the Name text box.

7. Click OK. The Preview In Browser dialog box reappears, and you see the name of the new browser in the Browser box.

8. Click Preview if you want to go ahead and preview a page in the selected browser, or click Close to close the Preview In Browser dialog box.

You can keep adding browsers as you see fit. When you delete a browser or upgrade from one version of a browser to another, FrontPage will *probably* detect the changes. "Probably" is the operative word. You might want to double-check by doing a quick preview after you upgrade. If FrontPage doesn't get it, you can repeat the steps above to select the new version of your browser.

If you'd like to remove a browser from FrontPage's list of available browsers, open the Preview In Browser dialog box, select the name of the browser to be removed, and click the Delete button. To change the name or location of a browser in the Preview In Browser dialog box, open the dialog box, select the name of the browser in question, and then click Edit. The Add Browser dialog box appears, where you can make changes to the name or command line (path name) of the browser. Unfortunately, you cannot edit or delete browsers automatically detected during the installation by FrontPage.

You may have an older version of Internet Explorer on your computer that was automatically installed by either Windows 95 or another software program such as Office. Search your hard drive (Start ➜ Find ➜ Files or Folders) for files called `iexplore.exe` (Internet Explorer 1) or `ie20.exe` (Internet Explorer 2). If these browsers are still on your drive, you may as well add them to your preview list so you can check for backward compatibility.

Testing in Other Environments

Even if you have access to only one computer, you can certainly ask your friends to look at your pages using their machines. This can be especially helpful if you're designing a site from inside the comfort of a high-speed direct connection. You might never know that your page takes an hour to download unless you talk to someone who has done just that over a 14.4Kbps modem.

Here's a checklist of test environments. This checklist describes how to create an ideally accessible Web site. If you know your audience, you may not need to consider all of these items:

- Load your entire site using a 14.4Kbps modem. Would *you* wait that long to see your site?

- Check the number in the lower-right corner of the window—it is an estimate of how long this page will take to download using a 28.8Kbps modem. Is the time shown acceptable?

- Test your design against as many browsers as possible. Do the tables break? Are the images okay? How are the fonts?

- Resize your browser window a half dozen times. Does the site look okay in small windows? How fast do the images refresh?

- Look at your home page on a PC, a Mac, and a Unix (or Linux) workstation, using either Netscape Navigator or Internet Explorer (or both). How are the colors? Is anything horribly out of whack?

- Run all your Java and JavaScript past both Internet Explorer and Netscape Navigator. Does it all function smoothly? Did the browser crash or freeze? Now try it again on the *other* platform, either Mac or PC.

- If you have alternate pages (such as a no-frames or text-only version of your site), make sure that they work, too.

- View a sampling of your pages with Lynx. Can you follow all the links? Do all the buttons have ALT tags?

- Visit your site at least once from a computer other than the one you designed it on. Are all the images still there? Do all the links still work? Do the forms respond properly?

- Try out your site on a gray-scale monitor. Is it legible?

Even if you don't get a chance to test every single option on this list, make sure you pay special attention to older browsers, text browsers, and the "other" platform. Your users surely will. And if you pass the test, your users will thank you for putting the effort into remembering that they exist.

Up Next

This chapter has helped refine your sense of what is and isn't supported in the variety of Web browsers your site visitors might be using. While some of the guidelines in this chapter might appear to be tedious because they add more work to your already busy schedule, they make the right sense if you want to have a more sophisticated brand of Web site out there.

Now it's time to shift gears from technology and challenge your creativity for a bit by delving into Part III. Chapter 17 looks at the basics of visual design and how they apply to the Web—helping you create Web sites that are not just technically interesting and cross-platform, cross-browser compatible, but that look great, too! The subsequent chapters in Part III introduce you to professional graphics programs and show you how to combine your advanced design skills with FrontPage to build a site from start to finish.

Part III
Advanced Web Graphic Design

In This Part

Understanding
Advanced Web Design

FRONTPAGE

Chapter 17

Many people come to FrontPage with little or no design experience. FrontPage does a good job of addressing design needs by providing themes and helpful wizards, but everyone needs to understand a handful of key design concepts if they want to create customized, professional-looking Web sites.

Chapter 1 offers basic design guidelines. It shows how design elements are used on the Web. Other chapters, such as Chapter 6 and Chapter 9, examine how to use basic type principles and how to work with graphics.

But this chapter and the following chapters in Part IV depart from the basics of Web design and lead you into the realm of the professional designer. The idea here is to challenge you to think about the elements of design—space, shape, and color. In this chapter, you discover how to manage these elements within the context of FrontPage. Topics include:

- Working with space

- Understanding color

- Using shapes

- Adding typographic designs

Space

What is space? In our day-to-day lives, space is both the physical and emotional perception of room. In design, space is the absence of visual elements such as text or graphics. This absence of visual elements is referred to as *white space*.

Don't let the term white space *confuse you. It doesn't mean that the space in question is literally white. It can be black, or green, or purple, or even a texture. White space is what is left when no graphic or text element is there.*

We need space. We use it as a cushion upon which to rest our eyes. Space is necessary to help lead us from one element to another or to help separate elements logically and attractively from other elements. Space is part of what makes a section of text readable; what makes a graphic interesting within the larger design; what makes a design flow naturally, without restriction.

Here is an interesting paradox: While space is the absence of certain visual elements, it is an element in and of itself. What this means in simple terms is that you need to think about and use space as conscientiously as you do *all other elements* on your Web pages.

The next handful of pages demonstrate how to gain the space you need.

Margins

Margins pull text and objects away from the sides of the screen—the virtual walls—of the page. Margins provide white space on the left, right, top, and bottom of a page. The white space of the margins is necessary to help the page be more friendly and approachable.

If you're creating a site in which tables are not the primary layout method, you need to ensure that the margins are set correctly. You can do this in a number of ways—with blockquote tags, margin attributes, and style sheets. Read on.

Blockquote

The *blockquote* tag offsets the text from the edge of the browser. The tag is an effective way of gaining precious margin space and is particularly useful on pages that are text-heavy, such as reports, research articles, and long FAQs.

The blockquote element is not part of the HTML 4 strict standard. It has been set aside in favor of style sheets, which create very effective margins, as you'll soon see. Style sheets, however, are unpredictable even in contemporary HTML 4 and later browser versions. Using the blockquote gives standard HTML pages the margins they need. Popular browsers will have no trouble interpreting them.

We advise using blockquotes to manage text margins whenever you don't use tables. Figure 17.1 shows a standard HTML page without blockquotes. Notice how the text runs from one end of the visual field to the other. In Figure 17.2, by contrast, the blockquote is in use. Notice the nice margins on either side of the text. The page looks better and is easier to read, too.

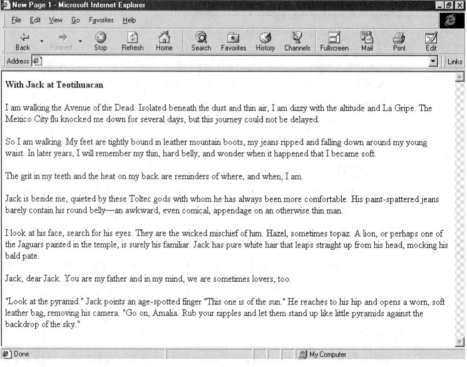

Figure 17.1 *With no margins, text runs to the extreme ends of the browser window.*

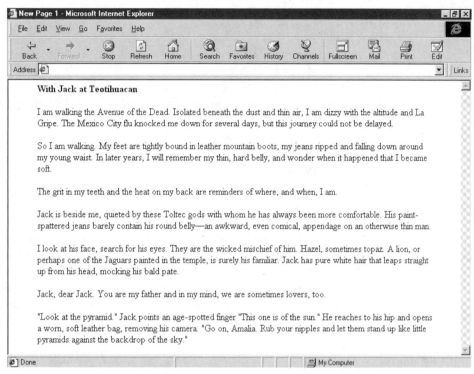

Figure 17.2 *Margins help a page look better and make it easier to read, too.*

Follow these steps to add blockquotes to your text:

1. Open the page in Page view.

2. Switch to HTML mode by clicking the HTML tab at the bottom of the Page view window.

3. Go to the top of the page, where your text begins, and enter the HTML tag: **<blockquote>**

4. Go to the end of your text and enter the HTML close tag: **</blockquote>**

5. Choose File ➜ Save.

6. Preview your work by clicking the Preview tab in Page view.

White space appears to the right and left of the text. Looks a *lot* better, doesn't it?

Here's an example of FrontPage code with the blockquotes added:

```
<html>
<head>
<meta http-equiv="Content-Type" content="text/html;
  charset=windows-252">
<meta name="GENERATOR" content="Microsoft FrontPage 2002">
<meta name="ProgId" content="FrontPage.Editor.Document">
<title>New Page 1</title>
</head>
<body>
<blockquote>
<h3>Web Graphic Formats</h3>

<p>
There are two dominant and useful file types used on the Web, the
  GIF and the JPG (also known as JPEG). Understanding the
  difference in how these file formats compress data is extremely
  key in ensuring that the end product is speedy and attractive.
  Furthermore, there are special considerations regarding each
  format.</p>
<p>
For example, GIFs can be transparent, interlaced, or used to
create
  animations. JPGs can be progressively rendered, and enjoy the
  distinction of using a compression method that does not reduce
  the number of colors in an image.</p>
<p>
<i>Are there other file formats that can be used on the Web? The
  answer is yes, but they are either limited in that they require
  a plug-in to view with the browser, or only a few browsers
  support them inline. One such file, the PNG, has received some
  attention in recent months. But PNG is Not ready for prime
  time.</i>
</p>
<p>How and when to use each of these types of files is critical
to
  optimization, as you will soon see.</p>
</blockquote>
</body>
</html>
```

Suppose you want to further offset text within a blockquoted section of text. To do so, *nest* the tags. Nesting simply means to place another set of open and close tags around a section of text within a blockquote. Take a look at this code:

```
<html>
<head>
<meta http-equiv="Content-Type" content="text/html;
  charset=windows-252">
<meta name="GENERATOR" content="Microsoft FrontPage 2002">
<meta name="ProgId" content="FrontPage.Editor.Document">
<title>New Page 1</title>
</head>
<body>
<blockquote>
<h3>Web Graphic Formats</h3>

<p>
There are two dominant and useful file types used on the Web, the
  GIF and the JPG (also known as JPEG). Understanding the
  difference in how these file formats compress data is extremely
  key in ensuring that the end product is speedy and attractive.
  Furthermore, there are special considerations regarding each
  format.</p>
<p>
For example, GIFs can be transparent, interlaced, or used to
create
  animations. JPGs can be progressively rendered, and enjoy the
  distinction of using a compression method that does not reduce
  the number of colors in an image.</p>

<blockquote>
<p>
<i>Are there other file formats that can be used on the Web? The
  answer is yes, but they are either limited in that they require
  a plug-in to view with the browser, or only a few browsers
  support them inline. One such file, the PNG, has received some
  attention in recent months. But PNG is Not ready for prime
  time.</i>
</p>
</blockquote>
```

```
<p>How and when to use each of these types of files is critical
to optimization, as you will soon see.</p>
</blockquote>
</body>
</html>
```

Now the margins on either side of the center paragraph are larger than they are elsewhere on the page (see Figure 17.3). There's a lot of nice white space here that adds to the visual interest of the page. Using blockquotes this way is exactly what you're after when formatting pages that are text-heavy. However, don't overuse the blockquote. Apply it once to the primary text area and then use it sparingly to emphasize specific passages of text.

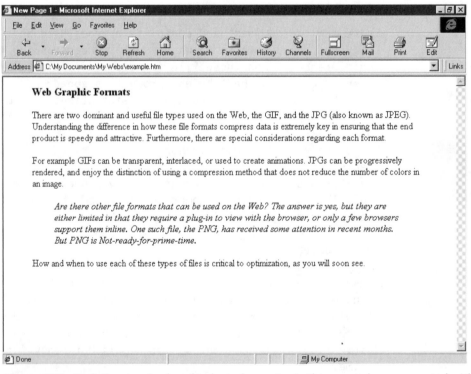

Figure 17.3 *Both the standard and indented margins in this example were created with the blockquote.*

Margin Attributes

A handful of Internet Explorer–specific attributes allow you to set margin controls within the <BODY> tag. These options are worth using when you know that your audience is only using Internet Explorer—perhaps in a corporate intranet, where the software is consistent across the network.

 If you're designing for Netscape Navigator or other browsers, the <BODY> tag attributes discussed here will not work.

One of the best aspects of margin attributes is that they can be used to set top margins as well as margins on the left and right sides of the page. Even if you're using tables for layout purposes, you can control the margins around the table.

Here are the four Internet Explorer-specific attributes:

- **bottommargin** Fixes a certain amount of white space, in pixels, on the bottom of a page.

- **topmargin** Sets the margin at the top of the page.

- **leftmargin** Provides margin space on the left side of the page.

- **rightmargin** Provides margin space on the right side of the page.

Interestingly, FrontPage 2002 only provides a tool to add topmargin and leftmargin. If you want to use bottommargin or rightmargin, you have to add them manually by following these steps:

1. Open the page of interest in Page view.

2. Right-click and choose Page Properties on the shortcut menu. The Page Properties dialog box appears.

3. Click the Margins tab (see Figure 17.4).

4. Check both boxes and add a numeric value in pixels for your top and left margins.

5. Click OK.

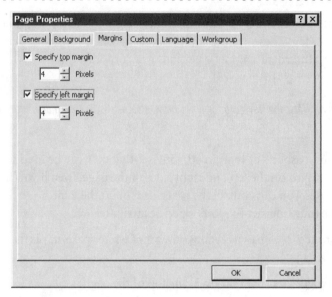

Figure 17.4 *The Page Properties dialog box*

FrontPage adds the following information to the opening <BODY> tag on the page:

```
<body topmargin="100" leftmargin="100">
```

Now follow these steps to add a bottom or right margin:

1. In Page view, click the HTML tab to see the HTML code for your page.

2. Find the opening BODY tag, position the cursor next to the last margin attribute and value, and press the spacebar once to add a space.

3. Enter **bottommargin="value"**, where *value* is a numeric value in pixels.

4. Press the spacebar to enter another space, enter **rightmargin="value"**, where *value* is once again a numeric value in pixels.

Your screen should look something like this:

```
<body topmargin="100" leftmargin="100" rightmargin="100"
   bottommargin="100">
```

Now, if you enter 100 as the pixel value, the entire page has a 100-pixel margin of white space around it when viewed in Internet Explorer (see Figure 17.5).

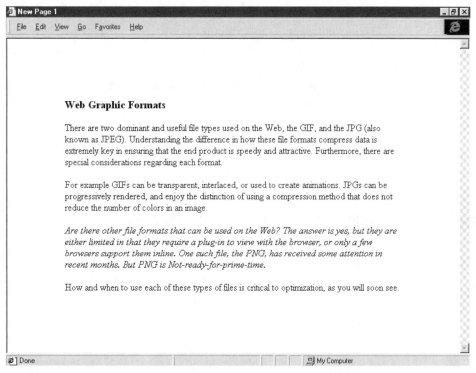

Figure 17.5 *Internet Explorer allows you to use margin attributes based in the* <BODY> *tag.*

Style Sheets

Style sheets are a way to add margins to a page, and they're growing in popularity because they offer the ultimate control. Not only can you choose values for the top, bottom, right, and left margins, but you can also choose among different ways of measuring margin sizes. Besides the standard pixels, you can choose pixels, points, inches, or centimeters.

Pixels are the default measurement unit for style sheets. FrontPage doesn't permit you to choose a different measurement type, but you can do it manually. We'll show you how shortly.

Chapter 13 explored all the types of style sheets that are available in FrontPage. The two types that we'll focus on here are *embedded* and *external* (or *linked*) styles. Following is a quick review of these approaches followed by instructions for changing margins by way of style sheets.

To control the appearance of every element on a particular page, you can use embedded style sheets, which are stored in a special HTML tag at the beginning of the page. Use the Format ➜ Style command to create or edit an embedded style sheet.

To use a single file to control the styles throughout your Web site, use external (also known as linked) style sheets, which are style sheets stored in separate files. The joy of an external style sheet is being able to update your Web site by changing just one file. An external style sheet must be linked to some or all of the pages on your site so that its effects are applied to those pages.

See Chapter 13 for a complete review of style sheets.

Whether you are using embedded or external style sheets, three style sheet properties are used to manage margins:

- **margin-left**   For a left margin, measure the distance in points (pt), inches (in), centimeters (cm), or pixels (px). The following sets a left margin to three-fourths of an inch: {margin-left: .75in;}

- **margin-right**   For a right margin, choose an options measurement and value: {margin-right: 50pt;}

- **margin-top**   For the top margin, use the same measurement values that you use for other margin attributes: {margin-top: 20pt;}

FrontPage assumes you want the measurement to be in pixels. If you want to use another measurement, simply change it manually.

Follow these steps to set up page margins by way of an embedded style sheet:

1. In Page view, choose Format ➜ Style. The Style dialog box appears.

2. In the Style list, choose the selector that you want to modify. In this case, BODY is an excellent choice because margin settings are applied to the entire body of the page.

3. Click the Modify button. The Modify Style dialog box appears (see Figure 17.6).

Figure 17.6 *Make style decisions in the Modify Style dialog box.*

4. Click the Format button and choose Paragraph on the drop-down menu. The Paragraph dialog box appears.

5. In the Before Text and After Text text boxes, enter the number, in pixels, of the right and left margins.

6. Click OK to close the Modify Style dialog box.

7. Click OK to close the Style dialog box.

8. Click OK and save your changes.

Click the HTML tab and you will see that FrontPage has added this style sheet code to the page:

```
<style>
<!--
body  { margin-left: 100; margin-right: 100 }
-->
</style>
```

Notice that the new code is added to the HEAD section of the Web page.

Now, follow these steps if you want to add the `margin-top` property or just change the value type:

1. With the page you just modified open in Page view, click the HTML tab to view the HTML code.

2. Place your cursor right after the opening curly quote in the style rule.

3. Type in the property and value you want.

4. Choose File ➜ Save to save your file.

Now that you know how to create an embedded style sheet that controls the margins of your page, you can create an external style sheet that you can use to control the margins of countless pages within your Web site. To create this style sheet, you will save it as a Cascading Style Sheet (a CSS file). Follow these steps:

1. In Page view, choose File ➜ New ➜ Page Or Web. The New Page Or Web task pane appears.

2. Click the Page Templates dialog box. You see the Templates dialog box.

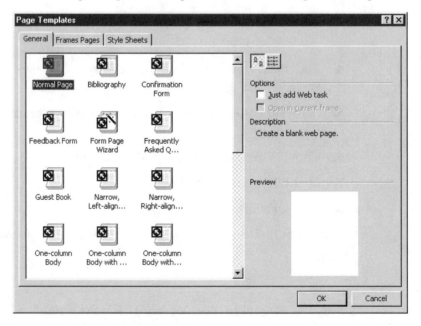

3. Choose Normal Page and click OK.

4. Manually type in the rulesets.

5. Save the file with a .CSS extension. To do so, choose File ➔ Save As, and, in the Save As dialog box, give the style sheet a name such as **margin-style.css**.

Your style sheet should look something like this:

```
body  { margin-top: 0; margin-left: 100; margin-right: 100 }
```

You can add many style sheet rules (syntax modifying a selector such as a paragraph, division, or spanned section of a page) to a single style sheet. We're focusing on the single rule that controls margins right now, but know that any style you want to add to the sheet can be added at any time.

Follow these steps to link the page to any pages in your site that require this margin style:

1. Open the page or Web site to which you want to apply the style sheet.

2. From the main menu, select Format ➔ Style Sheet Links. The Link Style Sheet dialog box opens:

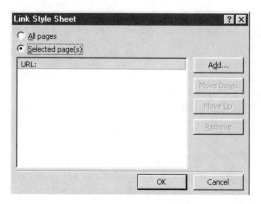

3. Choose how you want to apply the style sheet to your Web pages:

    All Pages Click this option button if you want to apply the style sheet to all of the pages in your Web site.

    Selected Page(s) Click this option button and, one by one, click the Add button and choose the pages in the Select Style Sheet dialog box. Each page you select appears in the Link Style Sheet dialog box.

4. Click OK. FrontPage now automatically links the style sheet to the pages you've chosen.

At this point, it's always a good idea to check your pages in different browsers to make sure the results you get match your intentions!

Graphics and Space

FrontPage offers several ways to ensure a nice balance of space beyond using margins. Putting space above, below, or to the side(s) of a graphic is always a wise idea. Figure 17.7 shows what happens when text and a graphic are too close together. This page is hard to read and is unprofessional as well.

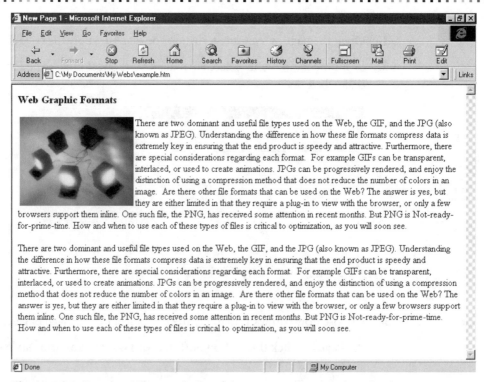

Figure 17.7 *Too close! The proximity of these page elements disturbs the eye.*

Small sections of text can be forced to the left or right of a graphic by using HTML code. Similarly, text can wrap around a graphic to create a flow of three elements of interest to the eye: type, image, and space.

Text that wraps around a graphic is referred to as *dynamic text*. This term shouldn't be confused with other uses of the word "dynamic." Dynamic text simply means that the text will wrap around nearby graphics when called upon to do so. How the text and graphic appear together on the page depends on the screen resolution of the computer—that's why they call it "dynamic" text. To fix graphics, space, and type, refer to the upcoming "Tables and Space," a bit later in this chapter.

To ensure that text flows well around a graphic, you can make use of three image tag (IMG) attributes and a variety of related values for each attribute. These attributes and values are as follows:

- `align=""` In this case, alignment values relate to vertical or horizontal alignment. Because you can choose only one type of alignment per image, we encourage you to be most concerned with the horizontal values of left and right. (See Appendix E for complete alignment options.)

- `hspace=""` Horizontal space takes a numeric value in pixels. Typically, somewhere between 5 and 10 pixels is necessary to gain the desired effect.

- `vspace=""` Vertical space corresponds to the image's placement on the vertical axis. As with `hspace`, it takes a value in pixels.

Follow these steps to examine how these attributes can be applied in FrontPage and what results are gained by using them:

1. Click the New Page button on the Standard toolbar (or press Ctrl+N) to create a new page.

2. In Page view, enter some text either by typing it or copying it from another Web page.

3. Click where you want to insert an image.

4. Choose Insert ➔ Picture ➔ From File and, in the Picture dialog box, locate and select an image.

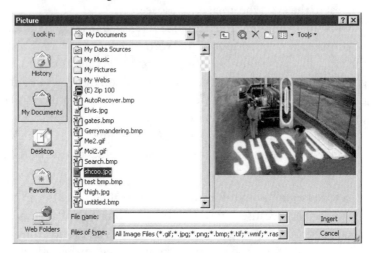

5. Click the Insert button. FrontPage inserts your image at the left margin.

6. Either double-click the image or right-click the image and choose Picture Properties on the shortcut menu. The Picture Properties dialog box opens.

7. If necessary, click the Appearance tab (see Figure 17.8).

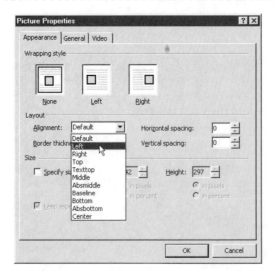

Figure 17.8 *Align images in the Picture Properties dialog box.*

8. In the Layout section, open the Alignment drop-down menu and choose an option. A number of options are available, but for text flow and space management, choose either Right or Left.

9. In the Horizontal Spacing box, enter a value, in pixels, of the horizontal space you desire. Doing so sets up the hspace attribute.

10. In the Vertical Spacing box, enter the value of your choice to add vertical spacing.

11. In the Border Thickness text box, leave the 0 to eliminate any disruption between the image and the text.

12. Click OK.

Now there is ample white space to distinguish the image from the text. This technique creates a sophisticated look and is easy on the eye (see Figure 17.9).

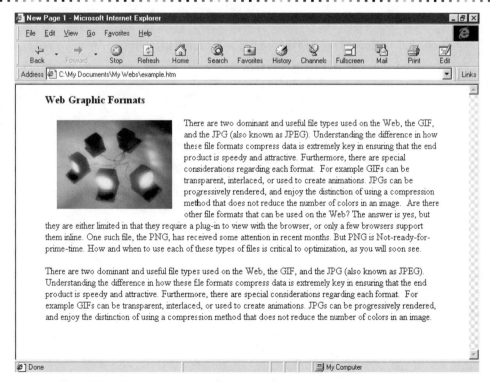

Figure 17.9 *Whew! More space, much easier to look at.*

After you insert an image, you can drag it to a new location on the page. Being able to drag an image is convenient, but you gain more control by managing the position of the image in the Picture Properties dialog box.

Tables and Space

Tables are especially handy for controlling and balancing a variety of elements on a Web page. When it comes to negotiating the eccentricities of different browsers and platforms, tables are the most effective method for handling space. To put space around your text and images and position images with precision, tables are the way to go.

Cell Padding and Spacing

Cell padding is the addition of space around the fixed parameters of a given table cell. *Cell spacing* determines the amount of space between table cells. By adjusting cell padding and cell spacing, you can put the right amount of white space around the content in table cells and thereby make your Web page easier to look at and read.

Is it necessary to use both cell padding and spacing? Of course not! Depending upon your individual needs, the choices you make will vary.

Follow these steps to create a table and adjust its cell padding and spacing values:

1. Choose File ➜ New ➜ Page Or Web. The New Page Or Web task pane appears.

2. Under New, click the Blank Page hyperlink.

3. Choose Table ➜ Draw Table. The Tables toolbar appears.

4. Click the Draw Table button and drag across the screen to create the outline of a table. You can now add as many cells and rows as you want using the options on the Tables menu.

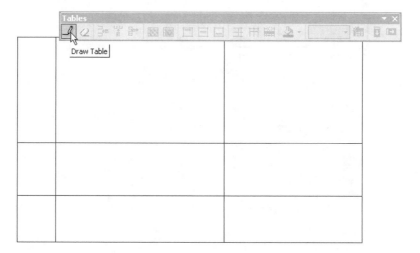

5. After you've drawn the table to your taste, choose Table ➜ Table Properties ➜ Table or right-click a table cell and choose Table Properties. The Table Properties dialog box appears (see Figure 17.10).

6. In the Layout area of the dialog box, enter a measurement in pixels in the Cell Padding text box.

7. In the Cell Spacing text box, enter a measurement in pixels.

8. Modify the table in any other way necessary to suit your design (see Chapter 11 for details).

9. Click OK.

You can now enter text and insert images in different cells. Cell padding will control the space between the elements in the cells and the table cell perimeter. Cell spacing will add space between cells.

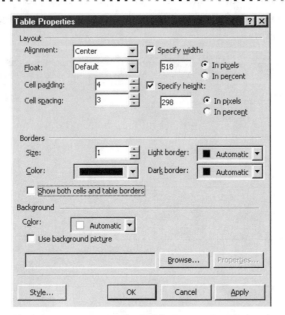

Figure 17.10 *Go to the Table Properties dialog box to adjust cell padding and cell spacing.*

If you're using borderless tables (and in most cases of layout design, you should be), you can always set the border to a value of 1 when you're working. This gives you an idea of exactly where your elements, space, and table perimeters are. Using the Table Properties dialog box, simply switch back to 0 when you're finished.

Single-Pixel GIFs for Width and Height

The good news about cell padding and cell spacing is that they represent a fast way to enter white space on a Web page. The bad news is that cell padding and cell spacing don't offer complete control over each individual area. The only way to control space with precision is to fix every cell element on a page. You can do that by fixing both the width of the table and the width of every individual cell. No cell padding or cell spacing is used, and of course, there are no borders.

To be precise about the amount of space between elements, insert a single-pixel GIF in a table cell and spread out the GIF to the desired width. This way, the width of the cell is fixed and the table can't be collapsed as the person who views your Web page changes the size of his or her browser window. Single-pixel GIFs require a lot of planning—and a little bit of math.

First, you need to decide exactly how many pixels wide your table is going to be. For a full-page layout, tables are typically set at 595 pixels. That's the recommended width to accommodate as many browsers and platforms as possible.

After you know the width of the table, have a look at the elements—graphics, text, and/or any other media—you want to include on your page. What exact widths are they going to require? It's a good idea to write all of this information down. For example, if we have an image that is 200 pixels wide and want that image placed to the right of any text, you have to subtract 200 from 595 to know what remaining space you have to work with, 395 total pixels. But say you want to put some space between the text and the image, maybe 15 pixels. Subtracting that from 395, you're left with 380 pixels for text.

At this point, you know you need three table cells as well, one in which to place the text (this cell is 380 pixels wide), another for the space (15 pixels), and another to hold the 200-pixel-wide image.

Draw the table by following these steps:

1. Choose Table ➔ Draw Table. The Tables toolbar appears.

2. Click the Draw Table button and drag to draw the outline of the table.

3. Click the Insert Columns button on the Tables toolbar twice. Now the table has three columns.

4. Right-click in the table and choose Table Properties on the shortcut menu or choose Table ➔ Table Properties ➔ Table. The Table Properties dialog appears.

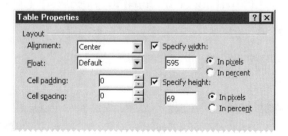

5. In the Layout section of the dialog, check the Specify Width check box if it's not already checked.

6. In the Specify Width text box (directly beneath the Specify Width check box), enter **595**.

7. Make sure that the In Pixels option button is selected.

8. Click OK.

Your table is now 595 pixels wide. Follow these steps to change the width of individual cells:

1. Right-click in the first cell and choose Cell Properties on the shortcut menu. The Cell Properties dialog box appears (notice that the Cell Properties dialog box is very similar to the Table Properties dialog box).

2. Check the Specify Width check box in the upper-right corner of the dialog box.

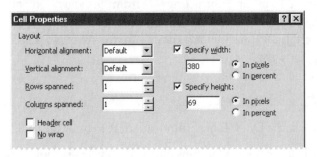

3. In the Specify Width text box, enter **380**, the width in pixels for the cell in the sample table.

4. Check the In Pixels option button if it is not already checked.

5. Click OK.

Repeat this process with each of the cells, specifying the exact width, in pixels, that is necessary for the layout of this page.

Notice the Specify Height option in both the Table Properties and Cell Properties dialog boxes. In any case in which you enter text on the page, do not specify the table or table cell's height. Reserve this option for those occasions when all of the cells in a table contain graphics—and then be sure both the width and the height of the graphic matches the width and height specifications of the given cell. In all other instances, make sure that the Table and Cell Height check boxes are unchecked.

In the example table, you can now add the text to the first cell and the graphic to the final cell. But what about the middle cell? This is where the single-pixel GIF comes in.

Using a transparent, single-pixel (1 × 1) image, you can invisibly fix the width of the empty cell so it doesn't collapse. Some browser types and versions are very fastidious with table cells—when they see a fixed-width cell, they respect it! But others are not so precise and may collapse the cell if there's nothing in it to hold it up.

To make a transparent GIF image, use your favorite image editor. In the editor, create a new single-pixel image. Fill the image with a single color (black or white is good) and export it as a transparent GIF. Your image file should be completely clear on any background or color. Typically, designers name this file `clear.gif` *or* `spacer.gif`.

You'll use this transparent GIF to hold the empty cell in place. In the example table, the cell is 15 pixels wide, but the GIF is only one pixel. Therefore, you have to modify the width of the image within the image tag by following these steps:

1. In Page view, click once in the cell where you want to insert the single-pixel GIF.

2. Choose Insert ➔ Picture ➔ From File. The Picture dialog box opens.

3. Find the GIF file and click the Insert button. FrontPage inserts the GIF into the cell.

4. Either double-click the GIF image or right-click it and choose Picture Properties. The Picture Properties dialog box appears.

5. Click the Appearance tab, if necessary.

6. In the Size section of the dialog box, check the Specify Size check box.

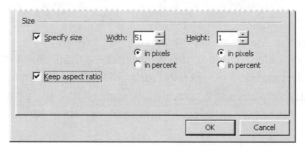

7. To the immediate right of the check box, you'll notice that the width and height values are filled in and read 1 and 1, respectively. Change the width *only*

to read 51 (or whatever the width of your spacing cell requires). Leave the height value at 1, and be sure that the In Pixels option button is selected.

8. Click OK.

You now have a table with fixed cells that will not shift or collapse. You've got text, an image, and your desired goal: space! You can use this technique to lay out almost any design. We highly encourage you to plan, fix, and lay out your advanced designs in this way.

Color

Color is as important to a design as the other major aspects—text, graphics, and space. Color creates a mood. It makes you think and feel at a deeper level. Color has undeniable psychological and social impact. If you want to think like a designer, think about color in terms of how it represents your site in an appropriate fashion. Here's a quote from color consultant J.L. Morton that sums up the importance of using correct color on a Web site:

> "Color plays a powerful role in that critical first impression—those first 5–10 seconds that either capture the viewer's attention and successfully communicate your message or fail miserably. Background colors and all link colors will either reinforce and enhance the site's theme or contradict it."

Suppose you're creating a site for a home-based resume and reports business. Your clients are in need of a professional, timely, precise, and neat service. How does color help or harm? Well, if you want to express precision and professionalism, you need a sedate color palette with muted earth tones or subtle blues. If you go with something too wild, such as neon green and yellow, or too soft, such as pastels, you won't project a neat and precise image for your business.

As you consider color, not only do you have to think about it carefully, but you also need to understand how color really works on the Web from a technical standpoint. The color utilities in FrontPage are helpful and can save you a lot of time and trouble, but without the proper knowledge, you can conceivably run into problems.

Mastering What's Online

Want to conjure up powerful responses to your Web sites? Visit J.L. Morton's Color Voodoo at `www.jiffyart.com/cvoodoo.html`.

About Web Color

In most aspects of Web design, the limitations that the designer faces make good design a challenge. With color, you're faced with many different variables—the visitor's hardware (computer, video card, monitor, and settings) and software (operating system and Web browser).

Never forget that Web color is derived from computer color. Computer displays manage color using a technology known as *additive synthesis.* Think of your monitor as having three little paint guns. One of these paint guns fires red, another blue, and the other green. Depending upon the needed color, the guns fire a certain amount of each at the screen, where the color is then displayed. In effect, the computer is *adding* color from its supply of red, green, and blue (RGB) to create any number of colors.

Depending upon an individual's hardware, anywhere from a handful to millions of colors can be displayed on the screen. Software such as operating systems and browsers can reduce or alter the way screen color is viewed. HTML also requires specific information to properly manage color.

In order to deal with all of these variables, the Web designer needs to know several important things. An awareness of the way computer color—and the resulting Web color—works is helpful. Understanding the way HTML interprets color and how to best work with that is imperative. Finally, because you are working with the restrictions born of an array of operating systems and browsers, understanding *Web-safe* color helps make sure that all your color designs are as stable as possible.

The amounts of red, green, and blue that go toward creating a single color are determined by a mathematical formula. In the formula, three numbers represent, respectively, the amount of green, red, and blue that are needed to create the color. For example, the formula 255 green, 102 red, and 0 blue create a certain color.

Web browsers require a standard way of measuring these colors so that HTML can recognize the numeric values and display the results to Web surfers. The numeric system that browsers use is known as *hexadecimal* (or just *hex*).

Recent browser versions do read RGB values without hex conversion. When working with Cascading Style Sheets, many designers—confident that if the browser can read the sheet, it can also interpret the hex code—use RGB values instead of hex. See "Controlling Color with Style Sheets" later in this chapter for an example of this approach.

Hexadecimal is the base 16 number system. Base 16 is an *alphanumeric* system, meaning that it uses both numbers and letters to represent values. Hexadecimal uses the numbers 0–9 and the letters A–F. You should always end up with a pair of three combinations (a total of six characters) for hex-based color.

You can figure out all RGB colors by converting each individual color from our standard decimal system to the hexadecimal system using a scientific calculator. Simply enter each individual red, green, and blue value and switch from standard decimal to hexadecimal. For example, enter 255 for green, and switch to hex mode. The result is FF. If red is 102, the hex number is 66. Blue is 0, and the corresponding hex number is also 0. Because a total of six letters is required, the value of blue is 00. The hexadecimal color is FF6600 (a bright red-orange, incidentally).

Using Safe Colors

It is important to understand what a Web-safe color palette is. Computers can read RGB and browsers read hexadecimal values best, but the number of colors that are really, truly safe to use from browser to browser, across platforms, and with different monitor color capacities is limited.

The so-called safe palette is made up of 216 colors. These colors have been determined to be the most stable colors as regards browsers, platforms, and the range of computer monitors and video hardware that Web surfers use. It's important to use the safe palette in almost all instances. Use a color from the safe palette and you can rest assured that your soft pastel yellow won't become neon yellow on some poor soul's system.

FrontPage is somewhat helpful in providing you with easy access to Web-safe, hexadecimal color. Its palette can be viewed as both limited or extreme, depending upon your take.

To understand what we mean, right-click any Web page in Page view and choose Page Properties on the shortcut menu. When the Page Properties dialog box opens, click the Background tab (see Figure 17.11). Select any option from a drop-down menu in the Colors section and you can choose a color from the standard color palette (or click More Colors to open the More Colors dialog box). If you choose an option on the drop-down menu, however, you run the risk of using an unsafe color, because Front-Page doesn't pay close attention to safe color in most cases.

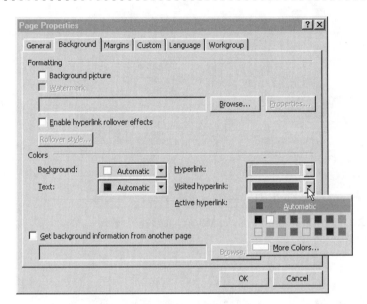

Figure 17.11 *A drop-down menu in the Colors section of the Page Properties dialog box*

If you choose More Colors, however, the More Colors dialog box appears (see Figure 17.12) and offers safe colors. This is good! However, not all 216 colors are available in the More Colors dialog box. This is bad—it means you have to put the lessons learned about RGB and hexadecimal color in this chapter to work rather than rely on a FrontPage utility.

After you know which colors you want for your Web pages, you can set up the pages using the More Colors dialog box. For each color option available to you, simply type the desired value in hex directly into the Value text box.

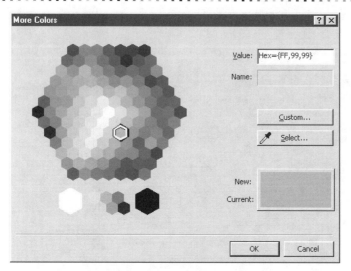

Figure 17.12 *While incomplete, the More Colors dialog box offers Web-safe colors.*

Using Color Intelligently

Earlier, we explained that color has psychological impact and that you have to use colors from the Web-safe palette when you choose colors for your Web pages. Your choices as far as color is concerned may seem quite limited. But the truth is that the Web-safe color palette can be empowering because it requires you, the Web designer, to think in precise terms.

First, you have to consider your goals carefully. Are you creating a home page for yourself or are you building a client site? Either way, you want to think about how colors best represent the expression you're after. If your client has chosen the colors, work from those colors to get a look and feel that is consistent with your client's goals. If you don't have much to go on, use your instincts and the information you've gathered from analysis (see Chapter 1). A conservative organization wants a conservative look—not neon greens and reds! Similarly, for a Web site that is energetic and on the edge, color can help you achieve that goal.

When you have a firm idea as to what you want to do with color, creating a custom palette for the site in question can be very helpful. To do this, simply choose up to seven colors for use in the background, in text, and in hyperlinks on the page. Then, either create a swatch of these colors by using your favorite image editor or make a list of the colors along with each one's name, its RGB values, and its hex value.

Controlling Color with Style Sheets

Style sheets offer ways of including color information on a site. You can control everything from backgrounds to links using a basic style sheet. If you're new to style sheets, we recommend looking into one of FrontPage 2002's style templates. You can use them intact or modify them as you please.

Follow these steps to work with style templates:

1. Choose File ➜ New ➜ Page Or Web. The New Page Or Web task pane appears.

2. Click the Page Templates link in the task pane. The Page Templates dialog box appears.

3. Click the Style Sheets tab. You see a variety of templates.

4. Choose the template of your choice and click OK. The style sheet appears on-screen.

You can now modify the style sheet by changing colors, removing undesired properties, or altering typographic elements. In the following section of code (a modification of the "Arcs" style template), notice how the style sheet uses RGB values to apply color to links and headers:

```
a:link
{
 color: rgb(51,153,255);
}
a:visited
{
 color: rgb(51,102,204);
}
a:active
{
 color: rgb(255,153,0);
}
```

```
h1
{
 font-family: Times New Roman, Times;
 color: rgb(153,153,51);
}
h2
{
 font-family: Times New Roman, Times;
 color: rgb(204,153,0);
}
```

You can use hex code instead of RGB in style sheets. Instead of RGB values in the a:link ruleset of the previous code, the hexadecimal style looks something like this:

```
a:link
{
 color: #3399FF;
}
```

Deciding which method to use is up to you. We prefer hexadecimal color because we believe it is safer across multiple browsers. However, FrontPage uses RGB, so if you're working in a FrontPage– and Internet Explorer–dominant environment, using the RGB method is a reasonable choice.

Be sure to visit Chapter 13 for helpful instructions about modifying style sheets and adding them to Web pages.

Shapes

Wander around the Web for a while and you will notice a variety of shapes. But if you watch carefully, you'll notice that one shape dominates the Web. The rectangle, by its nature, is the king of the Web. We view the Web through a computer monitor, which is a rectangle. The browser window is rectangular. The shapes we can create with HTML using tables or frames are all rectangles. So it makes sense for rectangles to dominate.

However, the dominance of rectangles is precisely the reason to think about other shapes! Using shape to create visual impact can really help set your Web site apart from the standard variety.

Shape, like color, has psychological impact. Here's a brief look at what primary shapes represent:

Rectangle   The rectangle represents stability, reliability, and longevity. If you're looking for a way to impress upon visitors that your product or company is there for the long-term, rectangles can help.

Circle   Circles evoke a sense of community, warmth, and wholeness. Circles are also considered feminine. If you want to make people feel at home or express a sense of strong ties, family, security, and safety, circles are the way to go.

Triangle   Energy, movement, and intensity are suggested by triangles. They are related with the masculine. Triangles are a great choice when you're suggesting progress and movement.

Want to mix your messages? Mix your shapes!

Playing with Shapes

Have some fun with shapes! Open your favorite image editor (see Chapters 9 and 18) and make shapes. Combine shapes. Fill shapes with color.

Another cool exercise is to take a piece of paper and cut a particular shape out of it. For example, cut a triangle out of a paper. Now, walk around your house, office, even an outdoor area, and look through the shape at the view. Move the shape close to an object, then far away. You'll begin to see how shape alters the way we see things. This exercise can help you gain a designer's-eye view of the world.

Using Graphics to Add Shape

So how do you get shapes onto a Web page? Primarily, by means of graphics. HTML can't handle shapes, although there are some unofficial DHTML methods of adding dimension or special treatments to page elements. For the most surefire method of adding shape to pages, rely on graphics.

Also, you need to start using the shapes that appear as the result of various images, including items from nature (a leaf, a cat's face) as well as items from the imagination. Any time you blend such an image with the flow of space, you end up with shapes!

So don't be limited—really get in there and work out your ideas. There are ways to combine the straight, flat edges of standard designs with interesting shapes. Figure 17.13

is a student project that combines the familiar left-margin navigation bar with the imaginative head of a dragon. Notice how the design is much more interesting to look at than a plain margin.

Figure 17.13 *A shape wrought from a standard and not-so-standard graphic.*

Type Tour

Chapter 6 introduced the important elements of Web typography. But now that you're beginning to think like a designer, it's important to mention how type plays a role in creating interesting space and shapes on the page. What's more, you can use color to add impact or interest to typographic designs.

The following visual examples from real Web sites demonstrate exactly how type can work to create designs with punch. Type in and of itself can become a fine art. And depending on your goals, you may employ type as a method of going beyond the simplistic into the realm of cutting-edge design.

Tiro Typeworks (see Figure 17.14) has a simple but effective approach to the design of its home page. There's nothing particularly overwhelming or difficult in what they've done—in fact, it's the simplicity of the design that makes it so effective. The beautiful headline text is in and of itself interesting to look at. The body font, which is standard Times New Roman, works well to provide a simple but compelling look.

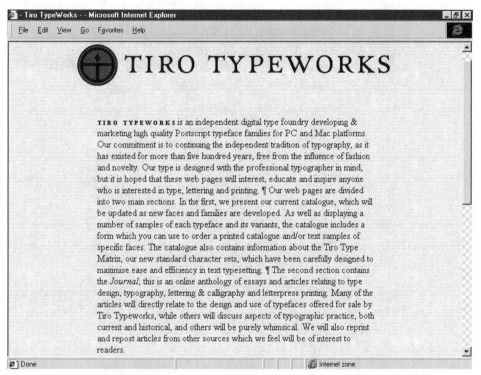

Figure 17.14 *Tiro Typeworks' understated and effective type design*

The designers had a little fun here. Notice that they entered paragraph marks (¶) instead of actual paragraph breaks to mark the end of paragraphs. This is not only clever, but an appropriate method of expressing the message of the Web page. The page is about type, after all.

Matthew George (see Figure 17.15), a personal branding firm in Oakland, California, approaches type, shape, and color in a confident and secure fashion. Pay special attention to the combination of serif and sans-serif titles.

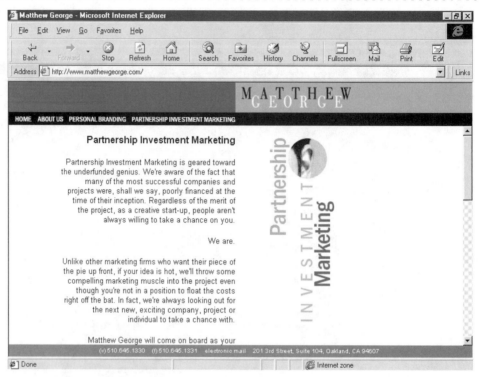

Figure 17.15 *Matthew George: type direction at work*

Especially important is the way the site uses direction to make the space, as well as the type, very exciting. The combination of confidence and movement are very appropriate for the site's intent: to market marketing! Potential clients feel that if they need rock-solid representation, it's there. But if they want to be more progressive, that option is available, too. Think about this design as a way to expand your options when designing with type.

Joel Neelen, a Belgian graphic designer, uses a great deal of edgy color, positioning, and type to achieve a very eclectic effect for his home page (see Figure 17.16). This example page demonstrates how designers can, in certain instances, take elements of design to the cutting edge and still manage to express ideas effectively.

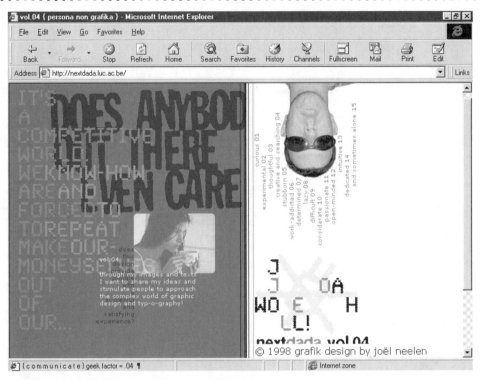

Figure 17.16 *Joel Neelen's edgy but fun home page*

Up Next

Now you're thinking like a designer! You have an understanding of what shape, space, color, and type mean to professional design, and you're ready to apply your ideas. Moreover, you're beginning to see how they each work together to create *design*.

While FrontPage 2002 helps you add these elements to your sites, developing an awareness of how these design elements work together takes your Web pages from the ordinary to the extraordinary.

To be truly professional in your approach, you also need to work in tandem with a variety of sophisticated graphic programs to gain the impact you're after. Chapter 18 surveys both the imaging and imaging-support applications that you need to make your design ideas real.

Working with Professional Graphics Programs

FRONTPAGE

Chapter 18

Chapter 9 introduced you to the programs that Microsoft offers along with FrontPage and the Office suite. Those programs can be very useful, but if you're looking for power and design on a par with professional graphic designers, you might decide to explore a variety of other imaging, illustration, and optimization programs.

Is it necessary to have professional tools to create high-quality graphics? Of course not. Tools don't make the designer. But newcomers to Web page design—especially those interested in taking their sites to the professional level—need to know how the pros do what they do.

If you're an experienced designer, much of the information in this chapter will be familiar. However, you may run across some gems that you'd not been aware of, so we encourage you to read it, and enjoy. Topics include:

- Imaging and illustration programs overview

- Macromedia Fireworks

- Compression utilities and filters

- Scanning techniques

- Tips for finding stock materials on the Web

- GIF animation programs

Understanding Imaging and Illustration Programs

To best understand the features of the programs mentioned throughout this chapter, it's good to know the difference between two important types of graphics: vector and raster.

Vector graphics These graphics are created mathematically in such a way that each plotted point relates to quantity and direction at the same time. When you create a vector graphic and save it for future editing in vector format (native format to a vector program, such as Illustrator), you can reopen and modify that file in terms of quantity and direction. Simplified: Within the vector application, you can make a vector graphic larger and smaller without losing quality, because you are simply altering the math involved.

Raster graphics A raster graphic is a bitmapped file. In order to be portable across platforms—and readable by Web browsers without special plug-ins—vector files have to be rasterized. You're probably familiar with raster graphics. They include BMPs, GIFs, and JPEGs. They use the x/y axes to create a predefined grid of information. The space in which they are created is specific in terms of quantity and direction. In other words, raster graphics are composed of a grid of colored dots. They can't be modified as elegantly as vector graphics.

Think about a grid. Color is placed in each of its little squares. It's a map of bits. Because a grid doesn't require the more complex mathematical statements of quantity and direction, raster graphics are fixed in quantity and direction. For that reason, they're larger and they're harder to modify. You can make them smaller without losing quality, but make them larger and you force each bit to stretch out, which results in blurry, blotchy graphics.

Programs that output and edit proprietary or popular bitmapped images are raster programs. Vector programs are more mathematically complex. Typically, the graphic results are much smaller than raster graphics. If file size is a concern for you, stick with vector programs.

Imaging and Illustration Programs for the Professional

If you want a career as a Web professional, you are expected to be familiar with Photoshop and Illustrator. These programs are the graphic-design industry standards for imaging and are used by most top Web design groups the world over. Photoshop is a raster program, whereas Illustrator is vector-based. As we describe their unique features, you'll see why this distinction is important.

Along with the esteem associated with these two programs comes a steep learning curve. While the interfaces are intuitive, to use Photoshop and Illustrator with speed and power takes time and care to learn. There's also the high price tag—around $500 per program for a single license. Yet there are ways of getting software at a discount (if you are an educator or a student, you'll find very affordable alternatives to shelf-priced software). Also, you can download demos of the programs in order to find out if you want to make a longer-term commitment to them. Adobe also offers Adobe Elements, a stripped-down, friendlier, and cheaper version of Photoshop.

The techniques with which graphics are created and manipulated are undergoing a change. High-end software developers such as Adobe and Macromedia recognize that Web designers don't need some of their offerings. So, in order to focus the applications environment and specific tools for Web design, new programs are being developed that are more sensible both for the individual working on the Web and for the budget-wise purchaser of these programs. The end result is a happy one: great new software that has the power and professional flexibility of its forebears, but with a price tag and learning curve that are much more attractive.

Adobe Photoshop

Adobe Photoshop is both a general graphic-design and Web-design industry standard. What this means is that if you plan on looking for employment in the design profession, you'll want to have Photoshop skills to be attractive to your potential employers.

Photoshop is extremely powerful—far beyond the scope of what is needed for the Web. However, a good user can quickly learn how to use Photoshop to maximize his or her design work.

Want to get the most Web knowledge from Photoshop? Check out Mastering Photoshop 6 *by Steve Romaniello (Sybex; January, 2001).*

There are many reasons why Photoshop is appealing and why you'll want to seriously consider it as a tool to demo yourself, with the intent to eventually purchase. First of all, being an industry standard, there's plenty of support for Photoshop—and plug-ins galore. Second, Photoshop is a raster-graphics program, which makes it easy to output Web-ready graphics. No need to mess with a vector program first, although you may want to use Photoshop in tandem with a vector program in order to get better control over shapes and type—which naturally can be altered much more easily without quality loss in a vector environment.

Layering

Another key component of Photoshop is the ability to work in layers (see Figure 18.1). While other programs such as Jasc's Paint Shop Pro have included layer functions in their imaging software, Photoshop has the most power and control. Essentially, you can create a file in Photoshop that contains different information on each layer, and save that file in native Photoshop format. Later, when you want to make a change to only one aspect of the design, you can simply go to the layer and change it. No need to redo the entire graphic.

Figure 18.1 *Working in Photoshop layers*

Layering is one of the reasons Photoshop is so extremely useful in professional design. Many times a client wants a color or text style altered. Using Photoshop, you simply go back to your initial files and make the change in the appropriate image layer. In Chapter 19, we'll look at some layout techniques that put you through your paces using Photoshop layers to maximize your work.

Specialty Features

With Photoshop, as with many raster-graphic programs, you can create transparent and interlaced GIFs. No need for extra tools—it's all right there in the software. Another feature that exists right within the application (versions 4 and above) is that the Web-safe palette we discussed in Chapter 17 ships with the program and requires no additional filters or plug-ins to work.

Not only can you create all kinds of standard graphics such as buttons and backgrounds with Photoshop, but you can scan art, photos, and objects directly into the program and use Photoshop to enhance and manipulate your work.

Photoshop offers a variety of powerful type options and filter features that allow you to quickly enhance your graphics with effects applied to the edges such as bevels, drop shadows, inner shadows, and light sources (see Figure 18.2).

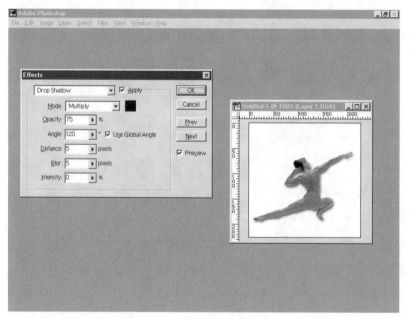

Figure 18.2 *Adding a drop shadow using Photoshop*

Mastering What's Online

If you're looking for Photoshop demos, support, and help, visit www.adobe.com/. You might want to check out other layer-based image editing programs, such as Jasc's Paint Shop Pro, available at www.jasc.com.

Adobe Illustrator

Illustrator is another Adobe program used by graphic design professionals that has an important place in the creation of professional Web graphics.

Unlike Photoshop, Illustrator is a vector-based program. This means that while it's not the most efficient tool for outputting Web-ready graphics, it allows you to create and work with graphics.

Remember: Vector graphics work on a mathematical principle that allows for changes in quantity and direction simultaneously. What this means in real terms is that if you want to take type and vary its direction with finer precision than you can get with a raster program, do it in Illustrator (see Figure 18.3). Using advanced intelligence within the program, you can create lines in the vector program and direct type along those lines. You can't do this with raster-based graphic applications.

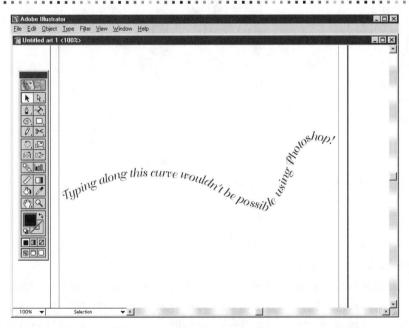

Figure 18.3 *Using Illustrator to set directional type*

Mastering What's Online

Demos, support, and information about Adobe Illustrator can be found at www.adobe.com/.

Because Illustrator is a drawing program, shapes are much more easily created and manipulated in Illustrator (see Figure 18.4). Illustrator allows you to draw shapes using the intelligence of vector graphics. You can create your own lines for the shape to follow or use several preset shapes that Illustrator provides.

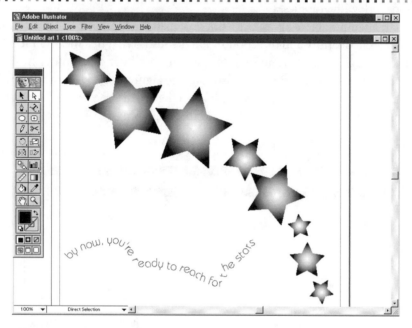

Figure 18.4 *Shapes in Illustrator*

Other Vector Programs

There are a variety of other popular vector-drawing programs. The two most common are Corel DRAW! (`www.corel`
`.com/`) and Macromedia's Freehand and Flash (`www.macromedia.com`). Interestingly, Flash is vec tor-based.
That's one of the reasons it requires a special plug-in—because the vector graphics have to be interpreted in order to
be visible within supporting browsers.

Macromedia Fireworks

Fireworks was specifically developed to give Web designers an easy interface to create Web-ready graphics, as well as provide specialty tools necessary to create great-looking Web sites. The program allows you to create image maps and slice graphics for positioning within tables. What's particularly impressive about Fireworks is that not only does it slice up your graphics, but it generates the appropriate table code. This makes your life with FrontPage so much easier, because you can combine the code generated from Fireworks with the page design you're working on in FrontPage.

An interesting fact about Fireworks: While you're working in it, you're working in vector format. However, because you can use Fireworks to export files to GIF or JPEG formats (which are raster graphics), in the end, Fireworks is really a raster program.

Suppose you have Fireworks and you want to use it to slice up a graphic so it fits properly on your page. Here's how you can begin to incorporate the Fireworks code into the FrontPage code:

1. Use Fireworks to create your graphic. To slice your graphic, select the Slice tool from the Fireworks toolbar.

2. Draw over an area you want to slice. Remember, slice wherever it makes sense to slice. Are you going to update a portion of the graphic? That should be a separate slice. Is another portion fitting precisely over a background? Fireworks helps you slice the page after you make your initial selection, creating a grid from your design (see Figure 18.5).

3. Choose File ➜ Slice Defaults. Select the default file types for the slices.

4. Click Save and Close.

5. From the main Fireworks menu, choose File ➜ Export Slices. Fireworks now exports the slices to a specific HTML file. It also saves the individual GIF files to a folder that you can specify—be sure it's the one where you're keeping the graphics for the FrontPage Web site you're working on.

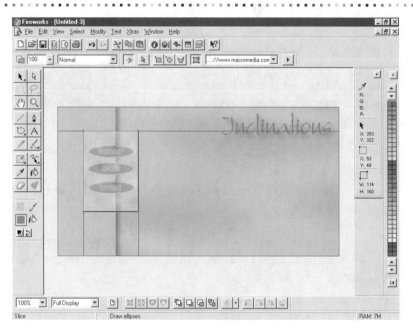

Figure 18.5 *Sliced areas in Fireworks*

Now that Fireworks has generated the necessary graphics and the HTML for you to copy into your FrontPage Web site, follow these steps:

1. Open the FrontPage Web page to which you'd like to add the table and associated graphics.

2. In Page view, open the specific HTML page where the table and graphics will go.

3. Select the HTML tab so you can see the code of the page.

4. Load the Fireworks HTML page into your Web browser.

5. Choose View ➔ Source. The source code appears (see the following "Viewing the Code from Fireworks" sidebar).

6. Look for the table section generated by Fireworks. Select the code with your mouse, and press Ctrl+C to copy it to the Clipboard.

7. Switch back to FrontPage. With the HTML code of your Web page open in Page view, paste the Fireworks code right into your FrontPage code.

8. Save your work.

Viewing the Code from Fireworks

You'll notice that the following code uses comment tags (tags that are hidden from the browser) to help you work with it easily:

```
<!------- BEGIN COPYING THE TABLE HERE -------------------------->
<!-- Image with table -->
<table border="0" cellpadding="0" cellspacing="0" width="297">
<tr><!-- spacing row, 0 height. -->
 <td><img src="images/test_00.gif" width="6" height="1" border="0"></td>
 <td><img src="images/test_00.gif" width="141" height="1" border="0"></td>
 <td><img src="images/test_00.gif" width="150" height="1" border="0"></td>
</tr>
<tr><!-- row 01 -->

 <td rowspan="2" colspan="1"><a href="http://www.macromedia.com">
   <img name="Ntest_01_01" src="images/test_01_01.gif"
   width="6" height="137" border="0"></a></td>
 <td rowspan="2" colspan="1"><a href="http://www.macromedia.com">
   <img name="Ntest_01_02" src="images/test_01_02.gif"
   width="141" height="137" border="0"></a></td>
 <td rowspan="1" colspan="1"><a href="http://www.macromedia.com">
   <img name="Ntest_01_03" src="images/test_01_03.gif"
   width="150" height="77" border="0"></a></td>
 <td><img src="images/test_00.gif" width="1" height="77" border="0"></td>
</tr>
<tr><!-- row 02 -->
 <td rowspan="1" colspan="1"><a href="http://www.macromedia.com">
   <img name="Ntest_02_03" src="images/test_02_03.gif"
   width="150" height="60" border="0"></a></td>
 <td><img src="images/test_00.gif" width="1" height="60" border="0"></td>
```

```
</tr>
</table>


<!-- This table was automatically created with Macromedia Fireworks -->


<!-- http://www.macromedia.com -->
<!-------- STOP COPYING THE TABLE HERE -------------------------->
```

If you've been careful to save the graphics to the correct directory, you should now be able to view your Web page, complete with the new graphics and code generated by Fireworks.

Other special features of Fireworks include the ability to create bevels and drop shadows with ease, as well as to create mouseover images and the JavaScript to go with them.

More from Macromedia

Aside from Fireworks, Flash, and Freehand, Macromedia makes several other programs that Web page enthusiasts are sure to want to learn more about. They include:

Macromedia Director   The Director Shockwave Internet Studio is the professional standard for creating and delivering powerful multimedia for the Internet, CD-ROMs, and DVD-ROMs. Rather than serving simple graphics and text such as you would find on a basic Web page, Director lets you combine graphics, sound, animation, text, and video into compelling content. For the Web, these presentations are delivered using the Shockwave player. Shockwave Web sites are highly interactive.

Macromedia Authorware   Authorware is a visually rich multimedia authoring tool for creating Web and online learning applications. It's especially useful for training developers, instructional designers, and subject matter experts to develop trackable learning applications and deploy them across the Web and on CDs.

Macromedia Flash   Flash is a tool for creating and delivering low-bandwidth animations. You can also use it to create Web site interfaces and training courses.

Macromedia Dreamweaver   If you like FrontPage, you might want to take a look at Dreamweaver. As with FrontPage, Dreamweaver integrates with other products in its family to create dynamic and interesting Web content.

Helpful Utilities

Whether as plug-ins compatible with your imaging and illustration software or as stand-alone applications, there are two kinds of utilities you will find very, very helpful: compression utilities and filters. This section talks about some of the best compression utilities and filters available, where to get them, and what kind of results you can expect when using them.

Compression Utilities

Compression utilities allow you to make very specific decisions about how to optimize your graphics. These utilities vie to make your files smaller for the Web, while keeping the best visual integrity possible. While you can use any raster imaging program to create GIFs or JPEGs, it takes a fine hand to do so with the best compression results. What's more, it's time-consuming!

Compression software can often make comparisons for you and help you decide which file format is best for the look you want. Furthermore, compression applications can batch-process numerous files at a time, making large jobs easy to manage. (Some programs, including ImageReady and Fireworks, include their own compression features.)

DeBabelizer Pro

Used in a variety of media applications including TV and multimedia presentations, DeBabelizer Pro is a very sophisticated optimization program that can be used to optimize and batch-process graphics for the Web.

Because DeBabelizer is such a high-end program, it's expensive. If you already have it, great. You can use it to optimize your Web graphics. But if you don't have it, we recommend first looking to some of the other easy-to-use and affordable options below. However, be aware that if you are looking for employment as a professional designer, you may be expected to have or learn DeBabelizer Pro skills.

Ulead SmartSaver

Ulead creates impressive products at very cost-effective prices. SmartSaver lets you do everything DeBabelizer Pro does for the Web but eliminates the overhead. In Figure 18.6, you can compare images to see which results will be most effective for your needs, and you can output batches of optimized files, too.

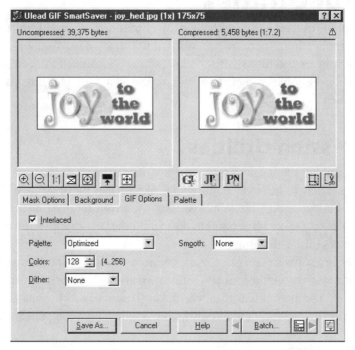

Figure 18.6 *Comparing images in Ulead's SmartSaver*

Optimization Tools

Downloads, tutorials, and support for our favorite optimization tools can be found at these Web sites:

DeBabelizer Pro: www.debabelizer.com

Ulead SmartSaver: www.webutilities.com

Filters

The way you present a graphic is as important as the graphic's quality itself. A well-processed image, while strong on its own, is rendered even more classy when enhanced with drop shadows, feathered edges, and geometric edge designs, just to name a few effects.

A *filter* is a small program, usually run right within your graphics program, that will help add these and innumerable other special effects to your page. Special effects can be achieved through the use of plug-ins to Photoshop or Photoshop-style imaging programs.

Alien Skin Software

A very popular suite of plug-ins, Alien Skin offers some cool filters including its Eye Candy and Xenofex packages. You can use Eye Candy with Photoshop and related raster-based programs to add shadows, glows, motion trails, jiggles, weaves, and water drops to your images. Examples of Xenofex's Baked Earth and Puzzle effects are shown in Figures 18.7 and 18.8, respectively; Figure 18.9 shows Eye Candy's Chrome effect.

Figure 18.7 *Xenofex Baked Earth effect*

Figure 18.8 *Xenofex Puzzle Effect*

Figure 18.9 *Eye Candy Chrome Effect*

Auto F/X

One of the best ways to make a Web site look polished is to enhance images with professional edges (see Figure 18.10). Auto F/X offers three wonderful packages of edge effects for photos. You can also create interesting type effects with Auto F/X's Typographic Edges feature.

Figure 18.10 *Adding an edge effect with Auto F/X*

Where to Get Graphic Filters

Use these helpful Web sites to get graphic filters and learn how to apply filter techniques:

Alien Skin: www.alienskin.com

Auto F/X: www.autofx.com

Scanning Techniques

Undoubtedly, you're going to want to scan photos, art, or objects at some point. Ideally, you'll be equipped with a good color flatbed scanner. They're very reasonably priced these days, and you should have no trouble finding one that will meet your needs.

And what might those needs be? Well, to start off with, scanners are excellent ways to get images from the everyday world into digital format. For the Web, this simply means good quality at low resolution. That's good news for your pocketbook. What's more, being able to scan images means not having to invest the time and energy needed to become a power user of Adobe products.

Scanning is simple, but scanning carefully means your results will be clearer, crisper, and more professional-looking. Here are a few basic scanning rules you should follow to help make your scans the best possible quality:

- Begin with your imaging software. Adobe Photoshop, Microsoft PhotoDraw, Microsoft Image Composer, Adobe ImageReady, and Macromedia Fireworks all allow you to scan images.

- Ever seen the acronym GIGO? It means "garbage in, garbage out." Ideally, all of your source materials will be of high quality to begin with. If your photo is blurry or your drawing has a coffee stain on it, these elements will be picked up by the scanner and make your job much more difficult.

- Your scanner bed should be free from dust and dirt. Clean it according to the manufacturer's directions.

- Similarly, your source material should be clean. Use any commercial canned air pack (available at office supply and most art stores) to dust photos without touching them directly.

- Graphics for the Web will always end up at 72 or 96 dots per inch (dpi). Many people like to scan at 300dpi and then reduce, claiming that this helps with quality. We're not convinced this is true, but try it and see if it doesn't work best. Either way, you should scan at 72, 96, or 300dpi and make sure your output image is set to 72 or 96dpi.

- After you've scanned your image, crop and size it accordingly. Use interesting cropping—perhaps a close-up of the face or eye is more interesting than the whole image itself.

- Add shadows, textures, edge effects, and other styles using filters for professional results.

- Always optimize your graphics properly. To do so, use one of the optimization applications discussed in this chapter.

Finding Stock Materials on the Web

Professional designers work from an assortment of stock photos, clip art, and type-faces, and there are many resources on the Web geared toward helping you achieve your goals of great-looking design. Whether you need professional-quality materials or are looking for good clip art for a personal site, you can always find what you need, right online.

If you're closer to the professional end of the spectrum, think about beginning a library of stock materi-als. For each project you do, write in the cost of a necessary typeface or photo set. Your client will foot the bill, and you can keep the materials for future use. If this sounds a bit awkward, remember that this is standard operating procedure for graphic designers—just be legitimate in your purchases.

Here are some recommended resources for your professional stock photos, art, and typographic needs:

- Adobe offers excellent typefaces at `www.adobe.com`.

- Eyewire houses an excellent line of quality stock materials including great clip art and fonts. You can get a regular paper catalog delivered via snail mail, or you can browse and purchase stock materials online at `www.eyewire.com`.

- Photodisc provides some of the cleanest, sharpest photographic images avail-able. A visit to their Web site, `www.photodisc.com`, will provide you with a shopping source for plenty of stock photos, backgrounds, and links to other sites of interest. Free membership entitles you to downloads of comp art and photos; you can also order a standard mail catalog.

- For an inexpensive alternative (albeit less professional in quality), check out ArtToday. For a very reasonable membership fee, ArtToday gives you unlim-ited downloads at `www.arttoday.com`.

If you're looking for casual, fun clip art, photos, backgrounds, and animations, you might try Caboodles of Clip Art, a perfect starting place for those new to design: `www.caboodles.com`

As with scanning, digital type and art demand that you work with the best images available; color, crop, and modify to suit your needs, and export at 72dpi.

GIF Animation Programs

GIF animations are extremely useful for a variety of reasons. Whether you're looking to spice up a page with a bit of visual intrigue or you need an animation for an online ad, you'll want to explore a variety of imaging programs that allow you to make GIF animations.

A few tips about working with animations:

- If you're considering using an animation on a page, stop and think first. What purpose does it serve? Is it really necessary?

- Too many items on a page that blink and move detract from rather than enhance a design. Stick to one animation per page, at most.

- GIF animations should still conform to small file size requirements. This means paying close attention to each individual cell of the animation.

- One way to avoid large file size is to restrict the number of colors to a handful and keep movement simple.

If you plan, design, and apply animations with care, you're bound to have excellent results. Of course, you'll need to have a great GIF animation program. Here's a few popular programs that you'll want to check out.

- GIF Movie Gear is an award-winning animation tool that has powerful palette control. This allows you to optimize each individual cell for maximum file optimization. Furthermore, it will throw out any repetitive colors or information.

- Ulead GIF Animator is another of Ulead's excellent, low-cost PC Web solutions. You can use it to create sweeps, fades, and fills without going to a lot of trouble to learn the program.

- GIF Construction Set is a popular shareware tool that will allow you to create animated GIFs using a wizard that walks you through the simplified process of creating an animated image. Advanced users can build individual images themselves.

Where to Get GIF Animation Tools

Use these Web sites to download GIF animation tools:

GIF Movie Gear: `www.gamani.com`

Ulead GIF Animator: `www.ulead.com`

GIF Construction Set: `www.mindworkshop.com/alchemy/gifcon.html`

Up Next

Now you're not only thinking like a designer, but you've got the tools to create professional quality design work. But how do you put this all together in the context of FrontPage? Not to worry—we'll show you how in the next chapter.

Creating Advanced
Sites with FrontPage

FRONTPAGE

Chapter 19

n the past several chapters, you've focused on understanding advanced design concepts and learning about a variety of tools that can help turn those concepts into reality. This chapter combines the lessons recently learned with the FrontPage knowledge you have gathered throughout this book and teaches you a process by which you can build your sites from start to finish.

At this point, it's important to look at the professional approach to site production. Even though some of this information is going to be familiar—we started you out with some of the same tips and tricks mentioned in this chapter—this time around we're going to give you the information in the context of all the things you already know. We'll take you from basic page creation to the development and management of Web sites on a refined level. Topics include:

- Pre-production planning

- Understanding your Web site

- Designing content

- Production and design procedures

- Post-production concerns and solutions

Pre-Production

The strategizing you do before you actually create graphics and use FrontPage to make your site come to life is possibly the biggest determining factor in the success of a Web site. The pre-production stage is where the critical issues of site intent, audience demographic, scheduling, procuring content, working with clients, creating a look and feel, planning technology, and building your site map are addressed.

Yes, that's a long list—as well it should be. It's very dangerous to go out into the wilds of the Web without understanding the reason you're doing a site and managing the procedural aspects of that site. This is especially true if your site has a commercial or promotional intent. If you fail to plan properly, there is no infrastructure upon which to build. Without a structure, the site is going to be more costly, time-consuming, and possibly more geared toward failure than success.

The best way to minimize risk is to *plan well*. We cannot overemphasize the importance of this phase! We've seen many instances where developers rush into the job only to find themselves spending a lot of time and money to go back and do it right. And, in all honesty, we've learned the importance of this by making the mistake of poor planning ourselves.

Understanding Your Web Site

As with any project, an understanding of the project's long- and short-term goals, general intent, and audience is necessary. Furthermore, there are issues surrounding scheduling and how to work with clients. In this section, we'll look at each of these issues in detail and give you insider tips on how to manage these first important steps in advanced site management.

Site Intent and Goals

What is your site's intent? In other words, what purpose does your site serve? If you're a typical Web surfer, you've visited many sites that seem to have no definite purpose or ideas to communicate.

From the get-go, you need to let your audience know who you are and what the site visitor will find on your site—and, of course, you need to give ample information about how to get from one place to the next with ease.

One reason why intent is often missing from a site is the failure on the part of the developers of the site to clarify their own goals before embarking on the design of the site. Developing a Web site takes time, and many people are in a rush to just get the site up and running. But whether you're designing a site for commercial purposes or for sharing pictures of your newborn baby, clearly understanding your specific intent is going to help you build a clear, concise site.

A good exercise is to take time out and brainstorm your site intent. If you're working with a group of people, schedule a few hours of meeting time—order lunch in and get a white board where someone can write down ideas as they are introduced into the conversation.

 If you are working in a company setting, refer to your existing business plan for guidance in terms of short- and long-term goals. Your company business plan is a powerful guide for your Web site intent— and, in turn, plans for your Web site can affect the company plan.

If you're working alone, take some old-fashioned tools (we like yellow legal pads and fine point pens) to your favorite spot—a coffee house or quiet outdoor area is perfect! The idea is to be in a place where you are comfortable and *away* from the computer. You want to be creative here and let the ideas flow.

Begin to talk or think about what it is you really want to *do* with your site. Begin with the short-term. Do you have a specific product you want to sell? Do you have a picture or sound file that you want to put on the Web? Maybe you have some ultra-sound pictures of your baby or audiotapes of the baby's heartbeat. Think about what you want and what you have right now. Write down everything that comes to mind, without thinking in orderly terms—there's time for that later.

Take a little break before moving on to the next phase: brainstorming long-term goals. The break is important because it will clear your head, and the long-term goals list is sure to serve you well. The information you gather regarding longer-term vision will help you determine how to prepare your site for future growth.

Sample Goal List

Here's a sample list of short- and long-term goals for a small company that sells handmade greeting cards and gifts.

Short-Term Goals:
- Showcase cards and gifts in our current inventory
- Add new real-time venues for our cards and gift items
- Sell inventory direct to online site visitors

Long-Term Goals:

- Add more artists and styles to our inventory

- Expand inventory to include other items, including T-shirts and hats

- Showcase the affiliated artwork of our contributing artists

From these simple lists, you can begin to see how this practice can clarify your site intent and plan. For the short term, you may find that you need space to show off current inventory; include a way to directly communicate with potential outlets; and include secure, online shopping for your site-based customers.

When you examine the long-term goals, you will see that you need to easily expand the existing Web site to include more inventory, diversify inventory, and finally, add an entire gallery section to show off the related work of contributing artists.

Consideration of short- and long-term goals not only helps visitors because your communicated intent is clear, but it helps you know how to design your site well from today's needs through tomorrow's vision.

Knowing Your Audience

Another critical step in the pre-production process is knowing who your audience is. We've made mention of this throughout the book, but now we're going to express in very clear terms just why this is so important.

Knowledge of audience, combined with site intent, creates the baseline from which *all decisions* you make about the look and feel, design, structure, and technology grow. Without this knowledge, the risk for failure is very high. This becomes especially true in team environments working under deadlines. Under a deadline, the risk is actually magnified rather than distributed.

Getting to know your audience is a complicated process. So how do you get to know your audience? Begin with what you have and what you know. Many businesses keep information about their customer base. If you're working in a situation like this, it's a great place to start—get out those statistics and write down exactly who has been buying or using your products and services. If your site is geared toward a personal page, it's still important to think about audience in general. Are children going to visit? Who do you really think is most interested in the site's information? Who definitely will *not* be visiting your site, at least intentionally?

Now, begin to question whether there are natural additions you can make to this existing group of people. For example, if your company has traditionally sold specialty auto parts to young males, it is possible that there are women online who might need or want to purchase these specialty parts? If the answer is yes, expand your demographic audience to include those women! Similarly, if you are putting up a site dedicated to the local bowling league, you might want to include information for bowlers outside of your geographical area. Any time you can expand your audience without straining your budget, you potentially add a new site visitor, client, or customer.

Finally, consider a demographics management program for your Web site. This is particularly important if you are doing electronic business, are managing an online community, or are in any way concerned about tracking where your visitors are geographically, what kinds of browsers and technology they are using, and how often they visit your site. Keeping statistical information like this will help you modify your site as the demographics change.

Setting Up a Schedule

Scheduling the construction of your site is important if you have a deadline to meet. You'll want to fairly address time concerns and allow for adjustments, changes in direction, and team members getting sick or taking vacations. Planning for risky situations can help minimize the problems you might encounter under heavy deadlines. And, even if you're on your own, setting up a schedule can sometimes help keep you organized and on track.

Schedules should be committed to. If you're working with a client, schedules should be written into the service agreement or contract. If you're planning for yourself, set your own goals and stick to them as best as you can.

There are many software products on the market that manage schedules. Users of FrontPage most likely have Microsoft Outlook as well. Outlook has excellent calendar-management capabilities. You can also use FrontPage's Tasks view to set up and manage tasks in a timely fashion.

Working with Clients

For those of you designing sites for others, working with your client(s) can be a joy and a headache! Here are some tips for client management that might help you out:

- *Always* treat clients with respect—and expect the same in return.

- Always keep the lines of communication open.

- Professional sites should be backed by a service agreement or formal contract. What's more, the contract should include wording to the effect that either party can cancel the contract. If a client proves troublesome, you need to be able to cancel the contract without jeopardizing your reputation or getting into a legal tussle.

- Be clear and specific about your goals and timeline.

- Be precise about milestone dates and payment—on both ends! The client will need to know what he or she must provide to you in terms of content, and you will need to turn that content into a product in a timely fashion. Billing statements should be sent out as previously agreed upon, and your client should pay on time.

- Always let a client know what you provide and what they will have to go elsewhere to get, and put this stuff in writing. For example, you should be happy to incorporate a pre-existing logo into a Web design, but you shouldn't design that logo unless you are getting paid appropriately and unless you are willing to provide this service.

- Provide clients with ample information and time to address needs. However, if a client is taking an unusual amount of time, clearly communicate boundaries in a supportive way.

- Know that sometimes the client is going to want to include design elements that you know are out of line or problematic. If a client wants you to do something that doesn't make good design sense, explain that in respectful terms to the client. If he or she still wants you to comply, try for a compromise. If all else fails, defer to your client.

- Never sell yourself short. Clients who pay less for professional work are often the ones who complain the most. Offer quality, honest, professional work in turn for fair and timely compensation.

- Meet your deadlines! If you see a problem with a deadline, be sure to communicate this to the client immediately, and make appropriate arrangements.

Good luck! If you have trouble with a client, or if you hire a company to work with you and your relationship with the company turns sour, remember that you may have contractual rights allowing for the termination of the business agreement. In the best-case scenario, your project will run smoothly, because both the client and you, the designer, understand exactly what is expected every step of the way.

Designing Content

After you have laid the groundwork and you have a clear idea of your site's intent, goals, and target audience, it's time to use this information as a means of determining how the site content will be designed.

What is content? It's a Web designer's term for the elements of a Web site, including text, images, and technology. "Designing content" means to organize the content in such a way that it works logically and aesthetically.

To design content, you need to examine how the site will be formally structured, how it will look, and what technology it will require in order to function properly.

Building the Site's Structure

Later in this chapter, we'll examine how to use FrontPage to set up your site. But first, you need to organize your content into logical groups.

Begin by collecting your content. Assemble all the materials you'll use for the site. You should gather up printed and electronic text, photographic materials, digital artwork, and any other information you require to make the site work.

Using the research you've done regarding intent and audience to guide you, study the content. You need to set up areas of your site—list each relevant area by topic. Suppose your son has asked you to do a site for his alternative rock band, Cat's Eye. In this case, you might include main topics such as member bios, tour dates, audio files, video clips, fan club information, and a guestbook for site visitors to sign.

After you have the main areas figured out, make a list of the content you want within each area, including the text, graphics, other media, and any necessary technology. Here's a sample table:

MEMBER BIOS	TOUR DATES	AUDIO	VIDEO	FAN CLUB INFO	GUESTBOOK
Charlie's bio	East Coast	All Too True	Cat's Eye	Special deals	
Demi's bio	West Coast	This Moment	In the Heat	Posters, hats, T-shirts	
Alicia's bio	Pacific Northwest	Now and Then			
Steph's bio	Europe	Get it Goin'			
Marcus's bio	Asia				

Study this table for a moment and you'll see how a site structure begins to evolve. All of the main topic headers become the primary level of navigation. Within those main topics, you might have either a page or several pages in a second tier.

For example, each of the member bios can form a second tier of information, as can the tour dates and fan club info, with each subtopic becoming a separate page. In the case of audio and video, not too much is available at this point, so a single page should suffice. However, depending upon the short- and long-term goals of the site, you may anticipate adding sections as more information becomes available, and as the audience demands it.

Now that your information is organized, it's time to think about how the site will be visually designed.

Creating a Look and Feel

What *is* "look and feel?" Well, this is a design term used to describe the visual sense of a site. It encompasses the many issues discussed in Chapter 17, including color, shape, space, layout, and type, and how all of these elements look together to send a visually based message to your audience.

Because you have critical information from your intent and audience analysis, you're in a good position to begin determining what your site should look like. At this point, you're still in the brainstorming phase—nothing is being committed to hard graphics or HTML yet.

Now is the time to seriously consider your audience and intent in the context of what look and feel is appropriate and effective. This can take an experienced visual designer—or, at least, it demands that you do some serious looking into the way professional sites are managed.

Suppose you're working with a church to help create a Web site. Your primary short-term goal is to offer information on clergy, schedules, and special events. Your long-term goal is to add a discussion forum where church members can seek support, discuss church directions, and ask questions on religious matters. The audience is the church's existing membership, but you want to make other local, potential members feel welcome. When your community is built, you want to encourage affiliate churches to become involved and in so doing create a non-geographical community with input from a wide range of members and clergy.

Because the church is conservative, a neutral color scheme is going to be important. We'd keep our use of shape to a minimum, with religious symbolism being the exception. Navigation would be simple, as many of the members might be older and not as computer-savvy as the younger members. Furthermore, contrast would be high—probably black type on a white background to accommodate everyone's eyesight. From a technology perspective, a light hand is probably best—adding supportive technology where necessary, such as to create the community forum. There should be no other media such as animation or JavaScript. If you do choose to use some subtle mouseover techniques to add a bit of color, just be sure to keep them very simple. All told, this site should be very easy to use and functional, not distracting.

Want inspiration? Go surfing! Start at your favorite search site, such as Yahoo! (www.yahoo.com) or Infoseek (www.infoseek.com), and look for sites that are similar in content and purpose to your own. Browse them and jot down notes. Which sites are strong? Which are confusing, and why? This experience will help you strengthen your ideas and avoid pitfalls.

Now, if your 19-year-old tattoo-loving, pierced son wants that Web site for his alternative rock band and comes to you for help, you've got a different story on your hands! A conservative, quiet, and mainly functional Web site isn't going to go over well with the audience here. You'll want to have some fun, be a bit wild in your color scheme, more liberal in your use of technology, more creative and inventive in terms of interface.

But does this mean that you won't approach the site with a process? Of course not! After all, this site could mean the launch of your son's successful music career. Sit down and go over the short- and long-term goals with him. Have him brainstorm with you. What is the site's intent? Who is the obvious audience? What about secondary audiences? Working through this process will ensure that your colorful and even edgy site will have the strong foundation it needs.

Sketching and Mocking Up Your Site

With the research you've gathered regarding site intent and audience, you can now begin to sketch out ideas and thereby take your Web site from the concept stage to the Web-page stage.

Gather your materials and study them hard. Now, instead of jumping right to the computer, it's helpful to the creative process to pick up a sketchpad and begin drawing the various sections of your site.

On many Web sites, a main page serves as the gateway through which all navigation of the site will occur. The *splash page*—a visual first page that sets the tone of the site but contains little, if any, textual information—is not necessary, but it is often helpful in establishing the look and purpose of the site. If you decide you want a splash page, begin by sketching out ideas for it. Be sure to include navigation related to each main topic area. Try out different ideas for this page before moving on to sketches for subsidiary pages. Don't worry about perfection here—the idea is to get your creative juices flowing and come up with some general ideas.

After you have a sketch that you really like, you can move to the imaging program of your choice (see Chapter 18). For this sophisticated level of design, we prefer using Photoshop, because we can place each element on a layer. However, other programs, including Paint Shop Pro, Fireworks, and ImageReady, allow you to work in layers.

Because the concept is a global one, we'll use Photoshop as our example, and you can adapt it to your preferred image editor's unique tools. Follow these basic steps to begin mocking up your site:

1. In your image editor, select File ➜ New. The New dialog box appears.

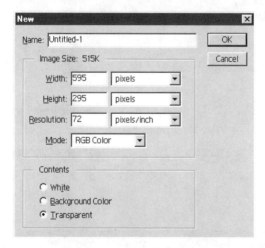

2. Create an image size that is no more than 595 pixels wide and at least 295 pixels high (the height will depend upon how long you expect the page to be; 295 is one screen) with a resolution of 72 in RGB mode. Be sure to select the Transparent button. (Note: This setup will vary from image program to image program.)

3. Click OK. Your work area is now set to the first layer.

4. To this layer, add your background color or design your background graphic look:

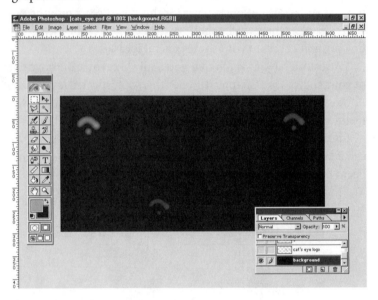

5. Now create a new layer by selecting Layer ➔ New ➔ Layer. On this layer, create the main logo or title, as shown next.

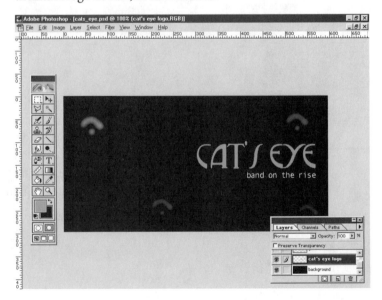

6. Add any navigation you'd like for this page. Typically, each button should be on its own layer (see Figure 19.1). This allows you more control later on. For example, if you want to duplicate the buttons but use a different color for mouseover effects, keeping each button on a separate layer allows you to do that.

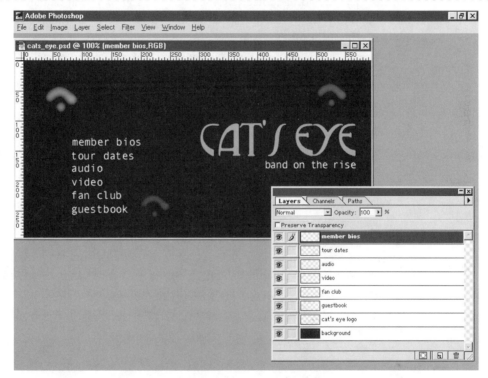

Figure 19.1 *Each of the navigation elements is on its own, individual layer.*

7. After you've added all the elements you want on this page, save the file by selecting File ➜ Save As. The Save As dialog box appears. Name the file and save it in the native layer format of your imaging program.

Do not merge the different layers just yet. If you do, you will not be able to go back and access the individual layers later on.

Try a variety of designs, and when you find one that satisfies you and your client's needs, go ahead and build the images using the technique just described.

Planning Necessary Technology

Another excellent point in the process of designing content is to list any particular technology you're going to need for the site. By doing so, you anticipate what you'll need to add to your production schedule and you help ensure that both your front- and back-end technology is in place.

If we examine the rock band example, we know immediately that we're going to need to support a variety of technologies including:

- Animation or JavaScript to add lively, interactive components to the site

- Support for audio

- Support for video

- A guestbook

While the church example is less technology-laden, it is still important to note that eventually a forum will be necessary to manage the community discussions. If Front-Page is the desired format for this, make sure that the host server offers FrontPage extensions. If another method, such as CGI, is desired, it's important to make that decision *right now*. If the site is built and then hosted on a server that doesn't support the technology you wish to add down the road, this could wind up costing extra money as well as placing time demands on everyone involved: site developers, site managers, and site participants.

Production

The production phase of creating a site is where you roll up your sleeves and go to work. You'll work back and forth between applications, including FrontPage and your imaging program. Depending upon your site needs, you'll work on the server-side to set up any scripts or other required elements (see Chapter 26 for details).

Production work is all the labor that gears you up to actually publish your Web site on the Internet. The following sections walk you through exactly what you need to do to make a site move from the planning phase, through production, and on out to the Web itself.

Setting Up Folders, Files, and Tasks

As you've worked through the planning of your site, you've collected a lot of important data and set up a powerful structure upon which to build your pages. Now it's a good time to turn to FrontPage and create the physical structure of your site. By doing so, you will generate a site map, which you can use as your guide for the future of the site's life.

Follow these steps to set up folders for your site:

1. Choose File ➜ New ➜ Page Or Web. The New Page Or Web task pane appears.

2. Click the Web Site Templates hyperlink. You see the Web Site Templates dialog box.

3. Select One Page Web, choose a folder for storing the Web site, and click OK.

FrontPage creates the necessary FrontPage and images folders. Follow these steps to create the additional folders you need for your Web site:

1. Click the Folders icon in the Views bar to switch to Folders view. You see the Folder List with your directories and files:

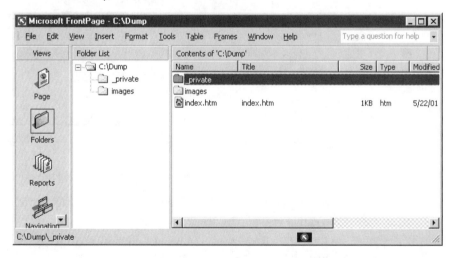

2. Highlight the root directory, the topmost directory in your Web site where the Index file is found.

3. Choose File ➜ New ➜ Folder. FrontPage adds an untitled folder.

4. Type a name for the folder.

5. Repeat steps 1 through 4 for each addition folder you need.

You can delete a folder that you do not want by right-clicking it and choosing Delete from the shortcut menu.

Now that you have created the folders you need, it's time to set up individual files by following these steps:

1. In Folders view, right-click anywhere in the interface. A shortcut menu appears.

2. Select New ➜ Page from the shortcut menu.

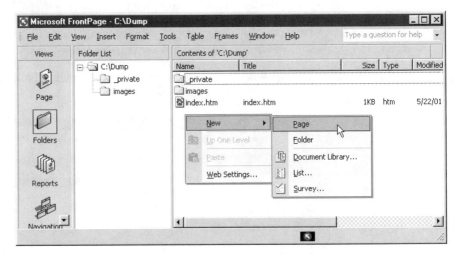

3. A new page appears in the root directory. Name the page appropriately.

Repeat this process until you have created all the pages you have planned for your site. You can always add or delete pages as necessary.

At this point, it's an excellent idea to set your work schedule. To do this, you can associate each file with a task by following these steps:

1. In Folders view, highlight the page you want to associate with a task.

2. Choose File ➔ New ➔ Task. You see the New Task dialog box. The name of the page you selected in step 1 appears beside "Associated With" in the dialog box.

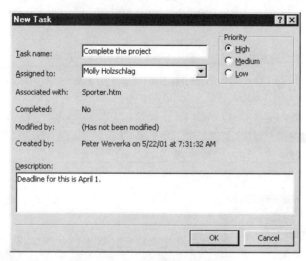

3. Enter a task name, the priority, and a description.

4. Click OK.

You can also set up tasks that are not associated with a page. These tasks will help you remember various stages of the production process. To set up a task without a page association:

1. Click the Tasks icon in the Views bar to switch to Tasks view.

2. Choose File ➔ New ➔ Task. The New Task dialog box appears. Notice that no page is associated with the task this time.

3. Fill in the task name, the task priority, and a description, and click OK.

You'll want to set up as many tasks as necessary to complete the production phase of each page.

Generating Site Graphics

Now let's move back to the image editor. If you've been able to work in layers, it'll be fairly easy to begin generating the various graphics for your site.

Suppose you developed the splash page for the band Cat's Eye during mock-up. Following the layer techniques, you've set various elements on individual layers. Now all you have to do is isolate those elements and optimize them accordingly by following these steps:

1. Open up the layered file in your imaging program.

2. Highlight the layer that has the image you want to process (see Figure 19.2).

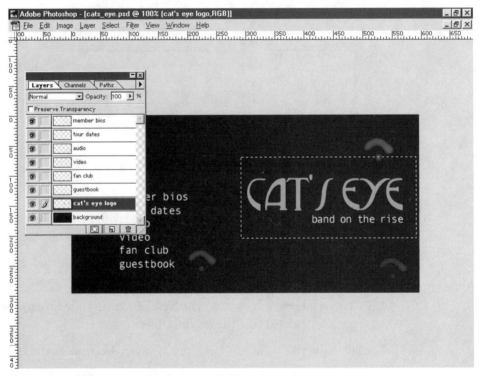

Figure 19.2 *Optimizing image elements layer by layer*

3. Using the marquee or selection tool (it will vary depending upon your program), draw a selection around the part of the image you want to keep, making sure you're on the correct layer.

4. Copy and paste the section into a new file.

5. Add any background or transparency color you wish and flatten the file.

Follow optimization techniques (see Chapter 18) to manage your graphics appropriately. Name the graphic you just created and save it to the folder you've set up for your site images, either the images folder created by FrontPage or a folder you created yourself.

You'll need to repeat this process for all of your site graphics. If you haven't mocked up all the pages, you may need to do so now, or create individual graphics. You may also need to scan and size photos, and then optimize them for the Web. If that's the case, now's the time to do so! Be sure to add interesting and appropriate design elements (see Chapter 18) and create any additional graphics you'll need for JavaScript mouseovers, backgrounds, and headers.

After you've got all the graphics you need, place them in the appropriate folder. Typically, this will be the images folder, the one that is created automatically when you create a new Web site.

Page-by-Page Design

You may be wondering why we're working page-by-page rather than with a Web wizard. If this seems a bit tedious, it's simply because you, rather than the software, are responsible for most of the work! For the many readers interested in creating a simple Web site, this may not be the right approach. However, for those interested in really taking sites *over* the top, this is how to gain absolute control of a site's integrity: one page at a time.

Here is the real meat of the production—adding the fun to your site, one page at a time:

1. In Folders view, highlight the file you want to work on.

2. Right-click and select Open from the shortcut menu. The page opens in Page view.

3. You can now begin to add the text, graphics, and technology you've prepared for this page.

When you've finished working on a page, be sure to return to Tasks view to either mark the task as complete or modify the task if more work needs to be done.

Keeping track of tasks is very important, especially if you're working in a team setting. This allows others working on the site to quickly see what's been done—and what needs to be done. For more information on how to use tasks to your advantage, visit Chapter 7.

Continue working on your pages until you've completed all the text and graphic work for each page. This process is the heart of Web site production—it will take the most time. If you've done your preparation well, the work will go much more smoothly than if you had just opened FrontPage and randomly went to work.

Preparing Your Site for Publication

After your text, graphics, and technology have been properly added to each individual page, you'll want to take several more steps before publishing your site to the Web.

Copyedit and spell-check all pages. This is an *extremely* important step and should be done for *every* Web site you design. FrontPage will help; it has a built-in spell-checker that you can use to ensure proper spelling. For high-end professional sites, it's a good idea to have a copyeditor on staff or hire a copyeditor to oversee your content and ensure that your text is well written and consistent.

Test all links. It's crucial to be sure that all of your links—whether within your site or to other sites on the Web—are working properly. Chapter 24 gives you step-by-step instructions on using FrontPage to check links.

Add META tags where appropriate. META tagging is a process by which you can aid your site in getting properly promoted on search engines. Adding META tag keywords and descriptions is commonplace for all commercial and hobbyist Web sites, although they may not be necessary in the case of private intranet and extranet publications. See Chapter 24 for more information on how to properly tag your pages for identification purposes.

Test your Pages. Using different browsers and platforms, check to be sure that all of your pages for Internet publication look good—whatever the screen resolution, the browser type and version, or the operating system.

See Chapter 16 for details on how to properly plan and test your site for a variety of browsers.

If you pass all of these milestones, you can confidently move on to publishing your Web site. Publication is the movement of all of your produced work onto the server where the site will reside. See Chapter 8 for a comprehensive look at the publishing process.

Post-Production

After your site is published, all of the hard work you've done preparing for it will have paid off. Your site will be well organized with clear intent, appropriate content for your audience, and attractive design. You'll also have tested the site locally to make sure that there are no spelling or grammar errors, that hyperlinks work, and that all issues having to do with browser compatibility have been addressed.

But now that the site resides on your server, live for the Internet audience, it's important to not forget that the site still requires your attention. Here are some matters you should address after your site has been produced and published:

Check content live. Be sure all your graphics, links, and technology are working properly on the server, and check these regularly.

Follow maintenance and promotion guidelines. In order to boost your potential success, you'll want to efficiently maintain and promote your site (see Chapter 24).

Prepare for the future. Using your long-term goals as a guide, decide when it will be necessary and appropriate to add content to your site, expand the site, and even redesign the site to keep it contemporary and interesting.

Up Next

This chapter has set you up with a process you can apply to any Web site project for management success. With this strong methodology behind you, you can now move on to setting the stage for fully maximizing your Web sites with Microsoft Office integration and a variety of programming, maintenance, and development techniques.

Part IV

Taking Your Web Site to the Top

In This Part

Integrating Sites with Microsoft Office

FRONTPAGE

Chapter 20

Because FrontPage is part of the Microsoft Office family, it is highly integrated with its siblings. And that means you can rely on other Office programs to do some of your Web development work.

There are many ways you can use Office to enhance your Web site building experience. You can convert tables you've made with Word or spreadsheets created with Excel into HTML tables at the drop of a hat. Anything you can make with Office, you can turn into a Web page—databases, annual reports, personal or company schedules, and multimedia presentations. In this chapter, you discover how to use FrontPage's officemates—including Word, Excel, PowerPoint, and Access—to create content for your Web site or company intranet. Topics include:

- Previewing an Office file in a browser

- Copying and pasting data for Web pages

- Using Word as an HTML editor

- Saving Excel worksheets as HTML tables

- Making PowerPoint presentations into Web presentations

- Posting Access datasheets and tables to the Web

- Linking to Office documents and Office viewers

Previewing an Office File in a Web Browser

In Word, Excel, Access, and PowerPoint, you can find out what your document, worksheet, database table, or slide will look like in a browser window. Before you use an Office file or part of an Office file in a Web page, see what it looks like in a browser by choosing File ➜ Web Page Preview. As shown in Figure 20.1, your default browser opens and you see the Office file.

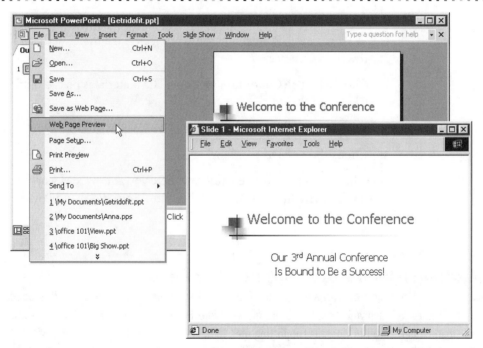

Figure 20.1 *You can see what any Office document will look like when viewed through a browser.*

In Microsoft Word, you can click the Web Layout View button or choose View ➜ Web Layout to see what your Word document will look like in a browser.

Copying and Pasting to Create Content

Here's some good news for users of FrontPage: HTML is now the native format for all Office files and documents. Copying parts of a Word document, an Excel worksheet, an Access database, or a slide from a PowerPoint presentation to FrontPage is easier than ever. When you cut or copy something to the Clipboard, Office saves it there in HTML. And when you paste it from the Clipboard into a Web page that is open in FrontPage, Office simply copies the HTML right onto the page.

You probably know the routine for cutting or copying and pasting material from one place to another:

1. In Word, Excel, PowerPoint, or Access, select the material that you want to borrow for a Web page.

2. Choose Edit ➜ Cut or Edit ➜ Copy. The material is placed on the Office Clipboard.

3. Switch to the Web page and, in Page view, click where you want the material to go.

4. Choose Edit ➜ Paste.

How the material arrives depends on where you got it. Excel worksheets and Access database tables arrive in the form of a table. Stuff from Word and PowerPoint arrives in the form of text.

Handling a Web Page's Supporting Files

As you know, a Web page is actually a composite of several different files, called *supporting files*, one for each component of a Web page. When you convert an Office file—a Word, Excel, Access, or PowerPoint file—into a Web page, Office creates a new folder to store the supporting files. To name the folder, Office tacks the word _files to the name of the Web page and makes the new folder subordinate to the Web page you just created. For example, if you turn a Word document into a Web page, name the Web page Jupiter, and store the Web page in the C:\Planets folder, Office creates a new folder at this location for storing the Jupiter supporting files:

```
C:\Planets\Jupiter_files
```

The problem with supporting files is that they can be a hassle to deal with. When you move the Web page, you have to remember to move its supporting files as well. The supporting files have to remain in the _files folder, where the browser software knows to find them.

Office, however, offers a couple of techniques for handling supporting files. You can keep the supporting files in the same folder or save them in Web Archive format:

- Saving in Web Archive Format: With this technique, the supporting files are folded into the Web page when you convert your Office file into a Web page. There are no supporting files. You only have to deal with one large file. The drawback with this technique, however, is that only the Internet Explorer browser can read the file and display the Web page.

  To save a file in Web Archive format, open it, choose File ➜ Save As, and, in the Save As dialog box, open the Save As Type drop-down menu and choose Web Archive (*.mht; *.mhtml). Then choose a folder for the Web page, give your Web page a name, and click the Save button.

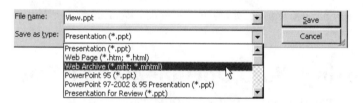

- Keeping supporting files in the same folder: With this technique, the supporting files are kept in the same folder as the Web page itself when you convert your Office file to a Web page. This makes moving the Web page around easier—you don't have to worry about bringing along the supporting files.

  To keep supporting files in the same folder, choose Tools ➜ Options, and, in the Options dialog box, select the General tab. Then click the Web Options button. In the Web Options dialog box, select the Files tab and uncheck the Organize Supporting Files In A Folder check box.

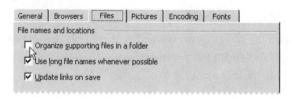

Using Word to Create HTML Documents

A Word document can be turned into a Web page very quickly—Word offers several commands for turning documents into Web pages. After the conversion is made, you don't have to worry about coding the page or reformatting the text because Word does that for you. Being able to convert Word documents to Web pages is especially convenient when you are working with tables, lists, and fancy formats. If you are comfortable working in Word, you can do most of the work in that program, save your work as a Web page, and then import the page into a FrontPage Web site. You don't have to start from scratch.

While it's possible to use Word as an HTML editor, Word is not nearly as robust or flawless an editor as FrontPage, so we're going to focus on converting content from Word format to HTML format.

Converting Word Documents to HTML

Follow these steps to convert a Microsoft Word file to a Web page:

1. In Word, choose File ➜ Save As Web Page. The Save As dialog box appears (see Figure 20.2). Notice, in the Save As Type text box, the words "Web Page (*.htm; *.html)." When you are finished saving the Word document as a Web page, the document will have the .htm file extension.

2. In the File Name text box, enter a Web-friendly name. Spaces and punctuation marks aren't generally allowed in the Web page filenames, although you can use underscores in place of spaces.

3. Click the Change Title button, and, in the Set Page Title dialog box, enter a name for the page and click OK. The name you enter will appear in the title of the browser when people look at the Web page.

4. Click the Save button.

You see your new Web page in the Word window. After you save the document as an HTML file, a new command appears on the View menu: View ➜ HTML Source. Choose that command to view the source code.

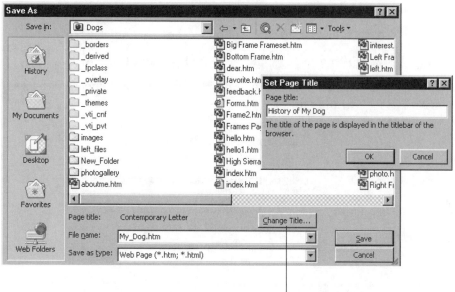

Click the Change Title button to enter a title for the Web page.

Figure 20.2 *Saving a Word document as a Web page*

Now that you've converted your Word document to HTML, you have several options:

- Continue to work with the document in Microsoft Word.

- Import the document into FrontPage and work with it there (see Chapter 2 for more on importing files).

- Choose File ➜ Web Page Preview to open the document in your Web browser and double-check its appearance.

Filtering to Remove the HTML Tags

When you save a Word document with the File ➜ Save As Web Page command, the command throws a handful of HTML tags into the file. The tags are thrown in so that you can continue to edit the file in Word. However, if you make the Word HTML file a part of a Web site, the HTML tags that Word throws in during the conversion are not necessary.

Follow these steps to convert a Word document to HTML without including the extra HTML tags:

1.   Choose File ➜ Save As. You see the Save As dialog box.

2.   Enter a name for the file in the File Name text box.

3.   Open the Save As Type drop-down menu and choose Web Page, Filtered (*.htm; *.html).

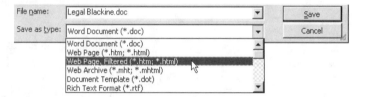

4.   Click OK.

Word versus FrontPage

There's plenty more you can do with Word as an HTML editor. In fact, most of the Word commands that pertain to Web page will be familiar to you if you've used FrontPage. FrontPage, however, does a much better job of creating Web pages than Word does. Briefly, here are some things you should note about Word as an HTML editor:

- The Templates dialog box (choose File ➜ New and click the General Templates link in the New Document task pane to get there) offers a tab called Web Pages. The templates available on this tab include a blank Web page, a Web Page Wizard, and some demonstrations of other Web tricks you can perform with Word. These templates and wizards are astonishingly similar to ones in FrontPage!

- You can create hyperlinks inside Word in exactly the same way you do it in FrontPage. Choose Insert ➜ Hyperlink or click the Hyperlink button and the Insert Hyperlink dialog box appears. It looks and works like the Insert Hyperlink dialog box in FrontPage (Chapter 4 explains hyperlinks).

Using Excel to Create Web Pages

Suppose you have an Excel spreadsheet file for the budget for an upcoming project. With Office XP (or Office 2000 for that matter), you can save this spreadsheet as an HTML table and post it to your company's intranet, where the project staff can review it. The staff will have access to the HTML files and can prepare their comments, which can save a lot of time during meetings.

You can also use Excel to create a new Web page from an existing spreadsheet, or to place HTML tables into existing pages. In this section, we're going to create brand new HTML files. In the next section, we'll cover adding a table to an existing Web page.

Converting Excel Worksheets to Web Pages

When you turn an Excel worksheet into a Web page, you have the option of converting a single worksheet or the entire workbook. Figure 20.3 shows what happens when you convert the entire workbook. Notice the buttons along the bottom of the page. Do they look familiar? Those buttons work exactly like the worksheet buttons in Excel. By clicking one, you can go to a different worksheet in the workbook.

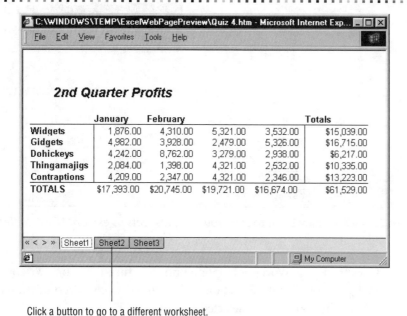

Click a button to go to a different worksheet.

Figure 20.3 *An Excel workbook converted to a Web page*

The next section in this chapter explains how you can insert a worksheet on a Web page in such a way that visitors to your Web site can use it to calculate worksheet data.

Follow these steps to turn Excel data into a Web page:

1. Open the Excel file whose worksheet or workbook you want to convert to HTML.

2. If you want to save a part of the worksheet as a Web page, select it. (If you want to save an entire workbook or worksheet, you're ready to go.)

3. Choose File ➜ Save As A Web Page. The Save As dialog box appears (see Figure 20.4).

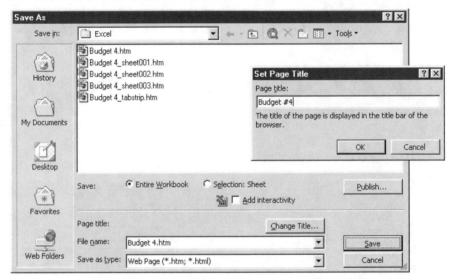

Figure 20.4 *Excel allows you to save your spreadsheets as elegant HTML tables.*

4. Click the Entire Workbook option button to turn the entire workbook into a Web page, or click the Selection option button to convert only the data you selected in step 2 (if you selected data in step 2).

5. In the File Name text box, enter a name for the Web page.

6. Click the Change Title button, enter a title for the Web page in the Set Page Title dialog box, and click OK.

7. Click the Save button to close the Save As dialog box.

To preview the way your page will look in Internet Explorer, select File ➜ Web Page Preview.

Now you can open this file in FrontPage, view it in your Web browser, or upload it to your FrontPage Web site. See Chapter 4 for more details on editing a Web page, Chapter 2 to find out about adding a Web page to your Web site, and Chapter 11 for details on the look and functionality of your tables.

Inserting a Live Excel Worksheet

As long as you have installed the FrontPage Server Extensions and you are sure that the people who will view the worksheet will do so with Internet Explorer 4 or higher, you can insert an Excel worksheet on a Web page that visitors can use to make calculations. Putting a live Excel worksheet on a Web page is not an option if you don't have the server extensions. And people without the proper browser can't view the worksheet, either.

Follow these steps to insert a live Excel worksheet on a Web page:

1. In FrontPage, open the page into which you want to insert a spreadsheet and click where you want the spreadsheet to appear.

2. Choose Insert ➜ Web Component. You see the Insert Web Component dialog box.

3. Under Component Type, select Spreadsheet and Charts, and, under Choose A Control, select Office Spreadsheet. Then click the Finish button. An empty worksheet appears on the Web page (see Figure 20.5).

There you have it—an empty worksheet. So how do you enter formulas and what all in the worksheet? To do so, click the Commands And Options button on the toolbar. The Commands And Options dialog box appears. It offers most of the standard Excel commands. Similarly, anyone who visits the Web page can click the Commands And Options button to play with the figures in the worksheet.

Because the Excel worksheet uses an ActiveX component (see Chapter 22), it's Internet Explorer–specific. This makes the component especially useful in intranet situations, or whenever you know your audience is using the IE browser.

Click the Commands And Options button to enter and format data.

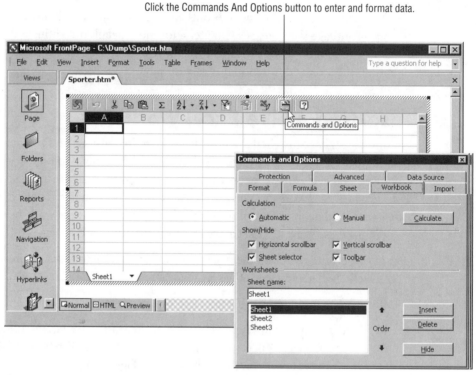

Figure 20.5 *Adding an Excel spreadsheet to a Web page*

Working with PowerPoint

Converting PowerPoint presentations into Web pages can be a great way to mobilize your office. You won't have to mess with bringing disks or overheads with you when visiting clients, because you can access your presentations through the Internet. You won't have to worry about the cost of fixing transparencies or slides that need revisions, because you can simply change the page digitally and upload it to the Web rather than reprint an over-head. And you can give colleagues and prospective clients previews of your presentations simply by sending them a URL. You can even do remote presentations!

Of course, before you visit a client armed only with a URL, you need to be sure that your client's office has Internet access, and that your site is accessible to your client. Check with your system administrator to learn where to post your Web files so they are not hidden behind a firewall, and give your presentation a test run from outside the office to make sure that loading the files isn't a painstakingly slow process.

Turning a PowerPoint Presentation into a Web Site

PowerPoint offers a very nice feature whereby you can turn a PowerPoint presentation into a Web site. When the conversion is complete, the Web site looks and acts very much like the PowerPoint screen (see Figure 20.6). Thumbnail images appear in a frame on the left side of the browser window. By clicking a thumbnail, you can go from slide to slide. Or, if you so choose, you can simply make the Web site work like a genuine Power-Point presentation. Each slide fills the screen. When you click a slide, the next slide in the presentation appears.

Click a thumbnail to go from slide to slide.

Figure 20.6 *When the conversion is complete, the Web site looks very much like a Power-Point screen.*

Only Internet Explorer 4.0 and later browsers can display PowerPoint presentations.

Follow these steps to make a copy of a PowerPoint presentation and turn it into a Web site:

1. Open the PowerPoint presentation and choose File ➔ Save As Web Page. The Save As dialog box appears.

2. Click the Change Title button, and, in the Set Page Title dialog box, enter a name and click OK. The name will appear in the title bar of the browser when you or someone else views the presentation.

3. In the File Name text box, enter a name for the file. Be sure to remember this name. When you open the presentation in your browser, this is the file you will open.

4. Click the Publish button. The Publish As Web Page dialog box appears (see Figure 20.7).

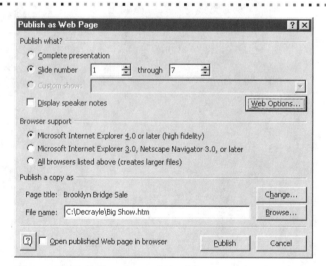

Figure 20.7 *Telling PowerPoint how to make the presentation appear in Web browsers*

5. Choose options in the Publish dialog box:

   Publish What?   Choose which slides to include on the Web site. Click the Complete Presentation option button to include all of them. Otherwise, select the Slide Number option button or the Custom Show option button and, using the text boxes, enter the numbers of the slides to include.

   Display Speaker Notes   If you want to include speaker notes as part of the presentation, check the Display Speaker Notes check box. The notes will appear in a horizontal frame at the bottom of the Web site.

   Browser Support   Choose which browsers you want to be able to display your presentation.

6. Click the Web Options button to open the Web Options dialog box.

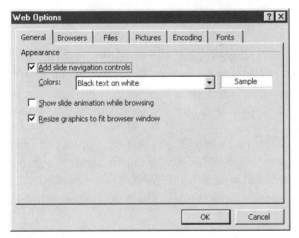

7. Choose options on the General tab:

   Add Slide Navigation Controls   Click this check box and a frame with thumbnail images of slides appears on the left side of the browser window. Choose an option from the Colors drop-down menu to decide the appearance of the frame. The Sample box to the right of the drop-down menu shows what your choice means in real terms.

To make the Web site work like a slide presentation, uncheck the Add Slide Navigation Controls check box. This way, the slide fills the entire screen—like a normal PowerPoint presentation. Choose this option if you intend to give the presentation over an Internet connection.

Show Slide Animation While Browsing If your presentation includes animation and you want it to appear on the Web site as well, click this option button.

Resize Graphics To Fit Browser Window Check this check box if you want the graphics in your presentation to fit nicely in the browser window.

8. Click OK to close the Web Options dialog box.

9. Click the Publish button in the Publish As Web Page dialog box.

Do either of the following to view your presentation in a Web browser:

- In Internet Explorer, choose File ➜ Open, and, in the Open dialog box, click the Browse button. Then, in the Microsoft Internet Explorer dialog box, locate and double-click the name you gave the .htm file in step 3 in the previous instruction list.

- In PowerPoint, choose File ➜ Web Page Preview.

 Suppose you want to copy a single slide and use it as a Web page. To do so, choose View ➜ Slide Sorter in PowerPoint to see all the slides in the presentation. Then right-click the slide you need and choose Copy on the shortcut menu. To paste the slide, switch to FrontPage, create a new page, and right-click and choose Paste on the shortcut menu.

You are now free to use FrontPage to edit these files and add any elements you'd like to spruce up the pages. When you're satisfied with your presentation, upload all the HTML documents and images to your Web site (as described in Chapter 8), and double-check the links and image locations before you announce your URL to the world.

Mastering What's Online

For more information on PowerPoint, be sure to drop by www.microsoft.com/powerpoint/. There you'll find news, demos, special offerings, and other resources to help you maximize your PowerPoint experience.

Displaying Access Data on a Web Page

You can create HTML versions of Access datasheets, database reports based on the information in your Microsoft Access databases, and management documents. For example, you can create a list of all your employees from your payroll database, a table of clients and their contact information from an accounts database, or even an online catalog from an inventory database. Any kind of information suitable for a database can be put onto an Access HTML datasheet.

Before you can export Access data to HTML, you need to have an HTML file available so that you can provide document and style information to your data (step 7 in the instruction list that follows will ask for the name and location of the HTML file). You can use *any* HTML file to fulfill this need—just be sure you have an HTML file that has the background, text, link colors, and any images or other information you want included within the Access data. If you don't have a file you'd like to use on hand, you can easily create one in FrontPage and save it to a folder.

If you plan on using the HTML file to format your Access data in the future, you can save the HTML file in a convenient location, such as within the Microsoft Office templates folder.

To output Access data as HTML, you need to use both the File ➔ Save As, and File ➔ Export options. These options let you create an HTML-based page from your Access database. Follow these steps:

1. With your database open in the Access window, choose File ➔ Save As. The Save As dialog box appears.

    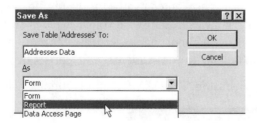

2. Enter a name for the file in the text box, and, from the As dialog box, choose how to present the data on a Web page—as a table form, report, or data access page. Access opens the file in the format you've selected. Check to make sure this is how you want your information organized.

3. Choose File ➔ Export. The Export To dialog box appears (see Figure 20.8).

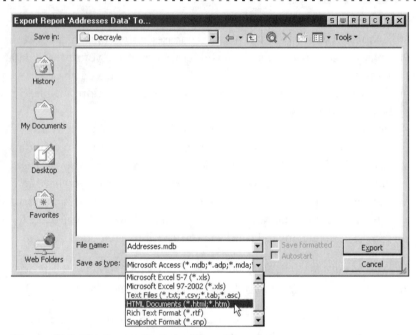

Figure 20.8 *The Export To dialog box allows you to export your Access data to HTML.*

4. In the Save As Type drop-down menu, choose HTML Documents (*.html; *.htm).

5. In the File Name text box, enter a name for the file. Be sure to choose an HTML-friendly name. For example, if your database name is Students And Classes, you can give it a short name (such as **sc.htm**) or a long name, using underscores to link the words: **students_and_classes.htm**.

6. Click the Export button. The HTML Output Options dialog box appears.

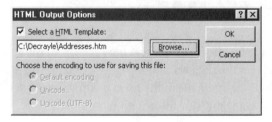

7. Click the Browse button and, in the HTML Template To Use dialog box, find and select the HTML file that you created to receive the Access data. Then click OK.

8. Click OK in the HTML Output Options dialog box. Access converts the data into HTML form.

You won't see your new HTML file right away—you'll have to open it with your Web browser to see the product of your export. To do this, open your Web browser. In your Web browser, choose File ➜ Open, click the Browse button in the Open dialog box, select the HTML file you created in the Microsoft Internet Explorer dialog box, and click the Open button. Then click OK in the Open dialog box.

Do you like the results? If so, great! If not, you can open this file in FrontPage and edit it any way you like, using the techniques described throughout this book.

Mastering What's Online

Want more information on Access? Visit www.microsoft.com/access/ for updates, troubleshooting, downloads, and product support.

Linking to Office Documents

Instead of converting Office documents to Web pages, you can simply provide links to the Office files themselves (DOC, XLS, PPT, and MDB files, in other words). In a corporate environment that uses Microsoft Office and has an intranet, your colleagues likely have the programs necessary to view Office documents. Even on the Internet, however, you can distribute Office documents that anyone can read using a free Office viewer. (A *viewer* is a very small piece of software that can be used to open documents, but not edit or change them.) If you'd like to make your Office documents available to your users, you can point them to the Office Internet page to download the free viewers for Word, Excel, and PowerPoint.

Version 3 or later of both Netscape Navigator and Microsoft Internet Explorer are capable of viewing—and even editing—Office documents within the browser window.

Linking to an Office document is the same as linking to any other document. Post it to your Web site as you would any other document, and make sure that links to it end in .doc (Word), .xls (Excel), or .ppt (PowerPoint), rather than the .htm or .html extensions you use for regular Web pages. (Chapter 2 discusses importing Web pages; the same process works here.)

It's a good idea to let people know that you're linking to an Office document rather than to a regular Web page. Your link and the surrounding text might read something like this: Download our 1998 Annual Report (MS Excel format).

When a user clicks a link to an Office document, one of three things might happen:

- If the user's Web browser is capable of opening Office documents, the document appears in the browser window.

- If the user has the appropriate Office program and his or her browser is configured to open Office documents, the document will be saved to disk, and the Office program will open and load the document.

- If the user's browser is configured to save Office documents to disk (the default for most people), he or she will be prompted to save the document to disk, and can then open it at a convenient time.

Don't Let Your Computer Get Sick!

You've got yourself some up-to-date anti-virus software, right? A certain type of virus, called a macro virus, inhabits Microsoft Office documents exclusively. Virus protection programs that do not specifically state that they detect macro viruses probably don't. Most of these viruses fall into the annoying category rather than the deadly one, but you should always be prepared to run regular virus checks to stamp them out.

Office programs include an automatic macro virus-scanning feature, but it isn't foolproof; the scanning software simply detects macro code created by a user other than yourself and warns you of its presence, but it doesn't destroy virus code. Earlier versions of the software do not have scanning included.

For information about macro viruses and how to detect and destroy them, visit the Microsoft Office Anti-Virus page at office.microsoft.com/assistance/9798/virusres.aspx. You'll find virus protection for Word templates, recommendations regarding other anti-virus software, and updates on virus solutions.

Up Next

In this chapter, you've learned a lot about how to make pages interactive. Office XP allows all of your Office documents to be linked to one another, as well as linked to, or from, a Web page. You've also seen how you can use Office programs to make or enhance your Web pages, which can then be improved upon using Microsoft FrontPage.

Your next step will be to take a look at JavaScript and Dynamic HTML. These technologies allow for a much broader spectrum of interactivity to be added to your pages, as well as offering a variety of management tools and cool special effects.

JavaScript, VBScript, and Dynamic HTML

FRONTPAGE

Chapter 21

So, you've got a fantastic-looking Web site. You're happy with the code, you're pleased with the look and feel, and the graphics are positively beautiful. You've even got some interactivity, such as forms. Perhaps you've gone so far as to add some features drawing from FrontPage's built-in suite of powerful tools. But you still feel you're missing something. Whether it's as simple as a mouseover effect, a pop-up window to aid in navigation, or a page transition, you can just sense that your site needs something more.

JavaScript is a powerful scripting language that not only allows you to add interesting effects to your pages but also empowers your site in both design and behavior. *Dynamic HTML*, or *DHTML*, is an umbrella name for a combination of technologies that include JavaScript and VBScript and work together to create powerful design options for your sites.

In this chapter, you will learn what JavaScript, VBScript, and DHTML are—and where they fit into the big picture of Web design. We'll also show you how you can begin using JavaScript, VBScript, and DHTML with FrontPage, and add that much-desired missing element to your pages right away. We will also take a look at the powerful Microsoft Script Editor, which can allow you to add complex, professional code to your Web pages. Topics include:

- What is JavaScript?

- What is VBScript?

- Scripting specifications and recommendations

- Choosing a scripting language

- Inserting a script

- Working with DHTML

- Using the Microsoft Script Editor

About JavaScript

JavaScript is a small-scale, easy-to-learn scripting language that allows you to add event-driven interactivity to your Web pages.

In the early days of the Web, common interactive Web elements such as fill-in forms, image maps, and features that automatically include such things as the "Last Modified on" line at the bottom of pages had to be added by the Web server. These *server-side* elements are still in use by many sites. But as you can imagine, the more work a Web server has to do in creating and serving these elements, the more bogged down it gets and the slower the entire site becomes. Luckily, JavaScript can help because it is a *client-side* application. This means it is downloaded to the browser right away, and then does its magic within the browser—it doesn't have to make a return visit to the server to get any more information after the initial handshake.

Let's say you have a form on your Web site that allows children to practice their multiplication tables. One way to evaluate the child's answers would be to use a *CGI* (*Common Gateway Interface*) script or *ASP* (*Active Server Pages*)—that is, the child would click the Submit button, and all of the answers he or she typed would travel back to the Web server. The server would run a little program to evaluate the answers, and then it would send back a Web page that showed how many were correct. That's three trips to the server—one for the child to get the page in the first place, one to send the answers in for grading, and one to send back the score.

If, however, you create the multiplication test with JavaScript, the user would communicate with the server only *once* to get the initial Web page. Contained on this initial page is the JavaScript program, which is actually run on the user's computer. The program itself collects the answers, evaluates them, and shows how many are correct. Because the user doesn't have to send data back to the server to get the results, the response is much, much quicker. And, as we all know, the faster your Web pages appear, the better.

Of course, JavaScript isn't always the appropriate choice for all applications. It does have its limitations. Because it is a script rather than a fully executable program, you can only get so fancy! Some of the things you can use JavaScript for include:

- Launching a new browser window when your Web page is first opened or when your visitor leaves your site. This script application can open a second, smaller browser window that might contain recent news and events or a list of URLs on your site. Unfortunately, some sites use this feature as a means of mass advertising, a purpose that is much less popular with visitors when done to excess.

- Validating the input from HTML forms without sending the data off to the server.

- Placing the current date and time on your page.

- Detecting which browser the user is running. You might use this function to identify users whose browsers don't support a feature you want to use on your Web site (such as frames, for example). Scripts can detect users who have older browsers and show them a version of your Web site without the advanced features.

- Playing sounds or displaying images when the mouse enters a certain part of the Web page.

- Navigating and generating pages in a frames environment. One example of this feature is an expanding navigation bar—similar to the Windows Explorer or the Macintosh Finder—on the left side of a two-frame Web page. You could use scripts to redraw the bar when a user asks for another level of detail, resulting in an instant change in the available navigation bar's links.

Understanding the Difference between JavaScript, Java, and JScript

A common misconception about JavaScript is that it is an easier-to-use, scaled-down version of Java. This can't be farther from the truth. The reason the two have a similar name has more to do with history than with any common features found within the languages.

JavaScript has its origins in a Netscape language known as LiveScript. Sun Microsystems, who is the developer of the Java language, teamed with Netscape to help bring LiveScript to sophistication. The name "JavaScript" was given to the end product to create a unity and familiarity between two products being developed with the Web in mind.

JavaScript runs inline, on the client side. Java is a full-fledged programming language that must be compiled in order to run. This is a world of difference, and the confusion about similarities between the two has come about largely due to the similarity in their names.

Interestingly, JavaScript has become a mainstay in the Web design world, used regularly to control a variety of features on Web sites. Java, on the other hand, has receded from the Web as a tool of choice. With the exception of a few small Java *applets* (mini applications), Java as a full programming language is simply too cumbersome to be as effective as the fast client-side JavaScript. Java itself has become more useful for general programming purposes—but its use as a tool to add design features to Web pages is fast going out of style.

So what about *JScript*? This is another name you'll run across, and you may wonder what the heck it means. JScript is, essentially, the Microsoft counterpart to JavaScript. It conforms fully to the *ECMA (European Computer Manufacturers Association)* 262 language specification. There is essentially no difference between JavaScript and JScript, but the browser support is somewhat different. We will learn more about the ECMA 262 language specification and JScript browser compatibility a little later on.

Microsoft's earlier versions of Internet Explorer were faulty in their adoption of JavaScript, but by the 4 generation of IE, most of the problems were solved. Where Microsoft has gained its competitive edge is with DHTML, as you'll see later in this chapter.

Ultimately, the most powerful aspect of JavaScript in terms of today's browser technology is that it addresses the need for cross-platform, multibrowser support. Netscape Navigator, Microsoft Internet Explorer, and Opera now support JavaScript, so if your audience uses any of these browsers, JavaScript is your best choice as a scripting language. In addition, JavaScript is fully supported on Windows 98, ME, NT, 2000, and XP, and can be supported on Macintosh, Linux, and UNIX platforms.

About VBScript

If JScript is the Microsoft counterpart to JavaScript, then VBScript, as used in Web pages, can be described as Microsoft's competitive product to JavaScript. When used with Microsoft Internet Explorer, VBScript is comparable to JavaScript. VBScript, or the Microsoft Visual Basic Scripting Edition, is a subset of the powerful Microsoft Visual Basic programming language. Programmers who are familiar with Microsoft Visual Basic will find using VBScript rather easy.

The use of VBScript is not limited to World Wide Web browsers; it can be used in other applications that use Microsoft ActiveX controls, automation servers, and Java applets. We will learn more about ActiveX and Java in Chapter 22. VBScript, being solely a Microsoft product and compatible only with other Microsoft products, has lost its ability to compete with JavaScript among Web designers. Where VBScript comes in very handy is behind the scenes. VBScript is quite often used along with databases, Microsoft Web-server configurations, and back-end products. Still, if you are designing your Web pages for a closed network, such as a corporate LAN, and you are certain that all your site visitors will be using Internet Explorer as their Web browser, then VBScript may be your preferred scripting language.

Specifications, Standards, and Recommendations

By now, you might be wondering why you need to be familiar with three different scripting languages—JavaScript, JScript, and VBScript. Is there a single, standard scripting language that we can use in our Web pages? Well, the long and the short of it is that there is! In this section we will take a look at the *ECMAScript* specification. We will also briefly cover other standards, specifications, and recommendations that relate to Web page design. First, we will take a look at why we need standards in the first place.

Why Use Standards?

Standards play a routine and important part in our everyday lives. Standardized weights and measures come from our need to standardize trade. The need for standards for our Web applications is essentially no different. If it weren't for standards and specifications, the reality of our Web experience today might pale in comparison to our dreams of a few years ago.

Compliance with Web standards and specifications makes it easier for people with special needs to use the Web. Blind people can have Web pages read aloud. People with poor eyesight can have Web pages magnified. People unable to use common interface devices such as a keyboard or mouse can use voice control or modified devices to activate standardized hyperlinks on our Web pages.

For Web page designers and developers, standards can make our work far less tedious. Our Web pages conform to a standardized layout. We can use standardized HTML tags in our pages. The use of standardized META tags and structured documents allows search engines to index our sites more rapidly. With applications such as FrontPage 2002, we can insert standardized Web page elements using a WYSIWYG interface with little or no knowledge of the underlying code.

In the context of this chapter, the use of a standardized scripting language ensures consistency in our scripts. In team projects and Web pages that undergo many development cycles, scripts conforming to a standardized scripting language enable others— and at times, us—to comprehend our scripts. Finally, the use of a standardized scripting language maximizes the compatibility of our scripts with the Web browsers used by our audience, *provided* those browsers support the standard.

Some Web designers fear that standards are limiting and restrictive. In reality, this is far from the truth. Standards remove much of the tedious labor required with Web site development. A good standard is both mindful of past technology and open to future enhancements.

The consequences of ignoring standards are apparent. The most basic consequence is that you will restrict access to your site.

The ECMAScript Standard

Microsoft and Netscape have competed aggressively for their share of our online viewing experience. Each has introduced features in their browser technology and implemented scripting support not supported by the other. If you've lived through the ongoing battle between Netscape and Microsoft, you will be well aware of these incompatibilities. While this healthy competition has allowed new features to be introduced into our Web experience, the need for JavaScript and JScript to conform to a single scripting standard has been apparent. Thus emerges ECMAScript.

ECMAScript, commonly referred to as *standardized JavaScript*, is a standardized scripting language based largely on Netscape's JavaScript and Microsoft's JScript. ECMAScript is more a standard than it is a scripting language on its own. The ECMAScript standard is defined by ECMA's Technical Committee 39, with the current specification being ECMA Standard ECMA–262, version 3. Both JavaScript and Microsoft's JScript are now conforming implementations of ECMAScript. VBScript does not comply with the ECMAScript standard. The JavaScript core used in Opera 5 mostly supports the ECMAScript 262 standard, version 3 specification.

Mastering What's Online

The ECMA Standard ECMA–262 continues to be under revision. To determine the level of compatibility of current, common browsers and for details on the current ECMA Standard ECMA–262, check out these useful Web addresses:

- Learn about the ECMA Standard ECMA–262 by downloading a copy from `www.ecma.ch/ecma1/STAND/ECMA-262.HTM`.

- For JScript and ECMAScript compatibility, take a look at the JScript FAQ at `msdn.microsoft.com/scripting/default.htm?/scripting/jscript/techinfo/jsfaq.htm`.

- Details on JavaScript compatibility with the ECMAScript standard can be found in Chapter 1 of Netscape's JavaScript overview at `developer.netscape.com/docs/manuals/js/client/jsguide/intro.htm`.

- Opera 5's support for the ECMAScript standard can be found in the Opera 5 specifications page at `www.opera.com/opera5/specs.html`.

- For information on the versions of JavaScript supported in some past, common Web browsers, take a look at `developer.irt.org/script/version.htm`.

- For some interesting articles on Web standards, visit The Web Standards Project at `www.webstandards.org`.

Other Standards, Recommendations, and Specifications

As you become more experienced with Web page development, you may want to look deeper into the underlying technologies and how they are evolving. Four main organizations are dominant in the proposal and adoption of new standards, recommendations, and specifications. These are:

The World Wide Web Consortium (W3C)   The W3C is a body that issues standards recommendations for the World Wide Web. While those recommendations are often referred to as standards, the W3C has no formal power as a standards body. The W3C was founded in October 1994 by Tim Berners-Lee, the inventor of the Web. The W3C is currently working on draft specifications for CSS3 and XML, amongst others. W3C Members include Microsoft, Sun Microsystems, RealNetworks, Opera Software, Nokia, Novell, and the National Institute of Standards and Technology. You can find out more information about the W3C and its recommendations at `www.w3.org`.

The International Organization for Standardization (ISO)   The ISO is an international organization and the source for over 13,000 international standards for business, government, and society. The ISO describes itself as a "network of national standards institutes from 140 countries working in partnership with international organizations, governments, industry, business and consumer representatives." The ECMAScript standard was submitted to the ISO for adoption and approved as international standard ISO/IEC 16262. You can find out more information about the ISO at `www.iso.ch`.

The Internet Engineering Task Force (IETF)   The IETF is an international community of network designers, operators, vendors, and researchers concerned with the smooth operation of the Internet. Visit `www.ietf.org` for more information about the IETF and its various working groups.

ECMA: European association for standardizing information and communication systems   The history of ECMA goes back to 1960. The formation of ECMA resulted from the necessity to have standardizations in operational techniques, such as programming, and input and output codes. We introduced the ECMAScript 262 standard earlier in this chapter. Visit www.ecma.ch for more information on the ECMA.

Choosing a Scripting Language

Now that you know a little about the scripting languages available with FrontPage 2002, you might be wondering which language you should choose. In this section we will take a look at the factors that influence your choice of a scripting language.

If you use the built-in features of FrontPage 2002 to insert any of its built-in scripts or components, you need not be concerned with the choice of a scripting language. FrontPage 2002 will seamlessly insert the script or component into your Web page. In some cases, you may need or want to edit the script or set the component properties. In those cases, some knowledge of the script language or component properties may be required.

When using the FrontPage 2002 WYSIWYG interface to insert scripts or components, FrontPage 2002 will only enable those technologies that are supported by your Browsers, Browser Versions, and Servers settings in the Compatibility tab in Tools ➜ Page Options.

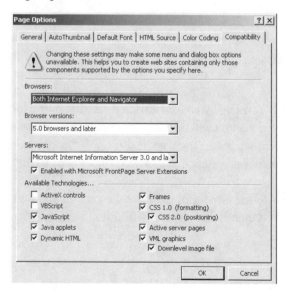

The settings shown above only disable some menu options available in FrontPage 2002. These settings have no effect on existing scripts or scripts you choose to insert directly into the HTML code. When developing your Web site for targeted browser audiences, remember to set these options before you begin adding components or scripts to your Web pages via the FrontPage 2002 menu commands.

If, however, you decide to extend your FrontPage Web pages with scripts you manually add to the HTML source code, your choice of a scripting language becomes vital.

If your site is intended for general access on the World Wide Web, be aware that your visitors will be using the browsers of their choice. You can assume that these will probably be Netscape, Microsoft Internet Explorer, and, possibly, Opera. In this situation, we recommend you use an ECMAScript-compatible language such as JavaScript or Microsoft's JScript.

Just because a scripting language is compatible with the ECMAScript 262 standard does not mean that all features available in that scripting language are supported by all browsers and browser versions. In an attempt to gain a competitive edge, browser manufacturers often introduce new features into their scripting languages that are only compatible with their latest browser versions. We cannot emphasize how important it is to install the latest versions of Netscape, Microsoft Internet Explorer, and, for completeness' sake, Opera, and then preview your Web pages in them. To preview your page in any installed Web browser, choose File ➔ Preview In Browser, select the desired browser in the Browser section of the Preview In Browser dialog box, select any required screen resolution in the Window Size section, and then press the Preview button. We also recommend you test your site (or have it tested) in earlier versions of the popular Web browsers.

If installed, Opera 5 may be recognized as Netscape Navigator 5.11 in the FrontPage 2002 Preview In Browser dialog box.

If you are developing FrontPage Web for restricted viewing over a local LAN and you can be sure that all your visitors will be using Microsoft Internet Explorer, then VBScript may be your client scripting language of choice. VBScript is particularly suited to those who have some experience with Microsoft's Visual Basic programming language.

Another alternative is to use JavaScript to detect the version and type of browser your site visitor is using and then redirect them to different versions of your Web pages.

You might, for example, have one page that has both VBScript and JavaScript support for Internet Explorer visitors and another that solely uses JavaScript for Netscape and Opera visitors, and redirect visitors to the appropriate page depending on their browser type and version. We don't recommend you use this alternative unless you are developing a site for general use and have some compelling reason to use VBScript for your Internet Explorer visitors or elements of JScript or JavaScript not supported by earlier versions of Netscape, Opera, or Microsoft Internet Explorer. Browser-detection scripts are readily available for download on the World Wide Web.

Most Web browsers will usually ignore scripting languages or elements of a scripting language that they don't understand. In Microsoft Internet Explorer, scripts that cannot be understood or are faulty will display a small error notification in the lower left corner of the Web browser—that is, unless they have Script Debugging enabled in Microsoft Internet Explorer. To disable Script Debugging in your own version of Microsoft Internet Explorer, select Start ➜ Settings ➜ Control Panel, double-click on the Internet Options icon in Control Panel to open the Internet Properties dialog box, select the Advanced tab, and check "Disable Script Debugging" in the Browsing section of Settings. Press OK to activate your changes.

If you intend designing Web pages for WebTV, your choice of a scripting language is easy—you can't use scripts.

Ever wonder what the PC-deprived WebTV users see when they browse the Web? You can download a WebTV Viewer that runs on a PC from `developer.webtv.net/design/tools/viewer/`*.*

Now that we know about the choice of scripting languages available, we will look at how to insert scripts manually into our FrontPage 2002 Web pages.

Inserting a Script

So, now that you know a bit about JavaScript, JScript, and VBScript, it's time to get down to the nitty-gritty of adding scripts to your Web pages.

Scripts are usually placed at the top of a Web page between the start and ending HEAD tags to make them easier to locate and edit. In general, if the script should display content when the page is first loaded, the script must be at the top of the Web page or embedded within the page where the script output should be displayed.

You may have noticed files in your FrontPage Webs with `.js` *extensions, such as* `animate.js`, *and wondered what they are. Well, these are JavaScript libraries. When you use external libraries, scripts need not be embedded in the HTML source code. They are accessed externally via the SRC attribute of the* `SCRIPT` *tag. External libraries are particularly useful if you need to access the same source code from many Web pages. VBScript, JavaScript, and JScript can all be accessed externally.*

It is sometimes not sufficient to simply add the script to your Web page. The script often needs to be activated or called by some type of *event*. Events that can activate scripts include when the Web page first loads, when your visitor leaves to access another site, when the mouse cursor is hovered over text or a hyperlink, and when a button is pressed on your Web page.

As an example of how to place and activate code, let's look at the following sample JavaScript code. This code will display a pop-up window when your site visitor leaves your Web page. The pop-up window displays the contents of a new Web page. You might use it say thank you to your site visitor for visiting your Web page.

```
<html>
<head>
<title>Sybex JavaScript sample</title>
<SCRIPT LANGUAGE="JavaScript">
<!- Begin
function leave()
{
window.open('http://www.Sybex.com','','toolbar=yes,menubar=yes,~CA
location=no,height=500,width=500');
}
// End ->
</SCRIPT>
</head>
<body onUnload="leave()">
</body>
</html>
```

The first thing to notice about the above code is that the main block of script is placed between the HEAD tags of the HTML document and is contained within starting and ending SCRIPT tags. This code would work equally as well if it was placed between the BODY tags. The LANGUAGE attribute of the SCRIPT tag in this example specifies that we are using JavaScript. The !- and - comment tags are used to prevent the script from showing up in the Web page.

Next note that the *leave* function in the script is called by the *onUnload* event by enclosing the call in the starting BODY tag. This means that the script is activated when the visitor leaves this Web page. The script is actually *loaded* into memory when the <BODY>...</BODY> of the Web page is loaded.

You might like to try the above code in your own Web page. Change the URL from http://www.Sybex.com to one of your choice and experiment with the values of toolbar, menubar, location, height, and width.

So that we don't leave our poor VBScript cousin out in the cold and to demonstrate a slightly different implementation of code, we will next take a look at a VBScript example. The following code, shown inserted into the HTML source code, displays a message box when the input button Click For Message is pressed.

```
<html>
<head>
<meta http-equiv="Content-Type" content="text/html;~CA
 charset=windows-1252">
<meta name="GENERATOR" content="Microsoft FrontPage 5.0">
<meta name="ProgId" content="FrontPage.Editor.Document">
</head>
<body>
<INPUT TYPE="button" NAME="btnSybexRulez"~CA
 VALUE="Click for message" >
<SCRIPT LANGUAGE="VBScript">
   <!-
   Sub btnSybexRulez_OnClick
       alert "Mastering FrontPage 2002 Rulez!!"
   End Sub
   ->
</SCRIPT>
</body>
</html>
```

Notice that, in the above example, we have included the SCRIPT block in the BODY section of the HTML document. This script would work equally well if placed in the HEAD section of the HTML document. This VBScript example will not work in either Netscape or Opera. Try manually adding the SCRIPT block and the INPUT line to the source code of a new FrontPage 2002 Web page. Preview the Web page in both Netscape and Internet Explorer.

There are multitudes of script samples you can download from the Web and try for yourself. You can add a downloaded script sample to the HTML source code of your Web page like this:

1. Download and save the script of your choice and any of its components. Be sure to read any online or included documentation about the script. Open the script file (preferably in Notepad) and copy the script to the Clipboard by choosing Edit ➜ Select All ➜ Edit ➜ Copy. In some cases, you might copy the code directly from an HTML Web page. In that case, it is important that you first paste the copied code into Notepad before proceeding to paste it into the HTML source code of your FrontPage 2002 document. Then, copy the script from Notepad to the Clipboard (again using Edit ➜ Select All ➜ Edit ➜ Copy). We do this so we can paste the script as unformatted text into the FrontPage 2002 document.

2. In FrontPage, open the Web page into which you want to insert the script and then select the HTML tab to view the source code.

3. Place the cursor where you want to insert the script (typically, this will go in the HEAD section of the document).

4. Paste the script into your Web page by selecting Edit ➜ Paste (or Ctrl+V). (See Figure 21.1). If necessary, make any additions to the HTML tags in your document, according to the script documentation, so that the script can be activated from an event.

5. Save the file.

Be sure to test your page in browsers that support the scripting language you are using to ensure that it works!

The script shown in Figure 21.1 is a sample JScript script obtained from the JScript samples at `msdn.microsoft.com/scripting/default.htm?/scripting/JScript/samples/welcome/explain.htm`. This particular script executes when the SCRIPT block is parsed and then writes directly to your HTML Web page. No further modifications to HTML tags are needed for this script to run. This script works equally well in Netscape 6, Microsoft Internet Explorer 5, and Opera 5. You may want to visit the above site and try this script for yourself in earlier versions of these browsers.

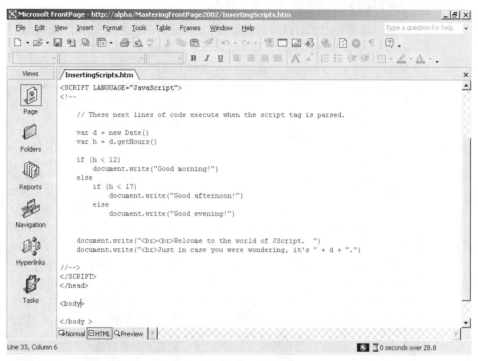

Figure 21.1 *Manually inserting an online script into a Web page*

Where to Get Scripting Help

If this section on scripting feels like a bit of a tease, it is! We encourage you to go out and find fun and functional scripts to use on your pages. There are numerous script archives and help sources on the Web. Here are a few favorites:

- Want to learn JavaScript from the ground up? Check out Voodoo's JavaScript introduction at www.webteacher.com/javascript/.

- JavaScript World: Articles, scripts, and discussion forums at www.jsworld.com/.

- Doc JavaScript: Improve your scripting health at www.webreference.com/js/.

- JavaScript Developer Central: Netscape's resource center for JavaScript developers at developer.netscape.com/tech/javascript/index.html.

- Microsoft Scripting Technologies: A reference for all things to do with Microsoft scripting. Includes VBScript and JScript, documentation, samples, and language references. Visit this site regularly at msdn.microsoft.com/scripting/.

Dynamic HTML

Dynamic HTML (DHTML) actually refers to using JavaScript, VBScript, JScript, Cascading Style Sheets (CSS), and internal browser technology to make pages more vibrant and active. Normally, in order to create Dynamic HTML pages, you'd have to understand each of these technologies and write scripts for each of your pages to perform tasks such as moving blocks of text around or changing images when the user points at them. But as luck would have it, FrontPage 2002 includes Dynamic HTML effects that you can incorporate into your pages without having to do any programming at all.

The availability of built-in DHTML effects in FrontPage 2002 depends on your page settings in the Compatibility tab in Tools ➜ Page Options. If, for example, you set your Browsers compatibility to Both Internet Explorer And Navigator and your Browser Version compatibility to 4.0 Browsers And Later, then only those FrontPage 2002 DHTML effects that are supported by *both* Internet Explorer 4 and Navigator 4 will be available to you. Naturally, those effects are also supported by later versions of these browsers.

DHTML in FrontPage 2002 is controlled from a special toolbar. You can get to this toolbar by selecting View ➜ Toolbars ➜ DHTML Effects. This toolbar will also become visible if you select Format ➜ Dynamic HTML Effects.

Using DHTML, you can actively modify just about any element on your Web pages—text, images, links, you name it.

Animating Text

To animate text, follow these steps:

1. With the page of interest open, select the text you want to animate. Ensure the DHTML toolbar is visible by selecting View ➜ Toolbars ➜ DHTML Effects or Format ➜ Dynamic HTML Effects.

2. On the DHTML toolbar, you'll see an arrow to the right of the On text box. Click the arrow to display a drop-down list. The options available in this drop-down list depend on your compatibility settings in the Compatibility tab of Tools ➜ Page Options.

3. You now have several options (here we will assume your Browsers Compatibility is set to "Microsoft Internet Explorer Only" with Browser Versions set to "5.0 Browsers and Later"), including:

    *   Click makes the animation occur when you click the text in question.

    *   Double Click makes the animation occur only upon double-clicking the text.

    *   Mouse Over makes the animation occur when your mouse passes over the text.

    *   Page Load makes the animation occur immediately upon page load.

    Choose an option to place it in the On text box.

4. The neighboring Apply text box also has a drop-down list, where you can now select the type of action you want to apply to the object. With text, you have two options:

    *   Fly Out will give you options to make the text move in a specified way across the page.

    *   Formatting will allow you to add borders or font changes to the selected text.

5. If you want to make your text fly out (leave the page), highlight Fly Out on the drop-down list and in the adjacent Effect drop-down list choose one of the following to occur upon the action you specified (click, double-click, mouseover, or page load) in the On text box:

    *   To Bottom-Left causes the selection to fly out from the bottom left of the page.

    *   To Bottom-Right makes the text fly out from the bottom right of the page.

    *   To Bottom-Right By Word causes the text to fly out from the bottom right of the page, one word at a time.

    *   To Left will cause the selected text to fly out from the left.

    *   To Top will cause the selected text to fly out from the top.

    *   To Top-Left makes the text fly out from the top left of the page.

- To Top-Right causes the selected text to fly out from the top right of the page.

- To Top-Right By Word causes the selected text to fly out from the top right of the page, one word at a time.

6. If you want to add a formatting change to your text upon the action specified in the On text box, select Formatting on the Apply drop-down list, and then choose an action from the adjacent Effect drop-down list. You can choose from the following:

- Font allows you to have the text change font face, color, size, or style and to apply any of the other text attributes available in the Font dialog box.

- Borders And Shading displays the Borders And Shading dialog box (see Figure 21.2), which allows a variety of borders and shading effects to be displayed.

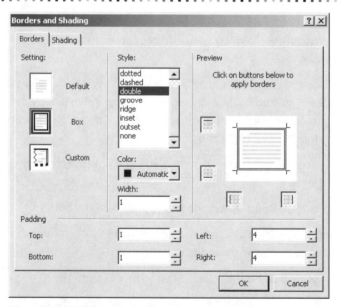

Figure 21.2 *Selecting borders for DHTML effects*

7. Save your page.

To remove any existing DHTML effects, select the text or image (covered shortly) that the effect is applied to and then press the Remove Effect button on the DHTML Effects toolbar.

You won't see any change on the editing screen itself, but if you select the Preview tab, the selected object will appear on screen and you can view the animation. For example, if you select a header (see Figure 21.3) and set it to fly to the bottom right, the header will fly out from the bottom-right side of the Preview window right off the page (see Figure 21.4)!

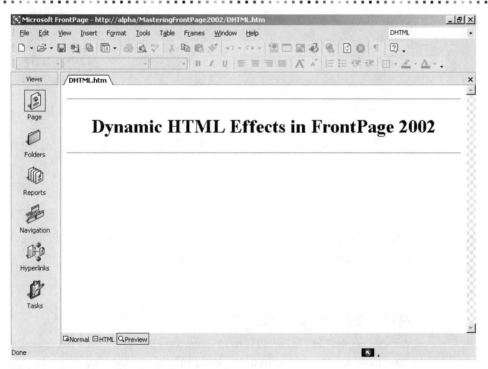

Figure 21.3 *A text header in its normal state*

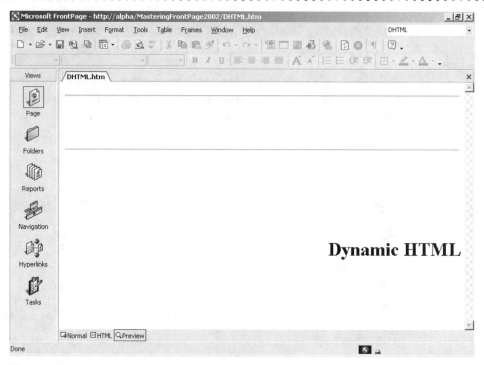

Figure 21.4 *The text after the DHTML effect*

To highlight all the DHTML text effects on your Web page in Normal view, select the Highlight Dynamic HTML Effects button in the DHTML Effects toolbar (it's the last button on the right).

Animating Images

You can apply DHTML effects to images, too! The DHTML effects available for images depend on the On selection in the DHTML Effects toolbar.

In this example, we're going to make our building change to a new one when we click it.

1. With a page open, select the image you want to animate.

2. On the DHTML toolbar, you'll see an arrow to the right of the On text box. Click the arrow to display a drop-down list.

3. You now have several options:

- Click makes the animation occur when you click the image in question.

- Double Click makes the animation occur only upon double-clicking the image.

- Mouse Over makes the animation occur when your mouse passes over the image.

- Page Load makes the animation occur immediately upon page load.

Choose an option to place it in the On text box and close the drop-down list. For this demo, we chose Click.

4. In the neighboring Apply drop-down list, select Swap Picture; Choose Picture will appear in the adjacent Effect drop-down list.

5. Reselect Choose Picture in the Effect drop-down list (use the drop-down arrow) and a new Picture dialog box will appear.

6. In the Picture dialog box, locate and select the image of your choice and then press Open to close the Picture dialog box.

7. Save the page.

8. View the page by selecting the Preview button, and you'll see the original image (see Figure 21.5) change to the image you chose in Step 6 when you click on it (see Figure 21.6). Keep on clicking the image and it continues to "swap."

9. Preview your Dynamic HTML effect in all of your installed Browsers to check that it works.

This particular Dynamic HTML effect was found to work in both Microsoft Internet Explorer 5 and Opera 5. It did not, however, work in Netscape 6 even though our compatibility settings were for both Netscape and Internet Explorer versions 5 or higher. Our advice to always preview your scripts and effects in your target browsers has paid dividends!

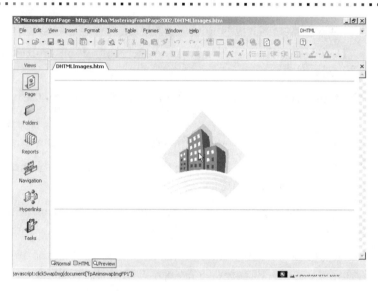

Figure 21.5 *The original image*

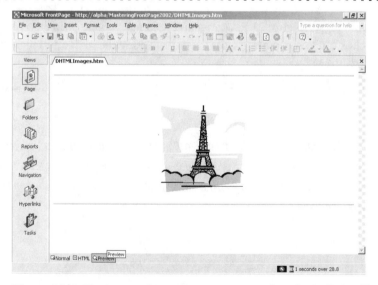

Figure 21.6 *The image changes to a new one after the DHTML effect is invoked.*

Are there other cool animation effects for DHTML? Absolutely! See the Mastering What's Online sidebar a bit later in this chapter, where we offer up some very helpful resources on using DHTML.

Setting Transitions between Pages

You can also use FrontPage's Dynamic HTML features to set the transitions that occur between pages. For example, you might want one page to dissolve as another appears. Other options are available, too—we've come a long way from simply jumping from link to link. To set the transition from one page to another, do this:

1. With a page open in Page view, from the menu bar select Format ➔ Page Transition. The Page Transition dialog box appears.

2. In the dialog box's Event drop-down list, select the transition for which you want to set a special effect. The transitions you can assign effects to are:

   • Page Enter, which occurs when the page is loaded by a user

   • Page Exit, which occurs when a user replaces the page with another page

   • Site Enter, which occurs the first time a user accesses a page from your site

   • Site Exit, which occurs when a user loads a page that is not part of your site

3. In the Transition Effect list box, select the effect that appeals to you. (The best way to learn about the effects is to try them all out.)

4. In the text box labeled Duration (Sec), type the number of seconds you want the effect to last.

5. Click OK. The dialog box closes.

You won't see any indication of that spanking new Dynamic HTML in Normal view. To best view the page transition effect, save or publish your Web page or site and then browse to its location in Internet Explorer, Netscape, or Opera. Depending on your choice of a page transition, you will need to enter or leave the Web page or site to see your new transition in all its glory.

Mastering What's Online

As with JavaScript, JScript, and VBScript, you can add DHTML to pages on your own—you don't have to feel restricted to what FrontPage offers. Furthermore, if you're interested in setting up your own DHTML that works across browsers, you'll need to spend time reading up on the subject. Here are some helpful Web sites for you to get started:

- The Dynamic HTML Zone. Macromedia's site, dedicated to all things DHTML, such as articles, tutorials, and a discussion group, at `www.dhtmlzone.com/`.

- DHTML Lab. Internet.Com's entrance, with tools, demos, articles, free newsletters, and discussion, at `www.webreference.com/dhtml/`.

- WebCoder. Ready-to-use DHTML scripts at `www.webcoder.com/`.

- DevEdge Online. Dynamic HTML in Netscape Communicator, including demos, samples, and a newsgroup, at `developer.netscape.com/tech/dynhtml/`.

- MSDN Library. Visit the Dynamic HTML section of this site for comprehensive articles, a FAQ, and references for DHTML. The DHTML Dude has some interesting articles. Visit `msdn.microsoft.com/library/default.asp?url=/workshop/author/dhtml/dhtml.asp`.

The Microsoft Script Editor

For adventurous FrontPage 2002 users who may wish to create their own advanced scripts and DHTML effects, Microsoft includes an advanced development environment known as the *Microsoft Script Editor* (shown in Figure 21.7). Those familiar with Microsoft Visual Basic or Microsoft Visual C++ may recognize a somewhat familiar interface in Figure 21.7.

To access the Microsoft Script Editor, choose Tools ➜ Macro ➜ Microsoft Script Editor from the FrontPage 2002 menu or press Alt+Shift+F11. You need a new or existing Web page open in Normal or HTML view for the Microsoft Script Editor to be available. Depending on the state of your Office XP or FrontPage 2002 installation, you may be prompted for your installation disks when you first access the Microsoft Script Editor.

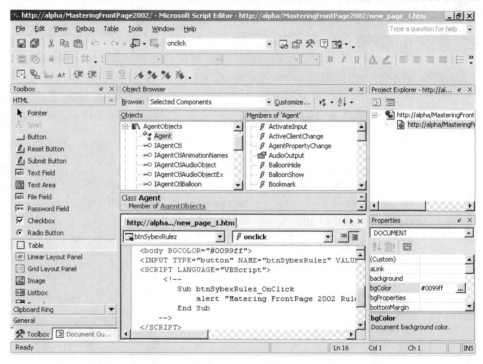

Figure 21.7 *Advanced coding with the Microsoft Script Editor*

The Microsoft Script Editor is certainly for advanced users and we cannot hope to cover its intricacies in a book of this size. Suffice to say, the Microsoft Script Editor provides the ultimate in HTML source and script creation and editing. It can also act as a powerful *script debugger*. For our purposes, we are mostly concerned with the excellent help that the Microsoft Script Editor provides. We encourage you to explore the Microsoft Script Editor more on your own.

Obtaining Help with the Microsoft Script Editor

The Microsoft Script editor provides comprehensive Help files and references on JScript, VBScript, HTML, DHTML, and CSS in addition to tutorials on VBScript and JScript. It also, naturally, includes help on using the Microsoft Script Editor. To access these Help files, open the Microsoft Script Editor and choose Help ➜ Microsoft Script Editor Help.

The Help files accessed above are installed on your computer (usually in the `C:\Program Files\Microsoft Office\Office10\1033` *directory for an English language installation of FrontPage 2002) as individual* `.chm` *files. You can open these files directly to learn more about these technologies. DHTML, HTML, and CSS help can be found in the* `HTMLREF.CHM` *file, JScript help can be found in the* `JSCRIPT5.CHM` *file, and VBScript help can be found in the* `VBSCRIPT5.CHM` *file. You may want to create desktop shortcuts to these files for quick and easy access. To create a desktop short-cut to any file, right-click on the file and, from the pop-up menu, select Send To* ➜ *Desktop (Create Shortcut).*

An extremely useful feature of the Microsoft Script Editor is to provide *context-sensitive help* for your HTML source and included scripts. This Help feature allows you to select any element of your Web page in the Microsoft Script Editor and obtain help on that element with a single press of the F1 key. Figure 21.8 shows the results of an enquiry on the INPUT button.

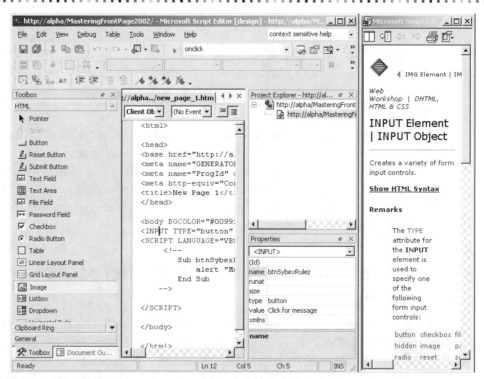

Figure 21.8 *You can obtain context-sensitive help using the Microsoft Script Editor.*

To obtain help on an existing Web page element using the Microsoft Script Editor, with the page open in FrontPage 2002 in Normal or HTML view invoke the Microsoft Script Editor, click the element you want help on in the code window, and press the F1 key on your keyboard.

The Hype about XML

If you've been living, working, or playing around the Net for a while you may have come across the term *XML, eXtensible Markup Language,* or, more appropriately in the context of this book, *XHTML,* or *eXtensible Hypertext Markup Language.* Modifications to the English language are commonplace here when we are talking about our new age of computer applications. Does EHTML have the same punch? So, what is XML and what does it mean to FrontPage 2002?

First we need to take a brief look at what HTML is. HTML is a language with a powerful and sometimes clumsy parent known as *SGML,* or *Standard Generalized Markup Language.* HTML is actually written in SGML and is, if you like, a child of SGML or an *SGML Application.* The complexity of SGML has deterred many users from trying it and thus from dis-covering its power—power that can be used to develop the next generation of applications for e-commerce, indus-trial, and personal use that transfer data in a standardized way. So, in an attempt to make a much more *user friendly* language, XML—based on SGML—has been developed and become standardized. XHTML is a child of XML or an *XML Application.*

At this stage, you may not need to be concerned about how the birth of XHTML impacts your HTML documents. The changes to HTML to make it comply with the XML rules and become an XHTML document are subtle. For example, our single <hr> (horizontal rule) HTML tag now becomes <hr /> when XML rules are applied. You can apply these new XML rules in FrontPage 2002 and take a look at the changes for yourself by opening a Web page in HTML view, right-clicking in the page, and choosing Apply XML Formatting Rules from the pop-up menu. Those who are intrigued by this new technology can find many articles on XML and XHTML and their continuing development at the W3C site at www.w3.org.

Up Next

Knowing when and why to use programming on your Web site is a big challenge for Web designers. Some of you are designing for the pure creative joy of it; others have a professional need. Each case is going to dictate how you use techniques such as JavaScript, JScript, VBScript, and DHTML.

But now that you've got a taste of Web programming, it's time to dish up some more! This way, you'll have plenty of choices when it comes to planning and weighing what is appropriate for your site needs.

In Chapter 22, "Specialty Programming Techniques," we'll take a look at the way FrontPage manages Java applets and ActiveX—two programming techniques that are powerful, yet highly specialized.

Specialty
Programming
Techniques

FRONTPAGE

Chapter 22

n addition to client-side techniques such as those discussed in Chapter 21, there are methods for inserting actual executable programs into your pages. These programs, however, can add to download time, so you're best off weighing the advantages and disadvantages of using them.

While FrontPage comes with some ActiveX and Java applets that anyone—even a nonprogrammer—can use (see Chapter 15), it is also possible to use many such applets and ActiveX controls from other sources in FrontPage Web sites. It is even possible (if you are a programmer) to create original ActiveX controls and Java applets for use in Web pages. This chapter is a quick introduction to all those possibilities. Topics include:

- What is active content?

- Locating ActiveX controls on the Web

- Tools for creating ActiveX controls

- Using ActiveX with FrontPage

- Locating Java applets and ActiveX controls on the Web

- Tools for creating Java applets

- Using Java with FrontPage

About ActiveX

ActiveX is a technology designed by Microsoft that enables software developers to create applications using *components*. Each component is a small piece of computer code that encompasses one part—or function—of the program. A number of components are then assembled into one big application, called a *container* application. By combining a bunch of components, in other words, one ends up with a real application. The most widely used application yet developed with this technology is (yes, you heard it here) Internet Explorer itself.

Internet Explorer consists of a container application and a bunch of ActiveX controls that perform such specific tasks as actually displaying Web pages. When all the components within the container application work together, you end up with (in this case) a Web browser. Similarly, one can use controls as parts of a Web page. ActiveX can be used by programmers to create controls (known, logically enough, as ActiveX controls) that you can then embed into your Web pages—whether you yourself are a programmer or not.

When we talk about active content *in this chapter, we are referring to compact computer programs you can incorporate into your Web pages. These are most often implemented to facilitate user interaction—typical examples might be an image that changes its look when the user moves a mouse cursor over it, or a calculator into which a user can enter numbers and from which a result is returned.*

Remember, when a user experiences an ActiveX control on a Web page, the control is actually made up of both what the user sees and some computer code that causes something to happen in response to the user's action.

ActiveX is a Microsoft technology and is only supported natively by Microsoft Internet Explorer. Use ActiveX controls in your Web pages only when you are certain your audience uses Internet Explorer.

Locating and Inserting ActiveX Controls

During your Internet travels you may have downloaded and installed many ActiveX controls. Whether the installation of these ActiveX controls is transparent and automatic or not depends on your Internet Explorer security settings and how you "trust" ActiveX controls from different publishers. Have you ever seen a dialog box similar to that shown in Figure 22.1? It's a prompt asking you to install an ActiveX control from the Web so that you can view and possibly interact with it. After you install the ActiveX control, it is added to your already impressive arsenal of controls and becomes available for your use. Some of these controls are, however, copyrighted.

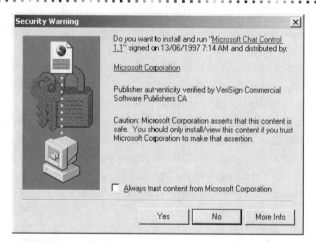

Figure 22.1 *Installing an ActiveX control from within Internet Explorer*

We advise you to keep Internet Explorer's default security settings (accessed via the Security tab in Tools ➜ Internet Options, from the main menu of Internet Explorer) unless you have a compelling reason to change them. If you do change any of these settings for, say, local testing purposes, be sure to change them back to their default values after your testing to ensure that you are protected from automatically installing potentially malicious ActiveX controls.

The ActiveX control shown in Figure 22.1 installs a version of the Microsoft Chat Control to your visitors' PCs and runs it right inside Internet Explorer—one application running inside another application. Just to whet your appetite for ActiveX, Figure 22.2 shows the installed Microsoft Chat Control running in Internet Explorer.

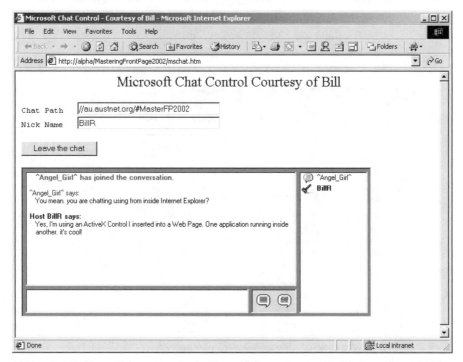

Figure 22.2 *One of the many ActiveX controls you can use with FrontPage 2002*

To locate ActiveX controls installed and available for use with FrontPage 2002, we'll run through the procedure of inserting an ActiveX control into your Web page. First note that since ActiveX is a technology supported only by Microsoft Internet Explorer, you will need your page compatibility in the Compatibility tab of Tools ➜ Page Options set to Microsoft Internet Explorer Only. Alternatively (but not recommended), you can use a Custom setting with the ActiveX Controls check box in Available Technologies checked. With a new or existing Web page open in FrontPage 2002 in Normal view, follow these steps to locate and insert ActiveX controls:

1. Click where you wish to insert the ActiveX control.

2. From the FrontPage 2002 menu choose Insert ➜ Web Component.

3. In the Component Type section of the Insert Web Component dialog box, select Advanced Controls (usually the last entry).

4. In the Choose A Control section of the Insert Web Component dialog box, select ActiveX Control and then press the Next button. You will be presented with the dialog box shown in Figure 22.3.

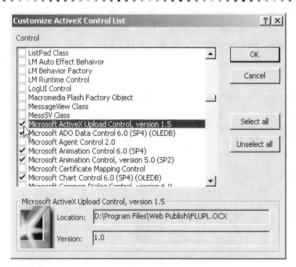

Figure 22.3 *Currently available ActiveX controls ready for insertion into your Web page*

5. Select the ActiveX control of your choice (scroll down to see more choices), then press Finish to insert it at the location you chose in Step 1.

Pressing the Find Components on the Web hyperlink in the lower left corner of the Insert Web Component dialog box in Figure 22.3 connects you to the Microsoft Office Tools On The Web online site where you may be able to obtain additional ActiveX controls provided by or recommended by Microsoft.

The list of ActiveX controls shown in the Choose A Control section of Figure 22.3 is but only a sample of the entire arsenal of ActiveX controls available to you. To explore the remaining available controls, press the Customize button in the Insert Web Component dialog box (refer to Figure 22.3) and you will be presented with a Customize ActiveX Control List dialog box. Scroll through the Control list and select any controls of interest. Press OK. All selected controls will then be available in the Insert Web Component dialog box shown below.

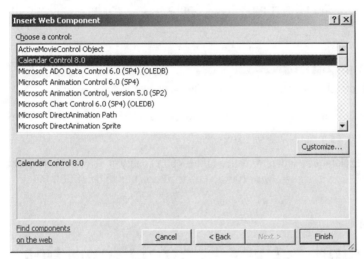

Obtaining Additional ActiveX Controls

There are many additional ActiveX controls available for download from the Web. Most of these are "home-grown" and come in prepackaged zipped files available for download. The packages often contain Help files and additional files that were used to create the ActiveX control. Be sure to read any documentation included with your newly downloaded ActiveX control.

Some of these controls are shareware and some are freeware. Installation of these controls can vary from file to file but usually involves registering an included file with an .ocx extension. Registration can be done from a DOS box (Windows 98 or Windows ME) or a command prompt (Windows 2000) with the Regsvr32.exe application often included in the zipped file (it is also included with Windows).

To learn how to use the Regsvr32.exe application, take a look at the Microsoft Support Online article located at support.microsoft.com/support/kb/articles/ Q249/8/73.ASP.

Some of the ActiveX controls you will discover are intended for use as components in executable and other projects and are not particularly suited for use in your Web pages. Be selective with your choices, but certainly download and experiment with controls to get the hang of it. Who knows—maybe you will be the first to develop a CD burner that runs from within Internet Explorer!

Once downloaded and registered, your newly discovered ActiveX control becomes available for your use with FrontPage 2002. Turn to the section earlier in this chapter titled "Locating and Inserting ActiveX Controls" to learn how to locate and insert it.

Mastering What's Online

To locate additional ActiveX controls that you can incorporate into your own Web pages, visit:

- BrowserWatch's ActiveX Arena at `www.browserwatch.com/activex.html`.

- CNET's dedicated ActiveX site at `www.activex.com`.

- Microsoft's Internet Explorer development section of the MSDN Library at `msdn.microsoft.com/library/default.asp?url=/nhp/default.asp?contentid=28000441`.

Changing ActiveX Control Properties

Often after inserting an ActiveX control into your Web page, you will need to change its properties. In some cases, included documentation will provide you with information on what properties can or need to be set. In other cases, you may need to consult an *SDK*, or *Software Development Kit*. Microsoft has a number of SDKs available for download. For example, the Net Meeting SDK can be obtained from `www.microsoft.com/windows/netmeeting/authors/sdk/default.asp`. The best place to search for a specific Microsoft SDK is at the MSDN online search at `search.microsoft.com/us/dev/default.asp`.

Some ActiveX control properties are relatively easy to set. Others can leave you scratching your head in frustration until you locate the appropriate documentation.

To access the properties of an ActiveX control, double-click the inserted ActiveX control in Normal view or right-click it and select ActiveX Control Properties from the pop-up menu.

The number of tabs you see in the ActiveX Control Properties dialog box depends on the ActiveX control you have inserted. There will usually be at least two tabs: the Object Tag tab and the Parameters tab.

For a "simple" control such as the Calendar Control, there are a total of five tabs, as shown in Figure 22.4. The use of most of these tabs (with the exception of the Object Tag tab and the Parameters tab) to change the Calendar Control properties is fairly self-explanatory.

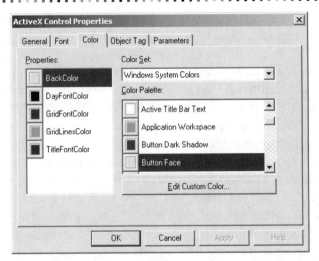

Figure 22.4 *You can change ActiveX Control Properties here.*

The Microsoft Chat ActiveX control we demonstrated earlier in this chapter, however, includes only the Object Tag and Parameters tabs in its ActiveX Control Properties, as shown in Figure 22.5.

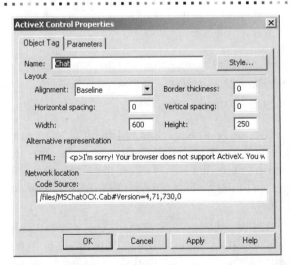

Figure 22.5 *There are usually at least two ActiveX Control Properties tabs—the Object Tag tab and the Parameters tab.*

The Object Tag tab shown in Figure 22.5 is the tab that often requires attention. Up until now, we have been assuming that the ActiveX control you have been using is installed on your site visitor's computer. If it isn't installed, we need to provide the *means* for the control to be installed. When your visitor accesses a Web page containing an ActiveX control, Internet Explorer first checks to see if the ActiveX control is installed on the client machine. If it isn't installed, Internet Explorer will attempt to install the control via the path you set in the Code Source section of the ActiveX Control Properties dialog box shown in Figure 22.5. The code source location may be an external path on the World Wide Web or may be the path to a file residing in your FrontPage Web.

The Code Source location in Figure 22.5 points to the MSChatOCX.cab cabinet file located in the Files folder of our FrontPage Web. The #Version= appended to the path denotes the version of the particular control. If Internet Explorer finds a previous version of the control installed, it will attempt to install the newer control. A site visitor using Internet Explorer without the Microsoft Chat Control installed or with an earlier version of the control installed will see the prompt to install this control, as shown in Figure 22.1 (turn back a few pages).

ActiveX controls are usually installed from within Internet Explorer via cabinet files, as shown in Figure 22.1 and Figure 22.5. There are, however, exceptions. If we were to insert the Net Meeting ActiveX control into our Web page, then the Code Source path in Figure 22.5 would point to the downloadable full version of Net Meeting as follows: http://download.microsoft.com/msdownload/netmeeting/3.0/x86/en/NM30.EXE. Be sure to check the documentation to determine the correct method to make an ActiveX control available to your site visitors who do not have it installed.

The Microsoft Chat room we have used as an example in this section requires additional scripting to enable it to operate as shown in Figure 22.2. Consult the documentation provided with your ActiveX control or the appropriate SDK to enable your control to function.

We have previously mentioned that ActiveX is a Microsoft product that is natively supported only in Internet Explorer. So, what do visitors who use other non-supported browsers see instead of ActiveX controls? This is where the Alternate Representation section in the Object Tag page of the ActiveX Control Properties dialog box shown in Figure 22.5 comes into play.

The Alternate Representation allows you to insert HTML code (including HTML tags) that will be run instead of the ActiveX control in browsers that do not support ActiveX. For example, if the page containing our Microsoft Chat Control shown in

Figure 22.2 is visited in Netscape 6, the Netscape visitor would see the following provided the Alternate Representation is as shown in Figure 22.5:

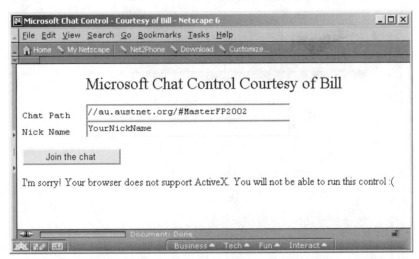

The HTML code inserted as the Alternate Representation to replace the ActiveX control need not be a simple text message as shown above. You can insert just about anything you like as long as it conforms to the HTML specification. For example, the Macromedia Shockwave Chat ActiveX control uses <embed> tags to attempt to install a plug-in for visitors not using Internet Explorer.

The Parameters tab of the ActiveX Control Properties dialog box (shown in Figure 22.6) is where you set specific parameters that control how the ActiveX control will work. You can add modify or remove parameters via the appropriate buttons in this dialog box. The documentation or samples that come with the ActiveX control or the SDK will usually help you to discover what parameters are needed and are under your control.

The properties of your ActiveX control can also be changed via the HTML source code by editing the source code of your Web page in HTML view in FrontPage 2002 or by using the Microsoft Script Editor. See the section in Chapter 21 titled "The Microsoft Script Editor" for details on how to access the Microsoft Script Editor. Also note the section in that chapter titled "Obtaining Help with the Microsoft Script Editor" for help with the tags associated with ActiveX controls. Parameter names and their values are contained in tags similar to `<param name="_cy" value="9260">`, *while the Code Source location shown in Figure 22.5 is contained in the* `codebase` *property of the* `Object` *tag.*

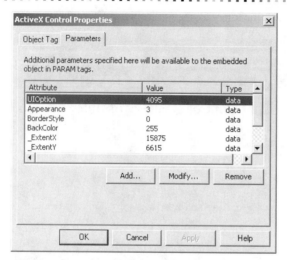

Figure 22.6 *You can add, modify, and remove parameters available to the ActiveX control via the Parameters tab in the ActiveX Controls Properties dialog box.*

Creating ActiveX Controls

While getting and using controls may be a fairly simple matter, actually creating an original ActiveX control is true programming, and best done by experienced programmers. If you are a programmer, you can use any of a number of languages to write code to create the control. Although how to turn your original idea into a new ActiveX control is beyond the scope of this book, we can offer a few words of advice about the popular programming environments used for this: Visual Basic and Visual C++. These tools were originally designed for writing Windows programs, so they are familiar to many programmers.

The Visual Basic Control Creation Edition is a special version of Microsoft's highly popular Visual Basic 5 software development system, modified for the sole purpose of creating ActiveX controls. Visual Basic is simple to use (again, assuming you are a programmer), and millions of people—even novice programmers—are familiar enough with it to succeed in writing controls.

While Visual Basic's strength is that it's no sweat to use, Visual C++'s strength is that it is complicated and powerful. It takes a lot longer to get up to speed in creating original controls using Visual C++, and novice programmers will find it a big challenge; but in general, it affords a broader range of possibilities.

The component development site from Microsoft offers resources for programmers, so take a run by it for more information and directions should you be interested in the idea of component development. Visit `msdn.microsoft.com/library/ default.asp?url=/workshop/components/activex/intro.asp` for articles, tutorials, and documentation on ActiveX component development. You can download a free copy of the Visual Basic Control Creation Edition along with samples and documentation from `msdn.microsoft.com/vbasic/downloads/cce/`.

About Java

Using Java (developed by Sun Microsystems), developers can create little applications called *applets*, which can be embedded into HTML documents or launched to run alongside your Web browser.

So how can you put Java to use? Let's say a programmer makes a Java calculator and you want to use it. Once you've downloaded the calculator *applet*, you can punch in numbers and the calculator doesn't have to ask the main server what the answer to "2 + 2" is; all the information it needs is right there in that little tiny program. The potential of Java applets is almost boundless, especially given the fact that Java is also theoretically *platform-independent.* This means that a Windows user, a Macintosh user, a Linux user, and a Unix user can all use the same applet and its appearance and performance will be *exactly* the same for all of those users.

Using Java, programmers can create other dazzling effects and applications: animation that might be used in games or for illustrations; tickertape feeds for news, sports, and stock data; applications that use real-time interactivity such as crossword puzzles, programs for the sharing of medical data, or programs that allow users to select airline seats; and handy gadgets such as mouse pointers that change shape, size, or color when you drag them over something.

Java is retreating as a programming method of choice on the Web. The primary reason is time—applets typically take longer to load, and often require a conversation between the browser and the server beyond the initial handshake. Java does have some good applications, so it's important to learn a bit about how to use it, but keep in mind its limitations and, especially, its differences from JavaScript.

FrontPage is not a Java-authoring tool, so it does not facilitate the actual writing of applets. FrontPage does allow you to embed existing applets into your Web pages. These can be original applets that you have written (see the following section, "Creating Java Applets") or applets you've acquired from other sources (see "Finding Java Applets" later in this chapter).

Creating Java Applets

As mentioned, Java applets are actually computer programs written in Java, which is a programming language. Java is much like those other popular languages, C and C++, but with "extensions" that make it adaptable to the Web.

When it comes to actually creating Java applets, you can use a programming environment that is designed specifically to create Java applets, or you can use one of a number of "point-and-click" tools that allow you to assemble applets out of existing components even if you are not a programmer. Let's look briefly at each of these options.

Java Development Environments

Working with a Java development environment is not for the faint of heart (or for those who want to quickly gain programming experience). Java development environments, such as Microsoft's Visual J++, are industrial-strength software development packages. If you are a programmer, for example, you'll find in them all the features you'd find in development packages aimed at developing Windows applications. When you use them, you'll bring into play a combination of existing Java elements—buttons and forms and more—along with original Java code you'll write yourself. In using one of these packages, there is no way to get around actual programming. That is, in fact, exactly what Java development environments are for—programming.

"Point-and-Click" Tools

As an alternative to developing your own Java code, you can build Java applets using so-called point-and-click tools, such as Jamba. For this you need not be a programmer. You are initially presented with a canvas on which you can draw your Java applet. You are then given a choice of elements to place onto the canvas—a container to hold a GIF file, a button, a drop-down list, and things like that. Everything is basically done for you, so all you really have to do is select which elements you want to use, point, and click. No programming is necessary. You can control some interaction between the elements you place on the canvas (for example, you can make it so that when a user clicks a given button, a specified image will appear). All this is done by entering information into a dialog box or two, without the need to actually write any Java code.

Once you have thus "described" the applet you want to create, you then select a menu option to actually generate the Java applet. The drawback in using these point-and-click tools is that they are very limited—they allow you little creativity as compared to actual programming. However, for the programming-impaired, they can be a very handy alternative.

Mastering What's Online
Check out Jamba's Web site at www.jamba.com/ for demos and applets, too!

Finding Java Applets

As we've said, you needn't actually write original Java applets in order to incorporate them into your Web site. Many existing applets are available for you to download from the Web and use. Some of these are freeware—meaning that you can nab them and use them as you like, without having to pay for them. Other applets are shareware—meaning you'll have to pay a specified licensing fee before you can use them. Still others are demos of commercial applets that you must purchase from their creators.

Mastering What's Online
You can find Java applets galore at Gamelan (www.softwaredev.earthweb.com/java). Sun Microsystems (the creator of Java) also offers applets for consumption at www.java.sun.com/openstudio/index.html.

Every Java applet exists as one or more files with the .class extension. To use an applet you find on Gamelan (or on any other online source of Java applets), you'll have to download the .class files for that applet. Java .class files are often available for download in prepackaged zipped files that contain documentation and other associated files. Once you have downloaded the .class files, you will want to copy them into a folder in the FrontPage Web that contains the Web page you'll be using them in. To copy the files into your FrontPage Web, open the Web in FrontPage 2002 and import them via the Add File button in the Import dialog box, accessed via File ➜ Import. You might want to create a new folder in your Web specifically for Java applets. Call it **applets** or **source**.

 Some Java applets package multiple .class *files into a single* .jar *file. If the working part of your applet comes as a* .jar *file, then import the* .jar *file into your FrontPage Web.*

The following section discusses how to incorporate a Java applet into a page on your Web site.

Inserting Java Applets

You can insert Java applets into your Web pages very quickly and easily; to do so, you must have downloaded or otherwise procured the applet, and placed it into a folder in the Web that contains the Web page you plan to use it in. Then follow these steps:

1. With the target Web page open in Normal view in FrontPage, click where you want to insert your Java applet.

2. From the menu bar, select Insert ➜ Web Component and then select Advanced Controls in the Component Type section of the Insert Web Component dialog box.

3. Select Java Applet in the Choose A Control section of the Insert Web Component dialog box and press Finish. The Java Applet Properties dialog box appears, as shown in Figure 22.7.

4. In the dialog box's Applet Source text box, type the Java applet's name. For example, for an applet called `ticker.class`, type **ticker.class**.

5. In the Applet Base URL text box, type the URL that leads to the location of the Java applet. If the Java applet is located in the root directory of your FrontPage Web, you can leave this field blank. If the Java applet is located in a directory of your FrontPage Web called `classes`, enter **classes** in this field.

6. Some Web browsers do not recognize Java. For users of those browsers, you can specify a message that will appear in place of the Java applet. In the text box labeled Message For Browsers Without Java Support, type an appropriate message.

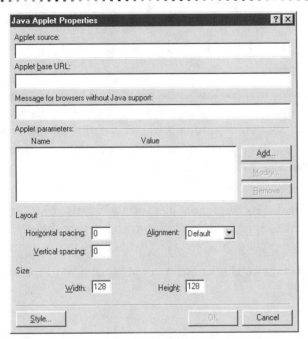

Figure 22.7 *You can easily insert Java applets into your Web pages, or make changes to the settings for applets you've already inserted.*

7. You can control the size of the applet as it will appear on screen. In the Size area, you'll see two text fields, labeled Width and Height. Specify the width and height (in pixels) you prefer.

8. In the Vertical Spacing text box of the Layout area, enter the amount of space, in pixels, you'd like to appear between the Java applet and any other elements to the left or right side of it.

9. In the Horizontal Spacing text box of the Layout area, enter the amount of space, in pixels, you'd like to appear between the Java applet and any other elements above or below it.

10. Finally, you can specify the applet's alignment as compared to other elements. In the Alignment drop-down list, select the alignment you prefer.

11. Click OK. The dialog box closes and the Java applet you have inserted appears as a small box with a huge bent "J" inside it in the Normal view of your Web page.

Setting Parameters

Many applets require you to specify parameters to indicate how the applet will work. For example, a tickertape applet would require a parameter to specify what text will appear in the tickertape as the applet runs. If you use an existing applet, such as one downloaded from Gamelan or elsewhere, it will come with some documentation telling you what parameters must be set.

To set parameters for an applet:

1. With the page that contains the applet open in FrontPage in Normal view, double-click the applet, or right-click it and select Java Applet Properties from the pop-up menu. The Java Applet Properties dialog box appears.

2. Click the Add button. The Set Attribute Value dialog box appears, as shown in Figure 22.8.

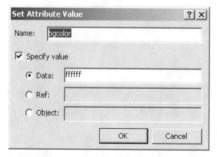

Figure 22.8 *You can set parameters for an applet here.*

3. In the Name text box, type the name of the parameter you want to set. (Get this info from the applet's documentation.)

4. Check the Specify Value check box and the Data option button will become selected by default (most applet parameters are data values). If your applet requires a Reference or Object value, select the appropriate option button.

5. Enter the required value for the parameter in the text box associated with the option button you have selected in step 4. (Again, find out your options from the applet's documentation.)

6. Click OK. The dialog box closes and the Java Applet Properties dialog box reappears. The parameter you just set will be visible in the middle of the dialog box.

7. If additional parameters are required, repeat steps 2 through 6 as needed.

8. Click OK. The dialog box closes.

Test your newly created Java applet by previewing it in Preview view in FrontPage 2002, but be certain to also test it in your installed Web browsers via File ➜ Preview In Browser.

 The above procedure creates <PARAM> tags in the source code of your Web page that is viewable in HTML view or by using the Microsoft Script Editor. See the section in Chapter 21 titled "The Microsoft Script Editor" for details on how to access the Microsoft Script Editor. As with ActiveX, these parameters and other properties of the Java applet can be inserted or edited directly in the source code. In some cases, the applet you download will contain sample code with default parameters that you can copy and paste directly into the source code of your Web page. You can then change these parameters directly in the source code or by following the steps in the next section, "Changing Applet Properties." If you intend to base an entire Web page around a single Java applet, you may want to import any sample HTML pages, applets, and associated files included with the applet into your page and edit the HTML file to your liking.

Changing Applet Properties

Having inserted a Java applet into one of your Web pages, you can then make changes to the applet's properties. You may want to do this, for example, to change the amount of screen space, the alignment of the applet, or any of the applet parameters.

Follow these steps:

1. With a Web page open in Normal view in FrontPage, double-click the applet, or right-click the applet and select Java Applet Properties from the pop-up menu. The Java Applet Properties dialog box appears.

2. You're home free. Well, almost. This dialog box is the same one you used originally to insert the applet. (See the earlier section, "Inserting Java Applets.") Use

the Add, Modify, and Remove buttons to make changes to any of the applet parameters and make any other changes you like.

3. When you've finished, click OK. The dialog box closes.

The changes you made will take effect immediately; if you've changed the size of the applet or its alignment, you'll see those results right away. However, some other changes may become apparent only when you view the page in a Web browser that supports Java, so if you don't see what you expect to see right away, check your page using a browser.

Dealing with Archived Java Applets

Some Java applets with multiple `.class` files come in archives such as `.jar` archives. To use these applets, you will need to import the archive into your FrontPage Web and add the `archive` property to the beginning applet tag, as shown below. To wrap up this section on Java, the following represents a complete applet including parameters. (You need the `.jar` file and images to use this.) Note that the main `Slideshow.class` file (along with other `.class` files) is included *within* the `Slideshow.jar` archive that is referenced via the `archive` property of the `applet` tag. This particular applet displays a stunning real-time cross-fade image transition. Try it for yourself! The applet, complete with documentation, can be obtained from www.waterlogic.com.sg/.

```
<applet archive  = "Slideshow.jar"
code = "Slideshow.class"
width = 400  height = 266>
    <param name = "image1"  value = "images/1.jpg">
    <param name = "image2"  value = "images/2.jpg">
    <param name = "image3"  value = "images/3.jpg">
    <param name = "image4"  value = "images/4.jpg">
    <param name = "image5"  value = "images/5.jpg">
    <param name = "image6"  value = "images/6.jpg">
    <param name = "image7"  value = "images/7.jpg">
    <param name = "image8"  value = "images/8.jpg">
    <param name = "image9"  value = "images/9.jpg">
    <param name = "image10" value = "images/10.jpg">
    <param name = "mask"    value = "images/mask.jpg">
    <param name = "frame"   value = "images/frame.jpg">
    <param name = "gradient"
           value = "images/gradient1.jpg">
```

```
<param name = "feather" value = "30">
<param name = "showtime" value = "250">
<param name = "fadetime" value = "4000">
<param name = "fademethod" value = "4">
I'm sorry but your Web browser does not support Java!
</applet></p>
```

Up Next

ActiveX components and Java Applets are often fun, and sometimes functional. As with any Web programming technique, it's important to think about your audience—can they see the effect, or will they end up reading a message that tells them their browser doesn't support it? Or will they find that the effect simply takes too long to download to be of real use? These questions are left to you—the designer—to answer. You've got the options now, and can make an educated choice regarding how these techniques are employed.

The next chapter shifts focus a bit to a growing and important area of Web development—databases. While we've focused a lot on the front end of Web sites, databases are the heart and soul of what goes on behind the scenes to add function and driving power to your FrontPage Webs.

Adding Databases for Maximum Impact

FRONTPAGE

Chapter 23

When it comes to rich content on the World Wide Web, there's never too much of a good thing. You can ride the top of the technology curve by adding scripts or applets to your site, but there's no substitute for providing useful, solid information—and lots of it! As Web developers, we understand the value of content, but we find that as we add more and more content to a Web site, it becomes increasingly difficult to keep everything current and well organized. Whether you start small by collecting user input or begin your Web project with a thousand-page catalog, you'll soon find you need a better way than static Web pages to keep everything organized and accessible to users. If you want to make a large amount of related data available on your site, you'll need the power and versatility of a database.

How can you be sure that you need a database? To help you decide if your site could benefit from the addition of a database, we'll talk about how other Web sites are using databases right now. We'll also discuss some database theory and explore some database jargon to help you understand what databases are all about. Finally, to assist you in adding the power of a database to your Web site, we'll give you step-by-step instructions for using FrontPage to create Web pages that will dynamically interact with your database. Topics include:

- Understanding how Web sites use databases

- Deciphering database lingo

- Deciding when to use a database

- Preparing a database for use with your Web site

- Inserting database data into Web pages

- Editing, saving, and viewing database-enabled Web pages

About Databases and Web Sites

Many Web sites use databases to organize and present all kinds of information. For example, sites that let you book travel arrangements, including Expedia and Travelocity, use databases to store and retrieve massive amounts of flight information.

Another common database-backed Web site application is the online catalog. One obvious example is Amazon.com, whose Web site is powered by massive databases of book information, users' shopping habits, and sales statistics.

In addition to providing travel or book title information, all of these sites let you purchase online. Online purchasing requires storing users' order information, billing information, and preferences. Once such a site gains popularity, you can imagine how quickly the size of these databases can grow!

Finally, there is the granddaddy of database-backed Web sites: the search engines. All of the key players—AltaVista, Yahoo!, Google, Excite, Infoseek, and others—rely on powerful databases to let you instantly search millions of Web pages.

As you can see, databases are essential for offering users convenient access to large amounts of data. Without them, many online projects would simply be impossible to create or maintain.

Can Your Web Server and Database Software Share the Same Machine?

As long as your server fulfills the requirements for the software, you can run both your Web server and database software on the same machine. However, if you expect your Web site and database to get a lot of use, you should consider running these two services on separate machines. Remember, "a lot of use" can mean different things, since how much your machine can handle before slowing down—or even crashing—depends on a number of factors, including your operating system, CPU, disk speed, and RAM. If you're unfamiliar with your server's general beefiness, consult your system administrator for a realistic idea of how much traffic your machines can take.

Whether you choose to use one server or several, make sure the machine that will host your database exceeds the minimum requirements for disk drive space and RAM. Plan for future expansion and newer versions of the product you choose, since software tends to be more resource-intensive with each new release.

As a general rule, it's always a good idea to include your system administrator in discussions regarding new software and services you plan to make available for your Web site. He or she will often have good suggestions and practical experience that can help you avoid problems down the line.

What Is a Database?

We've heard of them, we've talked about them, we use them—sometimes unknowingly—every day, but what is a database, really? Let's start by taking a look at the individual parts of a database. Like most other areas of computer technology, each part comes with its own set of descriptive jargon.

This chapter covers the basics about incorporating databases into your Web sites. To learn more about professional approaches to database design, dive into Chapter 28.

Learning More Database Lingo

A *database* is a system that lets you organize and store pieces of related information so that they're easier to find and use. Sounds simple, but what does it really mean? In the real world, we use systems to organize and store information all the time. For example, you may have a stack of business cards from associates or clients. The business cards usually hold the same information from card to card: the person's name, company name, office address, phone number, and e-mail address.

In normal conversation, the words data *and* information *can be easily interchanged. However, in the world of database jargon, data and information do not refer to the same thing. In database lingo,* data *is broken-down bits of stuff.* Information *is what happens to data when you organize it into a meaningful structure. Data would be a list of first names: Pete, Jill, Fred. Information would be a list of the first name followed by the last name: Pete McGill, Jill Greene, Fred Forrest. Without the context of a last name or a familiar face, a list of first names doesn't really mean very much to anyone. You must organize this data into information—in this case, by adding the last name—for it to be useful.*

Information is what is contained on each business card. That information is organized into several *fields*—in our example, the fields might be name, phone number, address, e-mail, and company name. Each single business card, with its fields of information, would be called a *record*. For a database to work properly, each record in it must contain exactly the same fields. Organize the records—business cards—alphabetically in a Rolodex and you have a *database*. The Rolodex full of business cards is a database because it fits our definition of a database—it is a bunch of information broken down into discrete pieces and organized in a way that's easy to use. Other real-life examples of databases include library card catalogs, dictionaries, and phone books.

Databases are extremely useful tools because organized information makes it easier to find a specific item in a search. A database search request is called a *query*. A database query is much more efficient than searching through random, unorganized data. For example, if you carry all of your customers' business cards around in a plastic bag, you must sift through *all* the cards each time you need to find John Smith's phone number. If, however, you've alphabetized those cards in your Rolodex, you know you can go directly to the *S* section to find John's information right at your fingertips.

Relational Database Basics

Computer databases have been around just about as long as computers themselves, and several different types of databases have evolved. Today, the *relational database* is the most popular and often the most useful.

In a nutshell, here's how a relational database works. Suppose you work for a company that supplies computer components. Your client list—represented by your stack of business cards—is stored in your database as a *table*. In this table, each customer's contact information is stored in a separate row, and each customer is assigned a unique ID.

But your company also has to keep track of who ordered what and when. So you need another table—one that contains data about each order, including the ID of the customer who made the order, the date and amount of the order, etc.

Now, one of your customers wants you to check on the status of his company's orders. If you don't have access to a database, you simply look up the customer in your Rolodex of business cards, find the name of his company, then search through your stack of printed invoices for orders by his company. In essence, you've just used relational database theory...although a database would do the job a lot quicker. But if all of your customer and order information were stored in a database, you could instantly *relate* these two different tables (the Rolodex and the stack of invoices) based on a shared field (the company name). This simple technique of linking tables with shared fields lets you create some very complex and elegant database queries to get information out of the database in any way you need.

When a Database Is What You Need

So how do you decide when your Web site needs a database behind it? When you have a lot of related information that changes frequently, you should think about organizing that data into a database. You'll know you should consider using a database if:

You collect data using surveys or contests. While you probably won't want visitors to your site to peruse this kind of data, you may find that several departments in your company want to access and search this data. Sending the survey or contest data directly into a searchable database can save you time and effort in the long run.

You have a catalog. To let your users browse through a selection of items or products, you'll want to use a database.

You plan to implement online shopping. You'll need a way to take shipping and payment information from your users, and you'll probably want to save their information so that they don't have to enter it each time they order from your site.

Your company already uses databases. If you're developing an intranet, or maybe you simply want to make company resources available to the public, you may want to access your company's existing database through a Web interface.

A great introductory book for Web site developers who are thinking of moving into the big leagues and implementing a database is Philip and Alex's Guide to Web Publishing *by Philip Greenspun. You can read it for free (or buy a hard copy) at* http://www.photo.net/wtr/thebook. *Chapter 11, "Sites That Are Really Databases," talks at length about when and why you need to use databases.*

Once you've identified your database application, it's time to move on to implementation. If you already have a database up and running, you won't need to pay much attention to the next two sections. However, if you are starting your database project from scratch, read on for some background information and design tips.

The Database Connection Wizard lets you pull data out of a database; it does not help you in entering data. You can use custom Active Server Pages (ASP) scripts to create a form for data entry; however, doing that is beyond the scope of this book. You can then use FrontPage's Form Page Wizard to store the data collected via such forms in a comma-delimited text file, which can be imported into a database. See Chapter 14 for more on forms.

Adding Database Information to Your Page

If you've never done it before, getting information from your database to appear on your Web pages might seem like a mysterious bit of black magic. In fact, what's going on is pretty straightforward: Whenever a visitor to your site requests a page that includes data from the database, your Web server does a little bit of work behind the scenes. It goes to the database for the information—for example, details about a product your company sells—and once it has it, the Web server inserts the data into the Web page and then sends the finished page to the user's browser. Luckily, FrontPage includes a wizard to make this process as painless as possible.

You must be working with a server-based Web (as opposed to a file-based Web) for FrontPage's database integration features to work properly.

If you've already got a database containing the information you want to publish, you simply need to figure out how to make the connection between your Web server and your database. Otherwise, you'll need to create a database. The first step is to choose a database product that is ODBC-compliant. *ODBC*, short for *Open Database Connectivity*, is a standard way to access different database systems. FrontPage uses ODBC to shuttle information between your database and Web site. Most professional database software, including Microsoft Access, Microsoft SQL Server, Sybase, and Oracle, is ODBC-compliant.

Step 1: Create the Database

If you don't already have a database, you'll need to create one. Microsoft Access, which is integrated into the Office family of applications, is a convenient tool for doing this. It offers a variety of wizards that should address most general database needs. See Chapter 20 for more information on Microsoft Access.

Step 2: Set Up a Database Connection

FrontPage 2002 has built-in support for four different types of database connections; the one you choose will depend on where and how your database is set up. Your options are:

- If you're using a simple database system like Access or FoxPro (or even an Excel spreadsheet), you can simply store your database file or folder in your FrontPage Web site.

- If your database lives on a Windows-based Web server, you can create a System Data Source Name on the server (we'll explain how to create a System DSN below) and connect to the database via that DSN. If you aren't the person in charge of the Web server, you'll need to talk to the server administrator about doing this.

- If you're using either a Microsoft SQL Server database or an Oracle database that is located on the same network as your Web server, you can create a network connection to the database server.

- For custom configurations, you can create a File DSN or Universal Data Link file and store it in your FrontPage Web site.

Out of these options, the first is by far the easiest to implement—but if you're building a serious site that will get any significant amount of traffic, or a site that will be built and maintained by more than one or two developers, it's probably also the worst solution.

The second option relies on Windows' built-in support for database access and is some server administrators' preferred method of controlling access to the database resources on their machines.

The third option—using a network connection to a dedicated database server running Microsoft SQL Server or Oracle—is probably the one you'll use if your project involves an existing enterprise database (e.g., a product information database, a human resources database, or a contact database). This is fairly simple to set up, provided you know or can find out the details about connecting to the database server.

And if none of the above applies to your situation, you can try to set up a custom database connection using a File DSN (`.dsn`) or Universal Data Link (`.udl`) file. To do this, you'll need to either create or get access to the file—and you'll probably need to talk to your system administrator about it.

Creating a System DSN on Your Web Server

A *Data Source Name* (*DSN*) points to your database—it's what allows your Web server and database to talk to each other. If someone else administers the server that hosts your database, you may need to contact your system administrator to obtain the DSN and an optional login and password for your database. Note that you need to perform this procedure on the computer that's running your Web server, not the computer you're using to run FrontPage. (Of course, if your Web server happens to be running on the same computer that you're using to run FrontPage, so much the better. Unfortunately, this often isn't the case.)

Be sure to close the database in any other applications such as Access before you follow these procedures.

If you're setting up the database yourself on Windows 95, 98, ME, NT, or 2000, you can take these simple steps to create a System DSN on the Web server:

1. From the Windows Start menu, choose Settings ➜ Control Panel. The Control Panel window appears.

2. If you're using Windows 95, 98, or NT, double-click the 32-bit ODBC icon. If you're using Windows 2000, double-click the Administrative Tools icon, then the Data Sources (ODBC) icon. The ODBC Data Source Administrator dialog box appears.

3. Select the System DSN tab. A list of the current system DSNs appears, as shown in Figure 23.1.

As you work through the steps in this section, you'll notice that there are several different kinds of Data Source Names (DSNs). The one that's most important to you at this stage of the game is the System DSN. However, so you'll understand the difference between the different kinds, a System DSN is available to all users, whereas a User DSN is only available to the user who creates it. All the details that are created when you set up System or User DSNs are stored in the system Registry. File DSNs are a bit more complex—instead of the Registry, information is stored in a file with a `.dsn` extension. The Web server then must look for the file in order to understand how to connect to the database. File DSNs are usually reserved for administrators and very advanced users with highly specific needs.

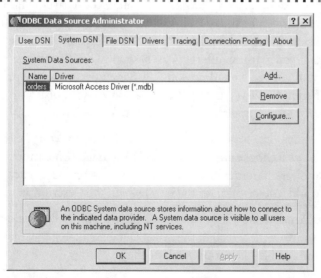

Figure 23.1 *The System DSN tab lists all current DSNs on your system.*

4. Click Add to add a new DSN. The Create New Data Source dialog box appears, as shown in Figure 23.2.

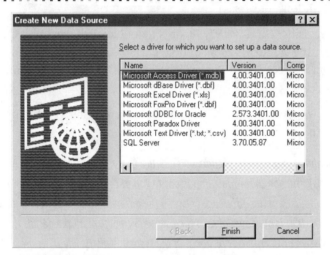

Figure 23.2 *Use the Create New Data Source dialog box to create a new DSN.*

5. From the list, select the driver for the database software that you're using. For our Access example, we'll choose Microsoft Access Driver (*.mdb). You should choose the driver for the specific ODBC-compliant database software that you're using. Then click Finish. The ODBC Microsoft Access Setup dialog box appears. If you're using different database software, the process will be slightly different. If you're using Microsoft SQL Server or Oracle, the process will be *very* different (however, the ODBC Data Source Administrator includes built-in Help for setting up database connections).

6. In the Data Source Name text box, type in a name for your DSN. For our example, we'll choose *orders*. It's a good idea to use something descriptive, short, and easy to remember, since you'll have to retype it exactly later on. You can also add a description of the new DSN in the Description text box.

7. Now you must associate your database file with the DSN. To do this, in the Database area click Select. In the Select Database dialog box that appears, locate and double-click your database file.

The DSN records the location of the database data file, so if your server administrator tells you where to put the data file, be sure to put it there and leave it there. If you're setting up your own DSN, put your data file some place where you expect it to stay, and don't move the file around. In either case, if you move your database file to a different directory after setting up your DSN, the DSN won't work and the Web pages that access the database will be broken.

8. Some databases are set up to require a username and password. If the database you are using requires this, click Advanced. In the dialog box that appears, fill in the login and password fields and click OK. The ODBC Microsoft Access Setup dialog box reappears.

9. Click OK to close the ODBC Microsoft Access Setup dialog box and return to the ODBC Data Source Administrator dialog box. You should see the name of your new DSN listed in the User DSN tab.

10. Click OK to close the ODBC Data Source Administrator dialog box. The Control Panel window reappears. (Or, if you're using Windows 2000, the Administrative Tools window reappears; you can click the Up button in the main toolbar to return the Control Panel window.)

Most ISPs prefer that you not develop your data-centric Web pages on their database server—they'd rather you do development elsewhere and then place your finished database on their machine. If this is the case for you and you're using System DSNs to connect to the database, make sure the System DSN for your local copy of the database has the same name as the System DSN on the ISP's server. The steps to create a System DSNs are discussed below. ODBC data sources on both of those machines use the exact same name.

Creating the Database Connection in FrontPage

Whenever you want to get your FrontPage Web pages to talk to a new database, you've got to set up a connection in FrontPage. You can do this from within the Database Results Wizard, or by accessing the Web Settings dialog box (shown in Figure 23.3) directly. The basic procedure is the same either way.

1. Open the FrontPage Web site you want to connect to the database.

2. From the menu bar, select Tools ➜ Web Settings.

3. Click the Database tab.

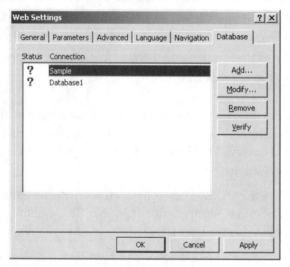

Figure 23.3 *The Web Settings dialog box*

4. To add your database, click Add. The New Database Connection dialog box, shown in Figure 23.4, appears.

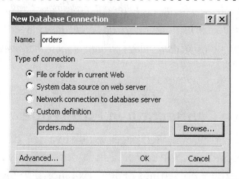

Figure 23.4 *The New Database Connection dialog box*

5. Type the name of your database in the Name text box. (We typed in **orders**.) Then click one of the Type Of Connection buttons. You will most likely be

linking to a file or folder in the current Web site. However, if you are trying to connect to a data source on a Web server, click the System Data Source On Web Server button. Similarly, if you are looking for a file that resides elsewhere on the network, click the Network Connection To Database Server button. To use a File DSN or UDL file, click Custom Definition.

6. At this point, you need to specify exactly how the Web server should connect to the database. First click Browse, and use the dialog box that appears to enter the details about your database. The dialog box you see will vary depending on which option you chose using the Type Of Connection buttons.

   File Or Folder In Current Web   You will see a simple dialog box asking you to locate the database file or folder; simply find the database file (or type its location into the URL field) and click OK.

   System Data Source On Web Server   You should see a dialog box listing the System DSNs on your Web server. Select the DSN you want to use and click OK. If the Browse button is disabled when you select System Data Source on Web Server option, or if you see an error saying "This Web server does not allow a client to list the server's data resources," see Microsoft Knowledge Base Article Q280392 (`http://support.microsoft.com/support/kb/articles/Q280/3/92.ASP`).

   Network Connection To Database Server   In the Network Database Connection dialog box, select the type of driver you will be using, enter the name of the server where the database is located and the name of the database, then click OK.

   Custom Definition   Locate the `.dsn` or `.udl` file you want to use. The file must be located in your FrontPage Web site. Then click OK.

7. Once you've completed the previous step, you'll return to the New Database Connection dialog box. If your database requires a user ID and password, click the Advanced button and enter the appropriate information. Click OK to close the New Database Connection dialog box.

8. When you return to the Web Settings dialog box, you'll now see the name of your database connection and its status. (If the Status icon is a question mark, simply select the connection and click Verify to see whether the connection is working properly.) Click OK to return to FrontPage.

Like any other HTML text, you can change the font of the database section, make it bold, or increase the type size. For more on changing the look of text on a Web page, see Chapter 5.

Your database is now linked, and you can modify it to your design tastes using the techniques learned elsewhere in this book. However, in order to make this database fully operational, you must save your HTML file with an `.asp` (Active Server Pages) extension, and upload all of the information to your ASP-compliant server. If you chose to include the database file or a custom connection file (a `.dsn` or `.udl` file) in your FrontPage Web, you need to upload these files as well.

Now you're ready to use the Database Results Wizard in Microsoft FrontPage.

Step 3: Use the Database Results Wizard

The Database Results Wizard allows you to do one of three things:

- Use a sample database connection, using a preexisting database named "Northwind."

- Use an existing database connection.

- Create and use a new database connection.

The sample database connection is helpful to you if you'd like to make a dry run through the process, and is especially useful if you've never designed database-backed Web pages before. Although our example below uses data (a list of employees from the Employees table) from the sample "Northwind" database provided with FrontPage, this section will teach you how to use the Database Results Wizard so that you can use it with your own databases later. To use a different database, simply select the connection you want in step 3 below. Or, if you need to create a new connection, see the section "Creating the Database Connection in FrontPage" above.

1. In FrontPage, open a new page to hold the information from the database.

2. Position the cursor at the place you'd like the employee list to appear, and select Insert ➔ Database ➔ Results.

3. The Database Results Wizard appears (see Figure 23.5). Choose the Use A Sample Database Connection (Northwind) option button and click Next. (To use a different database, simply choose Use An Existing Database Connection and select the connection you want from the drop-down list. Or, if you choose Use A New Database Connection and click the Create button, FrontPage opens the Web Settings dialog box, which is described in the previous section.)

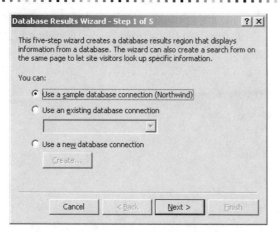

Figure 23.5 *The Database Results Wizard, step 1*

4. When the next window appears (see Figure 23.6), you'll have to wait briefly as FrontPage connects to the database to retrieve a list of the tables and views in the database. Click the Record Source option button and select Employees from the drop-down list. This tells FrontPage that you want to use records from the Employees table. Click Next.

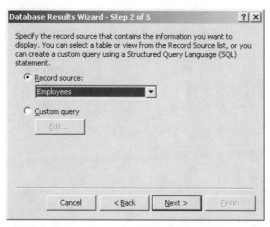

Figure 23.6 *The Database Results Wizard, step 2*

5. Step 3 of the wizard (see Figure 23.7) displays a list of the fields in the Employees table. By default, all fields are selected to be included in your page. For this example, we will exclude certain fields from the results; click Edit List.

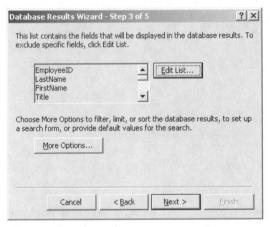

Figure 23.7 *The Database Results Wizard, step 3*

6. In the Displayed Fields dialog box (see Figure 23.8), you can choose exactly what fields should appear and the order in which they should be displayed. In our example, we've excluded everything but the LastName, FirstName, Title, Extension, and HireDate fields. Use the Add, Remove, Move Up, and Move Down buttons to organize the fields. Click OK to return to step 3 of the wizard.

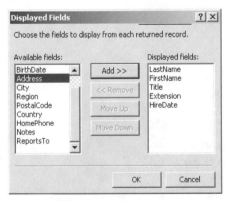

Figure 23.8 *The Displayed Fields dialog box*

7. Click the More Options button. In the More Options dialog box (see Figure 23.9), you can filter the results from the database (for example, we could choose to show only employees hired during the last six months), add a search form to your page to allow users to look up records on their own, change the sorting order of the records, and enter a custom message to display on your page if, for some reason, no records are found in the database. For our example, we'll change the sort order so that employee records are sorted by last name and first name, just like a phone book.

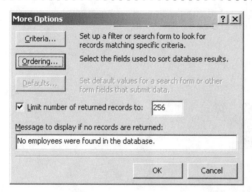

Figure 23.9 *The More Options dialog box.*

8. Click the Ordering button. FrontPage displays the Ordering dialog box (see Figure 23.10). Move the LastName and FirstName fields from the Available Fields list to the Sort Order list by selecting them and clicking the Add button. When you're done, click OK to return to the More Options dialog box, then click OK again to return to step 3 of the wizard.

9. Click Next to advance to step 4 of the wizard. Step 4 of the wizard (see Figure 23.11) allows you to change the way the records are displayed on the page. For this example, leave things as they are and click Next.

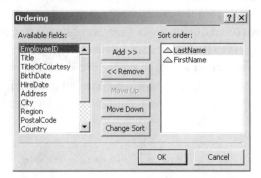

Figure 23.10 *The Ordering dialog box*

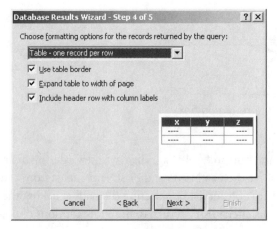

Figure 23.11 *The Database Results Wizard, step 4*

10. Step 5 (see Figure 23.12) allows you to choose whether to display all of the records from the database on a single page, or to break them up into smaller sets. Leave the default settings in place and click Finish.

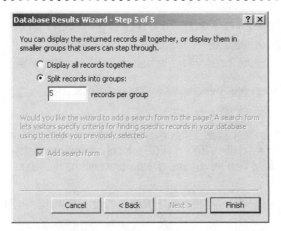

Figure 23.12 *The Database Results Wizard, step 5*

That's it. FrontPage adds a Database Results region to your page. Read on for instructions on saving your work, previewing the page with live data from the database, or modifying the properties of the Database Results region.

Step 4: Save Your Page

It's important to pay special attention when saving files that contain data that's dynamically linked to a database. When the Database Results Wizard is applied to a Web page, it actually turns that page into an Active Server Page. Active Server Pages are different from regular HTML pages in that they contain special scripts that must be processed by the Web server before they can be sent out to the user. To indicate to the Web server that these pages require special processing, you must do two things:

- Save the file in a folder that allows scripts to run.
- Change your file's extension to `.asp`.

Create an Executable Folder in Your FrontPage Web Site

Web pages that contain Database Results Wizard additions (or any other ASP pages, for that matter) must be stored in a folder that allows scripts or programs to be run. This is not the default setting for FrontPage Web site folders.

If you do not already have an executable folder in your Web site, it's easy to create one:

1. From the FrontPage menu bar, select File ➜ New ➜ Folder.

2. Give the new folder a name. Web folders that allow scripts or programs to run are usually called *cgi*, *cgi-bin*, or *scripts*, but you can choose any name you like. (The name *CGI* comes from Common Gateway Interface, which is a standard technique for getting Web servers and external programs on the server to work together to create dynamic Web pages.)

3. Right-click the folder you just renamed and choose Properties from the menu that appears. The folder's Properties dialog box appears.

4. At the bottom of the folder's Properties dialog box, select the check box labeled Allow Scripts To Be Run. Note that you must be using a server-based Web for this to work. If you're using a file-based Web (one that lives only on your hard disk rather than on a FrontPage-enabled Web server), this option will be unavailable.

5. Click OK. The Properties dialog box closes and your new folder will now allow any scripts and ASPs it contains to be run.

Front Page will attempt to remind you to save your ASP files correctly by showing you an alert box (see Figure 23.13).

Figure 23.13 *FrontPage will alert you to save your file as an ASP file.*

You can follow these simple steps to save your file properly:

1. The file you're preparing to save should be open in Page view.

2. From the menu bar, select File ➜ Save As. The Save As dialog box appears.

3. In the Save As dialog box's list of directories, select the directory you created to hold scripts. (See the sidebar "Create an Executable Folder in Your FrontPage Web Site," earlier in this chapter.) In the URL text box, type a filename. The name you give the file should end with the extension .asp (for example, whatever.asp).

4. Click OK. The dialog box closes and the file is saved to the location you specified. The Page view reappears.

Once you've saved your page as an ASP file, you're done. Read on to learn how you can modify the properties of the Database Results region in your page and preview the page.

ISP Issues

It's important to consider who's supporting your Web site when you're planning and implementing any interactive Web pages, including adding database interaction—especially if your Web site is hosted by an ISP. There are several issues to consider regarding a Web site hosted by an ISP:

- Your ISP may not be using the right operating system or Web server to support ASPs.

- For security reasons, your ISP may not routinely allow users to post Web pages that contain scripts—including ASPs.

- Your ISP may not allow you to use a database as part of your Web, or it may allow only certain database products.

It all comes down to this: If an ISP hosts your Web site, you absolutely must check with (and perhaps make special arrangements with) your ISP *before* you begin adding or uploading databases or ASPs.

Changing Database Properties

You've created this great new database-backed Web page, but nobody's perfect. What if you want to make a change to a database region once you've left the Database Results Wizard? Fortunately, FrontPage makes it easy to go back and edit the database you've added to your pages. Here's how:

1. In FrontPage, open the Web page containing the database templates. You'll see sections demarcating the beginning and end of the database regions (see Figure 23.14).

2. Right-click within the database area. A menu appears, as shown in Figure 23.14.

3. From the menu that appears, select Database Results Properties. The Database Results Wizard dialog box appears. All the values you typed in when you last used the wizard will still be in place.

4. You can now make any modifications to your database that you'd like.

Once you are done with the Database Results Wizard, you'll be returned to Page view, where you'll see the changes you made to the database.

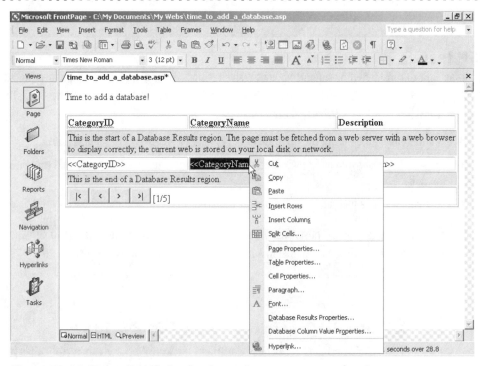

Figure 23.14 *Right-clicking the database gives you a menu of options.*

Viewing Your Page

After you've saved your database-enabled Web page, you can view it. One option is to view the page by selecting the Preview tab along the bottom of the window. You'll notice that the database values do not appear on the page as they should. Also, note that if you are using a disk-based Web site, you need to publish your page prior to pre-viewing it.

Database values do not appear in the FrontPage Preview window because the Web page must be served by a Web server.

It's easy to view your page as a user would see it. Follow these steps:

1. Make sure your Web page has been properly saved as an ASP file in a folder that allows scripts to be run.

2. Open the database-enabled page in Page view.

3. From the menu bar, select File ➜ Preview In Browser. The Preview In Browser dialog box appears.

4. Click the Preview button. The page appears in a Web browser window.

The resulting page looks quite different from the preview you looked at in Page view. Instead of placeholder text appearing where data from the database should appear, the actual data appears.

Notes on Database Maintenance

You've defined the project, organized the data, chosen a database product, and implemented the solution. But you're not done yet! Getting the most out of your database requires that you maintain the database and the information contained within it.

You or your staff can perform some of the regular maintenance that your database requires, but some changes may require calling in a *database administrator* (*DBA*) or consultant. Here are some items you can manage yourself, once the database is up and running:

- Adding new records to the database
- Editing existing records
- Deleting old or outdated records
- Making regular backups

Maintenance items that may require the assistance of a DBA or consultant include:

- Creating complex queries
- Adding new fields or new tables to an existing database
- Upgrading the database software
- Upgrading the hardware of the machine on which the database software runs

Up Next

Databases add functionality in a variety of ways, and entire books have been written that describe how databases can be used to enhance Web sites. While we can't address such a vast technology in one short chapter, we have given you the basics to get you started.

As mentioned, databases, like any advanced or interactive Web application, demand updates and maintenance.

In Chapter 24, "Site Maintenance and Promotion," we'll take a look at how you can apply professional techniques to help you get the most mileage out of your databases and Web site in general. We'll show you how to keep track of changes, make updates, and keep links fresh, as well as how to promote your site once it's on the Web.

Site Maintenance and Promotion

FRONTPAGE

Chapter 24

ongratulations! You have successfully constructed a well-thought-out, well-designed, robust FrontPage Web site. You've linked it up, brought it live, and taken your team out to lunch to celebrate. Now you find yourself charged with keeping your creation current and working like new. You need to be sure that your site's content is visually, textually, and technically up-to-date and that your fellow Webmasters and favorite search engines are paying attention. This chapter takes you through the basics of site maintenance and promotion. In this chapter, you make sure that your site gets the airtime it deserves. Topics include:

- Maintaining your Web site

- Verifying and fixing hyperlinks

- Promoting your Web site and building traffic

- Finding your target audience

- Getting listed with directories and search engines

- Getting retroactively linked

- Announcing your site in newsgroups and the press

- Taking advantage of e-mail publicity

- Buying and trading banner ads

Managing Maintenance of Your Web Site

Keeping a Web site going is a constant challenge, not unlike maintaining a house. A house can't keep itself in good repair. You have to scoop leaves out of drains and gutters, fix leaks in the roof, insulate the pipes to prevent freezing in the winter, and that sort of thing. Similarly, a Web site needs to be maintained on a regular basis.

Some tasks are pretty obvious. You have to check the hyperlinks on your site to make sure they're still live, fix the odd script or database query here or there, and refine navigational elements as you add new pages and areas to your site. You also have to do a certain amount of routine server maintenance, which basically consists of reading log files and dealing with what comes up. Luckily, FrontPage offers some handy tools that make site maintenance quite a bit easier than it might be otherwise.

Don't forget to use the handy Tasks view feature described in Chapter 7 to organize and track maintenance tasks.

Organizing and Assigning Maintenance Tasks

Maintenance doesn't tend to be at the top of a Web team's list of things to do. You'll find that a Web site is maintained only if the tasks involved are specifically detailed and then assigned to particular people. Almost everyone would rather have fun than clean their house, and it's really easy for Web site managers and worker bees to get caught up in the glamour tasks of creating new pages or adding zippy features to a Web site. Site maintenance can be a low priority until something breaks or users start to complain.

For every one person who complains about a broken link, half a dozen more don't bother and just leave the site. Don't wait for complaints. Find broken items on your site before visitors do, and fix them immediately.

Make yourself or your group an organized list—a *chore chart* of sorts—showing what maintenance needs to be done and who will do it. You might even consider keeping a log and having each person jot down his or her initials when a task is complete. For that matter, you could jot down notes for others who might do the task in the future. Often it is easier to trace the source of a problem if you have a history of events to consult.

Basic Web site maintenance includes:

Verifying that links work.   Later in this chapter, "Verifying Hyperlinks" shows you how to use FrontPage's Verify Hyperlink Status feature to painlessly locate and fix hyperlinks that may have died or otherwise gone sour.

Replacing outdated text and images.   FrontPage's search-and-replace function enables you to easily substitute new text for outdated content. (To replace images, you must find and replace them manually. See Chapter 4.)

Improving organization and navigation as needed.   Especially when new material is added to the site or old material is deleted, improving the organization of your site and the tools for getting here and there is essential. For navigation purposes, you may need to change your navigation bars (see Chapter 15) and button text (also covered in Chapter 15).

Repairing broken queries or scripts.   See Chapter 21, Chapter 22, and Chapter 23 for more on databases and scripts.

Conducting server maintenance.   This is a matter of reading and responding to log files, identifying broken scripts, monitoring disk and memory usage, predicting load levels, and generally taking steps to ensure that your Web site doesn't cause the server to crash.

Depending on the size, goals, and mission-critical status (or lack thereof) of your site, these tasks might be done often or rarely. The point is to do them *regularly*. The allocation of maintenance responsibilities among your team members depends on how your team is configured. To make sure that maintenance tasks are performed on schedule, those tasks must be assigned to specific people who will be accountable for getting them done.

Your graphically inclined team members, for example, are the obvious nominees for keeping your Web site's imagery up to date. Copywriters can be given the task of revising the content. Programmers can be relied on to parse server logs and regularly offer the reassurance that your site is (or will immediately be) bug-free. As for "grunge work" such as checking retroactive links and search engine placement, taking turns doing it is one option, but you may also consider hiring a willing high school or college intern to support your team. You'll appreciate the labor and the intern will appreciate the good reference on his or her resume. All of these services can also be outsourced to independent consultants if your budget permits, and if it seems to be the best alternative for your company.

You can see some examples of style guides on the Web. Some of these give certain matters more coverage than others, and some are easier to navigate or more attractively designed than others. Take a look at several and you'll get ideas about what should be in your own style guide.

Managing Style

If many different people handle different parts of your Web site, you need a way to communicate to all members of the group what's been decided about matters of *style*. (Even if you are the only person working on the site, you're better off jotting these things down for your own reference than trying to remember them from one month to the next.) Style is an important part of maintaining the look, feel, and general content integrity of a Web site. For example, you need to communicate exactly which colors compose your site's palette and which fonts are used for which elements. You should even document such nitpicky matters as how to spell certain words that have more than one spelling (such as *e-mail* or *email*) and how to punctuate (whether *U.S.* or *US* is correct when abbreviating *United States,* for example). Nothing looks more unprofessional than inconsistency, and the best way to maintain consistency is to create, maintain, and consult a *style guide*.

Your style guide can be an online document, a printed document, or both. It should include information about the following:

- The site's *mission*—for example, a brief statement that describes the site's goals or the product or service that the site offers, along with an indication of the style in which these aims will be pursued, the audience the site will reach, and how success can be assessed in the context of the goals set out for the site.

- The site's *look and feel*—including color and font choices, guidelines regarding the placement of art on the pages, where banners and navigation bars go, and even records of how certain design decisions were reached and who did the actual design work (so you can later reference that information instead of reinventing the wheel).

- Conventions you've established for *use of HTML*—for example, the screen size (in pixels) you design for, how and when to use META, ALT, and other tags, what types of headings go where, which browsers are supported, how tables are used (with specifics of cell size and so on), how to lay out tabular matter, and how to use art, captions, sidebars, pull quotes, and footers.

- Policies for *linking and cross-linking*—for example, how many links can appear on a page or in a paragraph, and which sorts of words or phrases to link on. (*Hint:* Linking on "Click here" is nowhere near as useful as linking on a word that describes what the user will actually find after clicking the link.)

- Standards for *editorial tone and conventions*—for example, whether the site's written text has a hip, playful, or "professional" tone, and whether to style certain phrases certain ways (again, is *e-mail* or *email* the correct spelling? What about P.M., pm, or p.m.?).

- Guidelines regarding *navigation and architecture*—for example, how the directory structure is organized and where things go in it, as well as (generally speaking) how the user is expected to make his or her way around.

- Conditions for using the company *logo and copyright notices*, as well as any other pertinent legal information—for example, what colors the logo is allowed to appear in and where it may be placed, as well as where copyright notices and other legalese must appear and what they must say.

- Processes and procedures you've established for *review and posting* of material—for example, who has the final say on which content is posted, how long they will have to offer feedback or consent, who decides which feedback to incorporate, and who may do the actual posting to the site.

Mastering What's Online

A great example of a Web site style guide is the Yale C/AIM Style Guide at `www.info.med.yale.edu/caim/manual/index.html`. Contrast its navigation and content with the Ball State guide at `www.bsu.edu/handbook`. Check out Lincoln University's University Outreach style guide at `www.outreach.missouri.edu/webteam/style`; for another example, see West Virginia University's guide (it offers at least some editorial information) at `www.wvu.edu/~telecom/wwwinit/guidelines.html`.

Verifying Hyperlinks

Dead links can kill a visitor's interest in a Web site faster than anything else. Links "die" when the Web page or site at the other end of the link goes down or its URL changes. You can't control that, and all too often, you know about it only because visitors to your site complain. Few things will chase users off your site faster than a lot of links that go nowhere. And yet, until recently finding and eliminating dead links on a big site was a big chore—in days of old, it involved a tedious process of clicking one link after another to be sure they all worked. Now FrontPage automates this process, making link maintenance so easy that there's just no excuse for not doing it.

Checking for Broken Hyperlinks

Before you can fix broken links, you must track them down. Checking links is a snap with FrontPage; the process is automatic and results in an easy-to-use list that shows the status of all the links in your Web site. You can then move on to the more entertaining part—fixing them.

If you use a dial-up connection to the Internet rather than connecting via a LAN or DSL line, FrontPage will give you the opportunity to log on to the Internet before verifying the links on your site. Otherwise, when you verify the links, all the links that go outside your site will appear to be bad. (The pages they point to were inaccessible, so they appeared dead to FrontPage.)

Follow these steps to check the hyperlinks on your Web site:

1. Switch to Reports view by clicking the Reports icon in the Views bar or choosing View ➜ Reports ➜ Site Summary. You see the summary list of all the reports you can run in FrontPage.

Name	Count	Size	Description
All files	54	497KB	All files in the current Web
Pictures	13	316KB	Picture files in the current Web (GIF, JPG, BMP, etc.)
Unlinked files	44	422KB	Files in the current Web that cannot be reached by starting from your home page
Linked files	10	76KB	Files in the current Web that can be reached by starting from your home page
Slow pages	1	137KB	Pages in the current Web exceeding an estimated download time of 30 seconds at 28.
Older files	0	0KB	Files in the current Web that have not been modified in over 72 days
Recently added files	23	90KB	Files in the current Web that have been created in the last 30 days
Hyperlinks	100		All hyperlinks in the current Web
Unverified hyperlinks	0		Hyperlinks pointing to unconfirmed target files
Broken hyperlinks	18		Hyperlinks pointing to unavailable target files
External hyperlinks	14		Hyperlinks pointing to files outside of the current Web
Internal hyperlinks	86		Hyperlinks pointing to other files within the current Web
Component errors	4		Files in the current Web with components reporting an error
Uncompleted tasks	3		Tasks in the current Web that are not yet marked completed
Unused themes	1		Themes in the current Web that are not applied to any file

2. Under Name, click Hyperlinks to generate a Broken Hyperlinks report.

3. If necessary, click the Status button at the top of the Status column to sort the links so that the Broken, Edited, and OK links appear together in the report.

You can also generate a Broken Hyperlinks report by way of the Reporting toolbar. To display the toolbar, right-click any toolbar and choose Reporting. Then click the Reports button on the toolbar and, from the drop-down menu, choose Problems ➜ Broken Hyperlinks.

In the report, every link in your Web site appears in a list, along with the URL associated with that link and the link's status. Each link's status is described with one of the following indicators:

This Status...	Means...
OK	The link works.
Broken	The link is broken.

This Status...	Means...
Unknown	The link has not yet been verified.
Verifying	The link is currently being verified.

If there are broken hyperlinks in your Web site, they are listed first in the Broken Hyperlinks report.

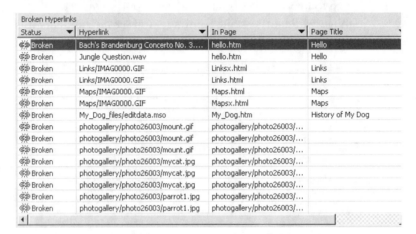

One by one, the status of all the links is updated in the Broken Hyperlinks report view. Now you can move on to fixing those broken links that you've discovered. Read on.

To return to the Site Summary reports screen after you have run a Broken Hyperlinks or other kind of report, choose View ➜ Reports ➜ Site Summary.

Mastering What's Online

If you're checking links from a computer where FrontPage isn't installed, you may want to try the venerated Doctor HTML. The Doc verifies links and HTML tags and even checks spelling; it also provides further information in the course of doing so beyond what FrontPage tells you. For example, Doctor HTML calculates how long a page will take for a user with a 14.4 modem to load. Consult Doctor HTML at www.imagiware.com.

Another site you'll enjoy is NetMechanic at www.netmechanic.com. If these sites don't suit you or you want to find others, do a search for HTML validators in your favorite search engine. Many great sites evaluate Web sites at no charge.

Fixing Broken Links

Okay, so you've checked the links on your site and found a few that were, to your dismay, broken. (If all the links on your site worked, don't forget to check again next week.) FrontPage offers two ways to deal with broken links:

- Change broken links: Change a particular URL (whether it appears in one instance or throughout the site).

- Edit broken links: Edit the page that contains the bad URL.

Changing links is a convenient technique in many instances, but if you have other work to do on a single page or if you want to delete the broken link instead of changing it, editing is the preferred route. Both techniques are discussed in the following pages.

Yet a third way to replace links is to simply find and replace them using the techniques described in "Finding Text and Replacing It Globally" later in this chapter. Finding and replacing is not always the most convenient method, but it is an option.

Changing Broken Links

Perhaps only one link showed up as broken. Or perhaps you found a lot of problematic links. A handy FrontPage feature enables you to change a broken link once and in so doing propagate the change throughout the site—a big time-saver. (You can actually use this method for a single broken link as well; this might be preferable to editing the page because it is such an easy operation.)

Follow these steps to fix one broken link or many:

1. In the Broken Hyperlinks report, double-click the link you want to change or right-click it and choose Edit Hyperlink on the shortcut menu. The Edit Hyperlink dialog box appears (see Figure 24.1).

2. Do one of the following to correct the target address of the hyperlink:

   - In the Replace Hyperlink With text box, type in the correct address. For example, if you made a typo when you typed in the old link, `http://www.acompany.cm`, and the new, good link is `http://www.acompany.com`, type the correct link into the URL text box.

   - Click the Browse button and enter the correct address by way of the Edit Hyperlink dialog box (see Chapter 4). You can click the Browse The Web button to open your browser to a Web page. The address of the page will appear in the Address text box in the Edit Hyperlink dialog box (see Figure 24.2).

Go to the page where the link is located.

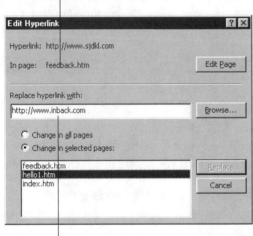

Change a broken link.

Figure 24.1 *Whether you want to fix a single broken link or many instances of that broken link, here's the place to do it.*

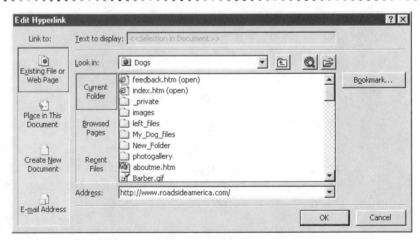

Figure 24.2 *Correcting the target address of a hyperlink*

3.   Change all of the occurrences or selected occurrences of the hyperlink:

   •   All occurrences: Click the Change In All Pages option button.

   •   Selected occurrences: In the box at the bottom of the Edit Hyperlink dialog box, Ctrl+click the links whose addresses you want to change. The box lists each page in your Web site where the link you are correcting is found.

4.   Click the Replace button.

In the Broken Links report, the replacement link appears in the list in place of the old one. The status of the link is Unknown (because it hasn't been checked in the most recent round of checking).

Editing Broken Links

Follow these steps to edit broken links:

1.   In the Broken Hyperlink report view, right-click the link that needs fixing and choose Edit Page on the shortcut menu. FrontPage opens the page where the broken link is located. The link is highlighted on the page.

2.   Right-click the link and choose Hyperlink Properties on the shortcut menu. The Edit Hyperlink dialog box appears (refer to Figure 24.2).

3.   Edit the hyperlink (Chapter 4 explains how this dialog box works).

To remove a hyperlink, click the Remove Link button in the Edit Hyperlink dialog box (refer to Figure 24.2).

In some cases, you might want to make other changes to a page in addition to fixing a broken link. Alternatively, you might want to simply remove the broken link. In those cases, editing the page is a good practice.

Finding Text and Replacing It Globally

As you build bigger and more complex Web sites, you'll find yourself wanting to make a single change across many, many pages. Maybe you want to change a name every time it appears on the Web site, or simply make a quick fix to a link. (A link is, after all, simply a piece of text.) The global search and replace features of FrontPage will save you a lot of time in doing this. They allow you to search—and make changes to—all of the pages that make up your Web site.

Finding Text

Follow these steps to search your entire Web site for a specific piece of text:

1. To search specific pages, select them in Folders view.

2. Choose Edit ➔ Find or press Ctrl+F. The Find and Replace dialog box appears.

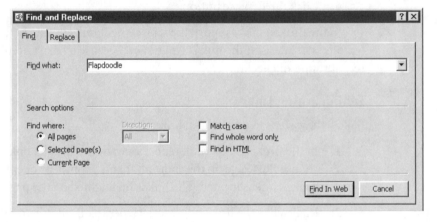

3. In the Find What text box, enter the text you want to find.

4. Click a Find Where option button: All Pages searches all the pages in the Web site, Selected Pages searches pages you selected in Folders view (if you selected pages in step 1), and Current Page searches the page that is on-screen.

5. Choose options to speed the search:

   Match Case   Searches for words with upper- and lowercase letters that match what you entered in the Find What text box.

   Find Whole Words Only   Searches for words, not fragments as well as words. Normally, a search for *bat* finds that word as well as *battle* and *wombat,* for example. Choose this option and you only get *bat.*

   Find in HTML   Searches for HTML codes.

6. Click the Find Next button (if you're searching a single page) or the Find In Web button (if you're searching more than one page or the entire Web site).

As FrontPage finds instances of the specified text, it highlights them on the page. Make any changes you like using the editing methods described in Part I of this book.

If you want to make changes to the found text globally (throughout the Web site), you'll use the Replace function. More on that in a moment.

Replacing Text

You can quite easily find and replace a specific piece of text on all of the pages that make up a Web site. Being able to do this is mighty convenient. When the company changes the official spelling of the name of a product, for example, you don't have to track down all instances of it on the site and edit them one by one. All you have to do is change them globally and save yourself the effort.

Watch out. We've seen it happen and done it ourselves. You make what you think should be a simple global change, and sometime later, in casually viewing your site, you see unexpected consequences. For example, the seemingly innocent change of hat *to* coat *can inadvertently give you occurrences of that changed to* tcoat. *Just be sure not to introduce a mistake when you search and replace.*

Follow these steps to make a global change to text:

1. Choose Edit ➔ Replace (or press Ctrl+H). You see the Replace tab of the Find and Replace dialog box.

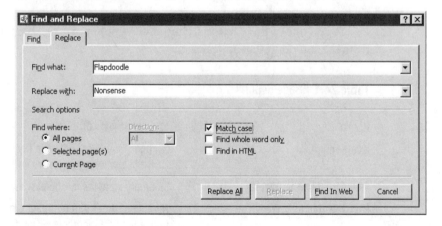

2. Enter the word or phrase that you want to replace (see the previous section in this chapter).

3. Enter the text you want to replace the found text in the Replace With text box.

4. Click the Find Next button (if you're searching a single page) or the Find In Web button (if you're searching more than one page).

5. To replace the text, click the Replace button. The highlighted text is instantly replaced with the text you specified.

To replace all instances of the text in one step, click the Replace All button. If you make a mistake, you can undo the replace by selecting Edit ➜ Undo or using the key combination Ctrl+Z to undo each instance of the changed items.

6. When you've finished, click the Cancel button. The dialog box closes and the Page view reappears.

Now you can resume other tasks, take a walk, or get a cup of coffee.

Reports for Seeing How Your Site Is Being Used

FrontPage offers a series of Usage reports for investigating who visits your site, how often visitors arrive, and one or two other things besides. Table 24.1 describes these reports. After your site has been up and running for a while, try running these reports. They can reveal a lot about your site.

To run one of these reports, choose View ➜ Reports ➜ Usage and a report name from the submenu that appears.

Table 24.1 Usage Reports

REPORT	WHAT IT REPORTS ON
Usage Summary	Summary statistics about the frequency with which your site is visited and which pages are visited.
Summary (Monthly, Weekly, or Daily)	Summary statistics for the past month, week, or day.
Page Hits (Monthly, Weekly, or Daily)	Number of times different pages in your Web site were visited in the past month, week, or day.
Visiting Users	The IP addresses of people who visited your site.
Operating Systems	Operating systems used by visitors to your site.
Browsers	Web browsers used by visitors to your site.

Table 24.1 continued Usage Reports

REPORT	WHAT IT REPORTS ON
Referring Domains	Names of domains where hyperlinks to your site are found.
Referring URLs	Web page addresses where hyperlinks to your site are found.
Search Strings	Search strings that people who visited your site entered in search engines.

Promoting Your Site and Building Traffic

If there are no links to your site, you will get no hits. This is a law of physics on the Web. You need many entry points to your site. You need *retroactive links* (links from other sites to yours) and prominent listings in directories and search engine databases. Your site needs all the attention it deserves. If no one knows it's there, how will they visit? Your job is to get out there and tell people that your site exists. You need lots of people visiting, lots of hits, and consistent *traffic.*

The best way to get publicity for a Web site is to make it such a whiz-bang piece of genius that no one can ignore it. Make sure your site includes outstanding original content presented in an appropriate style, with great design, easy navigation, and a healthy dose of wit. The combination of all of these elements will make your site appealing to those in the know who see so many and recommend so few. These individuals, when satisfied, are the best visitors to any site.

The stuff of real-world publicity includes press releases; newsletters; print advertising; direct mail or other distribution of flyers, postcards, or letters; public appearances; gala events; and so on. You may be surprised to find out how many of these common real-world publicity techniques transfer directly to the Net. A press release can easily go to selected online venues via e-mail; an electronic "mailing list" can be an avenue to distribute newsletters to your circle of associates; a chat might be thought of as an "event," and so on. Effective use of these techniques requires a combination of diligence and creativity.

The most important caveat in using online publicity techniques is basic: *respect the culture within which you're moving.* Online culture is not a grab-and-run environment and does not suffer a deluge of junk mail lightly. It's important to avoid "spamming," or flooding people with e-mail they're not interested in reading. Your goal is to center your online publicity on the values that citizens of the Web hold dear—choice, privacy, and content over form. Before we launch into specific techniques for publicizing your site, let's look at how to identify your target audience and how to choose which venues to use in your campaign.

Finding Your Target Audience

When marketing a product, you can go either *broad* or *deep*. You usually don't want to slam your message at everyone on the Internet (that's *broad*) unless your site is of overall interest to everyone. A search engine site or other online directory is one example of a site that has very broad appeal and would especially benefit from broad exposure; another example might be a site devoted to some piece of Internet software. For most topics, however, you do better to focus your efforts on reaching those who are most likely to respond to the topic of your site. That's *deep*—meaning that you deeply penetrate a narrower market. If your site is about cars, for example, you want to reach people with an interest in cars.

The content of your site will help you decide whether to go broad or deep. If you're going broad, look for venues that will reach a large number of people. If deep is the route you choose, look for venues that are trafficked by the folks you want to reach. Be creative about your target audience—if your site is about lunch boxes, your audience might be kids, pop culture fans, memorabilia collectors, and even fans of some celebrities who appear on lunch boxes. If your site is about rose gardening, your audience will not only be garden hobbyists, but also decorators, landscape architects, florists, and Valentine's Day gift-givers.

Take a minute to think through the topic of your site and brainstorm about what types of people might be interested in it. This preliminary demographic study will help you choose the best means of locating the audience you want to communicate with.

Planning Your Campaign

Organizing and carrying out a promotional campaign for your Web site is much like conducting promotional efforts for any other product, service, or company. Of course you need to know what your site is about and who your target audience is. To create your own campaign, you'll also need to get your message in order. Planning your promotional campaign will include:

- Gathering materials. For example, you need to have your site's mission statement and goals on hand, as well as any logos and other visual elements you can use in your marketing efforts.

- Writing up some key points (*talking points*) and a brief summary of your site's content (a *blurb*). These are, in a sense, just friendlier versions of your list of goals and mission statement.

- Researching how your site compares to others of its type, and what differentiates it or sets it apart from those competitors. (Be sure to cover this in your talking points and blurb.) You may also have to research what individual promotional options cost, who's who at a print venue you want to target, and so on.

- Considering your budget. You always want to get the biggest bang for your buck; how to accomplish the most economical and *effective* promotion is the name of the game.

- Targeting the venues most likely to reach your audience and reel them in.

The rest of this chapter offers pointers to addressing these action items. Let's start by looking at how people—most people, that is—locate Web sites they might find of interest. Most folks find what they're looking for on the Internet through just a few venues. The most common are:

- Search tools

- Retroactive links

- Newsgroups

- The press (magazines and newspapers)

Signature (sig) files, the hyperlinks that sometimes appear at the bottom of e-mail messages, and books are less common venues. However, don't write off these options—they are often the least expensive venues and sometimes reach extremely specific audiences; they also carry the weight of great authority—recommendations from a friend or a book, for example, are very persuasive, aren't they?

In considering which venues to tackle, your goal is to determine which are best for you and which will reach the largest percentage of your target audience.

You can choose to pursue any combination of venues. For example, you can pursue a presence in news-groups that are appropriate to your topic, and in the press, and in search tools, and so on. Don't overlook the "smaller" venue of placing a small notice of your site in a sig file that will appear at the bottom of every e-mail you send out. More on each of these options as we go along.

Your campaign should be as extensive as your time and resources allow. But it should also take into account which venues will be most likely to reach your target audience, and which are most cost-effective. For example, many people find out about Web sites via newsgroups. While frequenting newsgroups to evangelize your site seems easy enough, it is also time-consuming for you to do it, and it's not cheap to pay someone to sit around shuffling through Usenet, either. Should you choose to go the seemingly free newsgroups route (described in an upcoming section), consider the hidden costs involved, and rather than spreading your efforts around many newsgroups, *target those most likely to lead to success* given how you've envisioned your audience.

To focus your campaign, start by thinking about the benefits your site offers (not just the features, but the *benefits*). What will people get from a visit to your site? Will they get fast solutions to specific problems or challenges? Easy access to other Web sites? The product or service they've been looking for? A quality entertainment experience? Jot down a few talking points so you'll remember what features you really want to emphasize when writing the copy of your announcements and messages. Write up perhaps five phrases or sentences that describe the benefits of your site and/or the product you deliver via your site. Do this in a bulleted list, not paragraphs. Hone these phrases—your talking points— until they describe exactly what you want people to know at a glance about your site.

Keep your talking points near you or in a folder with records of your promotional efforts and how they panned out. These talking points can form the basis of any press releases you send out and ads you create. They can also help you in focusing the design or redesign of your site, since they are a sort of shorthand definition of your mission.

Remember to keep in mind the goals you've set for your site as you write up your talking points and focus your promotional campaign on the audience you plan to reach.

To actually plan your campaign, you will need to weigh the cost versus benefit of each potential venue you consider. Among the benefits to consider are:

- Will your message be intensely targeted (deep) or reach a wide variety of people (broad)? Which is more appropriate to your product, service, or site?

- How many users will you reach? A site that covers a popular topic is more likely to be visited than one that covers an obscure topic.

- What will it cost to reach each user? (If it costs you $1 to reach a single user, that's probably not very cost-effective.) You usually want to spend, at most, a few pennies per user. Generally speaking, the less you spend to reach a single user, the better.

- What hidden costs are involved? (Adding a sig file to the end of every e-mail message sent out by every employee in the company is obviously free, but the seemingly free venture of trading ads with another site may involve hidden costs. Think of the time it takes one employee to rustle up those ad trades as well as the time needed to create the ads.)

Consider these items carefully as you put together your promotional budget and your overall publicity campaign. Now, let's take a look at the most commonly accessed venues—those that users say they most often employ to find what they seek. Then you can determine which venues are right for you and attack those first.

Getting Listed with Directories and Search Engines

You can get your page listed in many big directories such as Yahoo! or Excite quite easily by submitting your URL via a handy form that you'll find at the directory's site. Or you can go to a central location (like "Pointers to Pointers" or "Submit It!"—see the sidebar in this section for more information on these sites) that lists a lot of different directories. Select as many or as few directories as you'd like your site to appear in, click an oh-so-easy-to-use Submit button, and—wham-o! An announcement of your site's birth will be blasted off to all the appropriate places in cyberspace in no time flat. Many of the Submit-It! type of announcement services used to be free but now charge a fee for making announcements to the major venues like Yahoo! and AltaVista, so you may just want to do the work yourself. It's quick and easy.

As always, consider your target audience when choosing where to list your site. For example, while Submit It! and other services list hundreds of search sites you could list with, will it really be an effective means of reaching your target audience if you list a site about lunch boxes in a medical research directory or search engine?

Just go, or send your intern, to the different search directories. Most directories offer a link that allows you to register your site. Keep in mind, however, that it is up to a given search engine or directory whether it will list your Web site. It also can take some time to get listed in these venues, which are overwhelmed with requests—you cannot expect to submit your site for consideration on Tuesday and see it listed on Friday. It actually may take weeks, so remember that patience is a virtue!

Part of your site's continuing maintenance consists of keeping sure that you're where you need to be in the search engine rankings. Many engines, directories, and link databases are updated every 24 hours. You don't want to look back a week later and find that your site has been eclipsed by your competitor's! More on optimizing your search engine ranking in the next section.

Optimizing Your Standing

Most Internet search tools—like AltaVista, Infoseek, Lycos, Google, and Excite—use small automated code-searchers called *spiders* to find your site. These spiders are released into the Internet, follow links, and index every site they find in the databases they service. Often they'll use the first few lines of text on your Web page as a description or as the basis of keywords to attach to your site. When a user searches for a given topic, the search tool usually lists whatever matches that search according to *relevancy*. So why does the spider think things are relevant that, to you, might not necessarily be so? Keep in mind that all the spider knows about your site is the description and keywords it "figured out" after running its automated processes on the beginning text of your Web pages.

You can control this all-important description and keyword list. Most of the big-gun search engines recognize the contents of a META tag—an HTML tag that resides in the HEAD area of a Web page and describes the page to spiders—that will aid in indexing Web sites in the database. You can use this tag and a few others to control the relevancy ranking of your site. Note that you ought to complete this exercise before listing your site with search engines. They don't come around looking for changes very often once they list you, so you want your house clean the first time they visit.

There are several types of META tags you can (and should) use. For example, you can specify a "title" META tag, which will identify the title of your page, a "keywords" META tag, which will allow you to specify keywords that describe your site more precisely than the automated Web crawlers will, as well as a "description" META tag.

You can easily insert META tags into your Web pages using the Page Properties dialog box. To start, write down a few items that describe your page:

- A couple of words that correspond to the topic of your page (place these in the title of the page, too)

- Some keywords (10 or 12 of them) that also correspond to the topic

- One short sentence (not two) that clearly describes the page

Follow these steps to insert META tags in a Web page:

1. In Page view, choose File ➜ Properties. The Page Properties dialog box appears.

2. In the dialog box's Title text box, type the "title" words you targeted. Note that the title must be understandable as well as include as many keywords as possible. Here's an example: **Horse Care and Riding**.

3. Click the Custom tab (see Figure 24.3).

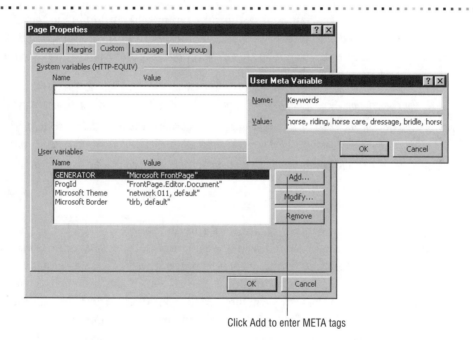

Click Add to enter META tags

Figure 24.3 *Inserting a META tag in a Web page*

4. Click the Add button to add a new META tag to the tags in the User Variables at the bottom of the dialog box. The User META Variable dialog box appears.

5. In the Name text box, identify the type of META tag you want to add. For example, type **keywords** now, so you can specify some keywords.

6. In the Value text box, type keywords that describe your site. For our example site about horse care and riding, you'd type keywords such as *horse, riding, horse care, dressage, saddle, bridle, horsemanship, thoroughbred, horses, rider,* and *horse riding.*

Because not all search engines are case-sensitive, always make your keywords lowercase, even if they are proper nouns. Also, remember to think up synonyms to include among your keywords. Finally, do not stack words to try to get the attention of search engines. Pages containing repeated keywords such as horse, horse, horse *will be tossed out or otherwise penalized.*

7. Click OK. The Page Properties dialog box lists the information you specified for your keywords META tag.

8. Repeat steps 5 through 7, this time typing **description** in the Name text box (instead of **keywords**) and adding the description you think best. In our example, this might be *Horse care and riding information for the serious amateur.*

In your description, avoid using "I" (as in "I teach horse care"). Instead, when necessary, use the third person ("horse care expert"). This will allow you to squeeze in additional references to keywords; it will also help users to understand what the site is about. A good description runs about 25 words or less, although you should be sure to check with search engines for their specific requirements.

9. Click OK.

The Page view window reappears, displaying your Web page. While visible signs of the META tags you just added won't be evident (META tags have no visible effect on a Web page), rest assured that they are now part of the HTML that defines your page.

Your META tags alone won't boost your relevancy score as much as you'd like. You also need to repeat the words you targeted for your title and keywords (*horse* and *riding,* for example) in the page's text at least once and preferably more than once. Make these mentions as close as possible to the top of the page. Then repeat them a few more times elsewhere on the page.

Your Web site is now enhanced in ways that will help it receive the ranking it deserves in search engine and Internet directory databases. This will be a big help to users in search of sites like yours.

Mastering What's Online

Search Engine Watch, by Calafia Consulting, offers good background information and tips for getting listed with the major search engines. It also offers a mailing list that announces major changes in search sites. Swing by www .searchenginewatch.com and sign up.

Retroactive Linking

Trust us, there are lots of other folks on the planet with businesses or hobbies that have things in common with the subject of your Web site. You can find sister Web sites by conducting a simple search via AltaVista, Yahoo!, Lycos, Excite, or Google; then contact those Webmasters by e-mail and offer to trade links. Having links to your Web site from other sites not only provides Web surfers with additional ways to reach your site, it also makes your site more visible to Web directories. Many Web spiders follow links from site to site, and the more often your site shows up, the higher it will be rated on the database.

If you're feeling creative, use a paint program or image composer to create a nifty little button or logo you can offer to Webmasters to use as a link to your site. Try to make the look of the button similar enough to the look of your site to create a connection in the minds of users. Try, too, to make the button or logo a size that is both small enough to be acceptable for others to place on their sites without your logo overwhelming everything else on their page, and large enough to be legible to users. Keep the size of the file for the button or logo small—don't use too many colors, avoid dithering, and stick to simple colors.

Finding Out About Retroactive Links to Your Site

AltaVista offers a quick and easy way to investigate whether your site has retroactive links. You can actually use this method to find out quite a bit about your retroactive links; in fact, you can learn just which domains and sites are backlinking to you. To find out what retroactive links lead to your site, follow these steps:

1. Open AltaVista (www.altavista.com) using your favorite Web browser.

2. In AltaVista's search box, where you would usually type a word or phrase to search on, instead type (in lowercase) link:http://www.yourdomain.com/-host:yourdomain.com.

Note that "−" here is a hyphen; also, replace *yourdomain* with (what else?) your own domain name. A list of retroactive links to your site will be returned.

Announcing Your Site in Selected Newsgroups

You can announce your site in various newsgroups and mailing lists via announcement services; just be sure to choose appropriate venues based on whether their topics are related to the topic of your page. Remember your Net value system here, though, and be discreet: no one wants to get junk mail in newsgroups any more than in real life. Make sure your announcement is timely, relevant, to the point, and respectful of a particular newsgroup's culture.

To find newsgroups that are related to your site's topic, you can search using a newsreader, such as Microsoft Outlook Express or Netscape Collabra. (These products come with Internet Explorer and Communicator, respectively.)

Avoid Spamming, but Get Your Message Out

Spamming—sending unwanted e-mail messages to multiple recipients—is the electronic counterpart to junk mail. Indiscriminately sending duplicate messages to every newsgroup and mailing list you can find is considered very bad form. Your Web site will not be well received if your promotional efforts are perceived as spam. But this doesn't mean you can't promote your site. You just need to use judgment and discretion in your electronic promotions. Here are some guidelines:

- Be selective. Post announcements only on newsgroups and mailing lists where the members are likely to have a genuine interest in your site.

- Before posting an announcement of your Web site on a Usenet newsgroup or a mailing list, monitor the group to get a feel for its tone and culture. Then tailor your announcement to the group.

- Check and respect the rules of the newsgroup or mailing list to which you plan to post an announcement. Some allow brief announcements; others explicitly forbid them. There is usually a FAQ file or charter available that spells out the rules for a given list or newsgroup.

- Be brief. Keep any announcements short and to the point, and give your message an appropriate subject that identifies its purpose.

- Include your Web site URL in a short signature at the bottom of each e-mail message you send. This subtle form of promotion is generally accepted by most places on the Net.

- Participate in relevant newsgroups and mailing lists. A little low-key self-promotion by a group regular is often accepted when the same behavior by a newcomer would be met with angry flames.

- Be helpful. Answer a question or suggest a solution to a problem being discussed on a mailing list or newsgroup, and refer the reader to your Web site for more information. If your Web site actually contains such helpful information, this is an excellent way to get the word out.

Getting Listed in Magazines and Newspapers

Your press release may not be greeted with overwhelming excitement. The sad truth is that each and every magazine and newspaper must constantly sift through thousands of unsolicited press releases. Some companies keep people or even whole departments on their staffs just to manage the company's relationship with the press and to get notice in the press for both the company's products and the company. Getting that notice often involves lots and lots of persuasion, cajoling, schmoozing, and sending of knick-knacks— if you've got the budget, go for it. Even magazines as diverse as *People* and *The New Yorker* now have columns devoted to recommending Web sites.

Mastering What's Online

Here are a couple of magazines devoted primarily to showing people what's online and how to get there:

Yahoo! Internet Life (www.yil.com)

Internet World (www.iw.com)

Your best bet in contacting any of these magazines is to take a look at their *mastheads* (the listing of information including who works at the magazine). Find the name of some person whose title includes the noun *editor* and send your press release to that person. (Don't go for the managing editor or anyone else too high up; they are busy people who throw lots of press releases right in the trash.) And before you write your press release, pick up a good book on the topic.

But remember: These magazines are in the business of making money, after all, and are usually twice as happy to notice paying advertisers as unsolicited press releases in search of attention. Unless you give them money to promote your site, you may find that the print press is largely uninterested in you. Here's where it comes in handy to flaunt an incredibly original, high-concept killer app—sexy things catch editors' eyes far more effectively than a niche market product or a message unlikely to be understood outside your target audience.

Get Listed with What's New or Purchase Premium Listings

Your page is new—and some special pages post links to other pages that have just launched. The criteria for acceptance vary; some are choosy, while others list anybody who's new. Anything goes at Internet Magazine's What's New page (www.whatsnew.com).

If you've got a big-ticket budget for promoting your page, you may want to invest in premium listings. Getting listed on Netscape's What's New page may be the priciest option; check their site for details. You can spend upward of $1,000 to have your site appear in Yahoo!'s Web Launch (www.yahoo.com/docs/pr/launchform.html). Other commercial announcement services include WebPromote (www.webpromote.com/) and PostMaster (www.netcreations.com/postmaster/).

Taking Advantage of E-Mail Publicity

E-mail publicity is free and easy. You can use every e-mail message you send to publicize your site—this may well be the simplest way to get publicity. (If your site represents your company, make sure every employee includes the company URL in his or her e-mail sig file.) You can also set up a mailing list or take advantage of existing mailing lists to announce your site and what's new on it.

Basically, you can and should treat your Web site's URL as part of your extended address—much like your telephone and fax numbers. Any place where you list information for customers, contacts, and friends is a potential place to promote your Web site.

Using a Signature File

Place your site address (URL) in a very brief signature file (in Netspeak, your "sig") that appears at the conclusion of all your e-mail messages. This will get the word out to those with whom you correspond on any topic. Your sig might look something like this:

```
Julie P. Ciamporcero, Yale '96
http://pantheon.yale.edu/~ciampor
ciampor@pantheon.yale.edu
```

Some e-mail programs provide menu options for creating a signature file within the program. Most e-mail programs can use any plain-text file as a sig. To create a text file to use as a signature file, first open your word processor and write a brief signature file for yourself. (Be sure to include your site's URL.) Keep in mind as you do this that it is generally considered bad form for your signature to be more than four lines long. Also, no single line of your signature should be more than 64 characters long—shorter lines are preferable, so that the text wrapping in different browsers doesn't leave your signature formatted oddly. Save the file (as a plain text file, of course) with a filename you'll remember (such as SIGFILE.TXT). Then open your e-mail program and follow its procedure for specifying a signature file. This should all take only a few mouse-clicks to accomplish. (If the procedure to use for your e-mail program is not obvious, you can search the program's online Help system for *signature*.)

Sigs, especially short ones, are perfectly acceptable in Internet culture. From this moment forward, whenever you send out an e-mail message, your Web site will be announced discreetly to the person with whom you're communicating. (And, if you subscribe to any e-mail mailing lists, it'll be announced publicly there, but *politely*, as well.)

Bonus! When you create a sig file this way and send messages using any of several popular e-mail programs (such as Microsoft Outlook Express, Netscape Messenger, or Eudora Pro), your URL will appear as a live link. When the recipient of your message clicks the link, a Web browser window opens and your Web page appears.

Creating a Mailing List

Another option is to create an e-mail *mailing list* so you can send out announcements to interested parties whenever you launch or update your page. Creating a mailing list is not difficult, but it does take some work. You can either create one just for occasional announcements, or create one that offers people interested in a given topic a place for discussion of that topic. A simple form page on your site will enable visitors to subscribe to your mailing list.

If you create a mailing list just for sending out announcements, be sure to offer people on the list a means by which to get off the list—a very prominent and easy-to-use "unsubscribe" option. No one wants to be bombarded with what they consider junk mail, and if you send out announcements they don't want, your desire for their interest in your site might backfire.

A very interesting way to build traffic for your Web site is to sponsor a mailing list discussion group on a particular topic. Subscribers to this sort of mailing list will get copies of all the messages distributed to the list. Some mailing lists are one-way affairs with announcements going out from the mailing list owner (you) to the list of subscribers. Some provide a forum for lively discussions by automatically forwarding all messages and replies addressed to the list to all members of the list.

Don't send e-mail to every e-mail address you run across. As we mentioned before, it's important to avoid the very rude practice known as spamming—*the unnecessary junking up of newsgroups or people's e-mail inboxes with messages of no interest to them.*

Announcing via Other Mailing Lists

You can also announce your page via Internet mailing lists like the venerable Net Happenings. Net Happenings, by the way, is also a wonderful way to stay current with what's happening on the Internet. To subscribe to Net Happenings, send e-mail to majordomo@lists.internic.net; in the body of your message, type **subscribe <net-happenings>**. The good people there will help you learn how to use Net Happenings to announce your site.

There are many, many mailing lists around on many topics. To find a topical mailing list likely to be frequented by your target audience, the best directory to search is at www.lsoft.com/lists/listref.html. As always, check the culture of a mailing list you've targeted before you barge in and start doing what is, in effect, "advertising"— some mailing lists allow it, and some don't.

Publicity through Your Plan File

A popular means of site (and personal) promotion commonly used in the programming culture is a plan file. E-mail users who log in through Unix-based shell accounts have access to a program called *finger*. When you finger a user, you retrieve information on that user that's stored on his or her computer. This package of retrievable information can be customized by altering a file called *plan*:

```
> finger ciampor@pantheon.yale.edu
[pantheon.yale.edu]

Login name: ciampor    In Real Life: Julie Ciamporcero
Directory: /home02/c7/ciampor Shell: /usr/bin/tcsh
Last login: [minerva/pts:75] Tues Nov 23 2000 09:16:25 from
   130.132.160.105

-Plan-

The design team at Sapiens Concepts is pleased to announce the
   launch of the Rachmaninoff Page v3.0! Check it out at
   http://www.rachmaninoff.net !
```

Savvy users will take advantage of every means available to promote their Web sites for minimal dollars. Plan files are one of these options. Using a plan file to communicate Web site or product updates is popular among game designers, for example. Check with your Internet service provider to see if you have a shell account with a functioning finger service. (Note: It's possible for an ISP to support both Unix features, like finger service, and Microsoft features, like FrontPage extensions. There's no reason why we all can't just get along.) If your ISP offers finger service, spend some time talking to their technical support staff about how to get your plan file up and running.

Using Assorted Other Media to Support Your Online Efforts

A relatively short time ago, a URL appearing on a business card or letterhead was a novelty, and many viewers might not have even recognized the strange-looking string of characters punctuated with periods. Now, Web site addresses are almost universally recognized and are commonplace on most business (and many personal) communications. In addition to business cards, stationery, brochures, and other printed pieces, URLs regularly show up on TV commercials. We've seen URLs on the sides of delivery trucks and have even heard announcements of Web site addresses while waiting on hold during telephone calls!

Some magazines list the addresses of Web sites, sometimes for a small fee—this is a different business than those magazines like *Yahoo! Internet Life* that review or recommend sites. In this case, we're referring to magazines that simply *list* site names and addresses, perhaps under a heading such as "Check It Out" or "What's New."

In some areas, you can get your Web address listed in the telephone book. It costs about the same as getting an additional listing. Also, if you have a display ad in the yellow pages, you need to include your Web address there.

The bottom line in publicizing your Web site is to be creative, seek opportunities, and weigh which venues are most cost-effective and suitable for your company, product, or site.

Up Next

Site maintenance and promotion is one of the most important means of getting your site in ship-shape and out into the public for the enjoyment of your site visitors. Whether your interests lie in self-expression or advertising, the information in this chapter will help you keep your sites fresh and gain plenty of exposure.

In the next part of this book, we begin an in-depth journey into the back-end, professional management concerns of Web sites. Chapter 25 describes the FrontPage Server extensions, special programs that make a Web server capable of handling certain FrontPage features. The chapter explains how to install the so-called server extensions on a Web server. It also looks at SharePoint Team Services, a set of collaborative tools for people who work on intranets. Using the services, you can set up a mini–Web site where colleagues can share documents, enter or take data from databases, and do one or two other things to make collaborating easier.

Part V

Back-End Applications and Professional Management

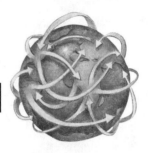

In This Part

Server Extensions
and SharePoint
Team Services

FRONTPAGE

Chapter 25

FrontPage asks a lot more of Web servers than most other HTML authoring tools do. FrontPage lets you upload and download files to and from Web servers directly instead of FTPing around; it also lets you incorporate active elements such as discussion groups, indexes, and search pages into a Web page instead of just standard HTML. This sort of thing goes well beyond what most Web servers were created to do; because of this, the Web server on which the site resides needs special *extensions* or programs that extend its capabilities. That's where the FrontPage Server Extensions come in. They add to many Web servers the functionality that FrontPage needs to do its thing.

With Office XP, Microsoft has added a new suite of collaboration tools, called SharePoint Team Services, that are built on top of the FrontPage server extensions. By installing the SharePoint Team Services software on your Web server, you can turn your Web site into an intranet where teams of people—whether they're members of the same department, partners on a project, or the staff of an entire company—can set up shared document libraries, calendars, task lists, discussion forums, and contact databases.

In this chapter, we'll describe how to install and use the server extensions and SharePoint Team Services. Topics include:

- What are the server extensions?

- What are SharePoint Team Services?

- Installing the extensions and SharePoint

- Configuring and customizing a SharePoint site

What Are the Server Extensions?

The FrontPage Server Extensions consist of a suite of programs that can be installed on the Web server. (The extensions are included in the servers that come with FrontPage; to use them with other servers, you have to install them.) When a Web server is running the server extensions, it is capable of responding to requests from users running FrontPage on their computers. For example, when you click Publish Web in FrontPage, FrontPage contacts your Web server and sends it the new files in your Web; the Web server accepts the files and copies them to the appropriate locations on the server. You can think of the functions provided via FrontPage Server Extensions as split into three general categories:

Authoring extensions allow you to save files directly to the Web server instead of FTPing them over there.

Administrating extensions allow you to assign Web team members the appropriate access to read or modify various parts of your site. Once access is allowed, team members can use FrontPage to make changes to their assigned portions of the site right from their desktops. These extensions also track what's what in the Tasks view, which is stored, logically enough, on the server. This gives all team members access to the Tasks view.

Browsing extensions allow you to include in your site such nifty elements as discussion groups, search pages, site indexes, and more—without the server extensions, many advanced features such as these simply would not work.

If you're not a Web server administrator, you probably won't need to worry about installing or configuring the extensions; someone else will have done it for you, and you can happily ignore everything that's going on behind the scenes when you use FrontPage's advanced site management tools. If you are a server administrator, this chapter will provide some basic information to help you get started. For a more in-depth look at the server extensions, see Microsoft's online documentation at `http://microsoft.com/technet/prodtechnol/sharepnt/proddocs/admindoc/ows000.asp`.

Mastering What's Online

As part of its FrontPage site, Microsoft offers information for Web site administrators at `www.microsoft.com/frontpage/`. There you'll find plenty of detailed information about running the extensions in general, along with information for ISPs that want to support the extensions, and other useful tips.

The FrontPage Server Extensions are available in a choice of languages, including English, German, and French. If the language you need is not on the CD, check for it on Microsoft's FrontPage Web site (www.microsoft.com/frontpage).

Which Servers Are Supported?

As mentioned, unless you're the administrator in charge of running your Web server you'll probably never have to deal with installing the FrontPage Server Extensions. If your site is hosted by an ISP, it will be up to the ISP's system administrator to install the extensions on their Web server. If you're working at a large company, another system administrator may be in charge of configuring servers. However, there are occasions when you'll want to install the extensions (for instance, if you want to test your ASP scripts on your desktop machine before uploading them to the server). Luckily, Front-Page makes it pretty easy to install the extensions either from the CD, or by download-ing an installer from Microsoft's Web site. In any case, you ought to know a bit about them, if only to have intelligent conversations with your ISP.

The FrontPage Server Extensions are available in Unix and Windows versions. The Unix version works with the following operating systems:

- Digital UNIX
- FreeBSD
- BSDI
- Red Hat Linux
- HP/UX
- IRIX
- Solaris
- SunOS
- AIX (FrontPage 2000 Server Extensions only)

There are two currently supported versions of the FrontPage Server Extensions for Unix: the FrontPage 2000 version and the FrontPage 2002 version. At this time, the

FrontPage 2002 Server Extensions are provided only for the Apache 1.3.19 Web server. However, if you're running a different Web server, you can still install and use the older FrontPage 2000 Server Extensions. Microsoft provides FrontPage 2000 Server Extensions installation scripts for the following Web servers at msdn.microsoft.com/library/default.asp?url=/library/en-us/dnservext/html/unixfpse.asp:

- Apache 1.3.12
- NCSA 1.5.2
- Netscape Enterprise Server 3.51
- Netscape FastTrack Server 2.0 and 3.01
- Stronghold 2.3

If your Unix Web server isn't listed above, you still may be able to obtain the server extensions for your server—but you'll have to get them from somewhere else.

The FrontPage 2002 Server Extensions for Windows are available only for Microsoft IIS 4.0 and higher. However, as with the Unix version, Microsoft still provides the older FrontPage 2000 Server Extensions, which you can obtain and run with the following Windows servers:

- Microsoft IIS 3.0
- Microsoft Peer Web Services
- Netscape Enterprise Server 3.51
- Netscape FastTrack Server 2.0 and 3.01
- O'Reilly WebSite Pro 2.0
- Microsoft Personal Web Server

Microsoft is constantly working on the FrontPage Server Extensions. If your particular variant of Unix or your Web server is not listed, check to see if it's available online at the FrontPage home page (www.microsoft.com/frontpage).

About SharePoint Team Services

SharePoint Team Services is one of Microsoft's newest efforts to fully integrate the entire Office suite of applications with the Web. SharePoint Team Services is an add-on to Microsoft's Internet Information Server 5.0 that allows you to quickly and easily set up collaborative Web sites where you and your colleagues can exchange information, hold discussions, set up group task lists and calendars, share contacts, and more.

It's a lot like having a powerful intranet built just for you—but instead of hiring consultants to spend months programming a complex, Web-based data sharing and collaboration system, you just run the installer and upgrade your Web server. SharePoint works right out of the box.

To use SharePoint, you must also install (or have access to a machine running) either Microsoft SQL Server 7.0 or the Microsoft Data Engine (MSDE). You also must ensure that the filesystem of the Web server is NTFS and not FAT; if necessary, you can convert the filesystem from FAT to NTFS using the convert.exe utility included with Windows 2000.

SharePoint Team Services is now included as part of FrontPage 2002 and Office XP, so if you've got access to a Web server that's capable of running it, it's worth giving SharePoint a try to see whether it can work for you.

One of its best selling points is that SharePoint is incredibly well-integrated with Office. Suddenly, it's as if your Web site were just another application in the Office suite. You can effortlessly upload and download contact and calendar information from Outlook to your SharePoint site. You can essentially copy and paste Excel data from your local spreadsheets into shared lists on your SharePoint site. And, of course, you can use FrontPage to customize the look and feel of your SharePoint site so that it works for your users.

Installing SharePoint Team Services and the Server Extensions for Windows

The FrontPage Server Extensions and SharePoint Team Services are included with FrontPage on the CD-ROM. To install the SharePoint Team Services, your server must be running Windows 2000 (any version) and Internet Information Server 5.0. If you are running your Web server on a computer that does not support SharePoint Team Services and wish to install only the server extensions, see `http://www.microsoft` `.com/frontpage/downloads/`.

You'll find the FrontPage Server Extensions and SharePoint Team Services for Windows in the FrontPage 2002 or Office XP CD-ROM's SHAREPT directory.

To install the FrontPage Server Extensions and SharePoint Team Services, simply run the SETUPSE.EXE program. The installer will walk you through the process of installing SharePoint on your computer.

When the process completes, the installer will launch Internet Explorer and load either the SharePoint Server Administration page (see Figure 25.1) or the home page for your newly configured SharePoint Team Services Web site (see Figure 25.2), depending on how your Web server is configured.

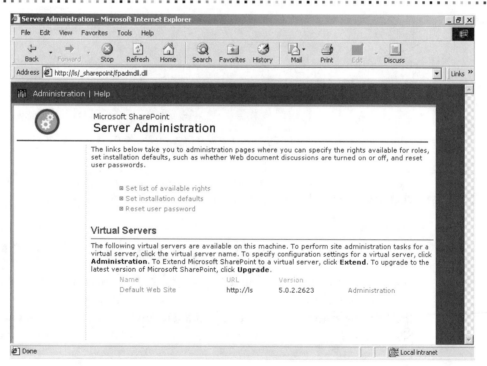

Figure 25.1 *Microsoft SharePoint Server Administration page*

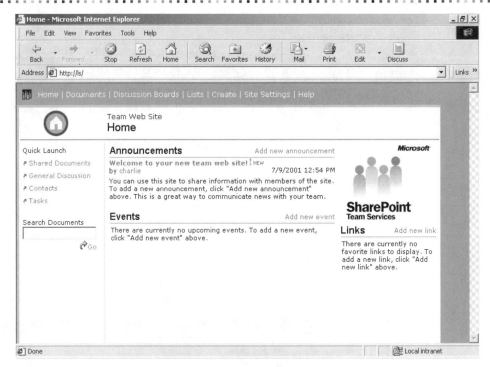

Figure 25.2 *The home page for a brand new SharePoint Team Services site*

For more information about installing SharePoint, see `http://microsoft.com/technet/prodtechnol/sharepnt/proddocs/admindoc/ows000.asp`

Configuring Your SharePoint Site

SharePoint Team Services includes a powerful Web-based configuration utility, the Administration interface, that you can use to customize your SharePoint site. To access the Administration interface, open your SharePoint site in your browser and click the Site Settings link in the navigation bar across the top of the screen to open the Site Settings page.

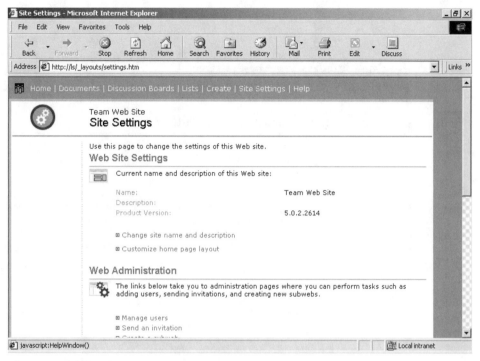

Figure 25.3 *The SharePoint Site Settings page*

From there, scroll down and click the Go To Site Administration link to open the Administration interface.

A complete discussion of all of the features of SharePoint Team Services sites is beyond the scope of this book, but you can click through the Administration interface to get a feeling for how SharePoint allows you to create a truly collaborative Web site in which many users can participate. You can add users, define roles for those users, add and remove features, schedule updates and notifications, and much more.

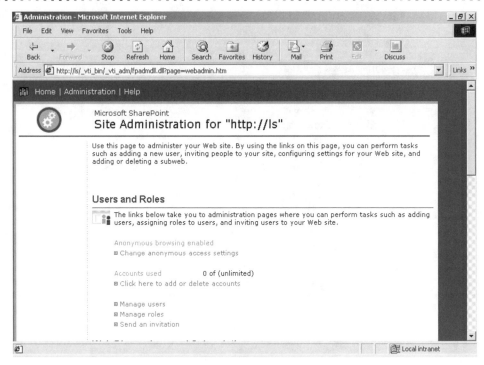

Figure 25.4 *The SharePoint Site Administration main page*

Customizing Your SharePoint Site With FrontPage

You can customize a SharePoint site with FrontPage just as you would customize any other page. To customize all or part of a SharePoint site, simply open the Web site from FrontPage, then open the page you want to modify in FrontPage, and make the changes you want. It's as simple as that. The only caveat is that if you modify your SharePoint pages too drastically using FrontPage, other users may lose the ability to modify those pages using the built-in, browser-based editing tools that come with SharePoint. Of course, if all of your users are also running FrontPage, that shouldn't be too much of a problem.

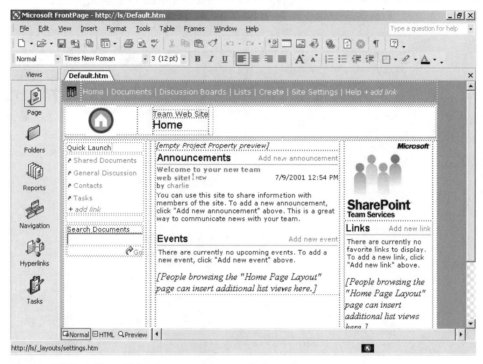

Figure 25.5 *A SharePoint home page open in FrontPage*

One common customization is to use FrontPage to apply a theme to your Share-Point site. Themes in FrontPage are much like the Desktop themes for Windows; they're a collection of visual elements—from icons and banners to color schemes and page layouts—that you can apply to your entire site, giving all the pages a unified look and feel. (For more about themes, see Chapter 4.)

To apply a FrontPage theme to your SharePoint site:

1. Open your site in FrontPage.

2. Open a page from the site.

3. Choose Format ➜ Theme from the main menu.

4. If you want to apply the theme to all of the pages in your site, make sure the All Pages option button is selected.

5. Choose the theme you want from the list, and click OK.

6.   FrontPage displays your page with the new theme applied.

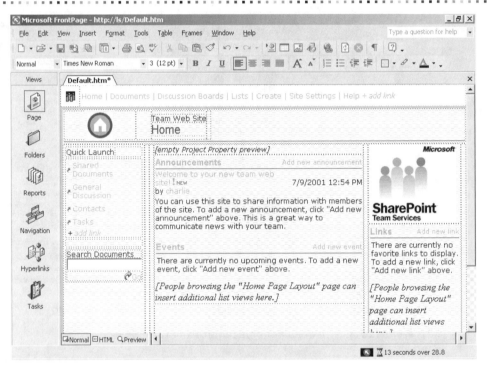

Figure 25.6   *A SharePoint Site with the Edge theme applied.*

That's all there is to it. You can use FrontPage to make whatever modifications you want to your SharePoint site pages.

For more information about SharePoint, see `www.microsoft.com/frontpage/sharepoint/`.

Up Next

Using FrontPage and SharePoint Team Services is a great way to easily make your Web sites more powerful. However, FrontPage technology can't do everything you want. In the next chapter, we'll show you how you can use CGI scripting—an old, time-honored technique for building interactive Web pages— to add the same features provided by the FrontPage Server Extensions and a whole lot more.

Understanding CGI

FRONTPAGE

Chapter 26

F rontPage can do a lot, but there are some things that simply extend beyond the scope of a WYSIWYG Web design application. One example of this is *CGI scripting*.

CGI scripting has been around longer than FrontPage, and longer even than many of the servers and related technologies that Microsoft has brought to the Web. This means that you can write and use CGI scripts on almost any Web server, and that you can find a wealth of resources, many of them free, to help you add CGI scripts to your site.

In this chapter, we explore what CGI is (and what it's not), how it works, what it can do for your FrontPage Web site, how and where to find valuable scripts and resources, and last but definitely not least, how to add CGI scripts to your FrontPage sites. Topics include:

- What is CGI?

- CGI and programming

- Getting the right servers

- Finding scripts

- Adding scripts to your pages

What Is CGI?

The answer is in the name: CGI stands for *Common Gateway Interface*, which is a standard, tried-and-true method of getting Web servers to interact with other programs on your server. Although CGI scripting is an old technique—and though it's not the most efficient or powerful way to add functionality to your Web site—the beauty of CGI scripting is that no matter what operating system, programming language, or Web server you use, your CGI scripts will always work the same way.

Contrary to what many might believe, CGI is not in and of itself a programming language. It's simply one way of enhancing the power and functionality of your Web server, so that it does more than just deliver HTML and image files to people who visit your site. In the end, CGI script is nothing more than a particular type of program— one that's designed to work in conjunction with your Web server.

Here are just some of the features you can add to your sites by using CGI scripts:

Search engines   Sophisticated search engines rely on technologies that work to get you the information that you need, fast. CGI scripts are frequently a key component of search engines.

Web community   Bulletin boards and forums can be delivered using CGI, without worrying about the portability problems that can come from relying on Front-Page extensions.

Shopping carts   Pile on those CD and book purchases! Look around and you'll find that there are plenty of good CGI-based shopping cart systems available; adding one to your site is easier than you might think.

Interactive forms   With CGI scripts and HTML forms, you can let your visitors communicate with you and with each other, and even allow them to use other applications on your Web server.

Page customization   Site visitors really like customizing favorite Web sites to behave in a way that best suits their needs. Take a weather site for example. Even though an individual lives in a given area—say, California—he or she might also be interested in the weather where family, friends, and business colleagues reside and work. You can allow your site visitors to make choices about what kind of information appears on a page by setting up custom scripts via CGI.

Page update comments   Another method of keeping sites current is allowing a page to reflect a "page last updated on" comment. CGI scripts can do this for you— you don't have to think about adding it by hand.

Timed updates   Instead of setting your alarm clock to make sure Monday's information is available across time zones, you can prepare the material in advance and rely on CGI to deliver the material to your site visitors while you get that precious extra hour of sleep!

Randomization   Undoubtedly, you've been to a site where content or images change upon a new visit, reload, or refresh. This is often delivered using CGI-based randomization scripts. You prepare a list of graphics and text options, and a discussion occurs between browser, server, and script to send back a random set of information upon the next viewing of the page in question.

Sequential events   If you want to set up changes that happen in a particular sequence rather than randomly, you can use CGI scripts to have your predetermined graphics, text, and Web elements sequentially delivered to the Web pages of your choice.

Games and fun features   You can please your Web surfers by providing a wide range of games and fun features such as crossword puzzles, community story telling—even online painting and coloring (see Figure 26.1).

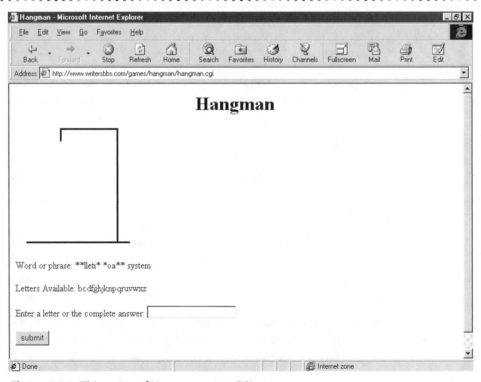

Figure 26.1 *This game of Hangman uses CGI.*

Impressive? No doubt! How on earth can CGI be so diverse, powerful, and reliable? The answer is that CGI is a server-side technology—meaning that unlike JavaScript or other client-site tools, it isn't limited to whatever the browser can do.

Furthermore, unlike FrontPage extensions, CGI is very flexible in terms of what kinds of scripts can be used. This means that there are more server and programming choices available. CGI takes the sting out of proprietary technologies and makes a lot of power available to the Web site builders, without the burden of FrontPage's proprietary and often browser-centric technologies.

Does this mean you should always choose to use independent server-side technologies like CGI over using FrontPage extensions? Not at all! You are going to perform more professionally if you understand your choices and why you would choose an individual technology over another. If you have a desire to be as portable, as browser-independent, and as varied in your applications as possible, CGI is probably going to be your best bet.

On the other hand, CGI scripting is an *old* technology, and there is considerably less support for writing CGI programs for Windows-based Web servers than for Unix machines. Newer technologies such as Microsoft Active Server Pages, Java servlets, and ISAPI extensions are, in many respects, better. See Chapter 27 for a brief introduction to Microsoft's ASP approach to server-side programming.

Still, CGI is a useful and versatile tool. To understand where CGI gets its power and how to tap into it, let's look at how servers and browsers relate to one another.

Web Servers and Browsers

In the very, very early days of the Web, Web servers were extremely simple things. Their role was remarkably basic: Whenever a Web browser requests a file, give it to them. On many sites, this is still their only function. Even the technical details are easy to understand. When you type a URL like www.foobar.com/contacts.html into your browser, your browser simply sends three words—specifically, GET /contacts.html HTTP/1.0—to the server named www.foobar.com. That's all. And if contacts.html is a simple HTML file, then the Web server at www.foobar.com locates the file, opens it, and streams its contents back to the browser. No magic there.

But as the Web has grown, two methods have developed to allow servers to do more than just deliver flat files to Web surfers: server-side programming and inline scripting.

Server-side programming allows for data management and processing using the resources of the server. Instead of just receiving the contents of a file on the server, browsers can now get access to actual applications running on the server. For example, when a browser sends a request for a CGI script—say, `www.foobar.com/cgi-bin/clock.pl`—the Web server actually runs a server-side program written in a language such as Perl or C. Once the program is run and the results are ready, the server sends them back to the browser.

The other method for managing programmed events, what we call *inline scripting*, lies on the side of the browser. A perfect example of this is JavaScript, which, as you may be aware, is entirely included *within* HTML documents. This means that the visitor gets to a page with JavaScript, and—presuming that he or she can support JavaScript and has it enabled—the browser will retrieve the HTML (including the script). Once retrieved, the JavaScript code in the page is executed by the browser, using the software and hardware resources on the visitor's machine.

At first, server-side programming was really the only existing method of managing programmed events. Browsers were the interface through which a Web page was viewed, and nothing more. But now browsers are more sophisticated and can easily manage a variety of programming events on the client side of the virtual fence.

Which is better, server-side programming or inline scripting? Even with the inconsistencies in browsers, that's a tough question to answer. Each technology boasts a set of features that make it attractive. Whether you choose proprietary FrontPage technology, ASP (see Chapter 27), CGI, JavaScript, or DHTML, the fact that you have a choice and a way of best solving the needs of your particular audience is very empowering.

In some cases, developers mix server-side and browser-side technologies for maximum effect.

Here are some server-side features worthy of note:

- Server-side programs rarely, if ever, cause problems for browsers. Because certain browsers do not support JavaScript or DHTML, and the browsers that do support them often allow users to turn those features off, many browser-side events will be lost on site visitors. Server-side programs are going to deliver the goods, consistently, to almost every browser in existence. (Note, however, that server-side programs can cause plenty of headaches for servers—if written poorly, they can drain the system's resources, crash the operating system, or even open up serious security holes.)

- Server-side programs allow you to work with databases and local files. Many times, you'll want to save information about your visitors, enable them to work with databases on your server (such as with search engines), and allow them to customize their pages. Browser technologies do not currently address these types of applications.

- Server-side programs do not rely on browser type and version to work. This is perhaps the most powerful aspect of server-side programming. Regardless of the browser—whether Microsoft Internet Explorer or Netscape Navigator; whether version 1.2 or 6, whether for Mac or for PC—CGI programs will work.

Of course, working on the server side is not for everyone. As you'll find out later in this chapter, there's a lot involved in getting even a simple script up and running. For the experienced Web developer or programmer, it won't be a big deal. To the novice, it might seem terribly overwhelming. There are so many variables regarding CGI that it's difficult to teach it step-by-step without writing an entire book! If you're a newcomer to the Web and dedicated to accessing the power that CGI scripting allows, we encourage you to stick with it and use the resources provided in this chapter to get additional help.

CGI Resources

Use these CGI sites if you'd like to learn more about CGI—we've included some Web-based listings of books and articles, too.

The Common Gateway Interface Overview:

`hoohoo.ncsa.uiuc.edu/cgi/intro.html` (introduction)

`hoohoo.ncsa.uiuc.edu/cgi/primer.html` (primer)

CGI City:

`icthus.net/CGI-City/references.shtml` (references)

`icthus.net/CGI-City/books.shtml` (books)

CGI Resources.com:

`www.cgi-resources.com/Documentation/` (tutorials and help)

`www.cgi-resources.com/Books/` (books)

In the following sections, we'll look at the specific languages that help create these server-side processes.

CGI and Programming

Let's revisit the familiar concept of forms. Forms very frequently use CGI scripts to shuttle information from one place to the next.

What kind of process happens when the script goes into action? Well, in the case of a common user-registration form, it's possible that the Web developer would want the name, address, phone number, and geographical location of the site visitor to be added to a file and organized into a sensible, line-by-line list. He or she can write a fairly simple script to do just that.

Once the information is properly organized, the Web developer also wants it delivered to a specific e-mail address. Furthermore, once the visitor has clicked the Submit button, the visitor should be shown a proper thank-you message for submitting the information.

What kind of language do you need to use to write a script that can pull off such jobs? As it turns out, you can use just about any language you want, although some choices are a lot more common than others. Perl is by far the most common language for writing CGI programs, although many other languages (including C, C++, TcL, and Python, to name just a few) are frequently used as well.

Perl

Perl is preferred by many Web developers because it's flexible, powerful, fairly easy to use, and free. What's more, there are hundreds if not thousands of freely available, already-written Perl scripts that you can simply download from the Web and—with a little skill—quickly put to work on your Web sites. Most Unix-based servers have Perl installed on them, and there is a Windows version of Perl available as well.

While today's Web is served up by a wide range of servers, Unix-based machines such as Linux, Solaris, and FreeBSD remain prevalent and, according to some surveys, dominant.

In addition to the program language and many of its scripts being free, Perl resources and help files are widely available. Whether you're only interested in one specific Perl script for your CGI needs or you really want to play around with the language, the information is all out there in substantial quantities.

With a fanaticism surpassed only by Macintosh users, the large community of dedicated Perl programmers has built an entire culture around the language. It's a little difficult to fathom that a programming language can inspire such intensity, but it happens. That's to the Web developer's benefit, really, since the books, resources, free script sites, and helpful newsgroups provide immediate support for newcomers and experienced Perl programmers alike.

Perl Resources

Learn more about Perl with a trip to the following Web sites.

What Is Perl? (And other frequently asked questions): `http://www.perldoc.com/perl5.6/pod/perlfaq1.html`

The Virtues of Perl: `http://www.webreview.com/1997/02_28/developers/02_28_97_1.shtml`

Perl.com: `www.perl.com` (the name says it all!)

Other Programming Languages

While Perl is extremely popular, you can write your CGI programs in any language you like, provided that your server is capable of executing them. Here's a selection of popular ones, with brief descriptions:

C   C is one of the world's most widely used languages, although it's not easy for beginners to learn. There are standard C libraries that allow you to efficiently write CGI programs with C.

TcL and Python   Two interpreted scripting languages that have been around for years and years, TcL and Python are well-established, full-fledged languages on the same level as Perl. Both are occasionally used with CGI.

AppleScript   Developed for Macintosh systems, AppleScript is also occasionally used for CGI.

In most instances, you'll be working with Perl. However, there may be times when you find a script written in a language other than Perl that really appeals to you. As long as the server you're working on supports the language in question, you should be fine.

Getting the Right Server

At this point, you should have a basic understanding of what CGI is and what it does. More importantly, in the context of this book, you know why you might want to choose it over options such as FrontPage server extensions.

As with those extensions, you need the right server to run CGI programs. Although it'd be a challenge to find a piece of Web server software that doesn't support CGI scripting, where you can run into trouble is in whether or not your Internet service provider will allow you to run scripts that you find on the Web or that you build yourself. For that reason, we've provided some guidelines to help you know what to look for when you're shopping around for the right server to support your CGI-driven sites.

If your current ISP isn't able to provide access to CGI and Perl or other languages, you may need to consider switching providers. Some options are provided later in this section.

To find the right server, start by finding out what Web server and operating system(s) your ISP offers. Most CGI and Perl scripts are fully supported on any Unix-based system such as Apache; they're a little less common on Windows-based servers, but finding a server that supports CGIs shouldn't be tough. Ask specifically what is being run and if CGI and Perl (or the languages your particular script calls for) are supported. Also find out what version of the language or languages is running.

Next, and perhaps most critical, you must find out whether the provider in question will allow you to run *your own CGI programs and scripts* with the account you currently have. While some ISPs do offer CGI, they only allow you to select from a few scripts that they have pre-approved. It's important to respect the ISP's choice, because usually these kinds of rules stem from past problems with abusive users. However, you'll ideally have full compliance to run whatever scripts you feel are appropriate for your site.

Some ISPs have a hard rule that says they will not accept user scripts. However, if you ask, you might find that your ISP will allow you to submit your script for review and, if it looks OK to them, to use it. Of course, if you have to constantly run scripts by the ISP, you might end up spending a lot more time and energy than is reasonable.

Once you've got a compliant ISP, you'll need to grab a pen and paper, or pop open Notepad, and jot down some important information, including:

- What directory should you store your CGI scripts in? Most servers have a specific directory set aside for CGI programs, normally /cgi-bin/ or /htbin/.

- What's the path to Perl (or your preferred language)? It should look somewhat like /usr/bin/perl.

- Are there any naming conventions of which you should be aware? For instance, many CGI programs use .cgi as their extension, and Perl programs often end with .pl. If you're on a Windows server, any programming language you use will definitely require a specific extension, so check out naming conventions for the script in question.

Unix servers tend to be case-sensitive. This means that your script must appear in the appropriate case in all instances (on the server, within your HTML) in order to run.

Once you acquire this information, put it in a safe place. It will be very helpful to you as you work with CGI, and having the information nearby will prevent unnecessary calls to your service provider.

Finding Supportive ISPs

Before seeking out any and all ISPs who will meet your needs, check with your local service providers first, or with the service provider you're already using. If you're still not satisfied, check out these ISPs for CGI and user-script support:

ProHosting Virtual Web Hosting: (www.prohosting.com)   This provider is very helpful; they even offer an online CGI FAQ that tells you everything you need to know about where scripts are located, what kinds of scripts are supported, extension names, and what to do in case of problems.

FASTNET (www.fast.net/hosting/)   This host supports both FrontPage extensions and CGI. They also provides some pre-installed CGI scripts.

Jumpline.net (www.jumpline.net)   Featuring FrontPage extensions and CGI, as well as a wide range of other attractive and affordable features, Jumpline.net is a good choice at a very reasonable price.

Pair Networks (www.pair.com)   This host offers FrontPage, shopping cart, and database access.

Pegasus Web Technologies (www.pwebtech.com)   CGI, FrontPage extensions, and commerce solutions are available here. An excellent choice for both novices and experienced developers.

Note that this list is to be used at your own risk—call or e-mail several on the list and be sure you go with the one that sounds most compatible with your individual needs.

Finding Scripts

The Web is rich with CGI and related scripts. Many are free; some of the more advanced are not. If you're just getting started with CGI, your best bet is to start with free scripts until you get the hang of working with them.

Once you feel confident, and your needs suggest it's time for a more advanced script, you can consider purchasing scripts if necessary. But before you do that, look around and compare—many of the free scripts are just as good as, if not downright better than, the ones you pay for.

Here's a look at some of our favorite script repositories, with a description of what's available and the URLs that will take you there when you're ready to get started:

CGI Resources (`www.cgi-resources.com`)   Our all-time favorite CGI script site. This Web site offers several thousand scripts in a variety of languages including Perl, C, C++, TcL, and AppleScript. Scripts are organized first by language, then by function. You can find scripts ranging from simple counters and utilities to complex shopping carts and auction software. Scripts also range in price—most are free, some are inexpensive, and some are for the higher-end developer. Aside from excellent scripts, CGI Resources is also home to a wide range of supportive resources including tutorials, books, magazine articles, and access to programmers—there's even a job database where skilled CGI programmers can find listings for work (see Figure 26.2).

Matt's Script Archive (`www.worldwidemart.com/scripts/`)   This site is another helpful stop along your CGI travels. Find Perl and C++ scripts written by book author and programmer Matt Wright, as well as contributions from other CGI enthusiasts.

CGI-World Professional Scripts (`www.cgi-world.com`)   This archive is a bit on the high end, offering professional CGI scripts for surveys, real estate Web software, search, discussion forums, and image management. Some of the scripts are pricey, but all are considered high-quality, and all have demos available.

CGI Script Center (`www.cgiscriptcenter.com`)   You can find shareware and commercial scripts at the CGI Script Center. The CGI Script Center keeps technical support representatives available, so when you run into problems, you can get personal troubleshooting help.

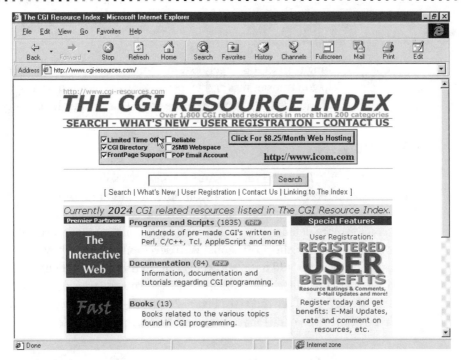

Figure 26.2 *CGI Resources is an excellent place to look for scripts.*

These resources will start you off well—all of the individual sites have links to other, related resources.

Getting Ready to Work with Scripts

If you've followed the advice in this chapter, you have a good idea of what you need before you start to work. Here's a quick checklist:

- A server that allows you CGI access

- A script or scripts that you'd like to add to your Web site

- An understanding of where your CGI and script information is housed on the server

Adding CGI to your FrontPage Web site typically requires some information that we can't cover in this book, since it requires a working knowledge of your server. However, we can get you started by helping you get all of the pieces in place.

Because working with CGI is largely external from FrontPage, you'll need some additional tools to help you transfer files and set permissions. The two most popular tools for accessing servers from a desktop, remote PC are an FTP client and Telnet software.

FTP Client

FTP stands for *File Transfer Protocol*. An *FTP client* is a software interface that allows you to send and receive files from your computer to a remote computer. Since Front-Page handles your Web transfers for you when you select File ➜ Publish Web (see Chapter 8 for more details), you might not have had a chance to work with FTP software directly. However, the professional Web developer or the hobbyist aspiring to diverse applications should have, and know how to use, an FTP client.

There are many FTP clients available for PCs. The one we like best is Ws_Ftp from Ipswitch, at www.ipswitch.com (see Figure 26.3). Ws_Ftp is a very powerful, low-cost tool that we have used daily for years, and we find it incomparable.

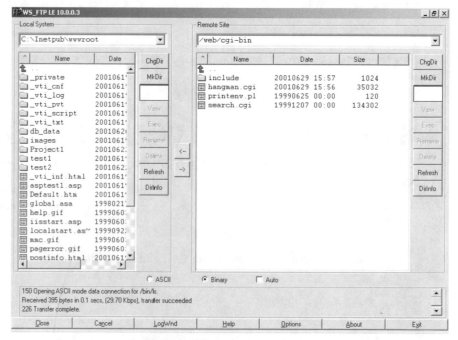

Figure 26.3 *Ws_Ftp is a powerful FTP client.*

There are many other reliable FTP clients. If you have another client that you'd like to use, note that the directions in this section will apply in general terms to that client. You can also find other FTP clients for your system by visiting www.download.com *and looking through what's available.*

To use Ws_Ftp, you'll need to set it up. Here's what you need to do:

1. Open Ws_Ftp. The Session Properties dialog box opens:

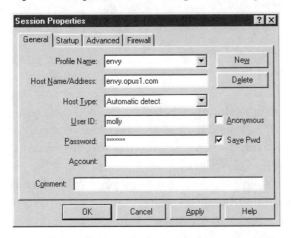

2. In the Profile Name text box, type in a name to identify the server you'll be connecting to. For example, if your server is called "greed.com," simply type in **greed**.

3. In the Host Name/Address text box, type in the exact name or IP address of your server, such as **ftp.greed.com or 192.168.1.4**. Be sure to check with your service provider for exact details.

4. In the Host Type text box, leave Automatic Detect selected (the default). Or if you know exactly what kind of server you are connecting to, use the drop-down menu to find it.

5. Type your user ID into the User ID text box.

6. In the Password area, type in your password. Note that it will echo back stars rather than distinct characters.

7. Click the Save Pwd check box, so Ws_Ftp will keep the password information for you. Leave the Anonymous check box unchecked.

8. Click OK. The client now connects you to your server.

At this point, you can highlight the files you want to send or retrieve, and then click the arrow button to transfer the files.

Be sure that all plain-text (ASCII) documents are transferred using ASCII, and all binary data is transferred using binary. Plain-text documents include HTML files, Perl scripts, and the like. Binary files include GIFs, JPEGs, zipped files, and executable programs such as compiled CGI programs. It's very important that you do this correctly! If you send ASCII data via binary, you can end up with a script that will not run.

Telnet

Telnet is a protocol on the Internet that, like FTP, allows you remote access to a server. You might need a Telnet client in order to access your server in command-line mode. The best example of this is when you want to change permissions of scripts—a necessary step in setting up CGI scripts.

Fortunately, Ws_Ftp allows you to change permissions on files using the FTP interface. This is a good thing, because working from the command-line using Telnet usually means dealing with Unix, which is a bit challenging for many newcomers and even some old hats at Web design. It's much more technical than a graphical user interface, demanding that you work with some confusing commands in order to make your changes.

If it turns out that you do require Telnet, or if you want extra options when working with your scripts that FTP can't provide, simply go to the Windows Start menu and select Run. In the text box, type **Telnet**, and the native Windows Telnet client will open (see Figure 26.4). You can use this to log on to your server and perform the required tasks.

As with FTP, other Telnet clients are available and can be found at software repositories around the Web. The step-by-step directions in the "Changing Permissions With chmod*" section below will apply, in general, to how you'll use other Telnet software.*

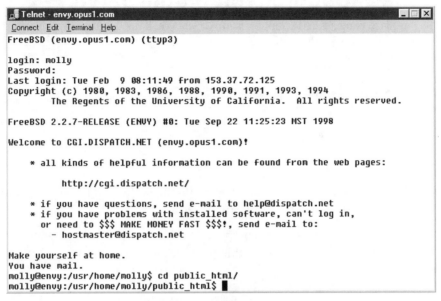

Figure 26.4 *Accessing a server with Windows Telnet*

Adding Scripts to FrontPage Webs

With the script you want to use close at hand, you'll need to follow a series of steps to get the script working with FrontPage. Here's a quick overview:

- Place the script on the server.
- Change the permissions of the script (using the chmod command).
- Point to the script from a page within your FrontPage Web site.
- Place the page on the server.
- Test your work.

Let's get down to it!

Placing Your Script on the Server

To place your desired script on your server, you'll need your FTP client and the script. Once you're set, follow these steps:

1. Open your FTP client.

2. Connect to your server.

3. Find the appropriate directory for your CGI script (check with your system administrator if you're unsure).

4. Locate the script you've saved to your local drive.

5. Checking to make sure the ASCII radio button on the Ws_Ftp interface is marked, transfer the file to the server.

When the file transfer is complete, Ws_Ftp will let you know by giving you a "transfer complete" message within the status window:

```
150 Opening ASCII mode data connection for '/bin/ls'.
Received 888 bytes in 0.4 secs, (2.45 KBps), transfer succeeded
226 Transfer complete.
```

Changing Permissions With *chmod*

The next immediate task is to ensure that the correct permissions are set on the script. On Unix servers, this is done with the chmod (change mode) command. If you're using another server, such as Microsoft NT or Microsoft IIS, check with the systems administrator for information relating to permissions.

To set permissions using Ws_Ftp:

1. If you're no longer connected to your server, connect now using Ws_Ftp.

2. Locate the script file on the server. Highlight the file and right-click. A menu appears.

3. Click chmod (UNIX). The Remote file permissions dialog appears:

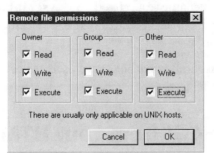

4. Under Owner, be sure the Read, Write, and Execute check boxes are marked.

5. Under Group, check the Read and Execute boxes only.

6. Under Other, check the Read and Execute boxes only.

7. Click OK. Ws_Ftp provides you with a "command successful" note in the status window.

If you want to be sure your chmod command has worked, click the DirInfo button to the lower-right of your Ws_Ftp interface. A list of all the files will pop open in Notepad, with a series of letters and dashes at the beginning of each line. The proper permission setting for most CGI scripts will look like this: -rwxr-xr-x.

To change mode using Telnet:

1. From your Windows Start menu, select Run.

2. In the Open dialog box, type **telnet *www.yourserver.com***, where *www.yourserver.com* is the name of the machine you'll be connecting to, and click OK.

3. The Windows Telnet client opens and connects to your server.

4. Your server will probably ask for your login name and your password. Type these in to access your server.

5. Once you're in the server, at a command line, you'll need to change directories to the directory in which your CGI script resides. On most Unix systems, this means typing **cd** and then the directory name.

6. When you're at the appropriate directory, if you type **ls** on most Unix systems you'll get a directory listing. You should, at this point, see your file.

7. From the command prompt of the directory containing your file, type **chmod 755** followed by the filename (e.g., **chmod 755 myscript.pl**) and press Enter. In *most* cases, this is the correct command. If you're unsure, check with your system administrator.

8. Your file permissions should now be properly set. Type **exit** and press Enter to disconnect and quit Telnet.

Pointing to the CGI from Your HTML

At this point, the server-side work is done. It's now time to point to the CGI from your HTML. This way, when a visitor gets to the particular page on which your script is to run, the CGI will initiate, and the interaction between the browser, the server, and the script can ensue.

There are a variety of ways you can point to a script within your HTML. In many cases, it will depend on the script, and we encourage you to consult the documentation that comes along with the script, or visit one of the resources in the "Getting Help" sidebar later in this section.

Often, you'll point to a script using the <FORM> tag—particularly when the CGI script requires some direct input from the visitor. For example, a game or a standard form requires that you click Submit, and it is through that action that your CGI script is located and executed using a variety of HTML attributes, including:

action   This attribute allows you to point directly to the script. Let's say it's a Perl script, residing in the cgi-bin of greedy.com. Here's what the action attribute will look like within the <FORM> tag:

```
<form action="http://www.greedy.com/cgi-bin/myscript.pl">
```

method   As its name suggests, this attribute controls the way in which information is sent to a server. There are two values for this attribute: GET and POST.

So what do you use—ACTION or METHOD, GET or POST? The syntax you'll choose will depend upon the script, the server, and your specific needs. There is really no way to globally tell you which is correct for your environment and circumstances. What you can do is check with the script author, ask the system administrator, or look to one of the Help newsgroups included in the "Getting Help" sidebar later in this section.

Once you know what syntax is necessary to operate your script, here's what you do:

1. Open FrontPage.

2. Select File ➜ New ➜ Page to begin with a fresh page. Or, to work on a file that contains a form ready to be pointed at your script, select File ➜ Open.

3. If you're working on a new page, use the Insert ➜ Form option and create a new form (see Chapter 14).

4. From Page view, click the HTML tab. The HTML code is now on-screen.

5. Locate the <FORM> tag. Add the attribute or attributes necessary to process your form, and add the path to the form on your server (check with the script author or your system administrator for the syntax relevant to your script).

6. Save the file.

7. Select File ➜ Publish To Web. FrontPage now sends the updated HTML to your server. If you've done everything properly, your script is ready to run.

Getting Help

If you're working with a script and don't know what to do, you can get help by posting a message to one of these helpful newsgroups and Web sites:

`comp.infosystems.www.authoring.cgi`
This newsgroup covers all topics related to writing and working with CGI scripts.

`comp.lang.perl.misc`
Here you'll find miscellaneous questions related to Perl scripts.

`comp.infosystems.www.servers.unix`
If you have problems with Unix servers, check here.

`microsoft.public.inetserver.misc, microsoft.public.inetserver.iis`
This is a helpful resource for CGI and scripting questions related to Microsoft Internet servers.

`comp.infosystems.www.servers.misc`
This site includes general questions related to World Wide Web servers.

`www.microsoft.com/office/frontpage/support/2002.htm`
This page lists resources for getting help with FrontPage and related issues.

`communities.msn.com/webdesign/`
This Web design community offers plenty of support for FrontPage and programming. An excellent starting point for newcomers to FrontPage and Web design.

Testing Your Script

To find out if your script is operating properly, simply open your browser, type in the URL of your site, and open the specific page you've just updated. Does the script run, or do you get an error? If the script runs, congratulations! If you get an error, don't despair. Start by going over these important questions:

- Is your server properly set up to handle the script you chose?

- Did you name your script with the right extension and the correct case?

- When you transferred your script, did you make sure it was transferred using the correct mode (i.e., ASCII mode for text files, Binary mode for compiled executables)?

- Did you place your script in the correct directory?

- Were the permissions for the script set accurately?

- Is the HTML pointing to your script using the syntax necessary to make it run?

If you've answered yes to all of these questions, and your script still isn't running, it's time to get help! Check the script's documentation for any special concerns or instructions, contact your systems administrator, or visit one of the newsgroups listed in the "Getting Help" sidebar.

Up Next

CGI is an extremely stable, portable, and powerful method of adding interactive and interesting events to your Web pages. While it demands knowledge and patience, the rewards are worth it.

As with CGI, Active Server Pages (ASPs) can add power to your Web sites. Whether it's a matter of interactivity or database connectivity, ASP is a potent Microsoft technology worth understanding. In Chapter 27, *Using Active Server Pages*, we introduce you to ASP, give you a look at how it works, and show you how to use it to add professional functions to your FrontPage Web sites.

Using Active
Server Pages

FRONTPAGE

Chapter 27

As you make the move from FrontPage technology to more advanced techniques that will take your Web sites to new levels, you will undoubtedly hear about Microsoft's *Active Server Pages* technology, referred to simply as *ASP*. Since its introduction several years ago, ASP has become extremely popular among developers who want to turn their Web sites into full-fledged Web applications.

As with CGI programming, putting ASP to work requires a base of knowledge beyond the scope of this book. Yet we want to give you an introduction to what ASP is, how it's used, why it's used, and where it's used. This chapter gives you enough preliminary information to make some technological decisions about your Web site or to move into more aggressive areas of Web development, should you so choose. Topics include:

- ASP structure

- Scripting in ASP

- ASP tools

- Adding ASP scripts to a page

ASP Overview

Like CGI scripts, ASP scripts run on the server rather than in the browser. ASP works by combining HTML and programming code to let Web pages do more. ASP scripts are capable of accessing databases to create on-the-fly Web pages, performing complex calculations, presenting pages in multiple languages or layouts depending on the user's choice, and interacting with other programs, just to name a few common uses. ASP scripts can also be used simply to make your Web site easier to maintain. For instance, using ASP you can define the content of the header and footer sections of all of your pages in a single location. Then, if you want to change your header or footer, you simply have to change it in that one location, rather than in every HTML page you've got.

If ASP and Dynamic HTML seem alike to you, you're correct. They work in a similar conceptual fashion to create dynamic pages. However, remember that ASP is a server-side technology, and DHTML is interpreted by the browser. It's interesting to note that they can be used together for maximum results.

At their most simple, ASP scripts are HTML pages with some added code that will be executed by the server. You'll save this HTML page with an extension of .asp rather than .htm, however, and you'll save it as a plain text (ASCII) file.

Here's a very simple look at an ASP script that, when served by an ASP-enabled Web server, will return a greeting depending upon the time of day. Note that our ASP script is basically an HTML document that combines standard HTML formatting, text, and programming code:

```
<html>
<head>
<title>My Site</title>
</head>
<body>
<%If Time > #08:00:00 PM# And Time < #12:00:00 AM# Then%>
<p>Good Evening!</p>
<%Else%>
<p>Good Day!</p>
<%End If%>
</body>
</html>
```

What's happening here? The text in between the special <% and %> tags is actually VBScript code that will be processed by the server every time this page is served. You don't even need to know how to program to understand this example. All we're doing is telling the Web server: If the current time is after 8 P.M. and before 12 A.M., then insert the HTML <p>Good Evening!</p> at this point in the page. Otherwise, display the HTML <p>Good Day!</p>.

ASP is an interesting approach to Web site development because, unlike CGI scripting, it allows server-side scripts to be written inside the HTML document itself but unlike DHTML or JavaScript code, which is also included inside HTML documents, ASP code is parsed by the server.

Many application developers consider ASP simple to learn. This is especially true if you take well to scripting and programming. If not, there are a few tools that can help you out. While no specialty tools are required to create ASP files, you need to have access to a server that supports ASP. Many servers do; check with your Internet service provider to be certain before selecting ASP as a method of delivering dynamic pages. ASP is a built-in part of Microsoft's Web servers and, as mentioned, now runs on a variety of non-Microsoft servers, including ones on Unix platforms.

ASP Structure

ASP uses five built-in *objects* to allow you to add complex programming to your Web pages, and allows you to install additional objects (which you can buy off the shelf and install on your own) as well.

The built-in objects used to create ASP pages are:

Request object A request object works to get information from the user, such as the data they've entered into a form, or information about who the user is and what browser is being used.

Response object The response object is the HTTP response that the Web server will send to the visitor's browser. ASP allows you to modify this response so that you can set cookies, redirect users to new pages, etc.

Session object The session object stores information about a single session in a cookie. This cookie can then keep track of each subsequent user session.

Application object Session objects relate to one user, but an application object shares information such as specific settings to all users throughout the life of the application (not the life of the session).

Server object   These objects control the relationship between a browser and the server's various components. The server object is the interface to Active Server Components—the pieces of ASP that make it work.

Installable objects come packaged with specific servers or can be obtained from third-party vendors (see the "ASP Resources" sidebar at the end of this chapter). For example, Microsoft IIS comes with a variety of very handy objects including an ad rotator and detailed browser-sniffing information.

ASP often works in tandem with databases. A good example of this is an ASP-driven discussion forum. The postings by bulletin board users must be saved in a database. The ASP, with its embedded script, pulls that information from the database and sends it to the site visitor's Web page. For more information on creating databases, see Chapter 23. If you'd like to learn more about database concepts, visit Chapter 28.

Scripting Choices in ASP

ASP scripts are *language-independent*. This means that, theoretically, you could write your ASP scripts in just about any language you know. In reality, however, your choices will be limited by the Web server on which your scripts will be run. To choose a language, simply include the one you'd like to use in the language tag:

```
<script language="JScript" runat="server">
```

You can use Perl (see Chapter 26) if you'd like, but most people use VBScript, which is a natural for ASP, or JScript, which works well too. But which languages you use to work with ASP will depend upon your given requirements for each individual project and environment.

Because JavaScript is widely supported, it is the language of choice any time a process is started on the browser side. VBScript is only supported by Microsoft browsers. However, any language can be used on the server side as long as the resulting information is readable by the widest range of browsers.

Obviously, because VBScript is a Microsoft technology, as are ASP and most of the servers with the best ASP support, using VBScript offers a variety of enhancements to ASP applications. Using a combination of VBScript and ActiveX controls, your server can carry on discussions with the site visitor's operating system via the browser.

Here's an example of an Active Server Page, written in VBScript, that creates a Web calendar. Note how the VBScript code and HTML are mixed together in the page.:

```
<%@ LANGUAGE="VBScript" %>

<%
Option Explicit

Dim dtToday ' Today's date
Dim dtCurViewMonth ' First day of the currently viewed month
Dim dtCurViewDay ' Current day of the currently viewed month
Dim  iDay, iWeek, sFontColor

REM This section defines functions to be used later on.
REM This sets the Previous Sunday and the Current Month.

'-------------------------
   Function DtPrevSunday(ByVal dt)
    Do While WeekDay(dt) > vbSunday
      dt = DateAdd("d", -1, dt)
    Loop
   DtPrevSunday = dt
   End Function
'-------------------------

REM Set current view month from posted CURDATE or today's date

dtToday = Date()

' if posted from the form
' if prev button was hit on the form
If InStr(1, Request.Form, "subPrev", 1) > 0 Then
   dtCurViewMonth = DateAdd("m", -1, Request.Form("CURDATE"))
' if next button was hit on the form
ElseIf InStr(1, Request.Form, "subNext", 1) > 0 Then
   dtCurViewMonth = DateAdd("m", 1, Request.Form("CURDATE"))
' any other time
Else
   dtCurViewMonth = DateSerial(Year(dtToday), Month(dtToday), 1)
End If
```

```
REM ----BEGINNING OF DRAW CALENDAR SECTION----
REM This section executes the event query and draws a
REM matching calendar

%>

<HTML>
<HEAD>
<TITLE>An ASP Calendar in VBScript!</TITLE>
</HEAD>
<BODY>

<CENTER>
<FORM NAME="fmNextPrev" ACTION="calendar.asp" METHOD=POST>
<TABLE CELLPADDING=3 CELLSPACING=0 WIDTH="95%" BORDER=2
BGCOLOR="#99CCFF"  BORDERCOLORDARK="#003399"
BORDERCOLORLIGHT="#FFFFFF">
  <TR VALIGN=MIDDLE ALIGN=CENTER>
    <TD COLSPAN=7>
      <TABLE CELLPADDING=0 CELLSPACING=0 WIDTH="100%" BORDER=0>
        <TR VALIGN=MIDDLE ALIGN=CENTER>
          <TD WIDTH="30%" ALIGN=RIGHT>
            <INPUT TYPE="submit" NAME="subPrev" VALUE="Prev"
            BORDER=0 WIDTH=18 HEIGHT=20 HSPACE=0 VSPACE=0>
          </TD>
          <TD WIDTH="40%">
            <FONT FACE="Arial" COLOR="#000000">
            <B><%=MonthName(Month(dtCurViewMonth)) & " " & ~CA
Year(dtCurViewMonth)%></B>
            </FONT>
          </TD>
          <TD WIDTH="30%" ALIGN=LEFT>
            <INPUT TYPE=submit NAME="subNext" VALUE="Next"
            BORDER=0 WIDTH=18 HEIGHT=20 HSPACE=0 VSPACE=0>
          </TD>
        </TR>
      </TABLE>
    </TD>
  </TR>
```

```
    <TR VALIGN=TOP ALIGN=CENTER BGCOLOR="#000099">

        <% For iDay = vbSunday To vbSaturday %>
        <TH WIDTH="14%"><FONT FACE="Arial" SIZE="-2"
COLOR="#FFFFFF"><%=WeekDayName(iDay)%></FONT> </TH>
        <%Next %>

    </TR>

<%
dtCurViewDay = DtPrevSunday(dtCurViewMonth)

For iWeek = 0 To 5
  Response.Write "<TR VALIGN=TOP>" & vbCrLf

  For iDay = 0 To 6
    Response.Write "<TD HEIGHT=50>"

    If Month(dtCurViewDay) = Month(dtCurViewMonth) Then

      If dtCurViewDay = dtToday Then
        sFontColor = "#FF3300"
      Else
        sFontColor = "#000000"
      End If

      '-- Write day of month

      Response.Write "<FONT FACE=""Arial"" SIZE=""-2"" "
      Response.Write "COLOR=""" & sFontColor & """><B>"
      Response.Write Day(dtCurViewDay) & "</B></FONT><BR>"

    End If

    Response.Write "</TD>" & vbCrLf
    dtCurViewDay = DateAdd("d", 1, dtCurViewDay)

  Next
```

```
    Response.Write "</TR>" & vbCrLf

Next

REM ----END OF DRAW CALENDAR SECTION----
%>
</TABLE>
<INPUT TYPE=HIDDEN NAME="CURDATE" VALUE="<%=dtCurViewMonth%>">
</FORM>
</CENTER>
</BODY>
</HTML>
```

In-Depth ASP

For in-depth documentation on ASP, visit
`http://msdn.microsoft.com/library/default.asp?url=/nhp/default.asp?contentid`
`=28000522`.

ASP Tools

A few tools exist to help people create Active Server Pages. One excellent application tool is Microsoft's Visual InterDev, a visual environment that will empower anyone building ASP pages. Figure 27.1 shows the InterDev interface.

Not only will Visual InterDev assist in programming, but it has a wide range of integrated uses, including integration with FrontPage (see Chapter 29).

Another useful ASP tool is the ASP Table Wizard. This Microsoft Access add-on allows you to created database-backed ASP scripts without writing a line of code (see Figure 27.2).

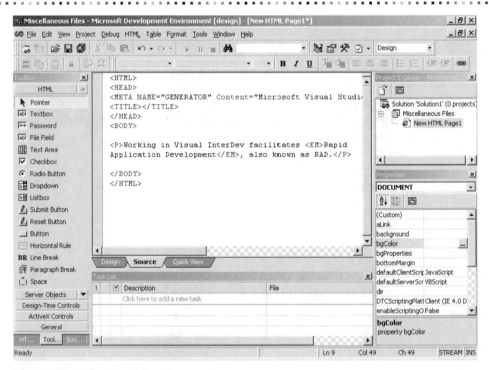

Figure 27.1 *The Visual InterDev environment*

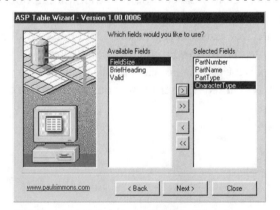

Figure 27.2 *Using the ASP Table Wizard*

Here's an example created by the program's developer; the VBScript that creates a formatted table, a section of which is shown in Figure 27.3:

```
<%

Option Explicit

'------------------------------------------------
'---- Generated by the ASP Table Wizard ----
'---- http://www.paulsimmons.com ----
'------------------------------------------------

Dim iCount
Dim sRowColor
Dim objDB
Dim objRS
Dim sDBName

'TODO: Verify database path...
sDBName = "driver={Microsoft Access Driver
(*.mdb)};dbq=D:\websites\fp\PaulSimmons\db\Northwind.mdb"
Set objDB = Server.CreateObject("ADODB.Connection")
objDB.Open sDBName

'TODO: Modify the next line to only return the records you
want...
Set objRS = objDB.Execute("select * from Products")

Response.Write("<html>")
Response.Write("<head>")
Response.Write("<title>Paul Simmons Dot Com</title>")
Response.Write("</head>")
Response.Write("<body bgcolor=white>")

Response.Write("<h3>ASP Table Wizard</h3>")
Response.Write("<a href=codebrws.asp?source=tablewiz.asp>")
Response.Write("<div class=tiny>Steal this code</div></a><p>")

If objRS.EOF Then
   Response.Write("<b>No matching records found.</b>")
   objRS.Close
   objDB.Close
```

```
      Set objRS = Nothing
      Set objDB = Nothing
      Response.End
   End If

   Response.Write("<table border=0 cellpadding=2 cellspacing=2>")
   Response.Write("<tr bgcolor=silver>")

   'COOL TIP: the <filter> tag is used by Excel 97
   'if your users save this file from the browser and open
   'it in XL 97, XL will parse all the table cells into XL
   'ranges and turn on filtering...

   Response.Write("<th filter=ALL>Productid</th>")
   Response.Write("<th filter=ALL>Productname</th>")
   Response.Write("<th filter=ALL>Supplierid</th>")
   Response.Write("<th filter=ALL>Categoryid</th>")
   Response.Write("<th filter=ALL>Quantityperunit</th>")
   Response.Write("</tr>")

   Do While Not objRS.EOF
      'this code alternates the color of the table rows...
      iCount = iCount + 1
      If iCount Mod 2 = 0 Then
         sRowColor = "skyblue"
      Else
         sRowColor = "#C4CEE5"
      End If

      Response.Write("<tr bgcolor=" & sRowColor & ">")
      Response.Write("<td align=right>")
      Response.Write(objRS("Productid"))
      Response.Write("</td>")
      Response.Write("<td>")
      Response.Write(objRS("Productname"))
      Response.Write("</td>")
      Response.Write("<td align=right>")
      Response.Write(objRS("Supplierid"))
      Response.Write("</td>")
      Response.Write("<td align=right>")
      Response.Write(objRS("Categoryid"))
      Response.Write("</td>")
      Response.Write("<td>")
```

```
        Response.Write(objRS("Quantityperunit"))
        Response.Write("</td>")
        Response.Write("</tr>")
        objRS.MoveNext
    Loop

    Response.Write("</table>")
    Response.Write("</body>")
    Response.Write("</html>")

    objRS.Close
    objDB.Close
    Set objRS = Nothing
    Set objDB = Nothing

    %>
```

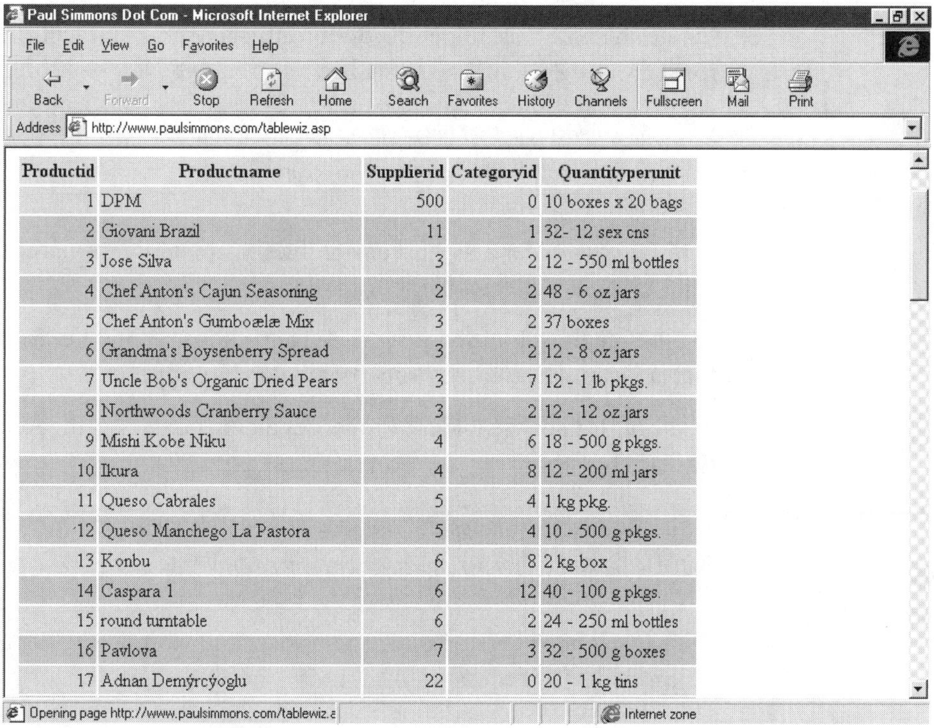

Productid	Productname	Supplierid	Categoryid	Quantityperunit
1	DPM	500	0	10 boxes x 20 bags
2	Giovani Brazil	11	1	32- 12 sex cns
3	Jose Silva	3	2	12 - 550 ml bottles
4	Chef Anton's Cajun Seasoning	2	2	48 - 6 oz jars
5	Chef Anton's Gumboælæ Mix	3	2	37 boxes
6	Grandma's Boysenberry Spread	3	2	12 - 8 oz jars
7	Uncle Bob's Organic Dried Pears	3	7	12 - 1 lb pkgs.
8	Northwoods Cranberry Sauce	3	2	12 - 12 oz jars
9	Mishi Kobe Niku	4	6	18 - 500 g pkgs.
10	Ikura	4	8	12 - 200 ml jars
11	Queso Cabrales	5	4	1 kg pkg.
12	Queso Manchego La Pastora	5	4	10 - 500 g pkgs.
13	Konbu	6	8	2 kg box
14	Caspara 1	6	12	40 - 100 g pkgs.
15	round turntable	6	2	24 - 250 ml bottles
16	Pavlova	7	3	32 - 500 g boxes
17	Adnan Demýrcýoglu	22	0	20 - 1 kg tins

***Figure 27.3** A portion of the table created with ASP Table Wizard*

ASP Tools

For more information on how to purchase Microsoft Visual InterDev, visit `msdn.microsoft.com/vinterdev/`. To download the ASP Table Wizard, check out `http://www.paulsimmons.com/tablewiz.html`.

Adding a Script to a Page

As you've seen with the code examples in this chapter, you can add your ASP-related script directly into your HTML page. Then, to save the file in ASP format, all you need to do is save it with the `.asp` extension.

Ask your server administrator to make sure that your Web server supports ASP scripts written in whatever language you choose to use.

Here is an exercise that walks you through adding and saving your ASP file:

1. Create an executable folder in your FrontPage Web. (This will allow scripts to run.) From the FrontPage menu bar, select File ➜ New ➜ Folder.

Since the default for a folder is not set to executable for security purposes (see the "Security Issues" sidebar later in this section), you'll have to set the permissions yourself.

2. Give the new folder a name. For ASP files, you can use the name *scripts* for your ASP-related script files.

3. Right-click the folder you just created and choose Properties from the menu that appears. The folder's Properties dialog box appears.

4. At the bottom of the folder's Properties dialog box, select the Allow Scripts To Be Run check box.

If you're using a file-based Web (as opposed to a server-based Web located on a Web server that's running the FrontPage Server Extensions), this check box will be disabled.

5. Click OK. The Properties dialog box closes and your new folder allows any scripts and ASP it contains to be run.

Now you need to open the page where you want to add your ASP scripts. To do so:

1. Add the script to the page by typing it in, or copy and paste it from another application.

2. From the menu bar, select File ➜ Save As. The Save As dialog box appears.

3. In the Save As dialog box's list of directories, select the directory you created to hold scripts. Type a filename in the URL text box. The name you give the file should end with the extension `.asp`.

4. Click OK. The dialog box closes, and the file is saved to the location you specified.

Security Issues

Security is a major concern for all developers. Security measures must be taken on *all* aspects of server-side applications.

All of your software will come with extensive security information. Be sure to follow guidelines to ensure that every tier of your servers, operating systems, and databases is free from holes. If you are purchasing service from an ISP, ask your customer service representative to describe, in detail, what security options are available and what security measures are taken to ensure the safety of your data.

Now that you have some of the basics of ASP down, we'd like to offer some good online resources so you can expand your knowledge. There are also many excellent books on ASP and related scripting technologies, such as JScript, VBScript, and Perl.

ASP Resources

4GuysFromRolla.com (www.4guysfromrolla.com): News articles, coding tips, FAQs and more. A key resource for ASP developers.

ASP.NET (www.asp.net): News and information about the forthcoming new version of ASP for Microsoft's .NET initiative, ASP.NET.

Active Server Pages.Com (www.activeserverpages.com): Tutorials, advice columns, and code.

The ASP Hole (www.asphole.com): Code, FAQs, consultants, demos, and book recommendations for ASP developers.

CNET Builder.com (www.builder.com): A great resource for all Web technologies.

Sybex Publishing (www.sybex.com): A wide range of supportive computer titles.

Up Next

ASP is an important Microsoft technology that is sure to appeal to you if you are interested in managing dynamic, data-driven sites. While it demands programming know-how, there are some good tools, such as Microsoft's Visual InterDev, that can get you started. More information on ASP is widely available should you find that you need to delve into it in more detail.

Up next is a look at databases—in detail. While we showed you how to work with databases in the context of FrontPage in Chapter 20, in the following chapter we'll help you learn a bit of the fundamental concepts that go into data management on a large scale. We'll also provide you with plenty of resources so that you can follow up any interest in databases with quality information.

Databases in Detail

FRONTPAGE

Chapter 28

Databases are the heart and soul of high-performance Web sites. Without them, we couldn't be making airline reservations through our favorite online travel agency, managing an online stock portfolio, or working with our company's intranet to stay on top of customer, manufacturer, or purchasing information.

Databases work with numerous other technologies discussed in this book, including CGI programs and ASP scripts, as well as other server-side technologies we haven't mentioned. In Web development, databases are almost exclusively used as server-side data stores, because they allow reliable, high-speed access to massive amounts of information.

High-end databases are not for everyone—while you can create a simple database with FrontPage and Access (see Chapter 23), database technology is a specialty field. This chapter looks at databases in detail and introduces you to key concepts so you'll be familiar with what databases are, what their internal structure looks like, and what they can do. Topics include:

- An overview of databases

- Popular database products

- Database structure

- Database modeling

- Applying database concepts

About Databases

The many brands of databases on the market fall into two categories: *file-server* and *client/server databases*. Each type has specific aspects that make it attractive to developers. Ultimately, you will have to choose your database using your desired goals and specific environment as your guides.

If your database (and your budget) is fairly small and is servicing a limited number of users on a single machine, you can choose from one of the file-server databases, which include Microsoft Access, Visual FoxPro, Corel Paradox, and Apple FileMaker Pro.

Serious databases with a large number of users and intensive application demands such as electronic commerce support are better served by a client/server system. High-end database systems like Oracle, Microsoft SQL Server, IBM DB2 and Sybase ASE—and even the free, open-source MySQL and PostgreSQL database systems—are all client/server systems. When you hear programmers and system administrators talking about their *RDBMS* (*Relational Database Management System*), chances are they're talking about client/server products like these.

What's so much better about a client/server RDBMS as compared to a file-server database system? In a nutshell, a "real" RDBMS like Oracle offers vastly increased speed, reliability, and scalability. But for that kind of power, Oracle and others also charge an arm and a leg. And large-scale RDBMSs like Oracle are notorious for demanding massive hardware resources, including gigabytes of memory, huge arrays of hard disks, and as many CPUs as you can throw at them.

A full-fledged RDBMS like Oracle is so much faster than a file-server database like Access because there's actually a piece of software called a *database server* to help speed things along. Just like your Web server handles all of the requests from Web browsers (its *clients*) to access files, the database server handles requests from *its* clients to read, write, and update records in a database. With file-server databases, each client directly accesses the shared database file; there's no database server acting as an intermediary. While it might seem like direct access to the database file would be faster than mediated access, it's not. Given the right hardware to run on, a client/server RDBMS will far, far outperform a file-server database.

On the other hand, file-server databases can be perfectly appropriate for small Web sites like a departmental intranet used by only a handful of people, or a small corporate Internet site that doesn't do e-commerce. Though they're not as reliable, scalable, or fast as client/server RDBMSs, file-server databases have two big virtues: They're easier for non-programmers to use and, when compared to something like Oracle, they're incredibly cheap to buy.

Manufacturers of file-server databases often offer products that will help you convert your file-server database to an enterprise-level RDBMS. But if you're serious about building a heavy-duty Web site, it's better to choose the right database for your needs from the start.

To help you make the right decision when planning for backend operation purchases, here is a list of some advantages and disadvantages of file-server databases and client/server RDBMSs.

File Server Database

Advantages	Disadvantages
User-friendly	Limited data storage
Affordable	Limited transaction processing
Available on all popular operating systems	Stores but does not manage data with advanced programming
Available as part of a suite of complementary tools	Limited management tools
Lower demand on system resources	
Easy to find support and information	

Relational Database Management System

Advantages	Disadvantages
Manages high-traffic situations easily	Greater cost
Easy access to support and tools	Significant learning curve
Highly configurable	Demands advanced hardware
Supports advanced technologies and programming languages	Demands extensive human resources
Built-in or add-on Web-related services	
Excellent security	

Manufacturers eager to sell their wares are typically happy to provide you with demonstration software, white papers, and support information. Try before you buy!

Popular Database Products

There are a wide range of databases in the marketplace today. The most common file-server databases and RDBMSs used by Web developers are looked at here.

File Server Databases

Although Microsoft Access is probably the most popular database in this class, there are a wide variety of other contenders including Microsoft's Visual FoxPro, Corel's Paradox, and Apple's FileMaker Pro. We'll take a look at what makes Microsoft Access appealing to some Web developers.

Microsoft Access

For those readers new to databases, Access may be your best choice in terms of a starting point, as you probably have the software and can take advantage of Office documentation to learn a bit about the program.

What's even more appealing to new and general audiences is that Access is equipped with wizards that will take you step-by-step through a variety of database development procedures (see Figure 28.1). This makes your job less stressful, as the learning curve is smaller than what you'll face with an RDBMS option.

Also, as we pointed out in Chapter 20, Access allows you to save documents directly to HTML for further editing in FrontPage. This is part of the powerful suite integration offered by Office, and it saves you a lot of steps when offering information culled from your database onto your Web site.

Of course, Access might not suit your needs—especially if they're more than Access's limited file-server architecture can handle. Still, it's a good place to start learning about how data is managed in the context of databases and Web-based applications.

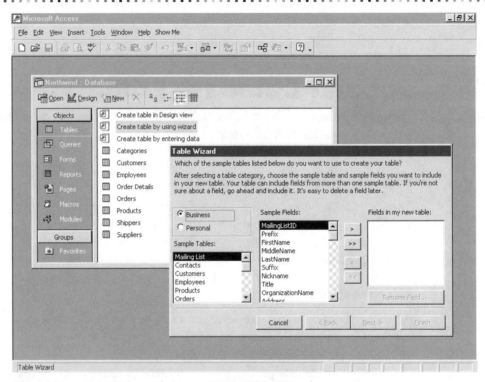

Figure 28.1 *Using Microsoft Access 2000's Table Wizard*

Microsoft Access

General information on Microsoft Access is available at www.microsoft.com//office/access.

For Access training in your area, visit https://www.microsoft.com/trainingandservices/.

You can get questions answered by looking for Office- and Access-related newsgroups at communities .microsoft.com/newsgroups/.

Client/Server RDBMSs

Let's move from the simple but user-friendly realm of file-server database systems into the more complex environment of the client/server Relational Database Management System. There are many contenders in this arena, and we've chosen to discuss those that best address Web-based applications and that are favored by Web developers.

Oracle8i and Oracle9i

Oracle has been very involved in the development of advanced RDBM systems. Of the various Oracle products, Oracle8*i* and Oracle9*i* offer very high performance along with tools that enable you to create databases from within a logical interface. Oracle is by far the leader in RDBMS sales, even though its products carry a hefty price tag. Its database products have been packed with Web-oriented features for years, and are considered the standard by major online players. However, using Oracle can be a laborious and expensive process. Often, just getting the software installed properly requires the assistance of a professional consultant.

Oracle Databases

Check out news, tools, community, and troubleshooting tips at Oracle's helpful Web site, www.oracle.com.

IBM DB2

IBM is making a big play for market share in the electronic commerce industry. DB2 has a legacy of reliability and speed that dates back to its days as the hands-down champion in the mainframe database market, and it now offers excellent support for Windows, Linux, and Unix systems.

With a variety of extended applications for the Web, DB2 sports very stable technology, including backup and recovery as well as replication options.

IBM DB2

Learn more about DB2 at the IBM Web site, www.ibm.com. You can even download a free trial of the software from www.ibm.com/software/data/db2/.

Sybase Adaptive Server Enterprise

This is Sybase's top contender in the realm of relational systems. Adaptive Server Enterprise is a favorite for many developers managing large e-commerce systems.

Database Structure

No matter what database you end up using, you'll find that there is a common structure and language applied to both the type of database and the brand. Let's examine a few of the key concepts.

Database   As the term implies, this is the central data repository. It is the file—or, more often, the large set of files—where all of your tables, indexes, views, procedures, etc. are stored.

Database schema   The *schema* of a database is its structure. When database programmers talk about schema, they're talking about its structural components minus the actual data it contains. You can think of the schema as an architectural blueprint for your database. The real database, including all of the information you enter into it, is the finished building.

In order to use databases effectively, you'll need to know more about the individual components that make up your database schema. Some schema components include:

Tables   Don't confuse database tables with HTML tables. Although both contain information, an HTML table is just a formatting tool. Database tables contain records, which are the meat and potatoes of a database. The information in a record is organized in columns, like the columns in a spreadsheet. Let's say you're tracking a list of stock purchases on your stockbroker Web site. You could store information about each transaction in records in a table, where each record would include the stock buyer's identification number, the stock buyer's name, the ID number of the stock purchased or sold, the price at the time of sale, and an ID number for the transaction itself.

Keys   Keys are used as a method of identifying information within a table. In our example, the key might be the stock buyer identification number.

Indexes   As with any method of cataloging information, an index is used to help quickly find specific information—in this case, records in the database.

Columns   Structurally speaking, tables are basically sets of columns. Each table is much like a spreadsheet, with individual rows (records) divided up into fields (columns). Each column should contain a distinct, basic piece of data, such as a person's last name or their telephone number. For instance, let's say you want to keep track of the stock buyers who use your stock trading Web site. Each record in your table might include the stock buyer's identification number as well as their name, address, and telephone number; each of those pieces of distinct data would go into a specific column.

Triggers   This is a block of code within a database that orders a specific operation to execute automatically upon a given command or action. Let's say a nurse updates his patient record. The trigger is the block of code that commands the database to update all the related information for that patient upon the completion of the nurse's update.

Stored procedures   Similar to triggers, stored procedures are blocks of code that order specific actions to occur. However, stored procedures are independent of user input and are related more to the function of the database and database performance.

Sequences   Sequences are aspects of database code that allow a database developer to organize an automatic increment in a given value. For example, if a customer record begins with 001, a sequence can be written to automatically add each subsequent customer record with the next logical increment (e.g., 002, 003, etc.).

Applying Database Concepts: A Closer Look

Now that you've got a basic idea of the parts that make up a database, it's time to investigate a few key concepts from the database programming world. The ideas discussed here are fundamental concepts for *designing and maintaining* your databases.

Normalization of Data

De-normalized environments have information stored in duplicate areas. For example, there might be a patient name in several areas of a database. But what happens when a change is made to one of the records? Without extra programming and accounting for the data, all of the records might not be globally updated.

Normalizing databases is the process by which data is stored in a non-redundant manner. Typically, this means storing given data *one time only*. If there are more instances of the same data, there is a higher risk for error, more demand on developers to manage each copy of the data, and more resources required from the software and hardware to manage the data.

Both environments have their place. Sometimes it's necessary to have redundant data in your database, but if you can avoid this and normalize your data, you're likely to have a smoother-running system.

Data Relationships

Relational databases are called *relational* for a reason: In addition to providing a place to store information, they provide a way for you to define the relationships between the bits of information in your database.

Why are these relationships necessary? They're needed to actually give meaning and context to *normalized data*—in other words, data that has been split up into many different tables. For instance, a purchasing database might have information about customers in the Customers table, information about the orders the company has received in the Orders table, and information about the details of each order (i.e., the products in the order, and the quantity of each product ordered) in the OrderDetails table. Individually, these tables are useful as lists, but they're more powerful if we can *relate* them to each other. For instance, to generate a report about all of the details for all of the orders placed by a customer, we've got to know that the product information from the OrderDetails table can be related to the order information in the Orders table, which can then be related to the personal information stored in the Customers table.

Here are some of the key relationships you'll encounter when designing and working with databases:

One-to-One   This refers to the relationship between data elements. In a hospital setting, there might be a main table comprising all the segments of the hospital (cardiac, surgery, neonatal) and another table where the patients are listed. Each table will have a relationship to the other, because each section of the hospital contains individual patients, and each patient is placed in a specific location within the hospital.

One-to-Many   Imagine two tables; one is a list of patients, the other, a list of medications. Each individual patient might be taking several different medications, although each medication on the list does not necessarily correspond to a single patient.

Many-to-One This is the reverse of a One-to-Many relationship. Let's say there's a table full of patient records and a table full of nurse records. In this case, many patient records will be related to a single nurse record.

Optimizing Database Performance

In order to make databases perform better, there are several steps developers take. This process is referred to as *optimization*.

In the "Database Structure" section of this chapter, we looked at various aspects of a database. One such aspect is the *index*. An index is especially helpful in allowing databases to find and retrieve information quickly. Well-designed indexes can make a huge difference in how efficiently a database performs.

Another aspect of optimization is called *caching*. This is similar in concept to what your Web browser does with Web information. If you visit a site with relative frequency, chances are your browser has cached, or stored, graphics and HTML from that page in its cache. This allows for faster load times. Similarly, in-memory database caches can hold data and other database objects that are used frequently, improving the speed of the database.

Almost any advanced RDBMS will allow you to spread the parts of your database across different drives. A database developer might opt to put some tables on one drive, indexes on another, and other components on still another. For high-demand systems, this reduces the load on a single machine's resources by balancing the demand across different drives.

 Database software typically offers a suite of tools to help developers fine-tune performance. There are also a number of excellent books and resources to assist you in learning how to maximize your database's performance potential.

Configuring Hardware

There are two important concepts to put to use when configuring database hardware:

RAID No, it's not a bug spray! In this case, it's *Redundant Array of Inexpensive Disks*. Essentially, this is a much-used method of increasing the speed and reliability of a server's storage. By combining several hard disks into an array, they can be used in parallel.

Replication and Clustering   In this case, an RDBMS breaks up the work among multiple computer systems. Though similar to RAID in a sense, the main difference between a clustered or replicated RDBMS installation uses not only separate disks but separate computers as well.

Database Resources

Enjoy these resources to help you understand more about the power of databases for Web development:

Philip and Alex's Guide to Web Publishing (`http://photo.net/wtr/thebook/`): A full-length book about building database-backed Web sites

DBASUPPORT.COM (`www.dbasupport.com`): Mailing lists, tutorials and tips for Oracle database administrators

About.com: Database Development (`http://databases.about.com/compute/databases/cs/development/`): A large compilation of feature articles, tutorials, and links for database developers

Database Resource (`www.unifx.com/links.html`): A long list of links about databases including manufacturers

Up Next

As you've seen in this chapter, databases are complex but powerful tools that can address big issues in high-end site development. Whether you're working on a site such as a customer service center that requires the storage, retrieval, and updating of data or working internally on an intranet or extranet and keeping track of clients, patients, or the progress of a corporate project, databases are the tool for helping you manage this information.

In the next chapter, we look at another important tool in Web site development related to the back end of sophisticated Web sites: Microsoft's Visual InterDev. This is a team-oriented development environment designed specifically for the rapid development of powerful Web sites.

Using FrontPage with Microsoft's Visual InterDev

FRONTPAGE

Chapter 29

While working in FrontPage is undeniably a convenient way to create Web pages and small sites, its team-oriented development tools mean that it can also be used by professional software developers to help build sophisticated Web applications. You've seen how FrontPage is well integrated into the Microsoft Office suite of tools (see Chapter 20). But FrontPage is also part of another group of applications specifically geared toward professional software developers. Included in this group is Microsoft's Visual InterDev.

In this chapter, we'll introduce you to the features of Visual InterDev, giving you an overview of why it exists, what it does, and how it integrates with FrontPage to create a work model for advanced Web site development. Topics include:

- Overview of Rapid Application Development (RAD)

- Avoiding mistakes and managing risk

- A close-up look at Visual InterDev

- The development team model

What Is Visual InterDev?

Visual InterDev is part of Microsoft's flagship visual Integrated Development Environment (IDE), Visual Studio. Visual InterDev is oriented toward Web application development and not only allows developers to create Web sites in a similar way to FrontPage—using a WYSIWYG page design tool and themes reminiscent of those in FrontPage—but can help the developer create and debug large, complex Web-based applications that combine ASP scripts, server-side applications, databases, client-side scripting, and more. Like most IDEs available for software developers, Visual InterDev is a big, expensive software package that aims to help reduce programming time by automating code generation (and thus reducing programming errors) and providing a unified view of all of the many components that make up a large software project.

For more information about how to purchase and use Visual InterDev, see Microsoft's home page for Visual InterDev at http://msdn.microsoft.com/vinterdev/default.asp.

Visual InterDev might sound like the big brother to FrontPage, and in many ways it is. But in the true spirit of software integration, Visual InterDev and FrontPage have been optimized to work together in a team environment with powerful results.

Rapid Application Development (RAD)

In order to properly describe the features of Visual InterDev, we first need to look at an important concept in project management: *Rapid Application Development (RAD)*. RAD is the *raison d'etre* of Visual InterDev.

For those readers who have a background in software development, the concept of RAD is likely to be very familiar. RAD isn't so much a technology as a way of doing things. Programmers who "do RAD" usually use sophisticated design and programming tools like Visual InterDev to speed up the software development process. The goal is to meet the high-pressure demands of the software industry: short deadlines, multiple platform concerns, user demand, and constantly shifting technologies.

The Web development environment is no different. The challenges are the same, and the argument could be made that Web sites are software products. Many features are indeed similar, and applying a management system to the development of Web sites makes complete sense (see Chapter 19).

The idea here is to create a streamlined production environment that effectively manages the job of a Web site in an organized fashion with precision and, ultimately, great expediency and meeting of deadlines.

RAD is often described as having three main themes that drive the system:

- Avoiding known mistakes
- Following good development practices
- Managing risk

Let's take a closer look at what each of these themes mean and how they pertain to working within the Web development industry.

Avoiding Mistakes

In an ideal production setting, each stage of the process would be handled without a glitch (see Chapter 19). But as everyone knows, that's not a very accurate state of affairs when it comes to real life.

RAD looks to common, or *classic*, mistakes for avoidance. These are the mistakes of hard-won experience. Just as the child must put her hand on a hot stove in order to fully understand what it means to be burned, so must we all learn from experience what *not* to do in order to protect ourselves. If we're very fortunate—and very wise— we'll listen to our elders and not make the same mistakes they did, helping us to avoid the common problems that can turn a development process into a stressful, even impossible, situation. Some of the classic mistakes to avoid include:

Planning ineffectively (or not at all) As mentioned in Chapter 19, planning is an essential part of Web site production. If you fail at this level, the consequences, particularly for large projects, could be disastrous. In order to accomplish the goals of RAD, a strong, effective plan must be in place.

Forgetting to include necessary tasks in the production plan It's easy to forget tasks necessary for a large project, and obviously you cannot anticipate every step you'll need from start to finish. However, if you are comprehensive at getting this phase done, potential problems will be minimized.

Adding inappropriate technology to a project Every time a technology is added to a given site, the amount of testing and potential failure rises accordingly. While it's fun to add Java applets, interactive forms, animations, guestbooks, and advanced scripts to Web pages, in professional development you must have a very strong rationale for having them there. Every component of a page must serve a specific purpose. Be sure that when you do your planning, you are extremely honest about what you need and, perhaps more importantly, about what you do *not* need on the site.

Changing tools mid-project   If you know your tools going into a project, there will be little need to change them later on. Changing a tool means loss in time and design control—you and team members are faced with having to learn or adapt to a new development environment. The time that this takes and the frustration factor can conceivably ruin a well-run production.

Selecting team members haphazardly   When you're working in a team, it's imperative that fast, clear, and effective communication takes place. Any known problems with colleagues should guide you to think carefully about selecting those individuals for rapid, team-oriented Web site development.

Not resolving team conflicts early on   Despite our best intentions, conflicts do arise. When they aren't resolved early on, they can become very serious risks to the maintenance of production flow.

Failing to maintain a good relationship with the client   One of the most critical problems that can come up during the production of a Web site is a major change in the climate between the Web team and the client. If communications fail or if the needs and responsibilities were unclear from the beginning, potential difficulties that affect the project's ability to survive can ensue.

Setting expectations that are unrealistic   All of us run the risk of being overly optimistic about scheduling and skill levels—particularly in the exciting, early stages of a project's life. This can lead us to set expectations both of ourselves, and others, that are unrealistic.

Is it always possible to avoid mistakes? Of course not. After all, they're inevitable by-products of humans and their technologies. However, as everyone knows, mistakes can help us learn how to be more effective in how we approach our work.

Following Good Development Practices

To address many of the classic production mistakes, employ these solid development practices:

Understand the complete nature of your Web site—intent, audience, and long- and short-term goals.   In Chapter 19, we explained the importance of planning. We'll say it again: Planning your site from birth to adulthood and beyond is your strongest ally in reducing problems.

Plan your production effectively and thoroughly.   Not only should the concept of your site be well-planned, but the individual tasks that you'll need to take each step of the way should be included in the production plan.

Map out your master plan on a large whiteboard. Leave this in a prominent place and mark off tasks as they are completed. Individuals on the project will then know exactly where in the project they are and where they need to go.

Determine all necessary tools before beginning production.   One of the concerns this chapter addresses is planning your site and site production. This includes choosing the tools you're going to use to plan, build, and maintain the site. Obviously, one of the tools in your toolset is FrontPage. In a large site development experience, there are going to be other software tools necessary to carry out the job: other Office suite members such as Word and Access, imaging utilities including specialty filters and optimizing programs, Internet utilities such as telnet and FTP clients, a plain text editor, database applications, and software development tools like Visual InterDev.

Develop a tools list and ensure that everyone on the team has the necessary skills to use those tools effectively. Keep the list public and provide it as part of a documentation set for the project. If your team has an intranet site, make sure it's available there, too.

Know the technological needs and direction of your site.   Understand what technology you need going in. This should be documented and clearly outlined in technical terms at critical points within the planning of the site, as well as in the master task list.

Pick an effective project manager   In a team environment, an efficient project manager is key. Whether you are that individual or you are a member of a team run by a project manager, knowing the role of such a manager is imperative. The project manager is the conductor—he or she takes the plan and ensures that each member of the team plays his or her part correctly, in a timely fashion, and with enthusiasm.

Use automated development tools   Automated software development applications like FrontPage and Visual InterDev help to eliminate bugs and mistakes. Just as using FrontPage helps you avoid writing sloppy or broken HTML, using Visual InterDev's built-in editor to write your ASP scripts will help you avoid many errors, from simple typographic errors in your VBScript code to more complex bugs. RAD tools like Visual InterDev also help you keep track of all of the components of a large software development (or Web site development) project, so that developers don't end up stepping on one another's toes or writing the same code twice.

Risk Management

Managing risk is such an important element that schools teaching computer science and information technology have at least one, if not several, courses dedicated to this area alone.

Risk management means exactly what it says. If you've avoided mistakes and followed good development practices, there's still going to be a potential for risk. That's life, after all—stuff happens! With critical projects, it's necessary to manage that risk.

Following is a list of ways to effectively address risk. Each suggestion here can help you know what to do in case of a problem:

Assess a project's potential risks.   This is a process by which the entire site's life is assessed in terms of what problems it potentially contains. This includes everything from a general awareness of classic mistakes to a specific personality challenge with a team member.

Create a plan to address each individual risk.   If you think you've exhaustively planned for your site, guess what? Your planning and assessment will clarify risk potential. For each of these potential problems, have a plan ready to go *should it become necessary*.

Prioritize any problems that occur.   Let's say one week you have a team member out of the office due to illness, the client calls up and wants to add something to the site right away, and there are problems with the computer network you're using to develop the site. Prioritize your problems by determining which problem will cause the most critical delay.

Track the resolution and monitor it closely for any new risk potentials.   Once a problem is resolved, don't turn away just yet—watch the situation to ensure that new problems don't come up.

Use all the risks and solutions you encounter as a reference for future risk management.   Keep a daily log of problems and effective solutions. For a professional development company, this practice will become invaluable. Each time you go through a project, you'll have new experiences and come up with new solutions. These experiences will help you prevent mistakes, improve development practices, and learn to manage risk more effectively.

By adequately planning your site's production, developing and following good production techniques, and successfully managing risk, you will create as smooth a production schedule and environment as possible.

 If you're very lucky, the RAD approach as applied to Web development environments will work on your first try. However, that's optimistic! RAD obviously becomes a more potent approach over time, when a given production team catalogs risk and learns from prior mistakes.

RAD Resources

Use these Web sites to gain a deeper understanding of RAD and to learn how to use it to effectively manage your Web development teams:

RAD Overview (`web.cs.bgsu.edu/maner/domains/RAD.htm`): An article examining RAD and why it should be used

Software Tech News' RAD Issue (`http://www.dacs.dtic.mil/awareness/newsletters/ tech-news2-1/`): Articles about RAD from the U.S. Dept. of Defense's software development newsletter

What Is Rapid Application Development? (`http://www.casemaker.com/download/products/ totem/rad_wp.pdf`): A white paper examining RAD by CASEMaker, a maker of software development tools

A RAD Review and Case Study (`http://www.comp.glam.ac.uk/SOC_Server/research/ gisc/RADbrf1.htm`): Briefing paper on RAD from the Glamorgan Information Systems Centre

Visual InterDev Close-Up

As you now are aware, RAD is a powerful method aimed at planning, organizing, and deploying projects. So how does Visual InterDev fit into the picture? Well, as a visual interface for Web site project management, it can give an eagle-eye view of a project in its entirety (see Figure 29.1).

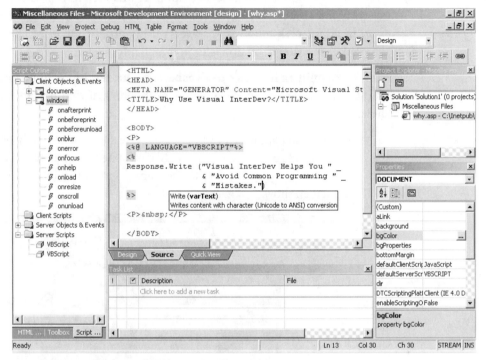

Figure 29.1 *The Visual InterDev Interface*

Visual InterDev is not only helpful to the Web development team using RAD as a development method; the software itself was developed to facilitate rapid deployment of integrated technologies. Think of the way your human team works: A project manager oversees team members and uses production techniques to ensure quality and timeliness. Visual InterDev is akin to the project manager—it oversees other applications, such as FrontPage, as well as its own internal facilities, to produce a good product within a set schedule.

Visual InterDev aids the RAD process from a conceptual point of view by:

Tracking tasks   Using a task manager, Visual InterDev can keep lists of what needs to be done as well as track tasks that are finished:

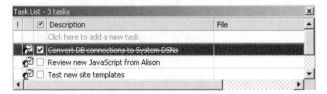

Working in tandem with related applications such as FrontPage   In the spirit of teamwork, Visual InterDev plays a major role in combining the efforts of multiple workstations and servers during production (see "The Development Team Model" section later in this chapter).

Providing a built-in interface to all aspects of the development process   Visual InterDev allows you to view the various components of your project as a unified whole.

- HTML and page design: While Visual InterDev is completely set up to work with FrontPage, it has a WYSIWYG page designer for those who use it as their primary interface to the team environment (as seen in the following screen shot).

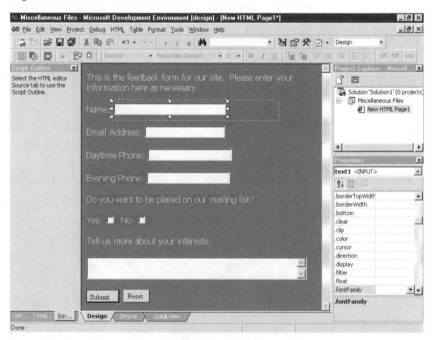

- ASP development: Using Active Server Page technology (see Chapter 22 and Chapter 27), Visual InterDev can help developers create server-side routines for on-the-fly Web site updates and changes, and advanced processes.

- Databases: Developers can use Visual InterDev to add database support to their Web projects (see Figure 29.2).

- Advanced programming: Using a variety of programming languages (see the "Programming Model for Web Developers" section later in this chapter), Web site developers use Visual InterDev to manage programming tasks related to site production.

Managing activities directly on remote Web servers   Visual InterDev has modules that allow developers to carry out debugging and other events on remote machines.

Visual InterDev has these practical elements embedded in the tool itself that assist in the ability of its users to work efficiently and productively by:

- Allowing for drag-and-drop between applications

- Automatically generating and completing programming statements through a point-and-click interface

- Employing modes such as Master mode, which allows team members to immediately see saved changes by other developers

Now let's look at some of the ways in which Visual InterDev approaches the management of Web sites.

Database Design

Database design is a critical piece of today's professional Web site. Visual InterDev allows for the same variety of approaches to database development as FrontPage offers to the Web page designer. Features include:

Database Designer   This is akin to Page view, where a range of controls are available to the user to design and develop databases.

Database wizards   Use these wizards for help creating various aspects of databases quickly and with ease.

FrontPage is fairly limited in what it can do database-wise, so this level of support is extremely helpful, particularly in environments where speed is essential. Supported databases include Microsoft SQL Server and Oracle.

Programming Model for Web Developers

Where FrontPage offers some support for programming, it's not an advanced programmer's tool. Visual InterDev, on the other hand, lets Web programmers work within its interface to develop with a variety of languages including:

- HTML
- CSS
- JavaScript
- VBScript
- JScript
- ActiveX

Support for ASP is a major focus of Visual InterDev. Since ASP uses a combination of the above programming languages, and since ASP is also a Microsoft product, it's a natural fit.

Unfortunately, CGI scripting and Perl are not well supported by Visual InterDev. For more information on using these technologies with FrontPage, see Chapter 26.

Visual InterDev Resources

The following online resources will provide you with technical support, developer insight, and additional references for working with Visual InterDev:

Microsoft Developer's Network (msdn.microsoft.com): Full range of support for developers using Microsoft products

Microsoft Visual InterDev (msdn.microsoft.com/vinterdev/): Articles and resources for Visual InterDev users

Developer Community (msdn.microsoft.com/vinterdev/technical/community.asp): Networking and newsgroups for Visual InterDev developers

The Development Team Model

Not only is Visual InterDev powerfully integrated with other Microsoft Web development tools such as FrontPage, but it works as the management center for a project. In order to understand how FrontPage fully works with Visual InterDev, it's necessary to describe the way Microsoft has used this product integration to assist developers.

Imagine that you're the project manager of a Web development team. You have a variety of very skilled individuals working with you. The team will likely include a content developer, a graphic designer, a database developer, and a Web programmer. Each is responsible for a very different but necessary aspect of the Web site.

Along with the people, you have the technology. At this level, you're probably designing on a network. Finished production will go to a staging server for testing before it's put into production: the live Internet, intranet, or extranet server. Then, the project is delivered over wide or local area networks to individuals via their Web browsers.

This process is a complex one, and it involves the ability of both people and technology to successfully communicate and create relationships with each other. While individual team members will have specialty areas, the project manager oversees those areas to combine them into a greater whole.

Herein lies the relationship of Visual InterDev and FrontPage! (Figure 29.4 shows this relationship in detail.) Earlier in this chapter, we described how Visual InterDev is the software equivalent of a project manager. If you are the project manager, you will likely be using management skills such as RAD to organize and maintain a smooth production schedule. But you'll also be ensuring that application production goes smoothly, relying on management software within FrontPage x Visual InterDev to track tasks and production milestones.

Your graphic designer will be using design theory to guide the thought behind a design, but will use a program such as Photoshop to render the graphics and FrontPage to render the design. Content developers will use tools including plain text editors, Microsoft Word and Excel, and Microsoft FrontPage to develop copy and manage content. Database engineers and ASP programmers will use Visual InterDev and other programming tools to work their magic.

Visual InterDev is the application that pulls together all of the parts of the team, and provides all the tools necessary to develop high-end Web sites within the concept of RAD: avoiding mistakes, working efficiently, using integrated tools, managing risk, and meeting deadlines.

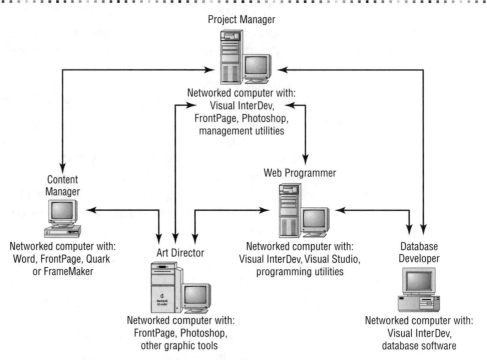

Figure 29.2 *The Visual InterDev team model*

Up Next

You've now seen FrontPage perform a very wide range of aesthetic and functional tasks. Whether it's used to design a personal home page or to develop an advanced Web application using suites of tools like those discussed in this chapter, the scope of the application is very broad—and very flexible.

The next part of this book focuses on using FrontPage to create Web sites from start to finish. Using the production techniques you've learned in Chapter 19 in combination with the rest of the information in this book, the next four chapters walk you through the development process of four Web sites including a personal Web page, a small business Web site, a community site, and a large-scale site.

Part VI

Step-by-Step FrontPage Sites

In This Part

Creating a Personal
Web Page

FRONTPAGE

Chapter 30

n this and upcoming chapters, you look at how FrontPage Web sites actually get produced. Using the method-based production concepts introduced in Chapter 19, this chapter examines different Web site types that you can design: personal Web pages, small-business Web sites, community sites, and large-scale sites.

This chapter offers useful tips and guidance to help you create powerful pages that are effective, stylish, and unique. Topics include:

- What is a personal Web page?

- Planning your page

- Building the home page

- Publishing the page on the Internet

What Is a Personal Web Page?

A *personal Web page*, or *home page*, is a site where people share information about themselves, their families, their interests, and their activities. Personal Web pages make up a significant portion of the Web sites on the Internet. A personal page is the perfect place for self-expression, and many people enjoy creating and visiting them.

A home page *can also refer to the welcome page of a commercial or private site. Both uses are accurate, but the meaning will depend upon the context in which the term is being used. Another term,* splash page, *is also often used to refer to the first page of a Web site, particularly if the page is graphical.*

What's more, building home pages is the perfect way to exercise your skills as you learn about Web design. Many of today's Web site designers started out designing their own personal pages and became enamored of the technology, art, and Web environment. Making a home page is probably the best opportunity to decide whether Web design is really for you! In fact, before moving on to creating more advanced sites, trying out a home page first is advisable.

Remember, however, that once you publish a page, it's there for the whole world to see! Here are some general guidelines to help you out:

- Only share things about yourself that you feel safe sharing. If something is very personal and private, the Web is *not* a good place for it.

- Potential employers may find your site, so be sure that anything you put up about yourself is acceptable to share with them, if you care about that kind of thing.

- Using the Web as an expression of personal beliefs and opinions is an exercise in freedom of speech. However, be careful that you do not slander or libel anyone (this protects *you*) or say anything that you would not be willing to say in person.

- Be sure that any graphics, multimedia, or written content that you put on a Web site belong to you or are in the public domain. Otherwise, without express permission of the original author to use it, you may be violating copyright laws.

- Avoid putting personal addresses and phone numbers on the Web. After all, you don't want every Tom, Dick, and Harry to know where you live and what your telephone number is.

Expressing yourself can be fun, but along with it comes responsibility. The Web can certainly be about freedom for many people, but with all freedom there comes the important need to think before you act.

A good way to learn more about home pages is to visit a wide variety of those done by other people. See what you like, what you dislike, and find guidance and inspiration from those sites that have succeeded in doing something along the lines of what you'd like to do.

In this chapter, we're going to work on a site called "Hallie is Horse Crazy." The fictitious young woman, Hallie, wants a home page that looks good and helps provide information about herself as well as her favorite thing in the world: horses!

Planning the Site

It's always important to plan out your site. You've got to think about audience, site intent, and site goals. From this information you can get ideas about what kind of a design you want to create.

Audience and Intent

Audience is always important—even in the construction of a personal page! This is something people often overlook, and it's a dangerous thing to miss. Why have a page if you don't want to share it with others? So you have to think carefully about who those others are going to be.

In Hallie's case, the audience will be made up mostly of young women who share her interests. Other groups she'll need to prepare for include:

- Family and friends
- Horse lovers of all ages
- Other individuals within her age group

Hallie's site is intended to share information about herself, her horses, her horse-related art and photo collection, and a great selection of horse-related links, as well as to provide a method for folks to get feedback to her regarding her site.

Short- and Long-Term Goals

Initially, Hallie wants a small site with a variety of information, but down the road she hopes to expand the links and possibly even add a forum for horse lovers to discuss their horses, display photos, and share favorite Web sites.

Knowing what we do about Hallie's audience, intent, and goals, we sketch out the actual structure of her Web site. The sketch will be our guide as we set up the structure of her Web site:

SPLASH PAGE

Me   Hallie's bio and some photos

My Horses   Stories and pictures about Hallie's horses

Horse Pics   Photos and drawings of horses

Horse Links   Favorite links to horse sites on the Web

Awards   Hallie's awards and Hallie's horse's awards

Guestbook   A place where people can say hello

Preparing for Production

Based on the audience and topic of the site, you want to create a look and feel that sets the tone for the Web site. You also need graphics that look good but don't take too much time to download.

Creating a Look and Feel

One of the first things to look at is color. For Hallie's site, we want to convey a sense of warmth, friendliness, and earth. So we created a palette of color to express these things:

Color Name	RGB Value	Hex Value	Expression
Dark brown	102 51 0	663300	Warmth
Deep gold	204 102 51	CC6633	Horses, earth
Light gold	255 204 102	FFCC66	A youthful, happy, upbeat color

We also included black for text and white for any accents.

Next, we looked at typefaces to see which are best for displaying the information. We wanted something fun and decided to mimic this approach in the way we laid out the Web page's type:

Type Family	Typeface	Expression/Use
Decorative	Whimsy ICG Heavy	Fun, playful look for headers
Decorative	Trackpad Letraset	Light, handwritten-style font for navigation and smaller headers
Sans serif	Arial	Easy to read for body text

We then examined the way to approach graphic accents. We decided that header text would have a drop shadow to add some depth to the pages. We created a similar drop shadow for the photos as well, adding interest to the page. The final decision was that navigation buttons would be graphic-based, flat text.

Preparing for Technology

We want to keep technology limited on this page, because typically a personal page is the first Web site a person does. The idea is to have fun, but keep it simple as you learn the Web site–design ropes.

In order to technologically challenge ourselves a little bit, as well as provide an opportunity for Hallie's visitors to send in feedback, we chose to use FrontPage's Guestbook. This means we'll need to make sure the Internet service provider we are using will support the Guestbook with the appropriate FrontPage extensions. To find this out for your site, you'll need to give the ISP you're working with a call or drop an e-mail and ask.

Production

With the planning of the site complete, we entered the hard-work phase. This means laying out the pages in our image editor, generating the site graphics, and using FrontPage to design the individual pages. We'll also be using FrontPage to help us manage our tasks as we work through the process and to set up the Guestbook.

Laying Out the Pages

Photoshop is our primary choice for page layout, but of course you may use the image editor of your choice. We do recommend you use an image editor with layering capabilities (see Chapter 18 for information about image editors).

Follow these steps to lay out the splash page:

1. In your image editor, select File ➜ New. The New dialog box appears.

2. Create an image that is 595 pixels wide by 295 pixels high.

3. Click OK. You now have your work area set to the first layer.

4. Add your background color to this layer. We selected Deep Gold (see the color chart earlier in this chapter).

5. Create a new layer by selecting Layer ➜ New ➜ Layer. On this layer, we added the page name:

6. Add the buttons one by one. They should be done on individual layers so that you can easily move, change, remove, or add to them in the future.

7. After you've added all the elements you want for this page, save the file by selecting File ➜ Save As. The Save As dialog box appears. Name the file and save it in the native layer format of your imaging program.

Figure 30.1 shows the completed splash page design.

Figure 30.1 *The completed splash page design*

Next, create the layout for an internal page by following these steps:

1. In your image editor, select File ➜ New. The New dialog box appears.

2. Create an image that is 595 pixels wide by 600 pixels high (higher if the page content needs to be more than two screens in height).

3. Click OK.

4. You now have your work area set to the first layer. To this layer, add your background color.

5. Create a new layer by selecting Layer ➔ New ➔ Layer. On this layer, create the header:

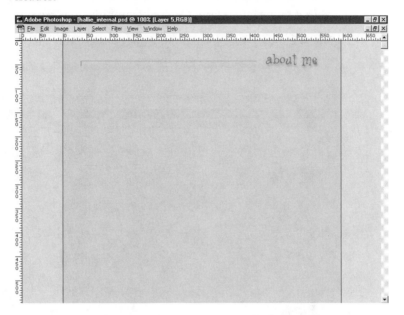

6. Layer by layer, add the graphic components of the page, including design elements such as sub-headers, navigation, and photos:

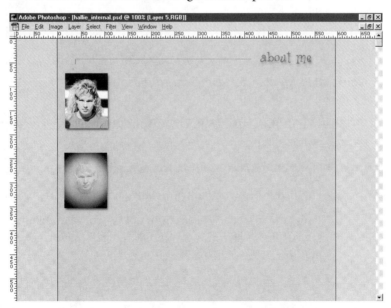

7. Once you've added all the elements you want for this page, save the file by selecting File ➜ Save As. The Save As dialog box appears. Name the file and save it in the native layer format of your imaging program.

Figure 30.2 shows a completed inner page design. You'll repeat this process for each and every page you've designed for the site.

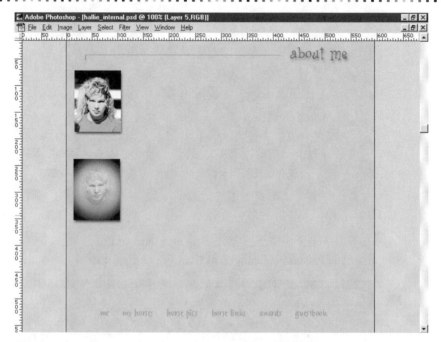

Figure 30.2 *The completed internal page design*

To generate the actual graphics for your site, move back to your imaging program and follow these steps:

1. Open up the layered file in your imaging program.

2. Highlight the layer that has the image you want to process.

3. Using the marquee or selection tool (it will vary depending upon your program), draw a selection around the part of the image you want to keep, making sure you're on the correct layer.

4. Copy and paste the section into a new file.

5. Optimize the file as a GIF or JPEG, depending upon the graphic.

6. Name the graphic and save it directly to the images folder within your Front-Page Web site.

Repeat the process for all of the buttons, headers, backgrounds, and spot art that you'll require.

Working with FrontPage

At this point, we turn to the wisdom of FrontPage to help us make folders, set up tasks, and begin the actual design of our Web pages. Start by setting up your folders:

1. Choose File ➜ New ➜ Page Or Web. The New Page Or Web task pane appears.

2. Under New From Template, click One Page Web. You see the Web Site Templates dialog box.

3. Make sure One Page Web is highlighted and click OK. FrontPage creates the necessary folder for your Web site, as well as subfolders named _private and images.

Because Hallie's is a small, manageable site, we use the root directory for all of the HTML pages and the images folder for all graphics.

To set up individual files in a root directory:

1. In Folders view, right-click anywhere and choose New ➜ Page on the shortcut menu. A new page appears in the root directory.

2. Type a name for the page.

3. Repeat this process until you have created all the pages planned for the site, using the chart prepared in the planning phase as a guide. You can always add or delete pages as necessary.

To add the Guestbook:

1. Select File ➜ New ➜ Page Or Web. You see the New Page Or Web task pane.

2. Click the Page Templates hyperlink. The Page Templates dialog box appears.

3. Select Guestbook and click OK. FrontPage adds the Guestbook and its companion files to your Web site

4. Save the file to the Web site. You'll customize it in just a bit.

Tasks are one of FrontPage's most helpful tools to guide you through building your Web site. To set up tasks using Folders view:

1. In Folders view, select the file you want to associate with a task.

2. Choose Edit ➜ Tasks ➜ Add Task. The New Task dialog box appears.

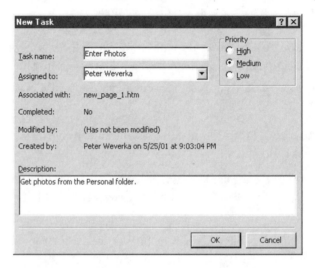

3. Fill in the task name, priority, and a description.

4. Click OK.

Whether associating a task with a page or without it, be sure to include as many tasks as you'll need to complete the production and post-production processes. For more information on tasks, see Chapter 7.

Creating the Splash Page

Now it's time to design the pages! Start with the splash (or home) page, as this will set the tone for the rest of the site.

1. In Folders view, highlight the `index.htm` file that you created earlier.

2. Right-click and choose Open on the shortcut menu. Your home page opens in Page view.

3. Right-click the empty page and select Page Properties from the shortcut menu. The Page Properties dialog appears.

4. Click the Background tab, and, in the Colors section, open Background drop-down menu and choose More Colors. The More Colors dialog box appears.

5. In the Value text box, type in the hexadecimal color you want for the background. Refer to the list you made in pre-production when you developed the look and feel of the Web site. In our example, we chose the Deep Gold, hex value CC6633, for the background.

6. Click OK to return to the Page Properties dialog box.

7. Click OK in the Page Properties dialog box.

Your page will now appear in Page view, with the background color you selected. Now you're ready to add the first graphic. To do this:

1. Place the cursor where you'd like to insert the graphic.

2. Choose Insert ➜ Picture ➜ From File. The Picture dialog box appears.

3. Select the image you want.

4. Click the Insert button.

FrontPage inserts the file into your page.

You can check the results of your work by saving the pages and selecting File ➜ Preview In Browser. In Figure 30.3, you see the results of our page design within the browser window.

Any time you're using consistent navigation from page to page, you have the option of using FrontPage's shared borders. For more information on this topic, see Chapter 15.

Figure 30.3 *The completed splash page design*

Designing an Internal Page

Typically, tables are needed to lay out most pages. Hallie's internal pages are no exception.

In Figure 30.4, you can see the page layout we did using our image editor. We set up some guides to show how we'd like to map out our table grid. Based on this information, we can turn to FrontPage and begin creating the actual table.

When planning a table, begin with vertical columns, only adding rows where necessary. Be sure to revisit Chapter 11 for more information about table design.

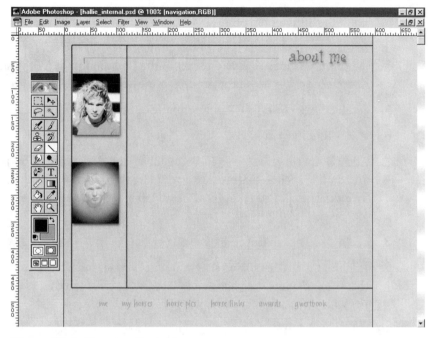

Figure 30.4 *Planning the table*

With your table in mind, follow these steps to lay out the page:

1. In Page view, choose Table ➜ Insert ➜ Table. The Insert Table dialog box appears:

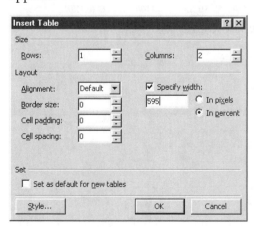

2. Enter the number of rows in the Rows text box (we entered 1).

3. Enter the number of columns (we entered 2) in the Columns text box.

4. In the Layout section, choose an alignment for your table. Typically, left alignment is used, but some people opt for the Default option. With this option, settings in the visitor's browser determine how the table is aligned.

5. Set the Border Size, Cell Padding, and Cell Spacing to 0.

6. Check Specify Width.

7. Add a numeric value for fixed-width tables and a percentage for dynamic. In an example such as this one, we want to fix the width so that all the content including images and graphics is neatly managed. We entered a total width of 595 pixels.

8. Click OK. The table appears on your page.

9. Add images and text using the techniques you learned in related chapters of this book to refine the page's look. Be sure to adjust table and table cell properties where necessary (see Chapter 11).

10. When you're finished adding images and text, save the page. Continue adding pages in this fashion until you've completed the full content of your site.

You can preview your new page(s) externally, or internally using the Preview tab, to see the way the page(s) will appear (see Figure 30.5).

When working with navigation, be sure to remember that you can use shared borders on appropriate pages if you will be using a server supporting FrontPage extensions. Check Chapter 15 for details, and be sure to ask your ISP if you have access to FrontPage.

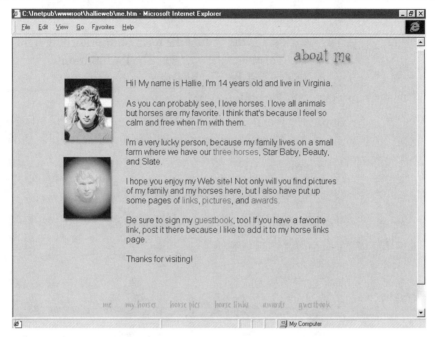

Figure 30.5 *The completed page in Preview mode*

Customizing the Guestbook

Because we want the Guestbook to match our design rather than the prefabricated look that FrontPage uses, we'll want to customize the form using our own colors and graphics. Here's how:

1. In Folders view, double-click your Guestbook page. The page opens in Page view.

2. Add the background and link colors to the page by following the directions we discussed in the "Creating the Splash Page" section.

3. Delete the comment and the horizontal rule from the top of the page.

4. Add your graphic header by selecting Insert ➜ Picture ➜ From File and choosing the appropriate header image for your page.

5. Customize the comments within the form field. Simply click within the field where you'd like to change the text and type in the new text.

6. If you'd like to change the text on the form buttons, simply right-click the button and choose Form Field Properties. The Push Button Properties dialog box appears. In the Value/label text box, type in the word or words you'd like to have appear on the button and click OK.

7. Customize any remaining text on the page, and be sure that the page is included in the shared borders if you are taking that approach to navigation.

8. Save your file to the Web site.

Your results should be similar to those in Figure 30.6.

 Have you marked off your tasks? If not, and if you are confident the work for a given task is finished, go into Tasks view and mark the task as complete.

Figure 30.6 *Hallie's Guestbook*

Preparing Your Site for Publication

After you've got all your pages designed, you're almost ready to upload them to the server so they can be live on the Internet. But there are a few things you should do before showing your creation to the world!

First, you'll want to spell-check all of the pages by following these steps:

1. Choose Tools ➜ Spelling (or press F7). The Spelling dialog box appears.

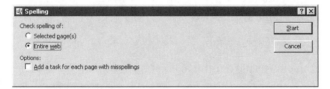

2. Click the Entire Web option button.

3. Click the Start button.

FrontPage will now spell-check all of the pages and report back any misspellings. Chapter 3 explains spell-checking in detail.

Now, check all of the links on your site by choosing View ➜ Reports ➜ Problems ➜ Broken Hyperlinks. The Broken Hyperlinks report appears. Each link's status is described with a particular indicator. (See Chapter 24 for a full list of these indicators.)

If one of the links on your Web site is no longer valid, or *broken*, you'll need to replace it with an updated one by following these steps:

1. In the Broken Hyperlinks Report view, double-click the link you want to change. The Edit Hyperlink dialog box appears.

2. In the Replace Hyperlink With text box, repair the hyperlink. See Chapter 24 for details.

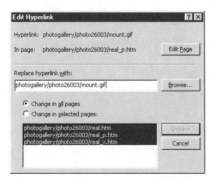

Continue to repair links as necessary. When you're finished, run through the process again to ensure no broken links remain.

The next step in the process is to add META-tag descriptions and keywords to the pages. To do this:

1. In Page view, choose File ➜ Properties. The Page Properties dialog box appears.

2. In the Title text box, type the "title" words you targeted. In our example, we used "Hallie's Horse Crazy."

3. Click the Custom tab.

4. In the lower part of the dialog box, locate the User Variables area. This area displays a list of all the META tags in the current page. To add a new META tag to the page, click the Add button. The User Meta Variable dialog box appears.

5. In the Name field, you need to identify the type of META tag you want to add. For example, type **keywords** now, so you can specify some keywords.

6. In the Value text box, type the keywords you think best for your site. For Hallie's site, try keywords and keyword combinations such as horse, horses, horse pictures, horse links, horse photos, hallie, hallie's horses, and so forth.

7. Click the OK button. Back in the Page Properties dialog box, your META tag is now visible.

8. Repeat steps 5 through 7, this time typing **description** (instead of **keywords**) and adding the description you think best. In our example, this would be: "Hallie's Horse Crazy is for all people who love horses. Links, guestbook, great horse pics!"

9. Click OK. Your site is now properly META-tagged.

Be sure to test the site using different browsers, platforms, and screen resolutions to ensure that you've done a good job at making the site cross-browser compatible (see Chapter 16).

Post-Production

After your site becomes a part of the Internet, it's important not to forget that the site still requires your attention. Here are some issues you should address after your site has been produced and published:

Check content live.   Be sure all your graphics, links, and technology are working properly on the server.

Follow maintenance and promotion guidelines.   In order to boost your potential success, you'll want to efficiently maintain and promote your site (see Chapter 24).

Prepare for the future.   Using your long-term goals as a guide, decide when it will be necessary and appropriate to add content to your site, expand the site, and even redesign the site to keep it contemporary and interesting.

Up Next

In this chapter, you became familiar with what it takes to make a personal Web page. The process is meant to be fun, and we hope you had fun doing it! Yes, there's work involved—planning, production, publication, and post-production techniques cannot be avoided if you want a strong site. However, the results are certainly worth it.

In Chapter 31, we look at a site geared toward aiding a small business to extend its sales and branding opportunities.

Designing a
Small-Business
Web Site

FRONTPAGE

Chapter 31

C ommerce on the Web is quite a deal. Major players such as MCI WorldCom and IBM are spending a great deal of money developing electronic commerce for high-end Web selling. But what about the talented native American artisan who lives in a rural community in the Southwestern United States? There's an enormous market for Southwestern art, pottery, and jewelry—a global demand, in fact. This artisan can conceivably use the Web to reach that audience, and in turn tap into a great way to improve the economy within the immediate area of his or her geographic location.

There's also the consultant who wants to take his or her talents to a larger audience. By using a promotional Web site, this consultant can make a resume and specialty list available, include a photo, client feedback, and contact information, and in so doing reach a much greater client base than before.

Then there's the small-goods manufacturer who has a successful small company with numerous employees and is looking at ways to expand its client base by placing a catalog online.

In this chapter, we're going to use the scenario of a manufacturer who wants to reach beyond the mom-and-pop type of shop and enter the international arena. Topics include:

- Understanding site intent and demographics

- Short- and long-term goals

- Product branding

- Using FrontPage to design a small-business Web site

Understanding Site Intent and Demographics

Chapter 30 demonstrated how site intent and audience is important to the way a site is developed. This is especially true for the small-business site. Whether the idea is to promote a person, service, or commodity, knowing your goals and audience is very important.

The imaginary manufacturer profiled in this chapter, Zapaton, specializes in a small, elegant selection of women's shoes and handbags made of the finest Spanish and Italian leather and natural fibers. At first glance, we see that an example such as Zapaton should appeal to an audience of older, well-heeled women, who are interested in the quality and style of their shoes and handbags and who have the finances to cover the cost. That's the natural audience and it's an important one.

But Zapaton is also looking to position itself in several other areas, including

- Making the competition aware of its existence

- Impressing potential corporate buyers and representatives in specialty boutiques the world over

- Expanding its client base to include younger women

Where does this information come from? Most businesses work from a detailed business plan. It is this plan that will guide and inspire the way you work day-to-day, as well as on the Web.

Think about Competitors!

One way to assist with market positioning is to check out what competitors are doing online. Visit Web sites of known competitors and do a more general search via your favorite search engine. Go to Web sites related to what you're doing, too. For example, if you sell women's shoes, see how companies specializing in men's footwear present their information. Take notes on the look and feel of sites, notice what is memorable and why, and think about how your site can make its own niche within the online marketplace.

Working the Business Plan

Why are you in business? What are your goals for quality, service, and financial growth?

This information should be readily available in your business plan. If you are in the early phases of thinking about your business, we heartily advise you not to jump in haphazardly, as planning is critical when it comes to a Web site—or any venture.

If you do not have a business plan, consider writing one. There are many helpful books in the business section of your favorite local and online bookstores. Check your favorite software source for helpful applications that can guide you through the task of creating such a plan.

If you already have a business plan, it's time to turn toward it for guidance and inspiration for what you are about to do on the Web. The business plan should tell you plenty about your product, your market, and the pathways to your audiences. You'll want to evaluate these factors in light of what the global perspective of a Web site can do for you. In a best-case scenario, you already have a Web marketing plan as part of your business plan; if you do not, you can easily add it as you go.

Use the following template to help guide you in making good Web site development decisions:

Describe the current product.   Your business plan should have a detailed description of your product.

> Zapaton shoes and handbags are handcrafted with attention to detail. Zapaton uses only the finest leather from Spain and Italy, and all-natural fibers for its more casual line.

Are there plans to expand the product line?   Look to your business plan for guidance here. Sometimes expansion is part of the product line, and sometimes adherence to existing standards is the name of the game.

> In Zapaton's case, the concern is not to expand, but rather to keep current with fashion trends. Each season, a new line is introduced.

How are products currently sold?   What avenues are you using for sales?

> Zapaton sells directly to the customer from one location. A small distribution deal allows Zapaton to sell its products in three boutiques located in New York, Los Angeles, and Scottsdale, Arizona.

Describe your current competition.   A business plan will have exhaustively examined product and service competitors. One of the purposes of a business plan is to help position your products and services in a competitive environment, carving a niche market from a specific audience to enable your survival and ultimate success.

> Competitors for quality shoes and handbags are numerous and include almost all major fashion designers.

How will your product be different from the competition's? Knowing the differences in your quality of product and service will help you find your distinct personality in the marketplace.

> Zapaton spares no expense in terms of quality materials. Each shoe is handmade, and each season sees an entirely new selection based on both style and comfort.

What is the current image of the business, and how can a Web site expand that image? This is an important question that can be answered by looking at what your current business plan calls for and by identifying what you hope to achieve with a Web site.

> Zapaton has a consistent but small clientele and distribution range. Within this environment, the image of the business is excellent and its name brand is well respected. However, the need is to expand the type of clientele and the range of distribution.

It is upon this template, and upon your business plan, that you'll want to base your short- and long-term Web site goals. Also, be aware that your Web site plan should be incorporated into your primary business plan now, if it wasn't before.

Short- and Long-Term Goals

Time and money are key here. You'll save more of both if you set your goals realistically, and you'll spend more of each if you don't. You want a clear idea of what you need immediately, what you want in the next few months, and what you expect to have down the road. These goals should always work in tandem with your business goals in general, too, so keep that business plan and your site-planning templates handy.

Short-Term Goals for Zapaton

Some of us make to-do lists on a daily basis. Lists are often an expression of short-term goals, the kind of goals you want to realize within a one- to six-month plan.

Immediate needs should be examined and met, certainly. But without looking at them in the context of short- and long-term goals, the results could be disastrous! For example, if an immediate need is to have a Web site up and running ASAP, and you spend a lot of money to develop a Web site in a week's time, it's highly likely that it will not be structured to meet your short- and long-term needs. This means scrapping what you paid for and starting over again! Remember that you can work in segments, deploying one aspect of a Web site for immediate needs, and later adding other areas that are important. This should not be done without incorporating all of your goals.

Using Zapaton as our guide, let's envision some short-term goals from what we know about the company:

- Create a good-looking site that appeals to potential suppliers and retailers as well as individual customers.

- Ensure that buyers and partners know how to get in touch with you.

- Make your current line available online in terms of both description and visual expression through photos and graphics.

Do You *Really* Need a Web Site?

Some companies think they need a Web site just because everyone has one! That's not always a wise move, because if you put up a Web site quickly, without thinking through your goals and needs, you could do yourself and your company a great disservice. Think carefully about logical reasons to have a Web site, and *be prepared* to have it updated and kept fresh in order for it to be of use to site visitors.

Mapping Long-Term Goals

Long-term goals should relate to the strategy your business plan sets to help grow your business. If you foresee an expansion in your products or services, or a shift from the storefront to a Web-based model, then address these issues immediately so your Web project can successfully manage the growth.

Zapaton eventually sees that the Web will be not only a primary point of sales to individual customers, but also a showroom to demonstrate current products to larger buyers and distributors. Eventually a network of those distributors will discuss business strategies regarding Zapaton's positioning, and as the company grows, more information about its activities—need for new employees, corporate success stories, and charitable activities—will help add to its favorable prestige.

Certainly your site will change over time, too. You will add technology, refresh the design, and expand the content. But the essential truth remains: If you create a model that is flexible and prepared for expansion, you'll have fewer limitations on expansion.

When building the site, you will focus on areas of current need—but be sure to incorporate a navigation format to which you can easily add new areas. If you make an image map rather than buttons, you lock yourself into having to redesign an entire map every time you add or remove an area. However, if you use individual buttons, you simply add or remove a button. Furthermore, sensible categories enable you to grow a site logically (see Figure 31.1).

next

Figure 31.1 *Using buttons rather than an image map*

Your brand should be strong and consistent with print and other campaigns from the start (see "Branding a Product" later in this chapter). Don't try out a "new" look on the Web just yet—if you have plans to update your brand, do it in a different test market. In order to be effective, a Web site must carry its brand to the online audience seamlessly.

What about Domain Names?

Should your site have a domain name? Effective branding means having a domain name that is an extension of your product name or mark. If you're in the business of promoting a person, product, or service, a domain name helps to reinforce your brand.

You can get a domain name in a number of ways. First, you need to see if it's available, and you can do this yourself by visiting Network Solutions (`www.networksolutions.com`) and using the search features offered. Type in the desired name of the business with an appropriate suffix, such as:

- `.com`: relating to a commercial business

- `.org`: usually a non-profit or religious organization

- `.net`: a network of related content

There are other suffixes, such as `.edu` *for education,* `.mil` *for military,* `.gov` *for government organizations, and* `.ws` *for Web site. For these suffixes, you will need to follow the guidelines of your organization for procuring the appropriate domain.*

So, the developer for Zapaton will visit Network Solutions and, using the search system available, type in **zapaton.com**. The results are as follows:

```
No match for "ZAPATON.COM".
```

This indicates the domain name is probably available.

If the domain is not available, the results of the search will be a page including the registrant's name and contact information. You always have the right to query the owner about the use of the name, and a fair agreement may be worked out for the purchase of that name. However, No means no, so don't harass someone who doesn't wish to sell. If they got there first, you may be out of luck. If you own a trademark on the name, however, you might want to consult an attorney who has Web-related experience.

You can fashion a domain name with up to 26 characters (letters, numbers, and dashes—no spaces or extraneous characters are allowed). The name will then be followed by a dot (`.`) and the appropriate suffix. Depending on your ISP, you may or may not have a www in front of the name; you may have another word, such as the name of the server: `molly.annex.com`.

Branding a Product

If you hear the name Coca-Cola, no doubt an image comes to mind. A product's success often comes from its ability to remain at the forefront of an audience's mind. This image is not happenstance—it is the result of calculated marketing on the part of the company and its advertising partners.

To brand a product, a company should have:

- A unique company name
- An appropriate and memorable slogan
- A logo that is simple but strong

Other methods of enabling a company to create a lasting and important image include:

- Positioning the company with some positive feature related to service or product, such as quality, price, or reliability.

- Company involvement in community success: Does the company participate in outreach programs, provide training and education for employees, or give money and time to charitable or humanitarian causes? These types of activities reflect a favorable light upon a company.

Many readers might have heard the term *presence* applied to a Web site. In a sense, it is the benefit of presence—the establishment and extension of a company's brand—that is the most beneficial aspect of a Web site.

Think of a billboard. No doubt you've seen effective billboard campaigns. Do they make you go directly out and buy a specific product? Not necessarily. What they do is embed a sense of that company or product's existence into your mind by reminding you what their image is and what they can offer you. Ultimately, this affects sales, but it doesn't usually do so in an immediate and obvious way.

The same is largely true for Web sites. Only a handful of site types have seen overwhelming success in direct online sales. These include sites that offer adult content, sites that sell books and CDs, and sites that provide travel-related services. And even if your product or service fits into one of these categories, you'll still want to be aware that *branding* and *presence* are the best benefits your site can help you gain.

Branding in Action

A company that has had enormous success in branding client products is Landor Associates, `www.landor.com`. Landor provides a detailed look at its branding strategies at its Web site.

Developing the Look and Feel

Chapter 30 walked through the creation of a look and feel for a personal Web site. We're going to do that here, too. It's important to develop the look and feel of your site using your business plan and, in the case of a company with a preexisting brand, the logo (see Figure 31.2) and other branding methods already in use.

Figure 31.2 *The Zapaton logo*

Let's examine, in terms of design, Zapaton's audience and intentions as far as marketing its product goes.

Assessing current demographics as wealthy women, aged 45 or older   The desire is to keep hold of this audience. An elegant and somewhat sedate look is in order.

Making competition aware of its existence   The competition should see the Web site as a well-designed, well-positioned site whose brand is consistent with other known brands in the same category.

Impressing potential corporate buyers and representatives in specialty boutiques the world over   This will be done using a sophisticated design, as well as by ensuring that the products are attractively displayed and well described.

Expanding client base to include younger women   Adding fashionable accessories and creating designs that appeal to younger women will help expand the product to this market.

One of the first things to look at is color. We want to convey a sense of elegance and sophistication, and we want to draw from any existing colors and design that a company might have in current advertising media. So we created a palette of color to express that elegance. We chose to use what is known as a *monochromatic* scheme (a theme based on one basic color—in this case, olive green), because that helps convey consistency as well as a sense of calm.

Color Name	RGB Value	Hex Value	Expression
Light olive green	204 204 153	CCCC99	Light, youth, refreshment
Medium olive green	153 153 102	999966	Elegance, refinement
Deep olive green	102 102 0	666600	Consistency, depth

We also included black for text and white for any accents. Black is typically an elegant color, and white is known for clean and crisp results.

Next, we worked with the typefaces that are used in the company logo to determine a nice method of displaying the information. The logo is done in Fritz Quadrata, and the sub-header of the logo uses Helvetica. We decided to mimic this approach in the way we laid out the Web page's type:

Type Family	Typeface	Expression/Use
Serif	Fritz Quadrata	Elegant, beautiful
Sans serif	Helvetica	Strong, easy to read

We then examined approaches to graphic accents. We decided graphic text should be flat, so as not to compete with the product images. We created a crumpled-paper look for the product photos, which add some texture and intrigue to the design. Buttons are graphic-based text with a subtle JavaScript mouseover.

Preparing for Technology

While we've decided to keep technology somewhat limited on the Zapaton site, there are three areas that require technology above and beyond what FrontPage can provide:

JavaScript mouseovers   While you could do mouseovers with a Java applet, we prefer to use JavaScript for this effect. JavaScript is very fast, is easy to use, and demands little resources from your server, or your visitor's hardware and software. While this means having to go in and add script, there are good copy-and-paste scripts available to make this process easy.

Feedback form   We definitely want a way for our prospective buyers and partners to get in touch. So we're going to ensure that a Feedback Form is made available, using FrontPage's Feedback Form template.

Ordering methods   This is an area that's less clear than the others. For larger product lines, a shopping cart would be put in place; however, this is a small product line. Instead of a shopping cart, we decided to rely on a secure commerce server to allow direct ordering of individual products from a single page. This keeps costs lower at the outset, and since there is *no expected expansion* of the number of products, but rather an expansion of the product type, we felt it would be the best route. However, for those of you interested in shopping cart technologies, we've provided a sidebar so you can investigate what's available to best suit your own situation.

Shopping Cart Technologies

There are several helpful resources that will aid you in making good decisions regarding your shopping cart needs. Some are free, others are inexpensive, and others can be very expensive. Be sure to research your needs well before jumping into a purchase.

For CGI scripts, see www.cgi-resources.com/.

Often, your ISP will be working with specialty back-end programs such as ColdFusion, which have built-in functions allowing for commercial transactions. It's possible they have or can write a custom script for your purposes. Checking with your ISP first is always a good place to start!

Understanding Secure Transactions

Secure transactions are those communications that take place in an environment using special Internet technologies called *protocols* or *encryption systems*. The concept is an important one for a number of reasons. First, it creates a way to protect site visitors with a very high level of security when they enter personal information such as home address, telephone number, and credit card numbers. Second, the *sense* of security that is conveyed is incredibly important, too. All too many users are afraid of hackers and fraud, and while there is always the possibility that an unfortunate incident can occur, the reality of it occurring is truly very rare.

Secure systems use methods including:

SSL Secure Sockets Layer was created by Netscape to manage secure transactions.

STT This is Microsoft's Secure Transaction Technology.

SET This is Secure Electronic Transaction. SET uses digital certificates to "sign" secure data.

RSA RSA is an encryption system typically used by SSL, STT, and SET to encode and authenticate digital data.

One of the biggest issues in security isn't that sites are insecure—but that people perceive them as being insecure. A note about your site's privacy can help site visitors feel more comfortable when making purchases online.

Laying Out the Pages

Once again, we turn to Photoshop as our primary choice for page layout. However, you may use the image editor of your choice. We do recommend you use an image editor with layering capabilities (see Chapter 18).

To start, you should lay out the splash page by following these steps:

1. In your image editor, choose File ➜ New. The New dialog box appears.

2. Create an image size that is 595 pixels wide by 295 pixels high.

3. Click OK.

4. You now have your work area set to the first layer. To this layer, add your background color. We selected Medium Olive Green (see the color chart earlier in this chapter).

5. Now create a new layer by choosing Layer ➜ New ➜ Layer. On this layer, create or add the company logo (see Figure 31.3).

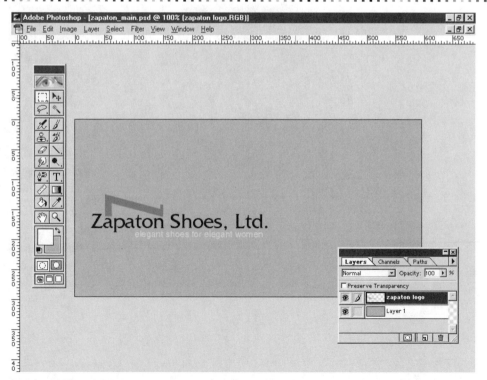

Figure 31.3 *Adding the main logo*

6. After you've added all the elements you want for this page, save the file by choosing File ➜ Save As. The Save As dialog box appears.

7. Name the file and save it in the native layer format of your imaging program.

Now create the layout for an internal page by following these steps:

1. In your image editor, choose File ➜ New. The New dialog box appears.

2. Create an image size that is 595 pixels wide by 600 pixels high (or higher if the page content needs to be more than two screens in height).

3. Click OK.

4. You now have your work area set to the first layer. To this layer, add your background color.

5. Now create a new layer by choosing Layer ➜ New ➜ Layer. On this layer, create the header.

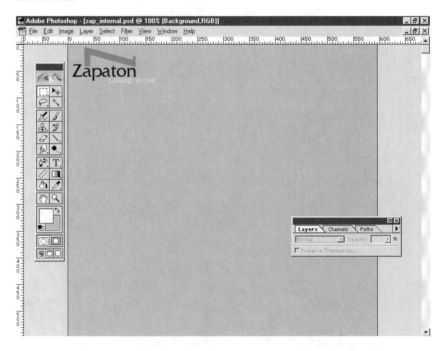

6. Layer by layer, add the graphic components of the page such as sub-headers, navigation, and photos.

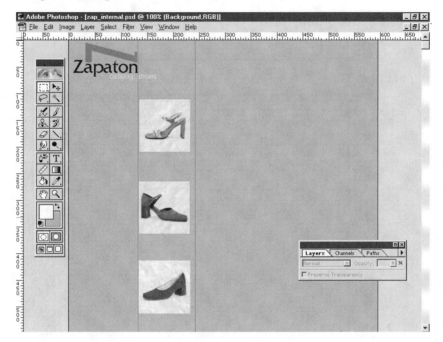

7. After you've added all the elements you want for this page, save the file by choosing File ➔ Save As. The Save As dialog box appears.

8. Name the file and save it in the native layer format of your imaging program.

Figure 31.4 shows a completed inner page design. You'll now repeat this process for each and every page you've designed for the site.

To generate the actual graphics, return to your imaging program to produce the site graphics, and then follow these steps:

1. Open the layered file in your imaging program.

2. Highlight the layer that has the image you want to process.

3. Use the marquee or selection tool (it varies depending on your program) to draw a selection around the part of the image you want to keep, making sure you're on the correct layer.

4. Copy and paste the section into a new file.

5. Optimize the file as a GIF or JPEG, depending on the graphic.

6. Name the graphic and save it directly to the images folder within your Web site.

Repeat the process for all buttons, headers, backgrounds, and spot art that you'll require.

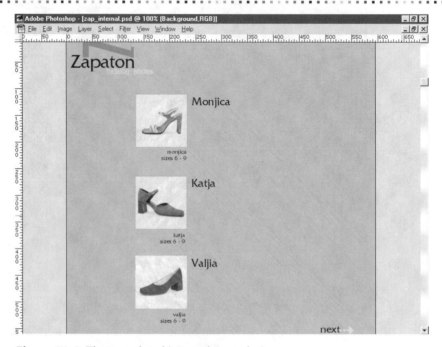

Figure 31.4 *The completed internal page design*

Working with FrontPage

Now that you've got the layout done, it's time to start working with FrontPage. We begin by setting up our directories in this way:

1. Choose File ➜ New ➜ Page Or Web.

2. In the New Page Or Web task pane, click Web Site Templates link. You see the Web Site Templates dialog box.

3. Select One Page Web, choose a folder to keep the Web site in, and click OK. FrontPage creates the necessary folders for your Web site.

Since ours is a manageable site, we use the root directory for all the HTML pages, and the images folder for all graphics.

Follow these steps to set up individual files in your root directory:

1. In Folders view, right-click anywhere in the interface. A menu appears.

2. Select New ➔ Page.

3. A new page appears in the root directory. Name this page.

Repeat the process until you have created all the pages planned for the site. You can always add or delete pages as necessary.

To add the Feedback Form:

1. Select File ➔ New ➔ Page Or Web. The New Page Or Web task pane appears.

2. Click the Page Templates link. You see the Page Templates dialog box.

3. Select Feedback Form and click OK.

4. Save the file as **feedback.htm**. You'll modify it later.

Tasks are one of FrontPage's most helpful tools to guide you through building your Web site. To set up tasks using Folders view:

1. In Folders view, select the file you want to associate with a task.

2. Choose Edit ➔ Tasks ➔ Add Task. The New Task dialog box appears.

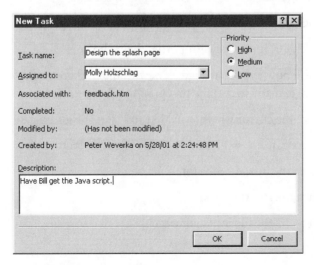

3. Fill in the task name, priority, and a description.

4. Click OK.

Whether associating a task with a page or without it, be sure to include as many tasks as you'll need to complete the production and post-production processes. For more information on tasks, see Chapter 7.

Designing the Splash Page

Now it's time to design the splash page for your site. Do so by following these steps:

1. In Folders view, select the `index.htm` file that you created earlier.

2. Right-click `index.htm` and choose Open on the shortcut menu. The page opens in Page view.

3. Right-click the empty page and select Page Properties from the shortcut menu. The Page Properties dialog appears.

4. Click the Background tab, and, in the Colors section, open the Background drop-down menu and choose More Colors. The More Colors dialog box appears.

5. In the Value text box, type in the hexadecimal color you want for the background. Refer to the list you made in pre-production when you developed the look and feel of the Web site. In our example, we chose the Medium Olive Green, hex value 999966, for the background.

6. Click OK to return to the Page Properties dialog box.

7. Click OK in the Page Properties dialog box.

Your page will now appear in Page view, with the background color you selected. Now you're ready to add the first graphic. To do this:

1. Place the cursor where you'd like to insert the graphic.

2. Choose Insert ➜ Picture ➜ From File. The Picture dialog box appears.

3. Select the image you want.

4. Click the Insert button.

FrontPage inserts the file into your page.

You can check the results of your work by saving the pages and selecting File ➜ Preview In Browser. In Figure 31.5, you see the results of our page design within the browser window.

Figure 31.5 *The completed splash design as shown in the browser*

Designing an Internal Page

Typically, tables are needed to lay out most pages. The Zapaton catalog pages are no exception.

In Figure 31.6, you can see the page layout we did using our image editor. We've set up some guides to show how we'd like to map out our table grid. Based on this information, we can turn to FrontPage and begin creating the actual table.

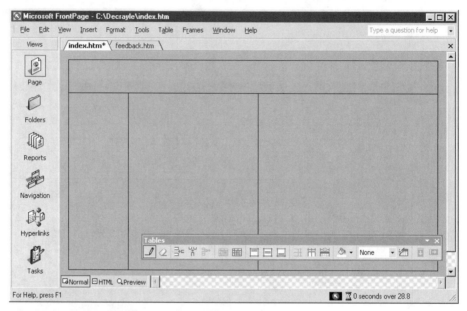

Figure 31.6 *Planning the table in FrontPage*

When planning a table, begin with vertical columns, only adding rows where necessary. Be sure to revisit Chapter 11 for more information.

With your table in mind, follow these steps to lay out the page:

1. In Page view, choose Table ➜ Insert ➜ Table. The Insert Table dialog box appears:

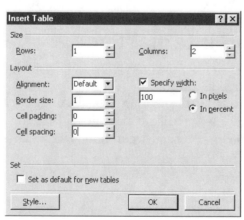

2. Enter the number of rows in the Rows text box (we entered 1).

3. Enter the number of columns (we entered 4) in the Columns text box.

4. In the Layout section, choose an alignment for your table. Typically, left alignment is used, although some choose the Default option. With this option, settings in the visitor's browser determine how the table is aligned.

5. Set the Border, Cell Padding, and Cell Spacing to 0.

6. Check Specify Width.

7. Add a numeric value for fixed-width tables and a percentage for dynamic. In an example such as this one, we want to fix the width so that all the content including images and graphics is neatly managed. We entered a total width of 595 pixels.

8. Click OK. The table appears on your page.

9. Add images and text using the techniques you learned in related chapters of this book to refine the page's look. Be sure to adjust table and table cell properties where necessary (see Chapter 11).

10. When you're finished, save the page. You can preview it externally, or internally using the Preview tab to see the way the page will appear.

When working with navigation, be sure to remember that you can use shared borders on appropriate pages if you will be using a server supporting FrontPage extensions. Check Chapter 15 for details, and be sure to ask your ISP if you have access to FrontPage.

Customizing the Feedback Form

Because we want the Feedback Form to match our design rather than the prefabricated look that FrontPage uses, we'll want to customize the form using our own colors and graphics. Here's how:

1. In Folders view, double-click feedback.htm. The file opens in Page view.

2. Add the background and link colors to the page by following the directions we discussed in the "Creating the Splash Page" section.

3. Delete the comment and the horizontal rule from the top of the page.

4. Add your graphic header by selecting Insert ➜ Picture ➜ From File and choosing the appropriate header image for your page.

5. Customize the comments within the form field. Simply click within the field where you'd like to change the text and type in the new text.

6. If you'd like to change the text on the form buttons, right-click the button and choose Form Field Properties. The Push Button Properties dialog box appears. In the Value/Label text box, type in the word or words you'd like to have appear on the button and click OK.

7. Customize any remaining text on the page, and be sure that the page is included in the shared borders if you are taking that approach to navigation.

8. Save your file to the Web site.

Your results should look something like Figure 31.7.

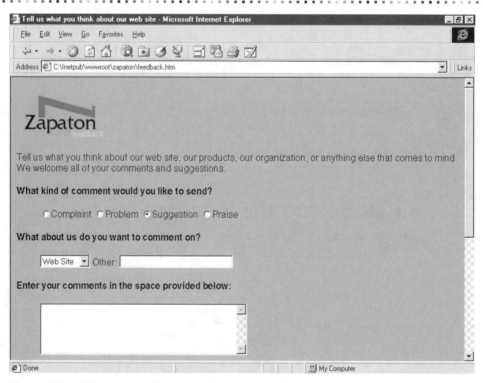

Figure 31.8 *The Zapaton Feedback Form*

Have you marked off your tasks? If not, and if you are confident the work for a given task is finished, go into Tasks view and mark the task as complete.

Adding the JavaScript

To achieve the mouseover effect, you'll want to add JavaScript. Certainly, this can be done with other methods, such as hover buttons, but JavaScript is a much faster method and is also less demanding on resources both on the client and server side.

Because FrontPage doesn't offer JavaScripts, you'll have to find your own. We're going to show you a great mouseover script here, and we'll describe how to add it to your pages. Be sure to check Chapter 21 for general guidelines and specific JavaScript resources.

To work with this JavaScript, you need to create two graphics, one each for the standard and mouseover states. In our example, we'll create two buttons; one will be a standard button, and the other will have some modification such as a highlight. We'll also name the graphics logically so we know which is the standard and which is the mouseover-state graphic.

This script is written to sniff and pre-load images if a supportive browser visits. If the browser is an older version without JavaScript, the standard state button will function just fine.

Here's the main portion of the script *before* customization. Note that the bold items are what you'll need to change.

```
<script language="javascript">
<!--
// browser test:
bName = navigator.appName;
bVer = parseInt (navigator.appVersion);
if (bName == "Netscape" && bVer >= 3) version = "n3";
else if (bName == "Netscape" && bVer == 2) version = "n2";
else if (bName == "Microsoft Internet Explorer" && bVer >= 3)
   version = "n3";
else version = "n2";

// end of browser test
// preload universal images:
// If it is Netscape 3 browser
```

```
if (version== "n3") {

b1off = new Image(); b1off.src = "path to standard image";
b1on = new Image(); b1on.src = "path to over image";
}
function hiLite(imgDocID,imgObjName) {
 if (version == "n3") {
  document.images[imgDocID].src = imgObjName;
  }
 }
function hiLiteOff(imgDocID,imgObjName) {
 if (version == "n3") {
  document.images[imgDocID].src = imgObjName;
  }
 }
//-->
</script>
```

Follow these steps to add the script to a page using FrontPage:

1. Open the page of interest in Page view.

2. Select the HTML tab to see the HTML code.

3. Locate the opening <HEAD> tag. Below any META tag information and before the closing </HEAD> tag, copy the script *exactly* as it appears here.

4. In the first bold area, replace the comment with the path and name of your standard image:

    ```
    b1off = new Image(); b1off.src = "path to standard image";
    ```

    becomes

    ```
    b1off = new Image(); b1off.src = "images/next.gif";
    ```

5. In the second bold area, replace the comment with the path and name of your mouseover image:

    ```
    b1on = new Image(); b1on.src = "path to over image";
    ```

    becomes

    ```
    b1on = new Image(); b1off.src = "images/next_over.gif";
    ```

6. To add additional images, add image sets directly beneath each other and rename the numeric values:

```
b2off = new Image(); b2off.src = "path to second standard
image";
b2on = new Image(); b2on.src = "path to second over image";
```

7. Continue this process until you've accounted for all images.

Save the file by pressing Ctl+S on your keyboard.
Now make these additional modifications to the image and the image link:

1. In Page view, select the HTML tab.

2. In the appropriate section of the body, add your image by choosing Insert → Picture → From File and selecting the *static* image file. The following code appears:

```
<img src="images/next.gif">
```

3. Select the code, right-click it, and choose Tag Properties on the shortcut menu. The Picture Properties dialog appears.

4. Click the Appearance tab, if necessary.

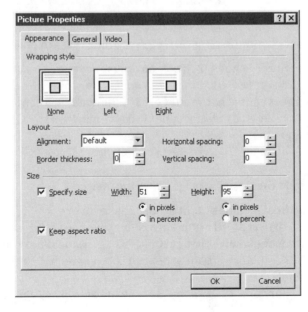

5. In the Layout section, make sure all settings are set to 0.

6. In the Size section, check the Specify Size check box (FrontPage will automatically have entered the width and height; do *not* change these numbers), and be sure the In Pixels option buttons are selected.

7. Check the Keep Aspect Ratio check box.

8. Click the General tab. In the Alternative Representations section, enter descriptive text into the Text text box.

9. Click OK. Your code looks like this:

```
<img src="images/next.gif" alt="go to the next page"
    border="0" width="32" height="32">
```

10. Now add the bolded information to the image:

```
<img src="images/next.gif" name="b1" alt="go to the next
page"
    border="0" width="32" height="32">
```

Continue adding images and corresponding names to your code until all your standard images are included.

Now add the proper link syntax and JavaScript code. We prefer you do this by hand. To do so:

1. In front of your first image, type everything that's in bold:

```
<a href="shoes_2.htm" on mouse-over=
    "hiLite('b1','images/next_over.gif')"
onmouseout="hiLiteOff('b1','images/next.gif')">
    <img src="images/next.gif" name="b1" alt="go to the next
page"
    border="0" width="32" height="32">
```

2. Now add the closing </a> tag after the image:

```
<a href="shoes_2.htm" on mouse-over=
    "hiLite('b1','images/next_over.gif')"
    onmouseout="hiLiteOff('b1','images/next.gif')">
    <img src="images/next.gif" name="b1" alt="go to the next
page"
    border="0" width="32" height="32"></a>
```

3. Continue to add the information as necessary for each image. Be sure your image names and numeric values match!

4. After you're finished, check your work in a browser by selecting File ➔ Preview In Browser.

Your mouseover script should now be in perfect working order!

Getting Ready to Publish Your Site

After you've got all your pages designed, you're almost ready to upload them to the server so they can be live on the Internet. But there are a few things you should do before showing your creation to the world!

First, you'll want to spell-check all of the pages by following these steps:

1. Choose Tools ➔ Spelling (or press F7). The Spelling dialog box appears.

2. Click the Entire Web option button.

3. Click the Start button.

FrontPage will now spell-check all of the pages and report back any misspellings. Chapter 3 explains spell-checking in detail.

Now, check all of the links on your site by choosing View ➔ Reports ➔ Problems ➔ Broken Hyperlinks. The Broken Hyperlinks report appears. Each link's status is described with a particular indicator. (See Chapter 24 for a full list of these indicators.)

If one of the links on your Web site is no longer valid, or *broken*, you'll need to replace it with an updated one by following these steps:

1. In the Broken Hyperlinks Report view, double-click the link you want to change. The Edit Hyperlink dialog box appears.

2. In the Replace Hyperlink With text box, repair the hyperlink. See Chapter 24 for details.

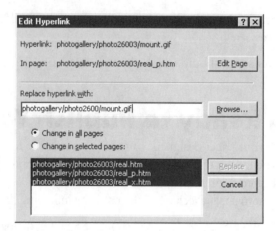

Continue to repair links as necessary. When you're finished, run through the process again to ensure no broken links remain.

The next step in the process is to add META-tag descriptions and keywords to the pages. To do this:

1. In Page view, choose File ➜ Properties. The Page Properties dialog box appears.

2. In the Title text box, type the "title" words you targeted. In our example, we used "Zapaton Shoes, Inc."

3. Click the Custom tab.

4. In the lower part of the dialog box, locate the User Variables area. This area displays a list of all the META tags in the current page. To add a new META tag to the page, click the Add button. The User Meta Variable dialog box appears.

5. In the Name field, you need to identify the type of META tag you want to add. For example, type **keywords** now, so you can specify some keywords.

6. In the Value text box, type the keywords you think best for your site. For Zapaton's site, try keywords and keyword combinations such as women, shoes, handbags, leather, leather goods, and so forth.

7. Click the OK button. Back in the Page Properties dialog box, your META tag is now visible.

8. Repeat steps 5 through 7, this time typing **description** (instead of **keywords**) and adding the description you think best. In our example, this would be: "Zapaton Shoes, Ltd. Features handmade shoes and handbags of the finest Spanish and Italian leather and all natural fibers."

9. Click OK. Your site is now properly META-tagged.

Be sure to test the site using different browsers, platforms, and screen resolutions to ensure that you've done a good job at making the site cross-browser compatible (see Chapter 16).

Post-Production Needs

A Web site should always be kept fresh. If it's not seeing changes and growth on at least a quarterly basis, it reflects to visitors that your business isn't dynamic. Continue to develop your site as your business develops. If you have a new product, or new job listing, or are offering an incentive or special—put it online!

Of course, this translates to human power. Many people make the mistake of thinking they can put a Web site up and the job is done—that's all that will ever be needed or necessary. This is like putting a shingle over the front door and believing the rest will take care of itself! It doesn't happen that way: effort and attention must be paid.

Whether you, someone in your organization, someone who comes in on a part-time basis, or a Web design firm does the updates and maintenance, the reality is that *someone* will have to do it. It might be cost-effective to train someone within your organization to manage updates, particularly if you don't expect too many changes over time. FrontPage can help you manage maintenance using tasks.

In any case, you should have a good idea of what it really means to be a "Webmaster." The following list includes qualities of a good Webmaster:

- Understands the business at hand. This way, the Webmaster not only can add to the site, but will be alert for potential problems and come up with helpful ideas, as well.

- Works with the technology. The Webmaster must be proficient in HTML and be able to use FrontPage and image editing programs.

- Understands the mechanisms by which to publish Web sites.

- Has good communications skills and an ability to discuss issues with the Internet service provider.

- Has a basic knowledge of branding and marketing concepts.

Sounds demanding? It is! Be confident that you can use this book and the resources within it, as well as many other books and Web sites, to supplement the education of your Webmaster.

Just because you have a Web site doesn't mean people are going to show up and suddenly start participating in your offerings. You've got to get the word out on the virtual street as well as within your preexisting marketing circles. Be sure to visit Chapter 24 for helpful guidance in this regard.

Up Next

In this chapter, you've not only extended your knowledge and practice of a process-oriented method of developing Web sites, but you've focused on how these practices apply specifically to the small business. Issues such as branding and identity were carefully demonstrated, and resources for additional ways to grow and manage your site have been provided.

In the next chapter, we take a look at how a community site is built and maintained. Communities are a powerful and growing force on the Web, and if you have interest in providing the ultimate user experience by building a community, be sure to read beyond the structural elements we've included, particularly the conceptual and management-oriented community issues also covered.

Building a
Community Site

FRONTPAGE

Chapter 32

In this chapter, we take a close look at what goes into the planning, production, and management of an online community. Community sites are popular, can offer opportunities for developers interested in building potential revenue sources, and are a great way to get people on the Web involved in special interests. Stretching beyond the standard offerings of a personal or small business Web page, a community site places significant demands on developer resources, technology, and human resources. An idea of what those demands are can help you decide if a community is in order and how to best manage a community once you decide to launch one. Topics include:

- What is online community?
- Why developing community is important
- Planning and producing an online community
- Management concerns

What Is Online Community?

Many readers will remember Bulletin Board Services, fondly referred to as BBSs. These typically single-line (although sometimes multiple-line) community boards allowed people to use their computers and modems and engage in communication, file downloads, and games.

Coupled with BBSs were commercial online services. You might remember GEnie, at one time the most popular online service. Other such services still in existence include Prodigy, Compuserve, and the still-thriving America Online (AOL).

BBSs and commercial online services were the first widely available online communities. Until the early 1990s, the Internet was restricted in its scope and access. So the home computer user interested in online life used these boards and services to find information and communicate with others who had shared interests.

When access to the Internet expanded, newsgroups became the focus of special interest communities, and Internet Relay Chat (IRC) became the free venue for chat-oriented folks to enjoy real-time community. The Web quickly became a locale for personal expression as well as business-oriented sites.

But creating a Web-based community has been challenging. This is largely due to the technology. Inline newsgroups and chats are inconsistent and difficult, and linking to existing resources from the Web often involves plug-ins and multiple software interfaces. Luckily, the technology is getting easier. And, as the technology becomes more accessible, Web-based communities are rising up with rapid force.

Why an Online Community?

The advantages of creating an online community are many. In some cases, online communities can extend a business. A great example of this is Saturn cars, a company that has very effectively used a community-oriented concept in all of its advertising. This has extended to its Web site, where community thrives.

Sometimes community is more utilitarian. You provide forums and chats as a way of handling outreach to company members who are out in the field. Or you may have an online fan club and provide forums and chats to talk about your favorite actor, musical group, or game.

Community sites are often funded by sponsors and advertisers. Larger communities can offer advertisers a pool of collected individuals with a specific demographic. This allows advertising to be more targeted and direct, and ultimately, more effective.

Planning the Community

Community sites are typically a combination of Internet and Web technologies that focus on human rather than technological activity. People meet in chat rooms to discuss issues in real time; use newsgroups to discuss projects, ask questions, and share art; or visit community Web sites for collected information on their favorite topics.

As a developer, you need to have a firm vision of what you want your community to be—both in structure and in content.

First, let's look at the components of a community. Then we'll take an example and walk you through the familiar pre-production activities of planning a site—defining intent, goals, and technology needs. While much of the process is similar to what you'll be doing in other chapters in Part VI of this book, the content is geared more specifically toward the subject of community sites. So this chapter will show you a familiar process, but with the individual look and feel, technologies, and production needs of a community site.

Community Structure

Communities can be made up of a variety of components, but they must have a common, central point. For a Web-based community, this is naturally the community Web site. Let's look at the aspects of a Web community in detail:

Web content Web content refers to articles, interviews, FAQs, and other information placed on a Web site. Typically, Web content will grow, with older articles getting archived and newer features moving to the front of the community.

Newsgroups and forums Much like BBSs, a newsgroup (also called a *forum*) is often the primary place where people choose to meet. A visitor leaves a message, and subsequent visitors respond to that message. The banter can be humorous, informative, and sometimes downright fiery! Newsgroups are best streamlined in their topical areas of interest. If your community is about women, your newsgroups might focus on women's health, romance, women and money, and so forth.

Chats While the majority of chats are populated by younger Internet users, chats within specialized communities are popular with more mature audiences, too. Special guests, specific topics, and chat hosts who can remove troublemakers all help to make chatting a very interesting real-time experience for visitors.

Ancillary content Depending upon the type of community you're developing, you might have a variety of related content. Some communities offer Web-based e-mail, games, and postcards for their visitors. This type of content can keep a community colorful and lively.

Figure 32.1 shows how these community components are structured within a Web site.

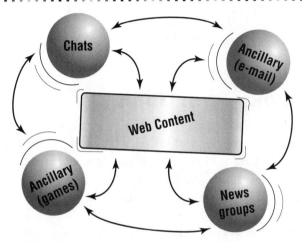

Figure 32.1 *Components of a community Web site*

Audience and Intent

When creating communities, these familiar issues are especially important. Communities can be broad in topical interest, such as automobiles, or they can be very specialized, such as The Mustang Convertible Club.

You might be developing a community as a hobbyist, in which case it's likely that you'll have a specialized audience. However, if you're building a community for commercial purposes, the community structure is likely going to be much bigger.

Defining how broad or specific you are going to be is critical to every aspect of site production and management. Knowing ahead of time how many newsgroups and chats (you may only have one of each, or you may have hundreds) and what kind of Web and ancillary content you want to have will help you make better site-design decisions. Also, the amount of potential traffic will help you and your Internet service provider choose the best technology in a given case.

We're going to use the example of Web Answers for Everyone, a community based on Web building. We want to be very broad in our scope, including design, programming, marketing, and other development interests, as well as appealing to a variety of audiences, including newcomers and professionals. We don't want to be technology-specific.

What all of this means is that we're planning a *big* community. However, for the purposes of this chapter, we're going to stick to the basic areas of development and show how FrontPage can help you produce the community in question.

For specialized information on the management of large Web sites, see Chapter 33.

Short- and Long-Term Goals

Our short-term goal for our Web Answers for Everyone site is to provide a content-rich, community-oriented environment for Web developers of all skill levels. Information will be completely free. For the long term, we want to amass members to draw the interest of advertisers and sponsors so the community can grow revenue, and eventually we'd like to create an online school where community members can get training in Web design and related topics.

We've sketched out the concept of our community, which you can see in Figure 32.2.

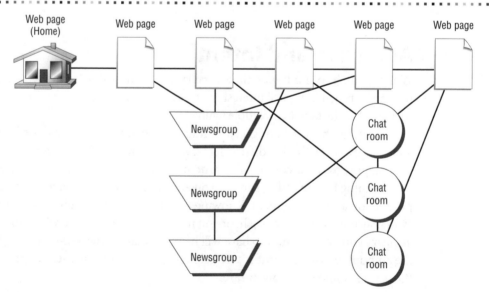

Figure 32.2 *Sketch of our proposed community*

Getting Ready for Production

While we've abbreviated the planning phase in terms of scope, once you have your community well planned in terms of intent, goals, and structure, it's time to get ready for production by creating the look and feel of your community and determining what technologies will be necessary.

Creating a Visual Design

Community look and feel should be fun, gregarious, bright, and welcoming. We first looked to color and shape to help us create the tone of the site:

Color Name	RGB Value	Hex Value	Expression
Dark orange	204 102 0	CC6600	Bright and warm
Light orange	255 153 0	FF9900	Fun and energetic
Dark blue	51 51 102	333366	Intelligent
Medium blue	0 102 153	006699	Another energetic color conveying "cool"
White	255 255 255	FFFFFF	Clean, crisp, easy on the eyes

We also included black for text and white for any accents.

Next, we worked with the typefaces to determine a nice method of displaying the information. We wanted something fun, and we decided to mimic this approach in the way we laid out the Web page's type:

Type Family	Typeface	Expression/Use
Decorative	Vienna Black	Chunky, humorous font for headers
Decorative	Architeqtura	Slender, decorative typeface for sub-headers
Serif	Times Roman	Common, cross-platform serif font good for body text

We then examined the way to approach graphic accents. We decided that header text would have a drop shadow to add some depth to the pages. We created a similar drop shadow for photos and illustrations, as well, and we employed a JavaScript mouseover animation for navigation (see Chapter 30).

Community Technology

When it comes to community sites, technology plays a critical role in how the site is managed and how needed functions are delivered. While we can't possibly demonstrate in one small chapter all of the ways community technology can be used, we will discuss the basics and help you see where FrontPage can be especially useful.

The following technologies are often used to create and enhance online communities:

Advertising banners   Because your site will likely be supported by sponsors and advertisers, planning for ad banners is a good thing. FrontPage offers an Ad Banner component, which you can learn to use in Chapter 15.

Forums   FrontPage allows you to create interactive forums. This is helpful, but for very big communities, FrontPage might not be sufficient for the kind of control or scope of forums you'll want to have. For our example, we'll walk you through how to set up forums effectively using FrontPage.

ASP   Active Server Pages can help keep your Web content pages dynamic. For more information about ASP, see Chapter 27.

Chats   Unfortunately, Microsoft FrontPage doesn't have a built-in chat component. However, there are a variety of ActiveX components and Java applets that you can use to create chats. Another method of chat creation is running your own chat server, or arranging with your ISP to let you have access to a chat server running on IRC technology. Then you can allow people to access the chat rooms using the software of their choice.

Technologies for ancillary services   Web-based e-mail, postcards, and games all have their uses. Many of these ancillary services are available in the form of free or low-cost scripts. Check resource sites made available in Chapter 21, Chapter 26, Chapter 27, and Chapter 28.

Producing the Site

As with the previous two chapters in this section, we're going to walk through aspects of producing the community site. First, we're going to create the design using our image editor, and then we're going to move on to FrontPage itself where, using a combination of wizards and templates, we'll get the community site going.

Laying Out the Pages

For this site, we decided not to have a splash page. We felt that a community site should have a sense of immediacy—where people can get to the information and interaction they want without a progression of visual and navigational information. So the first page we designed is our welcome page.

Follow these steps to lay out a welcome page:

1. In your image editor, choose File ➜ New. The New dialog box appears.

2. Create an image that is 595 pixels wide by 600 pixels high.

3. Click OK. You will now have your work area set to the first layer.

4. To this layer, add your background color. We selected white (see the color chart earlier in this chapter).

5. Create a new layer by choosing Layer ➜ New ➜ Layer. Here you'll add the areas of color to create the unusual feel. In our example, we build the arcs using Adobe Illustrator (see Chapter 18), a vector-based drawing tool, and then import them into Photoshop.

6. On subsequent layers, add the page title, navigation bars, and sub-headers.

7. After you've added all the elements you want for this page, save the file by choosing File ➜ Save As. The Save As dialog box appears. Name the file and save in the native layer format of your imaging program.

Figure 32.3 shows the completed welcome page design.

To generate the actual graphics for your welcome page, return to your imaging program and follow these steps:

1. Open up the layered file in your imaging program.

2. Highlight the layer that has the image you want to process.

3. Using the marquee or selection tool (it will vary depending upon your program), draw a selection around the part of the image you want to keep, making sure you're on the correct layer.

4. Copy and paste the section into a new file.

5. Optimize the file as a GIF or JPEG, depending upon the graphic. Name the graphic and save it directly to the images folder within your FrontPage Web site.

Repeat this process for all of the buttons, headers, backgrounds, and spot art that you'll require.

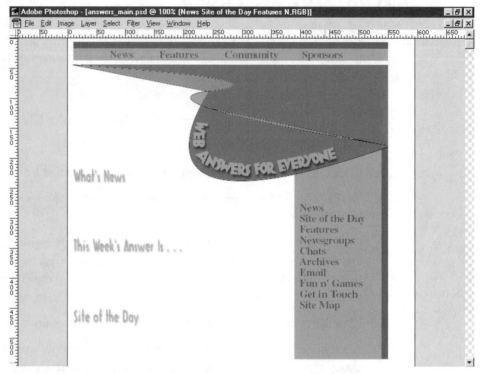

Figure 32.3 The completed welcome page layout

For detailed help optimizing and working with graphics, see Chapter 9 and Chapter 18.

Using FrontPage to Create the Community Site

We'll use the Discussion Web Wizard to set up a discussion Web page. The wizard makes it easy to set up the initial forums necessary for our site. From there, we can use templates to add the pages that will link to the discussion.

To set up your site using the Discussion Web Wizard:

1. Open FrontPage.

2. Choose File ➜ New ➜ Page Or Web. The New Page Or Web task pane appears.

3. Click the Web Site Templates hyperlink. You see the Web Site Templates dialog box.

4. Select Discussion Web Wizard.

5. In the Specify The Location Of The New Web text box, enter the local path to your new Web site. The Discussion Web Wizard dialog box appears.

6. Read the information and, when you're ready, click the Next button. The first question you are asked is which features you want for the discussion page:

7. Check the features that you want and click the Next button.

8. Enter a title for the discussion pages and a folder name; then click the Next button.

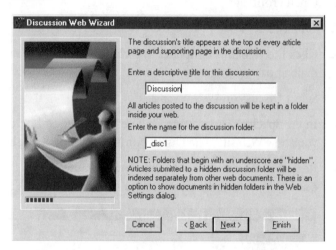

9. Set up the input fields. We chose Subject, Category, and Comments, but you should use what is best for your site. You can always add fields by hand later in the game. When done, click Next.

10. Choose between letting only registered users access your discussion or making it open to all. Choose what is best for you. We chose registered users only. When you've completed this choice, click Next.

11. Choose how you want the Table of Contents to sort messages. We chose Newest To Oldest. When you've chosen, click Next.

12. Choose whether you want the Table of Contents to be the home page. We don't, so we selected the No button. After you've made your choice, click Next.

13. Choose whether to use a Web theme or not. Because we are designing our own page, we simply clicked Next to move on to the next dialog box in the wizard.

14. The wizard offers configuration options. Choose what you feel is best for your site. We chose a dual interface using frames if available. When you have made your choice, click Next.

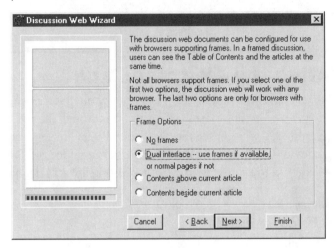

15. You see a synopsis of pages. Click the Finish button to have FrontPage set up the pages as you've requested them.

After FrontPage is finished with the discussion portions of the Web site, you'll want to go ahead and set up individual files in the root directory by following these steps:

1. In Folders view, right-click anywhere in the interface and choose New ➜ Page on the shortcut menu. A new page appears in the root directory.

2. Name the new page **index.htm**.

3. Repeat the process until you have created all the pages planned for the site, using the chart prepared in the planning phase as a guide. You can always add or delete pages as necessary.

Tasks are one of FrontPage's most helpful tools to guide you through building your Web site. To set up tasks:

Tasks are one of FrontPage's most helpful tools to guide you through building your Web site. Follow these steps to set up tasks:

1. In Folders view, select the file you want to associate with a task.

2. Choose Edit ➜ Tasks ➜ Add Task. The New Task dialog box appears.

3. Fill in the task name, priority, and a description.

4. Click OK.

For more information on tasks, see Chapter 7.

Creating the Welcome Page

Now that you have your site set up, it's time to lay out the welcome page. Because tables are needed to lay out most pages, we'll walk you through the process of building a table.

In Figure 32.4, you can see the page we laid out with our image editor. We've set up some guides to show how we'd like to map out our table grid. Based on our information, we can turn to FrontPage and begin creating the actual tables necessary.

When planning a table, begin with vertical columns, only adding rows where necessary. Be sure to revisit Chapter 11 for more information.

With your table in mind, follow these steps to lay out the page:

1. In Page view, choose Table ➜ Insert ➜ Table. The Insert Table dialog box appears.

2. Enter the number of rows in the Rows text box.

3. Enter the number of columns in the Columns text box.

4. In the Layout section, choose an alignment for your table. Typically, left alignment is used.

5. Set the Border, Cell Padding, and Cell Spacing to 0.

6. Check the Specify Width check box.

7. Add a numeric value for fixed-width tables and a percentage for dynamic tables. In our example, we want to fix the width so that all the content including images and graphics is neatly managed, so we entered a total width of 595 pixels.

8. Click OK. The table now appears on your page. If you need to stack or nest a table, go ahead and draw those tables as well (see Chapter 11).

9. Add images and text using the techniques you learned in related chapters of this book to refine the page's look. Be sure to adjust table and table cell properties where necessary (see Chapter 11).

10. When you're finished, save the page. You can preview it externally, or internally using the Preview tab.

Continue adding pages in this fashion until you've completed the full content of your site.

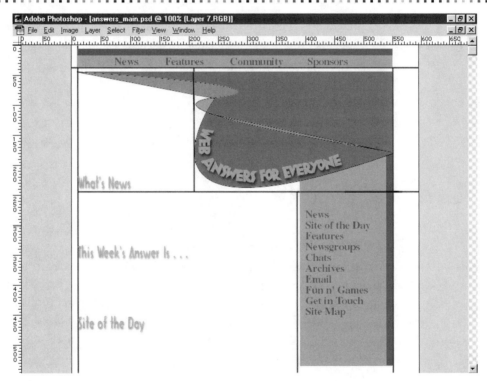

Figure 32.4 *Planning the table*

Customizing the Forum and the Table of Contents

Since we want the forum pages to match our design rather than the prefabricated look that FrontPage uses, we need to customize each of the forum pages using our own colors and graphics by following these steps:

1. In Folders view, double-click one of the forum pages (we began with the discussion welcome page, `disc1_welc.htm`). The file opens in Page view.

2. Add background and link colors to the page.

3. Add your graphic header by selecting Insert ➜ Picture ➜ From File and choosing the appropriate header image for your page.

4. Customize the comments within the page. Simply highlight the text you want to change and type in the new text.

5. Save your file.

You need to repeat this process for each of the individual discussion pages.

Adding Chats

There are a variety of ways to add a chat to a community site. First, you'll need to decide which method you want to use. The most common are ActiveX components, Java applets, and actual links to chat servers.

For the best compatibility for inline chats (*inline* refers to the fact that the chat runs in the browser and requires no extra software), Java applets are a good choice. ActiveX is an excellent choice if you're running chats to a private audience with Microsoft browsers. Relying on a chat server can be a daunting task—the server has to be maintained around the clock. This means human resources. However, if you are interested in very large community creation, it's a good option, as it gives people the most choice.

Depending upon your choice of chat, you can refer to Chapter 22, which discusses Java and ActiveX, or take the discussion up with an Internet administration specialist.

Preparing Your Site for Publication

Now that you've figured out all of the logistics and have completed everything from planning to design, it's time to prepare your site for production. This process, which includes spell-checking your pages, looking for and repairing broken links, and ensuring that your site is cross-browser compatible, is discussed at length in Chapter 30.

Managing Community

The ideal online community is well organized and well managed. For it to run smoothly, human resources are needed to help with the many day-to-day functions of the community.

Think about your online community just as you would your local, real-time community. People get along well most of the time, but problems arise. Sometimes these problems are as simple as straying from the topic when there's business at hand, or as complex as some people abusing others.

Managing a community is no easy task, but depending upon the resources you have and the general interest of people within your community, you might be able to hire or recruit volunteers to help keep things in order.

Moderated Forums

Because forums are subject to specific types of problems, moderating them is in order. Common problems include:

Topic drift   This is when conversation moves off of the specified topic. For example, if the newsgroup is about HTML, and people start talking about their children, the topic has drifted!

Unsolicited advertising   Unwelcome advertisers will often post their products, get-rich-quick schemes, and adult site advertisements on your forums. These can be very disruptive to the flow of conversation.

Inappropriate posts   Sometimes members get angry about an issue and will use language that is inappropriate or a tone that is argumentative.

Flame wars   Arguments can break out between community members. These can escalate into members taking sides and attacking each other.

You can approach these problems in several ways. First, you or community member volunteer moderators can work with topic drift to gently get it back on course. Unsolicited advertising should be removed from the forum quickly, and the same is true of inappropriate posts. When such a post is made by a regular member, typically the moderator will remove the post and write a short e-mail note to the member explaining why the post was removed.

Chat Hosts

Because of their real-time nature, chats are vulnerable to specific types of abuse. If you host a chat room, you may well encounter some of the following problems:

Scrolling   This is when a malicious user sends a script that scrolls messages too rapidly. In effect, the user sabotages the chat screen because the words fly by too fast to be read.

Inappropriate comments   Common offenses include sexual comments where they are not welcome, use of foul language, and harassment of other visitors.

Take-over scripts   These are scripts that actually take over the room, removing powers from moderators and chat hosts.

As with newsgroups, it's very helpful to have a moderator and tools that can help manage such incidents. Check with your chat software documentation or ISP for more information on management techniques appropriate to your type of chat environment.

Content Managers

Web content management is a big job! You may want to consider working with others to help develop and manage content. Here are some helpful tips:

- Generate content relating to conversations taking place in forums and chats.

- Recruit interested individuals to find or write content for the community site.

- Match content to calendar events such as holidays.

- Use contests to generate enthusiasm and involvement.

- Cross-promote activities in one area of a community with another.

- Cross-promote with other, related communities.

Another way to get ideas is to visit other community sites. What are they doing with their content? You may find a lot of inspiration from what other communities are doing—even if the community focus is very different from your own.

Creating Community Rules

The following is a bona fide community rule page taken from the Seniors' Community on the Microsoft Network (MSN). Use this as a guideline to building your own community regulations.

Seniors' Community Rules

In order to take full advantage of this Community, you must read and understand the following rules and operating procedures of the community and agree to abide by the rules and operating procedures in their entirety. This community was created and is administered by a Community Manager, an entity which is separate and apart from MSN. As such, rules and operating procedures of this community must also be followed. Your access to this community is a privilege, not a right. The act of joining the community and your use of the community constitutes your acceptance of and agreement to be bound by these Community Membership Rules.

These rules will be enforced and violators may, at the sole discretion of the Community Manager, be suspended or "Locked Out" of the Community. Certain behavior carries potential risks to the Community Manager and cannot be allowed.

Members are invited to call a community manager's or assistant's attention to a potentially problematic message.

While there is nothing wrong with a healthy argument, you must not use offensive language or engage in personal attacks on members (or nonmembers) or the staff of this Community. Personal attacks may subject you and the Community Manager to potential liability for defamation, contribute nothing to the free flow of ideas, and tend to inhibit rational discussion of the issues. The Community Manager is not limited in any way in deciding whether a particular message may be offensive to a particular member or the Community in general. Examples of potentially offensive messages include, but are not limited to, messages that denigrate, insult or ridicule another person, or that contain negative comments on the integrity, personality, honesty, character, intelligence, methods or motives of any person.

In addition, you must respect the privacy of the members (and nonmembers) of the Community. Do not publish private messages or e-mail messages without the permission of the sender (unless you feel a Community rule has been broken; if so, forward the message privately to a Community Manager for evaluation). Do not publish facts, rumors, or innuendo regarding anyone's personal life.

Members may not use profanity or sexually explicit language in the Community. Although these terms are not easy to define, the Community Manager and sysop staff may use its discretion to make this Community comfortable for members who may be sensitive to profane or sexually explicit language.

You may not use the community to promote or facilitate illegal activities.

Planning, inciting, promoting or facilitating illegal activities through the Community is strictly prohibited.

You may not post copyrighted, trademarked, or other proprietary material without the express permission of the owner.

Library uploads will be reviewed prior to posting in a relevant Library section to determine whether, in the sole discretion of the Community Manager, copyrighted, trademarked, or other proprietary material is included in the upload. The Community Manager cannot review messages prior to posting in the Message section. Reproduction and/or publication, whether knowing or inadvertent, of copyrighted, trademarked, or other proprietary material may result in liability to the Community Manager and/or the posting member and therefore cannot be tolerated. Your upload or posting of any material constitutes a certification by you to the Community Manager that the material does not make use of or infringe on any copyright, trademark, or other proprietary material of others. If you have any question as to whether your upload or post contains copyrighted, trademarked, or other proprietary material, please e-mail the Community Manager, prior to posting or uploading the material.

Because it is important that this Community is useful and enjoyable to all its members, we will take appropriate action, which may be a warning, a suspension, or a termination of membership rights in the Community, if a member breaks these Rules, or threatens the security or order of this Community. We don't plan on doing these things, but we will do them if we judge that we must.

Indemnification

Operation of this Community carries inherent risks to the Community Manager because the Community Manager literally cannot control all aspects of the Community at all times. Accordingly, by joining the Community, you agree to indemnify the Community Manager for any damages, costs, and expenses, including reasonable attorneys fees, that accrue to the Community Manager as a result of or arising out of your activities on the Community, including, but not limited to, any claims for violation of any copyright, trademark, or protected material, or any claim of defamation, slander, libel, disparagement, or the like.

Limitation of Liability

You join and participate in this community at your own risk. The Community Manager shall not be liable for any damages or losses which result to you from your use of or participation in this community.

Choice of Law and Community

In joining this Community, you agree that any disputes between you and the Community Manager will be governed by the law of the State of California for all disputes arising out of or related to your membership or participation in the Community.

Any and all actions and proceedings relating to this Community or activities on this Community shall take place in courts located in the State of California.

No Warranties

The Community Manager makes no warranty, express or implied, that access to the community will be available at any particular time; that operation of the community will be uninterrupted or error-free; or that any particular result or information will be obtained. Membership in the community is offered on a "AS IS" Basis without warranties of any kind, other than warranties which are incapable of exclusion, waiver, or restriction under the law applicable hereto.

Entire Agreement

The operating rules and procedures of this Community as described here constitute the entire agreement between you and the Community Manager concerning your participation in this Community. The operating rules and procedures of the Community may change from time to time and such changes will be posted in this Announcement. Only the Community Manager or MSN can change a rule or policy of this Community.

Severability

If any of the rules, promises, conditions or agreements described here are held to be void, invalid, or unenforceable it shall not affect the enforceability, effectiveness, or validity of any of the other rules, promises, conditions or agreements.

If you have read and agree to the terms of the foregoing rules and operating procedures, you may use the Seniors' Community.

Obviously, you will tailor the rules to your own needs. While many people will ignore your rules, it protects *you* to make them clear. Ultimately, the rules are in existence to help your community run smoothly and effectively. Be sure that any and all volunteers or staff members are familiar with the rules of conduct, too.

Up Next

Community sites are often fraught with challenges born of both the technological limitations of forum and chat applications and the management of people. In this chapter, we looked at some of the options available for dealing with these issues, as well as stepped through a mock site design to get you going conceptually.

Chapter 33 moves away from the page-by-page approach and examines site structure, advanced management, and what tools and technologies can be used to work with very large Web sites.

Constructing and Managing a Large-Scale Site

FRONTPAGE

Chapter 33

By now, it will be evident to you that the more you add to a Web site, the more critical the planning stages become. And, the more content you have to manage, the more demands are placed on resources, be they technological or human.

In this chapter, we discuss some of the ways large-scale sites are managed. We begin with details about Web site structure, then look at management of data, and then move on to demonstrate how FrontPage becomes the prototyping tool to manage and design individual pages within the site. Topics include:

- Web site structure

- Tier-based models

- Producing and publishing a large-scale site

- Managing large Web sites

- Your future in Web development

Web Site Structure

In order to create successful Web sites—particularly very large ones—an understanding of the medium from the technological ground up is necessary. While this knowledge can be very helpful when building a personal page, it's much less important in that context. However, when you have multiple sections with hundreds or even thousands of documents to manage—and new documents being added regularly—understanding the Web's infrastructure becomes paramount.

With this understanding, you gain control over the way documents are managed within the structure. And with this understanding, you can plan not only how your site visitors will interact with your Web site, but how back-end technology will work behind the scenes to make the process a powerful and effective one.

Historically, the Web was never specifically intended to be a graphical medium. The idea was to create a fast way to connect text-based documents for easy access. For example, if a doctor publishes the finding of a medical research study with references, she could, in the pure hypertext environment, link those references directly to her primary study.

Of course, today's Web might seem very different with its commercial sites, personal fan magazines, and online games, but essentially, the structure has not changed. It is to this structure that we go to gain our foothold when designing very large sites.

When you create a link, you're grabbing hold of the Web's structural power. This is the element upon which Web sites are built. Seem too simple? Well, the reality is that with all of the cool things we can do on the Web these days, we've easily overlooked that it is this simple concept that makes the Web a very different medium than almost any other with which contemporary individuals are familiar. And this linking is what brings the concept of *interactivity* to the Web.

This doesn't mean a page cannot be *static*. In fact, in many cases, static Web sites are necessary or even preferred. A static site is one that has very simplistic options and really is an extension of a printed page. It contains limited information, isn't updated, and offers no interactive opportunities for the site visitor. As with a TV program, the only real options for the visitor is to go somewhere else—to change the virtual channel.

Interactive sites are dynamic, moving content. If you can set aside what you've learned so far about dynamic this and interactive that and think of the most essential aspect of what makes a site interactive, you come up with one element: the hyperlink. Of course, we build from that, and the farther away we move technologically from just the link as an interactive element, the more compelling and visually interesting design can become. Unfortunately, this growth away from the essential can also make it difficult to explain how simple and fundamental the hypertext structure of the Web really is.

Interactive media has been called "new media." Essentially, it is this interactivity that separates it from familiar, static media such as newspapers, magazines, books, radio, standard animation and video, and even film.

The Web, and hypertext along with it, soon moved away from the purely textual and into the realm of the graphical. As soon as graphic file formats were supported inline using graphical Web browsers, the text link became the graphical link. Nowadays, that link might have all kinds of options added to it via HTML and style sheets, JavaScript, and Dynamic HTML. The options are growing, but we remind you that the *essential structure has remained the same.*

Linearity

What we can do with hypermedia—be it text-based, graphic-enhanced, or technologically dynamic—is pretty amazing. Not only can we present static information if we want to, but we can present information in varying degrees of what is known as *linearity*.

In the contemporary, dominant cultures of the Western world, we think of time in terms of a linear structure; 12:00 P.M. is followed by 1:00 P.M., Monday by Tuesday, January by February, and so forth. We also perceive life as being a line—beginning with birth and ending with death. It's interesting to note that this is not the way much of the world thinks! American Indian tribes have been described as having a spiral view of life, and many Eastern philosophies relate to time as a circular event, with birth and death simultaneously representing a beginning and an ending. Spirals, circles, and other conceptual or physical structures that move beyond the horizontal and vertical axes are referred to as *non-linear.*

Another comparison of linear and non-linear would be a prepared monologue versus a relaxed conversation. In a prepared monologue, the speaker is discussing an issue, followed by a sub-issue, and so forth. He or she is speaking in one direction: to the audience.

In a natural, relaxed conversation, people talk about different topics, and the topics can suddenly go off on a tangent and become something else. You might begin discussing the movie you saw last night and end up supporting a friend through his emotional challenges with an ill parent. And, in conversations, people talk at different intervals, and sometimes all at once!

The Web, interestingly enough, encapsulates all of these things. You can have a completely linear presentation, with one page following another following another and yet another. Or, another linear form common in the West is the *hierarchy*, which is essentially levels of lines. On the Web, you can have linear structures with some non-linearity, or you can have completely non-linear sites.

These structures offer many opportunities to the Web site developer—and many choices as well. Is there an ideal way to structure a Web site? We are convinced that the only way to make the best choice is to go back to that all-important determinant of what drives your site: your audience. If the audience wants very flat information, a linear site is in order. If the audience wants a wild ride, lots of linking and randomization will give them just the thrill they're after.

But in most cases, you want to create a balance. The more data you're working with, the truer this becomes! Usually you want to work with a familiar linear structure and only add tangential information where it is necessary and appropriate.

In order to achieve this balance when planning your site, you can follow these steps:

1. Begin with a simple, tier-based structure (see next section).

2. Add links within that site that are logical: navigation, references, indexes.

3. Add links to external but complementary sites where appropriate, but be careful not to let the links distract from your primary information.

Let's start by examining tier-based models. This will help you begin conceptualizing how to structure your large-scale Web site within the infrastructure of the Web itself.

. . . .

Great Big Web Sites!

Check out these sites to see how large sites are managed and designed:

Microsoft (`www.microsoft.com`): Microsoft's is an enormous site comprising all of the faces of the software giant. From individual applications to developer support to an extensive knowledge base, magazines, news, press releases, and communities, Microsoft is one of the largest sites on the Web.

Yahoo (`www.yahoo.com`): This ever-popular site started as a catalog of Web sites and grew into a vast Web event with community, news, shopping, services, electronic mail—the list goes on and on.

CNET is the premier Web site for technology-oriented individuals. It is broken into a series of individual sites such as `www.download.com`, where individuals can find thousands of files for download; `www.builder.com`, CNET's vast developer center; and `www.cnet.com`, where technology news is the buzz. The site also has community events, special reports, and even a career center.

. . . .

Tier-Based Models

A *tier-based model* is really a familiar hierarchy; information is structured on levels, or tiers. Simple tier models lean toward the linear, complex models add links that are based on logic, and shared-tier models begin to lean toward the more non-linear in that they add a wide variety of pathways within the site. Let's take a look at these model types in detail.

A Simple Tier Model

The simple tier model in Figure 33.1 shows two levels. The first is a point-of-entry page, or home page, and the second is the page's content. If you refer back to Hallie's site in Chapter 30 and the Zapaton site in Chapter 31, you'll see that they are both models based on simple tiers.

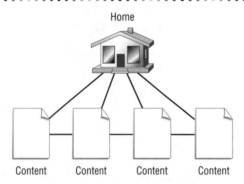

Figure 33.1 *A simple tier model*

A Complex Tier Model

The model in Figure 33.2 demonstrates three levels with multiple pages. Note how pages are linked to one another, creating a logical but slightly less linear set of navigational pathways.

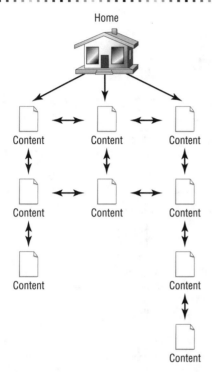

Home

Figure 33.2 *A complex tier model*

With complex tier models, it's important to provide some frame of reference for site navigation. This helps people reorient themselves should they become lost within the site (see Figure 33.3). Typically, this task is carried out by the addition of a site map, table of contents, or index that defines the various elements of the site and links directly to them individually.

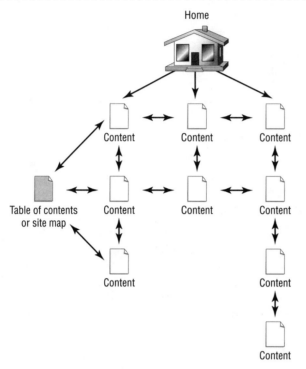

Figure 33.3 *A table of contents or a site map can anchor a site by providing links to all areas.*

As sites become more complex, orientation *becomes paramount. A site map can help with this, so be sure to include a link to it on every page of the site. Another important issue is that individual pages must be clearly identified. Use titles, headers, and footers to help reinforce visitors' understanding of where in the site they are.*

Shared, Complex Tiers

We begin moving away from the linear and into the more tangential, complicated structure when we create sites using shared tiers. Figure 33.4 shows how a shared tier works. Essentially, it looks like a complex tier, but instead of having sequential pages for every page on a given tier, pages are cross-referenced.

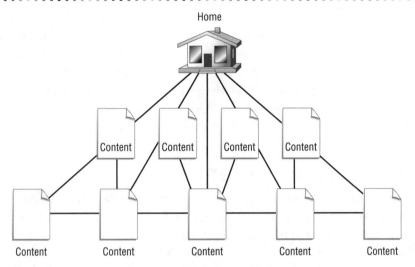

Figure 33.4 *Shared tiers cross-reference multiple pages.*

Not only does the shared-tier model provide a more interactive, choice-driven experience for site visitors, but it is often very helpful when managing large sites. For example, if you run a feature article and other articles on your site are related to that feature, you can links to those pages within the site, creating new pathways and corridors for people to travel.

At this stage, it also may become important to create *sub-sites*. This is true when a main site has so many subsections that each is in and of itself a Web site with related areas of information. We'll take a look at this in our chapter model, which we begin discussing in detail in the next section.

Planning a Large-Scale Site

So what is a large-scale site, really? We look at a large site as anything beyond 25 pages that is updated on a regular basis. Typically, large-scale sites range from corporate sites to e-commerce sites, and even to information or personal promotion sites.

The example used in this chapter is taken from real life. One of the authors of this book, Molly E. Holzschlag, often repeats the old saying "A painter never paints his house." She feels that her site is never up-to-date enough, nor does it offer enough information to site visitors who want details on books including code and graphics, access to articles, activities, Web design information, news, and personal information.

So Molly set about drawing up a site that fits into the large-scale model. The idea is to ensure that a lot of information is offered to site visitors and that a shared, tier-based model will enable cross-referencing where appropriate and keep information fresh.

The following sections detail Molly's progress in building her site. The first step, of course, is to define audience, intent, and goals. Then, we'll show how her site structure was sketched out and walk you through the actual building of some of the site's areas.

Audience and Intent

Both the audience and the intent of Molly's first site related to individuals interested in her books and design services. However, over time, audience needs have grown to include requests for support and FAQs for individual books, Web design tutorials, listings of upcoming courses, and personal information.

So, the intent and audience have broadened. It began to appear that numerous sites would need to be developed in order to accommodate these needs. And, in a way, that's what is being planned right now—a main site encompassing several sub-sites that focus on specific content concerns for each of these needs.

Short- and Long-Term Goals

Molly's short-term goal is to provide a content-rich, easy-to-navigate, personable yet useful site that can help individuals find current events, ancillary information, and personal information surrounding Molly's activities.

Long-term goals include expanding the resources on the site, adding community elements (see Chapter 32), and even adding online classes in Web design.

Site Structure

Based on the knowledge of audience, intent, and goals, as well as on a study of the Web's structure, Molly developed a site map showing the tier-based environment. Take a look at the aspects of the site in detail to gain an idea of the actual impact of each of the planned site elements:

News   This section is geared to highlight anything that is newsworthy for the month in question. The concept here is to point to other areas on the site for extrapolated information on activities. This makes good use of the shared-tier concept. News will highlight new Web site clients, new books, public appearances, classes, articles, and online events.

Books   This is a site unto itself but makes good use of the cross-referencing elements of shared-tier structures by linking to related areas such Web design and courses. The book area includes a section highlighting all books and provides ordering details. A book resource area offers code, errata, and other support information for readers. The reader's section has reader mail and a FAQ about which books might best suit an individual's needs.

Courses   The course section offers information on current and upcoming courses and appearances. There will also be a student gallery of selected student works.

Web Design   In this area, the focus is on all things pertaining to Web design. There will be tutorials in areas such as HTML, Web graphics, user interface design, and other Web-related technologies and resources. Also included is a site design portfolio.

Professional   This area encompasses professional and public information. Included will be a resume, publications list, publicity photos, and a summary of radio and television appearances.

Personal   The "home page" section of the site will include biographical information, photos, essays, poetry, music, and other items of a more personal nature.

Contact   This area can be used to provide feedback about the Web site or to write a personal e-mail.

While the News and Contact pages will likely be no more than one page, most of the primary areas of this site will contain at least 25 and possibly hundreds of pages, with new pages being added over time.

Preparing for Production

With the infrastructure firmly managed and a strong idea of what will be necessary to get this site rolling, the next major step is gathering the information and organizing it into appropriate areas.

At this point in the process, many site designers will use a white board or other large, erasable drawing area upon which they will begin sketching out how individual groups of content will relate to other groups of content on the site. This process is a fluid one and, in large-site production, is often subject to change. Feel good about your primary areas before moving on to creating a design appropriate to the site.

Creating a Look and Feel

Because the most significant aspect of this site is promotion of an individual's collected works and ideas, the site is going to be personal and warm, but express the bold and inventive nature of its creator. To accomplish this on her site, Molly chose a variety of warm, vibrant colors.

Color Name	RGB Value	Hex Value	Expression
Dark orange	255 102 0	FF6600	Deep and warm
Light orange	255 153 51	FF9933	Fun and energetic
Pale yellow	255 255 153	FFFF99	Vibrant
Light yellow	255 255 204	FFFFCC	Bright, warm, inviting

Molly also included black for text and white for background color and accents.

Next, Molly worked with typefaces. She wanted to ensure that information was readable and basic but still had a fun, bold appearance.

Type Family	Typeface	Expression/Use
Sans serif	Helvetica Bold	Thick, clean typeface for headers
Sans serif	Helvetica	Standard weight for sub-headers
Serif	Times Roman	Common, cross-platform serif font good for body text

Molly then examined the way to approach graphic accents. She decided that flat patches of bright color would give the site its visual impact. Playing off of that, she used color photos and spot art. She employed JavaScript mouseover animation for navigation, using a fiery design with a lot of movement to add excitement and vivacity to the pages (see Figure 33.5)

Figure 33.5 *Mouseover buttons in static and over states*

For more information about adding JavaScript to a page, see Chapter 21.

Preparing for Technology

Technology plays an important role in large-scale sites. Molly's example uses the following:

JavaScript   A JavaScript mouseover effect is used for navigation.

Feedback Form   Molly uses a standard set of feedback forms so individuals can get more information or write personal letters.

To learn more about working with forms, see Chapter 14 and Chapter 26.

Site Search   Because of the scope of the site, Molly used a Web site search. This will allow people to enter a keyword and find information on the site.

It's important to know that aside from commonly used technologies like these, large sites will often place large demands on back-end technologies including:

Active Server Pages   ASP helps keep a site dynamic and helps Webmasters manage updates and interactive aspects on a site. ASP is a natural extension of FrontPage, as it is a Microsoft product and is well integrated into Microsoft's suite of Web server and design applications. (For more on ASP, see Chapter 27.)

Common Gateway Interface   CGI programming is extremely helpful when managing large amounts of data. It can help manage updates and interactivity on a site as well as perform a wide range of Webmaster functions. (For more on CGI, see Chapter 26.)

Databases   Databases help Web developers store, retrieve, and manage all kinds of information about a site. Databases can help developers search, track site visitors, archive information, and enable electronic commerce events on a site. (For more on databases, see Chapter 28.)

Advertising banners   FrontPage has an ad banner rotator, which can be used to handle advertising on a large site. Other advertising methods are available, too. (Check out Chapter 24 to learn more about advertising-related techniques.)

No matter what technology you choose, large sites are demanding! You'll want to take special care in the planning stages to think clearly about what you want to do with your site so that you can make good selections when it comes to technology.

 You'll always be matching site intent, audience, and site goals with budget and availability. Be sure to research your options before settling on options that might be too time-consuming for your resources, or too under-budget for your true needs.

Production

As in the previous three chapters in this part of the book, we're going to walk through aspects of the large-scale site. First, Molly creates the design using her image editor, and then she moves on to FrontPage itself, where, using a combination of wizards and templates, she gets the large-scale site going.

Laying Out the Pages

As with the community site in the previous chapter, Molly decided not to use a splash page for this site. She felt that a personality- and information-oriented site should have a sense of immediacy—people can get to the information and interaction they want without a progression of visual and navigational information. So, the first page she designed was her welcome page.

Follow these steps to lay out a welcome page similar to Molly's:

1. In your image editor, select File ➜ New. The New dialog box appears.

2. Create an image size that is 595 pixels wide by 600 pixels high.

3. Click OK. You will now have your work area set to the first layer.

4. To this layer, add your background color. Molly selected white (see the color chart earlier in this chapter).

5. Create a new layer by selecting Layer ➜ New ➜ Layer. Here, you'll add the areas of color and shape to create the unusual feel. Molly built the arcs using Adobe Illustrator (see Chapter 18), a vector-based drawing tool, and then imported them into Photoshop to be optimized.

6. On subsequent layers, add the page title, navigation, and sub-headers.

7. Once you've added all the elements you want for this page, save the file by selecting File ➜ Save As. The Save As dialog box appears. Name the file and save it in the native layer format of your imaging program.

Figure 33.6 shows the completed welcome page design.

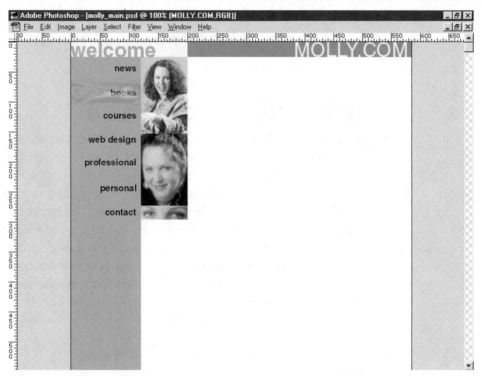

Figure 33.6 *The completed welcome page layout*

You'll need to repeat this process for each and every page you've designed for the site. To generate the actual graphics for your site, return to your imaging program and follow these steps:

1. Open up the layered file in your imaging program.

2. Highlight the layer that has the image you want to process.

3. Using the marquee or selection tool (it will vary depending upon your program), draw a selection around the part of the image you want to keep, making sure you're on the correct layer.

4. Copy and paste the section into a new file.

5. Optimize the file as a GIF or JPEG, depending upon the graphic.

6. Name the graphic and save it directly to the images folder in your Web site.

Repeat the process for all of the buttons, headers, backgrounds, and spot art that you'll require.

Working with FrontPage

As mentioned earlier, with very large Web sites you may find yourself using a range of development tools. Chapter 29 discussed how designers and content managers can use FrontPage in tandem with other team members to develop and maintain large sites. For the purposes of this chapter, we're going to use FrontPage to set up the site prototype. Depending upon how large a given site is, other members might use FrontPage, Visual InterDev, or other development tools to design and manage the site.

In the prototype for her site, Molly began by setting up a single-page Web and then added folders and files by hand. This gives her the ability to first demonstrate if the site looks good and behaves well. Eventually she'll set up a more detailed series of directories. For example, all of the sections discussed earlier will likely have their own directories, and it's possible that these directories will have subdirectories, and so forth.

When beginning to build your prototype, always look to your site structure in order to include all of the various aspects of your site.

Follow these steps to set up the Web site:

1. Choose File ➜ New ➜ Page Or Web.

2. In the New Page Or Web task pane, click the Web Site Templates link. You see the Web Site Templates dialog box.

3. Select One Page Web, choose a folder to keep the Web site in, and click OK. FrontPage creates the necessary folders for your Web site.

After FrontPage is finished building the Web site, you'll want to add folders and files as necessary. Molly used the root directory for top-tier HTML pages, but created subdirectories for the data that will go into those areas. She'll have one images directory for all graphics.

Follow these steps to set up individual files in your root directory:

1. In Folders view, right-click and choose New ➜ Folder on the shortcut menu.

2. A new folder appears in the root directory. Name the folder accordingly.

3. Repeat the process until you have created all the pages planned for the site, using the chart prepared in the planning phase as a guide. You can always add or delete pages as necessary.

Your next step is to set up individual pages. To do so:

1. In Folders view, right-click anywhere in the interface (see Figure 33.7). A menu appears.

2. Select New ➜ Page on the shortcut menu

3. A new page appears in the root directory. Name this page.

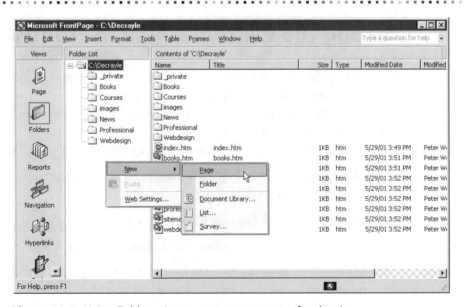

Figure 33.7 *Using Folders view to create new pages for the site*

Repeat the process until you have created all the pages planned for the site. You can always add or delete pages as necessary.

At this point, you'll want to get organized and allow FrontPage to help you manage the various production steps you'll be following. Follow these steps to set up tasks:

1. In Folders view, select the file you want to associate with a task.

2. Choose Edit → Tasks → Add Task. The New Task dialog box appears.

3. Fill in the task name, priority, and a description.

4. Click OK.

Whether you associate a task with a Web page or create a general-purpose task, be sure to include as many tasks as you'll need to complete the production and post-production processes. For more information on tasks, see Chapter 7.

In a large-scale site scenario, Task view is your friend! While this view is helpful in any site's development, it is invaluable when managing large sites. Task view can help you keep track of the project and allow different people to work on the project, start and stop at specific tasks, and even leave detailed messages for other team members about the status of a given task.

Creating the Welcome Page in FrontPage

The welcome page of any site is a critical one. It sets the tone for the entire site and gives people an idea of what's to come. We'll begin by laying out the welcome page. Typically, tables are going to be needed to lay out most pages.

To build your tables, begin with vertical columns, only adding rows where necessary. Be sure to revisit Chapter 11 for more information.

With your table in mind, follow these steps to set up your grid for the page's layout:

1. With the page open in Page view, choose Table → Insert → Table. The Insert Table dialog box appears.

2. Enter the number of rows in the Rows text box.

3. Enter the number of columns in the Columns text box.

4. In the Layout section, choose an alignment for your table. Typically, left alignment is used.

5. Set the Border, Cell Padding, and Cell Spacing to 0.

6. Check the Specify Width check box.

7. Add a numeric value for fixed-width tables or a percentage for dynamic tables. In Molly's example, she wanted to fix the width so that all the content including images and graphics is neatly managed. She entered a total width of 595 pixels.

8. Click OK. The table appears on your page. If you need to stack or nest a table, go ahead and draw those tables as well (see Chapter 11).

9. Add images and text using the techniques you learned in related chapters of this book to refine the page's look. Be sure to adjust table and table cell properties where necessary (see Chapter 11).

10. When you're finished adding images and text, save the page. You can preview it externally, or internally using the Preview tab, to see how the page will appear.

Continue adding pages in this fashion until you've completed the full content of your site.

Creating and Customizing a Site Map

The easiest way to create a site map is to put the Table of Contents template to work for you. The template not only makes life easier for you by providing you with a simple but effective outline, but it is also structured so that it will automatically update any pages added to the site if you are using FrontPage extensions.

Follow these steps to use the Table of Contents template:

1. In Page view, choose File ➜ New ➜ Page Or Web. The New Page Or Web task pane appears.

2. Under New from Template, click the Page Templates hyperlink. You see the Page Templates New dialog.

3. Select the Table of Contents template (see Figure 33.8).

4. Click OK.

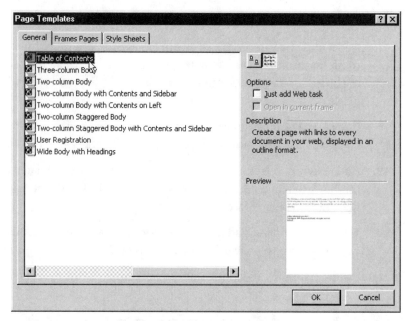

Figure 33.8 *Creating a Web page from the Table of Contents template*

Now, let's tap into the automatic updating power of the Table of Contents template. Follow these steps to customize the Table of Contents page to meet your individual needs:

1. Add background and link colors to the page.

2. Add any tables or design features to match the layout of the page.

3. Customize the comments within the page by simply highlighting the text you want to change and typing in the new text.

4. Save your file to the Web site.

Your Table of Contents page relies on FrontPage extensions to supply the information to the page. You'll need to publish the page in order for the Table of Contents to display with the appropriate information.

Adding a Feedback Page

If you've planned a contact page for people to use as a method of getting in touch, you'll want to create it using the Feedback Form template by following these steps:

1. In Page view, choose File ➜ New ➜ Page Or Web. The New Page Or Web task pane appears.

2. Under New from Template, click the Page Templates hyperlink. You see the Page Templates New dialog.

3. Select the Feedback Form template.

4. Click OK.

Molly wanted her form to match her design rather than the prefabricated look that FrontPage uses, so she customized the form using her own colors and graphics. Follow these steps to customize the feedback page:

1. Open the feedback page in Page view.

2. Add the background and link colors to the page.

3. Delete the comment and the horizontal rule from the top of the page.

4. Customize the comments within the form field. Simply click within the field where you'd like to change the text and type in the new text.

5. If you'd like to change the text on the form buttons, simply right-click the button and choose Form Field Properties. The Push Button Properties dialog box appears. In the Value/Label text box, type in the word or words you'd like to have appear on the button and click OK.

6. Customize any remaining text on the page, and be sure that the page is included in the shared borders if you are taking that approach to navigation.

7. Save your file to the Web site.

Your results should be similar to those in Figure 33.9.

830

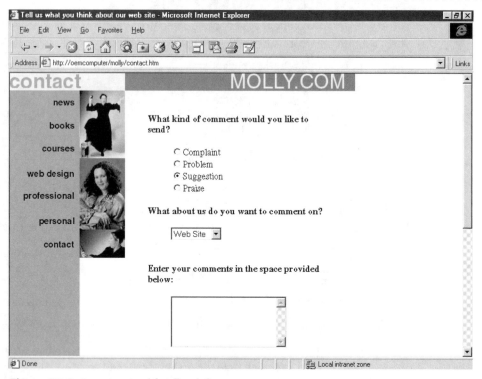

Figure 33.9 *A customized feedback form*

Just a reminder! Have you marked off your tasks? If not, and if you are confident that the work for a given task is finished, go into Tasks view and mark the task as complete.

Preparing Your Site for Publication

Now that you've figured out all of the logistics and have everything from planning to design completed, it's time to prepare your site for production. This process, which includes spell-checking your pages, looking for and repairing broken links, and ensuring that your site is cross-browser compatible, is discussed at length in Chapter 24.

Managing Growth

A critical issue with large publications is how to successfully and easily manage growth. This relates to the swell of content on your site, as well as to the growth in interest that your site can generate.

Managing growth involves looking carefully at what you have today, what you're planning to have tomorrow, and what you'll need to accommodate down the road. You want to think about archiving articles and keeping that information readily available by linking to it from current articles of interest.

It's helpful to organize your growth plans into current, past, and future areas. For example:

Current: News	Past: Archived News	Future: Upcoming Events
Recent book	All books	Books to be published and planned books
All courses, student gallery, relevant course materials	Planned courses and related materials	
Up-to-date resume and publicity information	Archived press releases and publicity	Planned area for new professional items of interest
Personal bio, creative writing, photos	Essays, poems, songs, and photos	New writing and photos

This table will be very valuable as your site expands. You can refer to it and modify it as necessary. Using it as a guide, decisions as to what you need to accommodate all of your current and past information, as well as how to manage future additions to the site, can be assessed.

Up Next: Your Future

As you've worked through this book, the exercises and knowledge have become increasingly complex. You've gained a solid base of FrontPage skills and have become aware of the wide range of technologies that are available to you.

Assessing your own needs is going to help you look to your future with FrontPage. If you're involved in the creation of an ongoing personal project, FrontPage will be an extremely valuable tool. Small businesses will benefit from using FrontPage to create and update sites. Communities can be built and maintained with FrontPage, and even large-scale, team-based sites can benefit from the prototyping power of the application.

But are you using FrontPage for your current personal and business needs, or are you examining a future in Web development? For those of you who are or who want to become professional developers, there's a lot of information yet to be learned. It will help a great deal to define your own interest and desired role in the Web-design world. Here's an overview of the variety of positions available to those interested in pursuing professional design options, and a rundown of the skills you might consider researching in order to achieve your goals.

Web Project Manager   If you want to manage Web projects, you'll need to know at least a little about a whole lot of Web-related technologies. Having a good foundation in management, human resources, and information technology is essential. Then you'll want to know a bit about all aspects of Web development—applications such as FrontPage, Visual InterDev, and Photoshop, and back-end technologies such as ASP, as well as general concepts involving site structure and user interface design.

Web Content Developer   A Web content developer is responsible for the collection and creation of Web site content. Typically, a content developer has a background in writing, with excellent communication skills, editorial knowledge, and an awareness of what kind of content works well on the Web. Content developers will need to be familiar with a variety of technologies and applications, including HTML, FrontPage, Word, and other members of the Microsoft Office suite.

Web Graphic Designer   Typically, the Web graphic designer will have a serious background in design. He or she will have studied the elements of design such as space, shape, typography, and color. The Web graphic designer also will be versed in multimedia development and have a good understanding of how to create useable, attractive, and appropriate visual interfaces. Graphic designers will be proficient in a range of design-oriented applications including Photoshop, Illustrator, and other utilities and tools related to Web imaging.

Web Programmer   Web programmers are interested in multiple languages. The Web programmer is fluent in HTML and aware of trends and standards. He or she will be familiar with a variety of technologies related to programming including JavaScript, Perl, CGI, and ASP, and will probably have a good understanding of various operating systems. Applications of interest to the programmer will include

Visual InterDev and Visual Studio when working from the Microsoft family of software.

Web Database Engineer   A database engineer is not only skilled with a range of database types, but is likely to be a proficient programmer, employing C, C++, Perl, Java, JavaScript, Visual Basic, and VBScript in his or her daily tasks.

Systems Administrator   If you're interested in operating and maintaining Web servers and Internet systems, you'll undoubtedly want strong familiarity with operating systems and related server software. Networking, including both hardware and software, will be the heart-and-soul of your work.

Obviously, the Web profession has grown from a fairly simple, one-person operation to a wide and deep field with numerous specialties. However, there are many opportunities, and if you have been inspired by this book to pursue Web development as a serious career, we are certain you will find an area of interest that is both suitable and personally gratifying.

Certification

If you're interested in pursuing certification in any of these Web design fields, visit Microsoft's Training and Certification Web site at www.microsoft.com/train_cert/.

Appendices

In This Part

Configuring
FrontPage 2002

FRONTPAGE

Appendix A

Since Microsoft FrontPage is now shipped as part of Microsoft Office XP, it's possible that you are installing it either as part of the Microsoft Office package or as a stand-alone program. In either instance, the program installs quite easily—and on its own—unless you decide to make custom decisions about installation. These decisions are typically for advanced users. We recommend you follow the instructions that come with your version of FrontPage 2002.

Once you've installed FrontPage on your computer, you probably want to get started right away. But wait! You can configure FrontPage to make it better suit your needs. For example, you can modify general settings to control the overall way Front-Page works, modify proxy settings to allow FrontPage to work along with a proxy server on your local area network, and modify settings to allow you to integrate other programs into the FrontPage environment.

To set these options, you must have FrontPage running. If FrontPage is not running, start it now. From the Windows taskbar, select Start ➜ Programs ➜ Microsoft FrontPage. FrontPage starts and its title window appears.

You can continue setting FrontPage options by following the steps outlined in the next sections.

General Customization

You can set a number of general FrontPage options, including options for modifying the interface, receiving warnings when your content needs updating, and receiving warnings when you apply a theme such that permanent changes throughout your site will occur. (You need not opt to set all of these; pick and choose, as you prefer.) Here's how:

1. From the FrontPage menu bar, select Tools ➜ Options. The Options dialog box appears, as shown in Figure A.1.

2. Click the General Tab. The contents of the dialog box change to reflect your choice.

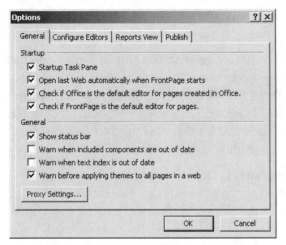

Figure A.1 *The FrontPage Options dialog box: your door to customizing FrontPage*

3. In the dialog box, you can control the following options by clicking the appropriate check boxes:

Startup Task Pane   This option controls whether the New Page Or Web task pane is displayed when FrontPage first starts. If the next option, Open Last Web Automatically When FrontPage Starts, is also selected and a FrontPage Web was open when FrontPage was last closed, then the New Page or Web task pane is not displayed when FrontPage starts.

Open Last Web Automatically When FrontPage Starts   This option allows you to decide whether FrontPage will automatically start exactly where you left off.

Check If Office Is The Default Editor For Pages Created In Office   This option determines which Office program created the page and whether it should be used to continue editing the page. If Office cannot determine the program that created the Web page, the default editor is used.

Check If FrontPage Is The Default Editor For Pages   This option makes FrontPage the editor for pages that Office cannot determine the editor for. This option is only available if the previous option is selected.

Show Status Bar   This option allows you to customize the interface to include the helpful status bar along the bottom of FrontPage, or to remove it to maximize your space.

Warn When Included Components Are Out Of Date   This option controls whether a warning appears when you open a page that includes out-of-date content. Examples of this are pictures and pages that have been included in a page as Scheduled Content via Insert ➜ Web Component ➜ Included Content and the display period for that content has ended. Refer to Chapter 15 for details on how to include scheduled content in your Web sites.

Warn When Text Index Is Out Of Date   This option controls whether a warning appears when the text index requires rebuilding. The text index is an index of words in your Web site and is only created if your server is running Microsoft FrontPage Server Extensions. The text index can be out of date if you delete a page from your Web site. The text index is rebuilt via the Tools ➜ Recalculate Hyperlinks menu option.

Warn Before Applying Themes To All Pages In a Web   This option controls whether a warning appears when you attempt to apply a theme that makes permanent changes.

You can turn any of these options on or off by clicking its check box.

4. Once you have made your selections, click OK. The dialog box closes and the FrontPage window reappears.

The changes you just made take effect immediately. To continue setting other options, read on.

Configuring FrontPage 2002 for Your Proxy Server

If your computer is on a local area network (LAN) that requires you to use a proxy server to access the Internet, you'll have to configure FrontPage to accommodate this. You can complete this process in a few short minutes.

You usually only need to enter proxy information if your computer is on a network that uses a proxy server and you are going to be publishing with FrontPage to Web servers that are not part of your LAN. Note that changes you make in this section also apply directly to your Internet Explorer connections.

1. From the FrontPage menu bar, select Tools ➜ Options. The Options dialog box appears.

2. In the General tab of the Options dialog box, click the Proxy Settings button. The Internet Properties dialog box appears, as shown in Figure A.2.

Figure A.2 *Here you'll enter information about any proxy servers your network uses to access the Internet.*

3. All of the connections available to you appear within this dialog box. If you want to enter a new proxy server, click LAN Settings, click the Use A Proxy Server check box in the Local Area Network (LAN) Settings dialog box, and type the Address and Port of the server in their respective text boxes. You can get the address and port of your proxy server from your system administrator.

If you can access local addresses (addresses on your LAN) without using the proxy server, check the Bypass Proxy Server For Local Addresses check box. Ask your system administrator if this is permissible.

4. For advanced configurations, click the Advanced button in the Local Area Network (LAN) Settings dialog box to open the Proxy Settings dialog box. If your proxy server uses a different port or address for the HTTP, Secure, FTP, Gopher, or Socks protocols than that entered in step 3, deselect the Use The Same Proxy Server For All Protocols check box and make any required changes in the corresponding text boxes. If you are capable of accessing any address without using your proxy server and want or need to do so, enter the corresponding address in the Do Not Use Proxy Server For Addresses Beginning With text box in the Exceptions section of the Proxy Settings dialog box. Wildcards are permitted here and you can separate multiple addresses with a semicolon. Provided your LAN is properly configured to use machine names for local computers, you can enter the machine name you wish to connect to directly in this text box.

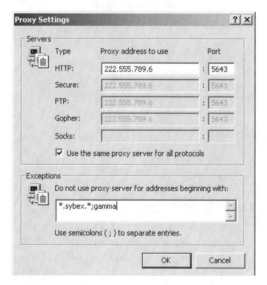

 We are primarily concerned with the HTTP and FTP proxy settings when publishing with FrontPage. All of the available proxy settings affect Internet Explorer directly. If you are uncertain of what to enter in any of the settings in the Proxy Settings dialog box, then leave them as-is or contact your system administrator.

5. When you're done, close all open dialog boxes and the FrontPage window reappears.

The changes you made take effect immediately. FrontPage is now set up to use your network's proxy server and is able to access computers on your local network as well as on the Internet.

Configuring FrontPage 2002 to Use Other Editors

FrontPage allows you to customize which editors will be used to edit different types of files. This is very handy if you want to edit JPEG files with Photoshop, for example, instead of with the default Windows viewer associated with that file type. Changing the application used to open a file type in FrontPage does not change the default application set to open or edit that file type in Windows. To change the editor that's associated with a specific type of file in FrontPage, just follow these instructions:

1. From the FrontPage menu bar, select Tools ➔ Options. The Options dialog box appears.

2. Click the Configure Editors tab. The contents of the dialog box change to reflect your choice (see Figure A.3).

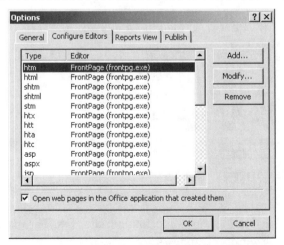

Figure A.3 *You can easily specify which editor will be used to edit different types of files in FrontPage.*

3. In the dialog box's list of file types, highlight the file type you want to work with (JPEG images, for example). Click the Modify button. The Modify Editor Association dialog box appears. Or, if you don't see the file type for which you want to specify an editor, click the Add button. The Add Editor Association dialog box appears. For file types not listed in the Configure Editors tab of the Options dialog box, FrontPage uses the default Windows application associated to open that file type when it is opened directly from the FrontPage Folder list.

If you intend to edit an image inserted in a Web page from within FrontPage 2002 by right-clicking on the image and selecting Edit Picture from the pop-up menu, you need to associate an editor with that file type using this procedure.

4. Regardless of whether you are modifying an existing association or creating a new one, a dialog box similar to the one displayed in Figure A.4 appears. Fill in or modify the following text boxes as appropriate:

    • File Type is the file extension for the type of file you wish to edit. For example, if the file is an image file of type JPEG, enter **jpg**.

    • Editor Name is the name of the editor you are setting up.

    • Command is the command to start the editor you are setting up. You can use the Browse button to locate the executable you wish to associate with that file type.

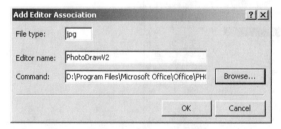

Figure A.4 *The Add Editor Association dialog box*

5. Once you have filled in the above information, click OK. The dialog box closes and the FrontPage window reappears.

The next time you edit or open a file of the type you just changed from within FrontPage, the editor you specified will be used. Note that, for supported image file types, the above procedure still allows you to use the powerful Pictures toolbar to edit images inserted into your Web pages. Access this by selecting the image and choosing View ➜ Toolbars ➜ Pictures. You don't need a fancy image editor to perform quite advanced image editing in FrontPage 2002.

Additional FrontPage 2002 Configuration

Before we finish this section, let's take a quick look at both the Reports View and Publish tabs in Tools ➜ Options.

The Reports View tab allows you to set the default options for when you generate Reports with FrontPage 2002. In most cases, you will keep these options as they are.

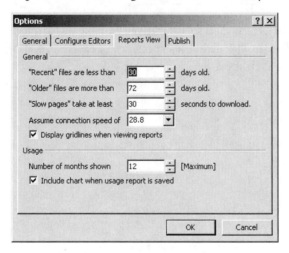

The Publish tab allows you to set whether you will publish changed pages only or all pages when publishing and allows you to decide how changes to pages are determined. The Logging option in the Publish tab of the Options dialog box enables you to create a log of the changes that have been made when a site is published. Press the View

Log File button to see the log of changes FrontPage made when you last published with FrontPage. Refer to Chapter 8, "Publishing Your Pages," for details on Web publishing.

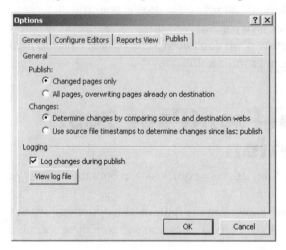

Now you have FrontPage 2002 all set up the way you like it. Turn to Chapter 1, "Introduction to Web Design," to begin the experience of creating, editing, and managing Web pages and entire Web sites.

Setting Up
Web Servers

FRONTPAGE

Appendix B

You are probably running FrontPage either on a stand-alone machine with a dial-up connection (via modem) or on a machine that's part of a corporate network (which implies that a firewall may be involved). In the first case, your connection is neither powerful enough nor round-the-clock enough for a real public Web server; in the other case, the firewall may pose security issues that make it impractical for your machine to function as a real public Web server. You may also be running FrontPage on a machine connected to the Internet via a cable or DSL connection. If so, the availability of a static IP address to host a real public Web server depends on the services you receive with that connection.

To run a publicly accessible Web server, you need to dedicate a powerful machine with a high-speed Internet connection (a T1 line, or possibly DSL or cable) and a static IP address exclusively for that purpose. That means you may have to post the live, publicly accessible site to such a dedicated server at your ISP or at your company, if your company hosts its own Web server.

FrontPage is designed to work as an authoring tool in tandem with different types of Web servers. To address your local needs, you'll want to install and set up the Microsoft Internet Information Services, or IIS, that is automatically offered with Windows 2000 and Windows 2000 Server to help make the process of building Web sites and/or pages easy. IIS 5 ships with Windows 2000 Professional and Windows 2000 Server, with some restrictions in the version supplied with Windows 2000 Professional. Having a server running on a machine will also, by the way, allow you to offer access to your FrontPage Web site to others on the same local network. You can use the server for a small intranet, or allow workgroups to access the site and work on different parts of it.

Using Web Services for Windows 2000 Professional and Server

If you plan on reaching beyond developing your Web sites for local use and offering them to others across a private intranet, or even right on the Internet itself, you'll need a powerful server. Microsoft's *Internet Information Services (IIS)*, is a powerful suite of services that can meet these needs.

The version of IIS that is included with Windows 2000 Professional is intended solely for peer Web services. It is restricted to a maximum of 10 simultaneous Web and FTP connections and will host only one main Web site and one main FTP server. Multiple Virtual Directories are, however, supported. Virtual Directories are discussed a little later on in this Appendix. For serious Web and FTP hosting, you will need access to the capacity provided by IIS and Windows 2000 Server. You may have FrontPage 2002 installed on the server or have network or Internet access to a machine dedicated to the purpose of serving your sites.

In this section, we'll talk about Microsoft's IIS and how you can configure and use its features.

Mastering What's Online

You can learn all about Microsoft's Internet Information Services at www.microsoft.com/iis.

Microsoft's IIS version 5 is very powerful; combined with the reliability of Windows 2000 Professional or Windows 2000 Server, it can actually afford you the *oomph* to host a public Web site on your machine. The restrictions in the preceding note on the peer Web services, of course, apply. For a site intended for public consumption or for a heavy-duty intranet site, you'd still have to have a high-speed connection, and you pretty much have to hand over a machine to the serving of your site, but given the power of the server software we're describing here, it is an option.

Microsoft's Internet Information Services is also more than just a Web server; it actually consists of three main Internet servers: the Web server, an FTP (File Transfer Protocol) server, and an SMTP (Simple Mail Transfer Protocol) server. The version of IIS that comes with Windows 2000 Server also includes an NNTP (News) server. We'll cover the basics of the first two types of servers.

IIS 5 comes with comprehensive documentation that can be conveniently accessed on the installed machine at localhost/iisHelp/iis/misc/default.asp. *This documentation is a valuable resource. The documentation is installed during a default installation of IIS 5. If this documentation is not installed on your machine, refer to the next section, "Installing the Web Services," and install the documentation as a subcomponent of IIS.*

Installing the Web Services

Before you can run and configure IIS 5, it needs to be installed. IIS 5 comes complete with FrontPage 2000 Server Extensions that are automatically updated to the 2002 version when FrontPage 2002 is installed. The procedure to install IIS is a generic Windows 2000 procedure specifically adapted to installing IIS. You can use the same basic procedure that follows to install (and uninstall) many Windows components. To install IIS 5 on Windows 2000 Professional or Windows 2000 Server, follow these steps:

1. From the Windows taskbar, select Start ➜ Settings ➜ Control Panel.

2. In the Control Panel window, double-click the Add/Remove Programs icon to open it.

3. In the left pane of the Add/Remove Components dialog box, select the Add/Remove Windows Components button. The Windows Components Wizard dialog box appears on-screen.

4. In the Components list in the Windows Components Wizard dialog box, select the Internet Information Services (IIS) check box to place a check mark in it.

5. You can control the subcomponents of IIS that are installed by selecting the Details button in the Windows Components Wizard dialog box while the Internet Information Services (IIS) entry is selected and then checking any required components in the new dialog box that appears on-screen. After the subcomponents you require have been selected, press OK to return to the main Windows Components Wizard dialog box.

 Subcomponents can also have subcomponents that are accessible via the Details button in the appropriate dialog box.

6. Press Next in the Windows Components Wizard dialog box to proceed with the installation. Respond to any prompts that may be given and, finally, press Finish when the installation has completed. Depending on the current state of your machine and the components you choose to install, you may be prompted for your Windows CD and to reboot your machine. Yes, even Windows 2000 still requires an occasional reboot!

Components of IIS or IIS itself can be uninstalled via a procedure similar to the above but by instead un-checking the component or the Internet Information Services (IIS) entry itself (if you wish to completely uninstall it). You can cancel any changes or the installation or removal of components or subcomponents via the Cancel button in the appropriate dialog box when the Cancel button is available.

Starting, Stopping, and Pausing Servers

A server, like any other program, can be running or not running, although they generally run all the time. (There are exceptions to this, but don't worry about them now.) The servers provided with Microsoft's IIS are usually configured to start automatically without any required intervention on your part. There may, however, be times when you want to stop or pause one, for maintenance or for some other reason. You can start, stop, or pause any of the Microsoft IIS servers—the Web, FTP NNTP (with Windows 2000 Server) or SMTP servers—by following these steps:

1. From the Windows taskbar, select Start ➡ Programs ➡ Control Panel, double-click the Administrative Tools icon, then double-click the Internet Services Manager icon to open the Microsoft Management Console with the Internet Information Services snap-in loaded.

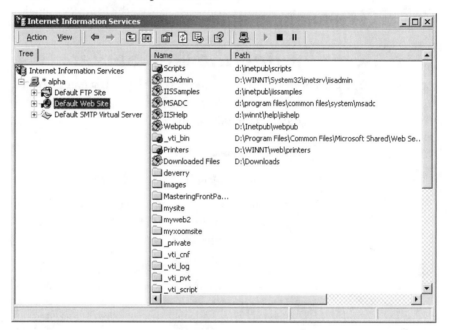

2. In this window, you'll see a console tree view of the services provided by IIS 5. From here you can manage just about every aspect of IIS 5. The plus sign next to any entry is used to expand the tree and display any available sub-entries. The display in the window to the right of the Tree pane changes according to the selection in the Tree pane. The servers we are concerned with here will likely be named by default as Default FTP Site, Default Web Site, Default SMTP Virtual Server, and Default NNTP Virtual Server (Windows 2000 Server only). If you don't see these services displayed, click the plus sign next to the icon that represents the computer name in question (likely your computer name if you are administering IIS installed on your own machine) to expand the tree and reveal them.

3. Select the server you wish to stop, start or pause.

4. With that server selected in the Tree pane, press the required Start Item, Stop Item, or Pause Item button on the far right of the Internet Information Services toolbar.

The change you make takes effect immediately. The availability of the Start Item, Stop Item, and Pause Item buttons reflects the current state of the server. If the Start Item button is unavailable, the server is currently running. You naturally cannot pause a server that is currently stopped (such are the beauties of logic).

Configuring the Web Server

You can control a number of aspects of the Web server provided with Microsoft's IIS, including which port the Web server listens to and the number of simultaneous connections that the server will handle.

Web Server Settings

To configure the basics of the IIS Web server, follow these steps:

1. With the Microsoft IIS console still open, right-click the entry for Default Web Site and then select Properties from the pop-up menu. The Default Web Site Properties dialog box appears.

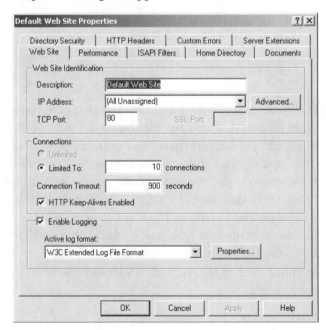

"Default Web Site" is the default name used by IIS 5; your "default" Web site may be named differently. Also note that with the version of IIS 5 shipped with Windows 2000 Server, you can host multiple main Web sites.

2. In the Description text box in the Web Site tab of the Default Web Site Properties dialog box, you can enter any name you want for your Server name. This name appears in both the Tree view of the IIS snap-in and in the title of the Properties dialog box for that server.

3. In the TCP Port text box in the Web Site tab of the Default Web Server Properties dialog box, you can change the port number the Web server listens to. This option is used to host multiple sites on a single server when that is necessary. The standard port for Web servers is 80, so you should leave this alone unless you have a good reason to change it and know what you're up to.

Changing the port number will affect the URL used to access material shared with the Web server. For example, if you change the port number from the default of 80 to 8080, you'll have to add :8080 to the URL (after your machine's name or Web site address) used to access the server. You may like to use a different port for your Web server so that only those who know the port address can access your site.

4. In the Connection Timeout text box, you can change the *timeout*—or how long the server will wait for a Web browser to receive a file. The default value of 900 seconds is a perfectly good choice. If people access your machine's Web server over a very slow connection, then increasing this value will increase the number of files the server can successfully serve. On the other hand, a large timeout number means your computer has to work harder and can slow down the whole process of serving Web pages (not to mention anything else you're doing with it while you're running FrontPage).

5. Each file request made of the Web server uses memory and can slow down the computer. To limit the number of files that can be requested at one time (and thus speed up the serving of that number of files), in the Maximum Connections text box enter the maximum number of connections your machine should handle at once. The version of IIS 5 shipped with Windows 2000 Professional is restricted to a maximum of 10 simultaneous connections. Once the server is handling the maximum number of requests that you specify, all additional requests will be refused. (Those people will receive a message that there

are too many users accessing the Web site at that time and will generally know to come back at a less busy time.)

6. Having changed what you must in the Web site tab of the Default Web Site Properties dialog box, press OK to return to the IIS console. The changes you made take effect immediately.

Access to your Web site and authentication methods are controlled via the Edit button in the Anonymous Access And Authentication Control section of the Directory Security tab of the Default Web Site Properties dialog box. Press this Edit button to display the Authentication Methods dialog box, shown in Figure B.1. Refer to the previous procedure for details on how to access the Default Web Site Properties dialog box.

Figure B.1 *Here you can enable anonymous access and set the authentication methods for the Web site.*

The Anonymous Access check box allows visitors to establish an anonymous connection with the publicly accessible areas of your Web site. When IIS was installed, it created a default user on the machine and called that user IUSR_*machine*, where *machine* is the name of the computer on which you installed IIS.

If you want IIS to use a different username and password than the default to access the local Web server, press the Edit button in the Anonymous Access section of the Authentication Methods dialog box (the Anonymous Access check box needs to be checked) and then type the preferred username into the Username text box. You can also use an existing Windows account for anonymous logins via the Browse button in the Anonymous User Account dialog box. To control the password used for access, you need to uncheck the Allow IIS To Control Password check box in the Anonymous User Account dialog box and enter the desired password into the Password text box. The password is only used within Windows.

You can control the method by which the server will *authenticate*—or identify—users who access content on the server. A username and password is required for these authentication methods when anonymous access is disabled or when access is restricted using NTFS access control lists. Your choices in the Authenticated Access section of the Authentication Methods dialog box (refer to Figure B.1) are described below:

- Basic Authentication (Password Is Sent In Clear Text) allows users to identify themselves using a nonsecure password mechanism. Enabling this option could potentially compromise your system security.

- Digest Authentication For Windows Domain Servers is a new feature of IIS 5. This authentication method is similar to Basic Authentication but with added security, using a *hash* (a number generated from a string of text, using a mathematical formula, in such a way that it is extremely unlikely that some other text will produce the same value) that is not feasible to decrypt. Digest Authentication is useable across firewalls and other proxy servers.

- Integrated Windows Authentication is a secure form of authentication and is enabled by default. Integrated Windows Authentication is used for private areas of your local intranet.

Sharing Folders with the Web Server

Once you have the IIS Web server installed, you can publish any folder on your machine, making it available as a Virtual Directory to other users as a Web Folder or via their Web browsers. (A Web Folder is a feature included in Windows 98 and later operating systems whereby you can work with files and folders served by a Web server in much the same way as you work with local files and folders using Windows Explorer.)

To publish a folder, follow these steps:

1. With the IIS console open, select the root folder for the Web site in question.

2. Select Action ➔ New ➔ Virtual Directory from the IIS console menu. The Virtual Directory Creation Wizard appears.

3. Press Next.

4. In the Alias text box of the Virtual Directory Creation Wizard dialog box, type the alias that will be used to access the folder and then press the Next button.

5. In the Directory text box of the Virtual Directory Creation Wizard dialog box, type the path to the *existing* directory that will become the Virtual Directory. For example, to make the folder C:\HOME available, type **C:\Home**. Alternatively, select an existing directory using the Browse button.

6. Press the Next button. The new Access Permissions pane of the Virtual Directory Creation Wizard appears.

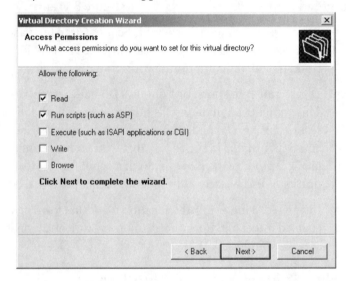

7. To restrict the type of access allowed to the folder to read-only, check the Read check box. Also, if the folder contains ASP scripts, check the Run Scripts check box. These two options are checked by default. To allow the execution of applications such as ISAPI applications or CGI scripts, check the Execute check box. To allow Web clients (applications that are capable of accessing resources provided by Web servers) to change file content and properties, check the Write check box. Enable Write access with caution. To allow the folder contents to be browsed in either a Web browser or as a Web Folder, check the Browse check box.

8. Press the Next button and, finally, in the new pane of the Virtual Directory Creation Wizard that appears on-screen, press the Finish button.

Virtual Directories created as subdirectories of the root Web site (Default Web Site if you have left this name unchanged and are hosting a single Web site) can be accessed via `http://hostname/alias/` where *hostname* is the local machine name and *alias* is the alias given to the shared folder. If your Web site is accessible via the Internet, then *hostname* is the Internet-assigned hostname for your server for external public access.

Virtual Directories can also be created as subdirectories of existing Web directories. To do so, select the existing directory instead in step 1 above. These are accessible via `http://hostname/directoryname/` *alias where* `alias` *is the alias you entered in step 4 above and* `directoryname` *is the alias of the existing directory you wish to make a subdirectory of.*

Setting the Default Document for a Virtual Directory or Web Site

When a visitor accesses your Web site or Virtual Directory *without* specifying a document in the URL, IIS serves a document according to a configurable search order. You can add documents to the search or change the order of the search. To configure the search order and add or remove documents from the search, follow these steps:

1. With the IIS console open, right-click the appropriate Web site or Virtual Directory of interest and select Properties from the pop-up menu.

2. Select the Documents tab in the Properties dialog box that appears on-screen.

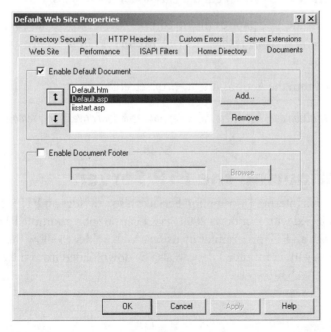

3. To enable the default document facility, check the Enable Default Document check box in the Directories tab of the Properties dialog box.

4. To add a document to the search, press the Add button, type the name of the document, and press the OK button. You might use this to add, for example, `index.htm` to the search.

5. To remove a document from the search, select the document in the list in the Documents tab and press the Remove button.

6. To change the search order that IIS uses, you can select any document in the list in the Documents tab and use the Up or Down arrows to the left of the list to move that document in the search order. For example, if you added `index.htm` to the list of searchable documents and wish `index.htm` to be served first (if it exists in the Web or Virtual Directory), then select `index.htm` in the list and keep pressing the Up arrow until it is at the top of the list.

7. When completed, press OK to return to the IIS Console.

Stopping the Sharing of a Folder

So, what do you do if you want to *stop* using the Web server to share a folder on your machine? Well, that's easy enough. Just follow these steps:

1. In the Tree pane of the IIS console, select the Virtual Directory you wish to stop sharing. If that Virtual Directory is not in view, expand nodes until you see it.

2. From the Actions menu entry, select Delete.

The Delete action does not delete the folder from your hard drive. It only removes it as a Virtual Directory.

Configuring the FTP Server

Microsoft's Internet Information Services also provides an FTP server. The version of IIS 5 shipped with Windows 2000 Server can support multiple FTP servers. FTP servers work with an FTP program or by using a Web Folder to allow the transfer of files to and from your computer. Files can also be downloaded from the FTP server using any common Web browser.

FTP Server Settings

To set options for the FTP server, follow these steps:

1. With the IIS console open, select the required FTP server in the Tree pane. This will likely be called Default FTP Site. If the FTP server is not displayed, expand the nodes (click the + signs) in the Tree pane until you see it.

2. Select Action ➜ Properties from the IIS console menu. The Default FTP Site Properties dialog box appears on-screen. (On your Web site, your default FTP site may be named differently.)

3. If not already selected, select the FTP Site tab in the Default FTP Site Properties dialog box.

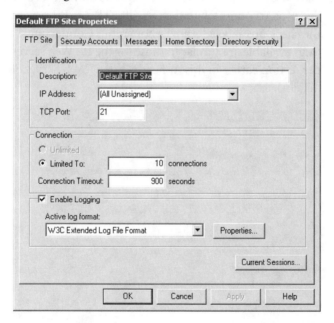

4. If you wish, enter a new description in the Description text box.

5. If required, change the port used by the FTP server. Port 21 is the universally used port for an FTP server. Only change the port number if you run multiple FTP servers on the same machine. If you change the port number, you will need to notify those who need to access this FTP server of the port used.

6. In the Maximum Connections text box, enter the maximum number of connections the FTP server should handle at one time. Again, this allows you to limit the number of people who access data on your server at one time and can help improve the machine's performance. The FTP server supplied with Windows 2000 Professional is limited to a maximum of 10 simultaneous connections.

7. The Connection Timeout text box allows you to change the same timeout value for the FTP server that you can change for the Web server with IIS. Refer to step 4 in the section in this Appendix titled "Web Server Settings" for details on this setting. The default timeout of 900 seconds is generally acceptable.

8. To allow that mainstay of "anonymous FTP," *anonymous connections* (that is, to allow access by people without accounts on your local machine), select the Security Accounts tab in the Default FTP Site Properties dialog box and check the check box labeled Allow Anonymous Connections. The user account settings available are similar to those for the IIS Web server. Refer to the end of the section earlier in this Appendix titled "Web Server Settings" for more details.

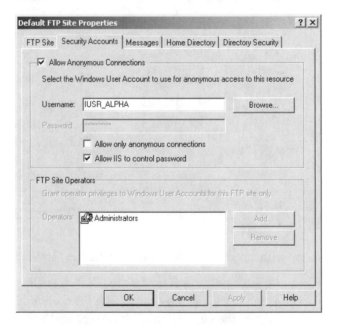

9. If you want to allow only anonymous FTP to the machine (in other words, you want people who actually do have accounts on the machine not to be able to

use their own usernames and passwords to access the machine), check the check box labeled Allow Only Anonymous Connections in the Security Accounts tab of the Default FTP Site Properties dialog box. (You actually may want to require people with accounts on the machine to use their own usernames and passwords so you'll know who's who and who's done what, but if it doesn't matter to you, use the anonymous FTP option.) If the Allow Only Anonymous Connections option is selected, only the account used for anonymous access is granted access.

10. In the Home Directory tab of the Default FTP Site Properties dialog box, you can change the location of the directory used for the FTP site and control its properties. To allow users to upload files to the directory, select the Write check box.

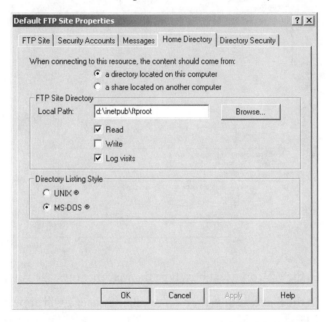

11. When the changes you need to make are completed, click the OK button in the Default FTP Site Properties dialog box to return to the IIS console.

Setting a Welcome Message

When a user connects to an FTP server using an FTP program, a message appears; usually the message conveys information about the company or organization that runs the FTP server. Sometimes it includes legalese that restricts the use of the FTP site. You can determine what this message will say and set additional departure and maximum connections messages by following these steps:

1. In the IIS console, right-click the entry for the FTP server and select Properties from the pop-up menu. The Default FTP Site Properties dialog box appears on-screen.

2. Click the Messages tab. The contents of the dialog box change to reflect your choice.

3. In the Welcome text box, type the welcome message you prefer.

4. In the Exit text box, type a farewell message; it will appear when a user ends the FTP connection.

5. In the Maximum Connections text box, type a message that will appear to warn users that the FTP server is already servicing the maximum number of simultaneous users. (You might want this message to suggest that they come back in a while.)

6. Click OK. The dialog box closes and you return to the IIS console.

The changes you made take effect immediately, though you won't see any evidence of that unless you test the FTP server using an FTP client.

Sharing Folders with the FTP Server

Sharing folders via the FTP server is very much like sharing folders via the Web server. To share a folder, follow these simple steps:

1. With the IIS console open, select the Default FTP Site entry or the FTP site in question in the Tree pane.

2. From the IIS main menu, select Action ➜ New ➜ Virtual Directory. The Virtual Directory Creation Wizard appears.

3. Press the Next button.

4. In the Alias text box, type an alias for the folder you wish to share and press the Next button.

5. In the Directory text box, type the path to the existing folder you plan to share. For example, to share the folder C:\PROJECT\FILES, type **C:\PROJECT\FILES**. Alternatively, locate and select an existing folder via the Browse button.

6. Press Next and the Virtual Directory Creation Wizard progresses to the new Access Permissions page.

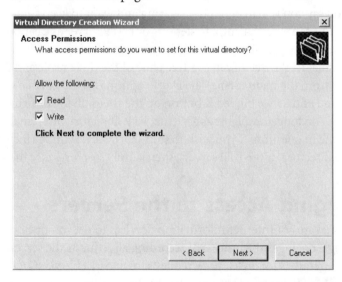

7. You can control the type of access allowed to the folder in the Access Permissions page of the Virtual Directory Creation Wizard. Your options are:

   • Read to allow read access, which allows people to download files from the folder

- Write to allow write access, which also allows them to change the folder contents and file properties and to upload files

Or you can select both, which allows people to have total access.

8. Press the Next button. Finally, in the new page that appears on-screen in the Virtual Directory Creation Wizard, press Finish.

The folder you just shared will be available via the FTP server immediately.

The method of accessing the new Virtual FTP folder depends on the FTP application used. For direct access via Opera, Internet Explorer, or Netscape, append /alias, where alias is the alias you chose in step 4 above, to the qualified FTP Internet server address (if the FTP server is accessed from the Internet) or the machine name of the FTP server (if the FTP server is accessed locally or from a LAN).

Virtual FTP folders can be created as subfolders of existing Virtual FTP directories. To do so, select the existing directory in step 1 and proceed normally.

Stopping the Sharing of a Folder

So, you say you've had enough of sharing and want to keep some things to yourself now? You can stop sharing a folder on your FTP server as easily as you can stop sharing a folder with your Web server. To stop sharing a folder as a Virtual FTP directory, select the Virtual FTP Directory in the Tree pane of the IIS console and then choose Action ➜ Delete from the main menu. The Delete option is also available via the right-click pop-up menu and a nice big red X button on the IIS toolbar Confirm the deletion. The folder is no longer available as a Virtual FTP Directory but remains intact on the machine in question. If you wish to stop sharing everything (including files in the home directory of the FTP server), then simply stop or pause the server!

Logging Access to the Servers

The final area of Internet Information Services to get you up and running with IIS is *logging*. Logging is the process of recording all requests the server receives. These can include requests for a Web page, requests to upload a file via FTP, requests to send e-mail via the SMTP server, and requests to post News messages to Newsgroups provided by the NNTP server (for Windows 2000 Server only when this Service is installed). Although each IIS server maintains its own log files, configuring the options you have for each is the same, so we'll cover all of 'em right here in one fell swoop. Follow these steps:

1. In the IIS console, right-click the entry of the server to be configured and select Properties from the pop-up menu. The Properties dialog box for the chosen service appears.

2. Select the appropriate FTP site, Web site, or General tab (for the SMTP or NNTP server), depending on which server you selected in step 1.

3. To enable logging, check the Enable Logging check box.

You can disable logging by deselecting the Enable Logging check box and clicking OK to close the dialog box. This stops all logging of that server on your machine.

4. In the Log Format drop-down list, you can choose a format for the log files. All formats available are ASCII text file formats. Of the three file formats available, only the W3C Extended Log File Format supports customizable fields. The NCSA Common Log File Format is a non-customizable format available only for Web and SMTP servers. The Microsoft IIS Log File Format is provided for backward compatibility with earlier IIS versions. Unless you are using custom third-party software to analyze your software or have a compelling reason to use another file format, use the default W3C Extended Log File Format. The NNTP server offered with Windows 2000 Server also supplies an ODBC logging option. We will not concern ourselves with ODBC logging in what follows.

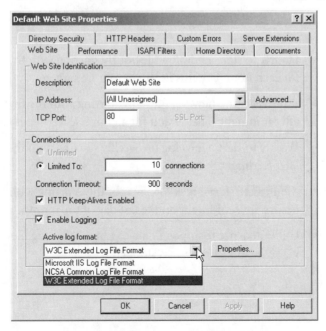

5. You can use a single log file forever—it will grow longer and longer as time marches on—or you can specify that new log files will be created at predetermined intervals of time or when a log file reaches a predetermined size. To control when new log files are created, press the Properties button adjacent to the Active Log Format drop-down list and ensure the General Properties tab is then selected in the Extended Logging Properties dialog box. Then check one of these options:

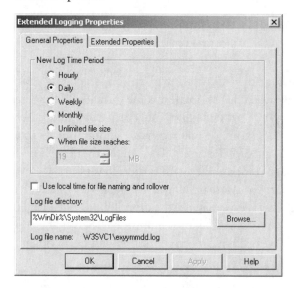

- Hourly to start a new log file hourly starting with the first entry that occurs for each hour. Use this for high-volume servers.

- Daily to start a new log file daily starting with the first entry that occurs after midnight. The default for all three server types is daily.

- Weekly to start a new log file weekly starting with the first entry that occurs after midnight Saturday.

- Monthly to start a new log file monthly starting with the first entry that occurs after midnight on the last day of the month.

- Unlimited Size to append data to the existing log file. This file can only be viewed while the server is stopped.

- When File Size Reaches to start a new log file when the current log file reaches the specified size. (You should enter the size at which you want a new file to start into the supplied text box.)

"Midnight" above refers to midnight on the host machine, with the exception of when the W3C Extended Log File Format is used. For the W3C Extended Log File Format, "midnight" refers to midnight GMT unless the Use Local Time For File Naming And Rollover check box is checked.

6. You can enter the path to a new location for the log file in the Log File Directory text box, or via the Browse button adjacent to it if you need to.

7. When completed, press OK and then OK again to return to the IIS console.

The W3C Extended Log File Format allows you to add and remove fields displayed in the log file. To do so, with the W3C Extended Log File Format selected as the file log format in step 4 above, press the Properties button adjacent to the Active Log File Format drop-down list and check any required fields in the Extended Logging Options section of the Extended Properties tab in the Extended Logging Properties dialog box.

Generated log files are saved in subdirectories of the directory you chose in step 6 above. These subfolders are prefixed according to the server type they are logging: W3 for Web servers, MSFTP for the Microsoft FTP servers, and Smtp for the logged SMTP servers.

For information on the naming convention used for the log files, refer to `localhost/iishelp/iis/htm/core/iiabtlg.htm#logsize`. The log files are simple text files that can be viewed in Notepad.

Alternate Web Servers and Platforms

While we have primarily been concerned with IIS 5 and Windows 2000 in this Appendix, if you are running Windows NT, Windows 98, or Windows ME, you aren't left totally out in the cold when it comes to hosting a Web server.

Windows NT 4 Workstation comes with Microsoft's Peer Web Services (PWS)— a server that may be capable of addressing your local needs. Peer Web Services, as supplied with Windows NT 4 Workstation, are intended for restricted use and are not capable of hosting FrontPage 2002 Server Extensions. For Windows NT 4 Workstation, you will want to download and install the Windows NT 4 Option Pack to update the Web services to IIS 4, which is capable of running the FrontPage 2002 Server extensions.

Windows NT Server 4 comes with IIS version 2. This is upgraded to IIS version 3 after the installation of Microsoft's NT 4 Service Pack 3 and can then be further upgraded to IIS 4 via the installation of the Windows NT 4 Option Pack. IIS 4 on Windows NT4 Server supports the installation of FrontPage 2002 Server extensions.

Windows NT 4 Option Pack requires Windows NT 4 Service Pack 3 and Microsoft Internet Explorer 4.01 or later.

Windows 98 comes with Microsoft's lightweight Personal Web Server. This server is supplied with FrontPage 98 Server Extensions and is capable of supporting only FrontPage 2000 Server extensions. It may, however, be adequate for your personal needs and to serve a small LAN.

Windows ME is not supplied with a Web server. Despite contrary assumptions, Windows ME is capable of supporting the same Web server that is supplied with Windows 98 along with FrontPage 2000 Server Extensions. Use this server for personal use or for hosting over a small LAN or home network. This Web server can be obtained by downloading the Windows NT Option Pack for Windows 95.

The Windows NT Option Pack, in its various flavors, can be downloaded via `www.microsoft.com/ntserver/nts/downloads/recommended/NT4OptPk/default.asp`.

If you have a connection to a Unix, Unix-like, or Linux machine, you may want to install and use the excellent Apache server as a cost-effective alternative to running a Windows server. The Apache server is an extremely common server that hosts the majority of Internet sites (although Windows 2000 Server use with IIS 5 is increasing). FrontPage 2002 Server extensions are available for installation with the Apache server when installed on a number of Unix, Unix-like, and Linux machines. For details on the availability of the FrontPage Server extensions with the Apache server, refer to Chapter 25: "Server Extensions and SharePoint Team Services." You can obtain information about the Apache server and download it for various operating systems via `httpd.apache.org/`.

Installing and Testing Network Connections

FRONTPAGE

Appendix C

For FrontPage to function properly, you must have TCP/IP (the *Transmission Control Protocol/Internet Protocol*) running properly; if you're connected successfully to the Internet, it probably is. There may be cases, however, where some trouble has occurred. For the sake of helping you out of such a quandary, we've provided this appendix, which is like one long "Mastering Troubleshooting" sidebar.

In this appendix, we discuss how to get TCP/IP running on a Windows ME or 2000 machine, how to run the FrontPage TCP/IP test application, and how to test your machine's interaction with other machines on an intranet. Then we finish off by demonstrating how, when your computer is connected to the Internet, anyone else on the Internet can access the Web server on it. Let's take a look.

Installing and Configuring TCP/IP

Installing TCP/IP correctly can be challenging. If you're lucky, you'll have access to a highly skilled network administrator who can install it on your computer for you.

 TCP/IP *stands for the* Transmission Control Protocol/Internet Protocol, *which is the method used to send information between computers on the Internet. Every computer that's connected to the Internet must be able to use TCP/IP. TCP/IP is installed during a default installation of Windows 98, Windows ME and Windows 2000.*

Sometimes, however, you might have to go it alone and install (or reinstall) TCP/IP yourself. We cannot hope to cover all of the permutations of networking and dial-up connections in an appendix of this size. Here we will show you how to ensure that the TCP/IP is installed and is properly *bound*. We will then show you how to access many of the configuration options for a TCP/IP connection if you need to enter this yourself.

First, you may need a few things:

- Your Windows ME or Windows 2000 installation CD. Ensure that you insert your Windows CD when prompted to and follow any prompts required to install the TCP/IP protocol. Reboot the computer if asked to.

- The IP addresses for a DNS server (contact your ISP or system administrator to obtain this information).

- The IP address of a gateway computer, if one is available (you can get this information from your ISP or from your network administrator).

- The IP address that has been assigned to your computer (if your computer is part of an intranet with a full-time connection to the Internet).

Installing and Binding the TCP/IP Protocol

Now, if you've got your propeller beanie on and you need to give TCP/IP a try, follow these steps:

For Windows 2000 Users

To ensure that TCP/IP is correctly installed and is used by existing connections, follow these steps:

1. No matter what you're working on, close all programs (saving your work if necessary). The Windows Desktop should be clear and visible.

2. From the Windows Start menu, select Settings ➜ Network And Dial-Up Connections. The Network And Dial-Up Connections window appears on-screen with a list of current network and dial-up connections

 Windows 2000 users must be logged on as an Administrator or as a member of the Administrators group in order to complete this procedure.

3. Right-click the dial-up or network connection of concern and select Properties from the pop-up menu. The Properties dialog box for that connection opens. The Properties dialog box contains a number of different tabs depending on the type of connection you are dealing with.

4. If the connection type is a LAN, select the General tab. For all other connection types, select the Networking tab.

5. Read through the list of network components that are installed and used by the connection of interest. A network component is used by the networking connection if it appears in the list and has a check placed in its check box. If Internet Protocol (TCP/IP) appears anywhere here, skip ahead to step 9. If TCP/IP does not appear in the list of available networking components, it will need to be installed—proceed with the next step.

6. Click the Install button. The Select Network Component Type dialog box appears, with a list of three different types of components: Client, Service and Protocol.

7. Double-click Protocol. The Select Network Protocol dialog box appears.

8. In the Select Network Protocol dialog box, select Internet Protocol (TCP/IP) and press OK to return to either the General or Networking tab of the connection you are dealing with. Internet Protocol (TCP/IP) should now appear in the list of available networking components.

9. Ensure the Internet Protocol (TCP/IP) check box is checked and then press OK.

 You may see a File And Printer Sharing For Microsoft Networks entry in the list of available network components. File and Printer Sharing enables you to share files and printers over a network connection, whether it is a local connection or one to the Internet. Enabling File and Printer Sharing over an Internet connection could allow unauthorized users to access your files and may compromise your system security. We recommend that you do not enable File and Printer Sharing over an Internet connection.

To ensure that TCP/IP is bound to existing LAN connections, follow these steps:

1. From the Windows Start menu, select Settings ➜ Network And Dial-Up Connections. The Network And Dial-Up Connections window appears on-screen with a list of current network and dial-up connections

2. From the Network And Dial-Up Connections main menu, select Advanced ➜ Advanced Settings. The new Advanced Settings dialog box appears on-screen.

3. With the Adapters And Bindings tab selected in the Advanced Settings dialog box, select Local Area Connection in the Connections list toward the top of this tab. The bottom pane will be named Bindings For Local Area Connection and will list the clients installed and the protocols they are bound to. Clients are presented with a computer icon and protocols appear as sub-entries of the client and are presented with a network icon. A client is active for the Network connection if its check box is checked. A protocol is bound to a client if the check box for its sub-entry for that client is checked. Most Microsoft Networks will use the Client for Microsoft Networks client.

4. Select the Client For Microsoft Networks client or the appropriate client for your network in the Bindings For Local Area Connection list of the Adapters And Bindings tab and ensure that its check box is checked.

5. Select the Internet Protocol (TCP/IP) sub-entry for the entry you selected in the preceding step and ensure that its check box is checked.

 Protocols bound to a service can be moved around in the order in which they are bound by selecting the protocol and using the Up or Down arrows to the right of the Bindings For Local Area Connection list. Changing the order in which protocols are bound can be done to improve performance. If TCP/IP is the primary protocol that you use, try moving it to the top of the list.

6. Press OK to return to the Network And Dial-Up Connections window.

For Windows ME Users

To install TCP/IP, follow these steps:

1. Close all programs (saving your work if necessary). The Windows Desktop should be clear and visible.

2. From the Windows Start menu, select Settings ➜ Control Panel. The Control Panel window appears, with a list of various Control Panel applets.

3. Double-click the Network applet. The Network dialog box appears on-screen.

4. Ensure that the Configuration tab is selected and then read through the list of network components that are installed. You should see Client For Microsoft Networks, Dial-Up Adapter (if you have a modem), and the brand of your network card (if you have one). If TCP/IP appears anywhere here, then it is installed and you can exit this procedure.

5. Click the Add button. The Select Network Component Type dialog box appears, with a list of three different types of components: Client, Protocol, and Service.

6. Double-click Protocol. The Select Network Protocol dialog box appears. Manufacturers are listed on the left side; network protocols are listed on the right.

7. Select Microsoft in the list of Manufacturers, select TCP/IP in the list of Network Protocols, then click OK. You'll return to the Network dialog box. Newly

listed should be one or two entries for TCP/IP. (It might say simply "TCP/IP"; if you have both a modem and a network card, you'll see "TCP/IP -> Dial-Up Adapter," and "TCP/IP -> NE2000," or whatever type of network card you have.)

8. Click OK in the Network dialog box to return to Windows.

To ensure that the TCP/IP is used for existing dial-up networking connections, follow these steps:

1. From the Windows Start menu, select Settings ➜ Dial-Up Networking. The Dial-Up Networking window appears, with a list of existing dial-up connections.

2. Right-click the dial-up connection of interest and select Properties from the pop-up menu. A Properties dialog box for that connection appears on-screen.

3. Select the Networking tab in the Properties dialog box and ensure that the TCP/IP entry in the Allowed Network Properties section is checked.

 You will also see the NetBEUI and IPX/SPX Compatible protocols listed in the Allowed Network Protocols section of the Networking tab. These protocols are usually not needed for dial-up connections to the Internet and may have a negative impact on your Internet connection. If you use a dial-up connection to the Internet, you can usually leave these protocols unchecked.

4. Press the OK button to close the Properties dialog box and return to the Dial-Up Networking window.

To ensure TCP/IP is bound to an existing network adapter, follow these steps:

1. From the Windows Start menu, select Settings ➜ Control Panel. The Control Panel window appears, with a list of various Control Panel applets.

2. Double-click the Network applet. The Network dialog box appears on-screen.

3. Ensure that the Configuration tab is selected in the Network dialog box and then double-click the adapter of interest. For network adapters, the adapter will be named according to network card you have installed, as shown below. The Properties dialog box for that adapter appears on-screen.

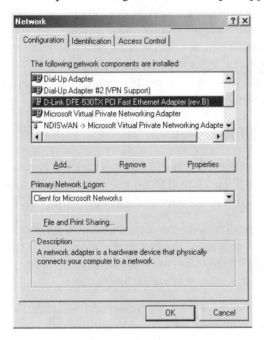

4. Select the Bindings tab in the Properties dialog box for the adapter selected above and ensure the TCP/IP protocol associated with that adapter is checked in the list of protocols used by that adapter. The TCP/IP protocol associated with that adapter will be prefixed with the TCP/IP -> prefix and followed by a descriptive name associated with your network card.

5. Press OK and then OK again to return to the Control Panel.

Setting TCP/IP Properties

Once you have ensured that TCP/IP is installed and correctly bound to the adapters in use, it's time to move on to configuring TCP/IP connection properties.

With the number of permutations of dial-up and networking connections in use, we cannot hope to fully cover all of the possible alternate settings in an appendix of this size. Automatic configuration utilities, such as the Home Networking Wizard in Windows ME and the Internet Connection Sharing options in Windows ME and Windows 2000, should be used when possible. Consult the online Windows Help system for details. If on a corporate LAN, check with your network administrator for the correct settings. Users with dial-up, DSL, or cable connections to the Internet should check with the provider of that service. The provider may have software that will set everything for you and may be able to advise you on the appropriate network settings should you run a LAN in conjunction with your Internet connection.

Here we will show you how to access the various TCP/IP settings should you need to change or enter them manually.

For Windows 2000 Users

1. From the Windows Start menu, select Settings ➜ Network And Dial-Up Connections. The Network And Dial-Up Connections window appears on-screen with a list of current network and dial-up connections.

2. Right-click the dial-up or network connection of concern and select Properties from the pop-up menu. The Properties dialog box for that connection opens. The Properties dialog box contains a number of different tabs depending on the type of connection you are dealing with.

3. If the connection type is a LAN connection, select the General tab. For all other connection types, select the Networking tab.

4. In the Components Checked Are Used By This Connection list, double-click the Internet Protocol (TCP/IP) entry to display the new Internet Protocol (TCP/IP) Properties dialog box for the connection you selected in step 2.

5. The options available on the General tab of the Internet Protocol (TCP/IP) Properties dialog box depend on the type of connection selected in step 2. There are two main sections in this tab. The first section relates to IP addressing while the second relates to DNS (Domain Name Search) addressing. Take some time to review the options presented to you and to acquire the information needed to configure these settings if you do not have it on hand.

6. If the connection you selected in step 2 is a dial-up connection to the Internet, it is highly likely that you don't have a permanent IP address. In that case, or when your network administrator requires it for a network connection, check the option button labeled Obtain An IP Address Automatically.

    If you have been assigned a static IP address for a dial-up connection or are using a networked connection that requires a static IP address, check the option button labeled Use The Following IP Address and enter the required IP address into the IP Address text box. The IP address entered here must be a unique one on your network or a unique address provided by your service provider. If Internet Connection Sharing has been enabled for a connection on the machine in question, the IP address for the LAN connection will likely be 192.168.0.1.

For a networked connection, there are two additional text box entries available in the IP addressing section of the General tab when Use The Following IP Address is selected: the Subnet Mask text box and the Default Gateway text box. Enter the required subnet mask address into the Subnet Mask text box. If Internet Connection Sharing has been enabled for a connection on the machine in question, the Subnet Mask address for the LAN connection will likely be 255.255.255.0. If the LAN connection requires a default gateway address, enter the IP address of the gateway into the Default Gateway text box.

7. The DNS section of the General tab of the Internet Protocol (TCP/IP) Properties dialog box has two mutually exclusive options: Obtain DNS Server Address Automatically and Use the Following DNS Server Address. In most dial-up cases, you will use the Obtain DNS Server Address Automatically option. If required by either your service provider or your network administrator, select the Use The Following DNS Server Address option button and enter the preferred and alternate (if available) IP addresses of the DNS server(s) into the corresponding text boxes.

8. The Advanced button in the General tab of the Internet Protocol (TCP/IP) Properties dialog box provides access to advanced TCP/IP properties. Only change the settings there if you are required to by your service provider or network administrator. Via the Advanced button, you can change such things as the WINS and DNS settings, add and remove WINS and DNS servers from the list of those used, and change the order in which WINS and DNS servers are queried. You can also add additional gateways and set security options used with TCP/IP.

9. When finished with the Internet Protocol (TCP/IP) Properties dialog box, press OK to close it.

10. Press OK in the Properties dialog box of the connection in question to return to the Network And Dial-Up Connections window. Remember to reboot your machine if asked to!

For Windows ME Users

To configure TCP/IP for existing dial-up networking connections, follow these steps:

1. From the Windows Start menu, select Settings → Dial-Up Networking. The Dial-Up Networking window appears, with a list of existing dial-up connections.

2. Right-click the dial-up connection of interest and select Properties from the pop-up menu. A Properties dialog box for that connection appears on-screen.

3. Select the Networking tab in the Properties dialog box.

4. With the TCP/IP check box in the Allowed Network Protocols section of the Networking tab checked, press the TCP/IP Settings button. The TCP/IP Settings dialog box appears on-screen.

5. In the first section of the TCP/IP Settings dialog box, there are two mutually exclusive options for IP addressing: Server Assigned IP Address and Specify An IP Address. It is highly likely that you don't have a permanent IP address for a dial-up connection. In that case, check the check box labeled Obtain An IP Address Automatically. Otherwise, check the check box labeled Specify An IP Address and enter the assigned IP address into the IP Address text box.

6. The second section of the TCP/IP Settings dialog box allows you to enter Primary and Secondary DNS and WINS name server addresses if these are required. If required to by your service provider, select the Specify Name Server Address option button and enter the required DNS and WINS server addresses into the appropriate text boxes. Otherwise, select the Server Assigned Name Server Address option button. This is the most common configuration for dial-up connections.

7. Toward the bottom of the TCP/IP Settings dialog box are two check boxes: the Use IP Header Compression check box and the Use Default Gateway On Remote Computer check box. The Use IP Header Compression option optimizes data transfer via the connection. Ensure that this check box is checked. The Use Default Gateway On Remote Computer option allows for the routing of IP traffic to the remote computer by default. You can leave this option checked unless otherwise advised by your service provider or network administrator.

8. Press the OK button in the TCP/IP Settings dialog box to return to the Networking tab of the Properties dialog box for the connection in question.

9. Press the OK button to return to the Network And Dial-Up Connections window. Remember to reboot your machine if asked to!

To configure TCP/IP for existing network connections, follow these steps:

1. From the Windows Start menu, select Settings → Control Panel. The Control Panel window appears, with a list of various Control Panel applets.

2. Double-click the Network applet. The Network dialog box appears on-screen.

3. Ensure that the Configuration tab is selected and then double-click the TCP/IP entry in the list of installed network components corresponding to the network connection in question. The TCP/IP protocol associated with that network connection will be prefixed with the TCP/IP -> prefix and followed by a descriptive name associated with your network card. The TCP/IP Properties dialog box appears on-screen.

4. Ensure that the IP Address tab is selected. If you are required to, select the Specify An IP Address check box and enter an IP address for your machine over the local network into the IP Address text box, followed by the required subnet mask. Otherwise, if your IP address is assigned automatically, check the Obtain An IP Address Automatically option button.

5. The WINS Configuration and DNS Configuration tabs allow you to enable or disable these processes and to add or remove servers from the respective search. WINS and DNS servers are searched in the same order in which they are added. If you are required to use DHCP (Dynamic Host Configuration Protocol) for WINS resolution, check the Use DHCP For WINS Resolution option button toward the bottom of the WINS Configuration tab. When this option is selected, Windows obtains necessary WINS configuration information from a host machine acting as a DHCP server.

6. If you are required to specify a default gateway, select the Gateway tab in the TCP/IP Properties dialog box and enter the appropriate addresses for gateways you have access to.

7. Press the OK button in the TCP/IP Properties dialog box when you have finished and then press the OK button in the Network dialog box.

8. Remember to reboot your machine if asked to!

Identifying Your Computer on a Network

In order for your computer to connect to another over a local connection using the TCP/IP protocol and to use FrontPage and Web servers over that connection, your machine must have a unique identity or *machine name* and belong to the same *domain* (for Windows 2000 machines only) or *workgroup* as the machine you wish to connect to.

For Windows 2000 Users

To set your machine name and designate the workgroup or domain that your machine belongs to, follow these steps:

1. No matter what you're working on, close all programs (saving your work if necessary). The Windows Desktop should be clear and visible.

2. Right-click the My Computer icon on the Windows Desktop and select Properties from the pop-up menu. The System Properties dialog box appears on-screen.

3. Select the Network Identification tab in the System Properties dialog box.

4. Click the Properties button in the Network Identification tab. The new Identification Changes dialog box appears on-screen.

5. In the Computer Name text box of the Identification Changes dialog box, enter a unique name for your computer.

6. In the Member Of section of the Identification Changes dialog box, select whether you are a member of a domain or workgroup by selecting the appropriate option button and then enter the name of the domain or workgroup you belong to. This domain or workgroup name must be the same as the computer you wish to connect to.

In Windows 2000, you must be logged on as an Administrator to change domain membership or to join a domain.

7. Press OK in the Identification Changes dialog box and acknowledge the prompt that you will need to restart Windows for the changes to take effect.

8. Press the OK button in the System Properties dialog box, and when prompted to restart your computer, reply with a resounding Yes!

The changes you have made will take effect once your computer has been restarted.

For Windows ME Users

To set your machine name, workgroup, or computer description, follow these steps:

1. No matter what you're working on, close all programs (saving your work if necessary). The Windows Desktop should be clear and visible.

2. From the Windows Start menu, select Settings ➔ Control Panel. The Control Panel window appears, with a list of various Control Panel applets.

3. Double-click the Network applet. The Network dialog box appears on-screen.

4. Select the Identification tab in the Network dialog box.

5. In the Computer Name text box, enter a unique name for your computer.

6. In the Workgroup text box, enter the name of the workgroup you belong to. This workgroup name must be the same as the computer you wish to connect to.

7. In the Computer Description text box, you can enter a "friendly" name for your computer.

8. Press the OK button in the Network dialog box and, when prompted, press the Yes button in the System Settings Change message box to restart your computer.

The changes you have made will take effect once your computer has been restarted.

Running the FrontPage TCP/IP Test Program

Every time you use FrontPage, it refers to your computer by its URL (which is simply http:// followed by your computer's name or address). While computer names are easier to type and remember, you may need to use the *IP address* if you're accessing your computer remotely, across the Internet.

An IP address is a series of four numbers separated by periods (each number ranges from 0 to 255). Every computer on the Internet has an IP address. While we're all used to referring to Web sites by name (such as http://www.yahoo.com/*), we could refer to them by IP address instead (such as* http://204.71.200.66/*).*

The first time you run FrontPage, it detects the name and IP address of your computer. Every time you run FrontPage after that, it verifies that your computer's name and IP address are still valid. To see your computer's name and IP address, you can run the FrontPage TCP/IP test.

To run the FrontPage TCP/IP test, follow these steps:

1. From the FrontPage menu bar, select Help → About Microsoft FrontPage. The About Microsoft FrontPage dialog box appears.

2. Click the Network Test button. The FrontPage TCP/IP Test dialog box appears.

3. Click the Start Test button. After a few seconds (or perhaps a few minutes, if your computer has an unusual configuration or if you're not connected to the Internet), the test results and information appear (see Figure C.1).

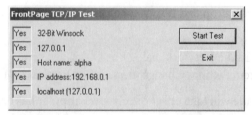

Figure C.1 *In addition to verifying that the networking options are installed correctly, the TCP/IP test gives you valuable information about the name and IP address of your computer.*

4. When you're finished looking at the results of the test, click the Exit button to return to the previous dialog box. Then click OK in the About Microsoft FrontPage dialog box to return to FrontPage. The dialog box closes and you'll see the normal FrontPage window again.

As shown in Figure C.1, FrontPage's TCP/IP test performs five tests, and the word *Yes* should appear next to all five. (If any of the tests fail, you'll need to check your Windows Network configuration and make sure that all of the networking protocols are installed and configured correctly; we'll give you some troubleshooting tips after describing the tests.)

Here's an explanation of each of the five tests:

- The first test makes sure that a 32-bit Winsock is correctly installed. Winsock (Windows Socket) is the interface used by applications on your computer to work with TCP/IP. Windows provides a 32-bit version of Winsock (usually installed along with TCP/IP). This supplied Winsock is sometimes updated by the way of Service Packs or Internet Explorer updates, depending on the operating system.

- The second test makes sure that the default IP address is working. The special *loopback* address 127.0.0.1 is shorthand for referring to the current computer, no matter what computer you're working on. FrontPage must be able to use 127.0.0.1 to refer to the computer it's installed on. If this test fails, there is a serious problem with the way TCP/IP was installed on your computer. You may need to reinstall TCP/IP in the Windows Network control panel if using Windows ME.

- The third test determines the hostname of the current computer (established in the Windows Network Control Panel under the Identification tab for Windows ME, or in the Network Identification tab in Properties under My Computer on your desktop if using Windows 2000). If this test fails, you may need to set a name for your computer. Refer to the preceding section in this appendix titled "Identifying Your Computer on a Network" for details on how to set your computer name. If your computer is assigned a qualified Internet hostname, this test determines that hostname.

- The fourth test determines the IP address for this computer. In general, every computer has to have its own unique IP address; no two computers on the entire Internet or on a local network can share the same IP address. If this test fails, then your computer either is not connected to the Internet or does not have a network IP address.

- Finally, the fifth test makes sure that the special name *localhost* is working. Local-host, just like 127.0.0.1, should always refer to the current computer. If this test fails, then there may be a serious problem with your TCP/IP installation.

By default, if your computer has a Web server installed, FrontPage uses your computer's name when you create FrontPage Web sites. Whenever you save a Web site, FrontPage saves the Web site to your local computer's Web server. Whenever you open a FrontPage Web site, you'll see your computer's name listed in the URL of the Web site address.

You should also verify that your computer is accessible by its name and that your local Web server is running properly. If your computer has a Web server installed, follow these steps:

1. From the Windows Start menu, choose your usual Web browser (such as Internet Explorer or Netscape Navigator). The browser window appears.

2. Now that you've fired up your browser, in the browser's location box type **http://localhost** and press Enter. The default IIS Web site, referred to by FrontPage as <Root Web> (local), should appear in the browser, as shown in Figure C.2.

3. Close your browser as you normally would (for example, by using the menu bar's File ➜ Exit command). You'll return to whatever you were doing before.

If this test was successful, great! You're well on your way to posting your FrontPage Web sites to your local machine. But if the test was not successful, you'll need to make sure that TCP/IP is installed correctly. You should review the TCP/IP installation instructions in this appendix and verify that, if running a Web server, it is installed and configured correctly.

*To further test TCP/IP, try pinging the loopback address of 127.0.0.1. To do so, type **ping 127.0.0.1** in a Windows MS-DOS Prompt box (if using Windows 98 or Windows ME) or in a Command Prompt (if using Windows 2000) and then press the Enter key on your keyboard. If the ping command fails, try restarting your computer and try the test again. If that new test fails, you may need to reinstall TCP/IP.*

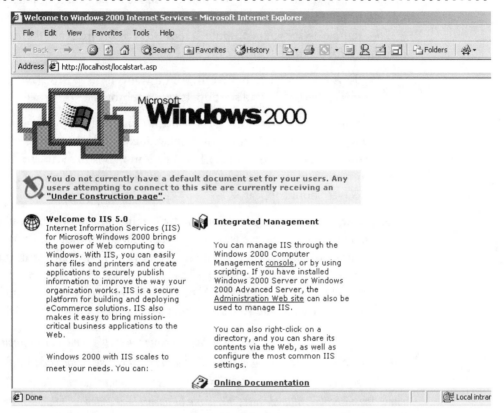

Figure C.2 *Internet Explorer displays the default home page for the local computer, known as "localhost." This page is installed by default along with the Microsoft's Internet Information Services.*

Testing Your Intranet Connection

Now for the tricky part: If your computer is part of an intranet, you'll need to test your connections on another computer located on the same intranet. When you run a browser on that remote computer, you should be able to reach your computer by using its IP address (not the localhost name or 127.0.0.1 address; those refer to *your* computer). You may also be able to reach it using its name; that depends on the way your intranet is set up or on whether your machine name is mapped to a static IP address in the hosts file on that computer.

For example, to see your computer's root IIS Web site from another computer on the intranet, follow these steps:

1. "Borrow" another computer on your intranet (your co-worker won't mind an extra coffee break) and start up its resident browser.

2. In the browser's location bar, type **http://** followed by your computer's IP address. For example, if the machine named has the IP address of 10.0.0.1, you would type **http://10.0.0.1** in the location box to see the root IIS Web site for your computer (named "fargo" in this example) and press Enter. The root IIS Web should appear.

3. Now in the browser's location bar, type in **http://** followed by your computer's name (for example, we would type **http://fargo**). If the root IIS Web site of your machine loads in the browser window, you know that your intranet is set up to use machine names as well as IP addresses. If you receive an error message, then you know that other people will have to use your machine's IP address to access the Web server on your computer, not your machine's name.

*If the above test fails, try adding an entry in that computer's hosts file to map your computer name to the IP address of your computer. For example, if your computer is called fargo and your IP address is 10.0.0.1, then, on a new line in the hosts file on that computer, enter "**fargo   10.0.0.1**" (without the quotes). The hosts file is a simple text file and can be opened and edited with Notepad. Perform a Windows search to locate it. In some cases, it may be currently named* Hosts.sam. *If so, then save it without the* .sam *extension after adding your new line.*

4. Once you've verified that you can access your computer's hosted FrontPage Web sites, close the browser as you normally would. The browser disappears and your co-worker can return to whatever he or she was doing before. (And be sure to thank him or her for lending you the computer.)

Accessing Your Web Server across the Internet

If your computer has an Internet connection, then your computer is on the Internet. That means that anyone may be able to see your computer's FrontPage Web sites, from anywhere on the Internet—if they know your IP address.

Before you get excited about this possibility, however, note that there are a few limitations to having your computer be a Web server. First, your computer must be turned on 24 hours a day and connected 24 hours a day to act as a permanent Web server. Second, your connection to the Internet must be fast. Don't even think about trying to host your Web site if your connection is through a modem. Third, any time that someone accesses your home page, your computer has to do work. If you're only getting a few visitors, you won't notice much of a slowdown. But if your site has lots of visitors, your computer may become too slow for you to use. Fourth, your computer must have a powerful processor and lots of memory to be able to serve lots of visitors.

To prevent these problems, most people use different computers for their development server and their live Web server, and they don't use their local machines as public Web servers.

If, after all our cautionary notes, you're still interested, try it out. Connect to the Internet (if you're not connected already), and determine your computer's Internet address by typing **ipconfig** in a Windows MS-DOS Prompt (if using Windows 98 or Windows ME) or a Command Prompt (if using Windows 2000) and pressing the Enter key on your keyboard. Take note of the IP address associated with your current Internet connection.

To run a Windows 2000 Command Prompt, select Start → Programs → Accessories → Command Prompt from the Windows taskbar. Windows ME users can run an MS-DOS Prompt by selecting Start → Programs → Accessories MD-DOS Prompt from the Windows taskbar.

Now call up a friend and have them browse to your computer. They'll simply use the URL of http:// followed by the four numbers of your IP address. After a few seconds, they should see the default Web page of your root IIS Web site.

If they can't see the default Web page of your root IIS Web site, it's probably because your computer is protected by your personal or corporate firewall. A firewall is a barrier that prevents outside access to an intranet, home network, or local computer.

If you're part of an intranet that is permanently connected to the Internet and has its own domain name, then other people outside the company on the Internet, might also be able to use your computer's name along with the domain name to reach it. For example, suppose you work for HappyFunCo, and your company's domain name is happy-funco.com. If your computer's name is fred, then people on the Internet may be able to see your computer's home page by using the URL of `http://fred.happyfunco.com/`.

For this to work, your network administrator must have set up your network properly, enabling it to resolve names on your intranet. In addition, he or she must place your computer on a special list of computers that are allowed to be accessed by the Internet. Most network administrators will not allow access for security reasons.

Using the Microsoft
Clip Organizer

FRONTPAGE

Appendix D

To help you manage and insert clip art files, sound files, and other multimedia files in FrontPage and the other Office XP programs, Microsoft offers the Clip Organizer. The word "clip" is kind of misleading because the Clip Organizer is a great way to handle other files besides clip art. The Clip Organizer can also handle sound files, movie clips, and photographs.

Appendix D explains how to search for a file in the Clip Organizer, insert a file, and organize files so you can find them easily. You also discover how to get files from Microsoft over the Internet.

Getting Acquainted with the Microsoft Clip Organizer

As Chapter 4 explains, you can choose Insert ➜ Picture ➜ Clip Art to open the Insert Clip Art task pane and obtain a clip art image, photograph, movie file, or sound file. The Insert Clip Art task pane is really just a doorway to the Clip Organizer. When you search for and insert files in the Insert Clip Art task pane, you are using the Microsoft Clip Organizer, whether you know it or not.

The first time you open the Microsoft Clip Organizer or the Insert Clip Art task pane, you are asked if you want to catalog the multimedia files on your computer. Click the Later button. As "Cataloging Files" explains later in this appendix, the Clip Organizer does a bad job of cataloging files on its own.

Under "See Also" at the bottom of the Insert Clip Art task pane is a hyperlink called Clip Organizer. By clicking that link, you can open the Microsoft Clip Organizer and do one or two things that you can't do in the task pane. You can, for example, organize the multimedia files on your computer and store shortcuts to files in folders so you can find the files quickly and easily. You can also, of course, insert files on Web pages by way of the Clip Organizer. Figure D.1 shows the Microsoft Clip Art Organizer.

Besides clicking the Clip Organizer link in the Insert Clip Art task pane, you can open the Microsoft Clip Organizer by clicking the Start button and choosing Programs ➜ Microsoft Office Tools ➜ Microsoft Clip Organizer.

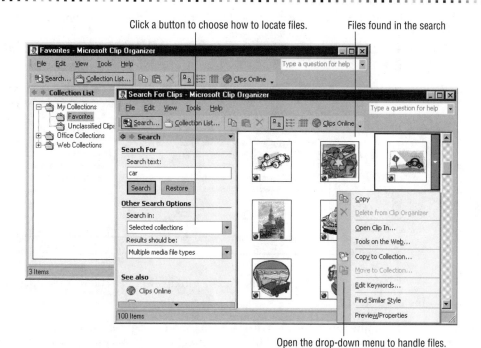

Click a button to choose how to locate files.   Files found in the search

Open the drop-down menu to handle files.

Figure D.1 *The two views of the Clip Organizer: Collection List view (left) and Search view (right)*

After you locate files, they appear in the window on the right side of the Organizer. A number in the lower-right corner of the Organizer tells you how many files were found.

Typically, the Organizer finds many files in a search. To find the one you need, scroll the list and examine the files. By clicking the Thumbnails, List, or Details button on the Standard toolbar, you can change views and examine the files in different ways:

Thumbnails view   Offers a small image of each file (refer to Figure D.1). Use this view when you are searching for clip art images and photographs.

List view   Lists file names only but displays the largest number of files in the window. Use this view when you know the name of the file you are looking for.

Details view   Lists file names, file sizes, and file types, among other information. Use this view when you are dealing with sound files and movie clips.

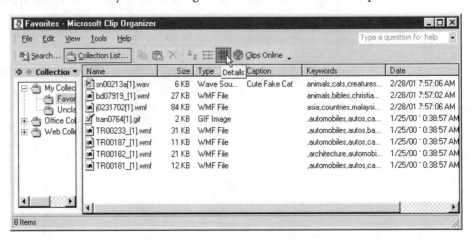

After you have found the file you are looking for, insert it in a Web page by following these steps:

1. Either open the file's drop-down menu or right-click its name and choose Copy on the shortcut menu. Doing so copies the file to the Clipboard.

2. Click in the Web page where you want the file to go.

3. Choose Edit ➔ Paste or press Ctrl+V.

The fastest way to insert a clip art file in a Web page is to drag it onto the page from the Insert Clip Art task pane.

Finding the File You Need

To search for files in the Microsoft Clip Organizer, you can start by clicking the Search button or the Collection List button (refer to Figure D.1):

- Click the Search button (or choose View ➔ Search) when you aren't sure which file you want. The Search pane opens. From there, you can search for files on your computer and the Microsoft Design Gallery, a Web site on the Internet. See the next section in this appendix.

- Click the Collection List button (or choose View ➜ Collection List) when you know that the file you want is kept in a My Collections folder, one of the folders where you can catalog and store your multimedia files. The Collection List pane opens. It lists the Favorites folder as well as folders you created for storing files. Click a folder to view its files. See "Getting a File from the Collection List" later in this appendix.

Searching for a File

Click the Search button (or choose View ➜ Search) to search for a multimedia file in the Search task pane (refer to Figure D.1). In the Search Text text box, the Search In drop-down menu, and the Results Should Be drop-down menu, make your choices and click the Search button:

Search For text box   Enter a keyword to describe the file you want. Each file has been assigned a handful of keywords. If a keyword you enter matches a keyword that a file has been assigned, the file turns up in the search.

To see which keywords have been assigned to a file, switch to Details view and look in the Keywords column. You can also right-click a file in the search results and choose Preview/Properties to see the list of keywords in the Preview/Properties dialog box.

Search In drop-down menu   Open the drop-down menu and select check boxes to tell the Clip Organizer where to search for files:

My Collections   Your Favorites collection, as well as other collections that you keep. Later in this chapter, "Organizing the Files so You Can Find Them Easily" explains how to place multimedia files in the My Collections folder and its subfolders (Favorites, Unclassified, and others).

Office Collections   Folders that hold the multimedia files that were transferred to your computer when you installed FrontPage and other Office XP programs.

Web Collections   Folders on the Design Gallery Live Web site, a Web site that Microsoft maintains. Your computer must be connected to the Internet to search Web collections.

By clicking the plus sign (+) next to folders, you can display subfolders and select them. In this illustration, the Web Collections subfolders are on display and the Academic and Backgrounds check boxes have been selected.

 To select all the subfolders in a folder, double-click the check box next to the folder's name. As the previous illustration shows, you can tell when all the subfolders in a folder have been selected when you see three overlapping check boxes instead of a single check box.

Results Should Be drop-down menu   To choose what kind of files you want, open the Results Should Be drop-down menu and click a check box. You can search for specific kinds of files by clicking the plus sign (+) next to a media type—Clip Art, Photographs, Movies, or Sounds—and selecting more check boxes. Here, for example, is a search for certain kinds of photograph files.

 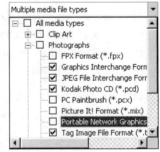

Getting a File from the Collection List

When you know where a file is located in the Clip Organizer, click the Collection List button (or choose View ➜ Collection List). Then, in the Collection List task pane, select the folder where the file is located. You see your file on the right side of the Clip Organizer window. The next section in this chapter describes how to organize files in the Collection List.

Organizing the Files so You Can Find Them Easily

The Microsoft Clip Organizer is a very handy place to store multimedia files so that you can find them easily. Whenever you come across a file and say to yourself, "I might be able to use that one later," store it in the Clip Organizer. The following pages explain how to place files in Organizer folders and create your own folders in the Clip Organizer.

By the way, the files whose names you see in the Clip Organizer are actually pointers to locations on your computer and the Internet where the files are kept. When you store a file in a Clip Organizer folder, all you are really doing is placing instructions in the Organizer for finding the file on your computer or elsewhere.

Cataloging Files

When you open the Clip Organizer for the first time, the Add Clips To Organizer dialog box asks whether you want to catalog the multimedia files on your computer. Don't do it! Click the Later (or Cancel) button and decline the offer.

Cataloging multimedia files automatically seems like a good idea, but all the Organizer does is list the multimedia files in the C:\Windows folder of your computer. Very likely, your C:\Windows folder contains any number of useless graphic files and tinny sounds, so cataloging these items isn't worthwhile.

Still, if you want to catalog them, you can do so at any time by choosing File ➜ Add Clips to Organizer ➜ Automatically. In the Add Clips To Organizer dialog box, click the Options button. Then, in the Auto Import Settings dialog box, check off the names of folders where useful multimedia files are found and click the Catalog button.

Copying Files to the Favorites or Another Folder

The Collection List task pane (click the Collection List button to open it) offers the My Collections Folder for storing files. This folder encompasses two subfolders, Favorites and Unclassified Clips, for storing multimedia files, and you can create folders of your own in the My Collections Folder as well (see the next section in this chapter).

Suppose you come across a file that you will need later. By placing it in the Favorites folder or a folder of your own making, you will know where to find it later on.

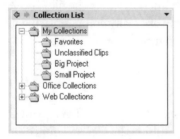

Follow these steps to place a file in the Favorites folder or a folder of your making:

1. In the results on the right side of the Clip Organizer window, either right-click the file to open its shortcut menu or open its drop-down menu (see Figure D.2).

2. Choose Copy To Collection. You see the Copy To Collection dialog box.

3. Select the folder where you want to store the file.

4. Click OK.

Choose Copy To Collection.

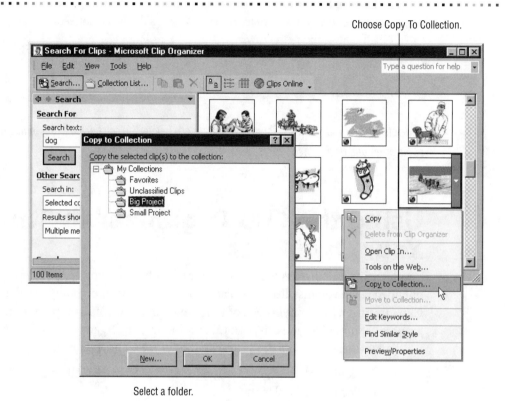

Select a folder.

Figure D.2 *Saving a file in a My Collections folder*

The fastest way to put a file in the Favorites folder is to drag it there.

Creating New Folders for Your Files

As the previous section in this chapter explained, you can copy files to the Favorites folder or a folder of your making. Follow these steps to create a new subfolder of the My Collections folder:

1. Click the Collection List button (or choose View ➔ Collection List) to display the Collection List task pane.

2. Choose File ➔ New Collection or right-click the task pane and choose New Collection on the shortcut menu. You see the New Collection dialog box.

3. Enter a name for the folder and select the folder that your new folder will be subordinate to.

4. Click OK.

To delete a folder you created, right-click it and choose Delete. You can't delete ready-made folders such as Favorites and Unclassified Clips.

Using the Clip Organizer to Store Your Own Files

Besides using the Clip Organizer to keep track of files you got on the Internet or obtained when you installed FrontPage, you can store your own multimedia files in the Clip Organizer. This way, instead of fumbling around in your computer to find a graphic or sound file, you can get it quickly in the Clip Organizer.

Follow these steps to store your own files in the Clip Organizer:

1. Click the Collection List button (or choose View ➔ Collection List) to see the Collection List task pane.

2. Select the folder where you want to store your files.

3. Choose File ➔ Add Clips To Organizer ➔ On My Own. You see the Add Clips To Organizer dialog box.

4. Select the file or files. Ctrl+click or Shift+click to select more than one.

5. Click the Add button.

Again, you can also drag files to store them in the Clip Organizer.

HTML Reference

FRONTPAGE

Appendix E

This HTML reference includes relevant tags and attributes for Web designers. It has been arranged alphabetically for convenient reference.

HTML Tags and Attributes

Tags	Attributes	Description
<!-- ... -->		SGML comment
<!DOCTYPE>		Public declaration
	HTML PUBLIC...	DTD conformance
<A>...</A>		Anchor
	ACCESSKEY=	Keyboard shortcut
	CHARSET=	Character encoding of link
	CLASS= ID= STYLE= TITLE=	Class(es), unique ID, style information, title
	COORDS=	Object coordinates of anchor
	DIR= LANG=	Text direction and language ID
	HREF=	Hypertext link
	NAME=	Name of hypertext link
	REL=	Forward link type
	REV=	Reverse link type
	SHAPE="rect | circle | poly | default"	Object shape of described anchor
	TABINDEX=	Explicit tabbing order
	TARGET=	Target frame name for rendering
	[events]	Core intrinsic events
<ACRONYM>...</ACRONYM>		Acronym content
	CLASS= ID= STYLE= TITLE=	Class(es), unique ID, style information, title
	DIR= LANG=	Text direction and language ID
	[events]	Core intrinsic events
<ADDRESS>...</ADDRESS>		Address content
	CLASS= ID= STYLE= TITLE=	Class(es), unique ID, style information, title
	DIR= LANG=	Text direction and language ID
	[events]	Core intrinsic events

Tags	Attributes	Description
\<APPLET>...\</APPLET>		Java applet
	ALIGN=	Alignment of applet
	ALT=	Alternate text description
	CODE=	Java applet name
	CODEBASE=	Location of applet
	DOWNLOAD=	Order of applet download
	HEIGHT=	Height of object
	HSPACE=	Horizontal space
	NAME=	Name of applet
	VSPACE=	Vertical space
	WIDTH=	Width of object
\<AREA>		Client-side image map area description
	ALT=	Alternate text description
	COORDS=	Coordinates
	HREF=	Hypertext link
	NOHREF	No hypertext link
	SHAPE="rect | circle | poly | default"	Shape of described area
	TABINDEX=	Explicit tabbing order
	TARGET=	Target frame name for rendering
	[events]	Core intrinsic events
\<B>...\</B>		Bold text
	CLASS= ID= STYLE= TITLE=	Class(es), unique ID, style information, title
	DIR= LANG=	Text direction and language ID
	[events]	Core intrinsic events
\<BASE>		Base URL
	HREF=	Hypertext link
	TARGET=	Target frame name for rendering

Tags	Attributes	Description
<BASEFONT>		Font setting for document
	COLOR=	Color of basefont
	FACE=	Typeface of basefont
	SIZE=	Size of basefont
<BDO>		Bi-directional override
	DIR=	Text direction required
	LANG=	Language ID
<BGSOUND>		Background sound
	LOOP=	Number of times sound repeats
	SRC=	Address of sound file
<BIG>...</BIG>		Big text
	CLASS= ID= STYLE= TITLE=	Class(es), unique ID, style information, title
	DIR= LANG=	Text direction and language ID
	[events]	Core intrinsic events
<BLOCKQUOTE>...</BLOCKQUOTE>		Block quote
	CLASS= ID= STYLE= TITLE=	Class(es), unique ID, style information, title
	DIR= LANG=	Text direction and language ID
	[events]	Core intrinsic events
<BODY>...</BODY>		Body of document
	ALINK=	Active link color
	BACKGROUND=	Location of background image
	BGCOLOR=	Background color
	CLASS= ID= STYLE= TITLE=	Class(es), unique ID, style information, title
	DIR= LANG=	Text direction and language ID
	LEFTMARGIN=	Create left margin
	LINK=	Link color
	TEXT=	Text color
	TOPMARGIN=	Create top margin
	VLINK=	Visited link color
	[events] onload, onunload	Core intrinsic events

Tags	Attributes	Description
 		Break
	CLASS= ID= STYLE= TITLE=	Class(es), unique ID, style information, title
	CLEAR=	Fixes text beside or below image
<BUTTON>...</BUTTON>		Form button
	CLASS= ID= STYLE= TITLE=	Class(es), unique ID, style information, title
	DIR= LANG=	Text direction and language ID
	DISABLED	Disables button
	NAME=	Name of button
	TABINDEX=	Explicit tabbing order
	TYPE=	Type of button
	VALUE=	Action desired
	[events] onfocus, onblur	Core intrinsic events
<CAPTION>...</CAPTION>		Table caption
	ALIGN=	Alignment of table caption
	CLASS= ID= STYLE= TITLE=	Class(es), unique ID, style information, title
	DIR= LANG=	Text direction and language ID
	VALIGN=	Vertical alignment
	[events]	Core intrinsic events
<CENTER>...</CENTER>		Centers text
	CLASS= ID= STYLE= TITLE=	Class(es), unique ID, style information, title
	DIR= LANG=	Text direction and language ID
	[events]	Core intrinsic events
<CITE>...</CITE>		Citation content
	CLASS= ID= STYLE= TITLE=	Class(es), unique ID, style information, title
	DIR= LANG=	Text direction and language ID
	[events]	Core intrinsic events
<CODE>...</CODE>		Code content
	CLASS= ID= STYLE= TITLE=	Class(es), unique ID, style information, title
	DIR= LANG=	Text direction and language ID
	[events]	Core intrinsic events

Tags	Attributes	Description
<COL>...</COL>		Column
	ALIGN=	Alignment of column
	CLASS= ID= STYLE= TITLE=	Class(es), unique ID, style information, title
	DIR= LANG=	Text direction and language ID
	SPAN=	Number of columns spanned
	VALIGN=	Vertical alignment
	WIDTH=	Width of column
	[events]	Core intrinsic events
<COLGROUP>		Column grouping
	ALIGN=	Alignment of column grouping
	CLASS= ID= STYLE= TITLE=	Class(es), unique ID, style information, title
	SPAN=	Number of column groupings spanned
	VALIGN=	Vertical alignment
	WIDTH=	Width of column grouping
<DD>		Definition data
	ALIGN=	Alignment of data
	CLASS= ID= STYLE= TITLE=	Class(es), unique ID, style information, title
	DIR= LANG=	Text direction and language ID
	[events]	Core intrinsic events
<DEL>...</DEL>		Deleted text
	CITE=	Change data
	CLASS= ID= STYLE= TITLE=	Class(es), unique ID, style information, title
	DATETIME=	ISO change date
	DIR= LANG=	Text direction and language ID
	[events]	Core intrinsic events
<DFN>...<DFN>		Definition content
	CLASS= ID= STYLE= TITLE=	Class(es), unique ID, style information, title
	DIR= LANG=	Text direction and language ID
	[events]	Core intrinsic events

Tags	Attributes	Description
<DIR>...<DIR>		Directory list
	CLASS= ID= STYLE= TITLE=	Class(es), unique ID, style information, title
	COMPACT	Compact representation
	DIR= LANG=	Text direction and language ID
	[events]	Core intrinsic events
<DIV>		Document division
	ALIGN=	Alignment of text section
	CLASS= ID= STYLE= TITLE=	Class(es), unique ID, style information, title
	DIR= LANG=	Text direction and language ID
	[events]	Core intrinsic events
<DL>...</DL>		Definition list
	ALIGN=	Alignment of list
	CLASS= ID= STYLE= TITLE=	Class(es), unique ID, style information, title
	CLEAR=	Clears list
	COMPACT	Compact representation
	DIR= LANG=	Text direction and language ID
	[events]	Core intrinsic events
<DT>		Definition term
	ALIGN=	Alignment of term
	CLASS= ID= STYLE= TITLE=	Class(es), unique ID, style information, title
	DIR= LANG=	Text direction and language ID
	[events]	Core intrinsic events
<EM>...</EM>		Emphasized text
	CLASS= ID= STYLE= TITLE=	Class(es), unique ID, style information, title
	DIR= LANG=	Text direction and language ID
	[events]	Core intrinsic events

Tags	Attributes	Description
<EMBED>...</EMBED>		Embedded object
	ALIGN=	Alignment of object
	HEIGHT=	Height of object
	HIDDEN=	Hides object
	PALETTE=	Sets color palette
	PLUGINSPAGE=	Sets plug-ins source link
	SRC=	Location of object source
	WIDTH=	Width of object
	[events]	Core intrinsic events
<FIELDSET>...</FIELDSET>		Form fieldset
	CLASS= ID= STYLE= TITLE=	Class(es), unique ID, style information, title
	DIR= LANG=	Text direction and language ID
	[events]	Core intrinsic events
<FONT>...</FONT>		Font
	COLOR=	Color of font
	FACE=	Typeface of font
	SIZE=	Size of font
<FORM>...</FORM>		Form
	ACCEPT-CHARSET=	List of supported character sets
	ACTION=	Server-side form handler
	CLASS= ID= STYLE= TITLE=	Class(es), unique ID, style information, title
	DIR= LANG=	Text direction and language ID
	ENCTYPE=	Encryption type
	METHOD="get | post"	Form data sent to server
	NAME=	Name of form
	TARGET=	Target frame name for rendering
	[events] onsubmit, onreset	Core intrinsic events

Tags	Attributes	Description
<FRAME>...</FRAME>		Frame within frameset
	BORDERCOLOR=	Color of border
	FRAMEBORDER=	Width of border
	HEIGHT=	Height of frame
	MARGINHEIGHT=	Height of margin
	MARGINWIDTH=	Width of margin
	NAME=	Name of frame
	NORESIZE	Prohibits resize
	SCROLLING="yes | no | auto"	Sets scroll
	SRC=	Location of frame source
	WIDTH=	Width of frame
<FRAMESET>...</FRAMESET>		Frameset
	BORDER=	Width of border
	BORDERCOLOR=	Color of border
	COLS=	Number of columns
	FRAMEBORDER=	Width of border
	FRAMESPACING=	Space between frames
	ROWS=	Number of rows
	[events] onload, onunload	Intrinsic events
<HEAD>...</HEAD>		Document head
	DIR= LANG=	Text direction and language ID
	PROFILE=	URL of metadata
<H1>...</H1>		Heading 1
	ALIGN=	Alignment of heading
	CLASS= ID= STYLE= TITLE=	Class(es), unique ID, style information, title
	CLEAR=	Fixes text beside or below image
	COLOR=	Color of text
	DINGBAT=	Adds defined dingbat
	DIR= LANG=	Text direction and language ID

Tags	Attributes	Description
<H2>, <H3>, <H4>, <H5>, <H6>	Same as <H1>	Headings 2 through 6
<HR>		Horizontal rule
	ALIGN=	Alignment of rule
	CLASS= ID= STYLE= TITLE=	Class(es), unique ID, style information, title
	CLEAR=	Fixes text beside or below image
	COLOR=	Color of rule
	NOSHADE=	No shading on rule
	NOWRAP	No wrapping of rule
	SIZE=	Height of rule
	WIDTH=	Width of rule
	[events]	Core intrinsic events
<HTML>...</HTML>		Document container
	DIR= LANG=	Text direction and language ID
	VERSION=	HTML standard version used
<I>...</I>		Italic text
	CLASS= ID= STYLE= TITLE=	Class(es), unique ID, style information, title
	DIR= LANG=	Text direction and language ID
	[events]	Core intrinsic events
<IFRAME>...</IFRAME>		Inline frame
	ALIGN=	Alignment of inline frame
	BORDER=	Size of border
	BORDERCOLOR=	Color of border
	FRAMEBORDER=	Width of border
	FRAMESPACING=	Space between frames
	HEIGHT=	Height of frame
	HSPACE=	Horizontal space
	MARGINHEIGHT=	Height of margin
	MARGINWIDTH=	Width of margin
	NAME=	Name of inline frame

Tags	Attributes	Description
<IFRAME>...</IFRAME> *(continued)*	NORESIZE=	Prohibits resize of frame
	SCROLLING="yes | no | auto"	Sets scroll
	SRC=	Location of inline frame source
	VSPACE=	Vertical space
	WIDTH=	Width of frame
<ILAYER>...</ILAYER>	(same as LAYER tag)	Inline layer positioning (behaves like text element)
<IMG>		Image
	ALIGN=	Alignment of image
	ALT=	Alternate text description
	BORDER=	Size of image border
	CLASS= ID= STYLE= TITLE=	Class(es), unique ID, style information, title
	DIR= LANG=	Text direction and language ID
	DYNSRC=	Dynamic source
	HEIGHT=	Height of image
	HSPACE=	Horizontal space
	ISMAP	Server-side image map
	LOOP=	Number of repetitions
	LOWSRC=	Location of low-resolution image
	NAME=	Name of image
	SRC=	Location of image source
	USEMAP=	Client-side image map
	VSPACE=	Vertical space
	WIDTH=	Width of image
	[events]	Core intrinsic events
<INPUT>...</INPUT>		Form input
	ACCEPT=	Accept input
	ALT=	Alternate text description
	CHECKED	Loads check boxes already selected

Tags	Attributes	Description
<INPUT>...</INPUT> *(continued)*	CLASS= ID= STYLE= TITLE=	Class(es), unique ID, style information, title
	DIR= LANG=	Text direction and language ID
	DISABLED	Disables input
	MAX=	Maximum number of input characters
	MAXLENGTH=	Maximum length of field
	NAME=	Name of form
	SIZE=	Size of field
	SRC=	Location of added images
	TABINDEX=	Explicit tabbing order
	TYPE="button | checkbox | file | hidden | image | password | radio | reset | submit | text"	Type of input method
	USEMAP=	Client-side image map
	VALUE=	Sets default value
	[events] onfocus, onblur, onselect, onchange	Core intrinsic events
<INS>...</INS>		Inserted text
	CITE=	Change data
	CLASS= ID= STYLE= TITLE=	Class(es), unique ID, style information, title
	DATETIME=	ISO change date
	DIR= LANG=	Text direction and language ID
	[events]	Core intrinsic events
<ISINDEX>		Document is a searchable index—Obsolete, use <FORM> instead
	ACTION=	URL
	CLASS= ID= STYLE= TITLE=	Class(es), unique ID, style information, title
	DIR= LANG=	Text direction and language ID
	PROMPT=	Prompt text
<KBD>...</KBD>		Keyboard
	CLASS= ID= STYLE= TITLE=	Class(es), unique ID, style information, title
	DIR= LANG=	Text direction and language ID
	[events]	Core intrinsic events

Tags	Attributes	Description
<KEYGEN>...</KEYGEN>		Form-generated security key
	NAME=	Required
	CHALLENGE=	Public key challenge string
<LABEL>...</LABEL>		Form field label
	ACCESSKEY=	Keyboard shortcut
	CLASS= ID= STYLE= TITLE=	Class(es), unique ID, style information, title
	DIR= LANG=	Text direction and language ID
	DISABLED	Disables labeling
	FOR=	Field ID
	[events] onfocus, onblur	Core intrinsic events
<LAYER>...</LAYER>		Layer positioning element (behaves like structure)

Note: Style sheets can also be used to control positioning of layer elements in a manner similar to but not the same as the W3C DOM and CSS-Positioning methods.

	ABOVE=	Relative stacking order
	BACKGROUND=	Background image
	BELOW=	Relative stacking order
	BGCOLOR=	Background color
	CLIP="n,n,n,n"	Coordinates of viewable area
	HEIGHT=	Height of layer
	LEFT=	Horizontal position of layer in layer
	PAGEX=	Horizontal position of layer in page
	PAGEY=	Vertical position of layer in page
	SRC=	Source of content
	TOP=	Vertical position of layer in layer
	VIEW="hidden | inherit | show"	Define layer visibility
	WIDTH=	Horizontal size of layer
	Z-INDEX=	Absolute stacking order
	onmouseover, onmouseout, onfocus, onblur, onload	Intrinsic events

Tags	Attributes	Description
<LEGEND>		Form fieldset legend
	ACCESSKEY=	Keyboard shortcut
	ALIGN=	Alignment of legend
	CLASS= ID= STYLE= TITLE=	Class(es), unique ID, style information, title
	DIR= LANG=	Text direction and language ID
	[events]	Core intrinsic events
<LI>...</LI>		List item
	ALIGN=	Alignment of items
	CLASS= ID= STYLE= TITLE=	Class(es), unique ID, style information, title
	DIR= LANG=	Text direction and language ID
	TYPE=	Numbering or bullet style
	VALUE="number"	Reset sequence number
	[events]	Core intrinsic events
<LINK>		Link
	CLASS= ID= STYLE= TITLE=	Class(es), unique ID, style information, title
	DIR= LANG=	Text direction and language ID
	HREF=	Hypertext link
	MEDIA=	Supported media list
	NAME=	Name of link
	REL=	Forward link type (application dependent)
	REV=	Reverse link type (application dependent)
	TARGET=	Target frame name for rendering
	TYPE=	Media type
<MAP>...</MAP>		Client-side image map
	CLASS= ID= STYLE= TITLE=	Class(es), unique ID, style information, title
	NAME=	Name of image map
<MENU>...</MENU>		Menu list
	COMPACT	Compact representation
	CLASS= ID= STYLE= TITLE=	Class(es), unique ID, style information, title
	DIR= LANG=	Text direction and language ID
	[events]	Core intrinsic events

Tags	Attributes	Description
<META>		Metadata
	CONTENT=	Content description
	DIR= LANG=	Text direction and language ID
	HTTP-EQUIV=	Server response
	NAME=	Name of document
	TITLE=	Title of document
	URL=	URL of document
<NOBR>...</NOBR>		Inhibits line breaking
<NOEMBED>		Inhibits embedding
<NOFRAMES>...</NOFRAMES>		No frames alternate document body
<NOLAYER>...</NOLAYER>		Inhibits layers
<NOSCRIPT>...</NOSCRIPT>		Noscript data
<OBJECT>...</OBJECT>		Object
	ALIGN=	Alignment of object
	BORDER=	Width of border
	CLASS= ID= STYLE= TITLE=	Class(es), unique ID, style information, title
	CLASSID=	Class identifier
	CODE=	Type of script
	CODEBASE=	Object code base
	CODETYPE=	Media type
	DATA=	Data type
	DECLARE=	References object name
	DIR= LANG=	Text direction and language ID
	DISABLED	Disables object
	HEIGHT=	Height of object
	HSPACE=	Horizontal space
	NAME=	Name of object
	SHAPES=	Name of shaped hyperlink
	STANDBY=	Standby message

Tags	Attributes	Description
<OBJECT>...</OBJECT> *(continued)*	TABINDEX=	Explicit tabbing order
	TYPE=	Media type
	USEMAP=	Image map
	VSPACE=	Vertical space
	WIDTH=	Width of image
	[events]	Core intrinsic events
<OL>...</OL>		Ordered list
	ALIGN=	Alignment of list
	CLASS= ID= STYLE= TITLE=	Class(es), unique ID, style information, title
	COMPACT	Compact representation
	DIR= LANG=	Text direction and language ID
	START=	Starting number
	TYPE=	Numbering style
	[events]	Core intrinsic events
<OPTION>...</OPTION>		Form option
	CLASS= ID= STYLE= TITLE=	Class(es), unique ID, style information, title
	DIR= LANG=	Text direction and language ID
	DISABLED	Disables option
	SELECTED=	Option selected at default
	VALUE=	Value to be returned
	[events]	Core intrinsic events
<P>...</P>		Paragraph
	ALIGN=	Alignment of paragraph
	CLASS= ID= STYLE= TITLE=	Class(es), unique ID, style information, title
	DIR= LANG=	Text direction and language ID
	WIDTH=	Width of paragraph
	[events]	Core intrinsic events

Tags	Attributes	Description
<PARAM>...</PARAM>		Parameter
	NAME=	Name of parameter
	TYPE=	Internet media type
	VALUE=	Sets value
	VALUETYPE=	Interprets value
<PRE>...</PRE>		Preformatted text
<Q>...</Q>		Inline quote
	CLASS= ID= STYLE= TITLE=	Class(es), unique ID, style information, title
	DIR= LANG=	Text direction and language ID
	[events]	Core intrinsic events
<S>...</S>		Strikeout text
	CLASS= ID= STYLE= TITLE=	Class(es), unique ID, style information, title
	DIR= LANG=	Text direction and language ID
	[events]	Core intrinsic events
<SAMP>...<SAMP>		Sample text
	CLASS= ID= STYLE= TITLE=	Class(es), unique ID, style information, title
	DIR= LANG=	Text direction and language ID
	[events]	Core intrinsic events
<SCRIPT>...</SCRIPT>		Script data
	LANGUAGE=	Script language
	SRC=	URL of script source
	TYPE=	Internet content type
	[events]	Core intrinsic events
<SELECT>...</SELECT>		Form selection list
	ALIGN=	Alignment of list
	CLASS= ID= STYLE= TITLE=	Class(es), unique ID, style information, title
	DIR= LANG=	Text direction and language ID
	DISABLED	Disables list
	HEIGHT=	Height of object

Tags	Attributes	Description
<SELECT>...</SELECT> *(continued)*	NAME=	Names of object
	SIZE=	Size of object
	TABINDEX=	Explicit tabbing order
	WIDTH=	Width of object
	[events] onfocus, onblur, onselect, onchange	Core intrinsic events
<SMALL>...</SMALL>		Small text
	CLASS= ID= STYLE= TITLE=	Class(es), unique ID, style information, title
	DIR= LANG=	Text direction and language ID
	[events]	Core intrinsic events
<SPAN>...</SPAN>		Generic text container
	ALIGN=	Alignment of container
	CLASS= ID= STYLE= TITLE=	Class(es), unique ID, style information, title
	DIR= LANG=	Text direction and language ID
	[events]	Core intrinsic events
<STRIKE>...</STRIKE>		Strikeout text
	CLASS= ID= STYLE= TITLE=	Class(es), unique ID, style information, title
	DIR= LANG=	Text direction and language ID
	[events]	Core intrinsic events
<STRONG>...</STRONG>		Strong text
	CLASS= ID= STYLE= TITLE=	Class(es), unique ID, style information, title
	DIR= LANG=	Text direction and language ID
	[events]	Core intrinsic events
<STYLE>...</STYLE>		Style sheet definition
	DIR= LANG=	Text direction and language ID
	MEDIA=	Supported media list
	TYPE=	Internet content type
_{...}		Subscript text
	CLASS= ID= STYLE= TITLE=	Class(es), unique ID, style information, title
	DIR= LANG=	Text direction and language ID
	[events]	Core intrinsic events

Tags	Attributes	Description
^{...}		Superscript text
	CLASS= ID= STYLE= TITLE=	Class(es), unique ID, style information, title
	DIR= LANG=	Text direction and language ID
	[events]	Core intrinsic events
<TAB>		Tab value
	ALIGN=	Alignment of tab
	INDENT=	
<TABLE>...</TABLE>		Table
	ALIGN=	Alignment of table
	BACKGROUND=	Location of background image
	BGCOLOR=	Background color
	BORDER=	Size of border
	BORDERCOLOR=	Color of border
	BORDERCOLORDARK=	Dark color for 3-D border
	BORDERCOLORLIGHT=	Light color for 3-D border
	CELLPADDING=	Space between table cell edge and content
	CELLSPACING=	Space between cell borders
	CLASS= ID= STYLE= TITLE=	Class(es), unique ID, style information, title
	COLS=	Number of columns
	DIR= LANG=	Text direction and language ID
	FRAME=	External border around table
	HEIGHT=	Height of table
	NOWRAP	Prohibits text wrapping
	WIDTH=	Width of table
	[events]	Core intrinsic events
<TBODY>...</TBODY>		Table body
	ALIGN=	Alignment of table body
	BGCOLOR=	Background color
	CLASS= ID= STYLE= TITLE=	Class(es), unique ID, style information, title
	DIR= LANG=	Text direction and language ID

Tags	Attributes	Description
`<TBODY>...</TBODY>` *(continued)*	VALIGN=	Vertical alignment
	[events]	Core intrinsic events
`<TD>...</TD>`		Table cell
	ALIGN=	Alignment of table cell
	AXIS=	Abbreviated cell name
	AXES=	AXIS values
	BACKGROUND=	Location of background image
	BGCOLOR=	Background color
	BORDERCOLOR=	Border color
	BORDERCOLORDARK=	Dark color for 3-D border
	BORDERCOLORLIGHT=	Light color for 3-D border
	CLASS= ID= STYLE= TITLE=	Class(es), unique ID, style information, title
	COLSPAN=	Number of columns spanned
	DIR= LANG=	Text direction and language ID
	HEIGHT=	Height of table cell
	NOWRAP	Prohibits text wrap
	ROWSPAN=	Number of rows spanned
	VALIGN=	Vertical alignment
	WIDTH=	Width of table cell
	[events]	Core intrinsic events
`<TEXTAREA>...</TEXTAREA>`		Form input text area
	ALIGN=	Alignment of text field
	CLASS= ID= STYLE= TITLE=	Class(es), unique ID, style information, title
	COLS=	Width of text input field
	DATAFLD=	Field of data
	DATASRC=	Location of data source
	DIR= LANG=	Text direction and language ID
	DISABLED	Disables text field
	ERROR=	Error message

Tags	Attributes	Description
<TEXTAREA>...</TEXTAREA> *(continued)*	NAME=	Name of text field
	READONLY	Read-only
	ROWS=	Height of text input field
	TABINDEX=	Explicit tabbing order
	WRAP=	Wrap text
	[events] onfocus, onblur, onselect, onchange	Core intrinsic events
<TFOOT>...</TFOOT>		Table footer
	ALIGN=	Alignment of footer
	BGCOLOR=	Background color
	CLASS= ID= STYLE= TITLE=	Class(es), unique ID, style information, title
	DIR= LANG=	Text direction and language ID
	VALIGN=	Vertical alignment
	[events]	Core intrinsic events
<TH>...</TH>		Table cell heading
	ALIGN=	Alignment of heading
	AXIS=	Abbreviated cell name
	AXES=	AXIS values
	BACKGROUND=	Location of background image
	BGCOLOR=	Background color
	BORDERCOLOR=	Border color
	BORDERCOLORDARK=	Dark color for 3-D border
	BORDERCOLORLIGHT=	Light color for 3-D border
	CLASS= ID= STYLE= TITLE=	Class(es), unique ID, style information, title
	COLSPAN=	Number of columns spanned
	DIR= LANG=	Text direction and language ID
	HEIGHT=	Height of table cell
	NOWRAP	Prohibits text wrap
	ROWSPAN=	Number of rows spanned
	VALIGN=	Vertical alignment
	WIDTH=	Width of table cell
	[events]	Core intrinsic events

Tags	Attributes	Description
<THEAD>...</THEAD>		Table header
	ALIGN=	Alignment of header
	BGCOLOR=	Background color
	CLASS= ID= STYLE= TITLE=	Class(es), unique ID, style information, title
	DIR= LANG=	Text direction and language ID
	VALIGN=	Vertical alignment
	[events]	Core intrinsic events
<TITLE>...</TITLE>		Document title
	DIR= LANG=	Text direction and language ID
<TR>...</TR>		Table row
	ALIGN=	Alignment of table row
	BGCOLOR=	Background color
	BORDERCOLOR=	Border color
	BORDERCOLORDARK=	Dark color for 3-D border
	BORDERCOLORLIGHT=	Light color for 3-D border
	CLASS= ID= STYLE= TITLE=	Class(es), unique ID, style information, title
	DIR= LANG=	Text direction and language ID
	HEIGHT=	Height of table row
	NOWRAP	Prohibits text wrap
	VALIGN=	Vertical alignment
	VSPACE=	Vertical space
	[events]	Core intrinsic events
<TT>...</TT>		Monospaced text
	CLASS= ID= STYLE= TITLE=	Class(es), unique ID, style information, title
	DIR= LANG=	Text direction and language ID
	[events]	Core intrinsic events
<U>...</U>		Underline text
	CLASS= ID= STYLE= TITLE=	Class(es), unique ID, style information, title
	DIR= LANG=	Text direction and language ID
	[events]	Core intrinsic events

Tags	Attributes	Description
<UL>...</UL>		Unordered list
	ALIGN=	Alignment of list
	CLASS= ID= STYLE= TITLE=	Class(es), unique ID, style information, title
	COMPACT	Compact representation
	DIR= LANG=	Text direction and language ID
	SRC=	Location of list source
	TYPE="disk|square|circle"	Bullet style
	WRAP=	Wrap text
	[events]	Core intrinsic events
<VAR>...</VAR>		Variable content
	CLASS= ID= STYLE= TITLE=	Class(es), unique ID, style information, title
	DIR= LANG=	Text direction and language ID
	[events]	Core intrinsic events
<WBR>		Conditional break

Index

Note to reader: **Bolded** page references indicate main discussions of a topic and definitions. *Italicized* page references indicate illustrations.

Make Learning Fun and Easy with

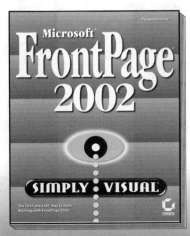

from **Sybex**®

The *Simply Visual* series of
books provides highly illustrated
introductions to the essentials of
Microsoft's Office suite. Goes
beyond the basics by covering
both the newest and most
essential features in a highly
visual easy-to-follow format.
The concise organization of the
book allows you to quickly find
what you need to know to get
up-to-speed fast.

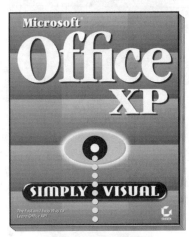
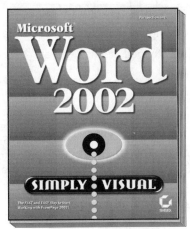

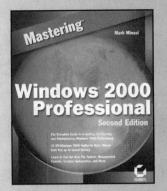

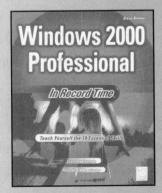

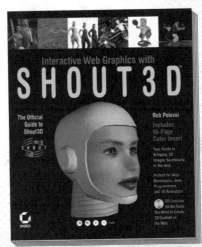
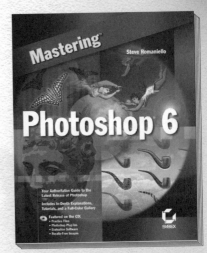